CMT LEVEL I

CMT LEVEL I

An Introduction to Technical Analysis

Readings Selected by

The CMT Association

WILEY

CONTENTS

■ The CMT Association

What We Do

The CMT Association, founded in the 1960s, is a not-for-profit professional association dedicated to advancing the discipline of technical analysis and the work of technical analysts worldwide. The Association pursues this mission through credentialing, ethics, education, and advocacy.

- Credentialing: The CMT Charter is the globally respected credential granted to Association members in good standing who complete the examination process. Charterholders have demonstrated mastery of a core body of knowledge in both the history and current practice of technical analysis. Their ongoing membership in the CMT Association is evidence of their commitment to the professional and ethical practice of the craft.

- Ethics: The CMT Association and its members are committed to maintaining the highest ethical standards in all their professional activities. The Association has adopted the CFA Institute Code of Ethics and Standards of Professional Conduct for its membership. In fact, questions on ethics appear on all three levels of the CMT exams. Furthermore, members risk disciplinary sanctions by the CMT Association including revocation of membership and the right to use the CMT designation for violating the Code and Standards.

- Education: The Association's dedication to education extends beyond the curriculum it maintains for candidates in the CMT Program. Through webcasts, local chapter meetings, and an Annual Symposium, the Association promotes ongoing learning and intellectual synergies among all those interested in technical analysis.

- Advocacy: The Association represents the technical analysis community to the public, to academia, and to regulatory bodies worldwide. This work is intended to secure the place of technical analysis as a recognized discipline alongside other modes of financial market analysis, and to make the public aware of its strengths and limitations.

Who We Are

The membership of the CMT Association includes technical analysts, portfolio managers, investment advisors, market-letter writers, journalists, and academics. With CMT charterholders in more than 50 countries, members are involved in global markets from currencies to commodities, equities to ETPs, and futures to fixed income.

The membership honors the long history of technical analysis of financial markets while generating new methods that incorporate the latest concepts in behavioral finance, quantitative analysis, and algorithmic applications.

Governance and Operation

The CMT Association is overseen by a Board of Directors elected from and by the membership. Additional work on behalf of the Board and the membership is carried out by committees composed of members who volunteer their time and expertise. Dozens of local chapters, found in many countries, offer opportunities to hear from renowned technicians and network with others who share a passion for technical analysis. New members as well as veterans are encouraged to become involved in chapters and on committees.

The staff of the Association, headquartered in New York, supports the Board and the membership in carrying out the mission of the Association. Members should feel free to contact staff for information related to the activities and workings of the CMT Association, volunteer opportunities, and the credentialing program.

■ The CMT Program

Purpose

The CMT Association initiated a professional credentialing program in technical analysis in the 1980s. This program is an essential part of the Association's work in advancing the practice of technical analysis and maintaining the highest possible professional standards for practitioners. By designing the curriculum and setting standards for examinations, ethics, and professional experience, the Association assures that candidates satisfy the stated requirements to be awarded the CMT Charter.

The CMT Program is overseen by the Curriculum and Test Committee of the CMT Association. The Committee is composed of volunteer charterholders who are distinguished by their dedication to technical analysis and their willingness to contribute to its advancement. The Committee approves the curriculum and monitors the exam content and administration.

Curriculum

The CMT Program curriculum is published in three volumes—one for each level of the exam series. The readings are drawn primarily from published texts written by recognized experts with additional content commissioned by the CMT Association.

The three levels of the curriculum are described as follows:

- Level I: Introduction to Technical Analysis: Basic knowledge of the terminology and analytical tools used in technical analysis.

- Level II: Theory and Analysis: Application of concepts, theory, and techniques.

- Level III: Integration of Technical Analysis: Integration of concepts with practical application.

The specific topics covered in each level of the curriculum have been determined by a job-analysis survey of technical analysis practitioners. The information from the survey, updated periodically, is used to create a list of knowledge domains, subdomains, and weightings for each level of the curriculum and exam. In addition, each of the three exams includes "ethics" as a knowledge domain.

Exams

All three levels of the CMT Association exams are administered during semiannual test windows in June and December. The exact dates for each test window are announced well ahead of time. Candidates complete the exams on computer terminals at Prometric Test Centers located worldwide or remotely, in a suitable location, using Prometric's ProProctor service. Candidates may sit for only one exam during each test window. Furthermore, candidates should be aware that the CMT Association exams are offered only in English, regardless of the candidate's location or the location of the test center.

CMT Exams

Level	Format	Duration	Content
I	Multiple choice	2 hours	132 questions: 120 scored, 12 trial
II	Multiple choice	4 hours	170 questions: 150 scored, 20 trial
III	Multiple choice and short answer	4 hours	Approximately 50, but varies at each administration

Receiving the CMT Charter

To be awarded the CMT charter, candidates must:

- Successfully complete all three exams. (CFA charterholders may request a waiver from Level I of the CMT exams.)

- Attain professional membership in the CMT Association, which requires:

  - Sponsorship by three members in good standing, and

  - Satisfying the stipulation for professional experience.

- Remain current on dues.

- Complete and maintain an accurate Personal Conduct Statement.

■ The Level I Textbook

As noted above, the CMT Level I exam is a 2-hour multiple-choice exam focused on basic knowledge of the terminology and analytical tools used in technical analysis. The knowledge domains listed in the table below, and their weightings, are covered in the Level I text and reflected on the exam. Although this may be a useful checklist for some readers, candidates may be best served by focusing on the Learning Objective Statements that appear at the start of each chapter. These are described in another section below.

Level I: Knowledge Domains and Weightings

Domain	Weight
Theory and History	9%
Markets	5%
Market Indicators	7%
Construction	5%
Trend Analysis	16%
Chart and Pattern Analysis	23%
Confirmation	3%
Cycles	5%
Selection and Decision	13%
System Testing	5%
Statistical Analysis	6%
Ethics	3%

The number of questions on the exam drawn from each knowledge domain approximates the percentages in the table above.

Ethics

The CMT Association has adopted the CFA Institute Code of Ethics and Standards of Professional Conduct ("Code and Standards") as its ethics guide. All three levels of the CMT exams include questions pertaining to ethics. All references to "CFA Institute," "members," "candidates," "CFA Program," and so on in the Code and Standards should be read to apply to CMT Association and its members, candidates, programs, and so on.

When preparing for the CMT exams, candidates are encouraged to review the Standards of Practice Handbook ("Handbook"). According to the CFA Institute,

"The Standards of Practice Handbook grounds the concepts covered in the Code and Standards for practical use. You can use this handbook for guidance on how to navigate ethical dilemmas you might face in your daily professional life." Reviewing the Handbook provides a more comprehensive study process and preparation for professional practice.

Study material regarding ethics is not in this text. Both the Code and Standards and the Handbook are available for download from the CMT Association website: https://cmtassociation.org/association/cmt-code-of-ethics/.

Learning Objective Statements

A list of Learning Objectives appears at the beginning of each chapter. These are intended as a guide to the most important concepts discussed in the chapter. An effective study method is to read the Learning Objectives as an introduction to a chapter before beginning study of the chapter. After completing the chapter, review the Learning Objectives again and write a few sentences that demonstrate competence on that topic.

Candidates should also be aware that the specific points mentioned in the Learning Objectives are prime material for the exams, but there may also be questions drawn from any part of the text.

THEORY AND HISTORY OF TECHNICAL ANALYSIS

My life seemed to be a series of events and accidents. Yet when I look back,
I see a pattern.

—**Benoît B. Mandelbrot**

Centuries of work in interpreting and understanding the movement of prices in financial markets brings us to today's technical analysis. Marks on paper and calculations by hand, pit traders and runners, have all given way to the speed and efficiency of computers and electronic information networks. Yet the goals remain the same: identify the trend as early as possible, capitalize on it for as long as possible, and manage the risks along the way.

It is traditional to examine price, volume, and indicator information in charts. To this day, understanding how and why charts are constructed as they are is critical not only to classical technical work—the need for a person to absorb and interpret large amounts of data—but also to the most modern applications of quantitative technical analysis.

This section introduces the core concept of "trend" and its components as used in technical analysis. This includes information on the fractal nature of price action, an important principle in the application of technical analysis across time horizons.

Charting—data visualization as practiced by technicians since before it became known as such—is introduced here with additional chart variations covered in the next section.

Of course, no discussion of the history of technical analysis would be complete without a primer on the work of Charles Dow and his successors, who gave us what we know as Dow Theory.

CHAPTER 1

The Basic Principle of Technical Analysis—The Trend

From Charles D. Kirkpatrick II and Julie R. Dahlquist, *Technical Analysis: The Complete Resource for Financial Market Technicians*, 3rd Edition (Old Tappan, New Jersey: Pearson Education, Inc., 2016), Chapter 2.

Learning Objective Statements

- Define what is meant by a trend in technical analysis
- Explain why determining the trend is important to analysts
- Identify primary, secondary, short-term, and intraday trends
- Describe the basic beliefs behind the art of technical analysis
- Define "fractal" as used in describing price action

> The art of technical analysis—for it is an art—is to identify trend changes at an early stage and to maintain an investment position until the weight of the evidence indicates that the trend has reversed. (Pring, 2002)

Technical analysis is based on one major assumption: Freely traded, market prices, in general, travel in trends.

Based on this assumption, traders and investors hope to buy a security at the beginning of an upward trend at a low price, ride the trend, and sell the security when the trend ends at a higher price. Although this strategy sounds simple, implementing it is exceedingly complex.

For example, what length trend are we discussing? The trend in stock prices since the Great Depression? The trend in gold prices since 1980? The trend in the Dow Jones Industrial Average (DJIA) in the past year? The trend in Merck stock during the past week? Trends exist in all lengths, from long-term trends that occur over decades to short-term trends that occur from minute to minute.

Trends of different lengths tend to have the same characteristics. In other words, a trend in annual data will behave the same as a trend in five-minute data. Investors must choose which trend is most important for them based on their investment objectives, their personal preferences, and the amount of time they can devote to watching market prices. One investor might be more concerned about the business cycle trend that occurs over several years. Another investor might be more concerned about the trend over the next six months, and a third investor might be most concerned about the intraday trend. Although individual investors and traders have investment time horizons that vary greatly, they can use the same basic methods of analyzing trends because of the commonalities that exist among trends of different lengths.

Trends are obvious in hindsight, but ideally, we would like to spot a new trend right at its beginning, buy, spot its end, and sell. However, this ideal never happens, except by luck. The technical analyst always runs the risk of spotting the beginning of a trend too late and missing potential profit. The analyst who does not spot the ending of the trend holds the security past the price peak and fails to capture all the profits that were possible. On the other hand, if the analyst thinks the trend has ended before it really has and sells the security prematurely, the analyst has then lost potential profits. The technical analyst thus spends a lot of time and brainpower attempting to spot as early as possible when a trend is beginning and ending. This is the reason for studying charts, moving averages, oscillators, support and resistance, and all the other techniques we explore in this book.

The fact that market prices trend has been known for thousands of years. Academics have disputed that markets tend to trend because if it were true, it would spoil their theoretical models. However, recent academic work has shown that the old financial models have many problems when applied to the behavior of real markets. Academics and others traditionally have scorned technical analysis as if it were a cult; as it turns out, however, the almost religious belief in the Efficient Markets Hypothesis has become a cult itself, with adherents unwilling to accept the enormous amount of evidence against it. In fact, technical analysis is very old, developed through practical experience with the trading markets, and has resulted in some sizable fortunes for those following it.

■ How Does the Technical Analyst Make Money?

Several requirements are needed to convert pure technical analysis into money. The first and most important, of course, is to determine when a trend is beginning or ending. The money is made by "jumping" on the trend as early as possible. Theoretically, this sounds simple, but profiting consistently is not so easy.

The indicators and measurements that technical analysts use to determine the trend are not crystal balls that perfectly predict the future. Under certain market conditions, these tools might not work. Also, a trend can suddenly change direction without warning. Thus, it is imperative that the technical investor be aware of risks and protect against such occurrences causing losses.

From a tactical standpoint, then, the technical investor must decide two things: First, the investor or trader must choose when to enter a position, and second, he must choose when to exit a position. Choosing when to exit a position is composed of two decisions. The investor must choose when to exit the position to capture a profit when price moves in the expected direction. The investor must also choose when to exit the position at a loss when price moves in the opposite direction from what was expected. The wise investor is aware of the risk that the trend might differ from what he expected. Making the decision of what price level to sell and cut losses before even entering into a position is a way in which the investor protects against large losses.

One of the great advantages in technical analysis, because it studies prices, is that a price point can be established at which the investor knows that something is wrong either with the analysis or the financial asset's price behavior. Risk of loss can therefore be determined and quantified right at the beginning of the investment. This ability is not available to other methods of investment. Finally, because actual risk can be determined, money management principles can be applied that will lessen the chance of loss and the risk of what is called **ruin**.

In sum, the basic strategy to make money using technical methods includes

- **"The trend is your friend"**—Play the trend.

- **Don't lose**—Control risk of capital loss.

- **Manage your money**—Avoid ruin.

Technical analysis is used to determine the trend, when it is changing, when it has changed, when to enter a position, when to exit a position, and when the analysis is wrong and the position must be closed. It's as simple as that.

What Is a Trend?

What exactly is this **trend** that the investor wants to ride to make money? An upward trend, or **uptrend**, occurs when prices reach higher peaks and higher troughs. An uptrend looks something like Chart A in Figure 1.1. A downward trend, or **downtrend**, is the opposite: when prices reach lower troughs and lower peaks. Chart B in Figure 1.1 shows this downward trend in price. A **sideways** or **flat trend** occurs when prices trade in a range without significant underlying upward or downward movement. Chart C in Figure 1.1 is an example of a sideways trend; prices move up and down but on average remain at the same level.

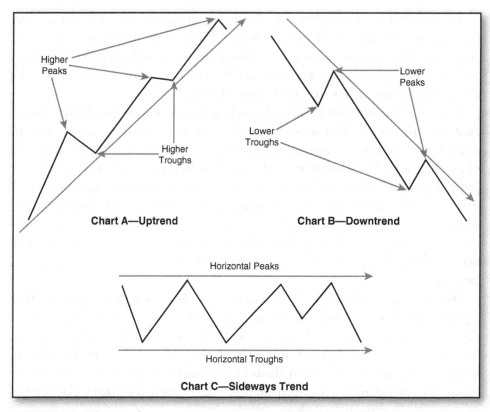

FIGURE 1.1 The Trend

Figure 1.1 shows a theoretical example of an uptrend, downtrend, and sideways trend. But defining a trend in the price of real-world securities is not quite that simple. Price movement does not follow a continuous, uninterrupted line. Small countertrend movements within a trend can make the true trend difficult to identify at times. Also, remember that there are trends of differing lengths. Shorter-term trends are parts of longer-term trends.

From a technical analyst's perspective, **a trend is a directional movement of prices that remains in effect long enough to be identified and still be profitable**. Anything less makes technical analysis useless. If a trend is not identified until it is over, we cannot make money from it. If it is unrecognizable until too late, we cannot make money from it. In retrospect, looking at a graph of prices, for example, many trends can be identified of varying length and magnitude, but such observations are observations of history only. A trend must be recognized early and be long enough for the technician to profit.

■ How Are Trends Identified?

There are a number of ways to identify trends. One way to determine a trend in a data set is to run a linear least-squares regression. This statistical process will provide information about the trend in security prices. Unfortunately, this particular statistical technique is not of much use to the technical analyst for trend analysis. The regression method depends on a sizable amount of past price data for accurate results. By the time enough historical price data accumulates, the trend is likely changing direction. Despite the tendency for trends to be persistent enough to profit from, they never last forever.

BOX 1.1   LINEAR LEAST-SQUARES REGRESSION

Most spreadsheet software includes a formula for calculating a linear regression line. It uses two sets of related variables and calculates the "best fit" between the data and an imaginary straight (linear) line drawn through the data. In standard price analysis, the two variable data sets are time and price—day d1 and price X1, day d2 and price X2, and so forth. By fitting a line that best describes the data series, we can determine a number of things. First, we can measure the amount by which the actual data varies from the line and, thus, the reliability of the line. Second, we can measure the slope of the line to determine the rate of change in prices over time, and third, we can determine when the line began. The line represents the trend in prices over the period of time studied. It has many useful properties that we will look at later, but for now, all we need to know is that the line defines the trend over the period studied. Appendix A, "Basic Statistics," provides more detailed information about least-squares regression.

Many analysts use moving averages to smooth out and reduce the effect of smaller trends within longer trends.

Another method of identifying trends is to look at a graph of prices for extreme points, tops, and bottoms, separated by reasonable time periods, and to draw lines between these extreme points (see Figure 1.2). These lines are called **trend lines.** This traditional method is an outgrowth of the time before computer graphics software when trend lines were hand drawn. It still works, however. Using this method to define trends, you must define reversal points. By drawing lines between them, top to top and bottom to bottom, we get a "feeling" of price direction and limits. We also get a "feeling" of slope, or the rate of change in prices. Trend lines can define limits to price action, which, if broken, can warn that the trend might be changing.

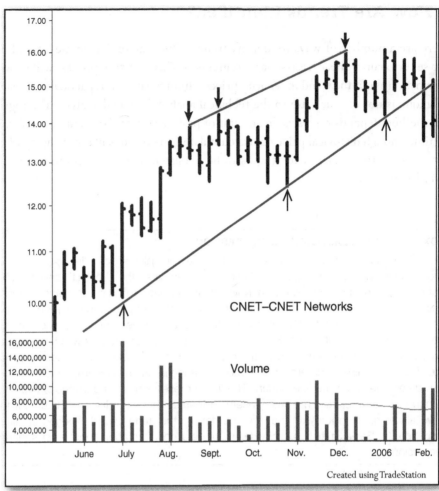

FIGURE 1.2 Hand-Drawn Trend Lines from Top to Top and Bottom to Bottom

■ Trends Develop from Supply and Demand

As in all markets, whether used cars, grapefruit, real estate, or industrial products, the economic principle of interaction between supply and demand determines prices in trading markets. Each buyer (demand) **bids** for a certain quantity at a certain price, and each seller (supply) offers or **asks** for a certain quantity at a certain price. When the buyer and seller agree and transact, they establish a price for that instant in time. The reasons for buying and selling can be complex—perhaps the seller needs the money, perhaps the seller has learned of unfavorable information, perhaps the buyer heard a rumor in the golf club locker room—whatever the reason, the price is established when all this information is collected, digested, and acted upon through the bid and offer.

Price, therefore, is the end result of all those inexact factors, and it is the result of the supply and demand at that instant in time. When prices change, the change is due to a change in demand or supply or both. The seller might be more anxious; the buyer might have more money to invest—whatever the reason, the price will change and reflect this change in supply or demand. The technical analyst, therefore, watches price and price change and does not particularly worry about the reasons, largely because they are indeterminable.

Remember that many players for many reasons determine supply and demand. In the trading markets, supply and demand may come from long-term investors accumulating or distributing a large position or from a small, short-term trader trying to scalp a few points. The number of players and the number of different reasons for their participation in supply and demand is close to infinite. Thus, **the technical analyst believes it is futile to analyze the components of supply and demand except through the prices it creates.** Where economic information, company information, and other information affecting prices is often vague, late, or misplaced, prices are readily available, are extremely accurate, have historic records, and are specific. What better basis is there for study than this important variable? Furthermore, when one invests or trades, the price is what determines profit or loss, not corporate earnings or Federal Reserve policy. The bottom line, to the technical analyst, is that price is what determines success and, fortunately, for whatever reasons, prices tend to trend.

■ What Trends Are There?

The number of trend lengths is unlimited. Investors and traders need to determine which length they are most interested in, but the methods of determining when a trend begins and ends are the same regardless of length. This ability for trends to act similarly over different periods is called their **fractal** nature. Fractal patterns or trends exist in nature along shorelines, in snowflakes, and elsewhere. For example, a snowflake is always six-sided—having six branches, if you will. Each branch has a particular, unique pattern made of smaller branches. Using a microscope to look closely at the snowflake, we see that the smaller branches off each larger branch have the same form as the larger branch. This same shape carries to even smaller and smaller branches, each of which has the same pattern as the next larger. This is the fractal nature of snowflakes. The branches, regardless of size, maintain the same pattern. Figure 1.3 shows a computer-generated fractal with each subangle an exact replica of the next larger angle.

The trading markets are similar in that any period we look at—long, medium, or very short—produces trends with the same characteristics and patterns as each other. Thus, for analysis purposes, the length of the trend is irrelevant because the technical principles are applicable to all of them. The trend length of interest is determined solely by the investor's or trader's **period of interest**.

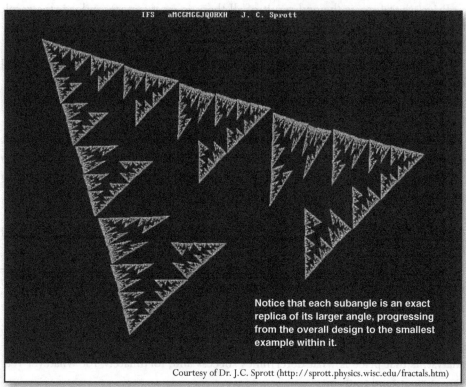

Notice that each subangle is an exact replica of its larger angle, progressing from the overall design to the smallest example within it.

Courtesy of Dr. J.C. Sprott (http://sprott.physics.wisc.edu/fractals.htm)

FIGURE 1.3   Example of Computer-Generated Fractal

This is not to say that different trend lengths should be ignored. Because shorter trends make up longer trends, any analysis of a period of interest must include analysis of the longer and shorter trends around it. For example, the trader interested in ten-week trends should also analyze trends longer than ten weeks because a longer trend will affect the shorter trend. Likewise, a trend shorter than ten weeks should be analyzed because it will often give early signals of a change in direction in the larger, ten-week trend. Thus, whatever trend the trader or investor selects as the trend of interest, the trends of the next longer and next shorter periods should also be analyzed.

For identification purposes, technical analysts have divided trends into several broad, arbitrary categories. These are the primary trend (measured in months or years), the secondary or intermediate trend (measured in weeks or months), the short-term trend (measured in days), and the intraday trend (measured in minutes or hours). Except for the intraday trend, Charles H. Dow, founder of the Dow Jones Company and the *Wall Street Journal,* first advanced this division in the nineteenth century. Charles Dow also was one of the first to identify technical means of determining when the primary trend had reversed direction. Because of his major contributions to the field, Dow is known as the "father" of technical analysis.

■ What Other Assumptions Do Technical Analysts Make?

That markets trend is the basic principle underlying the theory of technical analysis. Of course, the price of the securities that are being monitored form the trend. Supporting this notion of trending prices, technical analysts have made several other assumptions that we cover briefly.

First, technical analysts assume that price is determined by the interaction of **supply and demand**. As basic economic theory teaches, when demand increases, price goes up, and when demand decreases, price goes down. One of the factors that determine supply and demand is buyer and seller expectations. (You do not buy a stock unless you expect it to rise in price.) Expectations result from human decisions, and decisions are based on information (perceived, accurate, or otherwise), emotions (greed, fear, and hope), and cognitive limitations such as behavioral biases, emotions, and feelings that originate from the chemistry and electrical connections within our brains. A new field of study called **neurofinance**, an interdisciplinary study of the application of neuroscience to investment activity, is finding remarkable connections between how our brain functions, how we make decisions, and how we invest.

Second, technical analysts assume that **price discounts everything**. Price discounts all information, related to the security or otherwise, as well as the interpretation of expectations derived from that information. This concept was first articulated by Charles H. Dow, later reemphasized by William Peter Hamilton in his *Wall Street Journal* editorials, and succinctly described by Robert Rhea (1932), a prominent Dow Theorist, when writing about stock market averages:

> The Averages discount everything: The fluctuations of the daily closing prices of the Dow-Jones rail and industrial averages afford a composition index of all the hopes, disappointments, and knowledge of everyone who knows anything of financial matters, and for that reason the effects of coming events (excluding acts of God) are always properly anticipated in their movement. The averages quickly appraise such calamities as fires and earthquakes.

This sounds a little like Eugene Fama's (1970) famous statement related to the Efficient Markets Hypothesis (EMH) that "prices fully reflect all available information." However, Fama was referring more to information on the specific security and was presuming that all interpretation of that information was immediately and rationally determined. Although technical assumptions include the price discount assumption of EMH adherents, they go far beyond that simplicity. They include not only information, both about the security and about all other outside factors that might influence that security price, but also the interpretation of that information, which might or might not be rational or directly related, and the expectations derived from that information. Interpretation, according to technical analysis, is subject to "irrational exuberance" and will "drive men to excess" as well as to a "corresponding depression" (Hamilton, 1922).

Third, an important corollary to the notion that markets trend is the technical analyst's belief that **prices are nonrandom**.

Fourth, technical analysis assumes that history, in principle, will repeat itself (or as Mark Twain said, "History rhymes: It does not repeat") and that **humans will behave similarly to the way they have in the past in similar circumstances**. This similar behavior tends to form into patterns that have predictable results. These patterns are almost never identical and are, thus, subject to interpretation, with all its own bias problems, by the technical analyst. This is the most controversial aspect of technical analysis as well as its most long standing, and it is only recently being investigated with sophisticated statistical methods.

Fifth, technical analysts also believe that, like trend lines, these **patterns are fractal** (see Figure 1.4). Each investor or trader has a specific period of interest in which she operates. Interestingly, regardless of period, patterns occur with similar, although not identical, shapes and characteristics. Thus, an analyst who is watching five-minute bar charts will observe the same patterns that an analyst watching monthly bar charts will see. These patterns suggest that the behavior that produces them is dependent also on the participants' period of interest. A pattern in a five-minute bar chart, for example, is the result of other traders with a five-minute bar chart time horizon. Monthly investors would have very little effect on the five-minute bar chart, as five-minute traders would have almost no effect on the monthly bar chart. Thus, each group of participants, as defined by their investment horizon, has its own world of patterns that might or might not affect each other but will be similar in shape. Pattern analysis is, therefore, universal and independent of time.

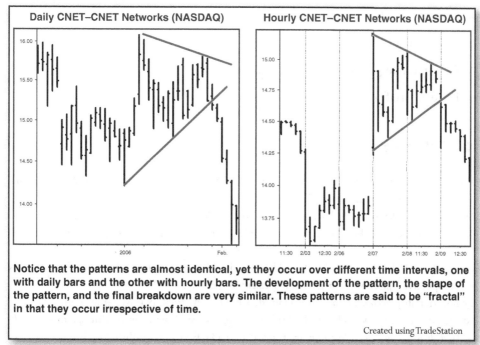

Daily CNET–CNET Networks (NASDAQ)   Hourly CNET–CNET Networks (NASDAQ)

Notice that the patterns are almost identical, yet they occur over different time intervals, one with daily bars and the other with hourly bars. The development of the pattern, the shape of the pattern, and the final breakdown are very similar. These patterns are said to be "fractal" in that they occur irrespective of time.

Created using TradeStation

FIGURE 1.4   **Daily and Hourly Charts in the Same Stock over Different Periods**

Sixth, technical analysis is also based on the notion that **emotions are affected by earlier emotions through emotional feedback**. If I buy a stock today and its price rises, I am happy and tell others to buy the stock, or others see its price rising and also buy it, thus causing the price to rise further. Action in the markets, therefore, is not independent but is related instead to how the market itself is behaving. Excessive feedback can cause "bubbles" when price behavior rises far out of proportion to value and can cause panics when price behavior declines sharply. Technical analysis presumes that prices will expand beyond equilibrium for emotional reasons, eventually will revert to the mean, and then expand beyond the mean in the opposite direction, constantly oscillating back and forth with excessive investor sentiment.

■ Conclusion

The focus of this chapter has been on the importance of understanding price trends to the practice of technical analysis. We have introduced some of the basic assumptions and beliefs of technical analysts. Some of the basic beliefs that technical analysis is built on and that we build upon throughout this book are as follows:

- The interaction of supply and demand determine price.
- Supply and demand are affected by investors' emotions and biases, particularly fear and greed.

- Price discounts everything.

- Prices trend.

- Recognizable patterns form within trends.

- Patterns are fractal.

■ References

Fama, Eugene. "Efficient Capital Markets: A Review of Theory and Empirical Work." *Journal of Finance* 25 (1970): 383–417.

Hamilton, W. *The Stock Market Barometer: A Study of Its Forecast Value Based on Charles H. Dow's Theory of the Price Movement, reprint of 1922 edition.* New York, NY: John Wiley & Sons, 1998.

Lo, Andrew. "The Adaptive Markets Hypothesis: Market Efficiency from an Evolutionary Perspective." *Journal of Portfolio Management* 30 (2004): 15–29.

Pring, Martin J. *Technical Analysis Explained.* 4th ed. New York, NY: McGraw-Hill, 2002.

Rhea, Robert. *The Dow Theory: An Explanation of Its Development of an Attempt to Define Its Usefulness as an Aid to Speculation,* reprint of 1932 Barron's Publishing edition by Fraser Publishing Co., Burlington, VT, 2002.

CHAPTER 2

Dow Theory

From Charles D. Kirkpatrick II and Julie R.
Dahlquist, *Technical Analysis: The Complete Resource
for Financial Market Technicians,* 3rd Edition
(Old Tappan, New Jersey: Pearson Education,
Inc., 2016), Chapter 6.

Learning Objective Statements

■ Describe the history of Dow Theory
■ Discuss the basic principles of Dow Theory
■ Identify the three basic types of trends identified in Dow Theory as defined by
  time: primary, secondary, and minor
■ Identify the three basic trend patterns of all prices: upward, downward, and
  sideways
■ Describe the "ideal market picture" according to Dow Theory
■ Express the concept of confirmation in Dow Theory
■ Explain the role of volume in Dow Theory

15

> Charles H. Dow was the founder of the Dow-Jones financial news ser-
> vice in New York, and founder and first editor of the *Wall Street Jour-*
> *nal*. He died in December, 1902, in his fifty-second year. He was an
> experienced newspaper reporter, with an early training under Samuel
> Bowles, the great editor of the Springfield [MA] Republican. Dow was a
> New Englander, intelligent, self-repressed, and ultra-conservative; and
> he knew his business. He was almost judicially cold in the consideration
> of any subject, whatever the fervor of discussion. It would be less than
> just to say that I never saw him angry; I never saw him excited. His per-
> fect integrity and good sense commanded the confidence of every man
> in Wall Street, at a time when there were few efficient newspaper men
> covering the financial section, and of these still fewer with any deep
> knowledge of finance. (Hamilton, 1922)

Charles Dow, the father of modern technical analysis, was the first to create an index that measures the overall price movement of U.S. stocks. However, he never specifically formulated what has become known as the "Dow Theory." Indeed, he likely never intended his disjointed statements and observations in the *Wall Street Journal* to become formalized. He wrote editorials about what he had learned from his experience as a reporter and advisor on Wall Street but never organized these individual pieces into a coherent theory. In fact, he only wrote for five years before his sudden death in 1902. The term "Dow Theory" was first used by Dow's friend, A. C. Nelson, who wrote in 1902 an analysis of Dow's *Wall Street Journal* editorials called *The A B C of Stock Speculation*.

After Dow's death, William Peter Hamilton succeeded him as editor of the *Wall Street Journal*. For over a quarter of a century, from 1902 until his death in 1929, Hamilton continued writing *Wall Street Journal* editorials using the tenets of Dow Theory. Hamilton also described the basic elements of this theory in his book *The Stock Market Barometer*, in 1922.

Alfred Cowles III (1937) performed the first formal test of the profitability of trading using the tenets of Dow Theory in 1934. Cowles was an early theoretician of the stock market and used statistical methods to determine if Hamilton could "beat the market." Cowles found that a portfolio based on Hamilton's theory lagged the return on a portfolio fully invested in a market index that Cowles had developed. (Cowles's index was a predecessor of the S&P 500.) Therefore, Cowles determined that Hamilton could not outperform the market and concluded that Dow Theory of market timing results in returns that lag the market. Cowles's study, considered a seminal piece in the statistical testing of market-timing strategies, provided a foundation for the Random Walk Hypothesis (RWH) and the Efficient Markets Hypothesis (EMH).

In recent years, however, researchers have reexamined Cowles's work using more sophisticated statistical techniques. In the August 1998 *Journal of Finance*, an article by Brown, Goetzmann, and Kumar demonstrated that, adjusted for risk (Hamilton was out of the market for a portion of his articles), Hamilton's timing strategies yield high Sharpe ratios and positive alphas for the period 1902 to 1929. In other words, contrary to Cowles's original study, Brown, Goetzmann, and Kumar conclude that Hamilton could time the market very well using Dow Theory. In addition, they found that when Hamilton's decisions were replicated in a neural network model of out-of-sample data from September 1930 through December 1997, Hamilton's methods still had validity. His methods worked especially well in sharp market declines and considerably reduced portfolio volatility.

After Hamilton's death, Robert Rhea further refined what had become known as Dow Theory. In 1932, Rhea wrote a book called *The Dow Theory: An Explanation of Its Development and an Attempt to Define Its Usefulness as an Aid to Speculation*. In this book, Rhea described Dow Theory in detail, using the articles by Hamilton, and formalized the tenets into a series of hypotheses and theorems that are outlined next.

Rhea presented three hypotheses:

1. The primary trend is inviolate.
2. The averages discount everything.
3. Dow Theory is not infallible.

The first of these hypotheses dealt with the notion of manipulation. Although Rhea believed that the secondary and the minor, day-to-day motion of the stock market averages could possibly be manipulated, he claimed that the primary trend is inviolate. The second hypothesis, that the averages discount everything, is because prices are the result of people acting on their knowledge, interpretation of information, and expectations. The third hypothesis is that Dow Theory is not infallible. Because of this, investment requires serious and impartial study.

BOX 2.1   SOME OF WILLIAM HAMILTON'S THOUGHTS ON THE STOCK MARKET AND THE DOW THEORY

The sum and tendency of the transactions in the Stock Exchange represent the sum of all Wall Street's knowledge of the past, immediate and remote, applied to the discounting of the future (Hamilton, 1922, p. 40).

The market is not saying what the condition of business is today. It is saying what that condition will be months ahead (Hamilton, 1922, p. 42).

The stock barometer [the Dow-Jones averages] is taking every conceivable thing into account, including that most fluid, inconsistent, and incalculable element, human nature itself. We cannot, therefore, expect the mechanical exactness of physical science (Hamilton, 1922, p. 152).

Let us keep in mind that Dow Theory is not a system devised for beating the speculative game, an infallible method of playing the market. The averages, indeed, must be read with a single heart. They become deceptive if and when the wish is father to the thought. We have all heard that when the neophyte meddles with the magician's wand, he is apt to raise the devil (Hamilton, 1922, p. 133).

These three hypotheses are similar to those of technical analysis today. They show how prescient Dow was and how universal and persistent his theories have been. As markets have become more efficient, there is some question about how much manipulation can and has occurred. Recent untruths by major corporations concerning their earnings have shown that the desire to manipulate still exists. Dow's tenet, however, stated that the primary direction of stock prices could not be manipulated and, therefore, should be the primary focus of all serious investors.

The concept that prices discount everything, including expectations, to the point that they are predictive of events is the most revolutionary of Dow's hypotheses. Until then, most investors looked at individual stock prices and studied what was available about individual companies. Dow believed that the averages of stocks foretold the shape of industry and were, thus, valuable in understanding the health of the economy.

Dow was under no illusion that he had found the magic formula for profit, nor were Hamilton or Rhea. Nevertheless, they did believe that by careful and unbiased study of the market averages, they could interpret, in general terms, the likelihood of the markets continuing or reversing in direction and thereby could anticipate similar turns in the economy. Their emphasis on study and lack of emotional reaction is still important today. Ignoring this point is one of the most widespread causes for investor failure.

■ Dow Theory Theorems

One of the theorems of Dow Theory is that the ideal market picture consists of an uptrend, top, downtrend, and bottom, interspersed with retracements and consolidations. Figure 2.1 shows what this ideal market picture would look like. This market picture, of course, is never seen in its ideal form. Consider Hamilton's quote, "A normal market is the kind that never really happens" (May 4, 1911, in Rhea, 1932; pg. 154). The purpose of the ideal market picture is to provide a generalized model of the stock market's price behavior over time. It is simple and resembles a harmonic without a constant period or amplitude.

From the modern standpoint of the EMH, this ideal picture is interesting because it presumes that prices oscillate over long periods based on the accumulated emotion of investors as well as the facts of the business cycle. Were market prices to duplicate the business cycle precisely, prices would not oscillate as widely as they do or lead the business cycle by as much as they do. Indeed, some theorists argue that the markets actually cause the business cycle, that confidence or lack of confidence from the markets translates into buying and selling of products (Szala and Holter, 2004). However, for Dow Theory, the picture of the ideal market remains the same regardless of cause.

A second theorem of Dow Theory is that economic rationale should be used to explain stock market action. Remember that Dow created both an industrial average and a railroad average. Although we have no record of Dow's precise reasoning for doing so, Rhea posited that Dow believed that industrial stocks represented the trend of industry profits and prospects and that railroad stocks represented railroads' profits and prospects. The profits and prospects for both of these sectors must be in accord with each other. For example, industry may be producing goods, but

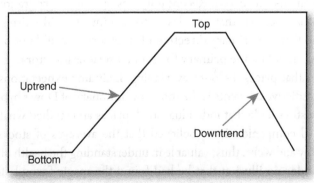

FIGURE 2.1 The Dow Theory Ideal Market Picture

if railroads are not shipping these goods, then industry must slow down. Goods produced must be shipped to the customer. Railroads must confirm that produced goods are being sold and delivered. Today, of course, the railroad average has been changed to the transportation average to represent airlines, truckers, and other means of shipping goods. Nevertheless, the economic rationale of goods produced and transported is still valid in the industrial sector of the economy. Where Dow's economic rationale differs from the present is in the service and technology sectors that have become larger in dollar volume than the industrial sector. Some analysts use representations of these newer sectors to form an economic rationale for stock market action.

A third theorem of Dow Theory is that prices trend. A **trend** is defined as the general direction in which something tends to move. Because we are talking about markets, that "something" is price.

BOX 2.2   SOME OF WILLIAM HAMILTON'S THOUGHTS ON TRENDS

. . . on the well-tested rule of reading the averages, a major bull swing continues so long as the rally from a secondary reaction establishes new high points in both averages. . . . (December 30, 1921, in Rhea, 1932; pg. 188)

An indication [of price trend] remains in force until it is cancelled by another. . . . (September 23, 1929, in Rhea, 1932; pg. 249)

A trend is the basic pattern of all prices. A trend can be upward, downward, or sideways. Obviously, a sideways trend is more difficult to profit from than an upward or downward trend. Technical analysts endeavor to forecast the direction of the market trend.

Dow Theory posited that there are three basic trends in price motion, each defined by time:

> There are three movements of the averages, all of which may be in progress at one and the same time. The first, and most important, is the primary trend: the broad upward or downward movements known as bull or bear markets, which may be of several years duration. The second, and most deceptive movement, is the secondary reaction: an important decline in a primary bull market or a rally in a primary bear market. These reactions usually last from three weeks to as many months. The third, and usually unimportant, movement is the daily fluctuation. (Rhea, 1932)

Figure 2.2 shows graphically how these three trends are interrelated. Let us look at each of these three types of trends—the primary, secondary, and minor—a bit more closely.

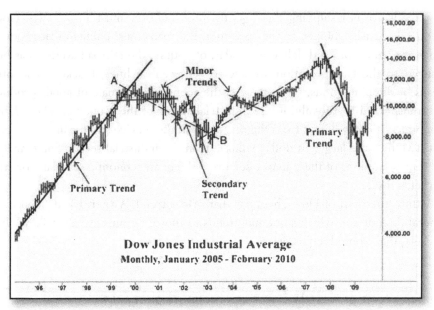

FIGURE 2.2 Dow Theory Three Trend Types (monthly)

The Primary Trend

> Correct determination of the primary movement (or trend) is the most important factor in successful speculation. There is no known method of forecasting the extent or duration of a primary movement. (Rhea, 1932)

The primary trend is the longest of the three trend types. It represents the overall, broad, long-term movement of security prices. The duration of this long-term trend can be several years. The primary trend may be an upward trend, which is known as a primary "bull" trend, or it may be a downward trend, referred to as a primary "bear" trend. The general long-run upward trend during the late 1990s in Figure 2.2 indicates a primary bull trend.

Primary bull markets are characterized by three separate phases. The first represents reviving confidence from the prior primary bear market; the second represents the response to increased corporate earnings; and the third is when speculation becomes dominant and prices rise on "hopes and expectations."

Primary bear markets are long downward price movements, interrupted by occasional rallies, that continue until prices have discounted the worst that is apt to occur. They, too, are characterized by three separate phases: first, abandonment of hopes upon which stocks were purchased; second, selling due to decreased earnings; and third, distress selling, regardless of value, by those who believe the worst is yet to come or who are forced to liquidate.

The Secondary Trend

> . . . a secondary reaction is considered to be an important decline in a bull market or advance in a bear market, usually lasting from three weeks to as many months, during which intervals the price movement generally retraces from 33 percent to 66 percent of the primary price change since the termination of the last preceding secondary reaction. (Rhea, 1932)

The secondary trend is an intermediate-term trend that runs counter to the primary trend. For example, during a several-year primary uptrend, prices may fall for a few weeks or a few months. During this secondary trend market decline, prices fall often, erasing 33% to 66% of the gain that has occurred since the completion of the previous secondary uptrend. Points A to B in Figure 2.2 represent a secondary downtrend.

Being able to anticipate or recognize secondary reactions increases profit capabilities by taking advantage of smaller market swings, but Dow believed this exercise was too dangerous. Because the primary trend and secondary trend reversal have similar characteristics, secondary reactions are often initially assumed as changes in primary trends or are mistakenly thought to be only reactions when the primary trend is changing.

The Minor Trend

> Inferences drawn from one day's movement of the averages are almost certain to be misleading and are of but little value except when "lines" are being formed. The day to day movement must be recorded and studied, however, because a series of charted daily movements always eventually develops into a pattern easily recognized as having a forecasting value. (Rhea, 1932)

> A line is two to three weeks of horizontal price movement in an average within a 5% range. It is usually a sign of accumulation or distribution, and a breakout above or below the range high or low respectively suggests a movement to continue in the same direction as the breakout. Movement from one average unconfirmed by the other average is generally not sustained. (Rhea, 1932)

> The portion of the Dow Theory which pertains to "lines" has proved to be so dependable as almost to deserve the designation of axiom instead of theorem. (September 23, 1929, in Rhea, 1932; pg. 249)

> The stock market is not logical in its movements from day to day. (1929, in Rhea, 1932; pg. 249)

Dow, Hamilton, and Rhea would likely be horrified at today's preoccupation with minute-to-minute "day trading" and would likely consider such activity too risky. (Based on the percentage of day traders who currently fail, they would be right.) Their observation essentially states that prices become more random and unpredictable as the time horizon shrinks. This is certainly true today as well and is one reason why, as during Dow's, Hamilton's, and Rhea's time, investors today should concentrate on longer-term time horizons and avoid the tempting traps in short-term trading.

Concept of Confirmation

> Dow always ignored a movement of one average which was not confirmed by the other, and experience since his death has shown the wisdom of that method of checking the reading of the averages. His theory was that a downward movement of secondary, and perhaps ultimately primary importance, was established when the new lows for both averages were under the low points of the preceding reaction. (June 25, 1928, in Rhea, 1932; pg. 238)

In line with the economic rationale for the use of the industrial and railroad averages as proxies for the economy and state of business, Dow Theory introduced a concept that also is important today, namely the concept of **confirmation**. Confirmation has taken new directions, which this book covers later, but in Rhea's time, confirmation was the consideration of the industrial and railroad averages together. "Conclusions based upon the movement of one average, unconfirmed by the other, are almost certain to prove misleading" (Rhea, 1932).

Confirmation in the Dow Theory comes when both the industrial and railroad averages reach new highs or new lows together on a daily closing basis. These new levels do not necessarily have to be reached at exactly the same time, but for a primary reversal, it is necessary that each average reverses direction and reaches new levels before the primary reversal can be recognized (see Figure 2.3). Confirmation, therefore, is the necessary means for recognizing in what direction the primary trend is headed. Failure to reach new levels during a secondary reaction is a warning that the primary trend may be reversing. For example, when there is a primary bull market, the failure of the averages to reach new highs during a secondary advance alerts the analyst that the primary trend may be reversing to a bear market. These are called **nonconfirmations**. In addition, if lower levels are reached during the secondary bear trend, it is an indication that the primary trend has changed from an upward bull trend to a downward bear trend. Thus, more extreme levels occurring during a secondary retracement in the opposite direction of the primary trend are evidence that the primary trend has changed direction. When confirmed by the other average, the technical analyst then has proof that the primary trend has reversed and can act accordingly.

Today, because the makeup of the economy is so different than in Dow's and Hamilton's time, with the advent of a wider base of industrial stocks and technology

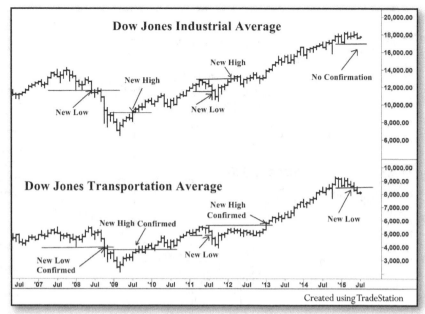

FIGURE 2.3 Dow Theory of "Confirmation"—Dow Jones Industrial Average and Dow Jones Transportation Average (monthly: June 2006–June 2015)

stocks, the usual method of confirming a primary trend is to use confirmation between the two indexes: Standard & Poor's 500 and the Russell 2000. The economic rationale is that the Standard & Poor's 500 represents the largest, most highly capitalized companies in the United States, and the Russell 2000 represents smaller companies with higher growth and usually a technological base. When these two indexes confirm each other, the primary trend is confirmed. Figure 2.4 shows the more modern application of Dow's theory of confirmation.

Importance of Volume

> Various meanings are ascribed to reductions in the volume of trading. One of the platitudes most constantly quoted in Wall Street is to the effect that one should never sell a dull market short. That advice is probably right oftener than it is wrong, but it is always wrong in an extended bear swing. In such a swing . . . the tendency is to become dull on rallies and active on declines. (Hamilton, May 21, 1909, as quoted in Rhea, 1932)

Although volume of transactions cannot signal a trend reversal, it is important as a secondary confirmation of trend. Excessively high market prices that are accompanied by less volume on rallies and more activity on declines usually suggest an overbought market (see Figure 2.5). Conversely, extremely low prices with dull declines and increased volume on rallies suggest an oversold market. "Bull markets terminate in a period of excessive activity and begin with comparatively light transactions" (Rhea, 1932).

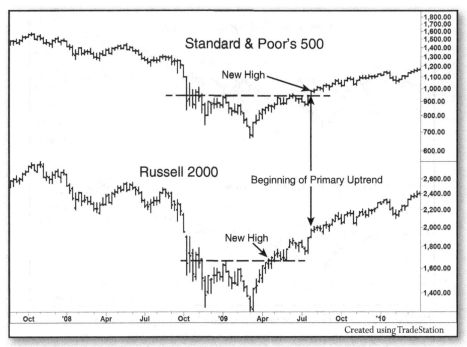

FIGURE 2.4 Confirmation between the Standard & Poor's 500 and the Russell 2000 (weekly: August 2007–March 2010)

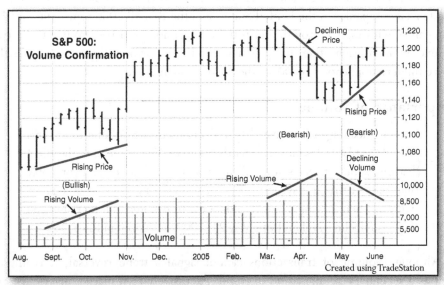

FIGURE 2.5 Volume Confirmation (weekly: August 2004–May 2005)

The originators of Dow Theory were quick, however, not to overstate the importance of volume. Although volume was considered, it was not a primary consideration. Price trend and confirmation overrode any consideration of volume.

> The volume is much less significant than is generally supposed. It is purely relative, and what would be a large volume in one state of the market supply might well be negligible in a greatly active market. (Hamilton, 1922, pg. 177)

■ Criticisms of the Dow Theory

Although Dow Theory forms the building blocks for modern-day technical analysis, this theory is not without criticisms. One of the criticisms is that following the theory will result in an investor acting after rather than before or at market tops and bottoms. With Dow Theory, there is an inevitable lag between the actual turn in the primary trend and the recognition of the change in trend. The theory does not recognize a turn until long after it has occurred and has been confirmed.

On the other hand, the theory, if properly interpreted, will recognize that primary trend change and will, thus, never allow a large loss. Dow's contention was that concentrating on any direction change of shorter duration than the primary trend increased the chances of having one's portfolio whittled away by high turnover, many errors in judgment, and increased transaction costs. Therefore, Dow Theory is biased toward late recognition of a change in trend to minimize the costs of wrongly identifying a change in trend.

A second criticism of Dow Theory is that the different trends are not strictly defined. Often the interpretation of price swings is difficult to assign to a specific trend type. Secondary trend beginnings often appear like primary trend beginnings, for example. This makes the determination of the primary trend unclear at times and can incite investment in the wrong direction.

Others, however, criticize Dow Theory for being too specific about the requirements needed to identify a change in trend. Requiring that only closing prices be used or that any break to a new level no matter how small is significant often places too much emphasis on a small change in price.

> . . . the Dow-Jones averages . . . have a discretion not shared by all prophets. They are not talking all the time. (December 17, 1925, in Rhea, 1932; pg. 224)

■ Conclusion

Although Charles Dow never formalized the Dow Theory, his work has formed the basis for modern-day technical analysis. Despite the many changes that have occurred in the securities markets over the past century, much of Dow's basic work and ideas remain pertinent today. Dow might be surprised at the analysis that more advanced tools and computer power allow, but his classic work provides the basic theory that these contemporary models build upon. Although the specific economic relationships that were valid in Dow's lifetime, such as the relationship between industrial stocks and railroad stocks, may need to be altered to represent today's economy, basic economic relationships such as these are still fundamental to market activity. Despite the fact that today's technical analyst can build sophisticated, complex mathematical models and run complicated computer tests of trading strategies, it is important to remember that a thorough grounding in the basics of market activity is necessary for any trading philosophy to stand the test of time and remain profitable.

■ References

Brown, Stephen J., William N. Goetzmann, and Alok Kumar. "The Dow Theory: William Peter Hamilton's Track Record Reconsidered." *Journal of Finance*, 53, no.4 (1998): 1311–1333.

Cowles III, Alfred and H. Jones. "Some A Posteriori Probabilities in Stock Market Action." *Econometrica* 5 (1937): 280–294.

Hamilton, W. *The Stock Market Barometer: A Study of Its Forecast Value Based on Charles H. Dow's Theory of the Price Movement, reprint of 1922 edition*. New York, NY: John Wiley & Sons, 1998.

Nelson, S. *The ABC of Stock Speculation, 1902*. Burlington, VT: Fraser Publishing Co., 1964 reprint.

Rhea, Robert. *The Dow Theory: An Explanation of Its Development of an Attempt to Define Its Usefulness as an Aid to Speculation*, reprint of 1932 Barron's Publishing edition by Fraser Publishing Co., Burlington, VT, 2002.

Szala, Ginger and James T. Holter. "Storm Warning! How Social Mood Drives Markets." *Futures* (November 2004).

CHAPTER 3

Introduction to Charts, Part 1

Julie Dahlquist, Ph.D., CMT
Professor of Professional Practice, Neeley School
of Business, Texas Christian University

Learning Objective Statements

- Explain how a technical analyst uses charts to summarize price action.
- Discuss the advantages of reviewing price information in chart format.
- Identify the four basic price points represented in charting.
- Describe how to construct line, bar, and candlestick charts.
- Identify the components of individual candles: real body and shadows.
- Review the information available in line, bar, and candlestick charts.
- Describe what is meant by "data interval."
- Define "range" as it applies to prices on a bar or candlestick chart.
- Define "fractal" and how it relates to chart construction.

■ A Brief History of Charting

Charts are the traditional tool of the technical analyst. Charts probably first came into use as an early form of record keeping. Consider a shop owner who was selling a commodity and wanted to record the selling price each time an item sold. The seller could write down $15.10, $15.00, $15.20, $15.10, $15.10, $15.20, $15.30, and so on as he sold the items. It would be much less time consuming simply to make a mark on a sheet of grid paper, as shown in Figure 3.1.

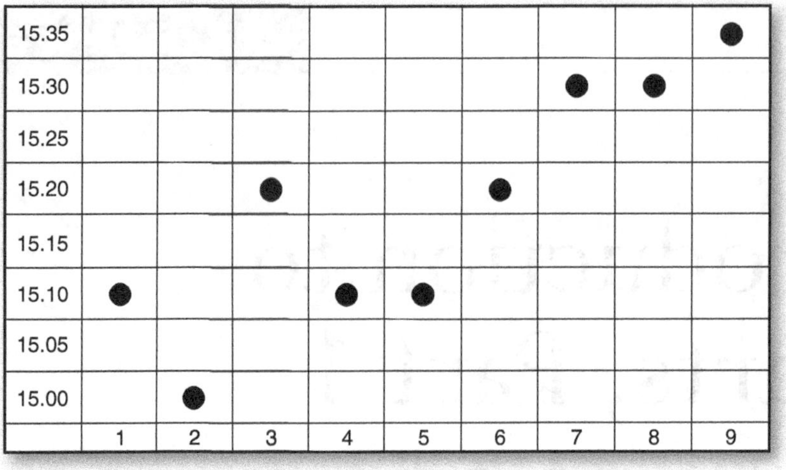

FIGURE 3.1 Recording of the Prices of a Seller's Sales

The seller realized that this chart was useful for more than just record keeping. The picture that developed when the information was recorded told a story. The seller could determine if the price was increasing, decreasing, or remaining the same. The seller's interest shifted from simply recorded data to the information contained in that data. The seller may have had a feeling that the price of the item in Figure 3.1 was increasing, but now that feeling was confirmed by a quick glance at the chart. The seller could not only see what had happened in the past; the seller could detect trends and forecast future price activity.

Likewise, traders on the floor of a stock exchange might have sensed when the demand for a stock was increasing. They would be aware that the price they were offering was higher than it had been, and they would notice that they were busier. Traders would feel a rush of energy and enthusiasm. Not only does a chart validate traders' intuition; it also gives them a way to communicate this dynamism to others who are not present at the exchange experiencing it for themselves.

Technical analysis is not so concerned with the record-keeping aspect of charting; technical analysis focuses on interpreting the information contained in the chart. Hand-drawn charts have become somewhat antiquated because computer-generated graphs are readily available. However, some analysts still produce hand-drawn charts. Many find that the activity of plotting the chart gives them more of a "feeling" for price action, allowing them to discern the fine points of price changes, trends, and patterns that they may not notice if they rely on computer-generated charts.

Remember that the price of a security at any particular point in time provides a summary of supply and demand for that security at that moment. A chart offers a concise price history and thus provides investors with essential information about market forces. Charts reflect market behavior that is subject to repetitive patterns, patterns that are discernible to experienced technicians. With experience, technicians also are able to spot periods of high and low price volatility, which is helpful in assessing risk.

Although charts are associated primarily with technical analysis, they can be useful tools for fundamental analysts. Long-term price moves of a security can be mundane, interspersed with brief periods of major price moves. Fundamental analysts viewing a chart can quickly spot the periods of major price moves, determine the fundamental conditions or events that were peculiar to those periods, and identify price-influencing factors.

Even if you will be relying on computer-generated charts, it is important to understand how those charts are constructed. In addition, spending a bit of time focusing on the mechanics of chart construction will help you gain perspective on the intuition that previous generations of technical analysts developed when they created their own charts by hand. Therefore, this chapter focuses on chart construction, with a discussion of line, bar, and candlestick charts.

■ Line Charts

Connecting the price data dots in Figure 3.1 produces a line chart, as shown in Figure 3.2. In early markets, when prices might have been reported only once or twice a day, the line chart was adequate to show the progression of price movement. Line charts still are valuable tools today.

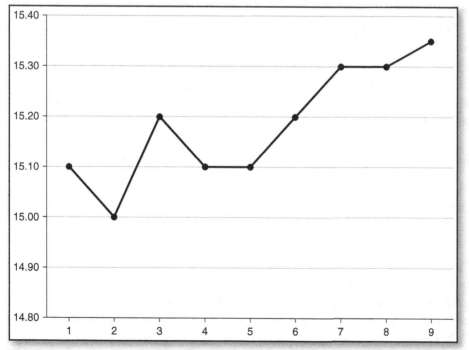

FIGURE 3.2 **Line Chart of the Prices of a Seller's Sales**

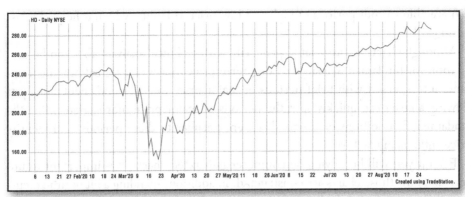

FIGURE 3.3   Home Depot Daily Line Chart

As securities were traded more frequently and prices changed throughout the day, price charting took two directions. One direction was to try to capture all the price data from each trade; this requires reliable access to a large amount of data. The other direction was to capture key prices at given time intervals, which is the focus of the charting methods in this chapter.

Figure 3.3 is an example of a line chart for Home Depot (HD) from January 2020–August 2020. This chart is created plotting only the daily closing price for the company. Although Home Depot stock is traded throughout the day, only one observation, the last trade of the day, is captured and plotted. Although this does not give a complete picture of what has happened to the price of Home Depot over that time period, it shows the underlying price trend.

This simple chart provides information about two variables: price and time. The price variable in Figure 3.3 is the daily closing price of HD, and it is placed on the vertical, or y, axis. Line charts are excellent ways to present time-series data, a sequence of observations presented in time order. Figure 3.3 represents discrete data observations: price, once per day. Later in this chapter we consider other time intervals for data representation.

To construct a daily line chart, only one data point is needed: the last price at which the stock traded each day. This makes data collection easy, but it ignores the fact that

BOX 3.1

The folk history of technical analysis offers several reasons for the importance placed on the closing price on many types of charts. Some reasons may no longer be valid in the modern era of digital data retrieval and electronic markets:

- Convenience—The ease of obtaining the closing price
- Consistency—A data point easily collected at the same time each trading day
- Capital requirements—The data point used to calculate traders' margin status and calls for capital
- Sentiment—The price at the time of day after which traders and investors had to "sleep with their positions" and were unable to modify them until the next day

the price may have been much different at other times during the day. The last price of the day is called the closing price (C). The regular trading day on the New York Stock Exchange (NYSE) ends at 4:00 p.m. Eastern time. The price that a stock sold for at 3:59 or 4:00 p.m. is not necessarily any more important than the price the stock traded for at 11:03 a.m. or 1:28 p.m., but it is the only price that is included on a line chart.

■ Bar Charts

Bar charts give analysts a way of displaying more information than line charts. In addition to the closing price, bar charts display at least two additional pieces of information: the highest price (H) at which the stock traded during the day and the lowest price (L) at which the stock traded during the day. A fourth piece of information, the opening price (O) for the day, is also displayed on some bar charts.

Figure 3.4 is an example of a daily bar chart. Price is plotted on the vertical axis, and time is measured on the horizontal axis, just as with line charts. Each trading day is represented by one vertical line, known as a bar. The length of the bar indicates the trading range for that day. The top of the bar records the highest price at which the security traded; the bottom of the bar records the lowest price at which the security traded that day. Thus, a longer bar represents a larger trading range, and a shorter bar indicates a smaller trading range. A small tick mark on the right side of the bar indicates the day's closing price. A small tick mark on the left side of the bar denotes the day's opening price, if that data is included on the bar chart. A bar chart displaying all four data points, as in Figure 3.4, is an example of an OHLC bar chart.

The second bar from the left in Figure 3.4 records trading information for Home Depot (HD) on August 3, 2020. The lowest point on the bar is 265.67, which is the lowest price at which HD traded on that day. The highest price at which HD traded that day was 268.58, represented by the highest point on the bar. The difference between these two prices, or 268.58 − 265.67 = 2.91, is known as the range. The left hash mark shows that the opening price was 266.73. The closing price for HD, 266.18, is recorded using the right hash mark.

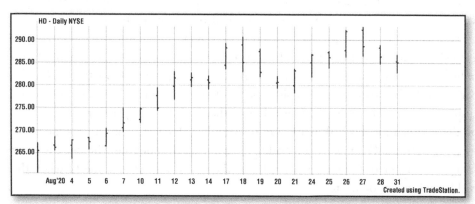

FIGURE 3.4   Daily Bar Chart, Home Depot, August 2020

■ Candlestick Charts

Candlestick charts are constructed in much the same way, and using the same data, as bar charts. This charting technique, which originated in Japan, was used as early as the mid-1600s to trade rice futures. Although it has been used for centuries in Asia, this type of charting did not become popular in the United States and European markets until the publication of Steve Nison's *Japanese Candlestick Charting Techniques*[1] in 1991. The popularity of candlestick charting has grown over the past few decades, and the method is available in virtually every technical analysis software package. Even Excel© provides an option for creating candlestick charts.

The candlestick records the three pieces of data that are always included in the bar chart: high, low, and close. The candlestick is more inclusive, however, in that it always includes the opening price, which is sometimes omitted from a bar chart. Price is plotted on the vertical axis and time is measured on the horizontal axis, just as they were for the line and bar charts we previously considered.

On a daily candlestick chart, each day of trading is represented by one candlestick, just as one day was represented by one bar on the bar chart. The low and high prices are plotted on a thin line, just as in the construction of a bar chart. The major difference between the bar chart and the candlestick chart is that a rectangle connects the opening and closing prices.

Horizontal marks are plotted at the opening and closing prices, and a rectangle is formed using these two horizontal marks. This rectangle is known as the *real body* of the candlestick. If the closing price is higher than the opening price, the real body is *white* or *open* (also known as *hollow* or *bullish*). If the closing price falls below the opening price, then the real body is shaded. These candlesticks are said to be *closed* or *black* (also known as *filled* or *bearish*).

Note: The terms "white body" and "black body" originated when most charts were created on white paper using black ink. Modern charting software often uses alternative color schemes or allows for custom colors, such as green for open (bullish) candles and red for closed (bearish) candles.

The thin line that shows the price range for the day forms the *shadows*. The shadow above the real body is called the *upper shadow*, and the shadow below the real body is known as the *lower shadow*. These shadows can also be referred to as *wicks*.

The candlestick chart for HD in Figure 3.5 contains the same price information as the bar chart in Figure 3.4. The difference between the two charting methods lies in how the relationship between the opening and closing prices is portrayed. On the bar chart, hash marks on the left side and right side of the bar record the O and C, respectively. Traders know the C was higher than O if the right hash mark is higher on the bar than the left hash mark. On the candlestick chart, a line across the bar is used for both the O and C, with shading or color used to denote whether the O or C was the higher of the two. Traders know the C was higher than the O when the real body is open, or white.

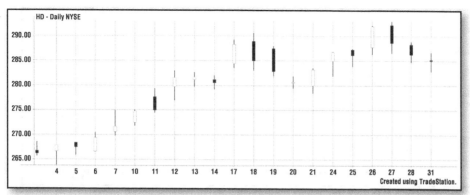

FIGURE 3.5 Daily Candlestick Chart, Home Depot, August 2020

Thus, candlestick charts provide a more nuanced display of four key prices for a trading day. Traders often find that it is easier and quicker to spot patterns and changes in trends on candlestick charts.

■ Data Intervals

The basic tools and principles of technical analysis can be applied to any time frame. Because of the fractal nature of trends—meaning that trends tend to act similarly over different periods of time—once analysts know the basic methods of charting, those methods can be applied in any time frame from very short-term intra-day trading to long-term investing. Investors and traders choose the length of time they are most interested in, given their time horizon, but the general principles of plotting the data and analyzing the information remain the same.

So far, we have looked at charts that summarize a trading day with one point, one bar, or one candle. However, the same types of charts can be constructed using different frequencies of data collection, such as 10 minutes, one hour, one week, or one month. "Data interval" is the term used here to refer to the units or intervals on the x-axis. The smaller the data interval, the more frequent the data collection and the more detailed but more cluttered the graph will be.

Consider Figures 3.6, 3.7, and 3.8. All show price data for Microsoft (MSFT) from August 2018 to August 2020. Figure 3.6 is constructed using the daily closing price of MSFT over the two-year date range. Figure 3.7 is based on the last price at the end of each trading week. Figure 3.8 is constructed using the last price at the end of each month. All three charts tell the same general story about MSFT over the two-year date range—the stock price more than doubled from about $100 per share in August 2018 to more than $200 per share in August 2020. Figure 3.6 provides more detail of exactly how the price got to that point than do Figures 3.7 and 3.8.

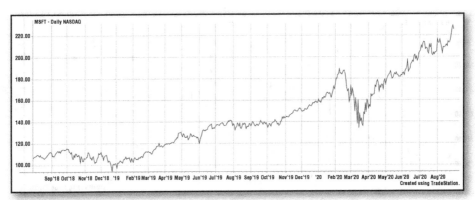

FIGURE 3.6   MSFT Daily, August 2018–August 2020

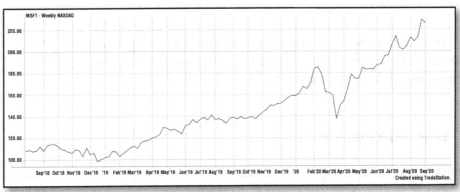

FIGURE 3.7   MSFT Weekly, August 2018–August 2020

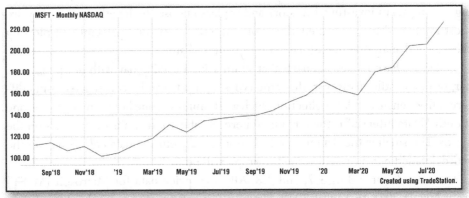

FIGURE 3.8   MSFT Monthly August 2018–August 2020

Line charts, such as those in Figures 3.6, 3.7, and 3.8, are especially useful when studying long-term trends. They provide a simple, concise way to view summary statistics. Analysts who are looking at the long-term trend of MSFT, for example, are concerned about the general direction of price movement over the past several years, not whether the stock opened higher than it closed on any particular day.

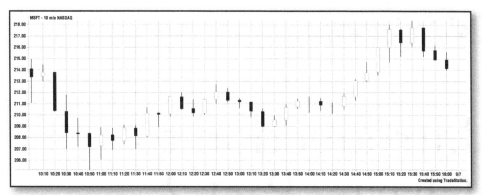

FIGURE 3.9   MSFT, September 4, 10-Minute Candlestick Chart

Although investors will be interested in the picture of the long-term trend of price movement for a stock such as MSFT, provided in Figure 3.8, day traders will be interested in the price movement throughout a particular day. These traders can use the same techniques discussed earlier to construct a line, bar, or candlestick chart to represent the price data with a smaller data interval.

Figure 3.9 shows a candlestick chart for MSFT constructed with each bar representing a 10-minute data interval. The real body of each candle shows the price at the beginning (open) and the end (close) of the 10-minute interval. The shadows, or wicks, of the candle show the range during those 10 minutes.

During a regular 6½ hour trading day on the NYSE, a 10-minute bar chart will produce 39 candles, each with four pieces of data, for a total of 156 price points. A chart comprised of daily candles would contain only four pieces of information: the same opening price as the first 10-minute candle of the day, the same closing price as the last 10-minute candle of the day, the lowest price that occurred at any point in the day, and the highest price that occurred at any time during the day.

CHAPTER 4

Introduction to Charts, Part 2

Julie Dahlquist, Ph.D., CMT
Professor of Professional Practice, Neeley School
of Business, Texas Christian University

Learning Objective Statements

- Identify the variables plotted on the axes in a conventional price chart
- Explain the differences between arithmetic and logarithmic scales and their uses
- Describe typical methods for displaying volume in a price chart
- Discuss volume as an alternative to time on the x-axis of a chart

In the previous chapter we looked at the basic construction of three types of charts: line charts, bar charts, and candlestick charts. The line, bar, and candlestick charts all record time series data with price on the vertical axis and time on the horizontal axis. In this chapter, we continue our study of these three types of charts, taking a closer look at when each of these charts might be used. In addition, we examine using a variable other than time for the x-axis.

■ Multi-line Charts

We begin by looking a little more closely at the line chart. Because line charts provide summary statistics, they are especially useful when information about several different time series is being plotted in the same graph. Viewing a line chart gives an analyst a quick, concise picture of the data being discussed. Consider Figure 4-1. By plotting three measures of inflation, the consumer price index (CPI), the producer price index (PPI), and the GDP deflator in the same chart, the viewer can quickly compare and contrast the three measures. For this reason, line charts are often used

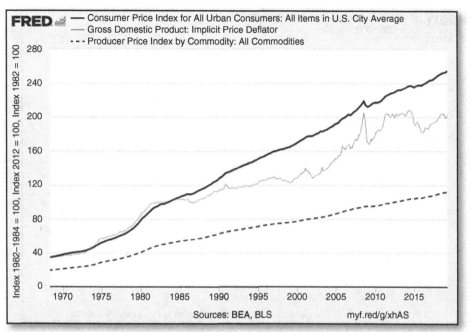

FIGURE 4-1 Line Graph of CPI, PPI, and GDP deflator

by economists to depict long-term trends in macroeconomic variables and by the media to convey simple relationships between variables in news articles.

Multiple Y-axes

Sometimes an analyst is interested in comparing the long-term trend of two variables that are of much different absolute values. For example, the Dow Jones Industrial Average (DJIA) has been above 20,000 in 2020, and the S&P 500 has been below 3,900 during the same time period. Attempting to plot these two variables on the same y-axis would result in a chart that is difficult to read. Because the level of the DJIA is expressed in terms more than five times greater than the level of the S&P 500, the S&P 500 would appear at the bottom of the graph and the DJIA would be plotted at the top of the graph with a lot of blank space in between. Because of the scaling of the graph, it would be difficult to detect moves in the S&P 500—it would appear to be an almost straight line. Because the y-axis scale would have to reach to 30,000, even a doubling of the S&P 500 would appear as a small move relative to the 30,000 unit size of the y-axis.

Using two different vertical scales, creating both a left y-axis and a right y-axis, allows for two variables with much different values to be plotted in the same graph, as is shown in Figure 4-2. The left y-axis begins at 10,000 and ends at 30,000 to measure the DJIA; horizontal lines mark 2,000-point increments. The right y-axis ranges from 900 to 3900 to measure the S&P 500; the horizontal lines mark 300-point increments when plotting the S&P 500. Time is still measured along the x-axis.

The DJIA and the S&P 500 plotted in Figure 4-2 tell similar stories of the U.S. stock market over the past decade. They both show a stock market that is higher in

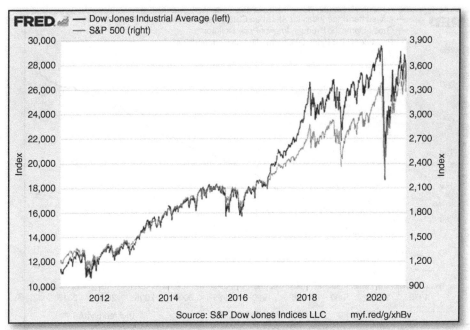

FIGURE 4-2 Line Chart of DJIA (Left Y-Axis) and S&P 500 (Right Y-Axis)

2020 than it was in 2011. They both show strong rises in 2017 and 2019, and they both record the tremendous downturn in the market in the spring of 2020 as COVID-19 hit. This type of chart allows the analyst to tell if two variables are generally moving in tandem and to spot periods of strength and weakness. However, one must be careful when looking at this type of chart and remember that the scaling is different. Notice that the left y-axis in Figure 4-2 ranges from 10,000 to 30,000, allowing for the value to increase threefold. However, the right y-axis ranges from 900 to 3900, allowing for more than a fourfold increase in the variable being measured on the right axis.

■ Vertical Scale

Because line charts are often used to track long-run trends in data, careful attention must be paid to the scaling on the vertical axis.

Consider the long-term line chart in Figure 4-3 which shows Apple's (AAPL) stock price since 2002. At first glance it is clear that someone who purchased AAPL in 2002 and held the stock until 2020 would experience significant gains. In fact, someone who invested $.25 in AAPL stock in late 2002 would have over $120 by late 2020. This chart shows a large dollar gain in AAPL stock during 2020, with a steeper slope of the line chart than in the previous years.

Arithmetic Scale

The y-axis in Figure 4-3 is an arithmetic (or linear) scale. The price units along the vertical axis are of the same price intervals. For example, the vertical plot distance

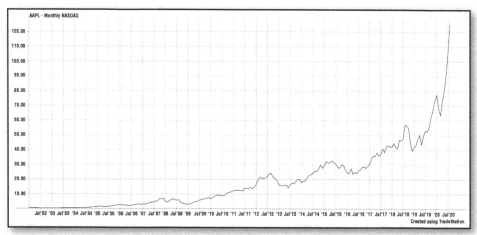

FIGURE 4-3 Long-term Chart with Arithmetic Scale, AAPL Monthly

of a change from $10 to $20 is the same as the plot distance from $50 to $60 or from $100 to $110. Using regular grid paper, each vertical box represents the same dollar amount. The arithmetic scale is the scale used most often for the vertical axis but when longer-term price movements are examined, adjustments to the vertical scale are sometimes necessary.

Compare Figure 4-3 to Figure 4-4. Both are line charts plotting AAPL from 2002 to 2020. Notice how both tell the same story of AAPL increasing in value from about $.25 per share in 2002 to $120 per share by 2020. During the 2002–2003 time period, when the price per share was about $.25, a $.25 increase would mean a doubling of price to $.50, and an investor would double her money. In 2002, a $.25 change in AAPL stock price was significant. Because the vertical axis spans more than $120, a $.25 move in price is a very small vertical change in Figure 4-3, making it difficult to discern the importance of a $.25 move in the early years represented on the graph.

By 2020, when AAPL was over $100 per share, a $.25 change in AAPL represented less than a 0.25% change and was not significant. However, on the arithmetic chart, a $.25 move is recorded at the same vertical difference when the stock price is $.50 as when it is $100.

Logarithmic Scale

Not only does the arithmetic chart make it difficult to perceive the significance of price moves at the lower price levels recorded on the chart, but it can also over-emphasize moves at the higher prices on the chart. A quick glance at Figure 4-3 shows an impressive price move from $80 to $120 per share in 2020; it appears as the steepest, most important price gain in the chart. However, in percentage terms, which is what determines the returns to an investor, this 50% gain in price is the same percentage gain that occurred when price rose from $50 to $75 per share in 2019. It is also the same percentage gain as the 50% gain that occurred in 2009 when

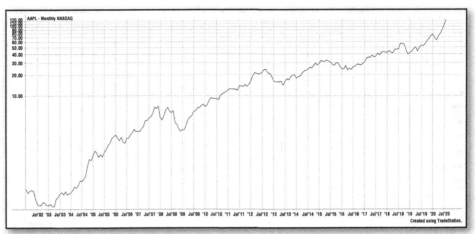

FIGURE 4-4   Long-term Chart with Logarithmic Scale, AAPL Monthly

the price went from $5 to $7.50 per share. In each of those time periods, an investor who began with $1000 invested would have ended with $1500.

The dollar amount of a 50% gain looks much more impressive on an arithmetically scaled chart when a stock is trading at a higher per share price than at a lower per share price. Don't let this steep slope deceive you. A logarithmic scale, which measures percentage change on the vertical axis, addresses this issue. Look at Figure 4-4. In this logarithmically scaled graph, the vertical distance between $1 and $2 is the same as the vertical distance between $11 and $22. The same vertical rise always represents a 100% increase in price, rather than a particular dollar increase in price as in Figure 4-3. As a rule of thumb, long-term charts that represent data exceeding a few years should be plotted on logarithmic scales. Also, many analysts find that when a graph is depicting a security with price movements of more than 20%, a logarithmic scale is more useful than an arithmetic scale.

■ Volume

The line, bar, and candlestick charts all portray time on the horizontal axis and price on the vertical axis, whether it is an arithmetic or logarithmic scale. Price is always the most important variable the analyst is considering, so it is always at the forefront of chart construction. However, charting techniques allow the analyst to consider more than just how price moves through time. Another common variable portrayed on a chart is volume. Volume is the number of shares or contracts traded during a specified data interval.

Volume is commonly portrayed at the bottom of the price chart, with its own scale, using a vertical bar to represent the total volume for each interval. Consider the candlestick chart in Figure 4-5 which depicts Twitter (TWTR) for the month of July 2020. The histogram at the bottom of the chart shows that, about 20,000,000 shares of TWTR changed hands on many days during the month. However, a couple

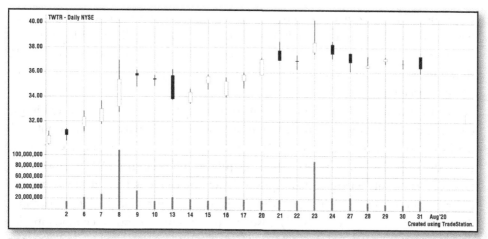

FIGURE 4-5 Candlestick Chart with Volume, TWTR Daily

of days in the month jump out. On July 8, volume exceeded 100,000,000 shares. July 23 also saw extremely heavy trading with approximately 90,000,000 shares changing hands.

Equivolume

In Figure 4-5, each candle represents one day of trading, with each progression along the horizontal axis representing one day. Each candlestick is the same width. Figure 4-6 displays the data for TWTR in a different manner to include volume in the same bar as the price information. This is known as an equivolume chart.

A rectangle is constructed for each day, with the height of the rectangle depicting the price range and the width of the rectangle depicting the volume. On July 8, for example, the price of TWTR had a range exceeding $4, from a low of $32.73 to a high of $36.98, leading to a tall bar. It also was a day in which volume was about five

FIGURE 4-6 Equivolume for TWTR

times the volume of other days shown in the chart; this heavy volume leads to a wide bar for the day. The rectangle for July 9 is smaller. It is not as tall, indicating a smaller trading range for the day, and narrower, indicating lower volume for the day. July 10 shows an even smaller rectangle. Then the rectangle for July 13 is taller, representing a larger price range.

The direction of the price movement from open to close is not recorded in the equivolume chart as it is in the color of a candlestick or with left and right hash marks on bar charts. Instead, color is used to compare the close one day with the close the previous day. The black box on July 9 indicates that TWTR closed at a higher level on July 9 than it did on July 8. Now, you can look back at July 8 and you can rule out any close higher than the top of the July 9 rectangle, but you cannot determine exactly where the stock closed on July 8, nor can you determine intraday directional movement on July 9. The rectangle for July 10 is gray which indicates the stock closed at a lower level on July 10 than it did on July 9; the only additional information that provides is that the stock could not have closed at the very bottom of the rectangle on July 9. Sometimes you can deduce ranges for where a closing price could have been by comparing the coloring of several successive rectangles, but this is time-consuming, cumbersome, and does not always result in useful information.

Like the line, bar, and candlestick charts we have considered before, the equivolume chart plots price on the vertical axis and time on the horizontal axis. However, time is not scaled in trading days or other units of time on the horizontal axis. Instead of a particular distance on the horizontal axis measuring a certain time increment, the distance is measuring volume. Therefore, on days with heavy volume, plotting moves a great distance on the horizontal axis. If the next few days see low volume, then it could be several days later before the same horizontal distance is travelled.

Volume-scaled Charts, or Volume Bars

Figure 4-7 presents an alternative charting technique for incorporating volume into a chart. This method creates one bar or candlestick for a particular number of shares or contracts, rather than for a set time frame. That is, the data interval is a unit of volume rather than a unit of time. The chart in Figure 4-7 uses 1,000,000 shares of volume as the interval for each candlestick. Instead of representing a day, or some other fixed period of time, each candlestick shows the range of prices while 1,000,000 shares of TWTR traded. If an extremely large number of shares of TWTR are traded in one day, as happened on July 8, then many candlesticks will be constructed that day. On days with lighter trading volume, such as July 9, fewer candlesticks are drawn. Like all the charts we have considered, price is measured on the vertical axis; but now volume, rather than time, determines the horizontal axis. New trading days can be determined only by notations along the bottom of the chart.

Volume-scaled charts and equivolume charts are similar in that a day with heavy trading volume will take up more horizontal space in the chart. Spotting extremely heavy trading intervals and extremely light trading intervals can be done quickly with

FIGURE 4-7   TWTR 1,000,000-Share Volume-Scaled Bars

the equivolume charts; the analyst simply looks for wide and narrow rectangles, respectively. The equivolume chart is designed to visually overweight the price range on heavy trading days.

Volume-scaled charts or volume bars, the charting method in Figure 4-7, places emphasis more on the progression of price over a unit of volume. A price range of $1 for 1,000,000 shares is visually the same in this chart whether it took one hour, one day, or several days for 1,000,000 shares to be traded. While the equivolume chart emphasizes heavy volume days, it does not distinguish whether price moves or trading volume were concentrated during particular parts of the day or occurred evenly throughout the day. Remember that the equivolume chart showed that TWTR's price ranged from $32.78 to $36.98 on July 8, but the analyst cannot tell if the price moved quickly during the day, or even where the price ended that day. The volume-scaled chart in Figure 4-7 shows that a few million shares of TWTR sold around the $33 price early in the trading day, but price quickly rose to over $35 per share and much of the volume that day was at a price over $35.

■ Conclusion

We have viewed a variety of charts in this and the previous chapter. While each has its own nuances, all the methods are ultimately about recording and summarizing price data in a format that makes analyzing the information easier. Examine the candlestick chart in Figure 4-8 and notice the type of information that is quickly discernable.

The chart is a daily candlestick chart, with daily volume displayed beneath the candlesticks, of Boeing (BA) for the month of September 2020. You can quickly see that price for the month ranged from about $145 to $180, that much of the time the price was between $160 and $170, and that the stock ended the month lower than where it began the month.

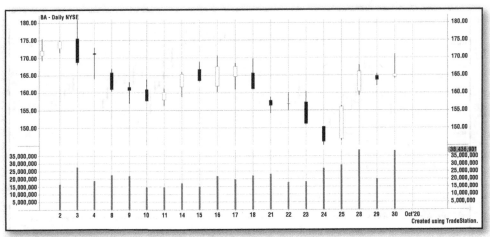

FIGURE 4-8 Daily Candlestick Chart for BA

Let's focus more specifically on the last week of the month and what information we can glean from the last five candlesticks. The September 24 candlestick has a closed real body, so we know that the stock opened at the price associated with the top of the real body and then closed at the price associated with the bottom of the real body. This candlestick has no upper shadow, which indicates the stock never traded higher than its open throughout the day. The small lower shadow indicates that the stock closed near its low for the day.

The following day shows different price behavior. The open real body indicates the stock closed higher than it opened. The short lower and upper shadows indicate that the stock did not trade much lower than its open throughout the day nor did it trade much higher than its eventual close. The taller candle on September 25 indicates a larger trading range than the previous day.

The next day we see that the stock opens at a price above the previous trading day and remains above the previous day's price the entire day. The lowest point of the lower shadow on September 28 is higher than the highest point of the upper shadow of the previous day's candle. We can also see that there was above average trading volume on September 28.

September 29 was characterized by both lower volume and a smaller price range. The entire price range for September 29 was within the price movement of the day before. The price closed a little bit lower than it opened, as indicated by the small, dark real body. Then, on September 30, volume was again heavy. The stock opened at a price near the previous day's closing price. Although the price surpassed $170 during the day, as indicated by the tall upper shadow, that price gain was not sustained throughout the day, with the price falling to close not much above the opening price.

With a simple chart we are able, visually, to discern a lot of information. The human eye can relay this information to the brain for processing much more quickly when it is presented in picture form rather than in paragraphs full of words or spreadsheets full of dates and data. The technical analyst gathers this information, processes it, and analyzes it, detecting patterns and noticing unusual price behavior that may be telling a story of things to come. Data visualization like this can also be the starting point for finding repeated patterns and events in price, time and volume that can then be tested and traded programmatically.

We have considered several options for plotting price information on a chart. The best method for a technician to use will depend on the security being traded and the investment horizon, as well as the technician's investment style. Remember that the chart is a tool. It is not the creation of the chart that is the end goal; we create the chart to organize market data so that it can be interpreted and analyzed. As we look at trendlines and the visual recognition of patterns in upcoming chapters, we will see how the issues of scaling on the x- and y-axes impact our analysis.

CHARTS, TRENDS, AND PATTERNS

History doesn't repeat itself, but it often rhymes.

—Attributed to Mark Twain

This section is a deep dive into examining and interpreting price action as it appears and is interpreted in a technician's charts. The first principle is the identification of the trend, critical price levels, and related tools such as trendlines and support and resistance. Finding these levels, projecting them forward, and managing entries and exits around them is a primary skill for the technician. Moving averages, arguably the most pervasive calculations in the world of technical analysis, are covered in their myriad variations and extensions.

The ensuing discussion of chart patterns respects their historical interpretations while also bringing them under the scientist's microscope. Instead of simply accepting the traditional notions, the text explains how computers allow for studies that provide insights into the validity of chart patterns. (Readers may want to reread the chapters on chart patterns after studying Section V on Behavioral Finance.)

Indicators such as momentum oscillators, used to better understand price action, are also covered in this section, along with volume and volume-based indicators. These are introduced for their value in confirming or denying the apparent trend.

Two additional methods for organizing price data into charts are also covered here: candlestick charting and point-and-figure charting. Candlesticks bring an additional price point to the customary bar chart and thereby open additional, and important, areas of analysis. Point-and-figure charts remove time from the *x*-axis of the chart and are instead built based on reversals in price. Both these approaches have long and storied histories and remain among the modern technician's techniques.

CHAPTER 5

Trends—The Basics

From Charles D. Kirkpatrick II and Julie R. Dahlquist, *Technical Analysis: The Complete Resource for Financial Market Technicians*, 3rd Edition (Old Tappan, New Jersey: Pearson Education, Inc., 2016), Chapter 12.

Learning Objective Statements

- Explain why trend identification is important to achieve profits
- Recognize an uptrend, a downtrend, and a trading range
- Describe the concept of support and resistance, and the underlying psychology
- Identify trends using most common methods
- Recall how significant reversal points are identified
- List general rules for trendlines

We are now entering into the more controversial aspects of technical analysis: the analysis of trends, and the analysis of patterns. This is the "fuzzy" aspect of technical analysis. Because the observations or rules are not specific, they discourage most students very quickly. Rules in technical analysis come from many observations by many traders and investors. In general, the rules have remained unchanged since Dow's time, and in reading some of the old masters back in the 1930s, one sees the same observations today. The advent of the computer has sped the process and has often eliminated rules that are quantifiable but turn out to be unprofitable. However, the basics remain essentially the same. The markets have near, intermediate, and long-term trends. Patterns still form in much the same manner as 50 or 100 years ago, and analysts interpret them in the same manner as in the past. The details may be different, and perhaps the methods of profiting depend on various trade-offs between risk and reward, but still the analyst must use the rules and decide on the entry and exit points. The difficulty of profiting from technical analysis is not with the rules themselves but with their application.

It is important to remember that the observations and statements we make derive from our observations and those of other practitioners of technical analysis. Most trends and patterns are not mechanical methods that can be easily programmed and tested on computers. Generally, they take long periods of practice to be fully utilized. One of the major criticisms of technical analysis is that it has yet to be thoroughly computerized and tested. Numerous relationships have been tested in the past but then break down as the future unfolds. The only constants, it seems, are that trends occur and that they are the source of profit when recognized and properly used.

All analysts occasionally make statements that appear to be fact, but in many cases, they are statements based on subjective observations and should never be blindly relied upon without a thorough investigation. Our discussion of trend, support and resistance, and pattern nuances will show where they can be in error or where interpretation can be particularly difficult. Rules have developed over the years that will help with interpretation. Nevertheless, the student, when he can, should test and experiment. Nothing in technical analysis, or any other investment analysis approach, is foolproof. Indeed, it is surprising how much money is invested using fundamental and technical theories that have not been tested or, when they have, have proven to be unprofitable. Most professionals, who have spent their lifetime in the study and practice of technical analysis, will assert, "There is no easy, magic formula for wealth!" Do not, therefore, expect the following observations and rules to be an easy means to profit. Study, have patience, and study some more. We suggest that the student trade on paper, and finally with small amounts of money. There is no need to rush. The markets are always there.

■ Trend—The Key to Profits

Remember that profit with minimum capital risk in the securities markets is the sole objective, and technical analysis is an effective way to profit as well as to control risk. The key to profiting in the securities market is to follow these three steps:

1. Determine, with minimum risk of error, when a trend has begun, at its earliest time and price.
2. Select and enter a position in the trend that is appropriate to the existing trend, regardless of direction (that is, trade with the trend—long in upward trends and short or in cash in downward trends).
3. Close those positions when the trend is ending.

Trending is simple in concept, but it is difficult in practice. Almost all successful mechanical trading systems that have made millions for their investors have been based on the simple concept of jumping on a trend and riding it to its inevitable end.

The principal caveat, however, in technical analysis, as mentioned previously, is that although the trend concept is easy to understand, its application is difficult largely because the determination of trend and trend reversal is, in many instances, a subjective decision that depends on one's skill and experience in the securities markets and one's ability to control one's own emotions. Practice and mental anguish are the background of any successful technical analyst. The most expensive education in the world is likely the money lost in incorrect, sloppy, and undisciplined decisions. All market participants make mistakes, but the regimented professionals correct theirs quickly.

■ Trend Terminology

Trends define a direction in prices. When we refer to a trend, we describe a directional trend, one of rising or falling prices from which a profit can be generated with a trend-following method. We refer to a sideways trend as a **trading range** or **neutral** area. These are the recognized terms for describing different types of trends. Trend-following techniques work poorly in nontrending markets. Most technicians prefer to use price oscillators and trade from outer bound of the range to the opposite bound when dealing with such patterns.

By that, we mean that when we discuss trends per se, we assume an upward trend (an uptrend). In most cases, the description and rules of a downtrend are exactly opposite from those of an uptrend. It does not make sense to duplicate every statement for both trend directions. Likewise, when we discuss support and resistance, we discuss support and make the assumption, unless otherwise noted, that resistance is the exact opposite but in an opposing direction. We do this for readability and because most investors prefer to look at rising prices anyway, even though there is no rational reason for doing so.

■ Basis of Trend Analysis—Dow Theory

Charles Dow was one of the first of the modern technicians to write about the fact that stock market prices trade in trends. Virtually all items that trade in free, liquid markets trade in trends. As noted by Dow, investors or traders must concentrate on the time horizon most favorable to their circumstances.

Trends are fractal in that their behavior is the same regardless of the period. Minute-to-minute trends behave exactly like day-to-day trends with only minor differences because of the understandable variation in liquidity over the shorter periods. Dow suggested there were three principal time horizons—the primary, the intermediate, and the minor—that he likened to tides, waves, and ripples. In fact, there are considerably more trend periods. Dow focused on the first two because he apparently believed no one could analyze the ripples. Today, some technicians recognize considerably more trends than Dow observed, but then he did not have the advantage of a computer that could track prices trade by trade.

Dow's final, and perhaps most important, observation was that, by their very nature, **trends tend to continue rather than reverse**. If it were otherwise, first, there would not be a trend, and second, the trend could not be used for profit. This seems like a silly and perhaps too obvious statement, but it underlies almost everything the technician assumes when looking for the beginning or end of trends. It also vexes the academic theoretician who believes that price changes are random.

Any particular trend is influenced by its next larger and next smaller trend. For example, in Figure 5.1, we can see a well-defined uptrend in the stock of AAPL (Apple Computer). It is not a straight line upward, however. Within the rising trend are many smaller trends, both down and up, and if we look more closely, there are even smaller down- and uptrends within these. This is the fractal nature of trends. Notice also that the next set of trends below the long uptrend have larger rises and smaller declines. This is the effect the larger trend is having on the smaller trends. It is why the analyst, when studying any particular length trend, must be aware of the next longer and shorter trend directions. The longer trends will influence the strength of the trend of interest, and the shorter trends will often give early signs of turning in the longer. By definition, short-term trends reverse before medium-term, and medium-term trends reverse before long-term.

FIGURE 5.1 Large and Small Trend (AAPL Apple Computer, daily: August 8, 2014–May 29, 2015)

■ How Does Investor Psychology Impact Trends?

As we know from basic economics, supply and demand establishes the price of any good. It is no different in the securities markets. Supply and demand, when sellers and buyers agree on a trade, determines prices. What does price, and especially price change, tell us? Presumably, if a substantial number of transactions occur at one price, the price is telling us that supply and demand are in a temporary equilibrium and that both buyers and sellers are satisfied. Of course, in the financial markets, long-term equilibrium is rarely reached. Prices constantly change, if only by miniscule amounts, as they move *toward* a theoretical equilibrium. They can oscillate in small increments or large; they can go up or down; or they can do both. Whatever the price movement, it is ultimately determined by the expectations and power of the buyers and sellers. If broad expectations are for a higher price in the future but with little or no capital to act, prices will remain as they are or even decline. Of course, expectations change, as does the power to act. Nothing is perfectly stable or constant in the markets.

When prices travel in a trend, called **trending**, they remain headed in one direction, and they tell us that there is an imbalance of demand and supply. Some will incorrectly say that there are more buyers than sellers or vice versa. However, in every transaction, there are an equal number of shares transacted, and, thus, there is always temporary equilibrium between buyers and sellers at that instant in time. What makes a trend is the power of the buyers or sellers—do they have enough stock or money?—and the aggressiveness or anxiousness of buyers and sellers—do they have specific information or deductions, rational or irrational, or are emotions of fear or greed propelling their action?

We know from behavioral studies that, psychologically, a positive feedback mechanism in our minds tends collectively to sustain a trend. In an uptrend, for example, buyers who have profited tend to continue being buyers, and new buyers, seeing what they have missed, also buy. The price trend continues upward. Eventually, over a longer period, prices revert to some kind of mean or value, but meanwhile, they trend up, down, or sideways. If, for example, prices are gradually rising, then buyers must have stronger positive expectations and be willing and able to place more money in the security. Contrarily, if prices are declining, sellers must have stronger negative expectations and larger positions to sell. The price trend, thus, tells us the amount of power, aggressiveness, and anxiousness there is in the marketplace to buy or sell each security. To the technical analyst, the basis for the expectations—and there are many—as well as the source of power, money, or stock, is largely irrelevant. The anticipating and "riding" a trend in prices, as long as it continues, is the way the technician profits.

■ How Is the Trend Determined?

Of course, the trend is never a straight line. Then it would be too easy to tell that it had reversed. Instead, the **trend is a direction rather than a line**. Many doubting participants often accompany this direction. Sometimes, it can be arbitrageurs who bet against the trend or who are merely trading the spread. More likely, it is investors or traders running out of money or stock or just holding back for a little while, hoping that the price will retrace back toward their orders. In other words, the security price oscillates back and forth in smaller trends along its travel in the larger trend. This makes determining when that larger trend is reversing a difficult decision because any signs of reversal may only be for smaller trends within the larger trend. Additionally, securities occasionally "rest" during a trend and move sideways as the earlier rise or fall is "digested" by all the different players. The psychology of what causes these spurts, stops, and retracements is an interesting study by itself, but again it is irrelevant for our present discussion. We simply want to know what our trend of interest is and whether there are signs of it ending or changing direction.

Peaks and Troughs

What is the simplest way to look at prices and determine the trend? The easiest is to look for peaks and troughs within a series of price oscillations. If the peaks tend to be higher than the earlier peaks, and the troughs tend to be higher than the previous troughs, the trend must be upward. As you see in Figure 5.2, it is that simple. If peaks and troughs are lower than previously, the trend must be downward. If the peaks and troughs are scattered, the trend is undeterminable, and if the peaks and troughs occur at the same relative levels, the trend must be a trading range.

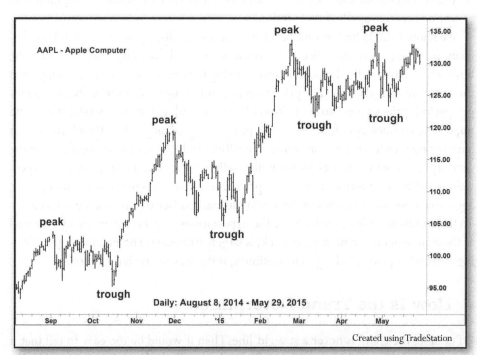

FIGURE 5.2 Peaks and Troughs used to Determine Trend (AAPL daily: August 8, 2014–May 29, 2015)

It is much easier to look at price trends on a chart. Most technicians use either bar or candlestick charts to draw lines representing trends. There are many ways to do this that are discussed later in the chapter. For now, let us begin with discussing sideways trends because they display very clearly an important technical concept called **support** and **resistance**.

■ Determining a Trading Range

Trading ranges (or sideways trends) occur when peaks and troughs appear roughly at similar levels (see Figure 5.3). The peaks cluster at a certain price level, and the troughs cluster at a certain price level below the peaks. The configuration usually occurs after a larger trend has come to a temporary halt. A trading range also is called a **consolidation** or **congestion area** or a **rectangle formation**. Charles Dow called small lateral patterns a **line formation**, and using it in the Dow Jones Averages had specific rules by which the averages had to abide for that designation. William Hamilton, Dow's successor editor at the *Wall Street Journal*, thought the line formation was the only price formation with any predictive power.

What Is Support and Resistance?

When prices have been rising and then reverse downward, the highest point in the rise, the peak, is referred to as a **resistance point**, a level at which the advance

FIGURE 5.3 Trading Range in AAPL (AAPL, daily: January–May 2015)

has met with selling "resistance." It is the level at which sellers are as powerful and aggressive as the buyers and halt the advance. When the sellers (supply) become more powerful and aggressive than the buyers (demand), the result is a subsequent price decline from the peak. A resistance level becomes a **resistance zone** when more than one resistance level occurs at roughly the same price. Prices rarely rise and stop at the same level. A single, high-volume price peak often defines a resistance point. Even then, however, because the high volume, especially if it is preceded by a sharp price rise, is a sign of speculation and emotion, and location within the price bar where large sellers actually begin to enter the market is unclear.

A **support point** is the opposite of a resistance point in that it is a single trough. At the support point, buyers become as powerful or aggressive as the sellers and halt a price decline (see Figure 5.4).

The concept of support and resistance presumes that in the future prices will stop at these recorded levels or zones and that they represent a remembered psychological barrier for prices. The zones will carry through time and become barriers to future price action. Not only will the zones carry through time, but once they are broken through, they will switch functions. Previous support will become resistance, and previous resistance will become support.

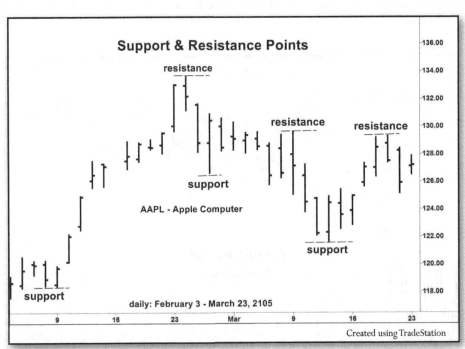

FIGURE 5.4 Support and Resistance in AAPL (daily: February 3–March 23, 2015)

Why Do Support and Resistance Occur?

> Have you ever bought a stock, watched it decline in price, and yearned to sell out for what you paid for it? Have you ever sold a stock, watched it go up after you had sold it, and wished you had the opportunity to buy it again? Well, you are not alone. These are common human reactions, and they show up on the stock charts by creating **support** and **resistance**. (Jiler, 1962)

Let us look at the presumed psychology behind a support level and see why it might carry into the future.

There is little question that a price trough is a point at which buyers overwhelmed sellers. In Figure 5.5, AAPL peaked at $133.60 on February 24, a potential resistance level, and then declined touching $121.63 on March 12, at which point it reversed upward but failed to reach the old supply level. Subsequently, the stock price fell back to $122.60 within a dollar of the earlier support on March 26, rallied to $134.54 within $0.86 of the first peak and resistance level, and fell again to the support level and halted at $123.36, only $0.76 from the previous trough. We now have two, well-defined resistance points and three support points: $133.60 and 135.54 resistance points and $121.63, $122.60, and $123.36 support points.

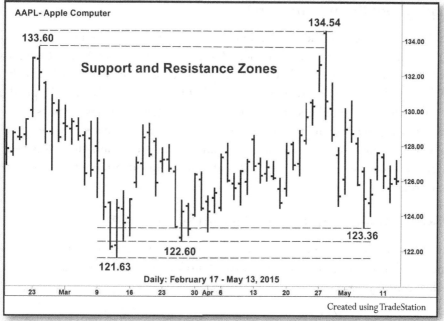

FIGURE 5.5 Support and Resistance Zones (AAPL daily: February 17–May 13, 2015)

We can assume there are potential buyers between $121.63 and $123.36 because

1. In the next sell-off, those who sold short at the $134 level will be covering because they have seen that the price halted its earlier decline at about $122 and do not want to take the risk that it will rally again to $134 and wipe out their profits.
2. Those who had been watching the stock but did not buy it at $122 earlier will be satisfied that the decline to $122 is back to where they earlier had wanted to purchase it but "missed it."
3. Those who sold the stock at the low of $122, when it declined from $134.00, saw the price immediately rise thereafter and wish to reenter a position at the price they sold it earlier.

Notice that none of these players is using a fundamental or other informational reason for buying the stock at $122. The reasons are purely psychological, but they are strong reasons by themselves. The presumption for technical analysts is that $122 has now become a support zone and that prices will stop declining at that level in the future. The presumption is that the more frequently prices halt at a zone, the stronger and more important that zone will likely be in the future.

A resistance zone will likely now also exist at $134 for similar reasons because sellers want to sell at that price: sellers who missed $134 before, sellers who bought at $134 and want their money back, and sellers who want to short the stock at $134 where it halted earlier. Support and resistance zones, therefore, are price levels where supply and demand reach equilibrium for unusual but persistent psychological reasons.

What About Round Numbers?

Ironically, when prices reach round numbers, the tendency to buy and sell increases. People think in terms of round numbers. Otherwise, why would Walmart sell a shirt for $29.95 rather than $30? They know people subconsciously will associate with the "29" and will believe they are getting a $29 shirt rather than a $30 one. People think in terms of round numbers and act accordingly in the securities markets as well. The current problem with the concept of round numbers is that knowledge of that tendency is widespread. From the standpoint of entering orders then, it is best to determine entry and exit points based on the technical situation rather than worry about round numbers.

How Are Important Reversal Points Determined?

The more important the reversal point, the more important the support or resistance level. There are a number of ways to identify a significant reversal point. Let us look at some of them.[1]

---

[1] In this section, we focus primarily on how to determine significant troughs and support levels. Of course, significant peaks and resistance levels would be determined in the same fashion, only in the opposite direction.

DeMark or Williams Method Tom DeMark and Larry Williams each have a method of determining a reversal point by using the number of bars (in a bar chart) on either side of a suspected reversal point. In a low bar, for example, the analyst may look for two bars with higher lows directly on either side of the suspected trough bar. The number of bars on either side can be increased to boost the importance of the trough, but the number of troughs will be sacrificed. The higher the number of confirming lows necessary, the more important but less common the trough.

As an example, look at Figure 5.6. Each of the two-bar lows and highs is marked with an arrow. Point (a) is not a trough because it does not have at least two bars on either side of it with higher lows. Likewise, Point (b) is not a peak. It does not have two bars on either side of it with lower highs. Is Point (c) a trough? We do not know because we can't see if there are two bars to the right of the low to judge Point (c).

Percentage Method Another method of identifying significant troughs is by deciding beforehand how much the price should decline into and rally from the trough. A percentage is usually used. Using 1%, for example, any time the price declines more than 1%, makes a low, and then rallies more than 1% would define a 1% trough. The larger the percentage used, the more important but less frequent the reversal point.

Gann Two-Day Swing Method W. D. Gann's swing method is similar to the DeMark's or Williams's method. To find a support point, or trough, a low bar is

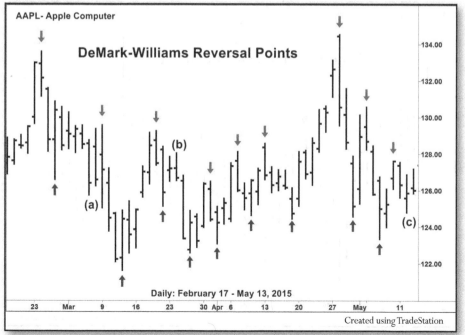

FIGURE 5.6 DeMark-Williams Reversal Points (AAPL daily: February 17–May 13, 2015)

identified. Once the low bar is identified, the two following trading days are observed. If these two days have higher highs than the low bar, the low bar is a support point. Originally, Gann used the three following trading days to determine a support point, but more recently, it has been switched to two days (Krausz, 1998). Likewise, a resistance point is defined as any high bar during an uptrend that is followed by two successive bars with lower lows. Figure 5.7 is identical to Figure 5.6 except that the reversal points are determined using the Gann rule. The difference between the two charts is that at Point (a), (b), (c), and (d), the reversal points as defined by the Gann rule do not occur at the DeMark/Williams reversal points. The reasons are that the days of the actual reversal points were not followed by the required two successive days. Thus, by Gann's rule, the reversal may not occur on the actual high or low bar as at (a) and (e) in Figure 5.7.

High Volume Method Very large volume can also identify a significant reversal point. High volume indicates that larger than usual activity occurred on that trading day. Figure 5.8 shows a one-day reversal on high volume at a high, creating a significant reversal point and resistance level.

Figure 5.8 illustrates a one-day reversal. One- or two-day patterns can occur at peaks or troughs. When these occur on high volume, they usually signify important reversal points. Because these formations usually occur at a stage of high emotion, they signify either a panic or a speculative bubble. As such, the actual price level at which the reversal took place is not identifiable on a large bar chart. Sometimes

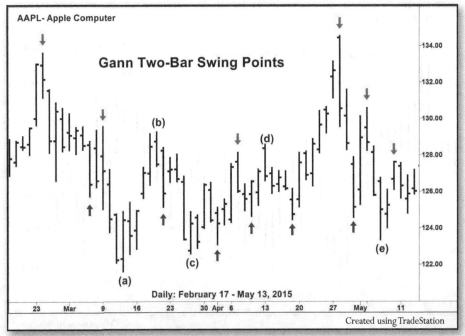

FIGURE 5.7 Gann Two-Bar Swing Points (AAPL daily: February 17–May 13, 2015)

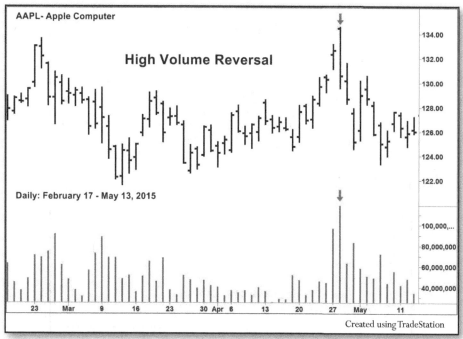

FIGURE 5.8 One- and Two-Bar Reversals (AAPL daily: February 17–May 13, 2015)

intraday action must be inspected to see at just what price level the majority of buying and selling occurred.

In Figure 5.8, the large spike in volume on April 28, 2015 occurred with a pattern called an **outside reversal day**, where daily range is large, the high is greater than the previous high, the low is lower than the previous low, and the close is near the low. These patterns can occur without the large volume, but when large volume is present, they are an excellent signal that the price rise has reached a speculative peak and will be a strong resistance in the future.

How Are Support and Resistance Zones Drawn? To construct a support (or resistance) zone, simply draw a horizontal line through each significant trough (or peak) into the future. These lines can be drawn through the respective bar lows or, as Jiler (1962) suggests, using the bar's close because this is what most investors read in the paper. These lines should also be extended into the past to see if earlier price declines stopped at the same price level. Where these horizontal lines bunch together, sometimes overlapping at the same price level is a support or resistance zone. This zone is usually stronger the more horizontal lines there are within it. In other words, the more times the price level has halted previous advances or supported previous declines, the stronger will be the resistance or support in the future. Because all previous significant troughs have not likely occurred at exactly the same price level, an area called a **zone** is constructed between the highest and lowest horizontal line. This defines the actual support or resistance area clearly.

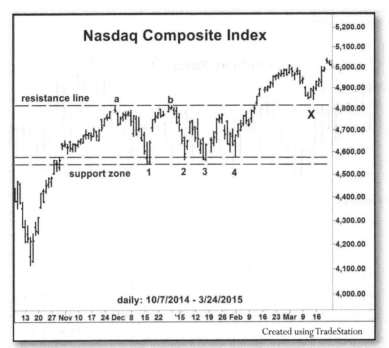

FIGURE 5.9 Support and Resistance Zones (Nasdaq Composite Index, daily: October 7, 2014–March 24, 2015)

Figure 5.9 shows how support and resistance lines are drawn. Notice that the line at Point 1 just under 4547 was the first support line. Points 2, 3, and 4 are also support levels but occur at slightly different price levels. The highest and lowest levels denote the support zone, a price area where declines tend to halt as buyers enter and reverse the downward direction. Points a and b also denote reversal points defining previous resistance levels and thus a resistance zone where prices can be expected to halt in a rally.

If a horizontal line is by itself with no other horizontal lines close to it, it is likely an independent support or resistance line. Such lines, unless accompanied by extraordinary volume, usually do not have the same strength in the future that a combination of horizontal lines might have within a zone.

In the future, prices will tend to halt at these zones, and occasionally at a single line. Prices will often enter the zone but will not break out of the outer horizontal line of the zone. If they do break that level, we have what is called a "breakout" that has important consequences. A price break above the resistance zone implies that sellers are satiated at that level and buyers are anxious. See the upward breakout in Figure 5.9 at the resistance zone in February. In this instance, the break left a vacuum of sellers, and the buyers, at least at that price, controlled the stock. If there is another resistance zone at some distance above the current broken zone, prices will generally trade up to that next higher zone. Thus, a resistance zone in an advancing market can become a price objective once a lower resistance zone is broken. Resistance zones exist at all horizons—day, week, or even minute-to-minute. Some traders only trade stocks or futures—especially e-mini futures—between these zones often on an intraday basis between very short-term support and resistance zones.

What we have said about resistance zones is equally applicable to support zones. Horizontal lines at significant troughs will show the existence of these zones, and extended into the future, they will become zones of support to price decline. In Figure 5.9, for example, the previous resistance zone became a support zone at Point X when the correction after the upward breakout halted at that same level. In addition, as time goes on, the importance of past horizontal lines diminishes for both support and resistance zones. More recent price reversals are more important. Human memory fades quickly.

How Do Analysts Use Trading Ranges?

Getting back to our earlier introduction of sideways trends, a trading range, as shown in Figure 5.9, is a price level where both support and resistance zones are relatively close together, and prices "bounce" between them until finally breaking out in one or the other direction. Some traders will trade the "bounces" between support and resistance, but this is usually dangerous and requires low operating costs and constant attention (Schwager, 1996). The most profitable and reliable way to use the trading range is to practice "breakout" trading. Let us look at each of these strategies a little more closely.

Range Trading   Trading within a range is difficult. Although many books suggest it as a strategy, it is almost impossible for the nonprofessional to profit through range trading. First, it is difficult to recognize that prices are trading in a range until after a considerable amount of trading and time has passed. It is, therefore, largely in retrospect that the opportunities are recognized. In addition, operating costs, such as commissions and slippage, must be small and execution efficient, or else any potential profit will be overwhelmed by transactions costs. Because the bounds of a trading range are often zones rather than specific price levels, the point at which an execution order, either buy or sell, should be placed is indefinite. Finally, the location for a protective stop-loss order to prevent a breakout from ruining trading profits is difficult to determine. By the time all these costs and execution levels are recognized, the potential for profit has diminished considerably, making any profit versus risk unlikely. Thus, most traders stay away from trading within a trading range and instead wait for the inevitable breakout and beginning of a trend.

The one exception to range trading is channel trading. A **channel** is a trading range tipped at an angle such that it trends upward or downward. Trend lines define the bounds of the channel just as support and resistance lines define the trading range. One can trade these channels back and forth but only in the direction of the channel trend. In other words, if the channel is trending upward, only long positions are taken at the lower bounds and sold at the upper bounds, but no short position is taken contrary to the channel trend. As mentioned earlier, upward trends have longer upward subtrends and shorter downward subtrends. To a certain extent, depending on the slope of the channel trend, the subtrends in the direction of the trend reduce the difficulty seen in trading ranges.

Breakout Trading **Breakout trading** is as old as technical analysis and likely the most successful. Remember that a trading range is somewhat like a battleground, where the buyers and sellers are warring for dominance. Most chart patterns are combinations of trend lines and, thus, are battlegrounds also. Before the battle is over, it is almost impossible to determine who will win. It is usually wiser, and more profitable, to wait rather than to guess. Once, however, prices break out of the trading range, the investor has information about who has won the war. If the breakout is to the upside, buyers are driving price up; if the breakout occurs to the downside, sellers are overwhelming buyers. Trading on this breakout is probably the most profitable and reliable strategy for the investor faced with a trading range or pattern.

Breakout trading can be used in many different ways other than for just trading ranges. One of the most famous is the **Donchian breakout method**, also called the "four-week breakout system," originated by Richard Donchian and later improved upon by Richard Dennis. It still appears to work. A recent study by *Active Trader Magazine* (Kurczek and Knapp, 2003) indicates that even though the method is popular and has been widely known for many years, it still produces profits, especially in the commodities futures markets. Its calculation is absurdly simple. Buy when the highest high over the past four weeks is broken, and sell when the lowest low over the past four weeks is broken. A "stop-and-reverse" strategy requires a position, long or short, at all times.

A breakout is a powerful signal. It indicates that the balance between demand and supply has been settled, usually violently, and, thus, is an indication of the initiation or continuation of a directional trend.

■ Directional Trends (Up and Down)

We have just considered trading ranges in which successive peaks and troughs occur at roughly the same price level. This results in a flat or sideways trend in prices. Whenever reversal points are occurring at higher (lower levels) than the previous reversal points, price is trending upward (or downward).

What Is a Directional Trend?

When a peak and trough occur at higher price levels than the immediately previous peak and trough, the trend has turned upward. Conversely, for a peak and trough lower than their previous peak and trough, the trend has turned down. The angle of the trend, therefore, is determined by the amount by which the peaks and troughs are higher or lower than their previous levels. To see this more clearly, a chart is almost a necessity. Figure 5.2 at the beginning of this chapter shows an upward trend in AAPL daily from August 2014 through May 2015. The principles of trends are applicable regardless of direction.

Quite obviously, the steeper the angle of the trend, the more powerful is the buyer or seller group. It means that the one group is overwhelming the other group at a faster pace. In a decline, sellers are willing to receive lower and lower prices before becoming temporarily exhausted at a trough. In an advance, buyers are more and more anxious and willing to pay higher prices. This is the time when an investor who is long the security is happiest. It is a trend and is what the technician is looking for in indicators and charts. The corollary, however, is that the steeper the angle of ascent or descent, the less sustainable it becomes.

An uptrend, therefore, is a display of the eagerness of the buyers versus the eagerness of the sellers. It is similar to the concept of support and resistance except that the support and resistance are changing in a specific direction. Because all the stock desired by the buyers and sold by the sellers is not transacted at one time and at one price level but over a time as news leaks out and positive feedback affects other players, the price trend continues until it has reached a point of exhaustion. At that level, the price trend either flattens out in a congestion or consolidation area or reverses direction into a declining trend. Some analysts argue that an actual trend lasts only a short time—approximately 20% of the trading period—and during the remaining time, prices remain in a consolidation or pattern formation with an indefinite trend. No one has demonstrated the validity of this percentage, however. It was estimated only by counting the time that an ADX indicator shows that a trend exists in varying markets, periods, and circumstances.

It is undeniable, however, that the majority of profits come from correctly anticipating and acting upon a trend. For this reason, almost all technical study is devoted toward early anticipation of a trend.

How Is an Uptrend Spotted?

In retrospect, a trend is easy to spot, especially on a price chart. Without being specific, it is usually easy to see reversal points and the general direction of historical prices. The difficulty, from an analysis standpoint, comes in being specific enough to determine when the signs of a trend change are occurring. To do this, the technical analyst uses several tools: (1) the regression line, (2) the trend line, and (3) moving averages. In this chapter, we discuss the regression line but focus the majority of our attention on the trend line.

Using a Regression Line   Mathematic formulas can fit two sets of data, such as price and time, to a straight line. This method is called **linear regression**, and the line derived from this formula is called a **regression line**. This line has two variables: its starting point and its slope. The technical analyst is interested in the regression line's location on the chart and to some degree its slope. In the example in Figure 5.10, the regression line from the first closing price to the last closing price

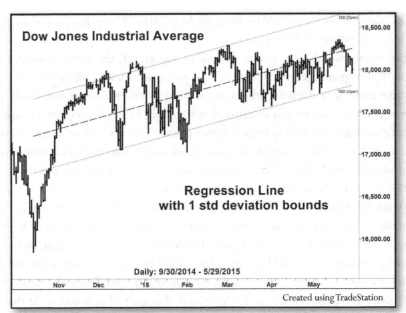

FIGURE 5.10 Regression Line and One Standard Deviation
(September 30, 2014–May 29, 2015)

travels through a majority of the data. Indeed, the mathematical equation used to determine the line minimizes the distance between all the data points and the theoretical line. The line is said to be the "best fit" to the data.

We can also calculate standard deviations about this best fit line that will encompass all the data. Outliers, those prices that occur outside of the standard deviation lines, are considered as either anomalies or, to the technical analyst, if they occur in the most recent data, signs that the trend may be changing. In Figure 5.10, the right-hand, most recent, price plots are inside the standard deviation of the line. These, having occurred recently, are a clue that the trend is still upward.

Using Trend Lines The oldest and easiest method of determining the trend of prices is with a trend line. Trend lines are drawn with just a ruler and the use of one's eyes rather than a fancy mathematical formula. All that is needed is two support reversal points or two resistance reversal points. A line is drawn between the reversal points, as shown in Figure 5.11.

The important lesson to learn is that the lines are generally drawn between troughs (support) when the price is rising and between peaks (resistance) when the price is declining. The lines that connect the lows or highs extend into the future so that the analyst can tell when the trend line is broken. Remember, the purpose of the trend line is to provide a signal of a change in trend. For example, in Figure 5.11, price movement appeared to be in the upward direction. Therefore, a trend line was drawn that connected the major troughs in September, October, and November and at peaks in December and January. In early December, when prices broke below the

FIGURE 5.11 Trend Line (May 17, 2013–March 26, 2014)

trend line, analysts had a clue that the trend was changing, but it took a breakdown through a second trend line (not shown) drawn through the December trough to show that prices had reversed downward.

Scale and Trend Lines The problem of scale sometimes arises in the plotting of trend lines as it does with prices. Generally, on an arithmetic scaled chart in which the prices are displayed within a 20%–40% range, a trend line can be drawn with accuracy. When price changes have occurred over a wider range, the logarithmic scaled chart is necessary. In this case, the trend line represents a percentage change in prices rather than a point change. Over long periods, this is the preferred method because it better represents how investors look at a stock price. Generally, over long periods, investors think in terms of percentages, whereas over shorter periods, they may think more in terms of points.

Accelerating Trend Lines Another problem with trend lines is that they might not be straight lines. Often prices, especially in a speculative bubble or in a panic, will accelerate upward or downward and run away from a standard, straight trend line. In this case, the trend line must be adjusted continually to account for the price action's acceleration. This phenomenon is shown graphically in Figure 5.12.

An accelerating trend line, of course, is unsustainable because eventually it would reach an infinite slope. If the acceleration can be calculated through mathematical means, the expected time for the infinite slope will be the time by which the price

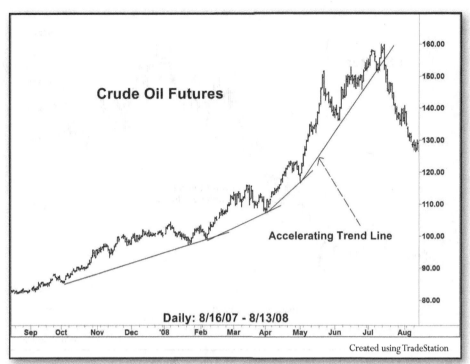

FIGURE 5.12 Accelerating Trend Line (Crude Oil Futures, daily: August 16, 2007–August 13, 2008)

must reach its zenith. It is a means of determining when the latest time for the eventual reversal will occur.

Decelerating Trend Lines The opposite of an accelerating trend line is the decelerating trend line. This is called a **fan line**. In the chart, the fan lines are shown as regular trend lines that are being broken without an obvious reversal in direction and then being redrawn to account for each new resistance level. Figure 5.13 shows the fanning effect that decelerating trend lines give.

These lines can go on forever in theory, but practitioners have generally stated that the maximum to be expected is three fan lines before a reversal in direction is to be expected. These three fan lines often are accompanied by some kind of standard pattern. Of course, if an earlier resistance zone is broken as well as a trend, it is a stronger implication that the trend has reversed direction.

General Rules for Trend Lines Several standard rules have been developed about trend lines. One is that the longer and the more times that the drawn line is touched by prices, the more significant it is when the line is finally broken. Another is that the steeper the trend line, the sooner it will be broken. This is obvious in an accelerating trend line but is equally true in a steep, straight trend line.

Sometimes a trend line is broken slightly by intraday price action, as shown in Figure 5.14. In this case, the trend line is adjusted downward because the breakdown

FIGURE 5.13 Decelerating Trend or Fan Lines (X, daily: December 3, 2012–December 6, 2013)

FIGURE 5.14 Adjustment in Trend Line (X, daily: February 3, 2014–February 2, 2015)

of trend #1 was an anomaly arising from bad news the previous week. The trend line #2 is then drawn through the trough of the earlier correction, and the breakdown through it in November is real. Obviously, this kind of action provides a problem for the analyst who must determine whether the break is permanent and indicative of a trend change or whether it is an anomaly. Should it be ignored, or should the trend line be adjusted slightly to accommodate the new level? The question here is whether the break of the trend line is significant or just minor. Trend lines should never be considered exact, largely because price action within a bar may be influenced for a short time by exogenous factors that have nothing to do with the trend. Some analysts, for example, draw trend lines between peak and trough closing prices rather than intraday highs and lows. They argue that because intraday traders usually must close their positions by day's end and are out of the market by then, the closing price represents longer-term players' determination of supply and demand and is, thus, a truer figure for drawing longer trend lines. By using the closing prices, the number of false breakouts is usually reduced.

Channels

Remember that uptrend lines should be plotted between support troughs, and downtrend lines should be plotted between resistance peaks. In other words, when prices are trending upward, the trend line will lie below the price action, and when prices are trending downward, the trend line will appear above the price action.

Sometimes, as in Figure 5.15, prices appear to travel in a "channel." A line is plotted through resistance reversal points and is parallel to the underlying uptrend

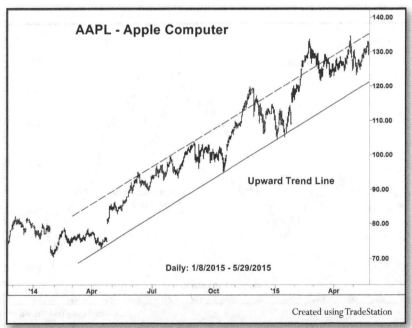

FIGURE 5.15 Trend Line with Channel Line (AAPL, daily: January 8, 2015–May 29, 2015)

line. This forms a channel. These channels often contain price motion just as the congestion area or rectangle formation contains prices when the trend is sideways. Remember that a trend is a direction of supply and demand. In an uptrend, the lower line represents the increasing demand for the security, and often the supply of the security is traveling parallel but above the demand. Thus, prices tend to "bounce" off this rising upper channel line as if supply were present at these moving intervals and rising at the same rate as demand. Indeed, when we see that a resistance reversal point is no longer parallel on the channel line but beginning to close closer to the underlying trend line, we know that supply is getting just a little more anxious and that the price is likely approaching a reversal point. Final proof that the channel has ended is when the price breaks the trend line. The same channel rules apply in downtrends.

A channel line can be drawn almost immediately after two troughs and their intervening peaks are recognized. A line is drawn parallel to the trend line through the intervening peak and projected into the future. This line now becomes a target line for subsequent rallies within the channel. In Figure 5.15, for example, the channel line (dashed line) could have been drawn as soon as the second trough in October had been recognized, by drawing a parallel line through the June peak. Projected into the future, that channel line was a level at which subsequent rallies would be expected to reach, just as the next one did at the peak in July.

Another potential signal with channel lines is when, in an uptrend, for example, the price breaks above the channel line rather than being contained by it as it was in November in Figure 5.15. This is a sign that the underlying trend is accelerating and that its end is nearing. In Figure 5.15, the subsequent correction declines all the way to the distance trend line where it halted. Such occurrences also occur during a downtrend and signal that a major price bottom is not far ahead. Any kind of acceleration is a sign of pure emotionalism and, thus, a potential sign of an impending reversal. Practically speaking, however, the investor or trader should never attempt to anticipate the reversal. A change in direction may occur soon, but because the price is changing so rapidly, an attempt to anticipate the actual price reversal can be disastrous. It is much wiser to watch for the actual reversal and then act with the comfort of trading with the new trend rather than against the old one.

Internal Trend Lines

There is also what is called an **internal trend line**. This line is more difficult to recognize and has only limited value. Generally, it is a line drawn through trending price action such that a large number of minor reversals touch the line both from above and below. An example of an internal trend line is shown in Figure 5.16. In some ways, it appears similar to a regression line that travels through the majority of prices, and in some ways, it appears like a midpoint line between the two boundaries of a channel. In any case, although it is interesting and occurs often, its use for trading or investing is limited. The observation that prices often bounce off an internal

FIGURE 5.16 Internal Trend Line (X, daily: September 20, 2010–July 27, 2011)

trend line may be somewhat useful for short-term trading, but moving averages provide a better means of measuring the midpoint in prices as they travel through time.

■ Other Types of Trend Lines

The concept of trend is central to the field of technical analysis. Therefore, analysts have developed a number of applications and variations of trend lines. Trend lines are not just useful with bar charts; analysts using point and figure charts make use of trend lines. Speed lines, Andrews' Pitchfork, and Gann fan lines are all example of types of trend lines that technical analysts use.

Trend Lines on Point and Figure Charts

A trend line may be drawn between successive lows or highs in the standard, old-style, point and figure charts, just as they are drawn in a bar or candlestick chart. There is one variation, however, that occurs in the three-box reversal method. For this type of chart' trend lines are drawn at 45-degree angles (see Figure 5.17). Upward trend lines, called **bullish support lines**, are drawn at a 45-degree angle from the lowest low, and downward trend lines, called **bearish resistance lines**, are drawn from the last peak. These lines are not really trend lines in the sense that we have covered earlier, but price penetration through them has a specific meaning.

FIGURE 5.17 Point and Figure Bullish Support and Bearish Resistance Lines on a Point and Figure Chart (LLY—Eli Lilly, through June 5, 2015)

Speed Lines

The late Edson Gould, an early proponent of technical analysis who did extensive market research, developed a means of estimating future support and resistance by what he called **speed lines**. Speed lines are calculated in the instance of an uptrend by taking the low point of the advance and the high point and creating a box whereby the low point is the lower-left corner and the high point is the upper-right corner (see Figure 5.18). Alternatively, during a downtrend, the beginning of the decline (the high point) is the upper-left corner of the box and the low point is the lower-right corner of the box. The vertical line from the high to the low straight down from the high is then marked at each third and at the halfway level, and a "speed" line is drawn from the actual low in the lower-left corner through each of the two marks on the right side and projected into the future. His hypothesis was that these speed lines were natural levels of support, and the prices would retrace to them. Modern methods have included marking the Fibonacci ratio numbers of 38.2% and 61.8% and drawing the speed lines through them. Because retracements do not seem to follow a consistent percentage, it seems doubtful that much merit should be applied to speed lines, but they are often seen in the literature on technical analysis.

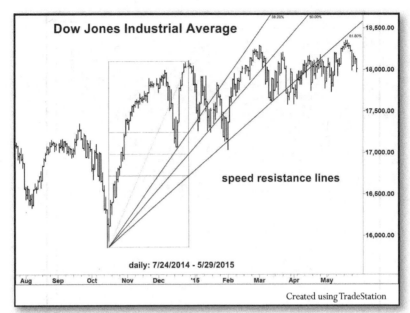

FIGURE 5.18 Speed Resistance Lines (Dow Jones Industrial Average, daily: July 24, 2014–May 29, 2015)

Andrews' Pitchfork

Developed by Dr. Alan Andrews, the pitchfork, in a downtrend (see Figure 5.19 for an example in an uptrend), takes the earliest high (1), the next minor low (2), and the first major retracement high (3) and then draws a line between the low and the retracement high (2–3). It then marks the halfway point on that line, draws a trend line through the earlier high and that mark, extending it into the future, and draws parallel lines to that new line from the minor low and from the retracement high. It sounds complicated, and like the speed line, apparently has limited value in projecting future support and resistance levels. Users claim that 80% of the time after the pitchfork is formed, prices will retrace to the middle line $(1 - A)$. This has not been tested, however. The method is often seen in press articles, likely because of the name (similar to candlestick patterns that also have catchy names), but its usefulness is suspect.

Gann Fan Lines

William Delbert Gann, known as W. D. Gann, was a famous commodities trader and book writer on trading tactics. He developed a number of technical methods that are still used by some practitioners. His invention of fan lines came from his belief that prices and time were related in a geometric pattern. To construct these lines, he used nine basic angles of trend lines based on the simple arithmetic relationship between the numbers 1, 2, 3, 4, and 8. By relating these numbers to a theoretical triangle beginning at an important price turning point, he could draw a series of trend lines that he thought had meaning. The angle of the trend line was always a ratio of the

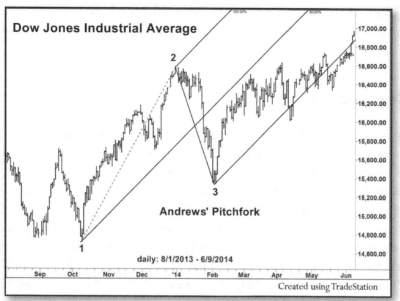

FIGURE 5.19　Andrews' Pitchfork (Dow Jones Industrial, daily: August 1, 2013–June 9, 2014)

numbers converted into degrees. For example, he believed that 1 by 1 was the most basic ratio and converted into 45 degrees. From there to 1 by 2 was 63.75 degrees; 1 by 3 was 71.25 degrees, and so forth. Figure 5.20 shows the Gann fan lines drawn on the Dow Jones Industrial Average daily chart used earlier for the Andrews' pitchfork. There is little statistical support for any of these methods, and you can see that

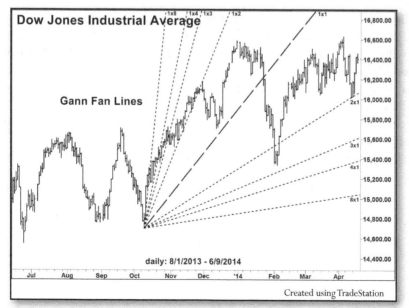

FIGURE 5.20　Gann Fan Lines (Dow Jones Industrial, daily: August 1, 2013–June 9, 2014)

the lines are similar regardless of the method used. There appears to be no foolproof method of anticipating trend lines. The best method is still to draw a line through the actual price data.

■ Conclusion

The trend of prices is the most important variable in profiting from technical analysis. The trend can sometimes be obvious and sometimes be elusive. The most useful trends are those identified the earliest, ridden as long as they last, and the inevitable end recognized. The first step in this process is observing what trends currently exist. Support and resistance zones determine when trends have reversed in the past and are a clue as to when they will reverse in the future. Support and resistance produces troughs and peaks. By connecting with a line from trough to trough and peak to peak, we can easily plot trend lines that represent past trends and extend them into the future. From the breaking of these extended trend lines, we can also spot when a trend may be changing direction.

■ References

DeMark, Thomas R. *New Market Timing Techniques: Innovative Studies in Market Rhythm & Price Exhaustion*. New York, NY: John Wiley & Sons, 1997.

Donchian, Richard D. "Trend-Following Methods in Commodity Price Analysis." *Commodity Year Book* (1957): 34–47.

Gann, W.D. *The Truth of the Stock Tape*. New York, NY: Financial Guardian Publishing Company, 1923.

Hamilton, W. *The Stock Market Barometer: A Study of Its Forecast Value Based on Charles H. Dow's Theory of the Price Movement, reprint of 1922 edition*. New York, NY: John Wiley & Sons, 1998.

Jiler, William. *How Charts Can Help You in the Stock Market*. New York, NY: Commodity Research Corporation, 1962.

Krausz, Robert A.W.D. *Gann Treasure Discovered*. New York, NY: Marketplace Books, John Wiley & Sons, 1998.

Kurczek, Dion and Volker Knapp. "Four-Week Breakout System." *Active Trader Magazine* 4, no.11 (September 2003): 74.

Schwager, Jack D. *Technical Analysis*. New York, NY: John Wiley & Sons, 1996.

CHAPTER 6

Breakouts, Stops, and Retracements

From Charles D. Kirkpatrick II and Julie R. Dahlquist, *Technical Analysis: The Complete Resource for Financial Market Technicians*, 3rd Edition (Old Tappan, New Jersey: Pearson Education, Inc., 2016), Chapter 13.

Learning Objective Statements

- Describe and identify breakouts
- List methods for confirming and filtering breakouts
- Explain the purpose of entry and exit stops
- Describe methods for setting entry and exit stops
- Define retracements, pullbacks, and throwbacks

We have discussed the importance of trends for profiting from price action, and we have observed several ways in which trends can be recognized. We also learned that to maximize profit, we must join a trend at its earliest, safest point and ride it until it shows signs of changing direction against us. To do this, we mentioned that a trend will begin often from a breakout of a support or resistance level and sometimes from a trend line. In this chapter, we discuss breakouts, stops, and retracements. They are never exact levels and require certain rules for us to have confidence in their validity. Once we're invested in a trend, the end of that trend is almost never anticipated, and the primary exits from trends are stops. Stops can also be useful for entries and are not limited to exit strategies alone. Breakouts and stops are somewhat similar, although stops need not be as stringent. Retracements are price actions that can follow breakouts and have their own peculiarities.

A breakout occurs most often when a price "breaks out" through a prior support or resistance level or zone. A breakout often but not always signals that a significant change in supply and demand has occurred and that a new price trend is beginning. For this reason alone, a breakout is an extremely important signal to the investor or trader. A breakout in the direction of the previous trend is a confirmation that the trend still exists, and a breakout in the opposite direction of a previous trend suggests that the trend is reversing and that a position should be closed and possibly reversed. Breakouts occur when prices pass through specific levels. Because these levels are often somewhat unclear zones and because false breakouts are common, the point at which a breakout occurs is extremely important. Often there must be a trade-off between speed and conviction. Speed of action is necessary just as a price breaks a level, and conviction is necessary to be sure that the breakout is real. There are a number of ways to accomplish both, but there is always the trade-off between risk and reward. Requiring more conviction that the breakout is real reduces the potential reward, and speed, although potentially more profitable, increases the risk that the breakout is false.

How Is Breakout Confirmed?

The first requirement for a breakout is a penetration of a trend line, or support or resistance zone. The next requirement is confirmation that the penetration is a real breakout, not a false one.

When the exact breakout level is not clear, as in a support or resistance zone, the extreme level of the zone is considered the **breakout level**. For example, in a trading range with a wide support zone of horizontal lines from previous support points, the lowest support line would be the breakout level. The other horizontal lines are also parts of the zone, but prices will often recede into the support zone without breaking through it entirely. Thus, a break of the lowest support point is evidence that the entire support zone has been penetrated. A trend line is a more definite breakout level because it is a line, but even with a trend line, a false breakout often occurs and requires redrawing of the trend line. In both these instances, a penetration of the breakout level or trend line requires confirmation. Penetrations often occur on an intrabar basis, and then the price closes back on the nonbreakout side of the breakout level or trend line. For an example of an intrabar penetration, see Figure 6.1, a trading range with two false, intrabar breakouts—one up and one down. Penetrations of this type are usually false.

Close Filter The major problem from the analyst's standpoint is that when the penetration is occurring, there is usually no other confirming evidence until after the close of trading. Some analysts will act immediately on the penetration and wait for the confirmation later. This is dangerous because the odds of a false breakout are greater with just an intrabar penetration, but the entry can be protected with a nearby stop. The less risky action is to wait for confirmation of the closing price to see if, perhaps, the penetration was just temporarily due to an intrabar exogenous occurrence that had little longer-term meaning. If the price closes on the nonbreakout side of the breakout level, it is plain that the intra-day penetration was likely false and new lines might have to be drawn to account for it. On the other hand, if the closing price is through the breakout level, the odds are higher that the breakout is real. Figure 6.2 shows the same prices as Figure 6.1 but advances time a few weeks to show when the true breakout occurred with a closing price below the support line.

FIGURE 6.1 Intrabar Breakout (GOLD, daily: November 7, 2012–February 13, 2013)

FIGURE 6.2 Close Breakout (GOLD, daily: December 10, 2012–March 15, 2013)

Some traders even wait for two bar closes beyond the breakout level for confirmation. This increases the risk that some part of the move subsequent to the breakout will be missed; on the other hand, it increases the possibility that the breakout is real.

Point or Percent Filter   Another confirmation method is to establish a breakout zone either a certain number or fraction of points or a percentage beyond the breakout level, as pictured in Figure 6.3, where both a filter and a close are required for a breakout. The theory in using a filter is that if the price can penetrate the breakout level and a prescribed zone beyond it, the penetration must be real. The number of points or percentage is determined before the penetration and is helpful in computerized models where a definite breakout price needs to be established. Waiting for the close after an intrabar breakout is more difficult to program. The number of points or percentage can be arbitrarily or empirically derived. Although the signal can use any percent or number of points, the most commonly used is a 1–3% rule, a level 1–3% from the ideal breakout point.

Time   Rather than looking simply at price, this method looks at time since the penetration. The basis is that if the penetration remains outside the breakout zone for a certain time, it must be real. The usual time period is two bars, but it can be any length of time. The price must remain beyond, or at least close beyond, the breakout level for the required number of bars. A combination of the time rule and the close rule uses both rules. This method requires a penetration and close beyond

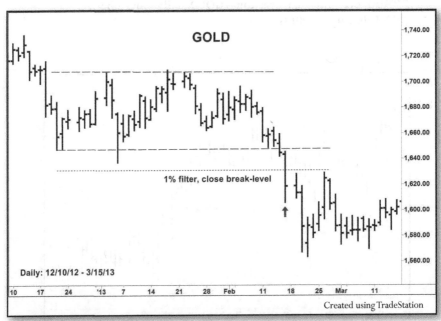

FIGURE 6.3   Filtered, Close Breakout-Level (GOLD, daily: December 10, 2012–March 15, 2013)

the breakout level, and then a second bar in which the price penetrates even further beyond the breakout level. For example, in a breakout down, the close must be below the breakout level, and the next bar must have a trade below the previous bar's low for confirmation of the breakout down. Figure 6.3 qualifies as a two-bar breakout with or without the filter or close constraint.

Volume Increased volume of trading often occurs with a breakout. Heavier trading demonstrates that other market players are acting in the direction of the new trend and that there is sufficient power behind the penetration. Jiler (1962), however, observes, and cannot explain why, that volume can dramatically decline on a breakout, and the breakout is still valid. Usually, however, volume increases as the trend develops.

Volatility All of the preceding price rules have obvious drawbacks. The principal drawback to most of these methods is that they don't account for the price volatility of the security. By nature, some securities tend to be characterized by more volatile trading; for these a more significant price move can be expected without it signaling a breakout. Remember that a filter using just the close doesn't require that the close be any distance from the breakout level. In highly volatile stocks, for example, the close can vary from a trend line or breakout level by a considerable amount and still not be a valid breakout.

A filter rule that uses some arbitrary point or percentage rule is likely to be broken by a highly volatile security before a true breakout occurs. In this case, analysts may consider the price volatility of the security when determining what the filter for a legitimate breakout should be. Three means of calculating volatility are most often used; these are beta, standard deviation of price, and average true range (ATR).

Beta is a calculation of the volatility of a security relative to a market proxy, usually the S&P 500. It is not useful in commodities because commodities have little useful correlation to the stock market or a commodity average. Indeed, beta's use has diminished over the years, as the underlying assumption that it is a valid measure of risk has been questioned. It does have one advantage in that it eliminates the trend of the market from the volatility calculation.

Standard deviation of returns, based on the percentage change in price, is the basis for most option and other derivative models and uses the complete set of prices over some past period in time. Its usefulness as a breakout filter is diminished by the fact that its value is influenced by the underlying trend of the security. The breakout filter must use the volatility about the trend and not include the trend itself. Otherwise, a strongly trending stock with little volatility about its trend would have a higher filter than a flat-trending stock with wide fluctuations about its mean.

Average true range (ATR) is a derivation of the **average range**, which is just the average of the difference between each bar high and low over some past period. The ATR is calculated using a special formula devised by Wilder himself to reduce the effects of older data. The ATR is an average of the **true range** of each bar (Wilder, 1978). It includes whatever effect a price gap between bars might have on the security's volatility. The true range is the greatest of

- The difference between the current bar high and low
- The absolute value of the difference between the prior bar close and the current bar high
- The absolute value of the difference between the prior bar close and the current bar low

The ATR is the average of the true range over some time period. Being dependent solely on the price of the security, the ATR is not influenced by any other average or security and is, thus, pure to the security's own action. It includes the recent trend only so far as the trend has had an effect on the range of prices. ATR is an excellent measure of volatility and is used in many indicators as well as breakout and stop-loss formulas.

As a price filter for confirmation of a breakout, by including a multiple of the ATR, the breakout level is adjusted for the volatility of the security. As you can see in Figure 6.4, an ATR filter expands and contracts over time as price volatility changes. For example, if price volatility increases, daily true ranges will expand, and the ATR will be larger, making it less likely to have a false breakout due to the increased price volatility. This means that a highly volatile security will have a wider filter to reduce its likelihood of making a false breakout just because of its higher volatility. On the other hand, a dull security that has few wild moves will have a narrow filter that will trigger the breakout with only a minimum deviation from its usual range.

Pivot Point Technique The pivot point technique is a method of determining likely support and resistance levels. It is widely used by day traders to establish potential price ranges for the day and rarely used as confirmation for breakouts (see Figure 6.5).

This technique uses the previous period's high, low, and close to establish support and resistance levels for the current period. Some formulas use the open as well. A series of points called **pivot points** for the current period are calculated from price points derived from the previous period. In other words, a day trader on a specific day would calculate the pivot points from the action the previous day. The theory behind using this technique is that as time goes on, the effect of past prices on current prices diminishes. Thus, the most recent, previous bar's action is the best predictor of the current bar's action.

This technique uses the following formula (Kaufman, 1998):

P (pivot point) = (Previous period: High + Low + Close) ÷ 3
R1 (first resistance) = (2 × P) − previous period Low
S1 (first support) = (2 × P) − previous period High
R2 (second resistance) = (P + previous period: High − Low)
S2 (second support) = (P − previous period: High − Low)

FIGURE 6.4 Average True Range (ATR) breakout filter (GOLD, December 10, 2012–March 15, 2013)

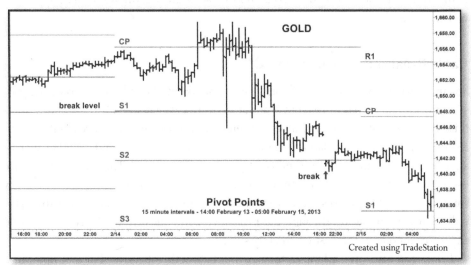

FIGURE 6.5 Pivot Point Technique Filter (GOLD, 15-minute bars, February 13, 2013–February 15, 2013)

These calculations establish upper and lower levels at which prices are expected to meet resistance or support based on the previous period's action. Floor traders will then enter or exit trades around these calculated pivot levels. The use of this formula is, of course, questionable because the logic behind it is questionable. The reason that so many intraday price reversals occur at pivot points is likely because so many traders use them, and, thus, they become self-fulfilling. Using 15-minute bars, Figure 6.5 shows intraday the gold price breakdown displayed using daily bars in

Figures 6.3 and 6.4. The pivot points are marked, as you can see, for the three days shown, and their labels correspond to the table above. The break level is the same as in the earlier figures and carried forward to these three days. As a swing trader, you would convert to a day trader and be looking for a break below S2 or S3 to execute your short sale. The break did occur on February 14 just after the stock market close at 16:00.

Traders looking for the validity of daily breakouts, on the other hand, will use the previous weekly or month action to establish current expected resistance and support levels; a price break through a current actual resistance or support level would be confirmed if it also broke a pivot resistance or support level. As a method of confirming breakouts, the logic behind their use is a little more solid. The formula is essentially a measure of the previous day's volatility projected into the following day. Volatility, as we have seen previously, is a useful method for determining accurate breakout confirmations.

Alternative pivot point calculations exist as well as the standard above. Tom DeMark developed a means of predicting support and resistance based on adding the relationship between the open and close price. There are also Woodie's and Camarilla pivot point formulas and a Fibonacci formula. When all these methods are compared, not one seems to be consistent or accurately estimate future support or resistance levels.

Can a Breakout Be Anticipated?

So far, we have looked at ways of confirming a breakout *after* it has occurred. Is it possible to determine that a breakout is about to occur *before* it actually does? Sometimes it is possible to anticipate a breakout. Often, volume is a clue that a breakout is about to occur. As we will learn later, volume often accompanies the trend. In other words, an increase in volume with a trend is supportive of that trend. Thus, when prices are oscillating, for example, beneath a resistance zone and volume increases on every small up leg and decreases with every small down leg, the odds favor that the price will eventually break up through the resistance zone because the increased volume expresses increased interest on the buy side.

Prices can also give a hint as to their next directional move. For example, in a trading range, if prices begin to reverse upward at a level slightly above the lower boundary of the range and then reverse downward right at the resistance zone, it indicates that buyers are becoming a little more aggressive with every minor correction and are willing to pay just a little more for the security when it corrects. If this tendency to have slightly rising lows is accompanied by increasing volume on the rallies, the probability of an upward breakout through resistance increases.

Figure 6.6 gives a hypothetical example of price activity hinting that a breakout may soon occur. Resistance has existed in the past and has stopped the first price rally. A downward reversal takes place to the point marked C. If volume increased on the initial rise to resistance but declined on the correction to C, C becomes a

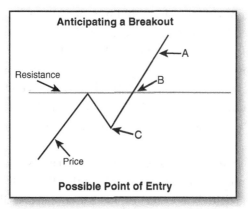

FIGURE 6.6 Anticipating a Breakout

possible entry point in anticipation of a breakout above resistance. This is a low-odds, risky entry point. The chances of its failing to follow with an actual breakout are considerably greater than after an actual breakout has occurred, but the price at which entry is made is lower, and, thus, the trade, if it works out, is potentially more profitable. A trade-off always exists between the higher risk of entry prior to the breakout and the higher reward of a cheaper entry price. At B, assuming again that volume has increased with the small rally, the odds of a breakout have increased over C, but the price is not quite as advantageous. At A, we know that a breakout has occurred, and, thus, our risk of a failure has diminished (but has not been eliminated because false breakouts can still occur), but the price of entry is considerably higher than the other possible entry points. This trade-off between risk and reward is a constant problem for the analyst, and the decision as to which breakout method to use is entirely at the analyst's discretion, based on individual reward/risk tolerance. Deciding on the most comfortable relation between risk and reward is a problem that will arise in almost every technical situation, from breakouts to money management, and it is one of the reasons that evaluating technical systems is so difficult.

■ Stops

A stop order is an order to buy or sell once a specific price has been surpassed. For example, a buy stop would be an order to buy a security at a specified price above the current price. Should the price rise to the specified buy stop price, it will be bought at the market. Conversely, a sell stop is an order to sell a security at a specified price below the current price when reached. The stop order can be further refined by adding a limit such that once the stop is triggered, the order becomes a limit order.

What Are Entry and Exit Stops?

Stop orders, also called "**stops**," can be used to enter a position or to exit a position. For example, if a price is approaching a resistance level above which a new trend is expected to develop, a buy stop order could be placed to be triggered if the resistance level is penetrated in a breakout. Or conversely, at a support level, the **entry stop** order could be placed to sell short once the specified level had been breached. These examples are entry stops. **Exit stops** are used either to protect capital from further loss, what Edwards and Magee (2007) call **protective stops**, or to protect profits from deteriorating back into a loss, usually called **trailing stops**. These stops are defensive in nature and are an absolute necessity once a trade entry has occurred.

Breakout levels and stop-loss levels or zones are similar. Exit stop levels are levels that signal the analysis might be incorrect or at least that the analysis is uncertain and that a position should be exited to protect capital but not necessarily reentered in the opposite direction. Entry stop levels are positioned using the rules for establishing a breakout level or zone or anticipation of a breakout through those levels or zones. The methods described previously for confirming breakouts are equally useful in confirming stop levels.

In an entry stop at a breakout level, an investor is committing new money and increasing the risk that the breakout is valid. In an exit stop, an investor is closing a position and, thus, decreasing risk. This is not to say that stops should be used carelessly. Indeed, by placing stops too close to current price action, an investor can be easily "whipsawed." A **whipsaw** occurs when an investor buys a security, the security price falls, the investor sells the security, and then the security price goes up above the original purchase price. The investor's original opinion was correct, but he still lost money. The word *whipsaw* comes from the timber industry, where a long, thin, two-man wood saw would often get caught in a log, if not properly handled, and whip the sawyers back and forth without cutting the wood and subjecting them to "two damaging and usually opposing forces at the same time" (www.Randomhouse.com). The whipsaw resulted from lack of analysis and lack of patience, just as in investing.

Changing Stop Orders

The most important underlying principle for defensive stops, because they protect one's capital but at the same time may imply the original analysis was wrong, is that they should never be moved away from the trend of the security. In other words, if one is long a security and has placed a stop at a reasonable level below the current price, he should never cancel or reduce the stop order. Its purpose is to keep the investor honest. By changing or canceling the stop, especially when the security is trading at a loss, the investor is losing discipline and reacting to emotional pressures having to do with not desiring to admit an error—a natural and strong human emotion, but unrelated to the rational assessment of the price action. If a decision about the security originally is made with the best logic and information available and a stop is placed when the analysis will obviously be incorrect, changing it or canceling it negates all the original thought and analysis. The stop may be adjusted along with price as a trailing stop or one that follows each successive change in support or resistance in the direction of the trend as the position progresses profitably, but it should never be canceled or changed against the trend.

Many investors and traders place stops too close to the current price of the security in which they have a position. This often causes whipsaws, even when the stop is adjusted for volatility. A defensive stop is a protection device. It is not necessary for short-term trading, but it's still preferred. Often, because they don't want to lose any amount of profit, investors will place a stop too close to the current price and be closed out too early in a longer move. A better method is to allow the security "breathing" room and place the protective stop below where the breathing room correction would be serious. We know that security prices retrace their advances in a progression of steps along the trend, and we know that we will never buy and sell at the absolute peak or trough. We also know that we have to decide upon what time horizon we want to play. Once that is decided, placing a stop based on a shorter time period only invites whipsaws. It is better to wait for the retracement and let the security "breathe."

On the other hand, if the overall market appears ready to reverse, and one's security has run along with the market but is also showing signs of fatigue, a trailing stop close to the current price is sometimes warranted. When a position will likely be closed soon anyway, for whatever reason, tightening the stop just allows the marketplace to make the decision rather than the investor or trader.

What Are Protective Stops?

Whenever a position is initiated, usually even before initiation, a protective exit stop level must be determined and placed with the entry order. The reasons are twofold. First, the protective stop protects capital. Not every entry is correct and ends up with a profit. Indeed, many traders have more losing trades than winning trades, but they are able to profit because of the judicious use of their stops. They place protective stops at a level where they know if the trade reaches that level, it will be unsuccessful, and when a trade works, they run with the profits until the trend appears to be reversing. The protective stop, therefore, is necessary in any investment endeavor. Even standard fundamental analysis should use some kind of stop. It is ridiculous to think that when entering a trade or investment, it will always be successful and risk of loss should be disregarded.

The second reason a protective stop is necessary is to determine what capital risk the trader or investor is accepting in the trade. By establishing a stop level (and placing an order to that effect), the investor now knows exactly what capital risk is being taken. Assume that a stock breaks upward out of a resistance zone at $20, and the entry stop is triggered so that the investor is now invested in the stock at $21. By analyzing previous support, trend lines, and other technical data, the investor determines that if the stock should sink to $17 (perhaps that is a support level or a trend line level adjusted for confirmation), there is something wrong with the analysis that suggested that the price would be rising. *The need to know what is wrong is unnecessary because the stock price action itself is suggesting that something is wrong.* Rational investment management would then get out of the stock until what is wrong is understood and evaluated. Technical analysis tells the investor at what price this exit should be made. Once the $17 price is determined as the exit point, the risk of the trade has been determined to be $4—the difference between the entry and potential exit prices. Knowing that the risk is $4 makes the money management problem considerably easier. Say the investor has $100,000 and never wants to risk more than 10% of capital in any one investment. A 2,500 share position with the risk of losing $4 is a $10,000 risk in a $100,000 portfolio, or 10%. No other investment method is as useful for measuring risk of loss. If the best exit point was $16 rather than $17, the risk would be $5 per share, and the ideal position to limit loss to 10% of the portfolio would be 2,000 shares. By knowing the risk level, the investor can thus adjust the amount of shares to be purchased to limit his risk to a predetermined acceptable level.

All stops should be placed based on the price action of the security and the level at which a reversal in trend is likely. Generally, these are trend lines or support or resistance levels. The methods using percentages or points from entry do not address the action of the price and are not adjusted to it. Instead, these levels are purely arbitrary. These rules will often stop out a position before a crucial level is reached or long after it has been penetrated. Exits always should be placed at logical levels of price based on the analysis of trend, support and resistance, volatility, and pattern, not on the peculiarities of a particular portfolio or on an arbitrary rule.

What Are Trailing Stops?

When a security is in a recognizable trend, a trailing stop can be used to avoid the potential loss of profits. Edwards and Magee called these stops "**progressive**" stops. These trailing stops are necessary because, for instance, in a significant uptrend, the prior support or resistance level may become a substantial price distance from the current price. For example, consider Figure 6.7. Assume that you initially enter a long position in March, with a protective stop placed at the March low price. As the stock continues trading in an upward trend over time, the price gets further and further from this initial stop point. By May, you have made a substantial profit. Setting a trailing stop will help you lock in that profit if the uptrend reverses. If you kept the stop at the original March level, you could watch the price fall by a large amount, and your profits would disappear before the protective stop was activated.

Trailing Stops Using a Trend Line The easiest method of establishing a trailing stop is to follow the trend line with a confirmation filter similar to those used in standard breakouts, as shown in Figure 6.7. For example, an uptrending stock has a definite, well-defined, standard trend line drawn beneath the recent price history. Setting a stop level below but parallel to the trend line, called a **stop line**, reduces

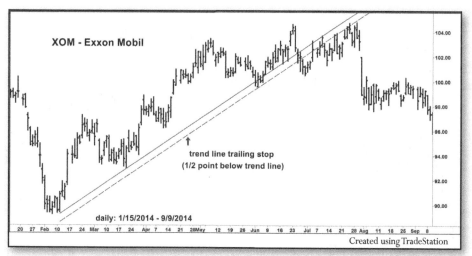

FIGURE 6.7 Trend Line Trailing Stop (XOM—Exxon Mobil, daily: January 15–September 9, 2014)

the number of false breakouts. The interval between the trend line and the stop line can be determined in the same manner as the intervals used earlier for breaks of support or resistance. The stop level must be adjusted with every new bar as it travels along the stop line. If it is triggered and the position closed, profits already accrued would not be appreciably affected, at least not as much as waiting for a previous support or resistance level to be broken would adversely affect them, yet the stop level is far enough away from the trend line not to be triggered with a false breakout.

Another method of trailing stop designed to account for the intrinsic volatility of the security is to measure some fraction of the security's ATR from its latest reversal point. This method is often called a "**Chandelier Exit**." For example, assume you are long a security rising on an accelerated trend that reaches a high of $50. The 14-day ATR for this stock is $2.50. Based on an evaluation of the market strength, you decide to place a stop three times the ATR below the recent highest high. (Usually a multiple of 2.5 to 4.0 times the ATR is used.) Therefore, you place a sell stop at $42.50. You don't consider the trend line or the previous support level, which may be considerably below the current price. This method provides a stop based purely on the price and volatility of the security. When price rises above $50, the stop moves up with the price rise to three times its new ATR below the new high. Figure 6.8 shows what using a limited ATR trailing exit stop looks like. This stop is called a **limited ATR trailing stop** because under the rule of not allowing a stop to move against the prevailing trend, we have adjusted the pure ATR stop to not decline below a previous stop. Using this method reduces the likelihood that a false breakdown will occur because you are adjusting the stop for the security's volatility. This method is especially useful when other levels such as a trend line or support level are considerably distant from the current price, and the security is following an accelerated upward trend whose end is difficult to predict.

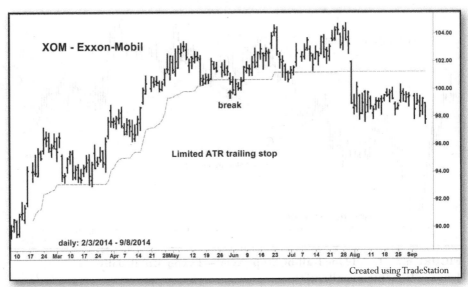

FIGURE 6.8 Limited ATR Trailing Stop (XOM—Exxon Mobil, daily: February 3–September 8, 2014)

Trailing Stops Using Parabolic SAR Another trend-following method for setting trailing stops is the **parabolic SAR**. (SAR stands for "**stop and reverse**.") Developed by Welles Wilder (1978), it was initially intended as a trading system because it required a long or short position. However, it has become not only a breakout confirmation rule, but also an excellent, but sometimes sensitive, stop rule.

The parabolic SAR is calculated by using an **acceleration factor** that increases as the price moves along its trend. Thus, the name *parabolic* is used because the stop level follows a parabolic curve, as shown in Figure 6.9. The weakness of the formula is that it doesn't include the security's volatility and is thus subject to many whipsaws, but since Wilder's original formula, an ATR component has been included in many parabolic systems. Nevertheless, the acceleration factor is arbitrary and requires some testing for each security to find the best level with the least whipsaws. The concept of a parabolic curve for a stop level is an interesting one, however, and now that it is adjusted for a security's volatility it may have more value.

Trailing Stops Using Percentage of Gain One final method of determining trailing stops is to place stops at a percentage of each leg in the direction of the trend. This requires that a profit is accruing. On the initial favorable leg, for example, a stop can be placed at 50% of the gain and moved with the gain until after the first retracement. The stop can then be raised as a higher fraction of each successive favorable leg. This method is generally inferior to those methods based on the actual price action.

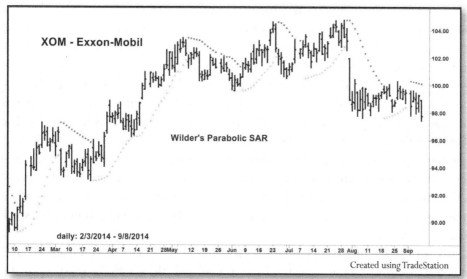

FIGURE 6.9 Parabolic SAR (XOM—Exxon Mobil, daily: February 3–September 8, 2014)

What Are Time Stops?

Time stops are exit stops used to close a position after a predetermined period of time has passed. *Time is an investor's enemy. Uncertainty increases in future time.* The longer we look into the future, the less accurate our projections are. This uncertainty is one reason why long-term interest rates are usually higher than short-term interest rates—to account for the risk of something adverse happening over time.

When a trading model or investment method determines that a position should be entered, for whatever reason, the longer that time goes on without a profitable reaction to the position entry, the higher are the chances that the entered position will be unprofitable. Technical analysis is a method of timing investments or trades. To maximize return on capital, capital should not be idle. For this reason, technical analysts often use a **time stop** to exit a position after a predetermined time, especially if the position is not profitable.

Time stops are also useful in testing mechanical trading methods. All positions must have an entry and exit. Often one is unrelated to the other, but without the ability to analyze both the entry and exit separately, their respective strengths and weaknesses are unknown. To analyze the signal entry, a time stop gives equal weight to all the entry signals being tested.

What Are Money Stops?

Instead of using price points at which risk of significant loss is possible, some traders and investors use a **money stop**. This stop is based on the risk one is willing to take in terms of money. For example, in the previous description of the protective stop, the investor was willing to risk $10,000. Instead of determining from the analysis at what point the security is at risk of major loss, the investor determines how far down the security may decline before the $10,000 is lost. With this method, investors enter into an arbitrary number of shares at their choosing without any analysis of the price point at which the position should be closed and then allow the balance in their investment account to tell them when to sell. From the strategic and money management viewpoint, this method is a poor way to establish a protective stop. The better method is to determine the risk points in the security and work from there. A money stop is based not only on the price change but also on the amount of securities or contracts entered. It is, thus, not a good method of determining when the chance of further loss has increased and will often cause expensive whipsaws, especially if the position has a large number of shares or contracts and is exited after only a small change in price.

As you can see, there are numerous variations of stops. The technical analyst usually tests a variety on the securities being traded and sticks with the most successful method.

How Can Stops Be Used with Breakouts?

A breakout above resistance or below support signals a change, usually in trend direction. A trend line breakout is a warning of change but not necessarily of a reversal in direction. The most used breakout is the breakout from support or resistance or from a trend line. Almost all patterns are made of trend lines and support or resistance lines. The most reliable chart patterns are completed on a breakout, usually through support or resistance. Most strategies utilizing chart patterns, therefore, must have a way of recognizing a breakout, measuring its importance, and confirming it.

Using Stops When Gaps Occur

Some traders act directly on the breakout and are willing to pay the extra price generated by the enthusiasm associated with the breakout. This is usually a wise decision when the breakout creates a gap (see gaps in Figure 6.10). A **gap** occurs when a security opens and trades at a range totally outside the previous day's range. In other words, there is no overlap between one day's trading prices and the previous day's trading prices, and a gap appears between the bars for the two days on a chart. A gap is usually a sign that important information was released during the period between the bars that had an extraordinary effect on the buyers and sellers. If the reason for the gap is legitimate, the price continues in the direction in which it broke out. When the gap is **closed** ("covered" or "filled"), however, there is the danger that the gap was false and prices will reverse their trend. Thus, a protection stop should be placed below the gap opening.

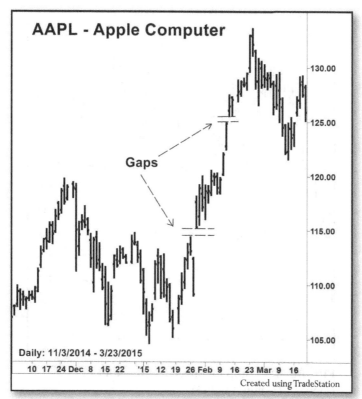

FIGURE 6.10 Gaps (AAPL—Apple Computer, November 3, 2014–March 23, 2015)

Placing Stops for a False (or "Specialist") Breakout

Figure 6.11 shows an example of an upward "specialist breakout." This false breakout triggers all the buy stops placed to protect against a loss from an upward reversal in a downward trend or to enter a new long position. Prices, with no follow-through, then reverse again, and they break back down through the earlier breakout level, leaving many investors with a loss. Those who bought to cover their shorts on a protective stop now have no position during the subsequent correction, and those who entered a long position now have a loss. The false upward breakout caught them. It is often called a **specialist breakout** from the days when specialists and market makers would buy stocks heavily at the edge of a resistance level and create a false breakout that, once it caught on and forced the public to buy after the breakout, they would sell into at a profit. Thus, the breakout upward shown in Figure 6.11 was preceded by heavy volume and an accelerating upward curve, giving the impression that the stock was soon to explode upward. Whether this false breakout was a manipulation is somewhat irrelevant today, but breakouts of this type do occur quite frequently and, if not protected against, can be painful.

To protect against these losses, the astute investor or trader who participated in the breakout will place another close sell stop slightly below the breakout level, as

FIGURE 6.11 Stop for Specialist Breakout
(January 27–June 12, 2015)

shown on the chart, and then an entry stop below the low of the bar preceding the breakout bar. If prices quickly reverse downward, the trader will cover losses and make a profit from the second stop being triggered. If the breakout is true, neither of the sell stops will be executed.

Thus, a specialist breakout is a tradable formation. In the chart example, should the trader have no position but see the upward breakout, rather than trade the breakout, she could place a stop below the breakout bar in case the breakout is false. If the breakout is false and triggers the trader's entry stop, she makes a quick profit, and if it does not trigger, she doesn't lose anything.

The most important point about trailing stops, or any kind of stop, is to test the method first. It is remarkable how much a stop, if properly placed, can improve performance over just an arbitrary stop placement.

■ Retracements

The final subject relating to trends is retracements. As mentioned and observed previously, a trend rarely follows a line without including a number of smaller trends. The smaller countertrends are called **retracements,** and several rules have been developed concerning them.

Retracements are always corrections to the principal trend. As prices rise, for example, in a strong uptrend, the rise is interrupted periodically by downward corrections. In an uptrend, the beginning of these corrections is always a resistance point, and the bottom of the retracement is always a support point. The lower support point is where a new trend line can be plotted from a previous support point. Thus, a retracement is a smaller trend itself and runs counter to the principal trend.

For example, consider the price movement pictured in Figure 6.12. Obviously, the principal trend for AAPL (Apple Computer) from late June is upward. However, from mid-August through mid-September, prices are trending downward in a countertrend, retracing a portion of the price gain. This retracement halts, as is often the case, at the downward trend line established before the upward trend began. Such a retracement is called a **throwback** and is an excellent level at which to participate in the upward trend. Not all retracements are as large. In early August, for example, a small throwback occurred right after the upward breakout through the trend line. A small throwback retracement such as this is also quite typical action after an upward breakout.

A retracement can be analyzed in the same way as the longer trend. It is, in fact, a trend in itself but with a direction opposite from the principal trend and with a shorter period and length. Within a trend, many retracements of different amounts and periods can occur. Because the end of a retracement usually is the support or resistance point for the longer trend, the length and time of a retracement can tell us something about the longer trend. For example, in a sharply rising upward trend,

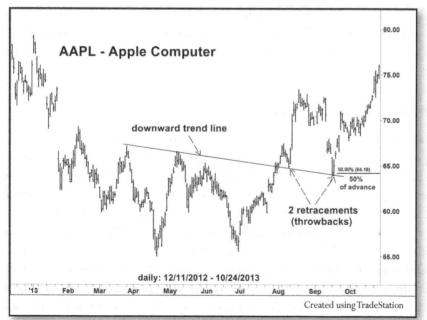

FIGURE 6.12 50% Retracement (throwback) from Upward Breakout (AAPL, daily: December 11, 2012–October 24, 2013)

you would expect the retracements to be short and not "retrace" a large percentage of the earlier rise. Indeed, the general rule is that a strong upward trend requires retracements of less than 50% of the previous trend. The same is true for downward trends. Should the retracement in an upward trend decline more than 50%, the trend line in the longer upward trend would be in jeopardy. Figure 6.12 shows a 50% retracement in the upward trend from July to late August. The retracement not only stopped at the 50% retracement level but also at the earlier downward trend line, thus, the amount of retracement indicates the larger trend's strength.

A retracement, in a healthy trend, can also present an opportunity for the trend follower who missed the earlier stages of the trend to jump on the longer trend. A retracement, as long as it holds above the longer trend line and does not retrace more than 50%, as occurred in Figure 6.12, is usually an opportunity for the trend follower to act in the direction of the larger trend.

Unfortunately, retracements rarely reach an exact percentage. Some analysts believe that percentage retracements provide a good entry point. Many articles and books have hypothesized that in an uptrend or downtrend, prices will tend to retrace a certain percentage. The most common mentioned are 33 1/3%, 50%, 66 2/3%, and the Fibonacci percentages of 38.2% and 61.8%. The late Art Merrill, a well-respected technical analyst, in a paper published in the *Journal of Technical Analysis* (August 1989), found that the amount by which prices retrace in the Dow Jones Industrial Average during an advance or decline did not concentrate about any of these percentages.

Anticipating retracement levels, therefore, can be somewhat hazardous, and the trade-off between the amount of retracement desired and what may actually occur is usually unanticipated. Thus, a rough estimate from previous retracements, support and resistance zones, and the location of the longer trend line is probably the best information for an estimate rather than the mechanical percentage numbers derived from various formulas.

Pullbacks and Throwbacks

Variations of retracements that occur after a breakout, usually from a horizontal support or resistance zone but sometimes from a trend line, are called **pullbacks** or **throwbacks** depending on whether the breakout was downward or upward. When the price retraces quickly back to the breakout zone from an upward breakout, it is called a **throwback**, and conversely, the quick retracement from a break downward is called a **pullback** (Edwards and Magee, 2007). Figure 6.13 shows a pullback in the gold market. These retracement variations will become more important when we discuss chart patterns, but they often are found in any breakout, especially in one from a rectangle formation or congestion area. These retracements may not abide by normal retracement percentages if they are blocked by the support or resistance level from which they broke. They tend to be very short in time and distance but often provide a second, lesser-risk opportunity for a breakout trader to enter a position.

FIGURE 6.13 Pullback (GOLD, weekly: October 4, 2013–June 11, 2015)

Waiting for Retracement

When a breakout occurs but a gap is not present, some traders will wait for the pullback or throwback before entering a position. To do this, they wait for the initial run from the breakout to exhaust itself, calculate a percentage—usually 50%—retracement from the breakout to the high or low, and place a limit order at that level. A breakout followed by a pullback is pictured in Figure 6.13. Studies have shown (Thom Hartle, *Active Trader Magazine,* March 2004) that the percentage retracement is not predictable and varies widely. Thus, these traders run the risk that the security will not retrace the percentage or will retrace the percentage and continue correcting back to the original stop level. To prevent this, once the percentage retracement level is determined and the limit order is placed, the stop is adjusted to just behind the limit order to prevent the retracement from becoming a large loss if it continues. Often the trader will also enter a partial position on the breakout and a partial position at the expected retracement level with a stop for the entire position just behind it. This way, the risk of missing the security continuing beyond its breakout without a retracement is reduced, and should the retracement occur, a full position will be entered at a lower average price.

Calculating a Risk/Return Ratio for Breakout Trading

Usually breakouts from support or resistance run to the next zone of support or resistance. This gives the investor or trader a price objective for the breakout. From that price objective, a risk/return ratio can be calculated. The return is the difference between the entry price and the price objective. The risk is the amount the price must go against the entry price before exited on a stop, usually some price on the other side of the breakout. Traditionally, the reward/risk ratio should be a minimum of 3:1. This gives the investor the odds of making money even when two out of three trades fail, assuming the third action provides a 3:1 gain. This 3:1 guideline, however, should always be the minimum reward/risk ratio. Anything less than 3:1 increases the odds of losing money beyond acceptable amounts.

■ Conclusion

Breakouts from support, resistance, or trend lines are the primary signal that the price has changed direction or is reaccelerating in its original direction. As such, breakouts are usually the first signal to act. Because breakouts can be false and often are, some means of confirming a breakout is necessary. We have covered a few methods, but none of them is foolproof. The technical analyst must experiment with different methods and find those most satisfactory to his method of trading or investing. The same can be said for stops. Although stops need not be as precise, they are always necessary when a position has been entered, and they must never be canceled or changed until they are triggered or the position is closed. Their purpose is to keep the investor honest and solvent. The rules for breakouts apply equally to stops. They should account for previous support or resistance or trend, should adjust for the security's volatility, and should not be placed too close to the current price as to invite a false signal or whipsaw.

■ References

Edwards, Robert, John Magee, and W.H.C. Bassetti. *Technical Analysis of Stock Trends*. 9th ed. Boca Raton, FL: St. Lucie Press, 2007.

Hartle, Thom. "Retracement Tendencies." *Active Trader Magazine* 5, no. 3 (March 2004): 32.

Jiler, William. *How Charts Can Help You in the Stock Market*. New York, NY: Commodity Research Corporation, 1962.

Kaufman, Perry J. *Trading Systems and Methods*. 3rd ed. New York, NY: John Wiley & Sons, 1998.

Merrill, Arthur A. "Retracement Percentage." *Journal of Technical Analysis* (Formerly *the Market Technicians Association Journal*) 33 (August 1989): 38–45.

Wilder, J. Welles, Jr. *New Concepts in Technical Trading Systems*. Greensboro, SC: Trend Research, 1978.

CHAPTER 7

Moving Averages

From Charles D. Kirkpatrick II and Julie R. Dahlquist, *Technical Analysis: The Complete Resource for Financial Market Technicians*, 3rd Edition (Old Tappan, New Jersey: Pearson Education, Inc., 2016), Chapter 14.

Learning Objective Statements

- Describe the basic principle of moving averages
- Explain how to calculate simple, linearly weighted and exponentially smoothed moving averages
- Identify trends and signals with moving averages
- Describe and interpret Directional Movement Indicators
- List common envelope, channel, and band indicators and their characteristics

One of the most successful methods of identifying and profiting from trends is the use of moving averages. A moving average is a constant period average, usually of prices, that is calculated for each successive chart period interval. The result, when plotted on a price chart, shows a smooth line representing the successive, average prices. Moving averages dampen the effects of short-term oscillations. Many of the most successful technical investment managers use moving averages to determine when trends are changing direction. Moving averages are especially useful in markets that have a tendency to trend.

Moving averages have been tested by academics and shown to have statistical significance. Brock, Lakonishok, and LeBaron (1992) were the first to demonstrate, using modern statistical bias-reducing methods, that moving average crossover signals have intrinsic value. As with most academic studies, the results of Brock, Lakonishok, and LeBaron's have been somewhat controversial. Even though some have since criticized their study, other researchers have validated their results. (Incidentally, the Brock, Lakonishok, and LeBaron study provides one of the more useful arguments against the Random Walk and Efficient Markets hypotheses.)

Although the Brock, Lakonishok, and LeBaron study focused on the Dow Jones Industrials, later studies have used moving average crossover systems for market data in other countries with generally the same positive results. Detry and Gregoire (2001) provided a summary of these studies.

There obviously is something to moving averages. Traders and trend investors, of course, have known all this for many years, but technical analysts now feel more comfort in what they have been doing. In this chapter, we discuss some of the moving average methods and strategies that technical analysts use, as well as introduce some variations on moving averages, such as Bollinger Bands, envelopes, and directional movement indicators.

■ What Is a Moving Average?

The moving average is one of the oldest tools used by technical analysts. Daily fluctuations in stock prices, commodity prices, and foreign exchange rates can be large. Moving averages tone down these fluctuations—deemphasizing but sometimes distorting fluctuations. Technical analysts use moving averages to smooth erratic data, making it easier to view the true underlying trend.

The principal reason that moving averages are used is to smooth out shorter fluctuations and focus on the trend that fits with the investor's time horizon. A moving average by its nature is just one number that represents a net of certain past numbers. For example, a 20-day moving average is one number that represents all the prices for the past 20 days. As such, it filters out each one of the prices during the past 20 days and tells us how the group of 20 days, rather than its separate parts, is behaving.

■ How Is a Simple Moving Average Calculated?

Table 7.1 contains the daily closing prices for WMT (Walmart) from November 18, 2014 through February 26, 2015. Most moving averages of prices are based on closing prices, but they can be calculated on highs, lows, daily means, or any other value as long as the price type is consistent throughout the calculations. We use closing prices.

TABLE 7.1	Price Data and Moving Average Calculations for WMT Daily Price Close between November 18, 2014 and February 26, 2015							
Date	Open	High	Low	Close	10-Day SMA	26-Day SMA	10-Day EMA	10-Day LWMA
11/18/2014	83.50	83.92	83.34	83.79				
11/19/2014	83.96	85.64	83.92	84.99				
11/20/2014	84.80	85.29	84.04	84.58				
11/21/2014	85.34	85.44	84.58	84.65				
11/24/2014	84.85	85.61	84.77	85.40				

TABLE 7.1 *(Continued)*

Date	Open	High	Low	Close	10-Day SMA	26-Day SMA	10-Day EMA	10-Day LWMA
11/25/2014	85.42	85.51	84.39	84.95				
11/26/2014	84.90	85.11	84.48	84.98				
11/28/2014	86.18	88.09	85.90	87.54				
12/1/2014	86.72	87.07	85.75	86.22				
12/2/2014	86.27	86.70	85.93	86.40	85.35		85.08	85.78
12/3/2014	85.96	86.00	84.68	84.94	85.47		85.05	85.71
12/4/2014	84.13	84.82	83.65	84.76	85.44		85.00	85.58
12/5/2014	84.90	84.90	83.51	84.12	85.40		84.84	85.34
12/8/2014	84.15	84.67	83.85	84.23	85.35		84.73	85.13
12/9/2014	83.65	84.21	82.65	83.56	85.17		84.52	84.80
12/10/2014	83.93	84.31	82.90	82.98	84.97		84.24	84.40
12/11/2014	83.18	84.50	83.16	83.83	84.86		84.16	84.19
12/12/2014	83.52	85.00	83.52	83.81	84.49		84.10	84.00
12/15/2014	84.26	84.70	83.05	83.94	84.26		84.07	83.90
12/16/2014	83.62	84.76	82.94	82.96	83.91		83.87	83.67
12/17/2014	83.28	84.26	82.95	84.23	83.84		83.93	83.73
12/18/2014	84.80	85.95	84.28	85.94	83.96		84.30	84.11
12/19/2014	86.26	86.34	85.16	85.16	84.06		84.46	84.33
12/22/2014	85.32	86.40	85.29	86.38	84.28		84.81	84.75
12/23/2014	86.69	87.08	86.36	86.66	84.59		85.14	85.18
12/24/2014	86.97	87.07	86.39	86.43	84.93	84.90	85.38	85.51
12/26/2014	86.18	87.14	86.01	86.91	85.24	85.02	85.66	85.87
12/29/2014	86.46	87.07	86.40	86.64	85.53	85.08	85.83	86.13
12/30/2014	86.52	87.13	86.48	86.79	85.81	85.17	86.01	86.36
12/31/2014	87.04	87.44	85.86	85.88	86.10	85.22	85.98	86.37
1/2/2015	86.27	86.72	85.55	85.90	86.27	85.24	85.97	86.33
1/5/2015	85.72	86.32	85.51	85.65	86.24	85.26	85.91	86.22
1/6/2015	85.98	86.75	85.79	86.31	86.36	85.31	85.98	86.23
1/7/2015	86.78	88.68	86.67	88.60	86.58	85.36	86.46	86.64
1/8/2015	89.21	90.67	89.07	90.47	86.96	85.52	87.19	87.35
1/9/2015	90.21	90.39	89.25	89.35	87.25	85.63	87.58	87.79
1/12/2015	89.36	90.31	89.22	90.02	87.56	85.83	88.02	88.29
1/13/2015	90.80	90.97	88.93	89.31	87.83	86.00	88.26	88.61
1/14/2015	87.65	88.52	86.50	86.61	87.81	86.10	87.96	88.39
1/15/2015	87.00	87.78	86.70	87.38	87.96	86.22	87.85	88.31
1/16/2015	87.20	87.46	86.23	86.77	88.05	86.34	87.66	88.09
1/20/2015	86.82	87.70	85.55	86.69	88.15	86.49	87.48	87.84
1/21/2015	86.10	86.91	85.71	86.64	88.18	86.59	87.33	87.57
1/22/2015	87.23	88.40	86.86	88.30	88.15	86.77	87.50	87.59
1/23/2015	88.42	89.26	87.89	88.51	87.96	86.94	87.69	87.66

(continued)

TABLE 7.1 (Continued)

Date	Open	High	Low	Close	10-Day SMA	26-Day SMA	10-Day EMA	10-Day LWMA
1/26/2015	88.31	89.16	88.12	88.63	87.89	87.16	87.86	87.78
1/27/2015	88.28	88.46	87.26	87.53	87.64	87.29	87.80	87.71
1/28/2015	88.02	88.23	86.77	86.82	87.39	87.32	87.62	87.56
1/29/2015	87.07	87.72	86.27	87.72	87.50	87.42	87.64	87.62
1/30/2015	86.66	87.36	84.90	84.98	87.26	87.37	87.16	87.17
2/2/2015	84.79	85.87	83.93	85.71	87.15	87.33	86.89	86.88
2/3/2015	85.83	86.53	85.66	86.19	87.10	87.32	86.76	86.71
2/4/2015	86.11	87.04	86.00	86.65	87.10	87.31	86.74	86.63
2/5/2015	87.11	87.36	86.56	87.28	87.00	87.33	86.84	86.66
2/6/2015	87.26	88.00	86.78	87.33	86.88	87.36	86.93	86.72
2/9/2015	86.97	87.19	85.64	85.91	86.61	87.36	86.74	86.54
2/10/2015	86.62	87.41	86.42	87.29	86.59	87.41	86.84	86.67
2/11/2015	86.63	87.12	85.92	86.34	86.54	87.44	86.75	86.62
2/12/2015	86.56	86.68	85.23	85.89	86.36	87.42	86.60	86.50
2/13/2015	85.84	86.16	85.32	85.81	86.44	87.31	86.45	86.40
2/17/2015	85.43	85.97	84.97	85.96	86.47	87.14	86.36	86.32
2/18/2015	86.00	86.30	85.52	86.29	86.48	87.02	86.35	86.28
2/19/2015	84.50	84.80	83.39	83.52	86.16	86.77	85.84	85.75
2/20/2015	82.73	84.38	82.55	84.30	85.86	86.58	85.56	85.41
2/23/2015	84.39	84.86	84.23	84.60	85.59	86.50	85.38	85.18
2/24/2015	84.52	84.82	83.92	84.57	85.46	86.39	85.23	84.99
2/25/2015	84.63	84.72	83.52	83.57	85.09	86.27	84.93	84.65
2/26/2015	83.85	83.86	83.27	83.80	84.83	86.16	84.73	84.42

Source: TradeStation.

The most commonly used type of moving average is the simple moving average (SMA), sometimes referred to as an **arithmetic moving average.** An SMA is constructed by adding a set of data and then dividing by the number of observations in the period being examined. For example, look at the ten-day SMA in Table 7.1. We begin by summing the closing prices for the first ten days. We then divide this sum by 10 to give us the mean price for that ten-day period. Thus, on the tenth day, the ten-day simple moving average would be the mean closing price for WMT for Days 1 through 10, or $85.35.

On Day 11, the moving average changes. To calculate the moving average for Day 11, we calculate the mean price for Days 2 through 11. In other words, the closing price for Day 1 is dropped from the data set, whereas the price for Day 11 is added. The formula for calculating a ten-day simple moving average is as follows:

$$SMA_{10} = \sum_{i=1}^{10} data_i / 10$$

Of course, we can construct moving averages of different lengths. In Table 7.1, you can also see a 26-day moving average. This SMA is simply calculated by adding the 26 most recent closing prices and dividing by 26.

Although a moving average can smooth prices over any desired period, some of the more popular daily moving averages are for the periods 200, 60, 50, 30, 20, and 10 days. These periods are somewhat arbitrary and were chosen in the days before computers when the calculations had to be done by hand or on a crank adding machine. Gartley (1935), for example, used the 200-day moving average in his work. Simply, numbers divisible by 10 were easier to calculate. Also, the 10-day, 20-day, and 60-day moving averages summarize approximately two weeks, one month, and three months (one fiscal quarter) of trading data, respectively.

Once calculated, moving averages are plotted on a price chart. Figure 7.1 shows a plot of the 26-day simple moving average for WMT. From early November through late January, the moving average is an upward sloping curve, indicating an upward trend in Walmart's price. The daily fluctuations are smoothed by the moving average so that the analyst can see the underlying trend without being distracted by the small, daily movements.

FIGURE 7.1 SMA—26-Day Simple Moving Average (Walmart [WMT] daily: October 14, 2014–February 6, 2015)

A rising moving average indicates an upward trend, whereas a falling moving average indicates a downward trend. Although the moving average helps us discern a trend, it does so after the trend has begun. Thus, the moving average is a lagging indicator. By definition, the moving average is an indicator that is based on past prices. For example, Figure 7.1 shows an upward trend in WMT prices beginning in late October. However, an upward movement in the SMA does not occur until approximately early November. Remember that according to technical analysis principles, we want to be trading with the trend. Using a moving average will always give us some delay in signaling a change in trend.

Length of Moving Average

Because moving averages can be calculated for various lengths of time, which length is best to use? Of course, a longer time period includes more data observations, and, thus, more information. By including more data in the calculation of the moving average, each day's data becomes relatively less important in the calculation. Therefore, a large change in the value on one day does not have a large impact on the longer moving average. This can be an advantage if this large change is a one-day, irregular outlier in the data.

However, if this large move represents the beginning of a significant change in the trend, it takes longer for the underlying trend change to be discernable. Thus, the longer moving average is slower to pick up trend changes but less likely to falsely indicate a trend change due to a short-term blip in the data.

Figure 7.2, for example, shows both a 13-day and a 26-day SMA plotted for WMT. Notice how the shorter, 13-day moving average shows more variability than the longer, 26-day moving average. The 26-day moving average is said to be the "slower" moving average. Although it provides more smoothing, the 26-day smoothing average is also slower at signaling underlying trend changes. Notice the 13-day SMA troughs in late October/early November, signaling a change in trend; a week later, the slower, 26-day SMA is flat but and gradually turning upward. Thus, the 26-day SMA is slower to indicate a trend change.

Because spotting a trend reversal as soon as possible maximizes trading profits, the 13-day SMA may first appear to give superior information; however, remember that the faster SMA has a disadvantage of potentially giving a false signal of a changing trend direction. For example, look at early December in Figure 7.2. The 13-day SMA flattens out, suggesting an end to the upward price trend. After the fact, however, we can see that a trend reversal did not occur until mid-January. The 13-day SMA was overly sensitive to a temporary decrease in price. During this period, the slower 26-day SMA continued to signal correctly an upward trend.

Using Multiple Moving Averages

Analysis is not limited to the information provided by a single moving average. Considering various moving averages of various lengths simultaneously can increase the

FIGURE 7.2 Two Moving Averages—Crossover as Support and Resistance Zone (Walmart [WMT] daily: October 15, 2014–February 26, 2015)

analysts' information set. For example, as shown in Figure 7.2, a support or resistance level often occurs where two moving averages cross. Where the shorter moving average crosses above the longer is often taken as a mechanical buy signal, or at least a sign that the price trend is upward. Likewise, it is considered a sell signal when the shorter declines below the longer. Many successful moving average strategies use moving averages as the principal determinant of trend and then use shorter-term moving averages either as trailing stops or as signals. In some instances, moving averages are used to determine trend, and then chart patterns are used as entry and exit signals.

Using these types of dual moving average signals during a sideways trend in prices, however, can result in a number of whipsaws. This problem can be seen in Figure 7.3. This is essentially the same problem that occurs during the standard sideways trend in a congestion area. It is difficult to determine from such action in which way prices are going to break out. Meanwhile, they oscillate back and forth within the support and resistance levels. A moving average provides no additional information on which way the trend will eventually break. Indeed, a moving average requires a trend for a crossover to be profitable. This means that the analyst must be sure that

FIGURE 7.3 Moving Average Crossovers Causing Whipsaws in a Flat Trend (Walmart [WMT] daily: October 15, 2014–February 26, 2015)

a trend exists before using moving average crossovers for signals. Otherwise—and some traders are willing to take the risk of short-term whipsaws so they don't miss the major trend—a plurality of signals will be incorrect and produce small losses while waiting for the one signal that will produce the large profit. This can be a highly profitable method provided the analyst has the stomach and discipline to continue with the small losses, and it often is the basis for many long-term trend systems. It also demonstrates how, with proper discipline, one can profit while still losing on a majority of small trades.

■ What Other Types of Moving Averages Are Used?

Although we have discussed various lengths of moving averages, up to this point our discussion has centered on the most basic type of moving average calculation—the SMA. Remember that each day's calculation of the SMA represents adding the most recent day's price figure and dropping the earliest day's price figure. When calculating the simple moving average, equal weight is given to each daily observation. For a ten-day SMA, the information contained in the stock price for each of the ten days is given equal importance. However, in certain situations, the most recent stock price may have more bearing on the future direction of the stock than the ten-day old stock price does. If observations that are more recent contain more relevant information than earlier observations, we want to weight data in favor of the most recent observation. By calculating a weighted moving average, the most recent day's information is weighted more heavily. This weighting scheme gives the most recent observation more importance in the moving average calculation.

The Linearly Weighted Moving Average (LWMA)

Let us refer back to the example in Table 7.1 to calculate a linearly weighted moving average. A ten-day linearly weighted moving average multiplies the tenth day observation by 10, the ninth day by 9, the eighth day by 8, and so forth. The total of these numbers is added up and divided by the sum of all the multipliers. In this case, the total will be divided by the sum $10 + 9 + 8 + 7 + 6 + 5 + 4 + 3 + 2 + 1$, or 55. In Table 7.1, we find that the linearly weighted moving average for the first ten trading days is 85.78.

When using this ten-day moving average weighting scheme, the most recent trading data (Day 10) is given twice the importance of the price five days earlier (Day 5) and ten times the importance of the price ten days earlier (Day 1). As we go on to calculate the ten-day linearly weighted moving average for Day 11, the prices for trading Days 2–11 again will be weighted. Therefore, just as with the simple moving average, as the moving average is calculated for each successive day, the earliest trading day information is dropped from the data set being used in the calculation.

The Exponentially Smoothed Moving Average (EMA)

For some analysts, dropping off the earliest trading day's data that occurs with an SMA or linearly weighted moving average is problematic. If the most recent price reflects little change, but the earliest price, now being omitted, shows considerable change, the moving average can be unduly influenced by the discarding of the older data. A large change in the moving average that results from the deletion of early data potentially generates a false signal. This is called the "drop-off effect" (Kaufman, 1998) and is probably the most criticized aspect of a simple moving average.

Although it is easy to see how this early data is not necessarily as important in determining future price movement as the most recent prices, it is still information that may have value. With both the simple moving average and the linearly weighted moving average, this older information, which lies outside the length of the moving average, is being totally ignored. To address this issue and maintain this older information in the moving average calculation, analysts use the **exponential moving average (EMA)**.

To see how the exponential moving average is calculated, let us again refer to the example in Table 7.1. The simple ten-day moving average on Day 10 was 85.35. The closing price on Day 11 was 84.94, a lower value than the mean value for the previous ten days. To calculate the exponential moving average, we will use both the ten-day moving average (which represents the mean exchange rate for Days 1–10) and the closing price for Day 11. Thus, we are now using 11 days of price information. If we were going to calculate an SMA using these 11 days of information, each day's price would have a weight of 1/11, or 9.09% in the calculation. Remember, however, that we want to place a larger weight on information that is more recent. If we want the price information from Day 11 to have a weight twice as great as it would have in a simple moving average, it would have a weight of 2/11, or 18.18%. Of course, the total of all the weights in the calculation of the exponential moving average must sum to 100%. This leaves 100% minus 18.18%, or 81.82% weight to be placed on the ten-day moving average.

The general formula for determining the weight of the current day's data in the exponential moving average calculation is as follows:

$$\text{WEIGHT}_{current} = 2 \div (\text{number of days in moving average} + 1)$$

In our example, the calculation gives us $\text{WEIGHT}_{current} = 2 \div (10 + 1) = 18.18$ percent. If we were using a longer moving average, this weight would decrease in value. For a 19-day EMA, the calculation would be $2 \div (19 + 1)$ or 10%; a 39-day EMA would have a weight of $2 \div (39 + 1)$, or 5%.

The general formula for determining the weight given to the moving average in the calculation of the exponential moving average is the following:

$$\text{WEIGHT}_{ma} = 100\% - \text{WEIGHT}_{current}$$

In our example, we have $\text{WEIGHT}_{ma} = 100\% - 18.18\% = 81.82\%$.

Once we have the weights, the formula for calculating the exponential moving average is as follows:

$$\text{EMA}_{day\ i} = \text{WEIGHT}_{current} \times \text{DATA}_{day\ i} + \text{WEIGHT}_{ma} \\ \times \text{Moving Average}_{day\ i-1}$$

The exponential moving average for Day 11 in our example in Table 7.1 is calculated as the following:

$$\text{EMA}_{11} = .1818 \times 84.94 + .8182 \times 85.08 = 85.05$$

To calculate the exponential moving average for Day 12, we need only two pieces of information—the exponential moving average for Day 11 and the closing price for Day 12. The EMA_{12} would be calculated as follows:

$$EMA_{12} = .1818 \times 84.76 + .8182 \times 85.05 = 85.00$$

Figure 7.4 shows both a 26-day SMA and a 26-day EMA for WMT. Generally, the EMA will change direction more quickly because of the additional weighting that is placed on the most recent data. However, these two curves will usually track each other closely.

The EMA is used in a number of indicators and oscillators. The McClellan Index uses a 19-day and a 39-day EMA. Because the 19-bar EMA has a smoothing factor of 0.10 and the 39-bar EMA has a smoothing factor of 0.05, these calculations are relatively easy. We will see later that a number of oscillators use an EMA, most prominently the MACD. The reason for the use of an EMA is that it is easily calculated and that it weighs more strongly the prices that are more recent. It is, thus, called an **exponential weighted moving average**.

FIGURE 7.4 Exponential versus Simple Moving Average
(Walmart [WMT] daily: October 15, 2014–February 26, 2015)

Wilder Method

Welles Wilder (1978) used another simple method to calculate a moving average that weights the most recent number more heavily. The formula for calculating Wilder's moving average is as follows:

$$MA_{day\ i} = ((n - 1) \times MA_{i-1} + Price_{day\ i}) \div n$$

For example, a 14-day Wilder moving average would be equal to the previous day's moving average figure times 13 (that is, $n - 1$, where n is the number of items to be averaged) plus the current closing price, all divided by 14 (that is, n).

Wilder's method of calculating a moving average should be used in the average true range (ATR), the relative strength index (RSI), and the directional movement indicator (DMI) calculations that he invented rather than the SMA or EMA. When using Wilder's indicators that are prepackaged in available trading and charting software, one must be sure that the calculations for moving averages are Wilder's. Some software programs use just an SMA or EMA and give results inconsistent with Wilder's methods.

Geometric Moving Average (GMA)

The geometric moving average (GMA) is used mostly in indexes. It is a simple moving average of the percent changes between the previous bar and the current bar over some past predetermined period. Using percentages rather than points does not change its range or dimensions like a price-based moving average. However, it still has all the other problems of equal weight and lag.

Triangular Moving Average

Taking a moving average of a moving average gives a doubly smoothed moving average. The triangular moving average (TMA) begins with a simple moving average of a predetermined number of bars and then, using those results, takes a moving average of a length of half the original number of bars. An example would be a 20-day SMA of daily closes smoothed in a ten-day SMA. The result is a smoothed line that emphasizes the weight of the middle of the price series. The benefit of this method is that it doubly smoothes the data and, thus, better represents the trend. However, the double smoothing also detracts from its sensitivity to trend changes.

Variable EMAs

The use of a variable moving average is suggested by Chande and Kroll (1994). This moving average is the same as an exponential moving average (EMA), but the weighting scheme is adjusted based on the volatility of the price data. This is done to make the EMA shorter during trading ranges when volatility is narrow and expand the EMA when price begins to trend. The desire was to reduce the number of adverse signals during a trading range.

There are a number of variations of this theme. For example, the Kaufman adaptive moving average (KAMA) involves an extremely complicated formula that adjusts an EMA for volatility and trend (Kaufman, 1998). The volume-adjusted moving average (Arms, 1989) is a somewhat complicated moving average, but its essence is that it emphasizes those bars with higher volume. In the September 2001 issue of *Stocks and Commodities Magazine*, John Ehlers presents MAMA and FAMA. MAMA, the MESA adaptive moving average, and FAMA, the following adaptive moving average, are EMAs that adapt to volatility using Hilbert's Transform based on the phase change of a cycle in the data. Needless to say, the calculation of these moving averages is complicated. A buy or sell signal is generated when the MAMA crosses the FAMA. In April 2004, *Active Trader Magazine* compared the effectiveness of using the MAMA-FAMA strategy to using an SMA for 18 stocks and found that the MAMA-FAMA strategy performed only slightly better than the simple method.

■ Strategies for Using Moving Averages

We have looked at a number of ways to calculate moving averages. Although each of these methods has its advantages and disadvantages, our main concern is not how to calculate a moving average but how to use moving averages to make money. Moving averages are widely used in the practice of technical analysis. They are a basic tool with a broad set of uses. Technical analysts use moving averages to determine trend, to determine levels of support and resistance, to spot price extremes, and for specific trading signals.

Determining Trend

Technical analysts use moving averages in four basic ways. First, moving averages are used as a measure of trend. The most common usage is comparing the current price with the moving average that represents the investor's time horizon. For example, many investors use a 200-day moving average. If the stock or market average is above its 200-day moving average, the trend is considered upward. Conversely, if the stock or market average is below the 200-day moving average, the trend is considered downward.

In Figure 7.5, you can see how the moving average tends to follow the trend line fairly well. The moving average then becomes a proxy for the trend line and can be used to determine when a trend is potentially changing direction, just as can a trend line. In the chart, for example, the later prices have held at both the trend line and the moving average.

FIGURE 7.5 Trend Line versus Simple Moving Average
(Walmart [WMT] daily: October 15, 2014–February 26, 2015)

Determining Support and Resistance

Second, the moving average often acts as support or resistance. As we have seen from Figure 7.5, a moving average often duplicates the trend line; therefore, it can be an easy trailing stop mechanism for determining when a position should be liquidated or reduced. In addition, prices seem to halt at the vicinity of moving averages. In Figure 7.5, for example, WMT halted its rally in late November at the moving average and again halted its decline at the moving average in early December.

Determining Price Extremes

Third, the moving average is an indicator of price extreme. Because the moving average is a mean, any reversion to the mean will tend to approach the moving average. For trading purposes, this reversion is sometimes profitable when the current price has deviated substantially from that mean or moving average. Price has a tendency to return to the mean. Thus, a deviation from the moving average is a measure of how much prices have risen or fallen ahead of their usual central tendency, and being likely to return to that mean, this deviation then becomes an opportunity to trade with and against the trend. As always, trading against the trend is dangerous and requires close stops, but the reversion also provides an opportunity to position with the trend when it occurs. In addition, when prices continue substantially away from the trend, they are often signaling that the trend is changing direction.

An example of the deviation about a 10-day SMA is shown in Figure 7.6. This is a ratio of the close to its 10-day moving average. It is a stock with a strong upward trend (the dominant trend for our purposes). When prices are trending strongly, they naturally will deviate from the moving average in the direction of the trend more than they will against it. In Figure 7.6, you can see that the advances carry much higher above the equilibrium level of 1.00 than they do during a correction in the upward trend. Action signal lines can thus be established, by testing, at the levels that optimize counter-trend signals. In Figure 7.6, we have arbitrarily used 1.0450 as the ratio below which we would sell WMT even in its upward trend and 0.9750 as the buy level above which we go long. Following this method, we go long on October 21 at 76.02 and sell at 86.40 on December 2. Again, we go long on the upward break of the ratio buy level on December 15 at 83.94 and sell at 89.35 on January 9.

FIGURE 7.6   Ratio of Current Price to Moving Average
(Walmart [WMT] daily: October 15, 2014–February 26, 2015)

We have made nice profits by trading along the trend. The last buy signal comes on February 3 at 86.19. Notice, however, that the trend line has been broken and that the trend may now be going sideways or downward. We sold at the high but hesitate to buy on the signal because of the potential trend change. What else can go wrong? Sometimes the trend is so strong that the ratio never reaches below the buy level. A buy entry stop should thus be placed above the bar where the sale took place. In the last example on the chart, where the trend may have changed, the buy may not work, but if it has a sell stop at its signal bar low, a breaking of that low would indicate a trend change downward and the buy and sell levels in the ratio would be the recipro-cals of the upward trend levels. Before you try this system, you should be sure to test for the optimal ratio levels under all trend directions including a flat trend. In this example, we did not optimize the levels; thus, they should not be used until tested.

Giving Specific Signals

Fourth, some technical analysts use moving averages to give specific signals. These can occur when prices cross a moving average, when a shorter moving average cross-es a longer moving average, and in some cases, when a third, even shorter, moving average crosses two longer ones. Generally, using two moving averages and their crossover as a signal has been successful, but with substantial drawdowns in capital in sideways markets because of the many unprofitable small trades that occur from the many false signals. Methods, such as using the ADX, described in the next section, have been developed to determine if prices are trending at a rate at which a moving-average crossover system will work. The MAMA-FAMA system described previously and other methods of adapting moving averages to changes in volatility are aimed at solving this drawdown problem. However, it will not go away, and thus, although the crossover methods are profitable over time, the investor must have patience and enough capital to withstand a series of small losses until a trend develops.

Of the four strategies, the most sensible use of moving averages is trend deter-mination. The trend is where the technical analyst profits. If the moving average can help in determining the trend, it is a useful tool. Indeed, it is only during a trend-ing market that moving average signals are profitable. A sideways market is costly in almost all cases, but it's especially so if the investor depends on moving average crossovers for signals. The deviation-from-trend method (see the section "Determin-ing Price Extremes" earlier and Figure 7.6) is about the only moving average method that can profit in a flat trend. Once a directional trend has been established and iden-tified, the next best method is to use price patterns and breakouts in the direction of the trend for timing of position entries. These methods will lag behind the major bottom and top of a price trend but will accrue profits and minimize losses while the trend is in effect. They are also the most popular method in professional trading systems, along with channel breakout systems such as Donchian's four-week rule that we discuss in the "Channel" section of this chapter.

■ What Is Directional Movement?

One of the great contributions to the concept of trend and direction is the concept of directional movement that Welles Wilder (1978) developed in his book *New Concepts in Technical Trading Systems*. Wilder compared a stock's trading range for one day with the trading range on the previous day to measure trend. Positive directional movement occurred when the high for a day exceeded the high of the previous day. As shown in Figure 7.7, the amount of positive directional movement (+DM) is the day's high minus the previous day's high, or the vertical distance between the top of the two bars. If the low for the day is less than the previous day's low, negative directional movement occurs. The value of the negative directional movement (–DM) is the difference between the two lows.

Days on which the range is completely within the previous day's range are ignored, and a zero is given to the range excess. In addition, one day's trading range is sometimes much larger than the previous day's trading range. This can result in both a higher high and a lower low. When this happens, the greater difference wins. In other words, only a +DM or –DM may be recorded for a particular day.

Constructing Directional Movement Indicators

A moving average is calculated for both +DM and –DM, usually over 14 days, using the Wilder method of averaging. In addition, a 14-day average trading range (ATR) is calculated. Two indicators are calculated using this data. The positive directional movement indicator (DI+) is the ratio between the smoothed +DM and the TR; this calculation gives the percentage of the true range that was above equilibrium for those 14 days. The second indicator is the negative directional movement indicator (DI–), which is calculated as the ratio between the smoothed –DM and the ATR.

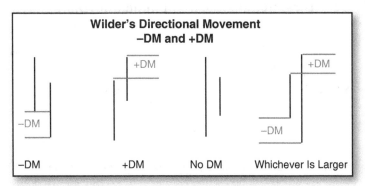

FIGURE 7.7   Calculating Directional Movement

Using Directional Movement Indicators

Figure 7.8 shows 14-day DIs for Walmart (WMT). Looking at this chart, an analyst sees a number of hints about trend. First, when one DI is higher than the other, the trend is in the direction of that DI. For example, from early November through late January, the DI+ was above the DI–, indicating that a majority of the 14-day ATR excess for WMT was on the upside during that period. The first major crossover occurred in early October when the DI+ crossed above the DI– (marked with "X1") indicating an upturn in the price trend, and the second occurred in late January when the DI– crossed above the DI+ (marked with "X2") and warned us that the trend had reversed downward. This confirmed the earlier downward break of the trend line. Thus, the DMI crossover is an important signal in analyzing trends.

Second, the minor crossover that occurred in early February (marked with a "mc") and lasted only a day is an important sign. It suggests that the direction of the trend is now sideways and, like a congestion area, it may break in either direction. Often, the two DIs come to equilibrium and then part in their original direction, as happened here, in which case the earlier trend resumes. At other times, the DIs

FIGURE 7.8 Directional Movement Indicator (Walmart [WMT] daily: October 15, 2014– February 26, 2015)

cross more dramatically and incisively, as they did in late January, and signal a trend reversal. When the two meet, therefore, is an important period. Wilder suggested placing a buy or sell stop at the price when the two first cross. In Figure 7.8, as the two DIs cross in early February, we do not know if this is a trend reversal. Thus, we place a buy stop at a price just above the price that occurred when the two initially crossed. If the trend is reversing, the price will hit our stop, and our position will be in line with the new upward trend. If the stop is not hit, the two lines will likely diverge again, and the old downward trend will continue without us.

Third, standard divergence techniques are valid in the DMI. In Figure 7.8, notice where the highest peak exceeded the earlier peak (price plot: dotted line from peak to peak) was not confirmed in the DI+, which failed to reach a new high at the same time (DMI plot: dotted line from peak to peak). This is a negative divergence that, although not an action signal, is a warning that the earlier upward trend is losing strength.

Fourth, the DIs can be used to create a directional index (DX). This DX then is used to create the average DX called the **ADX line** shown in Figure 7.9. The DX is calculated by taking the absolute difference between the values of the two DIs and dividing it by the sum of the two DIs. The DX is always positive and represents the tendency of the market to trend because it measures the DIs against each other. When one DI is very large compared to the other DI, the market is moving strongly in one direction and the value of the DX will be large.

The ADX is the smoothed value of the DX and is plotted on Figure 7.9. When the ADX is rising, the market is increasingly trending in either direction.

The ADX indicator is valuable in determining when to apply a moving average trend-following system. A rising ADX indicates an increasing tendency to trend in the corresponding prices. A low ADX or one that's declining indicates a flat or dull trend on one that is losing momentum. We know that the moving average cross-over systems have multiple whipsaws when the market is not in a directional trend but have profitable outcomes when the market is trending in either an upward or a downward direction. Many trend-following models use the ADX to determine when money should be committed to the markets.

Fifth, ADX peaks and troughs provide valuable information about the price trend. When the ADX peaks, it often signals a peak or trough in prices. In Figure 7.9, peaks in the ADX (marked with arrows) show how closely they coincide with up or down reversals in price. Because their pinpointing the end of trends is so accurate, ADX peaks are used as trading signals to close trend positions.

Troughs in the ADX are useful because they signify periods when the market has become dormant and trendless but is beginning to accelerate in a trend direction. When the ADX begins to rise, not necessarily from a low level, it signals a sudden increase in trending and is a time to look for entry into the trend. As we know from looking at congestion areas, a dormant period is usually followed by a dynamic period. This phenomenon can be seen in Figure 7.9 with the ADX troughs (marked with arrows within circles) associated with the dormant period turning into a trend with

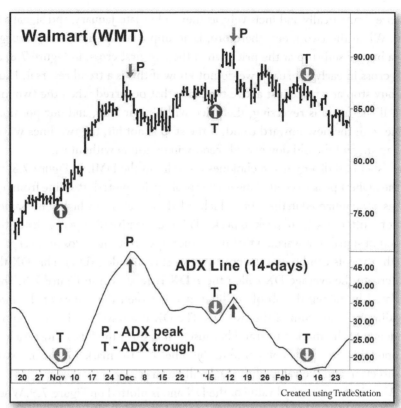

FIGURE 7.9 ADX Line (Walmart [WMT] daily: October 15, 2014–February 26, 2015)

increasing momentum. When an ADX trough occurs, the trader or investor should be watching price closely for a breakout in either direction.

ADXs and DMIs can be used on weekly, monthly, and even shorter-term, intraday charts for clues as to trend strength and direction.

■ What Are Envelopes, Channels, and Bands?

The simple moving average represents the center of a stock's price trend. Actual prices tend to oscillate around that moving average. The price movement is centered on the moving average but falls within a band or envelope around the moving average. By determining the band within which prices tend to oscillate, the analyst is better able to determine the range in which price may be expected to fluctuate.

Percentage Envelopes

One way of creating this type of band is to use **percentage envelopes**. This method, also known as a percentage filter, was developed in an attempt to reduce the numerous unprofitable signals from crossing a moving average when the trend is sideways. This is a popular method used in most of the academic studies on moving average crossover systems. It is calculated by taking a percentage of the moving average and plotting it above and below the moving average (see Figure 7.10)—thus the term *envelope*. This plot creates two symmetrical lines: one above and one below the moving average.

This envelope then becomes the trigger for signals when it is crossed by the price rather than when the moving average is crossed. The percentage used in the calculation should be large enough that it encompasses most of the oscillations around the moving average during a sideways period and, thus, reduces the number of incorrect signals, yet it should be small enough to give signals early enough to be profitable once a trend has been established. This percentage must be determined through experiment because a slight difference in percentage can cause a considerable difference in performance.

One of the major problems with fixed-percentage envelopes is that they do not account for the changing volatility of the underlying price. During a sideways trend, when volatility usually declines, price action can be contained within a relatively

FIGURE 7.10 Percentage Envelope about a Moving Average
(Walmart [WMT] daily: October 15, 2014–February 26, 2015)

narrow band. When the trend begins, however, volatility often expands and will then create false signals using a fixed-percentage envelope. To combat this problem, the concept of bands that are adjusted for volatility developed.

Bands

Bands are also envelopes around a moving average but, rather than being fixed in size, are calculated to adjust for the price volatility around the moving average. They, thus, shrink when prices become calm and expand when prices become volatile. The most widely used band is the Bollinger Band, named after John Bollinger (2002).

Bollinger Band As we mentioned earlier, there are two principal ways to measure price volatility. One is the standard deviation about a mean or moving average, and the other is the ATR. Bollinger Bands use the standard deviation calculation.

To construct Bollinger Bands, first calculate a simple moving average of prices. Bollinger uses the SMA because most calculations using standard deviation use an SMA. Next, draw bands a certain number of standard deviations above and below the moving average. For example, Bollinger's standard calculation, and the one most often seen in the public chart services, begins with a 20-period simple moving average. Two standard deviations are added to the SMA to plot an upper band. The lower band is constructed by subtracting two standard deviations from the SMA. The bands are self-adjusting, automatically becoming wider during periods of extreme price changes.

Figure 7.11 shows the standard Bollinger Band around the 20-period moving average with bands at two standard deviations. Of course, both the length of the moving average and the number of standard deviations can be adjusted. Theoretically, the plus or minus two standard deviations should account for approximately 95% of all the price action about the moving average. In fact, this is not quite true because price action is nonstationary and nonrandom and, thus, does not follow the statistical properties of the standard deviation calculation precisely. However, it is a good estimate of the majority of price action. Indeed, as the chart shows, the price action seems to oscillate between the bands quite regularly. This action is similar to the action in a congestion area or rectangle pattern, except that prices also tend to oscillate within the band as the price trends upward and downward. This is because the moving average is replicating the trend of the prices and adjusting for them while the band is describing their normal upper and lower limits around the trend as price volatility changes.

Keltner Band Chester Keltner (1960) introduced Keltner Bands in his book *How to Make Money in Commodities*. To construct these bands, first calculate the "Typical Price" (Close + High + Low) ÷ 3, and calculate a ten-day SMA of the typical price. Next, calculate the band size by creating a ten-day SMA of High minus Low or bar

FIGURE 7.11 Bollinger Bands (Walmart [WMT] daily: October 15, 2014–February 26, 2015)

range. The upper band is then plotted as the ten-day SMA of the typical price plus the ten-day SMA of bar range. The lower band is plotted as the ten-day SMA to the typical price minus the ten-day SMA of bar range. (When the calculation is rearranged, it is similar to the use of an ATR. These bands are sometimes referred to as ATR bands.)

As with most methods, different analysts prefer to modify the basic model to meet their specific needs and investment strategies. Although Keltner's original calculation used ten-day moving averages, many analysts using this method have extended the moving averages to 20 periods. The 20-period calculation is more in line with the calculation for a Bollinger Band.

STARC Band STARC is an acronym for Stoller Average Range Channel, invented by Manning Stoller. This system uses the ATR over five periods added to and subtracted from a five-period SMA of prices. It produces a band about prices that widens and shrinks with changes in the ATR or the volatility of the price. Just as with the Keltner Bands, the length of the SMA used with STARC can be adjusted to different trading or investing time horizons.

Trading Strategies Using Bands and Envelopes

In line with the basic concept of following the trend, bands and envelopes are used to signal when a trend change has occurred and to reduce the number of whipsaws that occur within a tight trading range. While looking at the envelopes or bands on a chart, one would think that the best use of them might be to trade within them from high extreme to low extreme and back, similar to strategies for rectangle patterns. However, the trading between bands is difficult. First, by definition, except for fixed envelopes, the bands contract during a sideways, dull trend and leave little room for maneuvering at a cost-effective manner and with profitable results. Second, when prices suddenly move on a new trend, they tend to remain close to the band in the direction of the trend and give many false exit signals. Third, when the bands expand, they show that volatility has increased, usually due to the beginning of a new trend, and any position entered in further anticipation of low volatility is quickly stopped out.

Bands, therefore, have become methods of determining the beginnings of trends and are not generally used for range trading between them. When the outer edge of a band is broken, empirical evidence suggests that the entry should be in the direction of the breakout, not unlike the breakout of a trend line or support or resistance level. A breakout from a band that contains roughly 90% of previous price action suggests that the general trend of the previous price action has changed in the direction of the breakout.

In Figure 7.11, a breakout buy signal occurs in early November, when the price breaks above the upper Bollinger Band, hinting that a strong upward trend is starting. The bands had become narrower during October. This band tightening, caused by shrinking volatility, is often followed by a sharp price move.

The only difference between a band breakout and a more conventional kind is that a band is generally more fluid. Because moving averages will often become support or resistance levels, the moving average in the Bollinger Band calculation should then become the trailing stop level for any entry that previously occurred from a breakout above or below the band. The ability of moving averages to be used as trailing stops is easily spliced into a system utilizing any kind of bands that adjust for volatility.

The other use for the moving average within a band is as a retracement level for additional entry in the trend established by the direction of the moving average and the bands. With a stop only slightly below the moving average using the rules we learned for establishing stop levels, when the price retraces back into the area of the moving average while in a strong upward trend, an additional entry can be made where the retracement within the band is expected to halt.

In testing band breakouts, the longer the period, it seems, the more profitable the system. Very short-term volatility, because it is proportionally more active, causes many false breakouts. Longer-term periods with less volatility per period appear to remain in trends for longer periods and are not whipsawed as much as short-term trends. The most profitable trend-following systems are long-term, and as short-term traders have learned, the ability of price to oscillate sharply is greater than when it is smoothed over longer periods. Thus, the inherent whipsaws in short-term data become reduced over longer periods, and trend-following systems tracking longer trends have fewer unprofitable signals. Bands are more successful in trending markets and are, therefore, more suitable for commodities markets than the stock market.

Another use for bands is to watch price volatility. Low volatility is generally associated with sideways to slightly slanted trends—ones where whipsaws are common and patterns fail. High volatility is generally associated with a strong trend, up or down. By watching volatility, especially for an increase in volatility, the analyst has a clue that a change in trend is forthcoming. To watch volatility, one should take a difference between the high band and low band and plot it as a line below the price action. Bollinger calls this line a **Bandwidth Indicator**. A rise in the bandwidth line, which results from increasing volatility, can be associated directly with price action. Any breakout from a pattern, support or resistance level, trend line, or moving average can be confirmed by the change in volatility. If volatility does not increase with a price breakout, the odds favor that the breakout is false. Volatility, therefore, can be used as confirmation for trend changes, or it can be used as a warning that things are about to change. This use of bands is more successful when combined with other methods of determining an actual trend change.

Channel

In discussing trend lines, we noted that a line can often be drawn parallel to a trend line that encompasses the price action in what was called a **channel**. For present purposes, that definition changes slightly by relaxing the requirement for a parallel line.

Channels have been described as something simpler than two parallel lines. We mentioned the Donchian channel method that has been so successful even though it's been widely known for many years. Signals occur with the Donchian channel when the breaking above or below a high or low over some past period occurs (see Figure 7.12). This method does not require the construction of a trend line; the only requirement is a record of the highs and lows over some past period. In the case of the Donchian channel method, the period was four weeks (20 days), and the rule was to buy when the price exceeded the highest level over the past four weeks and sell short when the price declined below the lowest low over the past four weeks. Such systems are usually "stop and reverse" systems that are always in the market, either long or short. As is likely imagined, the channel systems are more commonly used in the commodities markets where long and short positions are effortless and prices tend to trend much longer.

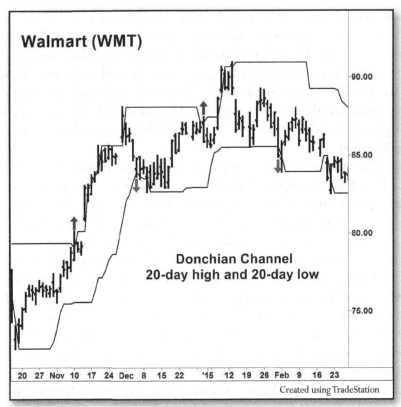

FIGURE 7.12 Donchian Channel on Daily Closes (Walmart [WMT] daily: October 15, 2014–February 26, 2015)

■ Conclusion

The basic way the technical analyst makes profits is by identifying a trend in prices and riding that trend. At times, daily fluctuations in prices make it difficult for the analyst to view the basic underlying trend in prices. Moving averages are tools used to smooth this erratic data, making it easier to discern the genuine underlying trend.

Although there are various methods of calculating a moving average, the basic idea is to give a summary of the average or normal price history of a particular period. Because the moving averages are based on historical prices, by nature, they will be a lagging indicator of trends. The shorter the period covered by the moving average, the less of a lag there will be. However, using a shorter period also leads to more false signals. As usual, when choosing a moving average system, there is a trade-off between early trend reversal recognition and certainty of trend reversal. The use of envelopes, bands, and channels around the moving average can minimize the number of false signals by providing a larger range of price movement before a signal is triggered.

Box 7.1 gives a list of basic principles that the technical analyst should keep in mind.

BOX 7.1 TRADING RULES

We have covered a good deal of material regarding trends. Here are some of the key points to remember when investing:

- Riding the trend is the most profitable use of technical analysis.
- Trends can be identified with trend lines, moving averages, and relative highs and lows.
- Always pick a security that trends up and down. Flat or random trends are usually unprofitable.
- Be aware of the next longer period and shorter period trends from the one being traded.
- Always trade with the trend:
  - "Trend is your friend."
  - "Don't buck the trend."
- Breakouts from support or resistance levels, patterns, or bands usually signal a change in trend.
- A trend line breakout is at least a warning.
- The longer the trend, the more important the breakout.
- Confirm any breakout with other evidence, especially when entering a position. In exiting, confirmation is not as important.
- Always use stops—protective and trailing.
- Do not sell profitable positions too soon; just keep trailing with stops.

■ References

Arms, Richard W., Jr. *The Arms Index: An Introduction to the Volume Analysis of Stock and Bond Markets*. Homewood, IL: Dow Jones-Irwin, 1989.

Bollinger, John. *Bollinger on Bollinger Bands*. New York, NY: McGraw-Hill, 2002.

Brock, W., J. Lakonishok, and B. LeBaron. "Simple Technical Trading Rules and the Stochastic Properties of Stock Returns." *Journal of Finance* 47 (1992): 1731–1764.

Chande, Tushar S. and Stanley Kroll. *The New Technical Trader: Boost Your Profit by Plugging into the Latest Indicators*. New York, NY: John Wiley & Sons, 1994.

Detry, P.J. and Philippe Gregoire. "Other Evidences of the Predictive Power of Technical Analysis: The Moving Averages Rules on European Indexes." European Finance Management Association Meeting, Lugano, Switzerland, 2001, http://ssrn.com/abstract=269802.

Ehlers, John. "MESA Adaptive Moving Averages." *Technical Analysis of Stocks and Commodities* 19, no. 9 (September 2001): 30–35.

Gartley, H.M. *Profits in the Stock Market*. 3rd ed. (1981). Pomeroy, WA: Lambert-Gann Publishing Co., 1935.

Kaufman, Perry J. *Trading Systems and Methods*. 3rd ed. New York, NY: John Wiley & Sons, 1998.

Keltner, Chester W. *How to Make Money in Commodities*. Kansas City, MO: Keltner Statistical Service, 1960.

Wilder, J. Welles, Jr. *New Concepts in Technical Trading Systems*. Greensboro, SC: Trend Research, 1978.

CHAPTER 8

Bar Chart Patterns

From Charles D. Kirkpatrick II and Julie R. Dahlquist, *Technical Analysis: The Complete Resource for Financial Market Technicians*, 3rd Edition (Old Tappan, New Jersey: Pearson Education, Inc., 2016), Chapter 15.

Learning Objective Statements

127

- Define what is meant by "chart patterns"
- List common characteristics of patterns
- Discuss opposing viewpoints over whether patterns exist
- Describe the influence of computer technology on price-pattern study
- Identify classic chart patterns such as triangles, and double and triple tops and bottoms
- Identify rounding chart patterns such as head-and-shoulders
- Identify "half-mast" chart patterns such as flags and pennants

Traditionally, technical analysis has been closely associated with price patterns, perhaps even more than it should be. Prior to the advent of the computer, hand-drawn charts of prices were the only technical resources available. Trend lines and patterns were the principal means of analyzing price behavior. The computer has diversified technical analysis because it has made other mathematical relationships easier to calculate.

After discussing some of the basic characteristics of patterns, we look at classic bar chart patterns—those used by the majority of technical analysts and having the longest history of use. In "Short-Term Patterns," we consider short-term patterns, candlesticks, one- and two-day patterns, and other patterns that are not so widely used. There are as many different patterns as the combinations of price open, high, low, and close can accommodate. Generally, shorter patterns are more common and less reliable, and longer patterns are more complex and less frequent. In addition, as a rule, the more complicated the pattern, the less likely it will be profitable, and the more frequent a pattern, the less likely it will be profitable. The best patterns seem to be in the middle of frequency and complexity. We address these. There are many reference books on other patterns that you can investigate, but most fail to give any special advantage over the classic patterns. However, the books by Thomas N. Bulkowski, used as a primary source here, are by far the most researched and detailed.

■ What Is a Pattern?

In the literature and usage of technical analysis, the terms **pattern** and **formation** are used interchangeably. We will do the same. A *pattern* is simply a configuration of price action that is bounded, above and below, by some form of either a line or a curve.

The lines that bind price movement in a pattern can be trend lines or support/resistance lines. In this chapter, we apply the concepts and terminology that we studied regarding these lines. When studying patterns, we add a new concept—prices being bound by a curve instead of a straight line. A *curve* is a less definite arc drawn with either a "smiley face" for a bottom curve or a "frown" for the top curve. The lowest level in a bottom curve is a support level, and the highest level in a top curve is a resistance level. Curves simply define a support or resistance level with curved rather than straight lines. A pattern can be bounded by any combination of curves or lines as long as the upper and lower bounds are defined well enough for a breakout level to be established.

Common Pattern Characteristics

The focus of this chapter is bar chart price configurations. Thomas N. Bulkowski has accomplished the most comprehensive modern study of bar chart patterns in his twin books *Encyclopedia of Chart Patterns*, 2nd edition (2005) and *Trading Classic Chart Patterns* (2002). Bulkowski observed more than 700 stocks over ten years on a daily basis and cataloged their results under varying conditions. In total, over two market periods he found and analyzed 12,385 chart patterns. Although his analysis of patterns was, of course, subject to his potential bias, it was consistent and included a significantly large number of examples. Much of the material—specifically the statistics—in this chapter relies on Bulkowski's work. Bulkowski has a Web site (www.thepatternsite .com) that explains in significant detail all the patterns we discuss and more. Before we begin discussing some of the particular patterns, however, we need to explain some vocabulary related to the general characteristics of bar chart patterns.

Entry and Exit All patterns have a combination of an entry and an exit. The entry describes the trend preceding the formation, and the exit is usually the signal for action. A pattern can occur after a decline, in which case, the entry is from above, or after an advance, in which case, the entry is from below. The exit, of course, can also be downward

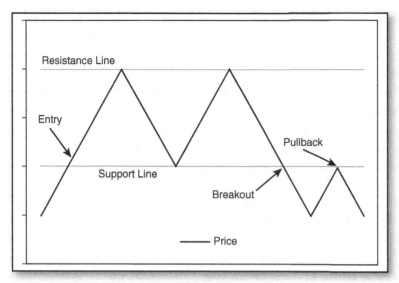

FIGURE 8.1   Double Top with Breakout Down

or upward. Figure 8.1, a double top, shows an entry from below and a downward exit. On the other hand, a bottom formation has an entry from above and an exit upward. A consolidation in a larger uptrend has an entry from below and an exit upward. Thus, all patterns are described with these four variables: entry from above, entry from below, downward exit, and upward exit. These variables are important because statistically, in each pattern type, some of these characteristics are more reliable, occur more frequently, or are more profitable than others.

Fractal   The bars in a bar chart can be any period: weekly, daily, minute, and so on. Bar chart patterns are fractal. This means they can occur in any bar chart, regardless of the bar period. A triangle formation, for example, can occur in hourly bars or weekly bars. The pattern is always the same type and will always have the same general characteristics. This is odd but true. Indeed, looking at a bar chart pattern without a specified time horizon, a technical analyst who is experienced in pattern recognition cannot tell the periods of the bars.

Pullbacks and Throwbacks   Pullbacks occur when prices break out downward and then "pull back" to their breakout level. Throwbacks occur when prices break out upward and then "throw back" to their breakout level (Edwards and Magee, revised 2007). Figure 8.1 shows an example of a pullback. Neither a pullback nor a throwback is easily or precisely defined, but you know one when you see it. The interesting aspect of this price behavior is that invariably a pullback or throwback will decrease the extent of the eventual move in the direction of the breakout. Thus, although each may provide a second opportunity for action at the breakout level, the subsequent rise or fall generally will be less than if there were no pullback or throwback. Tactically, this implies that a breakout should be acted upon immediately; waiting for the retracement will diminish profitability, and you may very likely miss the entire price move.

Pullbacks seem to occur more frequently on downward breakouts with less-than-average volume, and throwbacks occur more frequently with upward breakouts on above-average volume. Because pullbacks and throwbacks seem to undermine performance, the ideal situation, as a rule, is that on an upward breakout, less volume is preferred, and on a downward breakout, more volume is preferred.

Failures All breakouts can fail in any of the formations—some more than others. Remember that a breakout is a signal that prices are beginning to trend, either upward or downward. This is particularly frustrating to the beginner who desires perfection. As we have seen, however, perfection is not in the lexicon of technical analysis. It is favorable odds, or an "edge," for which we are looking. Bulkowski's definition of a failure, which we use, is when a breakout occurs and the price fails to move at least 5% in the direction of the breakout.

■ Do Patterns Exist?

Some academics and investors believe that patterns do not exist. They believe either that price action is completely random or, at least, is indecipherable. The concept of randomness is now being questioned, leaving open the possibility that order does exist in prices. However, even if order does exist in market prices, it is possible that it cannot be recognized with present mathematical models because it is so complex. The methods used in chaos theory, neural networks, and other esoteric mathematical models may prove useful sometime in the future, but not now. Thus, there is still the realistic question of whether patterns do exist in prices. Technical analysts swear they do, but in many cases, analysts are not mathematically sophisticated enough to demonstrate their validity.

As mentioned before, the unpublished article by Hasanhodzic et al. (2010) on a study of online video game players (http://arora.ccs.neu.edu) attempting to distinguish between financial market price statistics in moving chart form from random permutations of the same data with immediate feedback found that these people could "consistently distinguish between the two types of time series." This experiment seemed to give evidence that humans can learn to distinguish patterns and real data from random series whereas computers, so far, cannot.

If prices do have patterns, what causes them? This has been a debate for at least a century and has coalesced into a belief that patterns are the result of human behavior, which, conveniently, is indecipherable. It is, however, why technical analysts are very much interested in the new behavioral finance and neurological studies. They hope that the biases and tendencies in human behavior now being measured and gradually understood by behavioral finance students will eventually explain why price patterns seem to exist.

Behavioral Finance and Pattern Recognition

The first fact to acknowledge about chart patterns is that they have not been proven to exist or to be profitable. Although many investors and traders swear by certain formations, their evidence is largely anecdotal. Added to this is the tendency to see patterns in random data.

Humans have a tendency to want patterns in data and other information and to see them when they do not exist. Superstitions are derived from the erroneous and coincidental observations of patterns that do not exist but are created because of the desire to have a pattern. B.F. Skinner, a famous Harvard psychology professor, studied pigeon behavior in a number of stimulus-response situations to see if the pigeons would react to various stimuli and thus "learn" responses. The reward for the correct response was usually food. In one experiment, he decided to give pigeons just food without a stimulus to see what they would do. Invariably, in trying to make sense out of stimulus-response, the pigeons responded in different manners by creating their own stimulus, some bobbing, some developing strange head motions, thus creating their own superstition, when a real stimulus did not exist (Skinner, 1947).

Humans are similar in their desire to have some kind of stimulus, even if it is a black cat crossing the road, and develop supposedly predictive relationships when none actually exists. This is a special danger in price analysis because the desire to see a pattern can occur when no pattern actually exists.

Humans are also poor statisticians and tend to put more weight on recent history than what is statistically warranted. An experiment by Kahneman and Tversky (1982) showed that in flipping coins, which have a statistical probability of landing on their heads 50% of the time regardless of what side they landed on earlier, observers began to expect more heads in the future when the sequence of heads turned up more frequently, and they were surprised when that did not occur. Their subconscious brains expected more heads because that was the most recent history of flips, even though the odds had not changed. In the technical analysis of patterns, the analyst must guard against superstition or what is often called "market lore." Frequently these statements contradict other statements or are just plain wrong. An example is that "a descending triangle always breaks downward." You will see how this is not borne out by fact when we discuss triangles. Pattern and trend analysis must be based on evidence alone.

Humans also tend to see the future as the past and look backward rather than forward. This bias is likely the reason that trends in prices exist in the first place and why prices rise or fall until they reach some exhaustion limit rather than adjusting immediately as the EMH would suggest. For this reason, humans have difficulty in recognizing when past signs or patterns are no longer valid. Studies have shown that the human brain releases dopamine (a pleasure sensation chemical and, thus, a reward) when a human takes action that has worked before. Thus, the pleasurable action is desirable and overcomes any cognitive reasoning that might suspect the action is wrong. This problem is especially prevalent and potentially very dangerous in the financial markets where change is constant.

"In a world without change, the best way to find cheese is to return to the location where it was found previously. In a world with change, however, the best way to find cheese is to look somewhere new" Burnham (2005, p. 284), paraphrasing from Johnson (1998). In other words, the chart pattern and trend reader should look for failure rather than believe in the constancy of previous patterns. Schwager (1996) suggests that profitability from failed patterns is often greater than from correct patterns.

■ Computers and Pattern Recognition

Analysts began recognizing chart patterns in the days when prices were plotted daily by hand. Aside from trend lines, patterns were the beginning of technical analysis, and for this reason, many nontechnicians mistakenly believe that patterns are all that technicians study. Floor traders and market makers still plot intraday charts of prices for their use in trading short periods, but the computer has changed technical analysis considerably. On a computer screen, charts of minute-to-minute, even tick-to-tick prices can now be displayed, and from them, various patterns can be recognized. This has led to impersonal contact with prices, different from the days when each bar was plotted individually and the "feel" for price action was more easily learned. In addition, the time horizon for traders off the floor has become shorter. The ability to see almost instantly a change in price behavior combined with lower commission costs and less slippage, all due to the introduction of computers, has led traders to speculate on shorter-term trends and patterns.

The computer did not make the study of patterns any easier, however. Patterns change and adjust to new markets. Some of the old patterns do not seem to work very well anymore, and others have taken their place. Patterns are also subjectively determined, and in many cases they are perhaps invalid. Tests are being made currently on their validity—a difficult enterprise because patterns are more visually based than mathematically based. They are peculiar to humans in that, like recognizing a friend's face out of a collage of faces, a particular chart pattern must be recognized out of a series of patterns in prices. Like quantifying your friend's face, quantifying a chart pattern is not easily accomplished. Only through practice, many mistakes, and many correct interpretations that go wrong is the technical analyst consistently able to recognize patterns. This is how the art of technical analysis developed before the computer, and although the computer is now taking over both in plotting and in analyzing, the chart patterns still exist and are used by many practitioners. Recent authors of books on technical chart methods will attest to the longevity of certain patterns and their fractal nature. The analysis of price patterns remains, although less emphasis is placed on it.

The analyst using a computer is able to compute more quickly various ratios, averages, spreads, and so on. Computer usage also has the advantage of giving the technician the ability to test these new calculations as well as the old ones for accuracy and statistical significance. The old-time technical analyst had to rely on many years of experience to determine the reliability of formations and indicators and often, for example, stayed up late at night with a hand-crank adding machine calculating indicators and oscillators. As we know from studies of behavior, anecdotal experience can be deceiving, but with the advent of the computer, we can now objectively study many oscillators, averages, and other methods that before were impractical to study. The computer has "cleaned" up a lot of the folklore about patterns and trends and eliminated those that have little or no validity. It has made technical analysis more of a science than an art. Remarkably, although understandable from the previous discussion of human behavior, many of these old inaccurate methods are still used.

■ Market Structure and Pattern Recognition

The markets, of course, have also changed since the beginning of technical analysis and the first recognition of patterns, and with this change, patterns have changed and become less accurate. First, the proliferation of technical knowledge has led to the recognition of specific patterns when they occur. Of course, once a pattern is widely recognized and acted upon, its effectiveness diminishes. Thus, patterns in widely traded securities tend to be less accurate than in those quiet trading securities that few traders watch.

In the stock market, ownership has become concentrated in relatively few hands that tend to act in concert. These "hands" are the institutional holders of securities. They tend to act together when news is announced; thus, by their large positions and anxiousness to get in or get out, they cause patterns to self-destruct. Although it is difficult to prove, when a large institution is the dominant owner of a stock and has knowledge of technical principles, there is a temptation to "manipulate" a chart formation and cause false breakouts. This can cause havoc with the short-term trader who is watching the same patterns develop.

Finally, the advent of derivatives in large quantities has influenced the price and volume action in individual securities for reasons other than the prospects for the underlying company. Addition or deletion from a market index or basket can suddenly introduce buying or selling unrelated to the pattern developing.

■ Bar Charts and Patterns

A bar chart is the most common chart of price behavior and has been used ever since continuous trading data became available. Bar chart patterns form by combining support and resistance zones and trend lines. In all cases, a pattern finalizes when a breakout occurs from the pattern. In some instances, a pattern will just dribble into inactivity, in which case it should be ignored, but most patterns result in a legitimate breakout in one direction or the other. The breakout may be false, of course, and we look at how to handle that occurrence. We have observed the peculiarities of drawing trend lines and establishing support and resistance zones and the difficulties in recognizing patterns from imperfect data. Patterns are, thus, never exactly the same from example to example and are fit into generic categories with common characteristics based principally on the direction of internal trends and their intersections.

Traditionally, we divide patterns into two categories: continuation and reversal. This is a holdover from Schabacker (1930), and used by Edwards and Magee (revised, 2007), who needed to break patterns into easily understood and recognizable divisions. Unfortunately, as Edwards and Magee recognized, patterns cannot always easily be relegated to a specific reversal or continuation category, and such a description can often be misleading. Instead, patterns can occur in both modes. For this reason, we prefer to abandon the standard method of differentiating patterns into "continuation" and "reversal," and although we still use the terms when appropriate, we instead describe the simplest patterns first and progress to the more complex.

■ How Profitable Are Patterns?

Studies of chart performance and reliability are scarce. The problem, of course, is the difficulty in defining a chart pattern on a computer. In 1970, one of the authors of this book and Robert Levy (1971) devised a method to identify patterns by recording the sequence of reversal points relative to their immediate past reversal points. This sounds complex, perhaps, but using only five reversal points, almost all simple chart patterns can be identified and their results recorded. Arthur Merrill (1997) took this study method and with some variation tested it on the Dow Jones Industrial Average. In both studies, the results showed that chart patterns as defined had little predictive ability. Several patterns showed some statistical reliability, but not enough to prove the case for technical price patterns in general.

In a 1988 study by Lo and MacKinlay, more sophisticated statistical methods were used to see if patterns existed in individual prices. The study had mixed results. Although it did not negate the possibility of patterns, neither did it prove that patterns existed.

The most comprehensive study to date is that of Bulkowski (2005). Many of the statistics mentioned in each pattern section later in the chapter are taken from his more recent work on trading classic patterns (2002). The intriguing nature of Bulkowski's studies is that many of the old observations seen in the classic literature are turning out to be questionable, especially for maximum performance. As examples, volume trend within a pattern, slope of trends, and breakout volume may not be as relevant as others had originally thought.

Remember also that Bulkowski's observations are in retrospect. We can easily identify many chart patterns after they have occurred and when we have observed the results. The real talent comes in identifying a chart pattern while it is evolving in real time and profiting from its completion. For this ability, only study, practice, and experience will suffice.

Finally, the results from Bulkowski's observations are relative only. They cannot be assumed to be profitable in the future, as they appeared to be during the trial period. The value of his study is not in determining the value of chart pattern analysis itself but in determining which of the classic patterns are more profitable with less risk. From Bulkowski's studies, it appears that pattern analysis outperforms the market (S&P 500) on average in every instance. This might or might not be true, but for our purposes, we are more interested in which patterns to study as being the most likely to profit over others.

> **BOX 8.2 USING BREAKOUT PRICE TO SET PRICE TARGETS**
>
> Bar charts can project price targets once a formation completes with the breakout. Most targets are measured from the breakout price. Targets are infrequently used because most technicians are satisfied with just being on the right side of the trend, want only to ride that trend, and believe that targets are generally inaccurate. In many patterns, however, this is not so. Generally, the target is calculated by taking the height of the pattern and adding it to the breakout price. In each of the following trading boxes, we describe the target peculiarities for each pattern and the success percentages.

■ Classic Bar Chart Patterns

We begin by looking at classic chart patterns. These patterns generally have been recognized and used for more than a hundred years. Only recently have there been tests of their reliability and profitability.

Double Top and Double Bottom

A double formation is about the simplest of the classic formations. A double top consists of only three reversal points: two peaks separated by a trough (refer to Figure 8.1). For it to be a true double top, the initial price must enter the pattern from below the trough price, and the exit signal must occur on the breakout below the trough low price. The best performing of the double tops is the "Eve and Eve" double top patterns. The tops are rounded and wide with some irregularity. According to Bukowski, the two peaks must be at or within 5% of each other's price level, and the middle valley should be around 10% or more from the lowest peak. The double top, thus, resembles the rectangle formation (described next) with less detail. The pattern forms over 2 to 6 weeks: the longer, the less reliable. A projection from the break below the trough is under the **Measured Rule** that hypothesizes a decline equal to 73% of the distance in points from the highest peak to the trough. The double bottom is the mirror image of the double top.

Newspaper and media commentators who want to sound like technical analysts frequently use the term *double* formation often when it is not a true double pattern.

A true formation is only valid when the intervening reaction reversal point has been penetrated. The danger of acting prematurely is great; roughly 64% of these patterns fail to penetrate the breakout level and instead continue on their original trend. When the pattern is completed with a breakout, however, it is very accurate.

The failure rates are 11%. This means that the odds of making a profit from a double top downward breakout are minimally risky. Bulkowski ranks the overall performance rank at 2 out of 21, a very high ranking. This ranking is a composition of the pattern's failure rate, average profit, pullback/throwback rate, and percent of trades reaching a price target.

BOX 8.3 TRADING DOUBLE FORMATIONS

If one observes a double pattern, several important observations must be made before acting to improve the chances of profit. First, never buy until the breakout has occurred. Second, look for flat bases either at the same level as the twin bottoms or slightly higher and earlier. Third, look for an absence of a consolidation area above the formation. Fourth, look for what is called an "Eve & Eve" variety. Volume doesn't seem to be important, although it is usually higher on the first "hump."

Rectangle (Also "Trading Range" or "Box")

In the earlier discussion on trading ranges and sideways trends, we effectively described a rectangle pattern. It is one of the simplest of patterns, consisting of a resistance line above and a support line below (see Figure 8.2). Each resistance or support line must also be a trend line, which means that it must touch roughly the

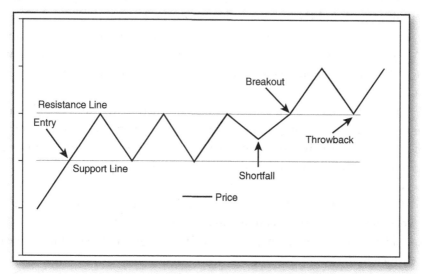

FIGURE 8.2   Rectangle with Entry Up and Breakout Up

same price reversal at least twice. This added requirement is what separates it from a double top or bottom formation, which only requires that three price reversals occur. Prices are bounded by and oscillate between the two lines, and they eventually exit, or break out, in one direction or the other. The pattern can have a slight tilt upward or downward, but the trend lines defining the support and resistance zones are always parallel. It appears similar to a horizontal channel. It often has false or premature breakouts, neither of which is predictive of the eventual breakout direction.

Within the rectangle formation, prices do not necessarily always reach the two zones but may fall short (a "shortfall" or "partial"). Sometimes this is a warning as to the direction of the eventual breakout. As an example, when well along the way of the formation of a rectangle, prices begin to reverse before declining all the way to the underlying support zone; buyers are getting a little more anxious and the odds increase for a breakout upward. Bulkowski reported that such a shortfall within the latter stages of the pattern is accurate 60% to 90% of the time in predicting the direction of eventual breakout depending on the breakout direction. More than half the time, prices throw back or pull back to the breakout zone, providing another action point but one with less profit potential. Edwards and Magee estimated that about 40% of the time, a pullback or throwback would occur. When the breakout occurs on a gap, the odds decrease that a retracement will occur.

Volume is often an important factor in any formation. In the rectangle pattern, however, a rising or declining volume trend within the pattern has little or no effect on the results after the breakout, although declining volume is more common. Results increase, however, when volume increases on the breakout itself.

Depending on the rectangle entry and exit (that is, whether it is a reversal or continuation pattern), the failure to reach 5% was between 9% and 16%. The worst was the declining coninuation pattern (entry from above, exit down). Bulkowski ranked the overall performance of rectangles in the middle of the classical pattern pack.

Edwards and Magee claimed that rectangles are more often continuation patterns, but as a reversal pattern, they occur more frequently at bottoms. This is likely why Bulkowski mostly found upward breakout rectangle patterns. An upward breakout, however, should never be assumed. Indeed, two out of three rectangles are continuation patterns, and the initial expected direction of the breakout should be in line with the previous trend.

Rectangles have the bad habit of producing false breakouts. Indeed, more than 75% of early breakouts are false. This is a large enough figure to hint as to the eventual final breakout direction, but it requires close breakout and stop discipline. Once the final breakout has occurred, the failure rate is very low. These failures are called **busted rectangles** and occur if the breakout fails to gain at least 10% before returning to the rectangle and breaking out in the opposite direction. Upward initial breakouts bust 22% of the time, and downward initial breakouts bust 42% of the time. Thus, it pays to be sure that the breakout is real. Another hint is the existence of shortfalls. Shortfalls occur later in the formation and can anticipate the breakout. The volume trend during the formation of the pattern gives no hint as to the breakout direction and has only a minor effect on performance.

Some traders will trade within a rectangle, buying at the support level and selling at the resistance level. This is not recommended, however, unless the rectangle is particularly wide from top to bottom. Trading has many costs inherent in acting on the buys and sells. The obvious costs are commissions, slippage, and width of the spread. Additionally, when trading within two bounds, the bounds are not exact, nor will a trade be executed exactly at the bound. Thus, sell orders must be placed a certain distance, a specified filter, below a resistance zone, and buy orders a certain distance above a support zone. To be able to absorb these costs and price filters, the trader is limited to rectangles that are sufficiently high, from support to resistance. One who attempts this kind of trading must be watching the price action incessantly and be ready to scalp the few points in between the bounds and filters in an instant. Most traders and investors are unable to do this.

A target can be calculated by adding the height of the rectangle formation to the breakout price. According to Bulkowski, in rectangles, the upward target is reached or exceeded 91%–93% of the time, and in downward breakouts, the target is reached or exceeded 65%–77% of the time. The difference in percentages is based on the entry, whether upward or downward, but in all cases, the target is a relatively accurate figure and can be used for risk/reward calculations.

Triple Top and Triple Bottom

The triple top and bottom formation is just a rectangle with the number of touches to the support or resistance line being three. It is, thus, more specific than the rectangle and is less common. Each peak in the top should be at the same level and have roughly the same shape. The middle peak can be slightly lower than the other two. As in the double formations, confirmation only comes with a price breakout below the two bottoms. Pullbacks are common (63% of the time) and diminish the breakout performance. Tops only project 40% of the formation width below the breakout

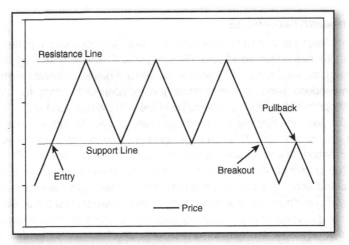

FIGURE 8.3 Triple Top with Breakout Down

level but reach the projection within the first two weeks. Figure 8.3 shows a triple top with a breakout down, and Figure 8.4 shows a triple bottom with a breakout up. As you can see, they are the mirror image of each other. Sometimes in a triple bottom, the second peak is slightly higher than the first. This is favorable, and the breakout is the line between the two peaks. The patterns are rare and usually depend on the underlying market trend. They rank in the top third of classic patterns. Their failure rates very low (10% for bottoms, 4% for tops).

Standard Triangles

The rectangle pattern is bounded by parallel lines. If the same general pattern has nonparallel boundary lines such that when extended into the future they cross each other, the formation is a *triangle* pattern. Triangles can be the result of an

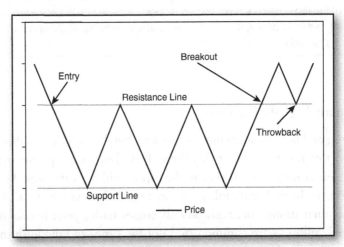

FIGURE 8.4 Triple Bottom with Breakout Up

upward-sloping lower bound or a downward-sloping upward bound. Thus, there are a number of possible combinations of the two lines.

In this section, we look only at the standard triangle patterns. In these triangles, the point at which the two lines extend and cross over each other is called the **apex** or the **cradle**, and the distance between the first high reversal point and the first low reversal point within the triangle is called the **base**.

When the lower bound is a horizontal support zone and the upper is a downward slanting trend line, it is called a **descending triangle**. When the lower trend line is rising and the upper bound is a horizontal resistance zone, it is called an **ascending triangle**. When the upper bound is declining and the lower bound is rising, it is called a **symmetrical triangle**. When both the upper bound and lower bound are slanting in the same direction and converging, it is called a **wedge**, and when the two lines are diverging regardless of slope, a reverse triangle, it is called a **broadening pattern**. When we combine a broadening pattern with a triangle, usually a symmetrical triangle, we get what is called a **diamond pattern**.

Descending Triangle

Figure 8.5 shows a descending triangle with a breakout down. Its bounds are a lower horizontal support line and a declining upper trend line; price should touch each line at least twice and should generally "fill" the triangle's space. It can be entered from any direction. The breakout is more common to the downside (64%), but the upward breakout is more reliable and profitable (47% to 16% average gain). This formation can be stretched high and wide and is sometimes difficult to recognize. The trend lines defining its boundaries are almost never exact and are loaded with

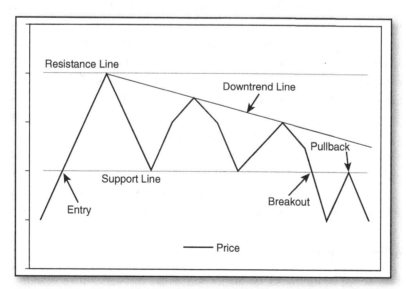

FIGURE 8.5   Descending Triangle with Breakout Down

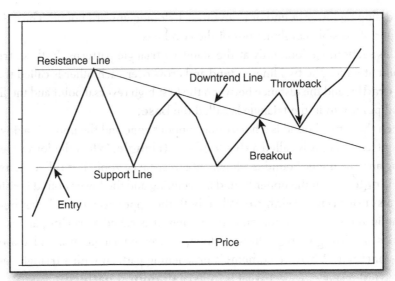

FIGURE 8.6 Descending Triangle with Breakout Up

false intrabar breakouts. However, prices often explode out of it and produce sizable gains. It can also be wild and guarantee an exciting ride. It will break out and run, break out and pull back to its trend line, break out and pull back to its cradle, or break back through the cradle, create a sizable trap, and then reverse back in its original breakout direction and run. In other words, when you enter on a breakout from a descending triangle, the subsequent action must be watched carefully.

Upward breakouts on gaps add considerably to performance and are definitely something to look for. On downward breaks, gaps seem to have little effect. Average breakout distance from the base to the cradle is 64%, most powerful at 80%. Entering from below and upward sloping volume equals better performance.

Figure 8.6 pictures a descending triangle with a breakout up. The typical pattern shows declining volume throughout its formation. However, increasing volume during the formation of an upward breaking descending triangle, although less frequent, is more favorable than declining volume. This contradicts the conventional opinion that advancing volume negates the pattern and represents a reason for screening it out for consideration. In the downward breakouts, declining volume during the pattern formation helps postbreakout performance only slightly. The amount of volume traded on the actual upward breakouts has little effect on the postperformance, but in downward breakouts, an increase on the breakout helps performance slightly. In many ways, the upward breaking descending triangle is similar to a failed head-and-shoulders top.

Ascending Triangle

A horizontal upper bound of resistance combined with an upward sloping lower bound of support defines an ascending triangle (shown in Figure 8.7 with a breakout

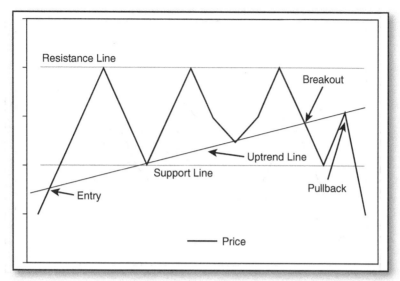

FIGURE 8.7   Ascending Triangle with Breakout Down

down). The characteristics in this pattern are just as erratic as in descending triangles—lots of action up and down. Breakout points must be chosen carefully because of the pattern's nature to have many small false breakouts, and declining volume is common but not necessary. Upward breakouts occur 77% of the time, and breakouts happen roughly 61% of the distance (time) from the base to the cradle. The overall performance rank is roughly in the middle of all patterns, with a little more favorable for downward breakouts. Failure rates are between 11% and 13% depending on breakout direction. This is about average.

Symmetrical Triangle (Also "Coil" or "Isosceles Triangle")

When the upper bound is downward sloping and the lower bound is upward sloping, a symmetrical triangle is formed (see Figure 8.8). The term **symmetrical** gives the impression that both lines should have the same angle but in different directions. However, the slope of the two boundaries being formed at congruent angles is not a requirement. Thus, "symmetrical" is not an accurate description but is the term most commonly in use for this pattern. The less commonly used term **coil** is often a more accurate description.

Like the other standard triangles, the prices must touch each border trend line at least twice and meanwhile cover the area of the triangle with price action. Volume usually trends downward during the pattern formation (86% of the time), and the breakout is usually upward (54% of the time). Symmetrical triangles have many false breakouts and must be watched carefully. A strict breakout system must be used that allows for such false moves. The breakout commonly occurs between 73% and 75% of the length of the triangle from base to cradle. This formation does not

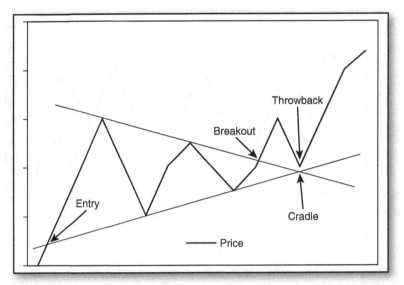

FIGURE 8.8 Symmetrical Triangle with Breakout Up

occur as frequently as the descending or ascending triangle, but it is still common relative to other chart patterns. Throwbacks and pullbacks occur 37% and 59% of the time, respectively, and, as in most patterns, when they occur, they detract from eventual performance. This implies that for actual investment or trading, the initial breakout should be acted upon, and if a pullback or throwback occurs, the protective stop should be tightened. It does not imply that a pullback or throwback should be ignored, but that instead, performance expectations should be less than if no pullback or throwback had occurred. Gap breakouts do not seem to affect the performance on the upside but do give a few extra percentage points on the downside. Increasing volume trend seems to be associated with better results once the breakout occurs. High volume on breakouts, both upward and downward, adds considerably to the performance of the formation and is something to look for. Overall performance is slightly below the mean for classic patterns.

BOX 8.6   TRADING TRIANGLES

The ideal situation for trading triangles is a definite breakout, a high trading range within the triangle, an upward-sloping volume trend during the formation of the triangle, and especially a gap on the breakout. These patterns seem to work better with small-cap stocks in a rising market.

Triangles are plentiful. For example, the upward failure of a head-and-shoulders top before any break through the neckline is a form of an upward-breaking descending triangle. This is one likely reason that such head-and-shoulder top pattern failures are so profitable.

Although triangles are plentiful, their patterns suffer from many false and premature breakouts. This requires that a very strict breakout rule be used—either a wide filter or a number of closes outside the breakout zone. It also requires a close protective stop at the breakout level in case the breakout is false. Once these defensive levels have been exceeded and price is on its way, the trader can relax for a little while because the failure rate after a legitimate breakout is relatively low. Trailing stops should then be placed at each preceding minor reversal.

There are many old rules about when a breakout should occur within a triangle. Some, such as Murphy, say that one-half to two-thirds the distance from the base to the apex is appropriate. Others, such as Edwards and Magee, use the one-half to three-quarters rule. In fact, the breakout can occur at any time once the triangle has been defined by legitimate upper and lower converging trend lines. Edwards and Magee do point out that the longer the distance, the more likely the performance will be less, but this also is not necessarily true. The highest percentage performance does come from breakouts generally around 60%–70% of the distance from the base to the cradle. However, in symmetrical triangles, the best performance comes from late breakouts in the 73%–75% distance. Thus, the old rules are partially correct but not strictly so.

Generally, the volume trend during the formation of a triangle declines, but in the case of an upward breaking descending triangle, an ascending triangle, and a downward breaking symmetrical triangle, an upward-sloping volume trend gives better results. Declining volume is not a reason to disregard the pattern, however. Volume on the breakout seems more desirable in symmetrical triangles, but it cannot hurt in others. Gaps are better predictors of performance in the upward-breaking descending triangle and the downward-breaking symmetrical triangle, but they are not necessary.

An initial target for these patterns is calculated by adding the base distance—the vertical distance between the initial upper and lower reversal point prices—to the price where the breakout occurred. In an upward-breaking descending triangle, for example, this target is reached better than 67% of the time. Other triangles have relatively the same success rate—higher in upward trends than in downward trends. This is why a wide trading range is preferred within the triangle—it suggests a higher target price on the breakout.

Broadening Patterns

A broadening pattern exists when we take the standard rectangle pattern and draw the bound lines diverging from each other into the future rather than converging as in a standard triangle. As pictured in Figure 8.9, the price range is increasing during the broadening pattern, as opposed to the narrowing price range that is associated with the standard triangle patterns. The terms **megaphone**, **funnel**, **reverse triangle**, and **inverted triangle** all refer to broadening patterns. The broadening pattern also comes in many variations. One is similar to ascending and descending triangles in that one of the bounds is horizontal. The other bound then slopes away from the horizontal line either above or below. A final variation is the broadening wedge. This pattern is similar to a wedge pattern (see Figure 8.9) except the bounds trend in the same direction but diverge instead of converge as in a wedge. None of these variations seems to have any above-average performance statistics except the

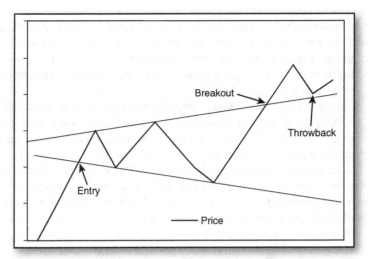

FIGURE 8.9 Broadening Formation with Breakout Up

ascending broadening wedge, which has both bounds rising and diverging. Upward breakouts in this pattern rank 6 out of 23 in Bulkowski's scale and have failure rates at 2%, which is almost negligible.

Broadening formations are the least-useful patterns for a number of reasons. First, they are relatively rare in occurrence and are often difficult to identify. Second, and more important, they are difficult to profit from. Because the boundary trend lines are separating over time, the breakout lines are constantly moving away from each other. In an upward breaking broadening pattern, this means the upper breakout level is getting higher and higher along the upper trend line (refer to Figure 8.9). By getting higher and higher, not only is it using up much of any potential gain after a breakout, but it is moving farther from any realistic protective stop level, thus increasing the risk. Finally, the raw performance statistics show that performance of a broadening pattern is average at best, and its failure rate is above average. One of the most profitable patterns utilizing a broadening pattern, however, is when it is combined with a symmetrical triangle into a diamond top, which we discuss next.

Diamond Top One of the less frequent but profitable patterns is the diamond (see Figure 8.10). It consists of a combination of a broadening pattern and a symmetrical triangle and usually occurs at the top of a sharp upward rise in prices. It is rare at price bottoms.

Because it combines two types of triangles, the diamond is the most difficult to observe. Remember that to establish a trend line, two extreme points that a line can be drawn between must be identified. In a standard broadening formation, the upper trend line slopes upward and must, therefore, have two peaks—the latter higher than the former. Likewise, the lower trend line must have two troughs—the latter lower than the former—and each line must be formed at the same time as

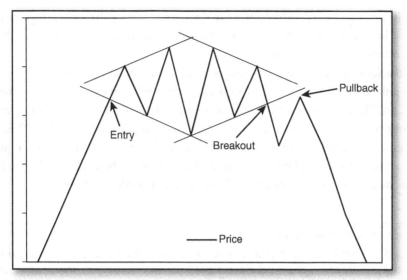

FIGURE 8.10 Diamond Pattern with Breakout Down

the other. The first reversal point depends on the entry direction, of course, and because diamonds are mostly top formations, the entry direction is generally from below. This means that the first reversal point will be a peak. After that, the first trough will appear, then the next higher peak, and then the next lower trough. When trend lines have been drawn to connect these reversal points, we have a broadening formation. Now we must observe a symmetrical triangle immediately after the broadening formation to establish a diamond pattern. The trend lines in a symmetrical triangle converge, as in all standard triangles, and must have at least two peaks and troughs to establish each trend line. The first reversal peak and trough may be the last reversal points in the broadening formation or the next reversal points following the broadening formation. Often the trend lines in the symmetrical triangle will be parallel to the trend lines in the broadening pattern, but this is not a requirement.

Bulkowski's figures show that around 58% of the time, the preceding price action in a diamond top was a steeply rising trend. When this occurs, the odds increase that the breakout from the diamond will be downward and will be equally as steep, and 82% of the time, it will retrace the entire prior rise. These figures are only valid for downward breakouts from a top, which occur 67% of the time. Upward breakouts from a diamond top have a poor performance history and should be avoided. Thus, action should only be taken once the pattern has been identified and the downward breakout has occurred.

Diamond bottoms have the same configuration as diamond tops and are the best patterns that Bulkowski ranks. They are number 1 in performance when they fail and break down (about 31% of the time). Even when they break upward, their ranking is 8 out of 23.

As in most patterns, volume usually declines (67% of the time) during its formation, but declining volume is not necessary. Indeed, rising volume is a plus for performance after the breakout.

Pullbacks are common in diamond patterns, occurring more than 53% of the time. These pullbacks tend to detract from performance when they occur but are not that significant. The best combination is when downward breakout occurs on below-average breakout volume and no pullback. The failure rate is relatively low at 4%–10%. These low numbers equate, to some extent, with risk. Combined with the above-average median return, these numbers suggest that, although rare, when a diamond top is identified, it has an above-average chance of being profitable with minimum risk.

BOX 8.7 TRADING DIAMONDS

The diamond formation, once properly defined, tends to have a fast-moving price run on the breakout. Indeed, if the postbreakout price behavior is sluggish, the position should likely be closed or a close trailing stop placed near the current price. The price objective is usually the distance that the entry price traveled to reach the diamond. A steep entry is usually followed by a steep exit.

Wedge and Climax

A wedge pattern is a triangle pattern with both trend lines heading in the same direction. A rising wedge has both lines headed upward, with the lower bound rising more quickly than the upper bound, as pictured in Figure 8.11. The declining wedge has both lines headed downward, with the upward bound falling more quickly than

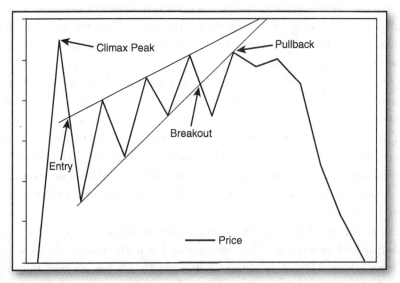

FIGURE 8.11   Rising Wedge with Breakout Down from a Climax Peak

the lower bound. The lines cross in the future, just as in a standard triangle, and the nomenclature for the crossover and height is the same.

Rather than the rectangle as the basis for this formation as it is with standard triangles, consider a channel. A **channel** is two parallel trend lines either rising or declining. In the earlier discussion of channels, we noted that when the channel line, drawn parallel to the trend line through the opposite set of reversal points, begins to slope toward the trend line, it suggests that players are becoming less enthusiastic with the trend line direction. For example, in an upward-sloping channel, the channel line above the trend line connecting the downward reversal points begins as a line parallel to the upward trend line. If a later rally within the channel fails to reach the channel line, the new channel line through the new downward reversal and the last downward reversal will have a lesser slope than the underlying trend line, and if projected into the future, it will eventually meet the trend line. This new configuration of channel and trend line is a **rising wedge**. It suggests in the example that sellers have become a little more anxious than before, and by implication, that the trend line will soon be broken. Indeed, the statistics bear this out. Almost all declining wedges (92%) break out upward, and most rising wedges (69%) break out to the downside (Bulkowski, 2010).

Wedges are one of a few patterns that can be consolidation patterns against the prevailing trend, consolidation patterns with the trend, or topping patterns, especially when accompanying a climax. They occur more often during consolidations but are more dramatic after a climax.

Let us look at rising wedges first. Rising wedges occur either during a long downward price trend or after an upward climax. The ones that occur during a downtrend appear as weak rallies against the trend. As mentioned previously, they invariably break again to the downside and continue the downtrend. Declining wedges are almost the same pattern and occur under similar circumstances, only in the opposite direction.

A market climax occurs when prices accelerate. At these times, the underlying trend line is gradually adjusted at a steeper slope in line with the direction of prices. In an upward accelerated trend, the support reversal points occur at levels higher than the projected trend line and cause that trend line to be adjusted to a steeper slope. This can occur several times as prices accelerate upward. The climax itself usually comes on extremely high volume and a sharp reversal. After a climax has occurred and prices have settled down, invariably a "test" occurs that attempts to rally back through climax extreme peak. The pattern most often associated with the failure of that test—in other words, when the test fails to exceed the climax extreme or only exceeds by a small amount—is a rising wedge (refer to Figure 8.11). In the case of a climax low after a panic, the test wedge is the declining variety (see Figure 8.12).

At a climax peak, when the test is a rising wedge pattern, the odds are extremely high that the breakout will be downward. Because the emotion and commitment

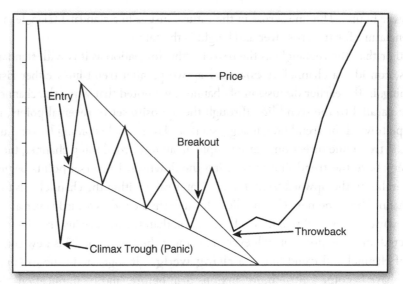

FIGURE 8.12 Declining Wedge with Breakout Up from Climax Trough

have been exhausted at the climax peak and are unable to return during the test, the downward break in the wedge pattern is the sign of a longer-term downward reversal. Thus, the wedge is a reversal pattern, even though it may not occur at the actual climax peak high.

Other rising wedges can occur as a consolidation during a sustained downward trend and occasionally will end at the top of a weakening upward trend.

Because trend lines often converge in the same direction when a wedge is not present, Bulkowski requires that at least five reversal points be touched to qualify the pattern as a wedge. This means three points on one trend line and at least two on the other. Otherwise, the pattern is not accurately identified and may fail to show the results seen in actual wedge patterns.

Another characteristic of wedges, in both the consolidation and the reversal varieties, is declining volume during the formation of the wedge. Declining volume occurs in three-quarters of the formations, and when it does, the post-performance improves over those wedges with increasing volume. Breakout volume seems to be irrelevant to postperformance. Pullbacks and throwbacks have high odds of occurring and when present detract from subsequent performance.

The performance rank for wedges is in the lower quartile of all the other classic patterns, and its failure rate is considerably lower for upward breakouts (8%–11%) than for downward breakouts (15%–24%). The rising wedge with a downward breakout is the least reliable.

BOX 8.8 TRADING WEDGES

It pays to wait for that breakout and to act immediately on it. In addition, because wedges have such a high percentage of breakouts in the direction opposite from the wedge direction, the direction of breakout is clear once the wedge is forming. A rising wedge invariably will break downward, and a declining wedge upward. Whenever a climax has occurred, whether up or down, look for a wedge to form on the test. This is one of the most profitable patterns of all. Just be sure that a wedge as described previously is valid before you take any action.

Patterns with Rounded Edges—Rounding and Head-and-Shoulders

The patterns we have considered up to this point have been defined by straight lines. When we begin to define patterns with curved lines, we become more indefinite than with using straight lines such as trend lines. This does not make the patterns any less useful, but it does make them more difficult to describe specifically.

Rounding Top, Rounding Bottom (Also "Saucer," "Bowl," or "Cup")

Rounding tops and bottoms are formed by price action that reverses slowly and gradually, rather differently from the spike with definite and sharp reversal characteristics. Volume in the bottoms seems to follow the same trend of lessening as prices gradually approach the bottom and increasing as they gradually turn upward again. In a rounding top, volume tends to follow the same pattern of lessening as prices decelerate and increasing as prices gradually turn down. Rounding usually takes time, and within its process, it has many minor up and down, short-term trends. Rounding is, thus, more conceptual than specific.

However, many formations depend on rounding for their description. The most famous is the "cup-and-handle" formation described in detail by O'Neil (1988) but referred to in many earlier publications. This formation, as shown in Figure 8.13, is a variation of the rounding bottom that shows a **lip** after the rise from the bottom and a small congestion area that reverses downward for a short while called a **handle**. The high of the lip establishes, in this type of rounding bottom, the resistance level to watch for an upward breakout. Sometimes the breakout never occurs, and prices keep declining in the handle, continuing to new lows. Traditionally, the cup-and-handle is considered to be a bottoming reversal pattern. However, Bulkowski has found that when it is a continuation pattern from an earlier low, it is much more reliable and profitable. It still only ranks 13 out of 23, despite its popularity.

Rounded bottoms are more common than rounded tops, but neither materializes often. They tend to be longer-term patterns, more easily identified in weekly or even monthly charts. They are reversal patterns, but they can also appear in long price consolidations. Shorter-term rounded formations, often called **scallops**, are usually

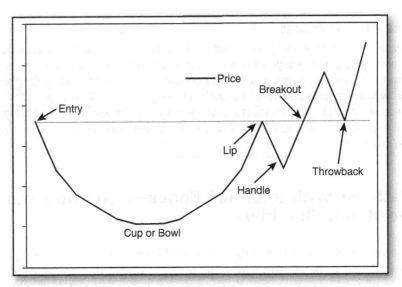

FIGURE 8.13 Cup or Bowl and Handle Variety of a Rounding Bottom with Breakout Up

continuation patterns that are equally difficult to define. Rounded bottoms rank 5 out 23 in performance and have a low 5% failure rate. Tops have the same performance rank, when breaking downward, but a slightly higher failure rate of 9%–12%. They are difficult to recognize and often require weekly or monthly charts to identify. They are also difficult to trade. First, the breakout level is not easily defined, except in cup-and-handle patterns. Second, they are slow to develop and often fail to break out.

Head-and-Shoulders

The head-and-shoulders pattern is probably the most famous technical pattern. Its name is often used when ridiculing technical analysis, yet its profitability is high, relative to other patterns, and it is one of the few that the Lo, Mamaysky, and Wang (2000) study showed had statistical significance.

Head-and-shoulders is a complex pattern because it combines all three potential characteristics of a pattern: trend lines, support or resistance lines, and rounding. It is most often seen at a top or bottom, but it can occur in its normal state or as a failed formation in a consolidation. Mostly, it should be traded only after it has formed completely. Its complexity causes many impatient analysts to anticipate its formation and to act prematurely. Its performance and success rate are high, but only after it has formed completely and satisfied all its requirements. We describe the traits of a head-and-shoulders top. The bottom formation (see Figure 8.15) is the reverse in every way except where noted.

An uptrend, but not necessarily a long-term trend, precedes a head-and-shoulders top. Thus, as shown in Figure 8.14, the head-and-shoulders top pattern is entered from below. (The head-and-shoulders pattern can also occur within a consolidation

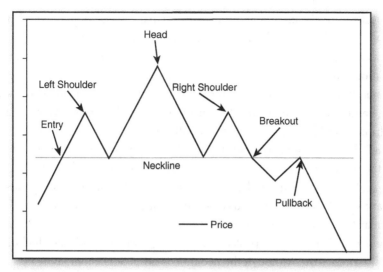

FIGURE 8.14 Head-and-Shoulders Top with Breakout Down

rather than at the end of a trend, but such occurrences are rare and more likely a series of triangles or a rectangle with a false downward breakout at the "head.")

The head-and-shoulders top pattern is a series of three well-defined peaks, either sharp or rounded. The second peak is higher than the first and third peak. This middle, higher peak is called the **head**. The first peak is called the **left shoulder**, and the third peak is called the **right shoulder**. Both the left and right shoulders must be lower than the head, but the two shoulders do not have to be the same height. In fact, a left shoulder peak slightly higher than the right shoulder peak adds a little to the postbreakout performance of a top formation. (A head-and-shoulders bottom is pictured in Figure 8.15. In the bottom pattern, a right shoulder low that is slightly lower than the left shoulder low adds to performance.)

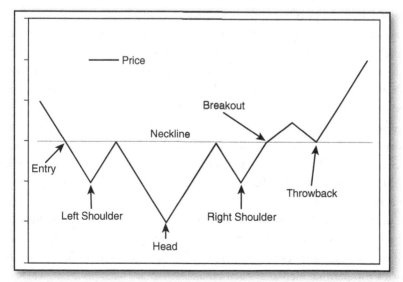

FIGURE 8.15 Head-and-Shoulders Bottom with Breakout Up

The peaks in the head-and-shoulders top formation are roughly equidistant from each other. The shoulders should appear roughly symmetrical about the head and should peak at roughly the same level. Symmetry is important and makes the formation more identifiable. Occasionally, more than two shoulders appear. These formations are called "complex head-and-shoulders" and have roughly the same performance and failure rates as the standard two-shoulder variety. As in the standard, the multiple shoulders appear symmetrically on both sides of the head. Rarely, a "two-headed" variety appears, and it, too, shows the same performance and failure rates as the standard. There is also the "unbalanced" version, as described by Edwards and Magee, but it is difficult to describe accurately and seems to fit only those formations that might be head-and-shoulders but cannot be formally categorized as such. The standard is the most common and the one to look for.

The bottoms between the peaks form a recognizable trend line. Technicians call this line the **neckline**. Although the neckline is often horizontal, as in a support line, it also can be downward or upward sloping. Indeed, there is some evidence that an upward-sloping neckline in a top formation produces better performance than the standard horizontal neckline. (In a bottom formation, the same rules hold except the neckline is now resistance rather than support. In a bottom formation, a downward-sloping neckline increases postbreakout performance over an upward-sloping neckline but not over the horizontal one.) Tilting the slope of the neckline to an extreme, however, destroys the head-and-shoulders pattern and its likely consequences.

Volume is usually highest on the rise into and at the peak of the left shoulder and decreases throughout the formation. This is not a requirement, however, because those formations with decreasing volume, although slightly less frequent, have a slight performance edge at tops. (Increasing volume has a slight edge in head-and-shoulders bottoms.) Higher volume on either shoulder does not affect performance at a top, but a bottom, higher volume on the right shoulder than on the left shoulder adds considerably to postbreakout performance.

Breakout and action signals occur when prices, after completing the right shoulder, break below the neckline. The breakout is a requirement for the formation. Second-guessing before completion of the pattern can be dangerous. Sometimes the right shoulder does not form completely, and prices fall short of breaking the neckline and rise to penetrate above the right shoulder peak. Not only is this a failure, but it also is an opportunity, provided the analyst had not anticipated a breakdown and acted prematurely. The head-and-shoulders failure of this type is profitable, according to Schwager (1996). The standard failure, however, is when prices break below the neckline and then reverse back upward through the right shoulder. This kind of failure is relatively rare.

The breakout often occurs on increased volume, but decreased volume is not a sign of an impending failure. It just occurs less frequently. Increasing volume on a bottom formation improves performance, whereas decreasing volume on the breakout from a top pattern increases performance.

Pullbacks or throwbacks are frequent—roughly 45%–63% for bottoms and 60%–67% for tops. In summary, the head-and-shoulders pattern—aside from being the best known, even among nontechnicians—is the most reliable and profitable of the classic formations.

The performance rank for the standard head-and-shoulders top is 1, the highest ranking possible. Complex tops have a rank of 3, standard bottoms a rank of 7, and complex bottoms a rank of 9. Both top and bottom patterns, therefore, are high on the list of performance.

We have seen in most other patterns that when a pullback or throwback occurs, the comparative performance suffers. This is also true in head-and-shoulders patterns. The failure rates for both top and bottom formations are low. Only 3%–4% failed a 5% gain or more from tops and bottoms. In short, the head-and-shoulders formation has a high rate of reliability as well as profitability.

BOX 8.9 TRADING HEAD-AND-SHOULDERS PATTERNS

Once a pattern has been observed using the preceding descriptive features, the neckline becomes the most important factor. The neckline is where the breakout level resides. Never should one act in anticipation of a break through the neckline. The risk of failure is too great, and as we have seen with the upward break of a descending triangle, the strongest upward formation, the rise from descending peaks and a flat neckline, can be substantial. This is equally true with head-and-shoulders bottom formations. The ascending triangle with a breakout down is also a powerful formation. Thus, breakout stops should be placed outside the right shoulder reversal point. Once the breakout is triggered, the risk of failure declines substantially. If the breakout is through the neckline, use the standard statistics as a guide, but if the breakout is a failed head-and-shoulders through the right shoulder extreme, use the appropriate triangle statistics as a guide.

The price target for a head-and-shoulders pattern is relatively accurate. It is calculated like the others by taking the height of the formation and projecting it up or down from the breakout price. The height is measured by drawing a vertical line from the peak of the head to where it intersects the neckline and measuring the number of points between the two. This holds for flat as well as sloping necklines.

Shorter Continuation Trading Patterns—Flags and Pennants (Also "Half-Mast Formation")

For efficient use of trading capital, consider trading with flags and pennants. They are frequent formations with extremely rapid and relatively reliable outcomes. After a breakout in either direction or either pattern, prices usually run immediately, having few pullbacks or throwbacks and low rates of failure. Some successful traders use only flags and pennants because of these advantages. Flags and pennants are really variations of the same formation. The flag is a short channel that usually slopes in the opposite direction from the trend. The pennant is a short triangle that does the same. Both of these patterns are pictured in Figure 8.16.

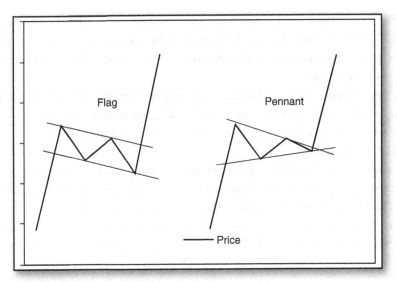

FIGURE 8.16   Flag and Pennant in Upward Trend

Both flags and pennants are preceded by a steep, sharp price trend, best at 45 degrees rather than straight up. Flags preceded by a rise of 90% or more have almost a zero failure rate and an average return of 69%. This variety is the best of all chart patterns. Two parallel trend lines in a small channel that resembles a flag form the pattern, and the slope of the channel can be in any direction, but most commonly the best performance comes when it slopes away from the preceding trend. Flag formations occur over a short period—usually a few days to a few weeks; the best flag is less than 15 days. Volume usually declines throughout the formation of the flag. In fact, this downward trend in volume is found in almost four out of every five flags that occur.

The pennant pattern is the same as the flag except that the trend lines converge, forming a miniature triangle, instead of being parallel. The direction of the formation is usually opposite from that of the immediately preceding price trend, but in stronger moves, it can be horizontal or even trending in the same direction as the underlying trend. Pennants differ from wedges in that they are shorter in time and require a sharp move preceding them. Wedges tend to be longer-term patterns. Falling volume throughout the formation is even more common with pennants; 90% of pennants are characterized by a downward trend in volume.

Two types of failures can occur. First, a breakout in the opposite direction from the previous trend can occur. Second, a failure can occur after breakout. Because a flag or a pennant is usually a continuation formation, the breakout should be expected in the direction of the preceding trend, provided it is steep and sharp. When the breakout goes opposite to that trend, the failure invariably returns to the earlier trend, but only after a few heart palpitations have occurred first and a few protective stops have been triggered.

BOX 8.10 TRADING FLAGS AND PENNANTS—MEASURED RULE

Because these patterns have low failure rates, few pullbacks or throwbacks, short time periods, and steep trends preceding and following their occurrence, they are very good trading patterns. One of the most important identification features is the steep trend preceding the pattern. It is important to be cautious to make sure that a complete formation has occurred and to wait for the breakout. The breakout occurs when a trend line is broken, usually in the direction of the preceding trend. The price target for these patterns is calculated by taking the distance from the beginning of the sharp trend, not necessarily the beginning of the entire trend, to the first reversal in the pattern and adding it to the breakout price. This method is called the **measured rule** (see Figure 8.17) and usually applies only to flags and pennants. It implies that the formation will occur roughly halfway through the entire steep price trend; because of this, these patterns are also called **half-mast patterns**. The projection of a target is only partially accurate (about 60% of the time), but because of the steepness of the subsequent trend, close trailing stops are the best manner of protecting profits.

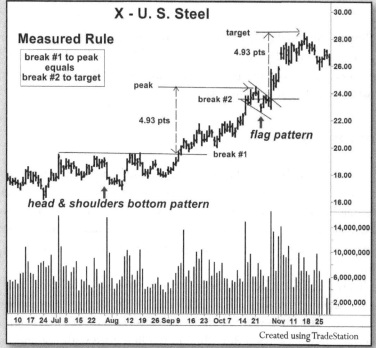

FIGURE 8.17 The Measured Rule (X—U.S. Steel, daily: June 4–December 2, 2013)

Long-Term Bar Chart Patterns with the Best Performance and the Lowest Risk of Failure

We have selected several patterns to highlight based on their combination of high gains and minimum failure rates. Other patterns can also be successful if monitored closely, but the "edge" appears to be in these patterns.

TABLE 8.1 **Comparative 3-Month Results in Classic Bar Chart Patterns**

	Overall Performance	Failure to Reach 5%	Average Performance	Tendency to Retrace	Reaches Target Price
High and tight flag, break up	1/23	0%	69%	54%	90%
Head-and-shoulders top, complex, break down	3/21	4%	23%	67%	53%
Head-and-shoulders top, break down	1/21	4%	22%	50%	55%
Triangle, descending, break up	5/23	7%	47%	37%	84%
Diamond bottom, break down	1/21	10%	21%	71%	63%
Diamond top, break down	7/21	6%	21%	57%	76%
Rectangle bottom, break up	11/21	10%	46%	53%	85%

Source: Bulkowski (www.thepatternsite.com).

According to Bulkowski (2015), the best-performing patterns, considering gain and risk, are the high-and-tight upward breaking flag, the head-and-shoulders top, top islands breaking down, and upward breaking descending triangles. A summary of these patterns is shown in Table 8.1.

■ Conclusion

In summary, the profitable use of chart patterns is not easy. The potential problems with recognizing and acting upon chart patterns that we have discussed in this chapter highlight the need to know thoroughly what we are doing. There are many variables in price behavior—mostly human—and being human ourselves and subject to the same biases, we must be adaptable and recognize that chart patterns are flexible.

It is unlikely that researchers will ever be able to prove definitively that patterns exist because the mathematics are so complicated and because the marketplace is always changing. In addition, many different patterns have been recognized, and, right or wrong, they have been described in the literature with nothing more than anecdotal evidence as to their reliability. If you see a pattern described with no background statistical evidence as to its usefulness, it is best not to bother with it. Today, most writers describing patterns will give some realistic evidence. Although this evidence might be flawed, it at least shows that it has been the subject of some serious study and, thus, is not merely a superstition.

The most reasonable approach for any chart reader is to take the classic patterns described in this chapter and become experienced in their use. Although the performance of these patterns will differ with different securities and with different trends in the general market, the behaviors of these patterns have remained relatively consistent for more than 100 years. We have discussed general attributes of patterns that in several studies show promise, but the analyst must always adjust parameters to fit the peculiarities of the security being analyzed. Profitable chart pattern analysis is the result of determined study.

■ References

Bulkowski, Thomas N. *Encyclopedia of Chart Patterns*. 2nd ed. New York, NY: John Wiley & Sons, 2005.

Bulkowski, Thomas N. *Trading Classic Chart Patterns*. New York, NY: John Wiley & Sons, 2002.

Bulkowski, Thomas N. "Bulkowski's Free Pattern Research." http://www.thepatternsite.com, 2010.

Bulkowski, Thomas N. www.thepatternsite.com/bestpatterns.html, accessed 2015.

Burnham, Terry. *Mean Markets and Lizard Brains*. New York, NY: John Wiley & Sons, 2005.

Edwards, Robert, John Magee, and W.H.C. Bassetti. *Techincal Analysis of Stock Trends*. 9th ed. Boca Raton, FL: St. Lucie Press, 2007.

Hasanhodzic, Jasmina, Andrew W. Lo, and Emanuele Viola. "Is it Real, or Is it Randomized?" A Financial Turing Test." Unpublished manuscript, 2010 (available at http://web.mit.edu/alo/www/papers/arorassrn.pdf).

Johnson, Spencer. *Who Moved My Cheese?* New York, NY: Penguin Putnam, 1998.

Kahneman, D. and A. Tversky. "Prospect Theory: An Analysis of Decision Under Risk." *Econometrica* 47 (1979): 263–291.

Kahneman, D. "Variants of Uncertainty." In *Judgment Under Uncertainty: Heuristics and Biases* (512), D. Kahneman, P. Slovic, and A. Tversky, eds. Cambridge University Press, Cambridge, 1982.

Levy, Robert A. "Predictive Significance of Five Point Chart Patterns." *Journal of Business* 44, no. 3 (1971): 316–323.

Lo, Andrew W. and Craig MacKinlay. "Stock Market Prices Do Not Follow Random Walks: Evidence from a Simple Specification Test." *Review of Financial Studies* 1 (1988): 41–66.

Lo, Andrew W., Harry Mamaysky, and Jiang Wang. "Foundations of Technical Analysis: Computational Algorithms, Statistical Inference, and Empirical Implementation." *Journal of Finance* 55 (2000): 4.

Merrill, Arthur A. *Behavior of Prices on Wall Street*. Published privately by the author, 1997.

Merrill, Arthur A. *Filtered Waves*. Published privately by the author, 1997.

O'Neil, William J. *How to Make Money in Stocks*. 3rd ed. (2002). New York, NY: McGraw-Hill, 1988.

Schabacker, R. *Stock Market Theory and Practice*. New York, NY: BV.C. Forbes Publishing Company, 1930.

Schwager, Jack D. *Schwager on Futures: Technical Analysis*. New York, NY: John Wiley & Sons, 1996.

Schwager, Jack D. *Technical Analysis*. New York, NY: John Wiley & Sons, Inc., 1996.

Skinner, B.F. "Superstition in the Pigeon." *Journal of Experimental Psychology* 38 (1947): 168–172.

CHAPTER 9

Short-Term Patterns

From Charles D. Kirkpatrick II and Julie R. Dahlquist, *Technical Analysis: The Complete Resource for Financial Market Technicians*, 3rd Edition (Old Tappan, New Jersey: Pearson Education, Inc., 2016), Chapter 17.

Learning Objective Statements

- Locate reversals in longer-term trends using short-term price patterns
- Describe the types of gaps that occur on price charts and their significance
- Recognize wide-range and narrow-range bars and their implications for volatility
- Identify one- and two-bar reversal patterns
- Identify common candlestick patterns and their significance within a trend

We have looked at longer-term patterns in bar charts and point and figure charts. We now turn our attention to short-term patterns. In this chapter, our focus is on short-term patterns on bar charts and candlestick charts. These patterns concentrate on the configuration and characteristics of individual bars, such as the height of the bar and the position of opening and closing prices on the bar. Some patterns also compare one period's bar with the preceding bar. Despite what their title suggests, short-term patterns are not limited to a particular short-term period, like one day. In this instance, "short-term" means a small number of bars. For example, on a daily bar chart, short-term patterns may form from one or two days of trading data, but on an hourly bar chart, a two-bar short-term pattern would include two hours' worth of trading data.

Although the longer-term patterns we have considered can be useful by themselves, they occur less frequently than shorter-term patterns. On the other hand, the shorter-term patterns we consider in this chapter are not useful by themselves but are common. Why do short-term patterns occur more frequently than longer-term patterns? Think of a common bar chart; four pieces of data are represented on each bar: an open, close, high, and low. With only four pieces of information, the number of various combinations in which these variables can occur is small. Even though stretching out the pattern to several bars increases the number of possible combinations, the number is still relatively small, and these combinations occur frequently.

Unfortunately, frequent patterns often give false signals. Although most market turning points include one or more of the short-term patterns covered in this chapter, these same patterns also occur at places where a reversal fails to follow. As Schwager (1996) states when referring to the one-day reversal pattern, it "successfully call(s) 100 out of every ten highs" (p. 89). Like Schwager, many others have been skeptical about the validity of short-term patterns. Just how useful and effective are they? Although some empirical tests suggest that these short-term patterns are not effective, many of the tests have covered longer testing periods than would be seen in practice. In most successful tests, short-term pattern entry signals are closed either at the close of the same day, the opening of the next day, the first profitable opening (called the **bailout** by Larry Williams), or the first profitable closing, which usually is only a few days later, barring the position first being stopped out. The ability to test over these short periods requires high-frequency data on a tick-to-tick basis and is usually beyond the capability of the normal investor or academic.

Nevertheless, once fully understood, short-term patterns are useful not only for trading but also for entering and exiting longer-term positions at more favorable prices. Although the average investor would not usually have the time or computer equipment and data feed to watch for short-term patterns, the professional trader certainly has the ability to watch intraday price behavior and can improve job performance and profits by understanding the nature of short-term patterns.

The basis for short-term patterns is to anticipate a sudden move, similar to the breakout concept in larger patterns, to take advantage of a period when prices have reached an emotion extreme, or to enter into a trend at an advantageous price as on a pullback or throwback. The methods usually have what is called a **setup**. A setup occurs when certain known factors needed to establish the pattern have occurred, and the trader is waiting for the action signal to occur. In larger charts, we have seen this concept in patterns. When the pattern, such as a triangle, forms, the setup is the pattern formation. If this pattern formation does not abide by the rules of triangle formations during its creation, it is not a setup, and we ignore it. If it does form correctly, we wait for the breakout, which is the action signal. Traders use the short-term patterns in the same manner, but over shorter time horizons, and they use tighter stops and exit signals.

Because short-term patterns are relatively frequent and usually depend on the previous trend as well as other factors, the prior trend must be known before short-term patterns can be used. A top pattern in a downward trend is obviously meaningless, for instance, and, thus, all top patterns can be disregarded from consideration during a declining trend. This leaves only bottoming patterns to consider during a downward trend. Also, a short-term reversal pattern should only be considered necessary when prices are at some kind of support level, resistance level, or trend line. Whenever many bits of evidence occur at a particular price and time, it is called a **cluster** of evidence. Once a cluster of evidence begins to form, the analyst should begin looking for a short-term pattern. It then can be useful in signaling when and where to act as well as what the price risk might be.

Short-term patterns can also be used to determine when upward or downward momentum is slowing. Remember that instead of using a momentum signal for action, using short-term patterns can often signal more precisely when to act and what risk exists once momentum begins to slow.

Although short-term patterns are usually reversal patterns, they can be used as continuation patterns in corrections within a trend. For example, in a strong upward trend, when the price corrects or retraces in a normal manner and a cluster of evidence forms that indicates the earlier, longer trend may soon continue, a short-term bottom reversal or continuation pattern may signal when to act. Usually, however, short-term patterns are best when they occur right at a peak or trough. Minimum action should be taken, however, unless there is a cluster of evidence that a longer-term reversal is due or that a strong trend is due to continue. For example, in an uptrend, if a price is near previous resistance, under but close to an important moving average, and has reached a price target, a short-term reversal top pattern is likely valid and worth acting upon. If a short-term reversal pattern of any kind occurs without supporting evidence, it might or might not signal an actual price reversal; it might simply signal that a slight consolidation period is next.

Short-term patterns are also the first sign that a reversal is nearing. They act quickly, often occurring on the actual peak or trough day. As such, they lead most other patterns, which take time and further price action to develop. In a head-and-shoulders top pattern, for example, the analyst must wait for the actual breakout below the neckline before acting, but a short-term reversal pattern might have already indicated a potential reversal right at the top of the head.

In experimenting with short-term patterns, the technical analyst should consider several variables:

- The more complex the pattern, the less frequently it is going to occur. Some analysts have libraries of hundreds of patterns they have found useful in the past and through experimentation and use a computer-screening program that will pump out all the relevant patterns before each trading day. This gives them an edge but is impractical for most traders.
- The relationship between bars in a pattern need not be just a matter of the position of the high, low, open, and close to each other. The relation can be a proportional one rather than an exact one (Harris, 2000) where, for example, the close

is in the lower 33% of the trading range, or the range that is three bars earlier is one-half the range of the last bar.

- The pattern may be split between two time periods, whereby one pattern appears at one time, and at some predetermined time later, another pattern must appear.
- The entry may be delayed by some predetermined time.
- The pattern may relate to another market entirely, whereby, for example, a pattern in the bond market may give a signal in the stock market or a currency.

These variables make the search for reliable patterns exceedingly complex and likely beyond necessity. The old principle of keeping things simple should be applied to any kind of pattern recognition search.

We divide the types of patterns into traditional bar chart patterns and candlestick patterns. Candlestick patterns portray the raw data of open, close, high, and low differently than a bar chart, but their patterns are similar to bar chart patterns. Part of the appeal of candlestick charts is not so much the patterns but the visual ease with which the analyst can "see" intraday pressures on price and the price trend. They also have peculiar but memorable names for specific patterns that make them engaging.

As in all patterns, experience will separate the winners from the losers. Anyone using such patterns should record in a notebook the successes and failures from interpreting short-term patterns. Reviewing this recording periodically will help the investor develop a better "feel" of his ability to act profitably and learn where mistakes more frequently occur. Every trading vehicle has its own "personality." Success is often a function of understanding the peculiarities of the trading vehicle most commonly traded.

■ Pattern Construction and Determination

The principal data used in short-term patterns—both traditional and candlestick, regardless of bar time—is open, close, high, and low. The opening price is traditionally considered the price established from any news, emotion, anticipation, or mechanical signals that have built up overnight. Most professional day traders, scalpers, and even swing traders prefer to avoid it. They wait for some action—a gap or opening range—to take place before judging the tone of the market.

Because the closing price is the final price of the day and the one at which most margin accounts are valued, it is like a summary of the bar's activity. If the close is up, the majority and most recent action was positive; if the close is down, the majority and most recent price action was to the downside. Professionals use it as a benchmark with which to compare the next day's price action. Most people reading the financial news remember and use it to value their accounts. The closing price becomes a benchmark for future action, both long and short term. Some traders consider it the most important price of the day, even though it is somewhat arbitrary.

The high is the upper extreme reached by buyers during the bar and is, thus, a measure of buying ability and enthusiasm. On the other hand, the low is the lower extreme reached by sellers during the bar and is, thus, a measure of selling ability and fear.

The configuration, length of the bar, position on the bar, preceding bar data, and price distance between each determine the pattern. As you might guess, there is a multitude of potential combinations, and all have been investigated for ways to profit. We present next just a few of the large array of short-term patterns that have shown promise in the past.

■ Traditional Short-Term Patterns

Let us look at some of the short-term patterns and their trading implications. These are patterns in use today that by themselves are warnings, at best, but not necessarily action patterns, that should be followed without a cluster of other evidence. You will notice that none of the patterns includes moving averages. Over short time periods, especially when the period is interrupted by inactivity, moving averages are not reliable. For example, when using five-minute data, the only moving average with any value would be short because the period from one day to the next is interrupted by a long period overnight when no trading activity occurs. In 24-hour markets, short-term moving averages have more value because the markets are open continuously.

Gaps

Gaps occur when either the low for the current bar is above the high for the previous bar or the high for the current bar is lower than the low of the previous bar. Figure 9.1 pictures a gap down. The "hole" or "void" created in the price history is a "price range at which no shares changed hands" (Edwards and Magee, 2007). A price gap might or might not have significance. We have seen them before in analyzing breakouts from classic patterns, trend lines, and support or resistance zones, and in those instances, the gaps were demonstrating the beginning of a new trend. However, gap types differ based on the context in which they occur. Some are meaningful, and others can be disregarded.

Gaps often do not occur in market averages that are not themselves traded. For example, the day following Saddam Hussein's capture on December 13, 2003, a majority of stocks opened strongly upward on gaps, while the Dow Jones Industrial Average showed an opening price roughly the same as that at the close of the previous day and then rose as the prices of the component stocks gradually opened. No gap existed in the DJIA because it is an average, not a security. On the other hand, the DJIA future showed a gap because it is a traded security.

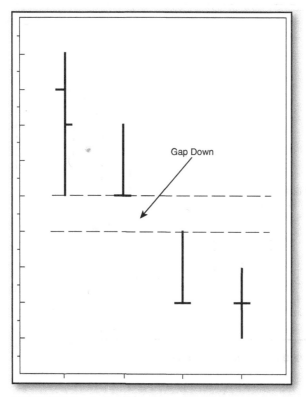

FIGURE 9.1 A Gap Down

Breakaway (or Breakout) Gaps The most profitable gaps are those that occur at the beginning of a trend, called **breakaway gaps**. We have seen these before when prices suddenly break through a formation boundary and a major change in trend direction begins. Breakaway gaps signal that a pattern is completed and a boundary penetrated. The size of the gap—the space between the two extremes in which no activity occurs—appears to be proportional to the strength of the subsequent price move. Heavy volume usually accompanies upward gaps but not necessarily downward gaps. The best manner of trading breakaway gaps is to wait a short while for the initial fading or profit-taking by the professionals to see if the gap is filled and, if not, to enter in the direction of the gap with a stop at the point where the gap would be filled. If the gap is filled immediately, a stop and reverse might be appropriate because a sudden failure in a gap is often followed by a large move in the opposite direction from the gap direction, similar to a Specialist's Breakout.

David Landry (2003) suggests a method of mechanizing the breakaway gap, known as the "explosion gap pivot." A reversal point, often called a **pivot**, establishes not only where prices have reversed direction but also where supply and resistance are likely to occur in the future.[1] In Landry's method, a pivot low is the low of a bar that

---

[1] This reversal "pivot" should not be confused with the "pivot point" used in intraday trading for anticipating potential support and resistance levels.

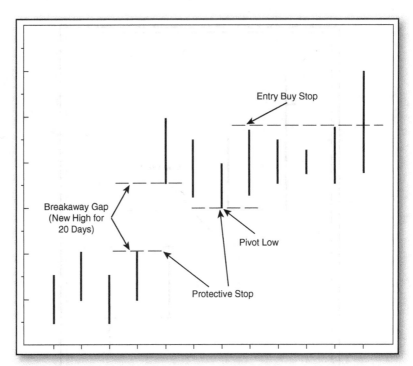

FIGURE 9.2 Explosion Gap Pivot

is surrounded on both sides by a bar with a higher low, as shown in Figure 9.2. This establishes a reversal point. Requirements that are more restrictive can be placed on the pivot point; for example, higher lows may be required for two or more bars on either side of the pivot point. For Landry's method, however, one on both sides is sufficient.

We know that a breakaway gap can be a false gap and that if it is "filled," the odds of it being false increase. Thus, we want a breakaway gap to establish a new high, for at least the past 20 days, and for the subsequent retracement not to fill the gap. If either of these requirements is not met, the gap is ignored. When the retracement does occur, eventually it will create a pivot low above the lower edge of the gap. Once this pivot low occurs, a buy entry stop is placed above the high of the next bar from the pivot low (the one that establishes the pivot), and a protective stop is placed just above the gap lower edge (or Landry suggests just below the pivot low). If the gap is then filled, the protective stop will exit the position. Occasionally, the pivot low will be penetrated again, but as long as the gap is not filled, the position should be kept. The reverse configuration is equally applicable to downward breakaway gaps.

Opening Gap   When the opening price for the day is outside the range of the previous day, it is called an **opening gap**. After the opening, prices might continue in the direction of the gap, and the gap becomes a breakaway gap, or prices might retrace from the opening and fill the gap. Figure 9.3 shows an opening gap to the downside,

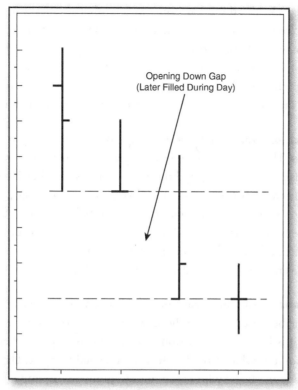

Opening Down Gap
(Later Filled During Day)

FIGURE 9.3 **Opening Down Gap**

with prices retracing and filling the gap during the day. This type of pattern is sometimes useful in determining a short-term trend reversal. The history of opening gaps in index futures suggests that they should be "faded" (or sold into) on large upward openings because they most often "fill" (retrace through the price vacuum) during the day. In downward opening gaps, a fill is not as common (Kaufman, 1998). In individual stock issues and commodities, a fill is a sign of weakness and should not occur in a breakaway gap. If the gap is not filled, usually within the first half hour, the odds of the trend continuing in the direction of the gap increase.

One potential way to profit from an opening gap is to watch the first three five-minute bars (a three-bar range) and determine the high and low of this range. A breakout of that range in the direction of the gap often indicates that the trend will continue in the gap direction; a breakout that moves in the direction of filling the gap will often continue to fill the gap. A danger is that the first run from the gap can last longer than the three bars. The three-bar range must, therefore, be obvious, not a continued run in the gap direction. In addition, the breakout from the three-bar gap range in the direction of the gap may be false. A tight stop is necessary, or a wait for a pull-back or throwback from the breakout, a narrow range bar break, or even a small cup and handle.

If the price breaks the three-bar range in the other direction toward the fill, the previous day's close, the fill line, will likely be the target. A bounce between the fill line and the range breakout line suggests that the longer-term move will be in the direction of the fill, a reversal of the gap. On the other hand, if the prices after a range break in the direction of the fill turn and retest the outer extreme of the three-bar range, the odds increase that the longer-term move will be in the direction of the gap.

Runaway Gaps (or Measuring Gaps) Gaps that occur along a trend are called **runaway gaps**. They can appear in strong trends that have few minor corrections and just keep rising or declining without retracements or other interruptions. They are also called **measuring gaps** because, like pennants and flags, they often occur at about the middle of a price run, and, thus, the initial distance to them can be projected above them for a target price. An upward runaway gap occurs on average 43% of the distance from the trend beginning and the eventual peak, whereas a downward gap occurs on average 57% of the distance (Bulkowski, 2010).

Exhaustion Gaps Exhaustion gaps occur at the end of moves but are not recognized at the time because they have the same characteristics as runaway gaps. If a gap is later closed, it is likely an exhaustion gap. These gaps appear when a strong trend has reached a point at which greed or fear has reached its apex. Usually they represent latecomers to the trend who are anxious to jump on or jump off. They can occur on light volume but more often occur on heavy volume.

The sign that such gaps are not runaway gaps is an immediate fill within a few bars of the gap. Remember that a runaway gap often occurs midstream in a price run. Prices should not immediately reverse and fill a gap unless the end of the run is approaching. Exhaustion gaps occur at the end of a move and signal a potential trend reversal. Usually more evidence of an exhaustion gap is necessary before an action signal can be justified. Sometimes prices reverse immediately, and sometimes they enter a congestion area.

Other Minor Gaps Common gaps are those that occur frequently in illiquid trading vehicles, are small in relation to the price of the vehicle, or appear in short-term trading data. They are of no consequence. Pattern gaps occasionally appear within the formation of larger patterns, and generally they are filled. Their only significance is to suggest that a congestion area is forming. Ex-dividend gaps sometimes occur in stock prices when the dividend is paid and the stock price is adjusted the following day. These have no significance and must not be misinterpreted. Often gaps occur in 24-hour futures trading when one market closes and another opens, especially if one market is electronic and the other open outcry. These are called **suspension gaps** and are also meaningless unless they occur as one of the four principal gaps described previously.

BOX 9.1   GAPS AND CLASSIC PATTERNS—A CASE STUDY OF APPLE COMPUTER

Figure 9.4 contains daily bar charts for Apple Computer (AAPL) for September 2009 through May 2010. What actions might we have taken in this stock, given our knowledge of classic patterns and gaps? Each paragraph number that follows corresponds to a number on Figure 9.4.

1. First we see a small pennant formation with an upward breakout at $167.28. We buy the stock on the breakout. Because we don't have the past history, we can't at this point make a measured move projection of the eventual target, and we decide to just hold the stock with a protective stop below the pennant's lower bound at $164.11. Upward gap1 and gap2 appear next. We use them to place trailing stops as the price progresses upward. The pivot low after the gap1 is the first trailing stop at $169.70. We now have a locked-in profit even if the stop is triggered. Gap2 is a runaway gap. A runaway gap should not retrace back into the gap, or it is not a runaway. We, thus, raise the trailing stop to the upper edge of the gap at $177.88. Because this is a runaway gap, we can now project the target with the measured move method. We do this by measuring the price difference between the move beginning ($167.28) and the midpoint in the gap ($176.77). This $9.49 we add to the gap2 midpoint to arrive at an estimated objective of $176.77 + $9.49 = $186.26. This price is reached two days later, at which point we can sell or hang on with a close trailing stop so we don't lose the gain we have already achieved. If we sell at the target price, we will have profited by $18.97, about 11.3% in nine days.
2. The price then goes into a flag pattern, and when it breaks out at $187.30, we buy it again. This breakout is accompanied by gap3, which is later filled. We place the protective stop at the low price of the flag at $180.70.
3. Gap4 occurs and has the initial appearance of a breakout or runaway gap. In neither case should prices fill such a gap, so we move our stop to the upper limit of gap4 at $197.85.
4. Our trailing stop is triggered by an unexpected price decline that negates the earlier interpretation of gap4. We profit by $10.55.

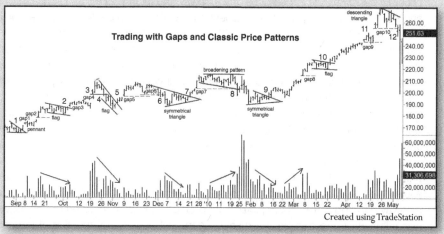

FIGURE 9.4   Case Study: Apple Computer

(continued)

5. The price then forms a downward flag pattern, and volume confirms as it declines with price. The break upward from the flag triggers another buy at $190.73. This is followed by gap5, another likely runaway gap. The measured move projection from this gap is $200.73, which is reached on the day following gap5. We can sell at this level and reap another gain, this time of $10.00.

6. Had we not sold at the target price, we still would have placed a trailing stop at the upper level of gap5 at $196.26 and sold the stock on the retracement. We might also have sold the stock short on the trailing stop because the filling of what's thought to be a runaway gap is often an exhaustion gap and, therefore, a price trend reversal.

7. Whether we sold the stock short or not, the upward breakout from a symmetrical triangle would require another entry buy at $196.05. Following that triangle, breakout gap7 forms. This also has the appearance of a runaway gap (strong price move closing near high on increased volume), and we move a trailing stop from below the triangle to the upper edge of the gap at $203.35. We also calculate the measured move target of $209.68, which is reached two days later. If we sell at the target, we achieve on the trade a profit of $13.63.

8. If we don't sell at the target, we certainly are forced to sell when the price breaks below our trailing stop at the upper bound of gap7. This breakout is not only through the gap but also through the lower bound of a broadening pattern. Indeed, with this combination, we will short the stock at the breakout price of $203.35 and place a protective stop at the upper bound of the broadening pattern at $215.55. Following the breakout down, the price rallies in a pullback to the breakdown level but fails to penetrate back through it on the upside. However, it also fails to continue downward after the pullback and instead forms a symmetrical triangle. We place a buy stop each day along the upper bound of the triangle as our trailing stop.

9. We get stopped out with the trailing stop at $196.60, and we buy the stock on the basis of the triangle pattern confirmed with declining volume. We place a protective stop at the cradle of the triangle where the two bounds meet at $189.48 in case the breakout is false. Indeed, the price throws back shortly after the breakout but doesn't penetrate the cradle, and we remain long the stock. Gap8 comes after a healthy rise in the stock price. This also has the appearance of a runaway gap (high volume, large price move), and we move our trailing stop to the upper bound of the gap at $219.70. The measured move target from this runaway gap is $234.02. It is reached 18 days later.

10. We could sell at the target price, but before the target is reached, a flag pattern formed. We move our trailing stop up to the lower edge of the flag at $220.15 to protect our profit. A flag pattern is also a measured pattern that will give an additional price target. The calculation in this instance is to take the high point in the flag at $227.73 minus the starting price of the move ($196.60) for an estimated price distance of $31.13 that we add to the level at which the price breaks out of the flat ($224.64). But prices broke upward from the flag and, thus, projected $31.13 to a target of $255.77, our new target.

11. Our price target is reached 21 trading days after the upward breakout from the flag pattern on a large upward gap (gap10). There was a small gap9 preceding gap10 and a few others along the way. Each of these gaps failed to show the characteristics of a runaway gap and were, thus, ignored. But gap10, aside from reaching our objective, was substantial and also likely a runaway gap, just because of the size of the gap compared with others. If we don't sell at the target price, we at least move the trailing stop to the upper level of the gap at $255.73.

12. As it turns out, gap10 was an exhaustion gap—something that can only be recognized in retrospect. However, we were stopped out of our trade at the trailing stop and perhaps went short on the exhaustion gap breakdown because this type of breakdown often indicates a trend reversal. That the exhaustion gap occurred at the price target from the earlier flag formation confirmed the likelihood of a trend reversal. The sell stop produced a profit of $59.13, a 30% gain, in less than 3 months.

The preceding example shows what can be done with just technical analysis alone. We did not act on any news or outside market behavior. We simply watched the price very closely. Stops were an important part of our strategy. If we had not moved stops when we did, we would have suffered at the upward breakout from the symmetrical triangle and from the failure of gap10. Risk control is sometimes more important than entry technique. Technical analysis takes knowledge, patience, and close watching of price action, but profits can be made.

Spike (or Wide-Range or Large-Range Bar)

Spikes are similar to gaps except that the empty space associated with a gap is a solid line (in a bar chart). Should a breakaway gap occur intraday, for example, the daily bar would not show the discontinuity from the gap but instead would show a long bar. The importance of a spike, as in a gap, depends on the context surrounding it. A spike can occur on a breakout from a formation, midpoint in a strong, accelerating trend, and as the final reversal day at the end of a trend. In the earlier discussion of breakouts, we demonstrated the Specialist Breakout. This is often a spike because it usually occurs intraday. At the ends of trends when either gross enthusiasm or panic appears, the last few bars are often spikes. At the end of an accelerated trend, the last bar within the trend is often a spike called a **climax** (see Figure 9.5). Thus, spikes can represent the beginning or the end of a trend. On the other hand, some stocks and commodities, especially those awaiting a news announcement, will have wide-range bars that subside almost immediately within the next few days with little net change in trend direction. This behavior is generally associated with a stock or commodity that will not follow standard technical rules.

Dead Cat Bounce (DCB)

"Dead Cat Bounce" is a graceless term for a failed rally after a sharp decline. Although the term has been used for many years on Wall Street and in Chicago, it was probably first used in print either in a 1985 *Financial Times* article by reporter Chris Sherwell in a comment on the sharp decline in the Singapore stock market or by Raymond Devoe Jr., research analyst and professional cynic, who advocated using a bumper sticker "Beware the Dead Cat Bounce" in 1986.

The DCB is most profitable and more easily recognized after a large downward breakaway gap or downward breakaway spike. The sudden downward motion is

FIGURE 9.5 Spike Peak and Buying Climax (X—U.S. Steel, weekly: November 8, 2013– June 26, 2015)

called an **event decline** because it usually occurs on an event such as a bad news announcement. It lasts just a few days (average of seven) and usually begins a longer-term downward price trend. The DCB's characteristics include a short rally of several days up to two weeks following the initial bottom from the sharp initial news event sell-off. Ideally, the rally should follow an event decline of more than 20%. Normally, the larger the first decline, the higher the bounce. A DCB is shown in Figure 9.6 of Hewlett Packard (HPQ). The "bounce" comes from bargain hunters and bottom-fishing traders who are second-guessing when the actual bottom will take place. It gathers momentum from short covering and momentum signals. The buyers are usually wrong. In more than 67% of DCBs (Bulkowski, 2010), the price continues to lower after the DCB and breaks the earlier news event low an average of 18%. The second decline in a DCB is characteristically less intense but equally deceiving. It also tends to be accompanied by much lower volume. Not all event declines include a DCB.

To trade the DCB, the event decline must first be recognized. This is usually easy because almost every day, somewhere, some bad news comes out about a company or commodity. Wait for the initial sell-off volume to decline and then look for a rally on lesser volume, sometimes back as far as the lower edge of the breakaway gap, and lasting only a few days. If the downward rush occurred as a spike rather than a gap, look into the intraday trading to see where the news event gap occurred, and

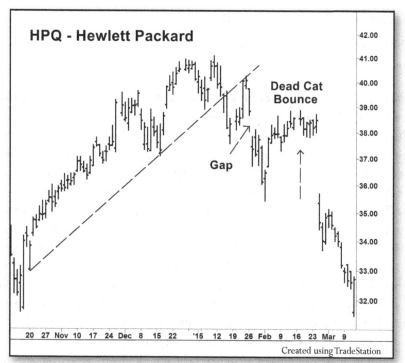

FIGURE 9.6 Dead Cat Bounce (HPQ—Hewlett Packard, daily: October 13, 2014–March 12, 2015)

use that gap just as if it had occurred between the daily bars. In the Hewlett Packard chart (refer to Figure 9.6), the rally filled the gap, just barely. The short-selling trading requirement then is for a topping of the bounce or a short-term top pattern, close protective stops above the entry, and a longer time horizon. For those wanting to purchase the stock, the odds are against profiting from a purchase for at least six months. Most bullish chart patterns fail during this period.

Island Reversal

An island reversal can occur at either a top or a bottom, and only after a relatively lengthy trend. It can happen in a congestion area, but only infrequently. It requires two gaps at roughly the same price: the first in the direction of the trend, an exhaustion gap, and the second in the reverse direction, a breakaway gap. The larger the gap, the more important is the formation. Between the gaps, low volatility trading can occur for a number of days or even weeks. Volume usually increases on the second gap from an island top but not necessarily from a bottom. The extreme price in the island must be either higher than previous highs at a top or lower than previous lows at a bottom. Pullbacks and throwbacks are frequent (65%–70%), and failures are low, around 13%–17%. This pattern is not common and has terrible performance results (Bulkowski, 2010).

One- and Two-Bar Reversal Patterns

The following one- and two-bar reversal patterns are common. Therefore, each of these patterns needs confirmation before use.

One-Bar Reversal (Also Reversal Bar, Climax, Top or Bottom Reversal Bar, Key Reversal Bar)   When a trading bar high is greater than the previous bar high and the close is down from the previous bar close, it is called a **one-bar reversal**. It is sometimes preceded by a gap, at least an opening gap, and its bar length is not as extreme or intensive as in a spike. It is not a spike, because a spike is not necessarily a reversal, but a combination of spike and reversal can elevate its meaning. This pattern will occur in reverse at a bottom. It is common, but unfortunately, its top and bottom version will also occur within a trend, making it practically useless as a signal by itself. To be useful, but also cutting down on the number of profitable signals, it needs more stringent requirements. For example, rather than just closing down, the close may be required to exceed the previous bar low or even the low of the two previous bars. Kamich (2003) argues that a close is more reliable after a sustained advance than after a short rally. This may require that it be the highest high or lowest low over a specified period or that a series of higher highs or lower lows precede it. When combined with a cluster of other evidence, a close's significance improves. Whatever signal it gives is completely negated once prices exceed its reversal peak or trough.

Two-Bar Reversal (Also Pipe Formation)   The two-bar reversal pattern, like the one-bar reversal, occurs at the end of a trend, upward or downward, but extends the reversal over two bars. Bulkowski calls it a **pipe formation**. A two-bar reversal formation is pictured in Figure 9.7. In the bottom pattern, the first bar usually closes in the lower half of the bar, and the second bar close ends near its high. Usually high volume is seen on both bars. In its extreme and more reliable version, it consists of two side-by-side spikes, but it can also be above-average length side-by-side bars of roughly equivalent length, peaking or bottoming at close to the same price, and occurring after a lengthy trend. Following and prior to the two-bar reversal, low bar prices should be in the vicinity of the top of the bars (in a bottom, the opposite for a top). It, thus, stands out quite easily in retrospect. It is preferable for the second bar to be slightly longer than the first bar, and volume is preferably higher on the left bar than on the right. Rarely this pattern acts as a consolidation area within a trend. Many pipes occur at the end of the retracement of a longer-term move. The directional clue is the direction of the breakout from it.

Failure rates are in the 5% range, which is low for a pattern (Bulkowski, 2010). Usually the failure occurs when the previous trend has been less than 5%. If the earlier trend is lengthy, the pattern rarely fails. Once the pattern has formed and prices have reversed direction, it is common for a test of the bars to occur soon thereafter. In most cases, the bars hold their extreme within a small percentage during the test, and this presents a good spot to place an initial protective stop. Both Kamich and

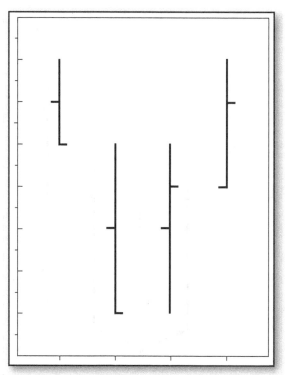

FIGURE 9.7   Two-Bar Reversal Bottom (or pipe bottom)

Bulkowski maintain that the formation in weekly bars is more reliable than in daily bars. Bulkowski ranks it 2 out of 23 for performance in a bull market.

Horn Pattern   Bulkowski describes the horn pattern as being almost identical in behavior to the pipe except a smaller bar separates the two lengthy bars. The two long bars become the "horns" of the formation (see Figure 9.8). As in the two-bar reversal, the formation is more reliable with weekly bars and otherwise has the same characteristics as the pipe. It is not as effective as the pipe at bottoms and tops, and its failure rate increases when the trend preceding the pattern is short.

Two-Bar Breakout   The two-bar breakout is an extremely simple pattern. Indeed, it is so simple that it is hard to believe it will work, but the testing column in *Active Trader Magazine* (November 2003) tested it and found it to be successful for stocks and commodities (more so with commodities). The rules they used and that could easily be experimented with are for longs: the next day buy on a stop one tick above today's high if (1) today's low is less than yesterday's low, (2) today's high is less than yesterday's high, and (3) today's close is less than today's open. Exit on a stop at the then-current day's low. The sell side is just the opposite. Results should be tested against a better exit strategy, but as it is, the pattern produced reasonable profits in commodities and an extremely low drawdown. In stocks, the results were not as favorable but likely could be improved upon with money management and a better exit strategy.

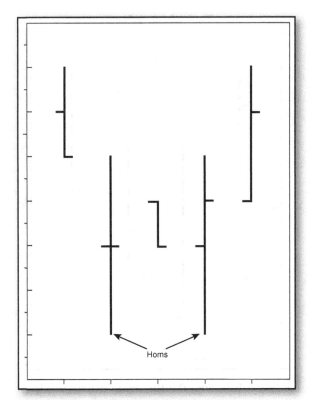

Horns

FIGURE 9.8 The Horn Pattern

Inside Bar An inside bar is a bar with a range that is smaller than and within the previous bar's range, as shown in Figure 9.9. It reflects a decline in momentum in a trend, a bar where a short-term congestion area is formed. As in most congestion areas, it reflects a pause, a period of direction-less equilibrium waiting for something to happen that will signal the next trend direction. During a larger congestion pattern, such as a triangle or rectangle, an inside bar has little meaning because it is just reflecting the lack of motion in the larger pattern. Some analysts plotting larger patterns delete inside bars, especially when determining pivots, because these bars fail to represent any important price action, similar to the way the point and figure chart eliminates dull periods. Within a trend, however, the inside bar provides some useful information and can generate profitable, short-term signals. As in the gap pattern, the context of the pattern's location is more important than the pattern configuration.

Toby Crabel (1989) found that without a cluster of other information, a number of inside bar combinations during the 1982–1986 period in the S&P futures achieved a better-than-average winning percentage. Crabel tested buying at the opening, if the opening price occurred above the earlier inside bar close, and selling at the opening, if it occurred below the earlier inside bar close (see Figure 9.10). This strategy produced a 68% winning percentage. This winning percentage could then be improved by adding even other requirements, mostly having to do with characteristics of the

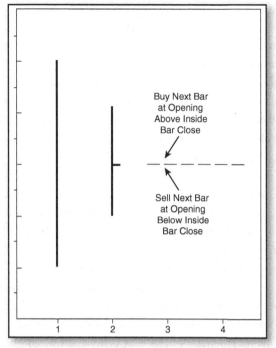

FIGURE 9.9 Inside Bar

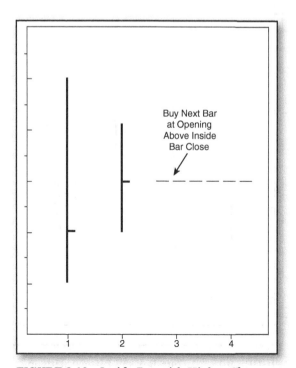

FIGURE 9.10 Inside Bar with Higher Close

bars preceding the inside bar and with the preceding trend. One strategy, for example, is to buy if the inside bar close was higher than the previous day close and there is a higher open on the current bar. Likewise, you'd sell when the inside bar close was below the previous day close and the opening on the current bar is below the inside close. For this slightly more complex strategy, a 74% winning percentage occurred.

Crabel took his inside tests a little further, looking for a four-day pattern. If Day 2 had a higher low than Day 1, Day 3 was an inside day, and Day 4 opened lower than the midrange and close of the inside day, a sell signal was generated. This strategy is pictured in Figure 9.11. During Crabel's test period, this strategy had an 80% winning percentage. The opposite strategy would occur when Day 2 had a lower high than Day 1, Day 3 was an inside day, and Day 4 opened above the inside day close, triggering a buy signal. This strategy produced a 90% winning percentage. Although these strategies had extremely high winning percentages, they only occurred on average twice a year.

What Crabel was demonstrating, regardless of the percentages, was that the opening of a bar after an inside bar shows a strong bias toward the new price direction. Granted, his testing was done during a bull market in the late 1980s and is somewhat dated today, but nevertheless, the tests showed some correlation to the inside day breakouts and future performance. His exit criterion was to close the position on

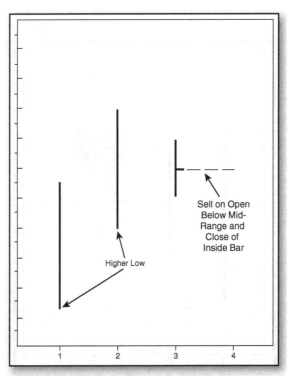

FIGURE 9.11   A Four-Bar Sell Pattern with an Inside Bar

the close of the day the trade was entered. This limits such trades to day traders. However, an inside bar can also occur on weekly bar charts and usually signifies a larger congestion area similar to a pennant or flag on a daily chart. In these cases, the inside week can be useful for longer-term trading.

Several other common patterns use the inside bar concept.

Hook Reversal Day Hook is a common term for a quick loss when a profit was expected. It comes from the fishhook that the fish bites thinking that the bait is a free meal. As outlined by Kamich (2003) and Crabel (1989), a hook reversal occurs after a series of upward thrust bars, called **run bars** when they occur right after each other (Schwager, 1996). Then suddenly, a narrow-range bar occurs with specific characteristics. The narrow-range bar must open at or above the previous high and close below the previous close. Kamich's variation is for an inside bar that opens at its high and closes at its low. This signals that the momentum built up during the run has reached a climax. A downward break would be an action signal.

Another hook formation occurs when traders are "hooked" into believing that the trend has reversed. This occurs when an open is above the previous high, but prices reverse direction and close down on the bar. This is the hook. It must have a narrower range than the previous bar, but it often fools traders into believing that a top has occurred. The action signal is when the price breaks back above the close of the first. It also works in reverse.

Naked Bar Upward Reversal A variation of the hook, a naked bar is one that closes below a previous low (suggested by Joe Stowell and Larry Williams) and is a down bar (close less than open). It is the most bearish close possible. If an inside bar follows a naked bar with open greater than naked bar close, it is a sign that the downtrend is reversing. An upward break from the inside bar would suggest the bears are caught.

Hikkake The hikkake is an inside bar signal that fails and becomes a signal itself (see Figure 9.12). As described by Daniel Chesler (2004), in Japanese, "hikkake" is a term meaning to trap, trick, or ensnare. It is a pattern that starts with an inside bar. When prices break one way or the other from an inside bar, the conventional belief is that they will continue in the same direction. The hikkake pattern occurs when the breakout fails to continue and prices in the following bars return to break in the opposite direction through the previous inside bar extreme. The reversal and opposite breakout must occur within three bars after the first breakout; the open and close of each bar seems to be unimportant.

Outside Bar An outside bar occurs when the high is higher than the high of the previous bar and the low is lower than the low of the previous bar. It is a specific kind of wide-range bar that "covers" all the previous bar's price action. In other words, the outside bar is longer than the previous bar and contains the entire price range of the previous bar. Traditionally, an outside bar is thought of as a bar of increased volatility,

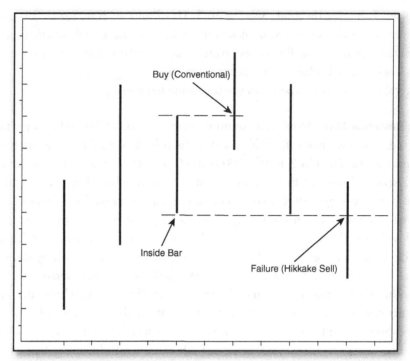

FIGURE 9.12 Hikkake Buy Failure

and, depending on the close, perhaps the beginning of a trend. Larry Williams (1988, 1995, 1999, 2000, and 2003) has done considerable study of outside bars, and the results are available in his various books.

When an outside bar closes near an extreme—that is, a high or low—and above or below the previous close and its current opening, it suggests further action in the direction of the close into the following bar. Bulkowski, using daily lows, observes that the close, if located within the upper or lower 25% of the range, tends to predict the future breakout upward about 66% of the time and downward 62% of the time. However, it often is a false signal. For example, one of the more reliable, although less frequently seen, setup patterns with an outside day is when the outside day closes at below the previous day's low and the next day opens lower than the outside day close. Buy the following day opening (Williams, 2000). Standard opinion would suggest that the series of lower closes was bearish, yet the setup is bullish.

Other Multiple-Bar Patterns

One- or two-day patterns are common, easily defined but not always reliable. Complex patterns are subject to interpretation by the analyst because their formation is not a perfect fit to the ideal. Between these pattern types are patterns with a few bars that have simple rules but require more price action than the short-term variety and are not as common as classic patterns.

Correction within a Trend Many studies have shown that acting in the direction of the trend is more advantageous after waiting for a correction to that trend. The reward of catching the trend at a cheaper price as well as having a closer stop level outweigh the potential opportunity loss of missing the trend.

There are at least two different types of trend correction patterns. One is to recognize a trend and act on a percentage pullback from that trend. *Active Trader Magazine* (March, 2003) tested on 18 stocks a long-only 6% pullback system. It demonstrated during the period 1992 through 2002, a generally rising period, that entering a buy at 6% below the previous bar close and exiting on the next open would produce an excellent equity curve when triggered. The gain over the period was the same as the buy-and-hold, but the market exposure was only 17% due to the limited number of trades and the quick exits.

Knockout Pattern The knockout (or KO) pattern is another trend correction method, used by David Landry (2003). (See Figure 9.13.) The first requirement for this pattern is that an extremely strong and persistent trend must be present. In an upward trend, Landry's criteria for a strong uptrend is that the stock must have risen at least ten points in the past 20 trading days and a trend line drawn through the prices touch almost all bars. Thus, if we think about a linear regression line, the bars should have a small deviation from that line, not wide swings back and forth. At some time, the stock will develop a throwback of two to five days in which two prior lows will be exceeded. Place a buy entry stop at the high of the bar with the

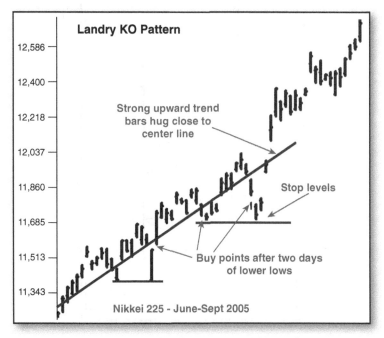

FIGURE 9.13 Landry KO Pattern

second low. If the next bar is lower, move the buy stop to its high until the position is executed. Place a protective stop below the last low, or use any reasonable stop method. According to Landry, the reverse is equally as successful in a downtrend using the criteria in reverse. Figure 9.13 shows a steady upward trend in the Nikkei 225 with occasional two-day sell-offs that fulfill the requirements of the KO pattern.

Oops!   Larry Williams (1979) uses the term **Oops!** to name an opening range pattern that profits from a sudden change in direction (see Figure 9.14). The setup for this pattern occurs when the opening price on today's bar is outside the previous day's range. Assume, for example, that a stock opens today at a price below yesterday's range. A buy stop is then placed just inside yesterday's range in case the market closes the gap, indicating a reversal. This pattern depends on other traders acting in the direction of an opening gap and being caught when prices reverse.

Larry Connors (1998) uses a 10% qualification variation of the Larry Williams Oops! pattern. The pattern is for the first day to have a close within 10% of the low. The second day must open on a downward gap. If these conditions are met, place a buy stop at the first day's low with a sell stop near the second day's opening. A sell pattern is just the reverse on a day when the close is within 10% of its high.

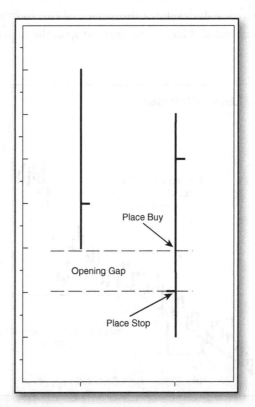

FIGURE 9.14 Oops! Buy Pattern

Shark   The shark pattern is a three-bar pattern. The most recent bar high must be lower than the previous high and the recent low above the previous low. In other words, the recent bar is an inside bar. The previous bar must also be an inside bar. The progression in bars, therefore, is one base bar and two successive inside bars, as shown in Figure 9.15. In effect, it is a small triangle or pennant. The name "shark" comes from the pattern's finlike shape.

In a *Stocks and Commodities* article, Walter Downs (1998) demonstrated that the short-term pattern called the **Shark-32** has implications for the longer-term as well as the immediate future. This study was an interesting approach to determining the success or failure of the pattern in that Downs questioned whether the symmetry of the pattern added to or detracted from its performance. Symmetry was measured by determining the amount by which the center of the final inside day range, called the **apex**, deviated from the center of the base day range. Although there can be many shark patterns, Downs limited his study to those patterns that fit a specified symmetry. The test was run on Harley Davidson stock from July 1986 to April 1998, a period of generally rising stock prices. The entry was to buy on the close of the first day after a day in which the close exceeded the widest point in the pattern—usually the base day. The exit was a trailing stop or a reversal on the opposite signal.

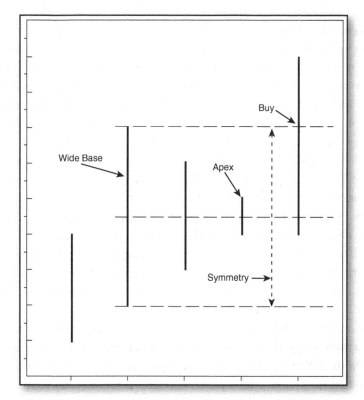

FIGURE 9.15   Shark Pattern with Break to the Upside

The results of Downs' study were useful in that they suggested that the more symmetrical the shark formation, the more likely prices would continue in the same direction and improve performance at least out to 30 days thereafter. As the symmetry became tight, the results did not change, but the number of patterns that fit into the requirements declined. One example was that if the symmetrical variance of the apex midrange was within 12% either side of the center of the base day range, the trend continued in the same direction as the prepattern direction 91% of the time, strengthened in 36% of the instances, and increased in momentum 34% of the time within 30 days.

Volatility Patterns

Most short-term patterns rely on an expansion in volatility. The inside bar strategies, for example, are based on the notion that inside bars represent low volatility and that when prices break one way or another, volatility expands. To take this concept of volatility further, many patterns look directly at volatility itself—either historical volatility as defined in the option markets, changes in trading ranges, or indicators such as the ADX. An expansion in volatility is used as a signal for action in most patterns, but sometimes a contrary action is suggested when volatility becomes extreme. Following are examples of some of these patterns.

Wide-Range Bar A wide-range bar is a bar in which the range is "considerably" wider than the normal bar. The bars are relatively long compared with the previous bar. How large does the range have to be to be considered "wide," and how far back must the comparison be made? There are no definitive answers to these questions. In any case, a wide-range bar is usually a bar with increased volatility. Increased volatility can imply the beginning of a new trend as in a breakout bar, or if the trend has been in existence for a long time and is accelerating, the wide-range bar may act like an exhaustion gap and warn of the trend's end. As a sign of impending trend reversal, it is more often seen at panic lows, as the emotions of fear accelerate prices downward. Emotional spikes and two-bar reversals are often wide-range bars. Otherwise, it is usually found on a break-out from a pattern, small or large, or as the base for a pennant or flag, indicating that the trend reached a very short-term peak and is about to consolidate. On the other hand, not all wide-range bars are meaningful. Consideration of trend, areas of support and resistance, patterns, and the relative location of opens and closes are necessary before a judgment of the significance of the wide-range bar can be determined.

Larry Connors (1998) gives an example of a wide-range pattern. Connors first looks for a wide-range day in which a stock experiences a two-standard deviation decline. On the following day, if the opening is a downward gap, place a buy entry stop at the first day's close with a protection stop at the first day's low. If the buy is near the previous day's low, lower the stop to give some room for the pattern to develop. The reverse set of signals is valid on the sell side at a top. The exit is to sell on the close, or if the close on the action day is within 10% to 15% of the high, sell on the next day opening.

Narrow-Range Bar (NR) Wide-range bars indicate high volatility; narrow-range bars indicate low volatility (see Figure 9.16). Determining narrow-range bars is useful because the low volatility will eventually switch to high volatility. As with the wide-range bar, the criteria for determining a narrow-range bar are not precise.

Toby Crabel designed one method of defining and using narrow-range days. In his method, he determines whether the current day has a narrower range than the previous day and, if so, over how many past days. For example, if the current day has a narrower range than the past three days, it is called an **NR4** day (to include the current day and the past three days); in other words, the current day represents the narrowest trading range of the four days. The common narrow days of this type are the NR4 and NR7 day. Their entry signal is a breakout from the most recent narrow-range day. Thus, if today is an NR7 day, we place a buy and sell entry stop on either side to be acted upon tomorrow or the next day.

Linda Bradford Raschke (www.lbrgroup.com) is one of the leading proponents of using narrow-range days to determine low-volatility setups. Raschke adds

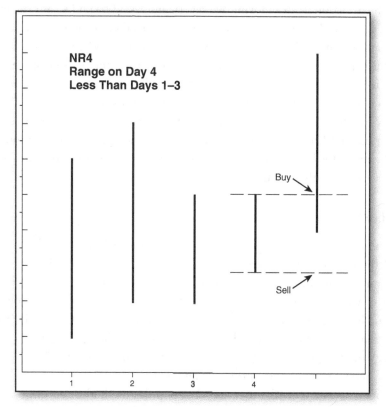

FIGURE 9.16   Narrow-Range Bar

another constraint to Crabel's method. She calculates the historic volatility of the vehicle over 6 days and over 100 days. If the 6-day historic volatility is 50% less than the 100-day, the conditions are right for either an NR4 day or inside day signal, provided today meets the criteria for each of these types of days. The buy and sell entry stops are placed at the high and low of the qualified NR4 or inside day. If the entry stop is executed, an additional exit stop is placed where the opposite entry stop currently exists. Exit the position at the close of the day if not already stopped out.

VIX Remember that the VIX is a reflection of anxiousness in the market. Traders and investors become anxious when the market declines and become complacent when the market advances. Thus, VIX becomes a sentiment indicator. Generally, when the market is bottoming, VIX is high because of the investor anxiousness. When the market is topping, VIX is generally low, indicating the complacency among investors.

Larry Connors (1998) introduced a number of short-term price patterns that were based on the behavior of the VIX. The principle behind these patterns was to watch for changes in VIX, as a measure of sentiment, at extremes, as for example, either after X number of days or combining with an oscillator formula to determine when VIX is overbought or oversold. A more general strategy for the VIX was to look at the deviation from a moving average (Connors, 2004). VIX has changed levels over the past decade, but a moving average dampens those changes. Connors used a 5% deviation from a 10-day simple moving average. If the VIX is below the SMA by 5% and the market is above its 200-day moving average, the odds favor a continuing upward trend but not necessarily a good time to buy except on throwbacks. When the ratio is above 5%, and even more so when it is above 10% of the SMA, the time is usually excellent to buy. Thus, the VIX in this instance gives general zones of when action in certain directions can be contemplated. The opposite relationship is valid when the market is below its 200-day moving average. Generally, bottoms are more reliably signaled by the VIX than tops.

Intraday Patterns

The opening range is the range of a daily bar that forms in the first few minutes or hour of the trading day (see Figure 9.17). It can be defined as either the high and low after a certain time, such as the high and low price that occur during the first 15 minutes of trading, or it can be a predetermined range about the opening price. A horizontal line is drawn at the opening range high and low on the intraday bar chart as a reference for the rest of the day. Other lines from the opening price, the close yesterday, the range yesterday, and so forth may also be drawn. These lines often become support or resistance levels during the day.

The opening range breakout (ORB) is a popular method of entering a position once a setup has been established from a previous short-term pattern. As reported

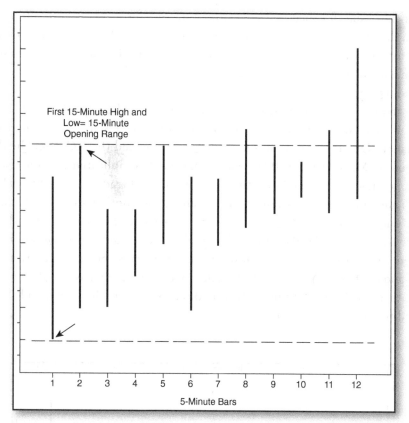

First 15-Minute High and
Low= 15-Minute
Opening Range

5-Minute Bars

FIGURE 9.17 Opening Range

in *Stocks & Commodities Magazine,* Toby Crabel experimented with NR days as setups and used an ORB defined by a specified, predetermined amount above or below the opening range. He compared these results with using a wide-range day setup. He found, first, that the wide-range day setup over both four and seven days vastly underperformed the NR days over the same period, thus confirming that more profit can be obtained from an expansion in volatility than contraction. Second, he found that once the price had moved away from the open in one direction after an NR2, it normally did not return to the opening.

In a series of articles for *Stocks & Commodities Magazine,* Crabel describes methods of trading from an ORB in considerable detail. In the first article, he described how he calculates the specified amount, called the **stretch**, above and below the opening that establishes the ORB. Crabel uses the ten-day average of the past differences between the open for each day and its closest extreme to the open for that day. Analysts use a number of other methods for calculating stretch, including specifying a number of ticks or calculating a range based on the ATR over some past period.

Crabel found that the use of ORBs worked well with NR4, NR7, inside days, and hook days. He found that the earlier in the day the ORB was penetrated, the better the chance for success. Even without the previously mentioned setups, trading on the ORB within the first five to ten minutes would also work, but after that short interval, if the prices have not penetrated out of the range, all orders should be canceled because the day will likely revert to a listless trading day rather than a trending day.

By analyzing the action around opening range levels, a good trader can find ways to take advantage of the tendency for these levels to act as support and resistance. One method of accomplishing this is called the **ACD method**, developed by Mark Fisher (2002). This some-what complicated method uses the opening range determined over the initial minutes of trading, an additional filter that is added to the upper bound of the range, and another subtracted from the lower edge, as shown in Figure 9.18. Entry signals occur when the outer bounds are broken during the day, and exit signals occur when the range bounds are broken. Fisher's method is not quite this simple because he uses numerous other rules and confirmations. However, Fisher, who reportedly has a trading room of more than 75 day traders using this method to make their daily bread, has appeared to be very successful.

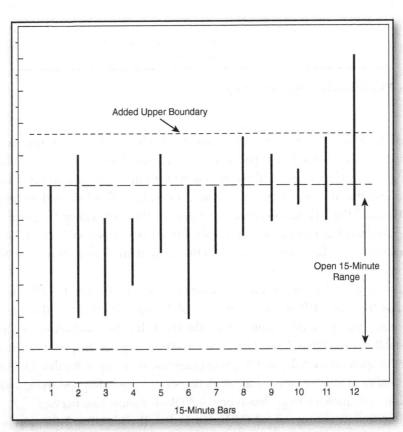

FIGURE 9.18 The ACD Method of Determining Opening Range

Summary of Short-Term Patterns

Although there appears to be value in short-term patterns, they are not immediate sources of wealth without study, experience, and trial-and-error testing. We have only touched the edge of methods being used. Others include performance around national holidays, days of the week, time during the day, and even the new moon. There seems to be no limit. The point in this exercise, however, is to demonstrate the many ways that prices are analyzed over the short term. If interested, you can continue to experiment on your own.

Candlestick Patterns

We have learned how to construct a candlestick chart. As you will recall, the raw data used in the candlestick chart is the same as the raw data used in the bar chart: open, close, high, and low price per specific period.

The candlestick chart has become popular because it represents price action in a more striking way; furthermore, the patterns that result have interesting and novel names. One advantage of the candlestick chart is that it can still use the Western methods of analysis—patterns, trend lines, support, and resistance—yet it has a set of unique patterns of its own. These patterns are mostly short term of only one to five bars, and by themselves they have not tested well. Many patterns have their Western equivalents that we have seen before. They are generally reversal patterns and can reveal price reversals early in overbought or oversold conditions, at trend lines, or at support or resistance levels. However, they are tools, not a system. Their disadvantage is that one must wait for the close before a pattern can be recognized, and they are useless in markets that do not accurately report the opening prices. The best resource on candlesticks is *Japanese Candlestick Charting Techniques* by Steve Nison (2001), the person who introduced this ancient method to the West.

The principal analytical difference between candlestick patterns and Western bar patterns is the emphasis on the opening and close. Western traders have recognized the importance of the opening and close, but bar charts treat them without special weighting. In candlestick charts, the "real body" is the wider area between the open and close. The "shadow" is the vertical line from the real body up to the price high and down to the price low. A long shadow indicates the inability for prices to maintain their highs or lows and is, thus, a warning of trouble. The real body is a heavy color, such as black, when the close is lower than the open, and usually white when the close is higher than the open. A black body denotes, therefore, a "down" day, and a white body indicates an "up" day. (This definition is different than in the West, where a down day is a day in which the close is lower than the previous close.) A large body (in relative terms) indicates strength in the direction of the trend, and a small body indicates indecision and a potential reversal, especially after a meaningful prior trend.

Patterns are made by the relative position of the body and the shadow, the location of the candlestick in relation to its neighbors, and the confirmation the next day. Because candlestick patterns usually are defined as top or bottom patterns, the analyst must be sure that the preceding price action is in a trend, either up or down. A single pattern may or may not be meaningful depending on the direction of the previous trend. Similar to Western short-term patterns, a candlestick pattern cannot predict the extent of the subsequent move or the significance of the pattern—that is, whether it occurs at a major or minor reversal. Thus, the pattern should always be used with other evidence before action is taken. For example, candlestick patterns are often reversal patterns and thus identify support or resistance levels when they switch direction. At first, the analysis of these patterns seems to be filled with an endless set of rules and names, but as you become more familiar with the nomenclature, you will see that the basis of these patterns is not much different from the basis for Western short-term patterns.

There have been few tests on the effectiveness of candlestick patterns. This is odd because the patterns are easily computerized. As with tests of other short-term patterns, many of the existing studies are flawed in that the signal outcomes are often assumed to last longer than they should. Measuring the effectiveness of patterns over weeks or months is useless because these patterns are only useful in short-term situations. However, even over shorter periods, the patterns do not test well. Their profit factors are relatively low, and their drawdowns are high and in all cases greater than net profits. Some of the variables in each pattern can be tweaked to improve performance, but the basic patterns, by themselves, are not outstandingly profitable.

Two relatively recent studies with short-term results are by Caginalp and Laurent (1998) and by Schwager (1996). The Caginalp and Laurent tests included eight three-day patterns in S&P 500 stocks from 1992 to 1996. Their purpose was to demonstrate that the patterns had value above what could be expected from a random walk; however, drawdowns were not considered. Schwager tested six major patterns in ten commodities from 1990 to 1994 and included a momentum filter to account for trend, an important factor in candlestick pattern analysis. A criticism, however, is that Schwager estimated commissions and slippage to be $100 per trade, considerably higher than what can be achieved now. Both studies suffer from the type of exit method in that they depend on a holding period that is arbitrary and not based on the behavior of prices. The results could be considerably improved with testing of each pattern in combination with others and the use of protective stops. At least stops and other exit signals would reduce the extremely large drawdowns. In our presentation of the patterns covered by Schwager, we average the results from the ten commodities for each pattern and give the relative ranking rather than the raw percentages. This avoids, to some extent, the problem of commissions and slippage.

Following are some examples of the more common candlestick patterns.

One- and Two-Bar Candlestick Patterns

Candlestick patterns are short-term patterns. In fact, a number of candlestick patterns are formed by only one or two bars. Thus, on a candlestick chart of daily data, only one or two days' worth of data would be necessary to form the pattern.

Doji   A doji pattern is formed when the open and close are identical, or nearly identical. This creates a candlestick with a real body that is simply a horizontal line, as shown in Figure 9.19. It suggests that the market is in equilibrium and affected by indecision. In some respects, it is like an inside bar in its meaning because in a trend, it shows a point at which the enthusiasm of the trend has stalled. It is, thus, often a warning of a reversal, but not necessarily a reversal pattern by itself. It can also occur about anywhere during a trend or within a trading range and is, thus, difficult to assess. As a result, its performance statistics were low (Schwager, 1996). It ranked at the bottom of our scale based on net profit, average trade, maximum drawdown, and percent winners.

Windows   Windows are simply the gaps that we discussed earlier in this chapter. Nison believes they are the most reliable formations, and evidence from short-term bar patterns tends to confirm his opinion. Because the interpretation of candlestick windows is the same as for Western gaps, we will not spend time discussing them.

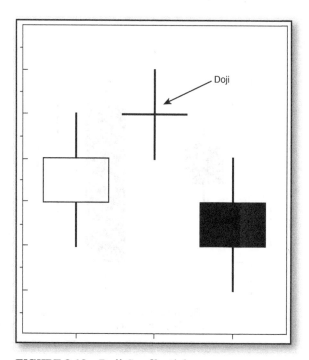

FIGURE 9.19   Doji Candlestick

Harami A harami pattern is a two-day pattern consisting of a large body of either color followed by a small body of either color that is completely within the boundaries of the large body. The harami pattern is pictured in Figure 9.20. The second candlestick pictured in the harami pattern in Figure 9.20 is called a **spinning top**. This second candlestick can also be a doji (resulting in a harami cross pattern), a hammer, a hanging man, or a shooting star; the only requirement is that the second candlestick body is within the first candlestick body.

The harami pattern is similar to the inside bar pattern; however, with the harami, the range, or wick, of the second bar does not have to be within the range of the first bar. The real body of the second candle must be within the real body of the first candle. Thus, the open and close range, rather than the range, determines whether the harami criterion is met.

We know that the inside day demonstrates a contraction in volatility, and the same can be said for the harami pattern. We also know from studies of short-term bar patterns that low volatility turns into high volatility and often begins a new trend. Thus, a harami pattern can be a powerful way of signaling either the reversal of a trend or an increase in velocity of the current trend, depending on which direction prices break.

Hammer and Hanging Man Both the hammer and the hanging man are candlesticks in which the real body is located at the upper end of the trading range, as

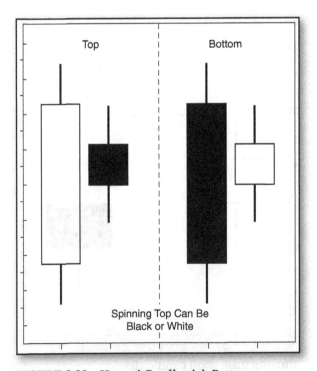

FIGURE 9.20 Harami Candlestick Pattern

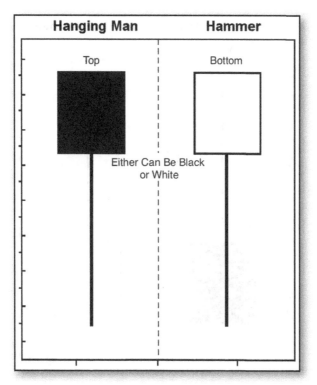

FIGURE 9.21 Hanging Man and Hammer

pictured in Figure 9.21. For these formations, the lower wick is at least twice to three times as long as the body, and the upper wick is small or nonexistent. In other words, both the open and close occur within approximately the top one-third of the bar's trading range, and either the open or close is, or nearly is, the highest price of the bar. The color of the body is irrelevant.

If this formation occurs at a peak, it is called a **hanging man**. A variation is called the **kasakasa** or **paper umbrella** when the body is shorter than the shadow. When the same formation occurs at a trough, it is called a **hammer**. These formations ranked best in our scale and were close to a tie with morning and evening stars.

Shooting Star and Inverted Hammer The shooting star and the inverted hammer can be thought of as an upside down hanging man or hammer. For these formations, the real body occurs in the lower end of the trading range. A shooting star occurs at peaks, and the inverted hammer occurs at bottoms. Both have long shadows above their bodies and short or nonexistent shadows below their bodies, as shown in Figure 9.22. Again, the color of the body is irrelevant. In our ranking of patterns, they fell into the middle, nowhere near the best-performing hammer and hanging man to which they are related.

Engulfing An engulfing pattern is a two-bar pattern in which the second body engulfs the first body (see Figure 9.23). This pattern is similar to an outside day reversal

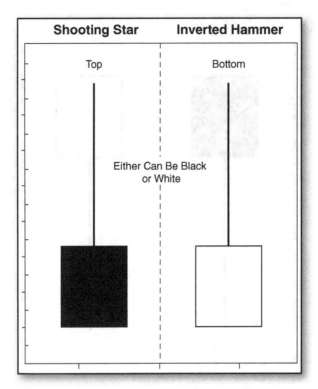

FIGURE 9.22 Shooting Star and Inverted Hammer

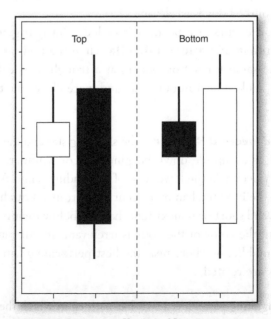

FIGURE 9.23 Candle Engulfing Pattern

in bar patterns. Because this pattern is designed to recognize a trend reversal, there must be a clear trend preceding the engulfing pattern. In a market uptrend, a bearish engulfing pattern would indicate a market top. The bearish engulfing pattern consists of a small white-bodied candle followed by a black body that engulfs the white body. The bullish engulfing pattern would indicate that a downward trend is reversing. This bullish engulfing pattern consists of a candle with a small dark body on one bar followed by a candle with a larger white body that engulfs the dark body. For both the bearish and bullish engulfing pattern, the signal is much stronger when the first body is small and the second body is large. However, performance of engulfing patterns is near the bottom of the six pattern types tested by Schwager. They had the worst net profits and the largest maximum drawdowns.

Dark Cloud Cover and Piercing Line   A dark cloud cover is a two-body pattern at a top. The first body is large and white, and the second body is large and dark. The second open should be above the upper shadow of the first bar, an opening gap upward, and the close well within the first bar's white body, preferably below the 50% level. The pattern resembles the Oops! pattern in bar charts. Performance of this pattern is supposedly enhanced by a deeper penetration of the white body. (A complete penetration would be an engulfing pattern.)

The opposite pattern, a piercing line pattern, would indicate market bottom. The piercing line follows the same rules as the dark cloud pattern, only in reverse. Both the dark cloud cover and piercing line formations are pictured in Figure 9.24. These patterns ranked in the lower half of the six types followed.

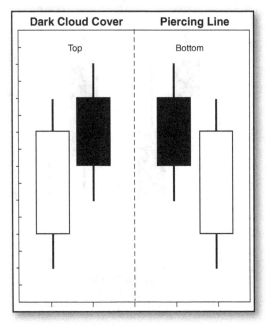

FIGURE 9.24   **Dark Cloud Cover and Piercing Line**

They had the second to least drawdown, the lowest average profit per trade, and the lowest winning percentage.

Multiple-Bar Patterns

Multiple-bar candlestick patterns develop over a time period of more than two bars. A quick glance at names such as "three black crows," "three white soldiers," and "three outside up" reveals that many of the multiple-bar patterns are three-bar patterns.

Morning and Evening Star   The evening star is a three-bar candlestick pattern that occurs at market tops, and the morning star is a three-bar, market bottom pattern. In each of these patterns, the second bar, or middle candlestick, is known as a star. A star is a candlestick that has a small body that lies outside the range of the body before it. It implies an opening gap, as does a dark cloud and piercing line pattern, but it can later cover part of the previous bar's shadow. The important point is that its body does not overlap the previous bar's body at all. It is similar to a doji in that it represents a sudden halt in a trend and some indecision between buyers and sellers. Indeed, a doji can be a star, called a **doji star**, if the doji body occurs outside the body of the previous bar's body.

The evening star pattern, pictured in Figure 9.25, starts with a long white body followed by a star of either color. If the third bar forms a large black body that closes

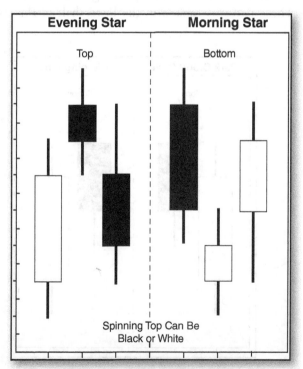

FIGURE 9.25 **Evening Star and Morning Star Candlestick Patterns**

well within the body of the first bar, the pattern is confirmed. Ideally, the third body should not touch the star's body, but this rarely occurs, and it is not a necessary condition for the pattern. The amount of penetration into the first white body is more important. The evening star is similar to the island reversal bar pattern without the necessary second gap.

The morning star, which occurs at a market bottom, is the opposite formation of the evening star. As shown in Figure 9.25, it begins with a black-bodied candlestick, followed by a star. The body of the star lies completely below the body of the previous candlestick. The pattern is then confirmed if, on the third bar, a white-bodied candlestick closes well within the range of the first candlestick.

The morning and evening stars were the second-best patterns in our ranking of Schwager's tests. They were first in net profits, had the least drawdowns, and were second in the percentage of winning trades. In the Caginalp and Laurent study, the morning and evening star pattern ranked third out of the four multibar types studied.

Three Black Crows and Three White Soldiers   White soldiers are white bodies and black crows are black bodies. Three black crows is a pattern with three consecutive, preferably long, black bodies, closing near their lows with openings within their previous day's body, and occurring after a meaningful upward trend. They are a top-reversal formation. As shown in Figure 9.26, three white

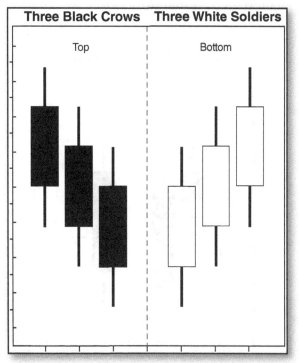

FIGURE 9.26   Three Black Crows and Three White Soldiers' Candlestick Patterns

soldiers is a bottom-reversing formation that requires the same parameters in the opposite direction.

Unfortunately, traders have difficulty profiting from these patterns because by the time they are recognized, a large portion of the new trend has already occurred. They are best played on a pullback or a throwback. Nison believes that the first or second bar in the pattern is the best location for entry on the retracement. That level is often accompanied by another pattern suggesting a short reversal in the direction of the trend signaled by the major pattern.

Three Inside Up and Three Inside Down   The three inside up pattern is a reversal pattern that occurs at the end of a declining trend. The first bar of this pattern has a large black body, and the second bar is a white spinning top (or doji) that forms a harami pattern. Then the third bar is a large, white candle that breaks and closes above the large black body of the first bar. Although the name may sound like it, the three inside up pattern does not imply that three inside bars in a row occur, as we saw with the NR3 pattern. Instead, the three inside up pattern is similar to an upward breakout from an inside bar in a bar pattern.

As shown in Figure 9.27, the three inside down pattern is the reverse of the three inside up pattern. The three inside down pattern consists of a large white bar followed by a black spinning top and a downward break by a large black body. This pattern signals that an upward trend has ended. From the Caginalp and Laurent study, we ranked this pattern type the best. It had the highest percentage of winning trades of the four pattern types studied.

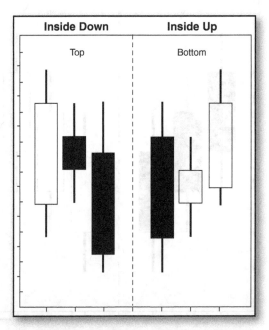

FIGURE 9.27   **Inside Down and Inside Up Candlestick Patterns**

From our look at short-term bar patterns, we know that outside bars are less predictable and less profitable than inside bars because the volatility has already expanded and is open to contraction at any time soon thereafter. The results of the three outside bar pattern types show the same decreased performance and were ranked fourth in our interpretation of the Caginalp and Laurent study.

Three Outside Up and Three Outside Down This pattern type starts with an engulfing pattern after a trend, just as the inside up and down started with a harami pattern. The three outside up version occurs at market bottoms. The first body is small, a spinning top, and the second body is large, engulfing the smaller previous body. The first is black and the second is white. A white body that closes above the second bar and reaches a new high above the previous two bars follows the engulfing pattern. This pattern is pictured in Figure 9.28.

Figure 9.28 also shows how the three outside down pattern is the same with opposite parameters. For the outside down pattern, the first bar is a small, white body, and the second bar is a black body that engulfs the first. The third bar is also a black body with prices moving lower than the second bar. Outside down bars occur at market tops.

Candlestick Pattern Results

We have described several of the most popular candlestick patterns. Bulkowski maintains a Web site (www.thepatternsite.com) with an extensive list of candlestick patterns. Table 9.1 highlights Bulkowski's ranking of the ten best-performing candlestick patterns.

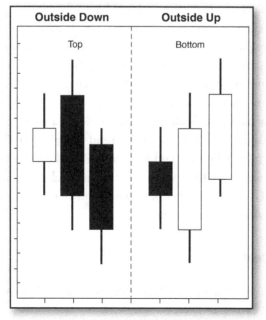

FIGURE 9.28 Outside Down and Outside Up Candlestick Patterns

TABLE 9.1	Bulkowski Ranking of Candlestick Patterns—Ten Best (Some are not shown but may be accessed from www.thepatternsite.com.)	
Pattern	**Reversal or Continuation**	**Percent Accurate**
Three-line strike	Bullish reversal	84%
Three-line strike	Bearish reversal	65%
Three black crows	Bearish reversal	78%
Evening star	Bearish reversal	72%
Upside Tasuki gap	Bullish continuation	57%
Hammer, inverted	Bearish continuation	65%
Matching low	Bearish continuation	61%
Abandoned baby	Bullish reversal	70%
Two black gapping	Bearish continuation	68%
Breakaway	Bearish reversal	63%

Source: www.thepatternsite.com © 2008–2009 by Thomas N. Bulkowski.

■ Conclusion

We have looked at a number of short-term patterns in this chapter on both bar charts and candlestick charts. To use these patterns successfully, a trader must be familiar with the underlying market trend. Remember that these short-term patterns are most often reversal patterns, giving the trader a hint that the underlying trend may be changing.

Short-term patterns forming as open, high, low, and close prices occur in particular combinations during a bar or over a few bars of trading. Particular short-term patterns occur frequently. Because of the frequency with which they occur, many times they are false patterns. Traders must be aware of this and not simply rely on a particular short-term pattern to make decisions. These short-term patterns can be useful indicators, but traders need to watch for a cluster of evidence instead of relying on a short-term pattern to make decisions.

Remember that the key to making money is riding a trend. Short-term patterns are a tool to help us determine when a new trend is beginning. These formations can also help us determine when a trend is ending. This allows us to participate in the trend as soon as possible and to exit the market as quickly as possible whenever the trend has ended. Using short-term patterns and protective stops can aid traders in maximizing their gains and minimizing their risk.

■ References

Bulkowski, Thomas N. "Bulkowski's Free Pattern Research." www.thepatternsite.com, 2008–2010.

Caginalp, Gunduz, and H. Laurent. "The Predictive Power of Price Patterns." *Applied Mathematical Finance* 5 (1998): 181–205.

Chesler, Daniel. "Trading False Moves with the Hikkake Pattern." *Active Trader Magazine* 5, no. 4 (April 2004): 42–46.

Connors, Laurence A. *Connors on Advanced Trading Strategies*. Malibu, CA: M. Gordon Publishing Group, 1998.

Connors, Laurence A. "Larry Connors on How the Markets Really Work." Interview by Editor Jayanthi Gopalakrishnan. *Technical Analysis of Stocks & Commodities* 22, no. 12 (2004): 74–79.

Crabel, Toby. "Inside Day Patterns in the S&P." *Technical Analysis of Stocks & Commodities* 7, no. 11 (1989): 387–389.

Crabel, Toby. "Opening Range Breakout Parts 1–8." *Techincal Analysis of Stocks & Commodities (1989–1990)*. The parts are in separate issues; 6, no. 9 (pp. 337–339); 6, no. 10 (366–368); 6, no. 12 (456–458); 7, no. 2 (47–49); 7, no. 4 (119–120); 7, no. 5 (161–163); 7, no. 6 (188–189); 7, no. 7 (208–210).

Downs, Walter T. "Combining Statistical and Pattern Analysis." *Technical Analysis of Stocks & Commodities* 16, no. 10 (1998): 447–456.

Edwards, Robert, John Magee, and W.H.C. Bassetti. *Technical Analysis of Stock Trends*. 9th ed. Boca Raton, FL: St. Lucie Press, 2007.

Fischer, Mark B. *The Logical Trader*. New York, NY: John Wiley & Sons, 2002.

Harris, Michael. *Short-Term Trading with Price Patterns*. Greenville, NC: Traders Press, 2000.

Kamich, Bruce M. *How Technical Analysis Works*. New York, NY: New York Institute of Finance, 2003.

Kaufman, Perry J. *Trading Systems and Methods*. 3rd ed. New York, NY: John Wiley & Sons, 1998.

Landry, David. *Dave Landry's 10 Best Swing Trading Patterns and Strategies*. Los Angeles, CA: M. Gordon Publishing Group, 2003.

Landry, David. *David Landry on Swing Trading*. Los Angeles, CA: M. Gordon Publishing Group, 2003.

Nison, Steve. *Japanese Candlestick Charting Techniques*. New York, NY: New York Institute of Finance, 2001.

Schwager, Jack D. *Schwager on Futures: Technical Analysis*. New York, NY: John Wiley & Sons, 1996.

Schwager, Jack D. *Technical Analysis*. New York, NY: John Wiley & Sons, 1996.

Williams, Larry. *How I Made One Million Dollars Last Year Trading Commodities*. Brightwaters, NY: Windsor Books, 1979.

Williams, Larry. *The Definitive Guide to Futures Trading*. Brightwaters, NY: Windsor Books, 1988.

Williams, Larry. *Futures Millionaire*. Manual published by Karol Media, Wilkes-Barre, PA, 1995.

Williams, Larry. *Long-Term Secrets to Short-Term Trading*. New York, NY: John Wiley & Sons, 1999.

Williams, Larry. *Day Trade Futures Online*. New York, NY: John Wiley & Sons, 2000.

Williams, Larry. *The Right Stock at the Right Time*. New York, NY: John Wiley & Sons, 2003.

CHAPTER 10

Introduction to Volume Analysis

Buff Dormeier, CMT

Volume is the steam in the boiler that makes the choo-choo go down the tracks.

—**Joseph Granville**

Learning Objective Statements

- Define volume
- Define open interest
- Define the terms related to volume as discussed in this chapter
- Describe how volume provides information on liquidity and participation
- Describe how volume adds perspective to price action

Even the most casual investor knows what matters about a stock: price. You are taught early on to "buy low and sell high." The mass media track the major indexes as if they were horse races, so most people naturally understand that a higher close is "good news" and a lower close is "bad news."

Price surely matters. But this is a market. Waiting for the final number on a given day or week will tell you what happened but not why or, more important, how. Picture a mall parking lot. Is it full or half empty? Is it Saturday or a weekday? How many people are walking the shops and sitting in the restaurants? Regardless of what they buy or how much they pay, what matters to investors in that mall is that customers are showing up and participating. To a smart trader, that's innately understood as "volume."

One can track volume for just about any stock or index or futures market easily enough but understanding it and using it to one's advantage is a skill few analysts possess. In this chapter we introduce basic definitions used in volume analysis. From there we begin breaking down the principal concepts behind volume analysis. As a technical analyst, you will be expected to understand how and why volume is an important data set in market analysis.

■ Volume Terminology

We begin by defining a few important volume and volume-related terms. "Volume" as a general term refers to the number of units of a given tradable item (shares of stock, futures contracts, options contracts, etc.) exchanged between buyers and sellers over a given length of time.

- *Market volume* or *trading volume*—The number of shares or contracts exchanged between buyers and sellers during a given time period, typically a day
- *Total volume* or *exchange volume*—The volume of all issues traded on an exchange, such as the New York Stock Exchange
- *Total trades*—The number of transactions recorded during a given time period, regardless of the volume of each transaction
- *Tick volume*—The intraday sum of volume on a per transaction basis; in other words, the total volume exchanged intraday during a specified number of "ticks" (transactions)
- *Open interest*—The number of open futures or options contracts. Open interest is technically not a volume statistic but is a companion statistic in the analysis of futures and options market dynamics.
- *Upside volume*—The volume traded on upticks, presumed to be from the demand side
- *Downside volume*—The volume traded on downticks, presumed to be from the supply side
- *Index volume*—The sum of the volume traded in all the components of an index, such as the S&P 500
- *Dollar volume*—The value of the shares traded during a given time period
- *Capital-weighted volume*—Index or exchange volume, weighted according to the capital weights of the index components
- *Float*—The number of shares of a corporation owned by the public and available for trading
- *Average volume* or *typical volume*—A moving average of volume that smoothes the peaks and valleys to show a more representative view of trading activity over time. Average volume is extremely important. It allows technicians to discern whether volume is increasing or decreasing relative to the past.

■ Importance of Volume in Market Analysis

A trade produces only two pieces of information: the price and price's oft-neglected sibling, volume. Perhaps the least appreciated piece of the puzzle, volume represents fertile ground for technical analysis. Proficiency in volume analysis is a rare skill. Properly understood, though, volume analysis can provide practitioners with the power to peer deeply into market mechanics.

Benjamin Graham, the father of value investing and a mentor to Warren Buffett, often called the market a "voting machine." If so, then volume is the ballot box. Volume is a literal illustration of the forces of supply and demand.

Volume is best understood as the validation of price and its cause, the source of liquidity, the substantiation of information, the fulfillment of convictions, the revelation of divergent opinions, the fuel of the market, the proponent of truth, and the energy behind the velocity of money. If you believe any of this information could be important in making investment decisions, then volume analysis is important to you.

Volume analysis attempts to expose the relationship between price trends and the corresponding volume information. Bernardo and Judd (1996) described this relationship: "Volume data is informational in this setting because prices alone do not fully reveal the magnitude of the private signals and their precision." Thus, by analyzing price and volume together, one can determine if the price-volume relationship confirms the price action or contradicts it, thereby giving notice of future price movements.

Volume Validates Price

Volume plays a critical role in the analysis of price action. Volume answers the deceptively simple question, "How many?" As discussed above, volume is the quantity of shares (contracts) traded. But here is the key: The more shares exchanged at a given price, the more the volume confirms price. More traders "vote," in the parlance of Graham, for that price at that point in time.

In the same way, low volume tells a different story. If fewer investors participate at a given price point, more doubt is cast on the validity of that price.

Perhaps you are looking to buy an item through an online auction site and found just one seller. How much confidence would you have that the listed price is fair and reasonable? Probably not much. However, if you found an item listed by a multitude of retailers with tens of thousands of transactions occurring at a similar price, you would reasonably conclude that the price being offered is a good representation of that item's value.

The same principle applies to trading volume. The more people participating in the price movement, the more the price movement is validated. For technical traders, volume dictates the "quality" of the price.

Volume Liberates Liquidity

We can glean another valuable piece of information from the online auction example. Assume that there was only one seller and no buyers. In that case, what is the probability of being able to exchange the item back into cash quickly at about the same price? In *Mind over Markets*, Eric Jones and James and Robert Dalton (2013) address this issue: "Volume is the truest and most reliable indicator of the market's ability to facilitate a trade...A market that is not facilitating trade will not survive long."

If volume is low, the odds of quickly selling a large block at a good price are not very high at all. In the high-volume scenario, though, where many transactions are happening in a narrow range of prices, the opposite is true. One is likely to sell a large block immediately at a fair price. High volume normally implies high liquidity, the ability to exchange an instrument or item for currency at a good price and without disrupting the market.

Volume Substantiates Information

Volume validates price, but it also contributes to forming price. As new information is disseminated to the public, volume reveals the flow of this information. By observing the change in volume as information is released, traders can tell how quickly new facts are being absorbed by market participants.

In this way, volume substantiates the importance of the new information. As volume rises, it equates to more emphasis being placed upon new information by investors. Similarly, news or information that does not greatly impact volume would indicate that the information has little significance to the market.

Volume Reveals Conviction

The volume of shares traded often reveals the market's true conviction. For example, perhaps you hear that a renowned investor has bought a certain stock. Upon learning this, you buy 1,000 shares of the same stock.

Later, though, you learn that the famous investor bought just 100 shares. This should change your view of the security considerably. You would expect a wealthy investor to buy a far larger quantity if he or she was truly acting with conviction.

Volume Expresses Interest and Enthusiasm

Market volume is money searching for a place to reside. There are only two reasons investors choose to transact. One is to seize upon an opportunity; the other is to reduce the risk of being positioned incorrectly. Rising volume reveals greater interest and enthusiasm, whether on the buying or selling side of a market. Falling volume shows that fewer investors see a need to participate, so they stay on the sidelines.

Volume Denotes the Disparity of Opinions

Volume can enlighten the savvy investor when there is a disparity of opinions. Often information and commentary in the media lead the investing public to choose sides, regardless of the underlying facts (or when no facts are evident). Trading activity expressed as volume is the empirical evidence that these diverging opinions are at work, with each side betting on its own beliefs. The greater the disparity of opinion, the greater return each side expects to realize from an investment. Thus, a wide divergence in those beliefs shows up as higher volume as the bulls and bears take positions in search of profit. Light volume, in turn, could denote equilibrium between supply and demand, a consensus that the price is "right," at least for the time being.

Volume Is the Fuel of the Market

For an engine to run, it needs fuel. The fuel of the market is provided by new supply (shares or contracts for sale) and demand (shares or contracts wanted for purchase). Volume is a measure of the total supply and demand being produced by market participants who have agreed on price. Volume, thus, is the fuel that allows markets to move. Trader Billy Williams (2006) put it this way:

> Volume is literally the fuel for stock values. Like the space shuttle when it is launched into space the majority of fuel is spent just to get to orbit. This explosive force of energy to propel the space shuttle into space or to new heights requires an above average reserve of the fuel but then the space shuttle can then use only a small portion of the remaining fuel reserve to carry out the rest of its mission. Volume is to stocks what rocket fuel is to the space shuttle."

Volume Exposes the Truth

If price is truth, then volume keeps prices honest. Large institutions would love to be able to buy or sell without drawing attention to their trades. The reality, though, is that they cannot. Large institutions must carefully assess the liquidity of securities in order to avoid adversely affecting price through their own operations. Once a security is chosen for purchase (or liquidation), a big institution must be cautious: If it tips its hand, others will try to front-run their trade (i.e., buy or sell early to "ride the wave" of the coming large transaction).

One way to hide a big trade is to sell at the "offer" or buy at the "bid," the publicly available price of the moment. But volume analysis sees through that trick. If a trade goes through, it must be reported. A significant increase in volume is a clear sign that a big institution is at the table, particularly if price movement is subdued.

Volume Gives Rise to Velocity

Market volume is a quantity that, when increased, tends to produce an acceleration of price direction. Charles Dow, founder of *The Wall Street Journal* and the namesake of the Dow Jones averages and Dow Theory, believed that high volume indicated a more accurate price and that, in turn, volume actually led price. In short, Dow felt that a substantial increase in volume often preceded significant price movements.

■ References

Bernardo, Antonio E., and Judd, Kenneth L. "Volume and Price Formation in an Asset Trading Model with Asymmetric Information." *UCLA: Finance* (July 1996).

Dalton, James F., Jones, Eric T., and Dalton, Robert B. *Mind Over Markets: Power Trading with Market Generated Information*. Hoboken, NJ: Wiley, 2013.

Williams, Billy. *Investment Helper*, "Trading with Price and Volume," 2006. https://www.investmenthelper.org/investment_guide/679078.shtml2006

CHAPTER 11

Volume: The Technician's Decryption Device

Buff Dormeier, CMT

Learning Objective Statements

- State the implications of volume changes for price trends
- Identify trends in price and volume in a chart
- Describe how volume is displayed in a Volume-at-Price chart
- Define VWAP
- Describe Equivolume charts
- Explain how open interest rises and falls
- State the implications of open interest changes for price trends

People have a burning need for the rational. We need explanations. It is interesting to hear various market pundits explain why the market did what it did. Then, with the next breath, they explain what the market should have done instead. Technical analysis focuses on understanding what a market is doing, allowing technicians to gauge what may be to come. A famous sports coach said, "We do what we do." Similarly, the market does what it does. Technicians build an understanding of markets by watching, observing, and listening to them.

■ Decoding Volume

Although the financial broadcasts would have us think otherwise, the market does not simply wake up and inform us of its mood each day. The market speaks to us through its behavior. In a real way, though, the mood of the market is encoded. Codes are

TABLE 11.1	Chart of Price–Volume Relationship		
Price	Volume	Meaning	Implication
Rising	Rising	Increasing demand	Bullish
Rising	Falling	Decreasing demand	Bearish
Falling	Rising	Increasing supply	Bearish
Falling	Falling	Decreasing supply	Bullish

messages containing hidden meanings. To the oblivious, a code might appear to be meaningless. Codes require decryption. Volume is our decoding device to decipher the meaning of price.

Extraordinarily high volume is the clearest technical indication that the market is poised to move. When volume is high, the market expresses firm conviction, like **BOLD CAPITAL LETTERS** in print. Such high-volume movement often signals a reversal from the present path or a fresh breath of new life in an existing trend. Table 11.1 shows the relationship between price and volume.

■ Displaying Volume

There are many ways technical analysts display volume. In discovering your own preference, keep in mind that volume gives meaning to price. As such, important visual depictions should illustrate how volume is relating to price. Volume is also relative; changes in volume trends and "low" and especially "high" volume outliers are particularly meaningful.

Volume Directly Under Price

Volume typically is displayed directly below the price data in time-based charts. This method may be applied to all time frames and even tick charts. Figure 11.1 is a chart of Tesla, Inc. (TSLA), daily price and volume.

Notice a high-volume move at point 1 closing near the low of the day.

From point 1 to point 2, the stock price consolidates. The volume declines from point 1 until price breaks through resistance at point 2. Notice the volume spike, confirming the price breakout.

This scenario plays out yet again between points 3 and 4, starting with a close on high volume at point 3.

At point 5, the stock surges higher on high volume but again closes near its low, leading to another price consolidation on low volume evident in points 6 through 7.

Finally, at point 7, price breaks out of its downward trendline, and the accompanying high volume confirms the price breakout.

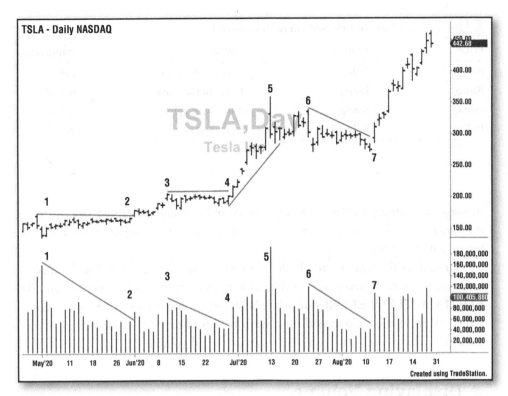

FIGURE 11.1 TSLA Daily Bars and Volume

Volume at Price (or Volume Profile)

Another way to depict volume data is to plot volume horizontally on the vertical axis. While price and volume are normally plotted in a time-based chart as they are in Figure 11.1, Volume at Price (also known as Volume Profile) plots volume horizontally, either from the left or right side of the chart, as a histogram. Volume at Price corresponds to the price levels at which the trading volume occurred. In this way, each Volume at Price bar represents how many shares were exchanged at various price levels. Also note the heavy line in Figure 11.2. This line is referred to as the point of control, the price level on the chart where the most shares changed hands. Volume at Price is very helpful in identifying potential support and resistance levels at which a large number of shares were traded.

VWAP—Volume Weighted Average Price

The volume-weighted average price (VWAP) is the average price, typically for one trading day, with each of the price points weighted by the volume traded at that price. The VWAP was first introduced to the trading community by Berkowitz, Logue, and Noser in a 1988 article. It typically is plotted on the price chart like a moving average.

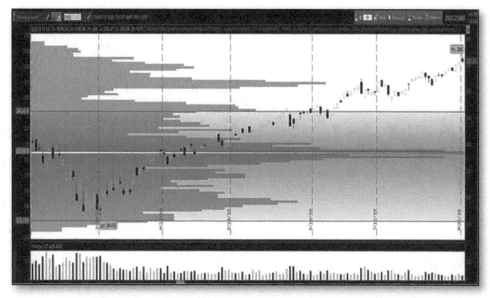

FIGURE 11.2   Invesco QQQ Trust (QQQ) Daily Bars with Volume at Price

This intraday "indicator" is calculated by multiplying each price tick by the corresponding volume, summing the results of all these trades, then dividing the total by the number of shares traded:

$$\text{VWAP} = (\text{Sum of (Tick Price} \times \text{Tick Volume)}) / \text{Trading Volume}$$

VWAP is used more as a statistic than a true indicator. It is the industry standard to determine the price at which a stock can be bought or sold throughout the trading session. It might be helpful to think of VWAP from the perspective of an institution. For example, say an institution needs to buy 200,000 shares of XYZ stock today. This quantity represents 2% of a typical trading day's volume. If the institution were to put in an order in at market, it is likely to move the market and thereby raise the price paid. An alternative strategy is to dollar-cost average the trades incrementally, throughout the day, based on the volume flow. A benchmark is needed to compare the prices paid for the stock throughout the day. This benchmark is generally the VWAP (see Figure 11.3). In this way, the VWAP assists institutions in reducing the market impact of their large trading operations.

Equivolume Charting

According to Richard Arms, "If the market wore a wristwatch, it would be divided into shares not hours." Arms epitomizes those thoughts with Equivolume charts (see Figure 11.4). Arms sought a way to show important volume information directly on price charts. The result is Equivolume charts, unique tools that illustrate volume's relationship with price. Equivolume employs a volume range methodology that alters the width of price bars based on volume. This is accomplished by plotting price on the y-axis as usual. However, the x-axis units, though time-based, are not of even distribution.

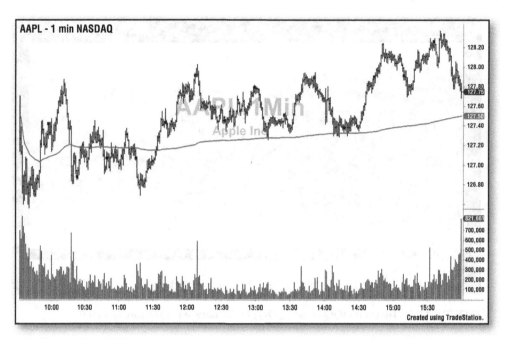

FIGURE 11.3 VWAP

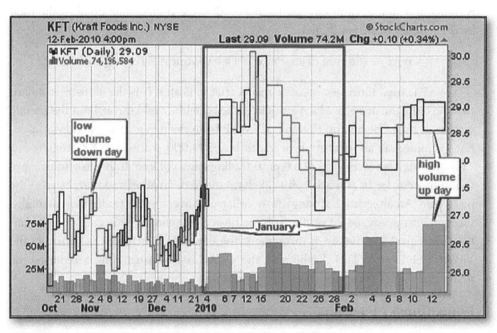

FIGURE 11.4 Kraft Foods (KFT) Equivolume Chart, Daily Bars

Equivolume charts set the width of the price bars by comparing the volume of the bar to the normalized volume of the range. Wide bars show stronger volume, whereas thin bars show weaker volume.

Arms called a tall and wide bar a "power box," indicating it has price movement and strong volume. Power boxes are of particular importance when a stock breaks through areas of resistance and support. The existence of such power boxes during a breakout or breakdown indicates a high probability of success. Equivolume is a useful charting application emphasizing the price–volume relationship.

■ Volume and Open Interest in the Futures Markets

Whereas volume is the number of contracts traded, *open interest* is the current number of outstanding futures contracts in a particular delivery month in a futures market. *Total open interest* is the sum of the open interest in all the delivery months in that market.

It takes a new buyer (long) and a new seller (short) to create a new contract or increase open interest. As contracts are closed, open interest declines: When a former buyer (current long) sells to a former seller (current short), a contract is closed and open interest declines. When contracts are traded between one party exiting a position and one taking a new position, that trade generates volume but does not affect open interest (see Table 11.2).

Table 11.3 outlines the conventional interpretation of volume and open interest.

Adding price to volume and open interest adds another dimension to the volume–price analysis. Table 11.4 shows the typical interpretation of price, volume, and open interest.

TABLE 11.2 Effect of New Positions and Offsets on Open Interest

Buyer	Seller	Open Interest
New long position	New short position	Increases
Current short position	Current long position	Decreases
New long position	Current long position	Unchanged
Current short position	New short position	Unchanged

TABLE 11.3 Interpretations of Volume and Open Interest

Volume	Open Interest	Meaning
Rising	Rising	Price trend is being confirmed
Rising	Falling	Interest is waning
Falling	Rising	Weak accumulation
Falling	Falling	Price trend is being contradicted

TABLE 11.4 Interpretations of Price, Volume and Open Interest

Price	Volume	Open Interest	Implication
Rising	Rising	Rising	New buyers
Rising	Falling	Falling	Short-covering rally
Falling	Falling	Falling	Bottoming
Falling	Rising	Rising	New shorts

Markets are formed by people and thus reflect how people behave. Decisions made today are based on what has happened to investors in the past. With that in mind, technical analysts should be cognizant of seasonal volume trends. Technicians will need to examine volume data in light of time and calendar-based trends.

Volume typically is weak during holiday weeks, especially preceding the Fourth of July, Thanksgiving, and Christmas. Overall, the volume in the North American summer typically is lighter than in the other seasons, with the North American winter typically being the most active season for trading.

Higher volume may be associated with beginnings and endings. Volume normally expands during the end of the quarter, whether it is "mutual fund window dressing," quarterly portfolio rebalancing, or index rebalancing. The third Friday of the month is option expiration. Generally, volume is higher on this day and the days leading up to it, especially when the market has been strongly trending higher or has previously been volatile. The end of the calendar and tax year and the beginning of a new year normally are associated with higher market volumes.

In addition, intraday volume is frequently "U" shaped. That is, volume is highest in the morning and at the close and weakest during midday lunch hours. During the weak-volume lunch hour, the price trend may also see a reprieve. If demand has been driving the market up, the absence of demand during the lunch hours may see the market trade temporarily lower. Likewise, if supply has been forcing the market lower in the early session, the market may drift up higher on low volume during the lunch hour.

Late-stage bear markets typically experience low volume as investors feel disenfranchised. As such, bull markets may be born in low volume and die on high volume. Secular bear markets typically are born in high volume and die in a low-volume state of apathy.

■ Reference

Berkowitz, Stephen, Dennis Logue, and Eugene Noser. "The Total Cost of Transactions on the NYSE," *Journal of Finance* (March 1988).

CHAPTER 12

An Introduction to Volume Indicators

Buff Dormeier, CMT

Learning Objective Statements

- List the seven types of volume indicators
- Describe the major differences among the types of volume indicators

Several elegant old homes in a local community supposedly were built by an old-time master carpenter who never used a tape measure. There are also a few old-school master traders successfully trading solely on gut feel and intuition. Yet I would not recommend so much as furnishing a house without the use of a tape measure. Likewise, through reading price and volume charts, tensions between supply and demand can be observed with the naked eye and the trained mind. That stated, quantifiable measurements through volume indicators are often much more useful tools for market analysis. As such, any discussion of technical analysis would be incomplete without a section on volume indicators. Thus far, we have discussed volume in conceptual terms. General volume principles include:

- High-volume movements confirm the trend.
- Low-volume movements contradict the trend.
- Volume declines in consolidation patterns.
- Volume spikes with the onset of a new price trend.

These volume principles have been doctrines of technical analysis since penned by H. M. Gartley in 1935. Yet all these principles assume that analysts are able to distinguish between normal, low, and high volume.

Volume indicators tabulate a running score of price and volume information. Through mathematical computations, volume indicators provide a quantitative assessment of the volume–price relationship. And unlike the art of tape reading, technical analysts can use scientific methods to test indicators, revealing how they perform in providing useful information under various conditions.

Volume indicators are informative in two critical ways. First, they should lead price, meaning that volume indicators often offer notifications before major price breaks and reversals. For example, when a volume indicator makes a new high or low while price does not, volume indicates in which direction price may move next. Second, volume indicators should confirm price. Volume confirmation occurs when volume rises as price trends. Should the volume indicator fall as the trend matures, this volume divergence is a warning that the price trend also may be poised to end.

Too often, though, investors and even analysts view indicators as a sort of magical phenomenon. They believe when a trigger line crosses the signal line, something in the underlying price is bound to happen. Another belief is that when indicators reach certain levels, the stock's trend will suddenly reverse or break out. In doing so, investors and analysts forget that technical indicators calculate information. Therefore, indicators should be used as information, not as absolute truth. Volume indicators should be viewed as tools, each designed to explain a distinct piece of information within the greater whole, helping to sort out the noise.

For any trade that takes place, three pieces of information are conveyed: the price at which the trade was executed, the time when it was executed, and the quantity of shares or contracts traded. It is from these three items that all market data is derived. Similarly, price indicators are further devised from five pieces of information: the open, the high, the low, the close, and time. This results in a high correlation between the price trend and price-only indicators. In contrast to the hundreds of price indicators all derived from similar forms of price data sets, volume indicators offer a fresh, often noncorrelating, alternative to price-only analysis. Technical analysts use volume indicators to gain fresh insights.

Volume indicators normally appear in a box below the price and volume chart. Typically they are set to their own scale of relative change corresponding to price, volume, and time, which enables users to make easy comparisons of price trend movements relative to the trends and movements of volume indicators. Interpretations of volume indicators generally are accomplished through either confirmation or divergence from price. To confirm, the volume indicator should trend in the same direction as price. This is called price–volume confirmation, and it gives notice that the present price trend is likely to continue. If the direction of the volume indicator diverges from the price trend, it is called price–volume contradiction, also known as divergence. Divergence is an indication that the present trend might be susceptible to correction.

■ Seven Types of Volume Indicators

It might be supposed that volume indicators simplify volume analysis, and they do. However, some confusion may arise in regard to the many varieties of volume indicators: Various volume indicators convey subtly different information. The objective of most volume indicators is to quantify the amount of money flowing into or out of the security. Popular terms to describe this are *money flow*, *accumulation*, and *distribution*. Each volume indicator represents the designer's own depiction of accumulation and distribution.

The marketing of volume indicators has led to volume indicators with similar or even identical names. Because of this, many practitioners assume that all volume indicators work essentially the same way. This is an incorrect assumption that amplifies the confusion surrounding volume indicators.

Astute technicians comprehend not only volume indicators' signals but also the type of information provided by different volume indicators. To help clear up some of the confusion, we offer seven categories of volume indicators based on the data they use and how they use it. In practice, some volume indicators fall into multiple categories (see Figure 12.1).

The seven ways to differentiate between price/volume information create seven categories of volume indicators:

1. Pure volume: volume indicators without price data
   Example: Volume rate of change
2. Volume accumulation based on bar-to-bar price change
   Example: On-Balance Volume
3. Volume accumulation based on intraday price movements
   Example: Chaikin's Money Flow

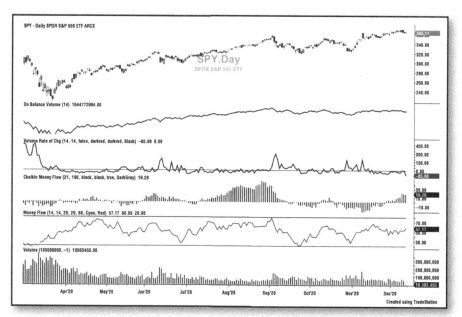

FIGURE 12.1   SPDR S&P 500 ETF Daily Candles with a Variety of Volume-Based Indicators

4. Volume–price range indicators: volume analysis based on intraday price range
    Example: Ease of Movement
5. Price accumulation based on volume change
    Example: Positive Volume Index
6. Tick volume: intraday accumulation of trades through tick data
    Example: Tick volume, also known as money flow
7. Volume-adjusted price indicators: volume-weighted price based on participation
    Example: MFI (Money Flow Index)

CHAPTER 13

Confirmation

From Charles D. Kirkpatrick II and Julie R. Dahlquist, *Technical Analysis: The Complete Resource for Financial Market Technicians*, 3rd Edition (Old Tappan, New Jersey: Pearson Education, Inc., 2016), Chapter 18.

Learning Objective Statements

- Define terms including overbought, oversold, failure swings, divergence, and reversal
- List the major indexes and oscillators designed to use volume as confirmation
- Describe open interest and how it might be used for confirmation
- Explain the concept of momentum in price action
- Identify characteristics and applications of indexes and oscillators such as MACD, RSI, and stochastics

The odds increase that a technical signal is correct if there is confirmation from another unrelated indicator. Charles Dow recognized this concept and used the confirmation of two different price averages before he recognized a legitimate market signal. In the days when only chart patterns were available as a means of interpreting price action, the technical analyst often used volume as the confirming indicator. Sometimes, depending on the calculating ability of the analyst, moving averages, rates of change, and momentum price, oscillators were also used. After the introduction of the computer, the ability to calculate more complicated indicators increased. Many analysts began to use more complicated indicators as the primary source of signals and deviated from the old price pattern analysis. The number of possible combinations of prices, volume, and other factors has become almost infinite. Indeed, there is some question as to whether all this computing power has increased the ability of technical analysts to interpret price action. Some would argue that most of the indicator calculations correlate with each other and that the market is no more understandable today than it was 50 years ago. Others maintain that the proper use of confirming indicators helps considerably in decision making and that many successful trading models depend almost exclusively on these complex calculations.

In this chapter, we look at volume. It's the oldest confirming indicator, but it has developed some problems recently from the increase in program trading and other mechanical trading systems. We look at open interest in the futures markets, and then we look at price oscillators, indicators, and the discouraging evidence for their reliability in giving stand-alone signals.

■ Analysis Methods

The methods for analyzing confirmation rely on two main tools: indexes and oscillators. **Indexes** are similar to the breadth line. They are cumulative sums of data, usually some variation of volume and price that continuously measure supply and demand over time rather than over a specific period. They do not have an upper or lower bound and are plotted with price charts where they can be compared with price action. The level of the index is irrelevant. What is relevant is the trend of the index relative to the price trend. The only useful indexes are those that begin to change direction before prices, signaling a change in trend. The analyst, thus, compares the prices with the index, looking for divergences between highs and lows in each. Although indexes can also be used with trend line, channel, and occasionally pattern analysis, their most important use is that of divergence analysis in trending markets.

Oscillators, on the other hand, are often bounded and limited to a specified past period. As shown in Figure 13.1, they tend to oscillate within these bounds and

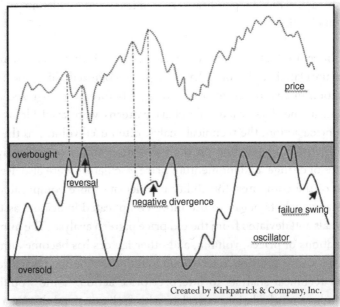

FIGURE 13.1   Example of Oscillator Analysis Methods

demonstrate when volume or prices are relatively high or low. These indicators show the relative changes rather than the absolute changes illustrated in indexes and are also amenable to divergence, trend line, and pattern analysis. Oscillators are used more successfully in trading range markets.

As with many technical indicators, research has not shown that indexes and oscillators are profitable on their own. The student must judge after thorough testing and experience whether to use them as secondary indicators to price analysis. They can be used to generate signals but must always be confirmed by actual and corresponding price action.

Various visual techniques have been developed to determine some meaning from these indexes and oscillators. They are divided into methods that are peculiar to indicators, such as divergences, and those that are just an extension of classical chart pattern analysis, such as trend lines and support and resistance. The principal methods unique to indicators are discussed in the following sections.

Overbought/Oversold

Oscillators can be bounded or unbounded. **Bounded** means that the oscillator swings back and forth within certain bounds or limits. These limits are the extremes to which the oscillator can reach. In most bounded and in some unbounded oscillators, a zone is chosen to represent the range near the extreme bounds. The oscillator might not reach the actual extreme bound, but it might come close and by doing so have the same implications. The zone then is the range that is close enough to the extreme bound to be important. The upper zone is called **overbought**, and the lower zone is called **oversold**. When a security has risen far enough that its oscillator reaches the overbought zone, it is said to be overbought, and when the price has fallen far enough that the oscillator reaches the oversold zone, it is said to be oversold.

In a trading range, the overbought and oversold levels are excellent indications of potential reversal levels, especially when the oscillator breaks out from the zone. The zones, however, can be deceiving in a trending market because the oscillator will remain in them during the period of the trend, and, thus, many breakouts from the zone will be false signals. In the following description of oscillators, we point out the conventional zone levels, but as always, the analyst must test for those most appropriate to the time and security being traded.

Failure Swings

A **failure swing** is a specific type of breakout from an overbought or oversold zone first described by Wilder (1978). A stronger version of the breakout, it often is the first sign of a potential reversal after a lengthy trend in which an oscillator has remained within or close to a zone. A **negative failure swing** is shown in Figure 13.1; it occurs when the oscillator breaks down out of an overbought zone, creates a reversal point, pulls back but fails to reenter the zone, and then breaks back down below the earlier reversal point. A **positive failure swing** is the opposite at an oversold zone.

Divergences

Although Wilder is also credited with discovering divergences, the concept is at least as old as Dow Theory. The basic concept is that to ensure a trend has begun or is still strong, all methods must be confirming the trend. If one index, for example, is breaking out upward but other indexes are not, the indexes are said to be diverging; in other words, they are not acting in concert with each other. A legitimate, strong trend, however, should have all indexes acting in concert. A divergence is, thus, considered to be a sign—especially after a trend has been in existence for a while—that the trend is slowing down and preparing to reverse. This is the same concept applied to oscillators and price charts.

The basic rule is that when a price reaches a new high, the oscillator should also reach a new high. Of course, this is subject to some interpretation, namely "what high is a new one?" but generally the relative highs should take place at the same time. A high on day 4 and another on day 20 should appear in both the price and the oscillator. If the price high on day 20 is higher than the high on day 4, but the oscillator high on day 20 is not higher than on day 4, the pattern is called a **negative divergence**. An example of negative divergence is shown in Figure 13.1. A **positive divergence** occurs at a series of price lows when the price reaches a new low unconfirmed by a new low in the oscillator. In a particularly strong trend, several divergences can occur and, of course, if the oscillator is bounded, it will occur more often because there is little room for the oscillator to keep making new highs or lows. This is why the first negative breadth divergence is often a false signal, but when two occur, back-to-back, the oscillator breakdown signal is more meaningful.

Reversals

Brown (1999) describes a variation of divergences known as oscillator **reversals** in detail. Like divergences, reversals have been used by technicians since oscillators were first used, but they have been popularized recently by Andrew Cardwell. A reversal differs from a divergence in that price leads the change instead of the oscillator. For example, **a negative reversal** occurs when, on day 20, the oscillator reaches a new high above that of day 4 but the price does not. As illustrated in Figure 13.1, it is sort of a divergence in reverse in that the price is showing weakness when the oscillator is not as opposed to the divergence when the price is still strong but the oscillator is not. Nevertheless, in keeping with the concept of confirmation, the two factors, price and oscillator, are not in sync and are, thus, no longer confirming the trend. A **positive reversal** is the same as the negative only at low bars. A reversal has the same implications as a divergence—namely, that the trend is beginning to show signs of stress and potential reversal.

Trend ID

Brown (1999) also describes what she calls "trend ID." In a trending market, oscillators will remain in one half of their range for long periods, and breakout signals from the standard overbought and oversold zones are often false. For example, when a price is trending upward, the oscillator can remain at or close to the overbought zone and never reach the oversold zone to give a buy signal during corrections. Brown suggests that the zones should be redefined with the zone parameters raised to include those corrections at a slightly higher level. Her work centers on what is called the "RSI," a bounded oscillator we look at later, that traditionally has an oversold zone below 30 and an overbought zone above 70. In a strongly upward trending market, the oversold price corrections at which opportune trades might occur are never reached by the oscillator. Thus, she suggests that during the rising trend, the oversold zone be raised to 40 and the overbought zone be raised to 90. Better signals then occur using these new levels as long as the underlying trend remains strong. In a downward trend, the zone levels can also be adjusted downward for the same reason. This adjustment of zones has no effect on divergences or reversals or any of the other chart patterns that might suggest an upcoming trend change. The analyst, however, must test for the best zones to fit the trend.

A variation of trend ID that is commonly used is the standard deviation of the oscillator, similar to the use of standard deviation in Bollinger Bands. The oscillator is calculated and two bands, upper and lower, surround its plot at the level of some multiple, usually one, of the oscillator's standard deviation. This gives a "moving" overbought and oversold that trend with the oscillator and adjust to changes in the oscillator's volatility. Signals are generated when the oscillator breaks out of the overbought or oversold zone toward the center just as with the classic zones.

Crossovers

Crossovers occur when the oscillator crosses over either a particular level or another oscillator. One level that is often important is the middle value, usually either zero or one, which bisects the range of the oscillator's travels. Almost by definition, when an oscillator reaches and remains above or below the midpoint in the oscillator range, it is defining the underlying trend. It is, thus, a potential trend indicator. Other oscillators have their raw figures smoothed through a moving average, and crossovers occur when the raw figure crosses over the moving average. These crossovers can either be signals to act or indications of trend change.

Classic Patterns

Strangely, oscillators and indicators often make simple patterns, such as triangles and rectangles, and produce support and resistance levels just as price does. They even have trends that can be defined by a classic trend line. These patterns have the same validity as price patterns, even when the oscillator is bounded, and can be additional evidence of trend change or short-term opportunity.

Which Indexes and Oscillators Incorporate Volume?

Let us look at some specific examples of indicators that analysts use when looking at volume as a confirming indicator. These indicators are divided into two principal categories: indexes and oscillators.

Volume-Related Indexes   Technical analysts have developed a number of volume-related indexes. On-Balance-Volume is probably the most well known of these.

On-Balance-Volume (OBV)   On-Balance-Volume (OBV) is the granddaddy of all volume indexes. Joseph Granville proposed OBV in his 1976 book, *A New Strategy of Daily Stock Market Timing for Maximum Profit*. The daily data that is cumulated into the index is the volume for the day adjusted for the direction of the price change from the day before. Thus, it is the total daily volume added to the previous day index if the price close was higher and subtracted from the previous day index if the price close was lower than that of the previous day. This index is a cumulative sum of the volume data and is plotted on a daily price chart. Figure 13.2 shows what a plot of OBV volume looks like.

The idea behind the OBV index is simply that high volume in one direction and low volume in the opposite direction should confirm the price trend. If high volume

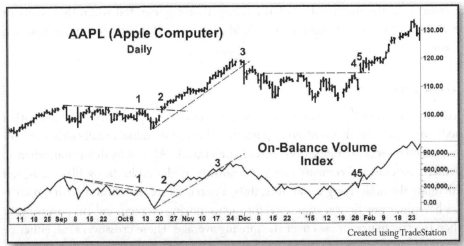

FIGURE 13.2   On-Balance-Volume (AAPL, daily: August 13, 2014–February 26, 2015)

is not confirming the price trend, then light volume in the price trend direction and heavy volume in the opposite direction suggests an impending reversal. Observing the OBV line by itself, therefore, is not helpful, but observing its trend and its action relative to price action is. For example, in a trending market, when prices reach a new high, confirmation of the price strength comes when the OBV also reaches a new high. If the OBV does not reach a new high and confirm price strength, negative divergence has occurred, warning that the price advance may soon reverse downward. A negative divergence suggests that volume is not expanding with the price rise.

How can the OBV be used in prices that are in a consolidation pattern or trading range rather than trending? When prices are in a trading range and the OBV breaks its own support or resistance, the break often indicates the direction in which the price breakout will occur. Therefore, it gives an early warning of breakout direction from a price pattern.

Let us look a little more closely at Figure 13.2. During September and early October 2014, a downward trend existed in both prices and the OBV. The OBV had a minor breakout upward at point 1, but the price did not confirm that breakout with one of its own. The suggestion was that the price was not ready to change trend direction. At point 2, however, both the OBV and price broke upward through their declining trend lines in a legitimate and confirmed breakout and initiated a month-long upward price trend. This demonstrates the importance of having confirmation from price when a signal is given by an index (or oscillator). At point 3, the OBV broke below its rising trend line signaling the volume was not keeping up with price. Nevertheless, price did not break its upward trend line to confirm this weakness until point 3 on the price chart, and it broke with a vengeance. During December and most of January, the price and OBV trend was flat. A small upward breakout occurred in the OBV at point 4 that was not confirmed by price until two days later when both the OBV and price broke upward on the same day, thus confirming each other's action. OBV is thus valuable in assessing the legitimacy of trend breakouts, and in this example actually led price breakouts, giving the analyst warning to watch for a directional change.

Price and Volume Trend   Another way of calculating a combination of price and volume is to determine daily the percentage price change, up or down, times the total volume for the day. This figure is then cumulated into an index called the price-volume trend. This index will be more heavily impacted when large percentage price changes occur on heavy volume. Signals are triggered in the same manner as for the OBV.

In Figure 13.3, notice that this method, using the same data as Figure 13.2, shows the price-volume trend confirming only after the upward gap breakout in November. In January, the Price-Volume Trend breakout above resistance coincides with a breakout in prices. And in February, the breakdown below support precedes a longer decline that doesn't begin until two weeks later with an equivalent breakdown in price.

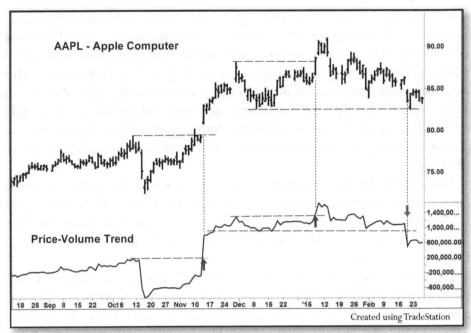

FIGURE 13.3 Price-Volume Trend (AAPL, daily: August 13, 2014–February 26, 2015)

Williams Variable Accumulation Distribution (WVAD)   Larry Williams believes that the open and close prices are the most important price of the day. The Williams Variable Accumulation Distribution (WVAD) calculates the difference between the close and the open and relates it to the range as a percentage. For example, if a stock opened at its low price of the day and closed at its high price of the day, this percentage would be 100%. The other extreme would be if a stock opened at P1, moved higher (or lower) during trading, but returned to close at P1, then the percentage would be 0%. This percentage is then multiplied by the daily volume to estimate the amount of volume traded between the open and close.

The new volume figure is then added or subtracted from the previous day WVAD and drawn on a price chart. It can also be converted into a moving average or oscillator. Interpretation of the WVAD is identical to the other volume indexes.

Chaikin Accumulation Distribution (AD)   In 1975, financial newspapers no longer published the opening prices of stocks. Marc Chaikin, using the Williams WVAD formula as a base, created the Accumulation Distribution (AD) index that uses the high, low, and close prices each day. The basic figure determines where within the daily price range the close occurs in the formula:

$$\text{Volume} \times ([\text{close} - \text{low}] - [\text{high} - \text{close}]) / (\text{high} - \text{low})$$

Thus, if the close occurs above its midpoint for the day, the result will be a positive number, called **accumulation**. Conversely, a negative number occurs when a stock closes below its midpoint for the day, and **distribution** is said to occur. Each daily figure is then cumulated into an index similar to the OBV, and the same general rules of divergences apply.

Figure 13.4 shows a plot of the AD index using Chaikin's formula. A negative divergence occurred in early October (point 1) that led to only a shallow correction. An upward trend line (point 2) in the AD line was broken in early December, long before the price trend line (point 2) was broken and missed the last upward surge, and another negative divergence developed in early January that warned of a decline that subsequently continued for several months.

Williams Accumulation Distribution (WAD)   Not to be confused with the earlier Williams Variable Accumulation Distribution (WVAD) or Chaikin's Accumulation Distribution (AD), the Williams Accumulation Distribution (WAD) also eliminates the use of the open price no longer reported in the financial newspapers. This indicator uses the concept of True Range that J. Welles Wilder developed during the same general period.

The True Range uses the previous day's close as a benchmark and avoids the problems that arise when a price gaps between days. The calculations for the True Range high and low are based on a comparison. The True Range high, for example, is either the current day's high or the previous day's close, whichever is

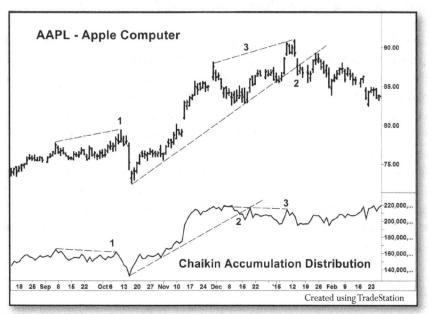

FIGURE 13.4   Chaikin Accumulation Distribution (AAPL, daily: August 13, 2014–February 26, 2015)

higher. The True Range low is either the current day's low or the previous day's close, whichever is lower.

In the WAD, accumulation occurs on days in which the close is greater than the previous day's close; the price move on these days is calculated as the difference between the current day close and the True Range low. Distribution occurs on a day when the close is less than the previous day's close; the price move on these days is the difference between the current day close and the True Range high, which will result in a negative number. Each price move is multiplied by the volume for the respective day, and the resulting figures are cumulated into an index, the WAD.[1]

Volume-Related Oscillators   Unlike indexes, volume-related oscillators are somewhat bounded. When an oscillator approaches the upper bound, an overbought condition occurs; when it approaches the lower bound, an oversold condition occurs. Oscillators are especially useful during trading ranges.

Volume Oscillator   The volume oscillator is the simplest of all oscillators. It is merely the ratio between two moving averages of volume. Its use is to determine when volume is expanding or contracting. Expanding volume implies strength to the existing trend, and contracting volume implies weakness in the existing trend. It is, thus, useful as a confirmation indicator for trend and for giving advanced warning in a range or consolidation formation of the direction of the next breakout. For example, if within the range, the oscillator rises during small advances and declines during small declines, it suggests that the eventual breakout will be upward.

Let us look at Figure 13.5. Like volume itself, the volume oscillator should confirm the price trend. In September 2014, the price is in a flat trading range but the oscillator is rising. This is unusual in that most trading ranges have declining volume until the breakout. October also had a mixed and unusual configuration. The price broke down heavily on large volume and volume continued on the rebound. This suggests that large buying stopped the decline. The volume oscillator then fell off while the price entered another trading range, and finally, in November, began to increase again along with price. This increase in volume was a confirmation of the new trend. The same confirmation occurred in late December and early January when rising volume confirmed the generally rising trend. You can see that this oscillator has a spotty record and generally is not as satisfactory in warning us of trend changes as others previously mentioned.

---

[1] Steven B. Achelis introduced a variation of the WAD in his book *Technical Analysis from A to Z* (2001). This variation eliminates the multiplication by volume and is thus not a volume index but a price index. Achelis's variation is often incorrectly identified in software programs on price indicators as the Williams Accumulation Distribution.

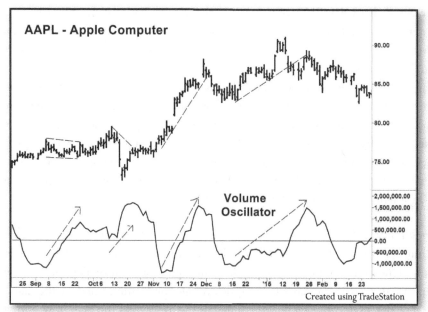

FIGURE 13.5 Volume Oscillator (AAPL, daily: August 13, 2014–February 26, 2015)

Chaikin Money Flow   The Chaikin Money Flow is an oscillator that uses the (Chaikin) AD calculation for each day. It is calculated by summing the ADs over the past 21 days and dividing that sum by the total volume over the past 21 days. This produces an oscillator that rises above zero when an upward trend begins and declines below zero when the trend turns downward.

Remember that each daily Chaikin AD calculation is based only on that particular day's high, low, and closing prices; therefore, if a gap occurs, it is not reflected in this oscillator. Another potential problem with this oscillator, as with all oscillators constructed using simple moving averages, is that simply dropping the number that occurred 21 days prior from the calculation can influence the current value of the oscillator. Remember that as an oscillator, this tool is used for confirmation, not signal generation.

Twiggs Money Flow   Colin Twiggs of www.incrediblecharts.com has adjusted the Chaikin Money Flow to account for the potential problems of gaps and the 21st-day drop-off. Twiggs eliminates the problem of gaps influencing the price strength by using Wilder's True Range, similarly to how Williams uses it in his WAD. In addition, using Wilder's calculation of an exponential moving average solves the problem of the drop-off figure affecting the current oscillator.

Chaikin Oscillator   Just to confuse things even more, Marc Chaikin invented the Chaikin Oscillator, as opposed to the Chaikin Money Flow. This oscillator is simply the ratio of the 3-day EMA of the AD to the 10-day EMA of the AD. Chaikin recommends that a 20-day price envelope, such as a Bollinger Band, also be used as an indication of when signals from the oscillator will be more reliable. Most signals are from divergences.

Figure 13.6 shows how well the Chaikin Oscillator signals short-term reversals within a trading range. The overbought and oversold levels in the chart are determined by a standard Bollinger Band. When the overbought (upper) band is broken from the outside, a sell signal is generated, and conversely when the oversold (lower) band is broke from the outside, a buy signal is generated. The narrowing of the bands shows a decline in volatility. Declining volatility precedes significant price moves and is, thus, a warning of change in direction if not intensity.

Money Flow Index (Oscillator)   Another method of measuring money flow into and out of a stock is the Money Flow Index (MFI). It considers "up" days and "down" days to determine the flow of money into and out of an equity. The money flow on any particular day is the day's typical, or average, price multiplied by the daily volume. The day's typical price is determined as the average of the high, low, and close. Therefore, money flow on Day i would be calculated as

$$MF_i = \{(High_i + Low_i + Close_i) / 3\} \times Volume_i$$

If Day i's average price is higher than the previous day's average price, there is positive money flow (PMF). Conversely, if Day i's average price is lower than the

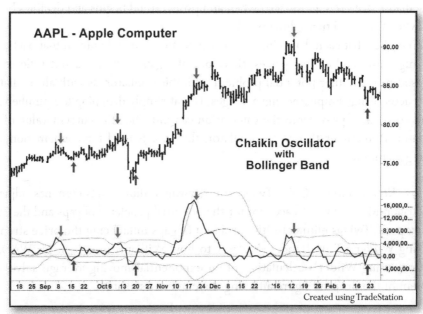

FIGURE 13.6 Chaikin Oscillator (AAPL, daily: August 13, 2014–February 26, 2015)

previous day's average price, negative money flow (NMF) occurs. The analyst chooses a specific period to consider and sums all the PMF and all the NMF for that period. Dividing the sum of PMF by the sum of NMF results in the money flow ratio (MFR):

$$MFR = \Sigma PMF / \Sigma NMF$$

The MFI is then calculated using the following formula:

$$MFI = 100 - (100 / (1 + MFR))$$

The MFI is an oscillator with a maximum of 100 and a minimum of 0. When positive money flow is relatively high, the oscillator approaches 100; conversely, when negative money flow is relatively high, the oscillator approaches 0. A level above 80 is often considered overbought and below 20 oversold. These parameters, along with the period, are obviously adjustable.

In addition, another variation of the MFI uses a ratio between positive money flow and the total dollar volume (rather than the NMF) over the specified period to calculate the money flow ratio. We used this method of calculation in Figure 13.7. Generally, the results of this method are not significantly different from the method we described earlier. In the example, we use a Bollinger Band to determine overbought and oversold. A break into the band is a signal, buy from below and sell from above. The chart shows the signals, which were profitable except the last one that needed a protective stop.

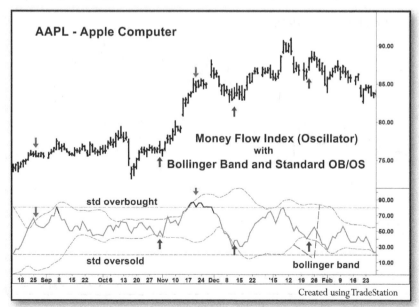

FIGURE 13.7 Money Flow Oscillator (AAPL, daily: August 13, 2014–February 26, 2015)

Elder Force Index (EFI)   The Elder Force Index (EFI) is an easy oscillator to calculate in that it uses only closing prices and daily volume. The daily price change is calculated as the daily closing price minus the previous day's closing price. This daily price change is then multiplied by the day's volume. The index is simply an exponential moving average over some specified period of the daily price change multiplied by the volume.

The purpose of this index is to measure the volume strength of a trend. The higher the level of the oscillator above zero, the more powerful the trend. A negative crossover through zero would thus indicate a weakening in trend power, and a deep negative would suggest strong power to the downside.

We have plotted the EFI in Figure 13.8. Elder suggests using either a 2-day EMA for trading or a 13-day EMA for trend determination. We used 13 days. You can see how erratic the EFI can be. In theory, a trade should be made whenever the centerline is crossed. As a mechanical method, this would have been disastrous as a number of whipsaws occurred. However, if we calculate a band of one standard deviation about the index number, as plotted in Figure 13.8, buy and sell signals can be generated with some accuracy. This oscillator succumbs to the classic problems with oscillators in a trending market. Trends tend to keep the oscillator at the extreme level; thus, it gives false closing signals and misses entry signals. Obviously, the entire Elder Force system should be optimized and tested with unknown data before using it, but there does seem to be some validity to the approach.

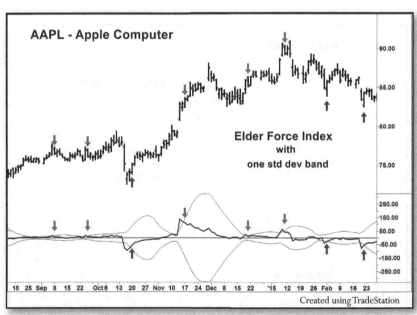

FIGURE 13.8   Elder Force Index (AAPL, daily: August 13, 2014–February 26, 2015)

Other Volume Oscillators   We have just studied the most commonly used volume oscillators. As always, a large number of variations exist, a few of which we mention here. Because these volume oscillators are variations of the more common ones we just discussed, the signals from overbought and oversold or divergences are similar.

Ease of Movement (EMV) is an oscillator developed by the volume expert Richard W. Arms. It uses a different calculation to determine daily price differences—namely, the average of the high and low for one day versus the average for the high and low of the previous day. The formula for calculating the EMV is the following:

$$EMV = [(Low_i + High_i) / 2 - (Low_{i-1} + High_{i-1}) / 2] \div Volume / [Low_i + High_i) / 2]$$

The result is a figure that measures the effect of volume on the daily range. The EMV is usually smoothed using a moving average because it can be erratic from day to day.

Volume Rate of Change is simply a ratio or percentage change between today's volume and the volume of some specified day in the past. For example, a ten-day rate of change would be today's volume versus the volume ten days ago. This method has problems because the drop-off number ten days prior, for example, will influence the current day's reading and might not have significance to recent trading. The ratio is used to identify spikes in volume (see the next section) but is not a reliable indicator by itself.

Volume Spikes

Volume spikes (not to be confused with price spikes) are most common at the beginning of a trend and at the end of a trend. The beginning of a trend often arises out of a pattern with a breakout, and the end of a trend often occurs on a speculative or panic climax. Higher-than-usual volume tends to occur with each event. By screening for volume, the trader can often find issues that are either ready to reverse or that have already reversed. The usual method of screening for a volume spike is to compare daily volume with a moving average. The trader can look for volume that is either a number of standard deviations from the average volume or a particular percentage deviation from the average. As for interpretation of the spike when it occurs, it is often difficult to determine which variety of spike has occurred until after the spike ends and you observe the subsequent price action.

Usually there is a reason for a volume spike, but the reason for the spike might be unrelated to the technical issues of price trends and behavior. Of course, heavy trading might be related to a news announcement made about the company. Or heavy trading volume in a stock can occur if the stock is a component of an index or basket that had a large institutional trade that day. Options expiring can also influence volume figures. In all spikes, any outside reason must first be investigated because it might have nothing to do with the issue's trend and price behavior.

Volume Spike on Breakout   Breakouts are usually obvious. High volume on a gap or on a breakout from a preexisting chart pattern is usually the sign of a valid breakout. Although breakouts do not necessarily require high volume, many analysts use a spike in volume as a confirmation of the breakout and ignore those without a volume spike.

Volume Spike and Climax   A climax usually marks the end of a trend and either a subsequent reversal or consolidation. Climaxes come in many forms, however, and are not always identifiable except in retrospect. Generally, climaxes occur with one of the short-term reversal patterns. These typically can be price spikes or poles, one- or two-bar reversals, exhaustion gaps, key reversals, or any of the other short-term reversal patterns.

Examples of Volume Spikes

A number of volume spikes appear in Figure 13.9. The first accompanies a breakaway gap, and the second is showing that large support exists at that price level, the same level as filled the earlier gap. The third instance occurred when prices tried to break above the resistance level at $215. It ran into heavy selling and turned down. Finally, a volume spike occurred on the runaway gap in early March. The high volumes at the support and resistance levels are often important clues as to changes in direction. If price meets those levels on heavy volume and then reverses direction, those levels are extremely important and must be recorded for future use. For example, the high volume low at marker 2 provided the support that also stopped the decline at marker 3. It told of huge buying pressure at that level. Likewise, the gap in March was caused by the realization that the earlier sellers who stopped the retracement to the resistance level at $215 were gone, and the stock price was free to rise to the next level of resistance at $240.

Shock Spiral   When we looked at the Dead Cat Bounce (DCB), we saw that a substantial volume spike occurs prior to the formation. Remember that the DCB occurs after a shocking news announcement causes a sudden and dramatic shift in price direction, usually accompanied by a large gap or a price spike. An extreme spike in volume accompanies that sudden shift. Tony Plummer (2003) uses the term *shock spiral* to describe the entire A-B-C pattern from the shock (A) to the DCB (B) to the final decline (C). The usual shock spiral is to the downside, but Plummer advocates that it can also occur on the upside.

Volume Price Confirmation Indicator (VPCI)   In a series of two articles in *Active Trader Magazine* and one in the *Journal of Technical Analysis,* Buff Dormier (2005) introduced a method of comparing a volume-weighted price moving average with a simple price moving average to determine whether volume is confirming price action.

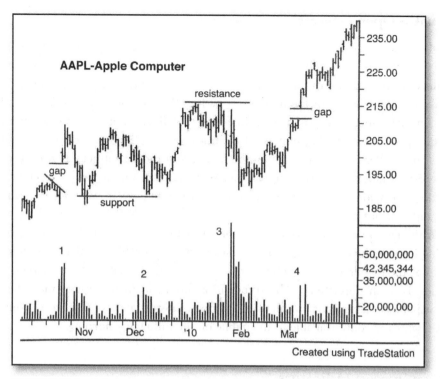

FIGURE 13.9 Volume Spikes (AAPL, daily: August 13, 2014–February 26, 2015)

A positive deviation in the Volume Price Confirmation Indicator (VPCI) suggested that the volume was confirming the price action, and a negative deviation suggested that the volume was contradicting price action.

Volume Dips Sharp declines in volume are usually not meaningful. For example, the low volume in Figure 13.9 at the end of December is due to the Christmas holiday. The decline in volume generally indicates a decline in interest in the security, which is usually accompanied by a decline in volatility. For that reason, the issue should be ignored during the period of low volume, but the trader should be watching for an increase in volume and volatility. A volume dip is also typical for action just before a sudden expansion in price and volume, as in a breakout from a formation. Declines in volume can also occur before holidays, on summer days, and at other times when general activity is low.

■ Open Interest

The volume-related indexes and oscillators we have just discussed are based, in part, on the number of shares or contracts traded over a specific period of time. In the futures market, the total number of contracts outstanding is another important factor. The number of outstanding futures contracts is called **open interest**.

What Is Open Interest?

In the futures markets, only contracts trade, not physical instruments or items. At the expiration of the specific futures market delivery month, the number of contracts reduces to zero as buyers and sellers "roll" their contracts into the next expiration or make or take delivery of the product or cash as the contracts require. The number of contracts outstanding at any one time in each delivery month is its open interest. Total open interest is the number of contracts outstanding in all delivery months. It is an excellent tool in estimating the liquidity of most contracts. However, open interest is a different figure from volume. **Volume** is the number of contracts traded during a certain period in a specific futures market delivery month, not the number of contracts outstanding.

Although open interest is a good tool for estimating the liquidity of a contract, using it for technical trading can be a bit tricky. One problem is that open interest rises at the beginning and declines at the expiration of each contract market. This action is often unrelated to the trend. In addition, in many futures markets, the clearinghouse takes time to calculate the open interest and actual cleared volume. The figures are only available to the public on the following morning.

Open Interest Indicators

Futures contracts are created as interest develops in the specific futures market and become eliminated as interest in the futures market recedes. Thus, the conventional interpretation of open interest is that expanding open interest confirms interest in the existing trend of the futures contract price. This expansion should also be accompanied by increasing volume. Expanding open interest and volume during an upward trend, for example, suggests buyers are creating more new contracts than old contracts. When the upward trend continues but open interest and volume decline, old contract holders are selling and absorbing any new buyers, suggesting that the trend may soon reverse direction. In a correction within an upward trend, declining open interest and volume suggest that the major trend is still healthy. In this sense, open interest is used similarly to volume.

Larry Williams believes that open interest reflects the commercials because they account for such a substantial percentage of volume activity. Commercials are generally short futures contracts used to hedge against inventory. Thus, a decline in open interest, he reasons, is a sign that commercials are covering shorts and that the price will likely rise. He warns that this strategy should only be used in a trading range, and that a 30% change in open interest is necessary before action is contemplated. Colby argues that Williams's strategy does not work in the stock index futures, but he did not test the requirement for a range only.

The Commodity Futures Trading Commission's Commitment of Traders Reports provide breakdowns in open interest by category of trader. Some analysts have compared this data with the data reported daily by the commodity exchanges and used the resulting ratios and changes as indicators of professional and amateur trading action (Greco, 2001). These relations and calculations are complicated and go beyond our present scope.

Herrick Payoff Index (Oscillator) John Herrick (1982) developed a complex oscillator based on price, volume, and open interest to show the money flow in and out of a commodity future. As in many oscillators, interpretation is based on whether the index is above or below zero and whether divergences exist between volume and open interest and price velocity. Thomas Aspray (*Stocks & Commodities Magazine* 6, no. 3: 115–118) has also found that in the Herrick Payoff Index, trend lines are often informative for warnings of a change in price direction, as are the penetration of support and resistance levels.

Figure 13.10 of soybean futures displays the Herrick Payoff Index (HPI) and its 48-week EMA. Signals traditionally were generated when the HPI crossed the zero line, but more recently an exponential moving average (EMA) has been used as the crossover line. Soybeans have some erratic moves over the period especially in 2013, and display several whipsaws. These losses were minimal compared to the large gains when the index caught the upward and downward trend in 2014. Minor crossovers

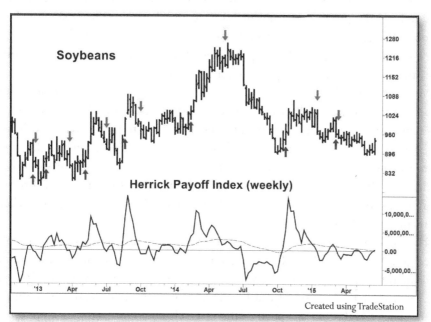

FIGURE 13.10 Herrick Payoff Index (soybeans, perpetual contract, weekly: May 2012–June 2015)

could be reduced by using a filter around the EMA. Overall, the results are favorable and can easily be optimized.

Other Open Interest Indicators   A number of combinations of open interest, price, and volume have been proposed. Most demonstrate what the Herrick Payoff Index displays, and the methods of analysis are the same as for other oscillators. One example is the On Balance Open Interest Indicator. William Painter proposed this indicator, which uses open interest instead of volume in a Price and Open Interest Index (POI), proposed by R. Earle Hadady (1989). This index is calculated similarly to the Price and Volume Indicator using the change in price times the change in open interest.

■ Price Confirmation

Confirmation is concerned with determining whether a price trend is continuing or coming to an end. One group of indicators uses measures based upon the movement of price itself to confirm the trend. Generally, these indicators are based on the concept of momentum.

What Is Momentum?

Momentum deals with the rate at which prices are changing. For example, in an uptrend, prices are rising and the trend line slopes upward. Momentum measures how quickly the prices are rising or how steeply the trend line is sloping. In high school calculus, you probably learned that the slope of a line is called the first derivative and that the change in that slope is called the second derivative. Momentum is, thus, the second derivative of price action over some period.

Momentum is similar to acceleration and deceleration. For example, let us assume that a car is initially traveling at a constant speed of 30 miles per hour; at this point, the car has a constant travel slope of 30. When the car starts accelerating, it is gaining momentum, and its travel slope is increasing. At some point, the car cannot maintain the level of acceleration, and the rate of increase in speed begins to decline. The car is then said to be decelerating, even though it is still traveling at an increasing rate of speed. The speed itself is not increasing as fast as earlier, so momentum is falling.

The same principle applies to markets. Speed is equivalent to the slope of the price trend—the number of points gained per day, for instance. Momentum is equivalent to the car's acceleration and deceleration and is the measure of the price trend's changing slope. Trend can be thought of as direction and momentum can be thought of as the rate of speed of the price change. For example, suppose that a stock is originally selling for $25 a share. If the same stock is selling for $30 a share five days later, then the stock price has increased by $5 in five days. The momentum would be $5 in five days (or $1 per day). If, over the next five days, the price continues to increase to $34, the trend is still upward. However, the rate of change (or momentum) has slowed to $4 in five days. A peak in momentum, therefore, is not equivalent to a peak in price. It leads a peak and is thus useful as a warning of a possible peak in the immediate future.

Technical analysts have developed many indicators to measure momentum, and these measures have become leading signal generators or confirmation gauges, telling us whether the trend slope is changing. When momentum is confirming the price trend, a **convergence** or **confirmation** occurs; when momentum is failing to confirm the price trend slope by giving a warning signal, a **divergence** occurs. As a sign of price trend change then, the technical analyst often looks for a divergence.

Confirmation also is used to identify **overbought** and **oversold** conditions. Remember that prices never follow a trend in an absolute straight line. Prices oscillate about a central trend, deviating above and below the trend. When prices are considerably above the trend, the expectation is that prices will return down to the central trend and perhaps even fall below the trend line. When prices are noticeably above the central trend, an overbought condition exists. When prices are considerably below the trend, they are to be oversold and are likely to return up to the central trend and, perhaps, above.

Analysts have developed many types of oscillators to measure what is overbought and oversold. These oscillators usually are based on price but can also be based on volume or other data. Mathematically, these oscillators eliminate the trend and look only at the oscillations about the trend.

Suppose that you are watching a particular stock and notice a breakout occurring. An oscillator can be useful in determining the validity of the breakout. If an oscillator is oversold, this breakout is more likely to be valid than if the oscillator were overbought. However, in some instances, buy signals are generated from an overbought oscillator accompanied by other indicators (as we will see with the popsteckle later in this chapter).

A word of warning about using oscillators, however, is warranted. Traders often incorrectly use oscillators to generate signals without respect for the underlying trend direction. This will result in many false signals. Remember, profits are made from anticipating and riding the trend. Indicators and oscillators should only be used as secondary evidence to confirm the trend; otherwise, the analyst is likely in for trouble.

To combat the tendency to focus on overbought/oversold signals while ignoring the underlying trend, analysts have developed a number of adjustments and filters to account for trend more mechanically. Adjustments include altering the oscillator parameters, such as the period over which the oscillator is calculated and the signal levels. Other adjustments are even more sophisticated, using digital filters or other mathematical means of filtering and smoothing. The bottom line, however, is that by and large the results are the same. In fact, some analysts argue that increasing the complexity of the calculations only produces a false confidence. They also argue that complexity breeds an increase in the possibility for error when one of the parameters changes and does not allow the analyst the opportunity to gain practical experience. The indicator or oscillator becomes too mechanical. Whatever the arguments, however, even in their simplest forms, indicators and oscillators are useful as confirmation of price behavior, once the quirks are understood and the dependence upon them is secondary.

How Successful Are Momentum Indicators?

Momentum indicators are based on price information. Most academic studies of technical indicators attempt to demonstrate whether price action is random and, if not, whether this apparent nonrandomness violates some of the principles of the Efficient Markets Hypothesis. As such, these studies are usually of little use to practicing technical analysts who introduce many more variables into trading or investment decisions.

It is difficult for academics to construct tests that take into account all the intricacies of real trading. When studying moving averages, for example, how would the requirement for protective stops around support and resistance be integrated? What kind of exit strategy should be used?

The trader must account for risk, as well as return, when considering the usefulness of an indicator. The academic concept of risk is considerably different from that which the practical investor must consider. Therefore, when we look at testing methods, the measurements of risk provided in academic studies are not the same measures that a practitioner would use.

Finally, we will note that any method tested by academia has likely already been discarded by the technical analysis world as outdated. By its nature, academia will always be behind the advances made in the more practical world. Nevertheless, academic studies are useful in determining the direction in which to look for means of profiting from technical analysis. For example, if a particular indicator shows no advantage over the random hypothesis, it should be treated with considerably more skepticism than one that does show some statistically relevant results.

Most academic studies of price indicators, so far, have focused exclusively on moving averages. Interestingly, there have been few studies of standard technical indicators. The two most recent studies of indicators are Bauer and Dahlquist (1999a, 1999b) and Thomas (2003). The Bauer and Dahlquist study covered 60 technical signals, including popular oscillators, for 878 stocks over the period from 1985 through 1996, a period of generally rising stock prices. The Thomas study included price and volume oscillators for 1,750 stocks over the five-year period from 1995 through July 2001, a time during which the stock market had a significant advance and decline.

Specific Indexes and Oscillators

Remember that because momentum indexes and oscillators are based on price data, they do not add new information to the analysis. They are simply manipulations of the same data. This means that they are less informative than other indicators, such as volume, that provide new and different information. The analyst, therefore, must be careful when using price indicators because confirmation may be more redundant than informative. This is not to say that a different manipulation of the data cannot be helpful, only that the base data itself is the same. For example, watching several price oscillators calculated over the same period is silly because by their nature, they will be providing roughly the same results. Watching several price oscillators over different periods or including volume or some other different information would be more productive.

We describe the most common price momentum oscillators next. There are many ways of calculating momentum, but because all of them arrive at essentially the same result, we describe only the most common and most popular.

Moving Average Convergence-Divergence (MACD)   Gerald Appel, publisher of *Systems and Forecasts*, developed the Moving Average Convergence/Divergence (MACD) oscillator. A variation of the moving average crossover, the MACD is calculated using the difference between two exponential moving averages. Traditionally, a 26-period EMA is subtracted from a 12-period EMA, but these times are adjustable for shorter and longer period analysis. This calculation results in a value that oscillates above and below zero. A positive MACD indicates that the average price during the past 12 periods exceeds the average price over the past 26 periods.

The MACD line is plotted at the bottom of a price chart along with another line—the signal line. The signal line is an exponential moving average of the MACD; a nine-period EMA is the most common. A histogram of the difference between the MACD and the signal line often appears at the bottom of the chart. You can see this type of plot in Figure 13.11. The chart displays the MACD (thin black line), the signal line (thick gray line), and the histogram of the difference between the MACD and its signal line for Apple Computer over the same period as the other charts in this chapter.

The MACD is useful in a trending market because it is unbounded. Crude signals occur when the MACD crosses the zero line, but these are just the same signals as would be generated from a moving average crossover. Other information can be gleaned from the MACD, however. For example, when the MACD is above zero, suggesting an upward trend, buy signals occur when the MACD crosses from below to above the signal line. Downward crossings are not at all reliable while the trend is upward. Through experimentation to determine overbought and oversold levels, analysts can use these levels as places to generate signals for price reversion to the central trend. These extremes showed good performance results in the Thomas study of oscillators.

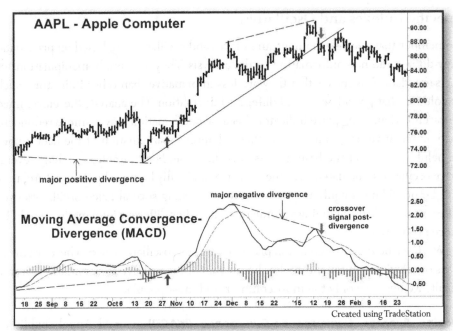

FIGURE 13.11 Moving Average Convergence-Divergence (AAPL, daily: August 13, 2014–February 26, 2015)

Additionally, some analysts compare the peaks and valleys in the MACD with the price line in a divergence analysis. Bauer and Dahlquist suggest that divergences can be useful, especially in a downward trending market. The peaks and valleys in the histogram provide two useful sets of information. They can be used for divergence analysis, and because they are sensitive to price directional change over short periods, they can also be used to signal shorter price trend changes within the longer trend.

Let us look a little more closely at Figure 13.11. The first observation is the two major divergences between the AAPL price and the MACD. Beginning on the left of the chart through mid-October, the price oscillated with only a slight upward trend and then collapsed to a lower low. Meanwhile, the MACD also advanced, but at the time of the collapse, the MACD failed to break below its previous low. This constituted a positive divergence and a warning of an upcoming advance. When the MACD (solid line) crossed above its signal line (dashed line), a buy signal was generated. Four days later the price closed above resistance, and the upward trend began. In early January another divergence occurred—this time a negative one where the price reached a new high but the MACD did not. This was a warning of a price decline that was triggered when the MACD crossed below its signal line. The crossover and close below the trend line were coincident, and the price began its decline. Notice the many times that the MACD crosses its signal line. These crossovers usually produce whipsaws unless other evidence supports their signals. This action is thus similar to our earlier discussion about moving average crossovers and how a filter of some nature is necessary to reduce the false crossovers.

Rate of Change (ROC)   Rate of change (ROC) is the simplest of all oscillators. It is a measure of the amount a security's price has changed over a given number (N) of past periods. The formula for calculating ROC is as follows:

$$ROC = \{(P_{today} - P_{N\ periods\ ago}) / P_{N\ periods\ ago}\} \times 100$$

With this calculation, ROC is zero if the price today is the same as it was N periods ago. It shows on a continuous basis how the current price relates to the past price.

It is simple to calculate, but the ROC has many problems as an indicator. Although economists often calculate ROC using macroeconomic data, usually on an annual basis to minimize seasonality, it suffers from the **drop-off effect**. Only two prices, P_{today} and $P_{N\ periods\ ago}$, appear in the calculation, and these two prices are equally weighted. Therefore, the older price that occurred N periods ago has the same effect on the oscillator as the current, more relevant, price. The ROC can, thus, have a current rise or fall based solely on what number drops off in the past. Some analysts will smooth the ROC with a moving average to dampen this effect.

Analysts use the ROC in the standard four ways. Its position relative to zero can indicate the underlying trend; it can be a divergence oscillator showing when the momentum relative to the past is changing; it can be an overbought/oversold indicator; and it can generate a signal when it crosses over its zero line.

Figure 13.12 shows a graphical representation of a 14-day ROC for Apple Computer. The following observations are marked with numbers: 1—downward sloping trend line upward break, 2—negative divergence, 3—small symmetrical triangle upward break, 4—upward trend line downward break, 5—negative divergence, 6—upward trend line downward break, 7—negative divergence, and 8—downward trend line no breaks yet. We didn't include the signals of moving out from overbought or oversold. Most of these signals proved worthwhile when confirmed by price action.

Relative Strength Index (RSI)   In June 1978, J. Welles Wilder introduced the relative strength index (RSI) in an article in *Commodities* (now known as *Futures*) magazine. The RSI measures the strength of an issue against its history of price change by comparing "up" days to "down" days. Wilder based his index on the assumption that overbought levels generally occur after the market has advanced for a disproportionate number of days, and that oversold levels generally follow a significant number of declining days.

Be careful to understand that the *RSI measures a security's strength relative to its own price history, not to that of the market in general.* Because of its name, a common misconception is that this indicator compares one security with other securities.

To construct the RSI, several calculations must be made, as follows:

$$UPS = (Sum\ of\ gains\ over\ N\ periods) / N$$
$$DOWNS = (Sum\ of\ losses\ over\ N\ periods) / N$$
$$RS = UPS / DOWNS$$
$$RSI = 100 - [100 / (1 + RS)]$$

The RSI can range from a low of 0 (indicating no up days) to a high of 100. In his original calculations, Wilder used 14 days as the relevant period. Although some analysts have attempted to use a time-weighted period, these methods have not been well accepted, and the 14-day period remains the most commonly used.

After calculating the RSI for the first 14 days, Wilder used a smoothing method to calculate RSI for future days. This process dampens the oscillations. For day 15 and after

$$UPS_{day\ i} = [(UPS_{day\ i-1} \times 13) + Gain_{day\ i}] / 14$$
$$DOWNS_{day\ i} = [DOWNS_{day\ i-1} \times 13) + Loss_{day\ i}] / 14$$

These measures for UPS and DOWNS are used to calculate RS and RSI. This method of smoothing the averages is now called the "Wilder exponential moving average" and is used in many other indicator formulas. We saw, for example, in the section on volume oscillators earlier in this chapter that the Money Flow oscillator uses the RSI formula.

The RSI has many characteristics that can generate signals. For example, when the RSI is above 50, the midpoint of the bounded range, the underlying trend in prices is usually upward. Conversely, it is downward when the RSI is below 50.

Overbought and oversold warnings are the same as with many other indicators. Wilder considered, for example, an RSI above 70 to indicate an overbought situation and an RSI below 30 to indicate an oversold condition. Analysts will often adjust these levels based on the underlying trend. Chuck LeBeau, for example, uses 75 and 25 as the overbought and oversold extremes, and Brown (1999) uses 90 and 40 in an upward trend and 60 and 10 in a downward trend. She calls these new levels trend IDs. Because the trend in Figure 13.12 is upward, we have drawn, in addition to the conventional overbought and oversold levels, the trend ID of 80 and 40. This gives us an oversold buy signal in August and in mid-October that would not have been available using the conventional method.

Similar to other oscillators, RSI divergences with price often give warning of trend reversal. The RSI also appears to have patterns similar to price charts. Triangles, pennants, flags, and even head-and-shoulders patterns occur, and support and resistance levels become signal levels. The rules for breakouts from these formations are used for signals from the RSI.

Another method of signaling is **failure swings**. A failure swing occurs when the oscillator exceeds an overbought or oversold level, corrects, reverses back toward the overbought or oversold, doesn't reach it, and then turns back beyond the correction. The oversold in August and in February are almost failure swings except the second swing in both cases did reach oversold. Nevertheless, they should be treated as a failure swing signal. Another short-term trading method using the RSI is to place a buy stop above the daily high when the RSI declines 10 points from a recent peak above 70. This should only be used when the trend is upward and never when a downward failure swing develops. The buy stop can be adjusted each day

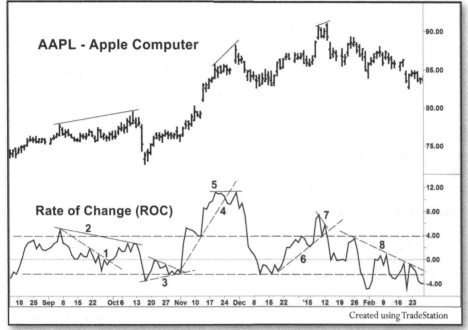

FIGURE 13.12 Rate of Change (AAPL, daily: August 13, 2014–February 26, 2015)

until either it is triggered for a day or two trade or the RSI continues to decline, suggesting that the trend is reversing downward.

There is also the method called the "RSI is wrong." In Figure 13.13, the RSI remains above or near the overbought level for a substantial period from early November onward, during which the AAPL price continued to rise. This method suggests that rather than looking for a top when the overbought level is penetrated, it would be better to buy the issue and use a sell stop. *Active Trader Magazine* (August 2004, pp. 64–65) tested an "RSI is wrong" system, not optimized, on 19 futures from 1994 through 2003 with the following rules: buy when 14-day RSI penetrates above 75; sell when RSI penetrates 25 or after 20 days. The opposite rules apply for sells using a break below the RSI 25 level as the initial short sale. The results showed a steady, straight equity curve especially for long positions.

Thomas (2003), in his testing of the RSI, found that none of the conventional signals had value except the positioning opposite from the conventional overbought/ oversold levels of 70 and 30. His testing showed promise for the "RSI is wrong" thesis. Bauer and Dahlquist found that the conventional use, called a "crossover" system, of selling on a break below the overbought 70 and buying on a break above the oversold 30 had marginal returns during the period tested. They also found that using peaks above 70 and below 30 had marginal returns, and that the opposite buying at peaks outperformed all signals. Their testing method, however, judged against the percentage of time in a position and did not account for the reduction in risk when in cash. Nevertheless, the results were "disappointing."

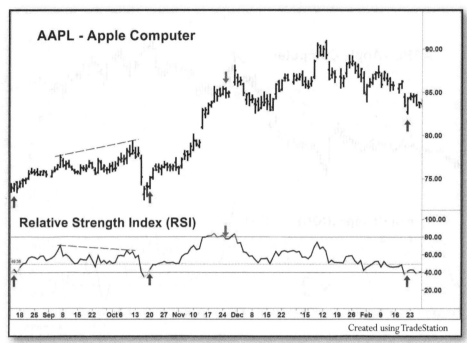

FIGURE 13.13 RSI (AAPL daily: August 13, 2014–February 26, 2015)

As the many warnings and signals that occur in Figure 13.13 suggest, the RSI cannot be interpreted mechanically and is, perhaps, why it does not test well. However, the action is informative and useful to many traders. In a survey of traders taken in 2002 (Charlton and Earl), the most popular indicator was the RSI. In short, traders have developed many methods. If you want to use the RSI as a confirming indicator, you must learn these methods, experiment with them, and always be sure of the underlying price trend.

Stochastic Oscillator All oscillators use a specific time over which they are calculated. The traditional periods for the MACD are 26 and 12 bars; the RSI traditionally uses 14 bars for its calculation. These oscillators depend on smoothing techniques that tend to dampen the most recent price action. The stochastic takes another tack. It looks at the most recent close price as a percentage of the price range (high to low) over a specified past "window" of time. This makes it sensitive to recent action. Analysts use the stochastic for trading or investing when the most recent close is the most important price.

It is not absolutely clear who was the inventor of stochastics. George Lane is known for promoting the concept since 1954 (Lane, 1985), and the concept is sometimes referred to as Lane's Stochastic (Colby, 2003), but others apparently preceded him. Two names mentioned are Ralph Dystant and a dentist friend of his and Richard Redmont. Dystant introduced the indicator as part of an Elliott wave course through his Investment Educators, and Lane, who lectured for that firm, took it over on Dystant's death in 1978.

Not only is the inventor of stochastics unknown, the origin of the term *stochastics* is not clear. The name of this oscillator has nothing to do with the scientific term *stochastic*, which means random or nondeterministic. Of course, traders would hope that this indicator did not produce random results. So, how did the name stochastic become associated with this indicator? According to Gibbons Burke (www .io.com/gibbonsb/trading/stochastic.html), Tim Slater, founder and president of CompuTrac, Inc., included this indicator in the company's software analysis program in 1978. He needed a name to attach to the indicator other than the %K and %D we will see in the indicator calculation. Slater saw a notation of "stochastic process" handwritten on the original Investment Educators literature he was using. The name stuck. Regardless of who the actual inventor might be or how it got its name, the stochastic oscillator is one of the most popular, both for long- and short-term momentum signals.

The formula for the stochastic is as follows:

$$\%K = [(C - L) / (H - L] \times 100$$
$$\text{fast } \%D = 3\text{-bar SMA of } \%K$$
$$\text{slow } \%D = 3\text{-bar SMA of } \%D$$

where   W is the time window (that is, 14 bars)
           H is the high for the window period (w)
           L is the low for the window period (w)
           C is the most recent bar close (w)

The "fast" stochastic, as seen in most trading software, refers to the raw stochastic number (%K) compared with a three-period simple moving average of that number (fast %D). This number is extremely sensitive to price changes. Because of the erratic volatility of the fast %D, many false signals occur with rapidly fluctuating prices. To combat this problem, analysts have created the "slow" stochastic. The slow stochastic is designed to smooth the original %D again with a three-period simple moving average. In other words, the slow stochastic is a doubly smoothed moving average, or a moving average of the moving average of %K.

Analysts often create their own variations of the stochastics formula. Lane, for example, smoothed the numerator separately from the denominator in the %K formula and then divided each rather than smoothing the %K itself (Merrill, 1986). He also used only five days in the time window.

The question of how many periods to use in the window is problematic. The volatility and cyclical nature of the issue traded, as well as the tendency for these factors to vary, are integral to choosing a window period. Larry Williams uses a composite of different time window periods and the True Range rather than the high and low for his "Ultimate Oscillator." Others adjust the window period, as well as the number of bars used in smoothing the %K based on their interpretation of the dominant cycle in prices. Many analysts just test the results of signals over different windows to see which works best.

As in most oscillators, the stochastic works better in a trading range market but can still give valuable information in a trending market. In a trending market, divergences, trend line breaks, and swing failures generate signals. During trading ranges, crossovers and swing failures generate signals when the stochastic reaches overbought or oversold, traditionally 80 and 20. Crossovers occur when the fast stochastic crosses over the slow stochastic. Following crossovers without other confirming evidence, however, can cause whipsaws.

As in the RSI and many other oscillators, chart patterns, such as triangles and pennants, can also evolve in the stochastic oscillator. Support and resistance levels, even without swing failures, can be useful signals or warnings, and trend lines often appear to warn of potential changes in momentum. All standard technical rules apply to oscillators. However, oscillators by themselves should never be used strictly for signals. The analyst must confirm any oscillator signal with price action—a breakout or a pattern.

Academic testing of standard stochastic signals has had the same mediocre results as with other oscillators. This is not surprising, of course, because the determination of trend or trading range is rarely included in academic studies. Indeed, the fact that some positive results have occurred is encouraging, considering the primitive definitions of signals and circumstances used. Thomas (2003) found that extreme levels of overbought and oversold were somewhat predictive of future price direction but that most standard overbought/oversold interpretations failed. Bauer and Dahlquist (1999a) found that acting at peaks and troughs above and below overbought and oversold respectively had better results on the long side than the short side. Unfortunately, trend was not a consideration in the testing, and the period tested (1985–1996) was one of a historically large upward trend when short signals would be expected to fail. Thus, the positive results for long signals were encouraging, considering that the signals had to keep up with the values in a generally rising market.

Figure 13.14 shows a 14-3-3 slow stochastic. This means that a 14-day time window was used; %D was smoothed once using a 3-day SMA and again using another 3-day SMA. Confirmed signals are shown on the price chart, and stochastic overbought/oversold and failure swing signals are shown on the stochastic chart.

AAPL is in a trending mode during the period considered but swinging in wide swings. In this case, the use of overbought and oversold levels is fruitful. Each time a buy or sell signal occurs from breaking toward the midpoint from oversold or overbought, an exit and reentry signal is given at the opposite extreme. This is not always the case. In a strong upward trend as developed during the later months of the period in Figure 13.14, the oscillator did not return to oversold. Thus, overbought breakdown sell signals in a rising trend must be suspect. They can signal the time to get out of a long trade, but they do not necessarily signal the time to enter a short trade.

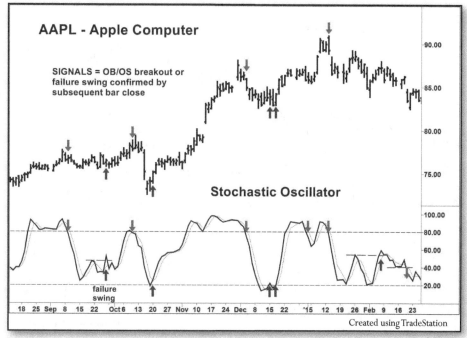

FIGURE 13.14 Stochastic (daily: August 13, 2014–February 26, 2015)

In addition to the overbought/oversold signals, three failure swings occurred in late November, late December, and late January. The downward signal in late November was timely, as was the upward failure swing signal in December. The January sell signal was less profitable.

Finally, we see that before the declines in late October and early January, negative divergences developed at the peaks when the stochastic failed to confirm the new price highs.

Other Oscillators, Similar to the Stochastics   Some analysts use oscillators that are similar to the stochastic oscillator. In particular, the Williams %R and the Commodity Channel Index are comparable indicators.

Williams %R   The Williams %R oscillator is almost identical to the stochastic. It can be thought of as an inverted stochastic. Instead of comparing the current close with the low that occurred during the time window, the Williams %R compares the current close with the high that occurred during the time window. Thus, the formula for the Williams %R is as follows:

$$\%R = [(H - C) / (H - L)] \times 100$$

The Williams %R tells whether a stock is at a relatively high point in its trading range, whereas the stochastic indicates whether a stock is at a relatively low point in its trading range.

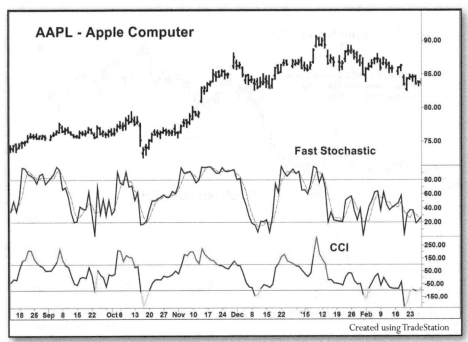

FIGURE 13.15 CCI and Fast Stochastic (AAPL daily: August 13, 2014–February 26, 2015)

Commodity Channel Index (CCI) The Commodity Channel Index (CCI) is also similar to the stochastic. Donald Lambert developed this indicator, describing it in the October 1980 issue of *Commodities* (now known as *Futures*) magazine. Do not be fooled by the name of the indicator; it can be used in any market, not just commodity markets. The CCI measures the deviations of a security's price from a moving average. This gives a slightly different picture than the stochastic, and in some cases, the signals are more reliable. However, the difference between the CCI and the stochastic is so miniscule that using both would be a duplication of effort and liable to create false confidence. Figure 13.15 shows how similar the CCI and the stochastic are.

The CCI is not bounded—that is, it can rise above +100 and fall below –100—as is the stochastic, and this bothers some analysts. To avoid this problem, some analysts use a stochastic calculation on the CCI, bounding the CCI to 0 to 100 and smoothing the CCI at the same time. Barbara Star reports in *Active Trader Magazine* (2004) that in trending markets, this bounded, smoothed CCI is often useful for entries in the trend direction, but not in a countertrend direction, and in trading markets, it often gives overbought and oversold signals.

Similarities between Oscillators Figure 13.16 shows a standard 14-day RSI compared with a 3-day to 10-day MACD. See how the two lines follow almost identical paths. It is, thus, redundant and nonproductive to use many oscillators that essentially tell the same story. This is why most analysts prefer to use just one, or perhaps

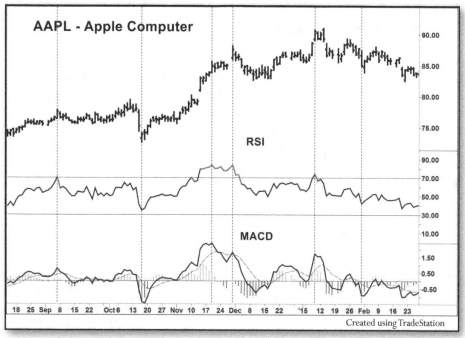

FIGURE 13.16 RSI and MACD (AAPL, daily: August 13, 2014–February 26, 2015)

two, oscillators and learn their complexities and intricacies well rather than depend on mechanical signals from many.

Combinations—Determining Trend and Trading Range: The ADX We have discussed trends, moving averages, and especially the use of the ADX and its component parts, the DMI+ and DMI–. We found that moving averages were only profitable in trending markets, just as we have found in this chapter that oscillators are more profitable in trading markets. The problem, then, is to be able to determine whether a particular market is trending or trading. Usually markets rotate from one to the other, but the signals generated by moving averages and indicators are not always quick to decipher the change. Because most profits come from trending markets, analysts focus on moving averages and oscillators to determine when a trend is beginning; the sooner they recognize the trend, the better.

The most common solution is the use of Wilder's ADX. Because it is smoothed through averaging, the ADX is a lagging indicator. However, its peaks and troughs give us important information. A peak in the ADX almost invariably occurs at a trend peak up or down. It is thus useful as an indicator to close a position established during the trend. A trough in the ADX occurs when a trend has begun and is beginning to accelerate. The period between a trough and a peak is a period of generally trending prices, and a period between a peak and a trough is a period of decelerating trend that can either be trending roughly with small oscillations or be trading in a range. In Figure 13.17, the up arrows in the ADX chart denote peaks. They are extended

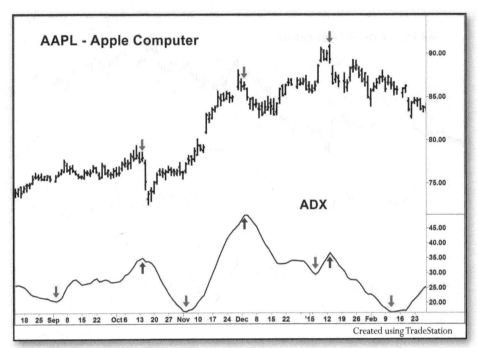

FIGURE 13.17   ADX (AAPL, daily: August 13, 2014–February 26, 2015)

up to the AAPL price chart to show how they occurred at each peak in prices, thus making them possible sell points. They work equally well pinpointing price troughs during a downward trend. The downward-pointing arrows in the ADX chart at ADX troughs. You can see in the price chart directly above each down arrow how the trend accelerates, upward or downward, once an ADX trough is formed. These are excellent entry points for several reasons: first, by the time of the trough, you know the trend direction and how to play it, and second, you know that once a trough has occurred, a peak must follow at some time that will tell you when to close the position.

Some analysts place importance on the level of the ADX rather than its trend, believing that they are constant across all securities. For example, an advancing ADX above 45 suggests the price will top soon. We know that is likely, but 45 is not a magic number. In Figure 13.17, for example, two of the three price peaks occurred when the ADX was below 45. However, it seems to be true that very low levels of ADX are periods of no trend and a high possibility of whipsaws. Indeed, we have seen trading models where a low ADX, determined through testing, is a time to stop trading entirely until the ADX begins to advance.

When developing trading systems, use of the ADX is helpful in switching between trending formulas and trading-range formulas. It defines the internal strength of direction and thus what formulas should be put into play.

Analysts have developed numerous methods of utilizing the ADX with oscillators and moving averages. Let us look at two of them: **David Steckler's popsteckle** and **Linda Raschke's Holy Grail**.

Popsteckle   In a 2000 article, appearing in *Stocks and Commodities*, David Steckler described a method of identifying stocks that are ready to "pop" upward using all three indicators. The name "popsteckle" is a contraction of "pop" and "Steckler," but Jake Bernstein (1993) is the originator of the method. Steckler's setup rules are as follows:

1. Recent price action shows low volatility (dull action).
2. 14-day ADX is below 20 (no trend).
3. Eight-day stochastic %K is greater than the day before and above 70 (upward trend beginning).
4. Eight-week stochastic %K is greater than the week before and above 50 (upward longer trend beginning).
5. Bullish market conditions exist (could be determined by market price above long-term moving average).
6. Stock breaks upward out of congestion on volume 50% above its 50-day simple moving average.

The popsteckle method monitors a low-volatility stock in a horizontal trading range for signs of positive trending action as displayed by changes in the various stochastics. No history of back testing this method is available, but the logic of the variables and indicators is consistent.

Holy Grail   Unlike the popsteckle, which looks for the beginning of a new trend, Linda Raschke's Holy Grail method takes advantage of an existing trend and uses the ADX in combination with a moving average. First, a 14-day ADX must be above 30 to indicate an existing trend. The primary trend is displayed by a 20-period EMA. An initial downturn in the ADX suggests a correction to the primary trend. When this occurs, enter in the direction of the trend when the price touches or comes close to that EMA. On the long side, the entry trigger would be a break above the high of the most recent declining bar, and it would be the opposite on the short side. The initial target that Raschke uses is the old price extreme, high or low, at which point the analyst must make a decision as to whether the price will continue in the primary trend direction or not.

■ Conclusion

To increase the odds that a technical price signal is correct, the technical analyst uses many other indicators as confirmation. The primary confirmation indicator is volume because it is a series of data independent of price. Unfortunately, volume indicators and volume itself do not always confirm a price pattern. Nevertheless, high volume at the appropriate moments does add value to the entry decision. Other means of calculating volume for comparison with past volume and price action have limited value in confirming signals, but they can provide warnings when not confirming price action. These divergences cannot be used as signals by themselves but do help the analyst by suggesting that trend change is soon likely.

The other major area of confirmation comes from momentum, or rate of price change, calculations. Strong momentum suggests a trending market, and weak momentum suggests a consolidating market. Naturally, the analyst principally looks for the beginning of a trending market, and because momentum indicators tend to lead price direction, they are often useful in warning of such a change. However, the reliability of these indicators is highly dependent upon whether the security is trading in a trend or in a trading range. By and large, these oscillators are more useful for signals in trading ranges as overbought/oversold indications. In trending markets, they are more useful as warnings of trend change. In strong trends, they tend to be skewed in the direction of the trend and, thus, fail to provide reliable entry signals.

Some of the problems with interpreting price and volume indicators can be ameliorated with the use of the ADX or other indicators of trend strength. Combining the ADX, a moving average, and an oscillator, for example, can improve timing results considerably.

■ References

Achelis, Steven B. *Technical Analysis from A to Z*. New York, NY: McGraw-Hill, 2001.

Arms, Richard W., Jr. *Profits in Volume*. 2nd ed. New York, NY: Marketplace Books, John Wiley & Sons, 1998.

Aspray, Thomas E. "Payoff Index." *Technical Analysis of Stocks & Commodities Magazine* 6, no. 3 (1988): 115–118.

Bauer, Richard and Julie Dahlquist. *Technical Market Indicators: Analysis and Performance*. New York, NY: John Wiley & Sons, 1999a.

Bauer, Richard and Julie Dahlquist. "Technical Indicators for Individual Stocks: The Quality Versus Quantity Tradeoff." *MTA Journal* 51 (Winter-Spring 1999b): 67–71.

Bernstein, Jake. *Investor's Quotient*. New York, NY: John Wiley & Sons, 1993.

Blume, L, D. Easley, and M. O'Hara. "Market Statistics and Technical Analysis: The Role of Volume." *Journal of Finance* 49 (1994): 153–181.

Bollinger, John. *Bollinger on Bollinger Bands*. New York, NY: McGraw-Hill, 2002.

Brown, Constance W. *Technical Analysis for the Trading Professional*. New York, NY: McGraw-Hill, 1999.

Chan, K., Y. Peter Chung, and W. Fong. "The Informational Role of Stock and Option Volume." *The Review of Financial Studies* 15, no. 4 (2002): 1049–1075.

Charlton, William T. and John H. Earl, Jr. "The State of Technical Analysis in Practice and in College Curriculums: A Survey of Technical Analysts." *Journal of Technical Analysis* (Summer-Autumn 2002): 5–9.

Colby, Robert W. *The Encyclopedia of Technical Market Indicators*. New York, NY: McGraw-Hill, 2003.

Dormeier, Buff. "The Volume Price Confirmation Indicator." *Active Trader Magazine* 6, no. 2 (2005): 21.

Dormeier, Buff. "Price and Volume, Digging Deeper." *Journal of Technical Analysis* 68 (2005): 19–25.

Gartley, H.M. *Profits in the Stock Market*. 3rd ed. (1981). Pomeroy, WA: Lambert-Gann Publishing Co., 1935.

Greco, Sal. "New Applications for Open Interest in U.S. Treasury Bond Futures: A Money Flow vs. Breadth Approach." *Journal of Technical Analysis* (formerly *The Market Technicians Association Journal*) (Spring-Summer 2001): 9–15.

Hadady, R. Earle. "The POI Index." *Journal of Technical Analysis* (formerly *The Market Technicians Association Journal*) (May 1989): 32–44.

Herrick, John. "Cyclic Timing." *Technical Analysis of Stocks & Commodities* 1, no. 3 (1982): 52–57.

Kaufman, S. Kris, and Marc Chaikin. "The Use of Price-Volume Crossover Patterns in Technical Analysis." *Journal of Technical Analysis* (formerly *The Market Technicians Association Journal*) 37 (Spring 1991): 35–41.

Lane, George C. "Lane's Stochastics: The Ultimate Oscillator." *Journal of Technical Analysis* (formerly *The Market Technicians Association Journal*) (May 1985).

LeBeau, Charles, and David Lucas. *Technical Traders Guide to Computer Analysis of the Futures Markets.* New York, NY: McGraw-Hill, 1991.

Merrill, Arthur A. "Stochastics ???" *Journal of Technical Analysis* (formerly *The Market Technicians Association Journal*) (February 1986).

Plummer, Tony. *Forecasting Financial Markets: The Psychology of Successful Investing.* 4th ed. London, UK: Kogan Page, 2003.

Star, Barbara. "The CCI Stochastic." *Active Trader Magazine.* September 2004, 52–54.

Steckler, David. "Trading Stochastic Pops." *Technical Analysis of Stocks & Commodities* 18, no. 8 (2000): 30–41.

Thomas, James D. "News and Trading Rules." PhD thesis, School of Computer Science, Computer Science Department, Graduate School of Industrial Administration, Carnegie Mellon University, January 2003.

Wilder, J. Welles, Jr. *New Concepts in Technical Trading Systems.* Greensboro, SC: Trend Research, 1978.

CHAPTER 14

Candlestick Charting Essentials

From Steve Nison, *The Candlestick Course* (Hoboken, New Jersey: John Wiley & Sons, 2003), Chapter 1.

Learning Objective Statements

- Describe strengths and limitations of candle charts
- Identify the components of individual candle lines—real bodies and shadows
- Explain how candles depict the high, low, open, and close of a trading period
- Identify candle confirmations of support and resistance

SECTION ONE

Candlestick Overview: Origins and Basic Applications

The financial markets represent some of the most exciting and challenging arenas on earth. Those who participate in these markets conduct research by utilizing two basic types of analysis: fundamental and technical. Fundamental analysts pore over fiscal statements and company reports, and technical analysts scan charts to assess a market, stock, or any other financial instrument.

Though the fundamentals are important, the shorter the time frame, the more important the psychological component of the market becomes. And the only way to measure the emotional aspect of the markets is through technical analysis. Indeed, there are many times when the emotional conditions of the market overwhelm the fundamentals. For example, how many times have we seen the appearance of a positive fundamental only to have that market descend? Even if we have a strong stock based on the fundamentals, what is likely to happen to that stock if the overall market is down sharply? Of course, the negative psychology of the overall market will influence that stock even if its fundamentals didn't change. As Bernard Baruch cogently put it, "What is important in market fluctuations are not the events themselves, but the human reactions to these events." The most potent way you can gauge the emotional state of the market is through candlestick charts.

In the pages that follow, you'll learn how Japanese candlestick techniques promote efficient and effective analysis. As your proficiency in interpreting candle charts evolves, the knowledge absorbed and its application should add to your success in the financial markets. Since the terms *candlestick charts* and *candle charts* are used interchangeably in the trading community, that is how they are used throughout this chapter.

In this section you will learn . . .

- Background of candlestick charting techniques
- Markets and time frames in which candles are utilized
- Limitations of candle charts
- Importance of risk/reward
- Significance of using other technical tools with candle charts

Key terms to watch for:

- Reversal signals
- Candle lines
- Price targets
- Risk/reward

The use of candlestick charts originated in Japan. Since little or no currency standard existed during those times, rice represented a medium of exchange. Feudal lords would deposit it in warehouses in Osaka and sell or trade the coupon receipts whenever they chose. Therefore, rice became the first futures market.

In the 1700s, Munehisa Homma, a rice trader from a wealthy family, studied all aspects of rice trading from fundamentals, such as weather, to market psychology. He subsequently dominated the rice markets and amassed a huge fortune. Homma's trading techniques and principles eventually evolved into the candlestick methodology used by Japanese technical analysts with the start of the Japanese stock market in the 1870s.

The greatest advantage to using candles on your charts, instead of bars, is that single candle lines and multiple candle patterns offer more reliable, earlier, and more effective reversal signals.

SIDELIGHT

Centuries ago, Japanese merchants were at the bottom of that country's social system, below soldiers, farmers, and artisans. By the 1700s, though, merchants moved up in prominence. Even today, the traditional greeting in Osaka is "Mokarimakka?" which translates to, "Are you making a profit?"

Reversal signals are the meat and potatoes of traders and investors. Major trend reversals represent the territory where the most gains are pocketed (and lost). In addition, the ability to identify possible reversal signals on the markets is invaluable for applying money-management strategies to improve profits and, equally important, preserve profits.

No single technical indicator, however, represents the holy grail. Like other indicators, candlesticks have limitations.

As will be detailed later, the candle line is constructed from the open, high, low, and close, which is the same data used in bar charts. Therefore, for a candle line or pattern to offer a proper signal, you must wait for the session's close to confirm it. To hasten the reading, however, rather than waiting for the end of a daily session (for a daily chart), you can look at a shorter time frame (i.e., an intraday chart) and obtain an earlier signal.

Let's say it's midday and you are focusing on a daily chart. Your view of the market is that it may be ready to rally. Rather than waiting for the end of the daily session to see if a bullish candle signal is confirming your outlook, you can switch to an hourly chart and see if any bullish candle patterns formed in the morning on the hourly chart.

Be aware that although candle signals can demarcate areas of support and resistance, they do not offer price targets. This is why it is so important to use classic Western techniques, such as pivot highs and lows, or trend lines, since these can be used to obtain a potential target. Before initiating a trade with a candle signal, always consider the risk versus the reward (risk/reward) of that trade. I repeat: NEVER PLACE A TRADE WITH A CANDLE SIGNAL UNTIL YOU HAVE CONSIDERED THE RISK/REWARD OF THE POTENTIAL TRADE. For example, if there is a bullish candle signal, such as a hammer, the risk (stop-out level) should be under the low of that hammer. Now that we have defined the risk, the next step is defining the potential target. Defining a target can be done in many ways, including a prior high or a falling resistance line. Now we have the risk/reward parameters defined, only then should you decide whether or not to place a trade. Bullish hammer or not, if the risk is $2 and the target is also $2 from the hammer's buy signal (which comes on the close of that session), this is not a trade that warrants action.

As a Japanese proverb says, "His potential is that of the fully drawn bow, his timing the release of the trigger." The timing of the release of the trigger depends on the risk/reward aspect of the trade.

Although candle lines and patterns may offer excellent signals, I advise using them in combination with other technical indicators. Just as several strands wound together are stronger than a single fiber, so is the combined power of several indicators all giving the same buy or sell signal.

In the next section of this chapter, we'll cover the construction of single candle lines. The basic formations are easy to learn. We'll start by placing emphasis on the length of real bodies, whether short or long, as well as the lengths of their accompanying shadows. With a little practice, you'll soon be able to decipher the important signals candles present.

SECTION TWO
Candlestick Construction

A Japanese proverb states, "Without oars, you cannot cross in a boat." This section will provide the oars you need to build your foundation of candle charts. We will address the actual construction of the candle lines, which have the same components as bars: a high, low, open, and close. We will also delve into basic candle applications and begin to harness the power of candle charts.

In this section you will learn . . .
- How to identify the components of individual candle lines
- How to discern the difference between real bodies and shadows
- How to construct a candle line

Key terms to watch for:
- Real body
- White real body
- Black real body
- Upper shadow
- Lower shadow

■ Getting Started

Technical analysts use three basic kinds of charts: line charts, bar charts, and candle charts. (Point-and-figure charts are an additional alternative, but they don't show a session's high, low, open, or closing prices.) Line charts are made up of points that usually represent the closing price of a financial instrument, connected by a single line.

> **KEY POINT**
> Because candles need open, high, low, and close, we can't use candle charts on mutual funds or tick-by-tick charts, since these have only closing prices.

Just as a bar chart uses the top and bottom of each bar to indicate high and low prices of the time frame indicated, so does a candlestick, or candle line (these two terms are interchangeable).

A single bar displays a small perpendicular line on its left to designate the opening price and another on the right to show its closing price. When using candlesticks, however, we draw in a real body to connect the opening and closing prices. This gives us a quick and complete picture of the stock's action and denotes prevailing sentiment.

The *real body*—the rectangular portion of the candle line—represents the range between the opening and closing prices. A white real body tells us that the close is higher than the open since the top of the white real body is the session's close and the bottom of the white real body is that session's open. A black (filled) real body shows that the close was lower than the open. The bottom of the black real body is the session's close, and the top of the black real body is that session's open. The session can be any time frame, from a minute to a month.

The vertical lines that extend above and below the real body are called the upper and lower shadows. The top of the upper shadow is the session's high; the bottom of the lower shadow is the session's low. The candlestick line uses the same data as a bar chart, but the color of the candlestick's real body and the length of the candle line's real body and shadows convey a snapshot of who's winning the battle between the bulls and the bears. For instance, when the real body is black, that means the stock closed *below* its opening price. This gives you an instant picture of a positive or negative close. Those of us who stare at charts for hours at a time find that candlesticks are not only easy on the eyes, they also convey strong visual signals sometimes missed on bar charts.

SIDELIGHT

When a real body, either white or black, closes at the high of the session, it has no upper shadow. Therefore, the Japanese say that candle has a "shaven head." When a real body closes at the low of the session and has no lower shadow, that candle has a "shaven bottom."

KEY POINT

The top of the upper shadow and the bottom of the lower shadow represent the highs and lows of a session, whether the real body is black or white.

Figure 14.1 shows basic candlestick formations. In (A), stock XYZ opens at 30 and closes at 35, with a high of 37 and a low of 29. In (B), XYZ opens at 35, closes at 30, and again has a high of 37 and low of 29.

Candlesticks, like bars, each represent a specified time frame. On a weekly chart, each candlestick represents one week; on a daily chart, each candlestick represents one day; and on a 15-minute intraday chart, each candlestick represents a 15-minute unit of time.

One of the most important benefits of using candles is that they give instant pictures of how traders and investors feel about a certain stock or market. A long, protracted real body translates into *very strong* opinion, either bullish or bearish.

Notice the long, white real body in Figure 14.1A. This white real body, showing the closing price multiple points *above* the opening price (in this case, 5 points), indicates

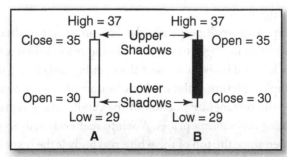

FIGURE 14.1   Constructing the Candlestick Line

extremely positive or bullish sentiment. In Figure 14.1B, the long, black real body, with the closing price several points *below* the open, reveals negative or bearish sentiment.

The upper shadow in Figure 14.1A tells you that buying pressure pushed XYZ up to a high of 37. Still, while the stock closed relatively high on the session, buyers were unable to hold it at 37 into the close. The lower shadow shows that selling pressure forced the stock to a low of 29. Nonetheless, buyers came in to offer support there and propelled it up to close at 35, 6 points higher than the low.

While we're talking about open and closing prices, we know that the Japanese place great importance on these critical time periods as they pertain to the trading day. They believe, as do most Western analysts, that the first hour of trading usually sets the tone for the day. One Japanese saying states, "The first hour of the morning is the rudder of the day."

On opening, the market has absorbed and digested the events that took place since the prior day's close. The results are often volatile. The impact of market reaction can cause radical price changes for equities, or even entire industry groups. By the hour's end, the flurry of activity may subside a bit, and market participants have a point of reference with which to work.

An American market adage contends, "The amateurs open the market, and the professionals close it." Although it's an overstatement to assume the market's open is populated strictly by novices, it's true that the close of the day usually produces heavy emotional involvement. During the last hour, many market players adjust their positions. This is the time when traders, investors, and institutional managers decide whether or not to hold positions overnight. Margin calls on the futures markets are calculated by their price at the close. No wonder the last hour can produce volatile price swings fueled by strong emotions and heightened volume.

Since both the opening and closing hours can be turbulent periods, if you choose to take part, remember to use caution and discipline.

In the next section, we'll discuss one of the most critical uses of candle charts: giving you early indications that the trend may be changing. Whether a mature, extended trend, or a shorter, intermediate-term trend is in place, candle lines and patterns display powerful clues that a shift in control from bulls to bears, or vice-versa, is in process or could be imminent. For a trader, this information is crucial. For an investor, recognizing these all-important signals could make the difference between keeping hefty gains or giving them back to the market. The material you learned in this section will aid you in learning how to interpret these potent signals.

SECTION THREE

Basic Market Strategies

Early recognition of potential trend reversals is one of the most important skills a trader/investor can cultivate. As you study candle charts and learn to recognize single candle lines and patterns, you will appreciate how candles offer an early heads up on possible trend reversals. In fact, most signals given by candle formations are reversal signals.

Candle charts often display reversal signals in a few sessions rather than over the longer time periods often needed for bar chart reversal signals. Using candle charts, you'll identify market turns quickly, which should help you to enter and exit the market with speed and accuracy.

In this section, we present the basics of trend reversals and how candles play such an important role. Also discussed are concepts inherent to trend changes and reversals: support and resistance levels and all-important breakouts and price closes above and below those levels.

In this section you will learn . . .

- How candles play a powerful role in recognizing early reversal signals
- How candle lines and patterns confirm support and resistance
- The importance of confirmation
- Why the closing price plays a key role in breaks above resistance and below support

Key terms to watch for:

- Trend reversal
- Uptrend
- Downtrend
- Consolidation
- Support and resistance
- Retracement
- Box range

■ Getting Started

The ability to recognize a potential trend reversal is one of the most important skills you can cultivate. Your ability to read candle lines and patterns will increase that skill many times over.

In this section we're going to get a topdown overview of candle lines and patterns and the signals they give in the contexts of uptrends, downtrends and trend shifts, or reversals.

To start with, let's examine the anatomy of a trend reversal. A Japanese proverb states, "Darkness lies one inch ahead." You need only watch the financial television networks to see the great degree of importance traders and investors place on foretelling market tops and bottoms to arrive at an early insight on upcoming moves. As you know, the common goal is to buy low and sell high or, in the case of selling short, to sell high, buy low.

On charts, Western trend reversal patterns include double and triple tops and bottoms, key reversal days, head-and-shoulders, cup-with-handles, and island tops and bottoms.

Although market cycles of alternating uptrends and downtrends interspersed with peaks and valleys are inevitable, you should remember that trends don't always end abruptly. In fact, trends usually occur slowly, in stages, as the underlying psychology shifts.

Remember the old market saying, "The trend is your friend." Successful trading entails staying on the right side of the trend (although most find this is easier said than done). Trend change or reversal signals are the market's way of warning. It means market psychology is in transformation and you need to adjust your trading style to reflect that environment change.

For example, if you see a reversal signal, you might consider initiating a new position only if that signal is in the direction of the major trend. Say your stock has been climbing in a strong uptrend. Then, it either consolidates sideways for a few sessions or moves down (retraces) to prior support. At this time you get a bullish candle signal. Since the major trend has been up, one can use the bullish candle signal to initiate a long position. A bullish candle signal in a bear trend should be used either to cover shorts or as an alert that the market may rally and to use that rally to sell since the major trend is down.

KEY POINT

When I say a bearish or bullish reversal with the candlesticks, it does not imply that the market will reverse from down to up (in the case of a bullish reversal) or from up to down (with a bearish reversal). It just means that the market has gone from up to neutral (with a bearish candle signal) or from down to neutral (in the case of a bullish candle signal). In other words, with these reversal signals, the odds of a turn have increased but are not assured.

Trend reversals or shifts are a modification in market psychology. In a strong uptrend, such as you see in Figure 14.2A, the bulls are in control. Shoulder-to-shoulder, optimistic bulls turn out in force, buying available supply and supporting ever-rising prices of stock XYZ. When a *retracement*, or sideways consolidation occurs (as it does from 1 to 2), the bulls stand aside, tucking their shares in their pockets. The stock rests for a time, then resumes its climb upward. Three shifts in psychology took place during each of these three movements in stock XYZ's strong uptrend.

In Figure 14.2B, the same bulls propelled XYZ higher with gusto. The market tops out at 3 (of course, we don't know it is a top until a few sessions later, when the stock descends). Again, those with long positions may have taken some or all of their profits. This time, however, the retracement turned into a trend reversal, barely stopping along the way.

Points 1, 2, and 3 in Figure 14.2 are reversals, and, as we don't know the extent of the move after the reversal starts, the candles will often be the first clue of a change in trend.

Besides scanning for possible trend changes, another critical component is asking, "Where are support and resistance?" Support and resistance on a chart can take

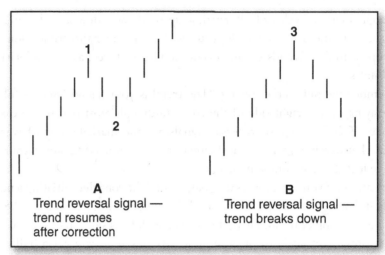

FIGURE 14.2 Top Reversals

multiple forms. It may be a prior high or low depicted in a price level or pattern. It may appear as a Western indicator, such as a trend line, moving average, or something as basic as the most recent high or low.

We know that a market often tops out at, or near, the same price range at which it pulled back at a previous time. It may also fall to a prior low price, then bounce off of that support level. If a candle signal confirms a support line, it would increase the potential bullish implications of that candle signal more than if that candle signal did not confirm support. Conversely, if a bearish candle signal emerges at a resistance zone, the chances of a turnaround have increased. As such, the rule is that the more technical signals—whether they are candle or Western or a combination of both—the more likely is a reversal. An example is shown in Figure 14.3 in which a bullish candle signal called a hammer confirms a support line.

In Section One of this chapter, we talked about the importance of the market's daily close. Let's take this a step further. Like most technical analysts, the Japanese place great emphasis on a security's closing price, especially if that price closes above resistance or below support. Think of it this way: If a stock, for instance, closes *above* a prior high, it means market participants are willing to pay more for it right then, *and* they are willing to hold it overnight. That means they are committed, and commitment is an extremely important factor in the movement of the financial markets.

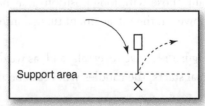

FIGURE 14.3 Candle Signal
Confirming Support

An intraday break of support or resistance does not have the same significance as a severing of support or resistance on a close.

Say you are studying a daily chart of a stock. Imagine it had moved sideways in a basing mode between $40 and $50 for the last five weeks or so. Suddenly, the bulls wrest control of the market, and the stock closes at $53. Do you see how important that closing price is? It means people are willing to buy and hold the stock at a higher price. The market has established new demand for the stock.

Conversely, if a market trades sideways in a *box range* (as the Japanese call consolidation patterns) for some period of time, then breaks down to close below that support area, it means that buyers were unwilling to step in and hold the price at that level. The bears are in control, and that market may fall to lower prices. If, however, a session's candle broke price support by dipping below it, but then closed inside the box range, that is not as bearish. This sort of session tells you that buyers stepped in before the close, and demand was strong enough to push the price back into the prior box range by session's end.

Now you understand how valuable tool candle formations are in the context of trend reversals, along with components inherent in those reversals, support and resistance.

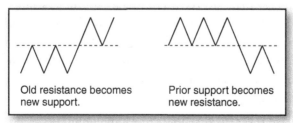

Old resistance becomes new support.

Prior support becomes new resistance.

FIGURE 14.4 Change of Polarity

CHAPTER 15

Point-and-Figure Charting

From Perry J. Kaufman, *Trading Systems and Methods, +Website*, 5th Edition (Hoboken, New Jersey: John Wiley & Sons, 2013), Chapter 5.*

Learning Objective Statements

- List three important characteristics of point-and-figure charts
- Define "box size" and "reversal"
- Describe how point-and-figure charts are constructed
- Explain the importance of box size to the sensitivity of point-and-figure charts
- Review the construction of various box size and reversal point-and-figure charts
- Identify common point-and-figure patterns
- Explain how trendlines are drawn on point-and-figure charts
- Locate basic signals on a point-and-figure chart
- Describe how price targets are obtained using a horizontal or vertical count on a point-and-figure chart

■ Point-and-Figure Charting

There does not appear to be any record of which came first, swing charting or point-and-figure charting. Both methods are very similar; however, point-and-figure has developed a much more extensive following. Point-and-figure charting is credited to Charles Dow, who is said to have used it just prior to the turn of the twentieth century. It has three important characteristics:

1. It has simple, well-defined trading rules.
2. It ignores price reversals that are below a minimum price move as determined by the *box size*.
3. It has no time factor (it is event-driven). As long as prices fail to change direction by the reversal value, the trend is intact.

---

* For Companion Website content access our Resources page at www.efficientlearning.com/cmt/resources/online-curriculum-materials/.

When point-and-figure charting first appeared, it did not contain the familiar boxes of Xs and Os. The earliest book containing the subject is reported to be *The Game in Wall Street and How to Play it Successfully*, published by Hoyle (not Edmond Hoyle, the English writer) in 1898. The first definitive work on the subject was by Victor De Villiers, who in 1933 published *The Point and Figure Method of Anticipating Stock Price Movement*. De Villiers worked with Owen Taylor to publish and promote a weekly point-and-figure service, maintaining their own charts; he was impressed by the simple, scientific methodology. As with many of the original technical systems, the application was intended for the stock market, and the rules required the use of every price change appearing on the ticker. It has also been highly popular among futures traders in the grain and livestock pits of Chicago. The rationale for a purely technical system has been told many times, but an original source is often refreshing. De Villiers said:[1]

The Method takes for granted:

1. That the price of a stock at any given time is its correct valuation up to the instant of purchase and sales (a) by the consensus of opinion of all buyers and sellers in the world and (b) by the verdict of all the forces governing the laws of supply and demand.
2. That the last price of a stock reflects or crystalizes everything known about or bearing on it from its first sale on the Exchange (or prior), up to that time.
3. That those who know more about it than the observer cannot conceal their future intentions regarding it. Their plans will be revealed in time by the stock's subsequent action.

The unique aspect of the point-and-figure and swing methods is that they ignore the passage of time. The point-and-figure chart differs from the swing chart in that each column representing an upswing is a series of boxes containing Xs, and each downswing is shown as a string of Os (Figure 15.1), and a mark is not placed unless a minimum price change occurs.

Silver									
854.0	X								
853.0	X	O	X						
852.0	X	O	X	O					
851.0		O	X	O	X				
850.0		O		O	X	O			
849.0				O	X	O			
848.0				O	X	O			
847.0				O					
846.0									

FIGURE 15.1   Point-and-Figure Chart.

[1] Victor De Villiers, *The Point and Figure Method of Anticipating Stock Price Movements* (1933; reprint New York, NY: Trader Press, 1966), 8.

The original *figure charts* were traditionally plotted on graph paper with square boxes, and only dots, or the **exact** price, were written in each box. The chart evolved to have prices written on the left scale of the paper, where each box represented a minimum price move. Some point-and-figure chartists then used a combination of *X*s and occasional digits (usually 0s and 5s every five boxes) to help keep track of the length of a move. In some cases the top of an upswing column was connected to the start of a downswing in the next column with a crossbar, and the bottom of a downswing column was connected to the beginning of the next upswing column. This gave the point-and-figure chart an appearance similar to the swing chart. Charts using 1, 3, and 5 points per box were popular, where each point represented a minimum price move. In the 5-point method, no entry was recorded unless the price change spanned 5 points.

Point-and-figure charts, which were commonly used on the floor of the Chicago Mercantile Exchange and the Chicago Board of Trade up to the late 1990s, are intended to show the greatest detail. Each box represents the minimum allowable price move, and reversals of direction use the traditional 3-box criteria. Floor traders use the charts to show only the short-term price moves, and leave a lot to the interpretation of patterns.

Plotting Prices Using the Point-and-Figure Method

To plot prices on a point-and-figure chart, start with a piece of square-box graph paper and mark the left scale using a conveniently small price increment. For example, each box may be set at $0.25 for Microsoft, $0.50 for IBM, 5.0 points for S&P 500 index, $1 for gold and platinum, 4/32 for 30-year bond futures, 1¢ for soybeans and silver, and so forth (as in Figure 15.1). The choice of a box size will make the chart more or less sensitive to changes in price direction as will be seen in later examples. The smaller the box size, the more changes in direction will be seen. This also corresponds to longer and shorter trends or major and minor trends. Therefore, a point-and-figure chartist looking for a long-term price movement will use a larger box size. Box sizes are often related to the current volatility of the markets.

Once the graph paper has been scaled and the prices entered along the left side, the chartist can begin. The first box is entered with the current closing price of the market. If the price of silver is 852.50 and a 1¢ (1¢ = 1.00) box is being used, a mark is placed in the box beside the value 852. An *X* or an *O* is used to indicate that the current price trend is up or down, respectively. Either an *X* or *O* may be used to begin—after that, it will be determined by the method.

The rules for plotting point-and-figure charts are easily shown as a flowchart in Figure 15.2. Preference is given to price movements that continue in the direction of the current trend. Therefore, if the trend is up (represented by a column of *X*s), the new high price is tested first; if the trend is down, the low price is given preference. The opposite price is checked only if the new price fails to increase the length of the column in the direction of the current trend.

The traditional point-and-figure method calls for the use of a *3-box reversal*, that is, the price must reverse direction by an amount that fills 3 boxes from the most extreme box of the last column before a new column can begin (it actually must fill

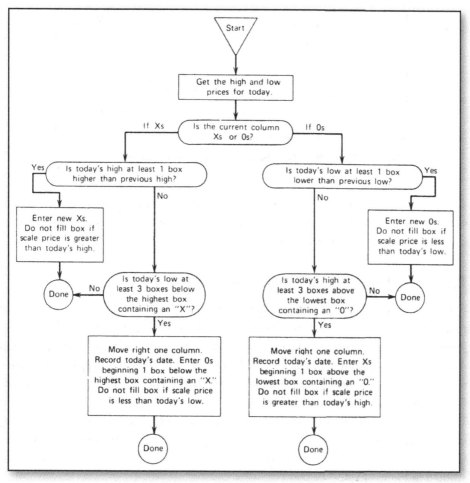

FIGURE 15.2 Point-and-Figure Daily Rules.

the fourth box because the extreme box is left blank). The importance of keeping the 3-box reversal has long been questioned by experienced point-and-figure traders. It should be noted that the net reversal amount (the box size times the number of boxes in the reversal) is the critical value. For example, a 5-point box for the NASDAQ 100 ETF (QQQ) with a 3-box reversal means that QQQ prices must reverse from the lows of the current downtrend by 15 points to indicate that an uptrend has started. The opposite combination, a 3-point box and a 5-box reversal, would signal a new trend at the same time, after a 15-point reversal. The difference between the two choices is that the smaller box size would recognize a smaller continuation of a price move by filling more boxes. Ultimately, the smaller box size will capture more of the price move; it is considered the preferable alternative. The choice of box size and reversal boxes will be considered later in more detail.

Painless Point-and-Figure Charts   There are a number of graphic charting and quote systems that allow a simple bar chart to be converted to point-and-figure automatically. It is still necessary to specify the box size and the reversal size. The reason for

```
Ascending Triple Top          Breakout of a Triple Bottom
            X ← BUY                    X   X
       X   X                      O X O X O
   X   X O X                      O X O X O
   X O X O X                      O   O   O
   X O X O                                      O ← SELL
       O
```

FIGURE 15.3   Best Formations from Davis's Study.

showing the construction in detail is that none of these services provide trading signals or performance results based on point-and-figure charting. For that, it will be necessary to code the instructions into a spreadsheet or a strategy development platform.

Point-and-Figure Chart Formations

It would be impossible for the average speculator to follow the original method of recording every change in price. When applied to stocks, these charts became so lengthy and covered so much paper that they were unwieldy and made interpretation difficult. In 1965, Robert E. Davis published *Profit and Profitability*, a point-and-figure study that detailed eight unique buy and sell signals. The study covered two stocks for the years 1914–1964, and 1100 stocks for 1954–1964. The intention was to find specific bull and bear formations that were more reliable than others. The study concluded that the best buy signal was an *ascending triple top* and the best sell signal was the *breakout of a triple bottom*, both shown in Figure 15.3 and with the other patterns studied in Figure 15.4.

Plotted using daily data, futures prices do not offer the variety of formations available in the stock market. The small number of markets and the high correlation of movement between many of the index and interest rate markets make the limitations of signal selection impractical. Instead, the most basic approach is used, where a buy signal occurs when an X in the current column is one box above the highest X in the last column of Xs, and the simple sell signal is an O plotted below the lowest O of the last descending column. The flexibility of the system lies in the size of the box; the smaller the size, the more sensitive the chart will be to price moves. In 1933, Wyckoff noted that it was advisable to use a chart with a different box size when the price of the stock varied substantially.[2]

Point-and-Figure Trendlines

Bullish and bearish trendlines are commonly used with point-and-figure charts. The top or bottom box that remains blank when a reversal occurs can form the beginning of a descending or ascending pattern at a 45° angle (diagonally through the corners of the

[2] Richard D. Wyckoff, *Stock Market Technique, Number One* (New York, NY: Wyckoff, 1933), 89.

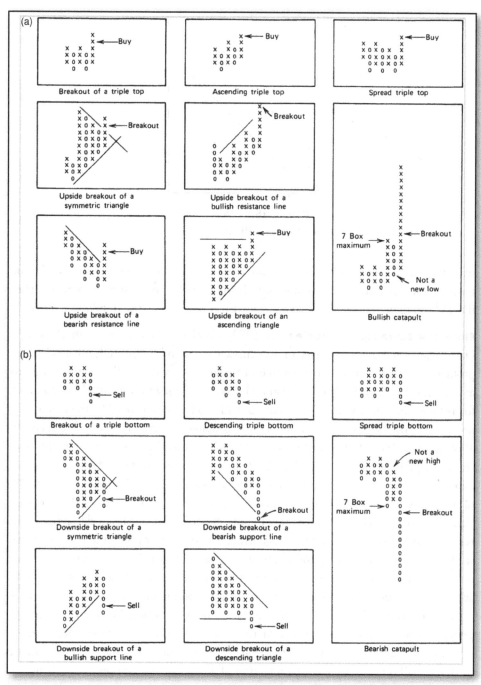

FIGURE 15.4 (a) Compound Point-and-Figure Buy Signals. (b) Compound Point-and-Figure Sell Signals.

boxes, providing the graph paper has square boxes). These 45° lines represent the major anticipated trends of the market. Once a top or bottom has been identified, a 45° line can be drawn down and to the right from the upper corner of the top boxes of *X*s, or up and towards the right from the bottom of the lowest box of *O*s (Figure 15.5). These

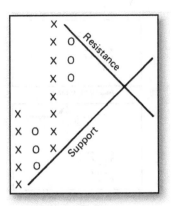

FIGURE 15.5 Point-and-Figure Trendlines.

trendlines are used to *confirm* the direction of price movement and are often used to filter the basic point-and-figure trading signals so that only long positions are taken when the 45° trendline is up and only shorts sales are entered when the trendline is down.

More Point-and-Figure Studies In 1970, Charles C. Thiel, Jr., with Robert E. Davis, completed the first purely futures market point-and-figure study[3] that calculated profitability of a reasonably large sample of markets by varying both the value of a box and the reversal criteria. With the standard 3-box reversal and only simple buy and sell formations, the tests showed 799 signals, of which 53% were profitable; the average net profit on all trades was $311 realized in approximately 50 days. The period studied was 1960 through 1969. In the mid-1970s, Zieg and Kaufman[4] performed a computerized study using the same rules but limiting the test period to six months ending May 1974, an extremely active market period. For the 22 commodities tested, 375 signals showed 40% of the trades were profitable; the net profit over all the trades was $306 and the average duration was 12.4 days. It is interesting to note that the most significant difference in the results of the two studies is in the average length of a trade, from 50 in the Thiel and Davis study to 12.4 days in the Zieg and Kaufman tests, indicating a change apparently induced by more volatile markets. Although the two tests varied in many of the details, the results are a strong argument for the consistency of the point-and-figure method as a trading tool.

In its current role, point-and-figure differs from traditional charting because it provides a rigid set of trading rules. Many of the formations are still subject to interpretation and are frequently used that way by floor traders. For the more systematic trader, it will tell exactly what penetration of a resistance or support level is necessary to generate a buy or sell signal and exactly where the stop-loss order should be placed to limit risk. It is this well-defined nature of point-and-figure charting that allows computer testing and evaluation.

[3] Charles Thiel and R. E. Davis, *Point and Figure Commodity Trading: A Computer Evaluation* (West Lafayette, IN: Dunn & Hargitt, 1970).

[4] Kermit C. Zieg, Jr., and Perry J. Kaufman, *Point and Figure Commodity Trading Techniques* (Larchmont, NY: Investors Intelligence, 1975). This book contains complete tabularized results of both point-and-figure tests.

A complete study of the point-and-figure method includes rules of charting, buy and sell signals, trendlines, geometric formations, and price objectives. They apply equally to point-and-figure charting. They have also been covered effectively in a book by Cohen and another by Zieg and Kaufman.[5] The following sections cover more advanced point-and-figure topics, including its relationship to bar charting, alternate plotting rules, risk-limited trading, and varying box size.

Point-and-Figure Box Size The box size used in a point-and-figure chart determines the sensitivity, or frequency of signals. The selection of the box size is critical to successful trading. For many years Chartcraft (Investors Intelligence) was the only major service that produced a full set of point-and-figure charts for the futures markets. A history of their box sizes is shown in Table 15.1. There are now a number of

TABLE 15.1	Point-and-Figure Box Sizes*							
		Prior to 1975[†]		1975[‡]	1977[‡]	1977[§]	1986[‡]	2002–2003
Futures Market	Units	Year	Box Size	Box Size	Box Size	Box Size	Box Size	Box Size
				Grains				
Corn	cents	1971	½	2	2	2	1	2
Oats	cents	1965	½	1	1		1	½
Soybeans	cents	1971	1	10	10	5	5	4¼
Soybean meal	pts	1964	50	500	500		100	200
Soybean oil	pts	1965	10	20	20		10	20
Wheat	cents	1964	1	2	2	2	1	1.5
				Livestock and Meats				
Live cattle	pts	1967	20	20	20		20	10
Live hogs	pts	1968	20	20	20		20	40
Pork bellies	pts	1965	20	20	20		20	75
				Other Agricultural Products				
Cocoa[¶]	pts	1964	20	100	100	50	10	2
Coffee	pts		(20)[†]	100	100	50	100	
Cotton	pts		(20)[†]	100	100		50	90
Lumber	pts		(100)[†]	100	100		100	170
Orange juice	pts	1968	20	20	100	20	100	100
Sugar	pts	1965	5	20	20		10	16
				Metals				
Copper	pts	1964	20	100	100	50	50	100
Gold	pts			50	100		400	200
Platinum	pts	1968	200	100	200	200	400	
Silver	pts	1971	100	200	200	400	1000	150

*All box sizes use a 3-box reversal and are in points (decimal fractions treated as whole numbers) unless otherwise indicated.
[†]Cohen (1972); parentheses indicate approximate values.
[‡]Courtesy of Chartcraft Commodity Service, Chartcraft, Inc., Larchmont, New York.
[§]Chart Analysis Limited, Bishopgate, London. Values are for long-term continuation charts.
[¶]Cocoa contract changed from cents/pound to dollars/ton.

[5] A.W. Cohen, *How to Use the Three-Point Reversal Method of Point and Figure Stock Market Trading* (Larchmont, NY: Chartcraft, 1972); and Kermit C. Zieg and Perry J. Kaufman, *Point & Figure Commodity Trading Techniques* (Larchmont, NY: Chartcraft, 1975).

services providing these charts, and they can easily be found by searching the Internet for "point-and-figure charts."

Since the 1970s, every traded commodity has had at least one major price move taking it to levels often greater than twice the normal price. Sugar and silver each topped at 10 times their value in 1970. By 2000 many technology stocks had surged 20 times their 1990 value only to retreat by as much as 90% in the next few years. These moves necessitate changes in box size in order to control the impact of the increased, and later decreased, volatility.

Table 15.2 shows the performance of the point-and-figure method from 2000 through 2010 for a selection of widely traded futures markets. When testing these markets, the first problem that surfaces is that each market needs its unique box size. For example, soybeans trading at $15/bushel will need a box size smaller than the DAX, trading at 6000. The box size reflects a sensitively to volatility during the period of the test data.

To solve that problem as simply as possible, the box sizes were initialized to a percentage of the price at the beginning of the test. These centered around 1%, so that gold at $1000/oz would have a box size of $10. All gold signals used the $10 box size and a 3-box reversal for a total directional reversal of $30. In Table 15.2a, all negative net profits are shaded in grey, and the best results for each market are outlined.

Results show inconsistency. The more trending markets, the interest rates and the euro, are generally profitable for all box sizes. The noisier markets, primarily the equity index markets, show consistent losing results. Eurodollar interest rates show few trades because a percentage of the price at 99.00 is far too big for a box size. To get the right box size, the series would need to be converted to yields. The same is true of the longer-term rates, even though both 10-year notes and 30-year bonds showed good returns. The grains were also inconsistent, with soybeans showing too many trades (see Table 15.2b) while wheat appears normal. This reflects the volatility of the individual markets.

Even during this 10-year test, the volatility of each market would have changed considerably. Systems that are event driven, such as swings, point-and-figure, and breakouts, are not bothered by low volatility for moderate periods of time. They typically hold the same position until something new happens. However, if at the start of the test the volatility was much lower than at the end, there will be few trades at the beginning and much more at the end. Results will be distorted, with greater importance given to the more volatile periods.

It seems reasonable to conclude that the change in price and, consequently, the change in volatility determine the most practical choice of box size. As an example, if we look at the best choice of box size for a selection of stocks and industrial groups for 2003, we get the results shown in Table 15.3. These are plotted as a scatter diagram in Figure 15.5. They show a clear relationship between price level and box size. We will use this pattern to create a more dynamic point-and-figure chart. Rules for varying box sizes and risks associated with these price and volatility changes are discussed later in the section, "Point-and-Figure with Variable Box Size."

TABLE 15.2a Net Profits for the Point-and-Figure Method. Initial box sizes range from 0.10% to 2.0% for a selection of futures markets, 2000–2010. Negative results are in grey, and the best results for each market are outlined.

Box (%)	Crude Oil	Cotton	DAX	EUR	Bund	Euro-dollars	S&P	Gold	Heating Oil	Japanese Yen	NASDAQ	Soy-beans	10-Year Notes	30-Year Bonds	Wheat
2.0	3540	-12540	31450	54538	0	0	-6838	-10200	22142	-925	4895	-8725	19641	-5188	-26200
1.9	-10510	-22970	80800	74600	0	0	-11325	3450	10580	14413	-2165	11150	16484	14813	-28813
1.8	-42370	44990	186225	74875	14360	0	11975	-24610	-55797	-9563	-11730	650	34672	2906	-32288
1.7	-9840	-45610	133513	89763	7240	0	-11500	25300	-122653	14100	-13985	18275	13953	26156	-32750
1.6	-28630	-67010	42425	104875	14580	0	-6875	-740	-97297	-14363	-21930	9700	24766	-3438	-26688
1.5	-34170	-47705	-4738	88325	2840	0	12225	-2860	-82555	-31538	-1215	8650	8328	17156	-7663
1.4	26410	-42895	74125	89125	-9120	0	2400	12480	-60967	-1263	-21130	10900	-2953	49563	-13363
1.3	6860	-53445	123688	105038	-6350	0	25850	16080	-60955	-11725	-29685	8000	-1766	20219	-13225
1.2	-13150	-53080	105950	128650	-9260	0	-20000	19980	-40110	-3488	-29150	-18000	16	2719	-1013
1.1	46420	-39220	92313	119838	710	0	-37300	33020	-23822	-5150	-43535	-5275	-1328	33688	2750
1.0	46420	-33535	175338	107063	20890	0	41250	-15280	-57464	-9175	-24410	-12550	-9609	23313	-15113
0.9	87410	-6700	-16375	117800	31980	0	-46500	9820	-61828	-66838	-12890	-22025	1828	10875	2538
0.8	32520	-3920	-15975	111700	22820	0	1250	-13020	-48313	-57213	-350	-7000	2078	60688	-24475
0.7	30770	2310	-8888	90063	16360	0	-1363	2500	56268	-90025	15010	1925	1016	52500	14963
0.6	-27060	25630	888	47263	21830	0	-40763	120	-82870	-50163	-16020	-11325	22766	31063	-2375
0.5	22460	31090	-21313	50988	6380	0	-42388	23880	-118335	-76950	-5540	-5575	16188	16188	20825
0.4	-31900	20820	22263	9000	17290	0	-55688	33300	-65814	-48463	-14380	3950	17813	24500	13350
0.3	-46300	6060	18913	34075	11760	0	-56163	12020	-71665	-25863	-25310	12875	-4063	-10375	20838
0.2	6640	13160	-48988	51250	-17960	7175	-54538	14340	-86684	-9213	-23160	14400	16031	3063	25788
0.1	-19020	9620	-15288	55525	-19500	8012.5	-44638	22920	-93848	25513	-27340	15700	-10438	10063	26663

CHARTS, TRENDS, AND PATTERNS

TABLE 15.2b   The Number of Trades Associated with the Performance in Table 15.2a

Box (%)	Crude Oil	Cotton	DAX	EUR	Bund	Euro-dollars	S&P	Gold	Heating Oil	Japanese Yen	NASDAQ	Soybeans	10-Year Notes	30-Year Bonds	Wheat
2.0	53	41	74	9	0	0	17	53	59	4	17	193	4	16	17
1.9	61	47	76	7	0	0	19	51	59	4	19	203	6	16	21
1.8	71	51	80	11	2	0	17	69	67	8	21	209	4	18	23
1.7	65	51	90	11	2	0	23	64	79	6	27	221	6	16	29
1.6	69	59	106	11	2	0	23	71	81	10	33	225	8	24	31
1.5	83	57	120	17	4	0	23	73	91	12	29	231	14	22	33
1.4	79	63	126	19	6	0	27	82	99	10	41	245	14	24	35
1.3	91	67	134	23	6	0	37	92	111	14	47	251	14	32	41
1.2	109	82	152	23	8	0	39	100	135	14	51	267	18	42	41
1.1	117	88	168	27	6	0	47	112	145	20	67	273	20	44	45
1.0	139	100	188	33	10	0	55	125	163	22	69	297	24	54	55
0.9	141	100	236	37	10	0	61	142	183	32	79	313	32	66	61
0.8	175	116	276	49	14	0	65	154	199	38	97	303	38	76	83
0.7	195	150	314	65	18	0	79	162	229	50	107	307	48	102	97
0.6	225	174	358	101	26	0	117	184	241	60	157	319	52	130	111
0.5	227	198	394	129	38	0	149	192	275	92	187	325	78	169	135
0.4	255	228	418	186	61	0	189	208	273	127	235	325	120	217	167
0.3	273	268	470	231	103	0	241	250	297	179	261	309	172	267	199
0.2	277	290	520	275	187	4	283	278	297	247	287	309	239	289	251
0.1	285	290	546	293	285	8	299	282	297	293	293	307	294	297	285

TABLE 15.3	Point-and-Figure Box Sizes— Stocks and Sectors 2003	
Market	Box Size	Average Price
AMZN	13	25
AMR	38	20
AOL	6	13.5
GE	25	27
IBM	143	72
INTC	80	17.5
MRK	162	52
XOM	50	34
Aerospace	17.5	1,800
Biotech	15	700
Large banks	8	1,000
Life Insurance	22	1,450
Semiconductors	1.6	300

Point-and-Figure Trading Techniques

The basic point-and-figure trading signals are triggered on new highs and new lows:

> *Buy* when the filled column of *X*s, the current upswing, rises above the previous column of *X*s by one box.
> *Sell* when the filled column of *O*s, the current downswing, falls below the low of the previous column of *O*s by one box.

Using the basic rules, you are always in the market, reversing from long to short and from short to long, unless you only trade stocks from the long side.

There are alternate methods for selecting point-and-figure entry and exit points that have become popular. Buying or selling on a pullback after an initial point-and-figure signal is one of the more common system entries because it can limit risk and still maintain a logical stop-loss point. Of course, there are fewer opportunities to trade when only small risk is allowed, and there is a proportionately greater chance that the trade will be stopped out because the entry and exit points are close together. There are three approaches recommended for entering on limited risk:

1. *Wait for a reversal back to within an acceptable risk, then buy or sell immediately with the normal point-and-figure stop.* Figure 15.6 shows various levels of risk in IBM with $2.00 boxes. The initial buy signal is at $150, with the simple sell signal for liquidation at $134, giving a risk of $16 per share. Instead of buying as prices reach new highs, wait for a reversal after the buy signal, then buy when the low for the day penetrates the box corresponding to your acceptable level of risk. Three possibilities are shown in Figure 15.7. Buying into a declining market assumes that the support level (at $134 in this example) will hold, preventing the stop-loss level from being reached. To increase confidence, the base of the formation should be as broad as possible. The test

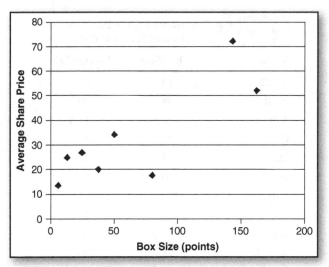

FIGURE 15.6 Point-and-Figure Box Sizes Are Larger When Prices Are Higher or Volatility Is Greater.

```
Price  _____
160
158  o
156  o
154  o
152  o  x
150  o  x  o        [x]  <----- Simple buy signal, standard risk of $16
148  o  x  o  x     x
146  o  x  o  x  o  x  <----- Enter on pullback to 146, risk $12
144  o  x  o  x  o  x
142  o  x  o  x  o  x  <----- Enter on pullback to 142, risk $8
140  o  x  o  x  o  x
138  o     o  x  o  x  <----- Enter on pullback to 138, risk $4
136        o     o
134                 [ ]  <----- Stop-loss and reversal at $134
```

FIGURE 15.7 Entering IBM on a Pullback with Limited Risk.

of a triple bottom or a spread triple bottom after a buy signal is a more reasonable place to go long than a simple buy after a small reversal in the middle of a move.

It is not advisable to reduce risk by entering on the simple buy signal and placing a stop-loss at the point of the first reversal (3 boxes below the highs). The advantage of waiting for the pullback is that it uses the logical support level as a stop. A stop-loss placed nearby following a breakout has no logical basis and will quickly result in a losing trade.

2. *Enter the market on the second reversal back in the direction of the original signal.* As shown in Figure 15.8, the first reversal following a signal may not reach the target risk level. Price movement does not often accommodate our expectations; therefore, a more flexible rule is needed. One technique is to enter a long position on the second upswing. That is, do not enter a long position on the initial buy signal but wait until a 3-box reversal has caused a downswing. As

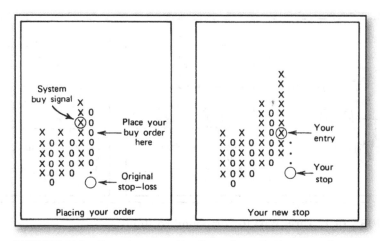

FIGURE 15.8 Entering on a Confirmation of a New Trend after a Pullback.

the downswing continues, place a trailing buy order at the point where the next upswing would begin, at the fourth box above the lowest box of Os. If the order is executed, then there is a new position in the direction of the trend; however, the risk has been limited to the value of four boxes, which is the new trend reversal point. In a wide-ranging, volatile market, this entry may be better than the original point-and-figure buy signal.

This technique is frequently used by traders, who firmly believe that a reversal follows immediately after a breakout, to prevent both high risk and false signals. If the pullback that follows the breakout continues in an adverse direction, penetrates the other support or resistance level, and triggers the original system stop-loss, then no entry occurs, thus saving a substantial whipsaw loss. These traders are essentially looking for a confirmation of direction. However, if prices continue upward, without a pullback, the trade may be missed entirely.

The reversal principle in Step 2 can also be effective for building positions. In bar charting, a pullback to a bullish support line or a bearish resistance line is a point for adding to a position with a risk limited to penetration of the major trendline. The equivalent procedure using point-and-figure is to add on each reversal back in the direction of the trend using the newly formed stop-loss point to exit the entire position (as shown in Figure 15.9).

3. *Allowing for irregular patterns.* Price patterns are not always orderly, and the price activity at the time of a trend change can be very indecisive. One basic trading principle demands that the market confirm a new high before buying; the first new high might simply occur during an erratic sideways pattern, or an expanding formation after a period of low volatility. If prices are required to make a new high by more than one box on the next upward thrust, and raise the lowest point of the reversal by another box on the third upward thrust, we are actually demanding that

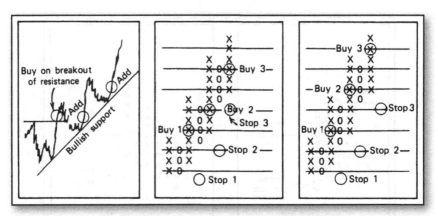

FIGURE 15.9 Three Ways to Compound Positions.

the momentum, or speed of price movement, increase before a position is set.[6] The pattern of higher highs and higher lows is similar to upwards acceleration.

This technique, which tends to minimize false breakouts, may be modified to increase the confirmation threshold from two to three or four boxes as market volatility increases. If the box size is changed according to volatility, as discussed later in this chapter, confirmation can remain at two boxes.

Point-and-Figure Trading Risk

I go long or short as close as I can to the danger point, and if the danger becomes real I close out and take a small loss.

—Jesse Livermore to Richard Wyckoff[7]

The point-and-figure method is a simple trend-following concept, yet in its normal use it is subject to interpretation using trendlines and geometric formations. Why is that necessary? The answer involves the risk of an individual trade. In the previous section, the risk of a trade was changed by using alternate entry points based on pullbacks; however, there are other choices.

The treatment of the same price move can be seen by looking at both a bar chart and a corresponding point-and-figure chart for the same period (Figure 15.10). The most basic bar chart trading method uses horizontal support and resistance lines to define a trading range; when the resistance line is penetrated, a long position is entered. This is the same concept used in the swing method. A stop-loss is placed below the resistance line in order to close out the trade in the event of a false breakout. An alternate placement of the stop-loss could have been below the support line, allowing the new bull move some latitude to develop.

---

[6] Adam Hewison, "The Will Rogers Theory of Point & Figure Trading," *Technical Analysis of Stocks & Commodities* (August 1991).

[7] Richard D. Wyckoff, *Stock Market Technique, Number One* (New York, NY: Wyckoff, 1933), 2.

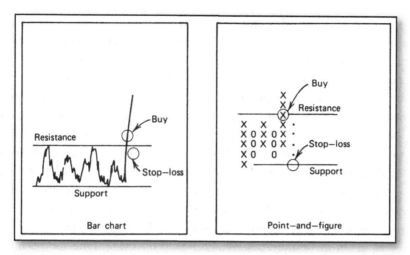

FIGURE 15.10   Placement of Point-and-Figure Stops.

Viewing this chart pattern in retrospect makes the selection of the entry point and the placement of stops or reversal of position seem obvious; however, when trading, the choice of the support and resistance lines is not usually as clear. The time to enter a trade after a breakout is never quite certain, and the position for the stop or reversal depends on the volatility of prices and the risk that you are willing to take. In contrast to the ambiguity of the bar chart, the point-and-figure method defines the support and resistance levels exactly, establishes a place to buy in advance, and designates the position for the stop-loss below the rectangular congestion area, always at the place where a long position would turn to a short sale. The rigidity of the method allows only one place for the stop-loss and fixes the risk as the difference between the support and resistance lines, a total of five boxes in the example shown in Figure 15.10. In the bar chart, the risk might have been held to the equivalent of two boxes using the closer stop-loss, where the trade is exited on a pullback into the range; however, a very small risk often results in being stopped out of the trend prematurely.

Take It and Run!   From time to time, you find yourself the beneficiary of a substantial price move where there is an uncomfortably large profit. It is normal to consider how much of the unrealized profits will be returned before the system finally generates an exit signal. At these times, some traders prefer to take the profits. These are decisions that go beyond the area of technical analysis, although they could be rigorously tested. If the profit currently held in open positions is enough to sustain a life of leisure, a home in the mountains, membership in a country club, and a small investment in a hotel or restaurant to occupy your time, then take it and run! A trading system should not depend on a single, very large profit to work over time. It should have a steady, successful profile. We can therefore reason that any extremely large profit is a windfall and should be taken. Occasionally, a price shock gives you a windfall profit that has nothing to do with a well-designed system or astute trading. It is another opportunity to take profits. If you are correct, prices will reverse after you have gotten out, and there will be an opportunity to reenter the trade at a much better level.

If you cannot sleep nights and the unrealized profits are just enough to satisfy some important obligations, but one or two adverse days would ruin the opportunity, then take the profits and begin again with a small investment. While it is important to follow a system in order to benefit from the long-term expectations, investor "risk preference" preempts the act of blindly following all rules. Sometimes you need to reduce the market exposure, whether the current position is a profit or a loss. If you have some risk latitude, a logical place to capture most of the current open profits and still have a chance of increasing those profits is to use the point-and-figure reversal value for your exit. If the 3-box reversal represents only 10% of the open profits, then you have a significant chance of profiting from a continuation of the price move. The *reversal value*, the box size times the number of boxes in a reversal (usually 3), is meant to indicate a significant contrary move and can be used as an objective indication of a change of direction. One approach to taking profits is shown in Figure 15.11.

In Figure 15.11a, a trailing 3-box reversal value is used for the stop-loss once there is a sustained move of at least 10 boxes. To reenter the move in the same direction, the same technique is used (Figure 15.11b), adding another 4 boxes of profits while keeping the new risk small. In Figure 15.11c, this method lost 4 boxes of the potential profits when the reversal was short lived.

In general, taking small profits in this way does not improve overall profitability because it most often misses the biggest moves. It may, however, reduce the risk of loss at a rate even faster than the reduction in profits, yielding a better reward-to-risk ratio. A new rule should be carefully tested to know its effect on different market conditions before it is used.

Control of risk can also be accomplished effectively using *volatility stabilization* methods. These continually adjust your position size to maintain a *target volatility*. If the volatility of either a market or your portfolio increases sharply, volatility stabilization will cause positions to be cut in order to bring your risk down to an acceptable level.

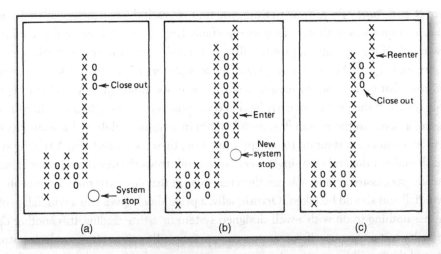

FIGURE 15.11 Cashing In on Profits.

Day	High	Low													
1	$8.02	$7.90	$8.40			X									X
2	$8.11	$7.95	$8.35			X									X
3	$8.13	$7.92	$8.30			X									X
4	$8.18	$7.96	$8.25			X						X			X
5	$8.25	$8.10	$8.20			X						X	O		X
6	$8.32	$8.08	$8.15			X						X	O		X
7	$8.40	$8.25	$8.10	X		X				X		X	O		
			$8.05	X	O	X				X	O	X			
			$8.00	X	O	X				X	O	X			
			$7.95	X	O					X	O				
			$7.90	X						X					
	(a)				(b)						(c)				

FIGURE 15.12 Alternate Methods of Plotting Point-and-Figure Reversals. (a) Sample prices for plotting. (b) Traditional method. (c) Alternate rule taken on day 6.

Alternate Treatment of Reversals Traditional point-and-figure charting favors the continuing trend. On highly volatile days, *broad ranging days* (also called *outside days*), it is possible for both a trend continuation and a 3-box reversal to occur. Point-and-figure rules require that the trend continuation be recorded and the reversal ignored. Figure 15.12 shows a comparison of the two choices. In the example, prices are in an uptrend when a new 1-box high and a 3-box reversal both occur on Day 6, as seen in Figure 15.12a. In Figure 15.12b, the traditional approach is taken, resulting in a continuous upward trend with a stop-loss at 7.90. Taking the reversal first as an alternate rule, Figure 15.12c shows the same trend with a stop-loss now at 8.05, 15 points closer.

Plotting the reversal first usually works to the benefit of the trader; both the stop-loss and change of trend will occur sooner. Subsequent computer testing proved this to be true. This alternative does not work when the reversal value is small and broad ranging days (that trigger the optional reversals) occur frequently.

Selecting Trades

Not all trades are profitable in any trading system. Some analysts prefer point-and-figure charts because both the profit objective and the risk can be identified at the time of entry. The profit objective can be calculated using the vertical or horizontal count, and the risk is the size of the price reversal needed to cause the opposite signal. Trades are then taken only if the return to risk ratio is greater than 2.0.

As with other trending systems, 45° trendlines can be drawn to identify the current dominant trend. Trades may be taken only in the direction of that trend. In a bull market, new short signals are ignored until the box is filled that penetrates the upwards bullish trendline. Then the bias switches to the short side.

Price Objectives

Point-and-figure charting has two unique methods for calculating price objectives: *horizontal counts* and *vertical counts*. These techniques do not eliminate the use of the standard bar charting objectives, such as support and resistance levels, which apply here as well.

The Horizontal Count   The time that prices spend in a consolidation area is considered directly related to the size of the subsequent price move. One technique for calculating price objectives is to measure the width of the consolidation (the number of columns on a bar chart) and project the same measurement up or down as the target of the move. The point-and-figure horizontal count method is a more exact approach to the same idea.

The upside price objective is calculated as

$$H_U = P_L + (W \times R)$$

where H_U = the upside horizontal count price objective
   P_L = the price of the lowest box of the base formation
   W = the width of the bottom formation (number of columns)
   R = the reversal value (number of boxes times the value of one box)

To use this formula, the *base* (width of the bottom or top formation) needs to be identified. Count the number of columns, W, not including the breakout column and multiply that width by the value of a minimum reversal, R; then add that result to the bottom point of the base to get the upper price objective. The base can always be identified after the breakout has occurred. For example, Figure 15.13 shows the March 74 contract of London Cocoa (£4 box) forming a very long but clear base. The reversal value is £12, and the width of the base is 19 columns (not counting the last column, which included the breakout). Added to the lowest point of the base (£570) this gives an objective of £798, reached on the left shoulder of the topping formation. Another alternative is the wider base, marked as $W_2 = 25$. Using this selection results in a price objective of £870, by adding $25 \times £12 = £300$ to £570, the lowest point of the base.

The downside objective is calculated in the same manner as the upside objective:

$$H_D = P_H - (W \times R)$$

where H_D = the downside horizontal count price objective
   P_H = the price of the highest box of the top formation
   W = the width of the top formation (number of columns)
   R = the reversal value

Some examples are given for downside objectives in the same Cocoa diagram (Figure 15.13). A small correction top could be isolated at the £720 level and two possible top widths, W_3 and W_5, could be chosen. The broader top, W_3, has a width of nine and a downside objective of £632. The shorter top, W_5, has a width of five and a downside objective of £680. Although the closer objective, calculated from W_5, is easy to reach, the farther one is reasonable because it coincides with a strong intermediate support level at about £640.

The very top formation, W_4, was small and only produced a nearby price objective similar to the first downside example; there would be no indication that prices were ready for a major reversal. The top also forms a clear head-and-shoulders pattern, which could be used in the same manner as in bar charting to find an objective. Using that technique, the distance from the top of the head to the point on the neckline

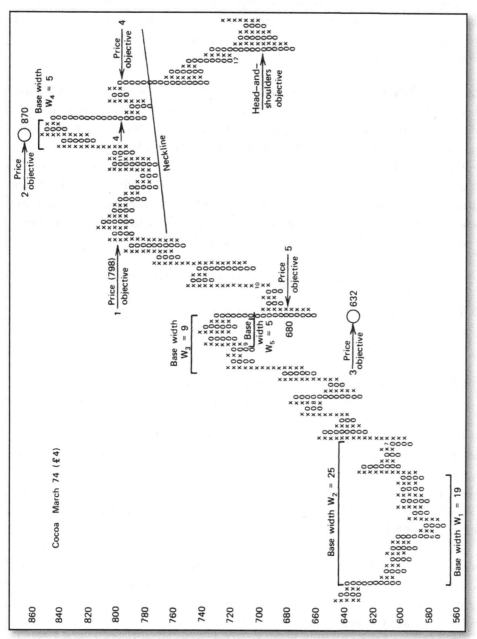

FIGURE 15.13   Horizontal Count Price Objectives.

directly below is 20 boxes; then downside price objective is 20 boxes below the point where the neckline was penetrated by the breakout of the right shoulder, at £776, giving £696 as the objective.

The horizontal count can also be applied to a breakout from a triangular formation, similar to the one on the very far right in Figure 15.13 (marked "Head-and-shoulders objective"). The width of the formation is the widest point in the center of the triangle, and the upwards objective is also measured from the center, rather than from the bottom of the triangle.

The Vertical Count   The vertical count is a simpler and more definitive calculation than the horizontal count. As with the horizontal count, there is adequate time to identify the formations and establish a price objective before it is reached. The vertical count is a measure of volatility (the amount of rebound from a top or bottom) and can be used to determine the size of a retracement after a major price move. To calculate the upside vertical count price objective, locate the first reversal column after a bottom formation. To do this, a bottom must be established with one or more tests, or a major resistance line must be broken to indicate that a bottom is in place. The vertical count price objective is then calculated:

$$V_{up} = Lowest\ box + (First\ reversal\ boxes \times Minimum\ reversal\ boxes)$$

The downside vertical count price objective is just the opposite:

$$V_{down} = Highest\ box - (First\ reversal\ boxes \times Minimum\ reversal\ boxes)$$

where   *First reversal boxes* = the number of boxes in the first reversal
            Minimum reversal boxes = the number of boxes needed for a chart reversal

Examples illustrating the vertical count are easy to find. In the QQQ chart (Figure 15.14), the NASDAQ low is clearly in early October 2002, followed by an upwards reversal of 13 boxes. Each box is $0.25, giving a total reversal of $3.25. Multiply the reversal amount by 3, the number of boxes in a reversal, and add that value, 9.75, to the low of $20.00 to get the target of $29.75. That value was reached during May 2003.

A secondary low in the QQQ chart occurs in February 2003 at $23.50. The first reversal that follows is seven boxes, or $1.75. Multiple 1.75 by 3 and add the result to the low to get the target of $28.75. The two objectives confirm each other. As a simple measurement tool based on recognizing key highs or lows, the vertical count relies on volatility to determine the extent of the move that follows. It can be quite accurate at times; otherwise it is likely to understate the expected price move.

In Figure 15.15, Intel is used to show frequent possibilities for the point-and-figure vertical count. As with QQQ, the chart uses a box size of 25 points ($0.25) and a 3-box reversal. The low in August 2002 at $19.00 gives a target of $27.25 reached at the end of October. The high in early January 2003 points to a very nice

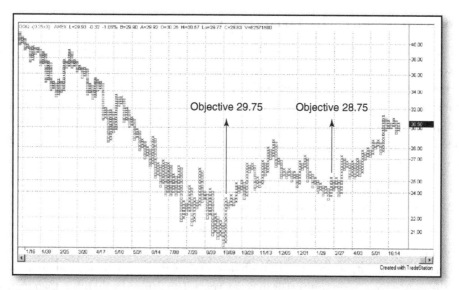

FIGURE 15.14 Point-and-Figure Vertical Count for QQQ. The major low in October 2002 had a reversal of 13 boxes, each with a value of 0.25, for a total of 3.25. Multiplying by 3 and adding the result, 9.75, to the lowest value $20.00, gives the price objective of 29.75. The second bottom in February 2003 shows a reversal of 7 boxes and gives a target of 28.75.

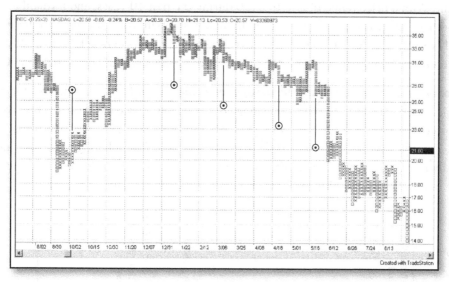

FIGURE 15.15 Intel Vertical Count Examples. This chart of Intel had many possibilities for the point-and-figure vertical count, all of which understate the actual price move. The vertical count is a good tool for setting initial objectives, but it is not a magic wand.

interim low in April, but falls far short of the actual low. Two other midrange price reversals could be used to find additional downside targets, each of which is successful but also fall short of predicting the true low of the stock. The vertical count can be very reliable but should not be expected to be a magic wand.

Point-and-Figure with Variable Box Sizes

In the section "Point-and-Figure Box Size," we looked at the results of various fixed point box sizes for a selection of markets. An optimization showed the net profits from boxes varying from 0.10% to 2.0%, all using a 3-box reversal (see Table 15.2). The inconsistency of results shows that each market must be treated uniquely, or that a more general approach to volatility-adjusting the box sizes is needed. Two possible solutions that would change the box size daily (or periodically) are based on

1. A fixed percentage of the current price
2. A fixed multiple of the average true range

These two methods will be applied to three futures markets, the euro, S&P, and gold, for the period from 2000 through 2010. That interval had every combination of price movement, strong trends, both down (after the tech bubble) and up, as well as the most severe economic crisis in many years. The price of gold more than tripled as well. Each showed very different results in Table 15.2.

To further support the need for a more flexible approach, consider crude oil, shown in Figure 15.16. The right scale shows the price of continuous futures (the cash price peaked near $150/bbl) and the left scale the annualized volatility in percent. With a price range of $30 to $150 during the past 10 years, and a volatility of less than 10% to near 60%, no one choice of box size will work. If you find a successful box size for 2007, it would be too large to generate any orders before 2000. If you used the best box size for the 1990s, it would be changing signals every day in 2007.

Boxes Based on a Fixed Percentage of Price Volatility is directly related to price; therefore, we can use a percentage of the current price to adjust the box size. For gold at $500, a 0.5% box size gives a $2.50 box and a $7.50 reversal criteria. At $1500, the box size is $7.50 and the reversal $22.50. With gold highly volatile, and daily ranges greater than $22.50, that seems a bit sensitive, so a 1% box size might be better. Prices may also have been represented on a log scale.

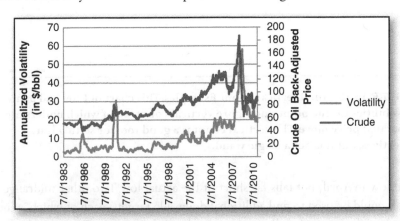

FIGURE 15.16 Annualized Volatility of Crude Oil in $/bbl Using Back-Adjusted Futures.

TABLE 15.4

TABLE 15.4 Results of Using Point-and-Figure with Variable Box Size Based on a Fixed Percentage Futures Data from 2000 through 2010

Box (%)	Net Profits or Losses			Number of Trades		
	EUR	S&P	Gold	EUR	S&P	Gold
2.0	0	19,538	13,770	0	21	6
1.9	0	30,650	51,160	0	19	8
1.8	0	−28,875	41,260	0	23	8
1.7	0	−29,038	11,4440	0	28	10
1.6	0	7,150	6,100	0	37	16
1.5	0	11,625	55,120	0	45	22
1.4	0	−14,300	89,540	0	45	24
1.3	54,900	56,050	−52,000	1	57	30
1.2	57,988	85,450	9,180	3	71	31
1.1	49,250	54,800	−33,800	4	77	42
1.0	71,013	58,875	45,520	7	101	62
0.9	15,575	81,525	−57,740	9	129	78
0.8	−100,200	100,200	−54,120	17	149	102
0.7	−73,000	85,400	−46,240	29	185	130
0.6	−30,288	111,500	−61,520	61	245	158
0.5	110,863	93,275	−87,640	110	305	230
0.4	−47,438	115,800	−13,8550	196	385	292
0.3	−55,750	89,075	−13,4300	317	449	380
0.2	46,475	106,650	−13,5380	461	553	498
0.1	46,225	111,100	−12,9900	553	593	556

When the box size is varied each day, and the point-and-figure chart is essentially redrawn, rising price will tend to hold the position longer because the reversal criteria get larger. On the other side, falling price will shorten the reversal and may generate a new signal where there was none yesterday.

Results in Table 15.4 are very different from those in Table 15.2. Where the euro was profitable everywhere in the original test, it has no trades for higher percentages and is profitable in only half of the remaining trades. The S&P, however, has the opposite result. Instead of erratic, mostly losing results, it is highly profitable for box sizes less than 1.4%. Gold has both better and worse results. Overall, this method changes the shape of the results but seems inconsistent.

Boxes Based on a Multiple of the Average True Range A clear problem with the percentage method in the previous section is that each market has a different level of volatility and that volatility changes. A percentage of the closing price is not sufficient to capture these variations. One measure that has proved valuable is the average true range. In this strategy, the average true range over the past 50 days

TABLE 15.5 Results of Using Point-and-Figure with Variable Box Size Based on a Multiple of the Average True Range (Factor) Futures Data from 2000 through 2010

Factor	Net Profits or Losses			Number of Trades		
	EUR	S&P	Gold	EUR	S&P	Gold
3.0	42,900	−1,800	85,590	5	9	8
2.8	24,913	−2,925	73,070	7	9	10
2.6	38,888	−9,563	76,410	7	11	12
2.4	38,788	3,625	71,030	7	9	8
2.2	−9,313	1,088	23,350	11	11	13
2.0	−77,363	−88	18,740	11	13	14
1.8	−17,538	−5,013	58,440	13	15	18
1.6	−23,688	4,763	33,980	13	15	22
1.4	12,538	5,713	24,070	21	17	24
1.2	31,088	21,150	19,30	31	21	26
1.0	16,963	39,538	−490	33	27	44
0.8	46,463	25,463	31,940	39	41	50
0.6	30,838	14,113	53,170	75	61	68
0.4	55,513	−18,163	14,320	121	127	126
0.2	18,538	−4,588	30,270	253	203	223

was multiplied by a factor, shown in the first column of Table 15.5. While the factor does not change, the volatility will vary considerably causing the box sizes to vary.

Results can be seen as much more uniform in both net profits and the number of trades. Rather than no trades in the euro, the three markets all show about the same pattern of trades based on the factor size. Profits also cluster. That is, the losing results are mostly adjacent to one another. All markets, on average, did very well. While this is intended to be an example of the way a strategy can adapt to changing volatility, it seems to show that there are some techniques that will succeed.

Finding the True Price-Volatility Relationship One other method must be discussed. The fixed percentage and ATR approaches were convenient and easy to program. But perhaps the best results will come from finding the true price-volatility relationship. As an example, we calculated the rolling 20-day annualized volatility of crude oil using futures from 1983 to 2010. Figure 15.17 shows that relationship as a scatter diagram. While there are sets of points near the top of the chart, the underlying relationship is very clear, clustering at about 7% when crude was $20 and reaching about 50% when crude was $140. This cannot be found using a linear regression because the higher outliers will cause the regression line to have a steeper ascending angle.

Stock Dividends and Splits When using point-and-figure charts for stocks, an adjustment must be made whenever a stock dividend is issued or the stock splits,

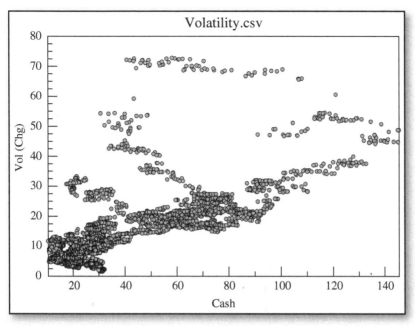

FIGURE 15.17 Volatility Relationship for Crude Oil, 1983–2010 (using PSIplot).

Activity	Stock Multiplication Factor
10% stock dividend	1.1
30% stock dividend	1.3
2 for 1 stock split	2.0
3 for 2 stock split	1.5

because the chart represents the price of one share. Splits and dividends result in stock multiplying factors:[8]

These multiplication factors can be used to correct the box size of a percentage or logarithmic point-and-figure chart by dividing all the boxes by the multiplication factor; therefore, the new box sizes represent the value of one share.

Recent Applications of Point-and-Figure

Not much new has happened to point-and-figure during the past 100 years; however, there has been renewed interest in using it. Two new books, *Power Investing with Sector Funds* by Peter Madlem and *Point & Figure Charting,* second edition, by Thomas Dorsey, show more recent examples of how this technique applies to stocks and sector indexes. There are also a number of websites with instructions and examples, most combined with advertising.

---

[8] William G. S. Brown, "Logarithmic Point & Figure Charting," *Technical Analysis of Stocks & Commodities* (July 1995).

ADVANCED CONCEPTS IN CHARTING AND TREND ANALYSIS

Is it a stock market or a market of stocks?

—Technical analyst's koan

The principles of chart construction covered in the previous section are a starting point for what follows in this section. Here, the discussion moves to more complex methods of interpreting the price data in the chart and even some additional data that can be charted in support of trend analysis.

The section offers a discussion of R.N. Elliott's Wave Principle. This approach to identifying and measuring price trends recognizes the rhythmic nature of price movement as evidenced in the technician's charts. Many years of work in this realm have produced a principles-based method of analysis, which includes mathematical relationships as guides to the ebb and flow of prices.

Identifying cycles in price action has been a pursuit of technicians for many years. Chapters in this section introduce the principles and nomenclature of cycle analysis, as well as some of the tools used to locate important points in a price cycle.

In addition, appropriate uses of traditional technical tools within the context of identified cycles is explained.

The general subject of "breadth" is also included in this section. Technical analysts must understand how to delve beyond the stock market indexes; while the indexes are intended to summarize the action of many stocks, how many of those stocks are actually providing impetus to the action in the indexes? The variety of breadth measures are explained here and are combined with divergence analysis as described in the previous section.

CHAPTER 16

Introduction to the Wave Principle

From Wayne Gorman, Jeffrey Kennedy, and Robert R. Prechter, Jr., *Visual Guide to Elliott Wave Trading* (Hoboken, New Jersey: John Wiley & Sons, 2013), Appendix A.

Learning Objective Statements

- Describe the basic operating theory of the Wave Principle
- Define motive waves and corrective waves
- Identify types of motive waves such as impulse, extension, and diagonal
- Identify types of corrective waves such as zigzag, flat, and triangle
- Label waves using standard Elliott Wave notation
- Describe Fibonacci relationships as applied to Elliott Wave analysis

In the 1930s, R.N. Elliott discovered that market price movements adhere to a certain pattern composed of what he called *waves*. He called the pattern's characteristics the Wave Principle. Every wave has a starting point and ending point in price and time. The pattern is continuous in that the end of one wave marks the beginning of the next wave. The basic pattern consists of five individual waves that are linked together and achieve progress as market prices move up or down (see Figure 16.1).

This five-wave sequence, labeled with numbers 1 through 5, is called a *motive wave*, because it propels the market in the direction of the main trend. Subwaves 1, 3, and 5 are also motive waves. Subwaves 2 and 4 are called *corrective waves*, because they interrupt the main trend and travel in the opposite direction.

Two Elliott wave rules govern motive waves: Wave 2 always retraces less than 100 percent of wave 1, and wave 3 can never be the shortest motive subwave (although it does not have to be the longest).

After a five-wave sequence is complete, the corrective wave begins. The corrective wave partially retraces the progress made by the motive wave. It follows a

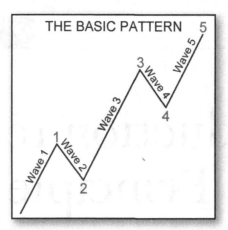

FIGURE 16.1
Source: Adapted from *Elliott Wave Principle.*

three-wave sequence or a specific combination of three-wave structures. Its waves are labeled using letters, for example A, B, and C (see Figure 16.2).

All waves are part of other waves at larger degree. They are also divisible into waves at lower degree, as shown in Figure 16.3. Motive and corrective waves can move up or down.

A number of rules and guidelines apply to wave formations. Guidelines differ from hard-and-fast rules in that they describe what is most likely to occur, even though it may not always occur.

■ Motive Waves

The two types of motive waves are *impulse* and *diagonal*.

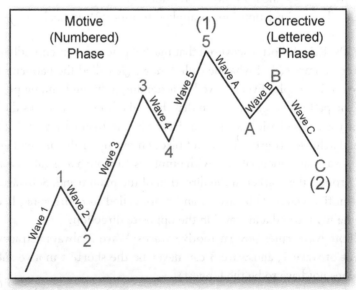

FIGURE 16.2
Source: Adapted from *Elliott Wave Principle.*

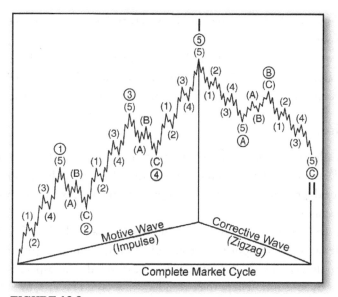

FIGURE 16.3

Source: Adapted from *Elliott Wave Principle.*

Impulse

The impulse wave, which is the strongest form of motive wave, follows these three rules:

1. Wave 2 never moves beyond the start of wave 1. In other words, it always retraces less than 100 percent of wave 1.
2. Wave 3 is never the shortest motive subwave, but it does not have to be the longest.
3. Wave 4 never enters the price territory of wave 1.

Add to these rules one strong guideline: Wave 4 should not enter the price territory of wave 2.

Rules are crucial to real-time application. In Figure 16.4, the first wave count is incorrect, because the end of wave 4 enters the price territory of wave 1. The second wave count is incorrect, because wave 3 is the shortest motive wave. The third wave count correctly displays the first three subdivisions of wave 3. The next wave count is correct because, even though wave 3 is not the longest motive wave, it is also not

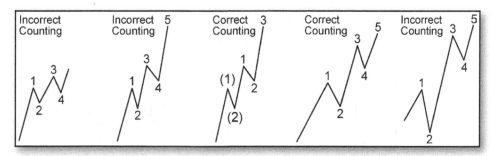

FIGURE 16.4

Source: Adapted from *Elliott Wave Principle.*

the shortest one. The last wave count is incorrect, because wave 2 here retraces more than 100 percent of wave 1.

In an impulse wave, waves 1 and 5 are always motive waves (that is, either impulse or diagonal), while wave 3 is always an impulse wave. Waves 2 and 4 are always corrective waves. Therefore, we call an impulse wave a 5-3-5-3-5 structure.

Extension

In an impulse wave, often one of the motive waves, usually wave 3 or wave 5, is extended. An *extended wave* is an elongated impulse wave whose motive subwaves at next lower degree are as large as or larger than the nonextended motive wave(s) of the same impulse wave.

Figure 16.5 shows diagrams of extensions for waves 1, 3, and 5. Sometimes the initial subwaves of an impulse wave are all about the same length, and therefore it is difficult to determine which motive wave is extended. This aspect is displayed in the diagram at the bottom, where the extended wave could be 1, 3, or 5. For all practical purposes, it does not matter which one is extended, as long as there is a total of nine

ADVANCED CONCEPTS IN CHARTING AND TREND ANALYSIS

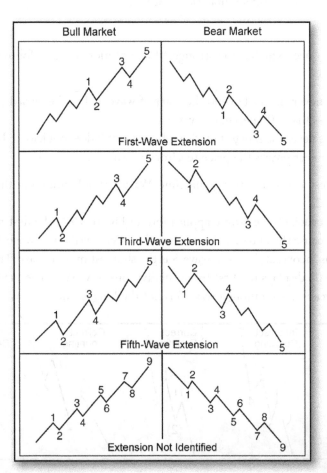

FIGURE 16.5
Source: Elliott Wave Principle.

waves. Third-wave extensions are often seen in the stock market, while fifth-wave extensions are often seen in commodity markets.

If wave 1 is extended, expect waves 3 and 5 to be about equal in length. If wave 3 is extended, expect wave 5 to be about equal to wave 1. If waves 1 and 3 are about equal, expect wave 5 to be extended. After a fifth-wave extension terminates, expect a swift and sharp reversal back to the second subwave of the extension. Rarely do two motive waves extend, but if that does happen, it is usually waves 3 and 5. We call that structure a *double extension*.

When an extension occurs within an extended wave, it is common for the extension at lower degree to be in the same wave position as the extension of which it is a part. For example, in a wave 3 extension, subwave 3 is often extended (see Figure 16.6).

Truncation

In an impulse wave, a *truncation* occurs when wave 5 fails to terminate beyond the end of wave 3. A truncated fifth wave still unfolds as a five-wave structure (see Figure 16.7). A truncated fifth wave, which is a sign of exhaustion in the main trend at next higher degree, is often preceded by an exceptionally strong third wave of the same degree. A truncated fifth wave is often followed by a swift and sharp reversal.

Diagonal

Although diagonal and impulse waves are both motive waves, diagonals differ significantly from impulse waves in that they follow the first two rules but not the third rule about wave 4 never entering in the price territory of wave 1. In a diagonal, in fact, wave 4 almost always enters in the price territory of wave 1.

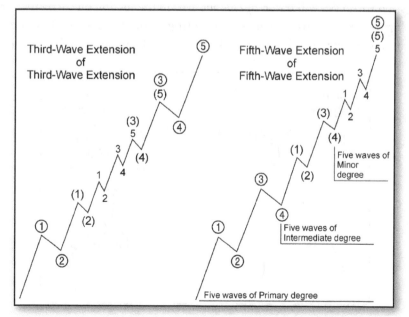

FIGURE 16.6

Source: Elliott Wave Principle.

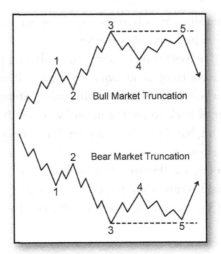

FIGURE 16.7

Source: *Elliott Wave Principle.*

A diagonal is typically contracting but, in rare occasions, expanding. In the contracting variety, wave 3 is shorter than wave 1, wave 5 is shorter than wave 3, and wave 4 is shorter than wave 2. In the expanding variety, wave 3 is longer than wave 1, wave 5 is longer than wave 3, and wave 4 is longer than wave 2. Since expanding diagonals are so infrequent, we will confine the rest of our discussion to the contracting variety.

The two types of diagonals are leading diagonal and ending diagonal, with the ending diagonal being more common. Within an ending diagonal, subwaves 1, 2, 3, 4, and 5 always take corrective-wave form, specifically either a single or multiple zigzag. Ending diagonals can form only as fifth waves of impulse waves and C waves of zigzags and flats. (We will cover zigzags and flats in the section on corrective waves.)

In Figure 16.8, wave (5) is a contracting ending diagonal. It is bounded by two converging trendlines, which gives the diagonal a wedge shape. One

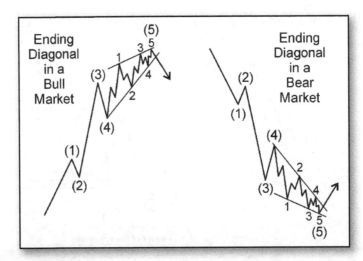

FIGURE 16.8

Source: Adapted from *Elliott Wave Principle.*

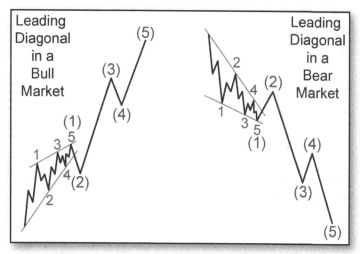

FIGURE 16.9

Source: Adapted from *Elliott Wave Principle.*

trendline connects the termination points of waves 1 and 3, and the other trendline connects the termination points of waves 2 and 4. Wave 5 can end either on or slightly above or below the 1-3 trendline. If wave 5 moves beyond that trendline, it is called a throw-over. A swift and sharp reversal usually brings prices at least back to where the diagonal began and usually far further. The reversal usually takes anywhere from one-third to one-half the time that it took the diagonal to form.

In a leading diagonal, waves 1, 3, and 5 are all impulse waves or all corrective waves in the form of zigzags. Waves 2 and 4 are always zigzag patterns. A leading diagonal can form wave 1 of an impulse wave and the first wave of a zigzag, which we call wave A. This formation is exceptionally rare.

In Figure 16.9, wave (1) is a contracting leading diagonal and has the same structural characteristics as the contracting ending diagonal. After a wave 1 leading diagonal terminates, expect wave 2 to retrace a significant portion of wave 1.

■ Corrective Waves

In markets, we have all heard the old adage, "nothing moves in a straight line." The Elliott wave model incorporates this observation. Market trends invariably encounter interruptions. In Elliott wave terms, we refer to these interruptions as corrective waves.

Corrective waves are either *sharp* or *sideways*. A sharp corrective wave usually has a relatively steep angle, never registering a new price extreme beyond the previous wave that it is retracing. A sideways correction's boundaries are closer to horizontal and, before terminating, it usually records a new price extreme beyond the previous wave that it is retracing. All corrective waves achieve some partial retracement of the preceding wave of the same degree. Because corrective waves come in many variations, it is a challenge to identify them in real time and to know when they are complete.

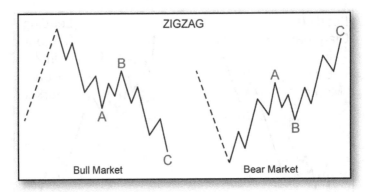

FIGURE 16.10
Source: Adapted from *Elliott Wave Principle.*

The three basic types of corrective wave patterns are *zigzag, flat,* and *triangle.* Elliotticians often use the word "three" as a noun, meaning a corrective pattern. When two or more of these patterns link together to form a sideways correction, they are called a *combination.*

Zigzag

A zigzag is a sharp, three-wave corrective pattern, labeled A-B-C. Wave A is always an impulse or leading diagonal, and wave C is always an impulse or ending diagonal. Wave B is always a corrective wave, that is zigzag, flat, triangle or combination. Therefore, we call the zigzag a 5-3-5 structure (see Figure 16.10).

In a zigzag, wave B can never go beyond the start of wave A, and wave C almost always goes beyond the end of wave A. If wave C does not go beyond the end of wave A, it is called a truncated wave C.

Zigzag corrections can take the form of one, two, or three zigzags. Three zigzags appear to be the limit. Whenever there is more than one zigzag, another corrective wave forms in order to link one zigzag to the other. In a double zigzag, the first zigzag is labeled W, the second zigzag is labeled Y, and the corrective wave that links the two zigzags together is labeled X. In a triple zigzag, the third zigzag is labeled Z. Wave X can form any corrective structure but is usually a zigzag. It always moves in the opposite direction of wave W (see Figure 16.11).

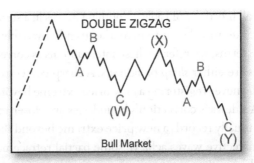

FIGURE 16.11
Source: Adapted from *Elliott Wave Principle.*

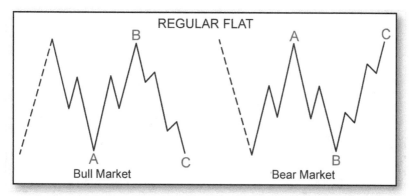

FIGURE 16.12
Source: Adapted from *Elliott Wave Principle*.

Flat

A flat is a sideways, three-wave corrective pattern, also labeled A-B-C. Waves A and B are always corrective waves, and wave C is always a motive wave. Therefore, we call the flat a 3-3-5 structure. In flats, waves A and B are never triangles and rarely flats. Wave B usually retraces at least 90 percent of wave A. There are three types of flats: regular, expanded, and running. The most common type of flat is the expanded flat. Running flats are rare.

In a regular flat, wave B ends at about the same level as the beginning of wave A, and wave C ends slightly past the end of wave A (see Figure 16.12).

In an expanded flat, wave B ends beyond the start of wave A, and wave C ends substantially beyond the end of wave A (see Figure 16.13).

In a running flat, wave B ends beyond the start of wave A, and wave C fails to reach the end of wave A (see Figure 16.14).

Triangle

A triangle is a sideways corrective wave with subwaves labeled A-B-C-D-E. In most cases, all the subwaves of a triangle are zigzags or multiple zigzag patterns. Therefore,

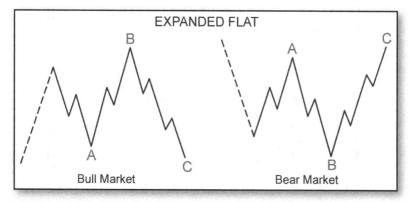

FIGURE 16.13
Source: Adapted from *Elliott Wave Principle*.

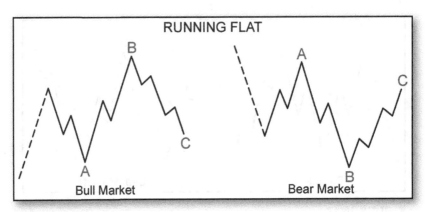

FIGURE 16.14

Source: Adapted from *Elliott Wave Principle.*

we call the triangle a 3-3-3-3-3 structure. On occasion, one of these subwaves takes the form of another triangle, and that subwave is usually wave E. Only one of these subwaves can be complex, meaning strung out over time, and that subwave is normally wave C, D, or E. Figure 16.15 shows the three types of triangles: contracting, barrier, and expanding.

In a triangle, the line that connects the termination points of waves A and C is called the A-C trendline, and the line that connects the termination points of waves B and D is called the B-D trendline. Wave E may terminate at, short of, or beyond the A-C trendline.

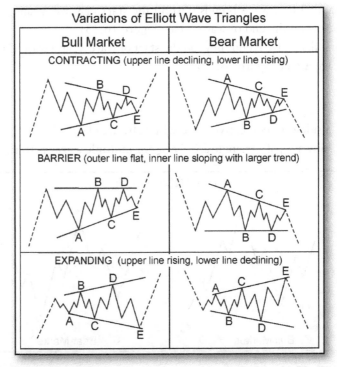

FIGURE 16.15

Source: Elliott Wave Principle.

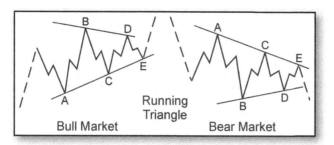

FIGURE 16.16

Source: Elliott Wave Principle.

In contracting and barrier triangles, the A-C and B-D trendlines converge. In barrier triangles, the B-D trendline is horizontal, and the A-C trendline points in the direction of the main trend at next higher degree. In expanding triangles, the A-C and B-D trendlines diverge.

In a contracting triangle, wave C never moves beyond the end of wave A, wave D never moves beyond the end of wave B, and wave E never moves beyond the end of wave C. Wave B may or may not move beyond the start of wave A. As shown in Figure 16.16, if wave B moves beyond the start of wave A, the triangle is called a running contracting triangle. Running triangles are common.

A barrier triangle has the same characteristics as a contracting triangle, with the following exception: In a barrier triangle, wave D ends at about the same level as wave B. In an expanding triangle, after completion of wave A, each new subwave moves beyond the starting point of the previous subwave.

A triangle always precedes the final motive wave in the direction of the main trend at next higher degree. That final motive wave normally makes a swift and sharp move, which is called the *post-triangle thrust* (see Figure 16.17).

For a contracting or barrier triangle, we can estimate the minimum termination point of the thrust by extending the A-C and B-D trendlines back to the start of wave A and then drawing a vertical line that connects those two trendlines. That vertical distance defines the "width" of the triangle. We then apply the width of the triangle

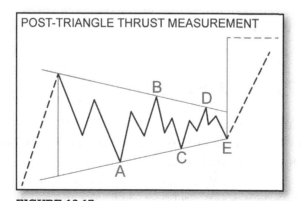

FIGURE 16.17

Source: Elliott Wave Principle.

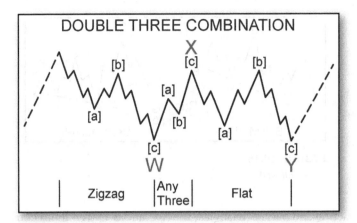

FIGURE 16.18
Source: *Elliott Wave Principle.*

to the end of wave E to give us an estimate for the next move in the direction of the main trend at next higher degree.

Within an impulse wave, a post-triangle thrust measurement estimates the minimum length for wave 5. If wave 5 goes beyond the estimated termination point, expect a prolonged fifth wave.

Combination

A combination is a sideways corrective pattern that includes two or more corrective structures. Three corrective structures appear to be the limit. Each corrective structure is linked by an X wave, which has three characteristics: It can be any corrective pattern; it always moves in the opposite direction of the previous corrective pattern; and it is usually a zigzag. There never appears to be more than one triangle in a combination, and, when one appears, it always seems to be the final corrective structure in the combination. The two types of combinations are double three and triple three.

A double three combination includes two corrective patterns—the first labeled W and the second labeled Y—that are linked by an X wave. Figure 16.18 represents one of many variations of a double three correction. A triple three combination includes three corrective patterns, labeled W, Y, and Z, each linked by X waves. Triple threes are rare. Within double and triple threes, X waves are usually zigzags and never triangles.

■ Fibonacci Relationships

Price and time aspects of wave patterns often reflect *Fibonacci ratios*. In wave formations, the key Fibonacci ratio is .618, which is known as the Golden Ratio or Golden Mean. It is represented by the Greek letter *phi* (ϕ), pronounced "fie." Its inverse is 1.618. *Phi* is the only number which, when added to one, is also equal to its inverse. If we square *phi* or subtract *phi* from 1, the result is .382, which is another Fibonacci ratio.

Fibonacci Ratios and Multiples		
Ratio	Inverse	Φ^N
.618	1.618	$(1.618)^1$
.382	2.618	$(1.618)^2$
.236	4.236	$(1.618)^3$
.146	6.854	$(1.618)^4$
.090	11.089	$(1.618)^5$

FIGURE 16.19

Figure 16.19 displays a number of Fibonacci ratios.

Each ratio can be expressed as *phi*—either .618 or its inverse 1.618—raised to a power. Other important Fibonacci numbers related to wave formation are 0.5 (1/2), .786 (square root of .618), 1.0 (1/1), and 2.0 (2/1).

In Elliott wave patterns, the key types of Fibonacci relationships are *retracements*, *multiples,* and *dividers*. Although these relationships are more commonly used to estimate the length of certain waves with respect to price, they can also be used to estimate the length of waves with respect to time.

Retracements

In impulse waves, second waves usually make deep retracements near .618 times the length of wave one. Fourth waves usually make shallow retracements that are often close to .382 times the length of wave three (see Figure 16.20).

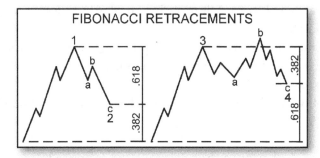

FIGURE 16.20
Source: Elliott Wave Principle.

Guidelines for Typical Retracements of Wave A by Wave B in Zigzags	
Wave B	Net Retracement (%)
Zigzag	50–79
Triangle	38–50
Running Triangle	10–40
Flat	38–79
Combination	38–50

FIGURE 16.21

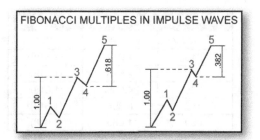

FIGURE 16.22

Source: Elliott Wave Principle.

In a zigzag, the retracement of wave A by wave B will depend on the structure of wave B. For example, in Figure 16.21, if wave B is a zigzag, it should retrace 0.5 to .786 of wave A. If wave B is a triangle, it should retrace .382 to 0.50 of wave A.

Multiples

In an impulse wave, wave 5 will often equal .618 or .382 times the net distance traveled of waves 1 through 3 (see Figure 16.22).

When wave 3 is extended, expect wave 5 to be related to wave 1 by equality or .618. When wave 5 is extended, expect wave 5, in price terms, to travel 1.618 times the net distance traveled of waves 1 through 3. If that length is exceeded, look for larger multiples as shown in Figure 16.22. When wave 1 is extended, expect the net distance traveled of waves 3 through 5 to equal .618 times the length of wave 1 (see Figure 16.23).

The most common Fibonacci relationship in single zigzags and multiple zigzag structures is *equality*—for example, C = A in the single zigzag, and Y = W in the double zigzag (see Figure 16.24).

When equality is not present, look for the other Fibonacci relationships, as shown in Figure 16.25.

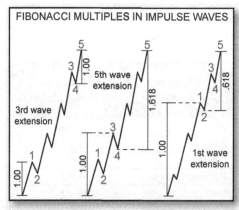

FIGURE 16.23

Source: Adapted from Elliott Wave Principle.

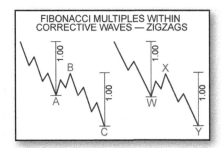

FIGURE 16.24

Source: Adapted from *Elliott Wave Principle.*

Fibonacci Relationships
Single Zigzag
Wave C = Wave A
Wave C = .618 Wave A
Wave C = 1.618 Wave A
Wave C = .618 Wave A past Wave A
Double Zigzag
Wave Y = Wave W
Wave Y = .618 Wave W
Wave Y = 1.618 Wave W
Wave Y = .618 Wave W past Wave W
Triple Zigzag
Equality for W, Y, and Z
Ratio of .618, i.e., Wave Z = .618 Wave Y

FIGURE 16.25

The relationships for multiple zigzags are analogous to those for a single zigzag.

In a regular flat, waves A, B, and C are generally equal to each other (see Figure 16.26).

In an expanded flat, expect wave C either to equal 1.618 times the length of wave A or to terminate at a price equal to .618 times the length of wave A past wave A. Expect wave B to equal 1.236 or 1.382 times the length of wave A (see Figure 16.27).

The alternate waves of a contracting triangle are often related to each other by the Fibonacci ratio of .618 (see Figure 16.28).

For expanding triangles, that ratio is 1.618.

Dividers

If we divide any length in such a way that the ratio of the smaller part to the larger part is equal to the ratio of the larger part to the whole, that ratio will always be .618 (see Figure 16.29).

This is called the *Golden Section*, which results in a .382/.618 split. Certain wave termination points will often divide wave patterns into the Golden Section or sometimes a .50/.50 split.

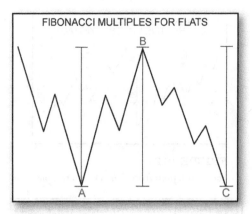

FIGURE 16.26
Source: Adapted from *Elliott Wave Principle*.

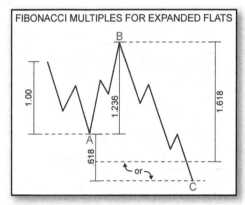

FIGURE 16.27
Source: Adapted from *Elliott Wave Principle*.

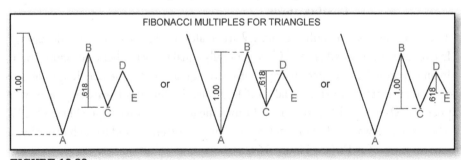

FIGURE 16.28
Source: Adapted from *Elliott Wave Principle*.

In an impulse wave, wave 4 (usually its origin or termination point) will often divide the entire wave into the Golden Section or into two equal parts (see Figure 16.30).

Clusters

Whenever possible, we prefer not to rely on just one Fibonacci relationship in forecasting market movements. The most powerful application of Fibonacci analysis is the identification of *Fibonacci clusters*. A Fibonacci price cluster occurs when two or

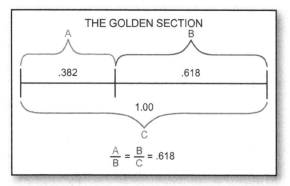

FIGURE 16.29

Source: Adapted from *Elliott Wave Principle*.

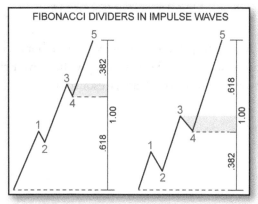

FIGURE 16.30

Source: Adapted from *Elliott Wave Principle*.

more Fibonacci price relationships project to approximately the same price level. (A Fibonacci time cluster occurs when two or more Fibonacci time relationships project to approximately the same time.) Since wave patterns unfold at all time frames simultaneously, there is often an opportunity to spot a Fibonacci cluster. The diagram in Figure 16.31 illustrates a Fibonacci price cluster.

Figure 16.31 identifies, at the same general price level, the following three Fibonacci relationships:

1. Primary wave [2] retraces .618 of Primary wave [1].
2. In the expanded flat, Intermediate wave (C) equals 1.618 times the length of Intermediate wave (A).
3. Within the Intermediate wave (C) impulse wave, Minor wave 5 equals Minor wave 1.

■ For More Information

Learn more at your exclusive Reader Resources site. You will find a free online edition of *Elliott Wave Principle* by Frost and Prechter, plus lessons on Elliott wave

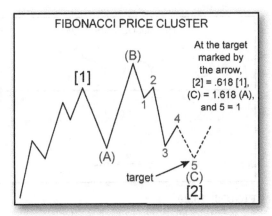

FIGURE 16.31

Source: Adapted from *Elliott Wave Principle*.

analysis, how to trade specific patterns, and how to use Fibonacci and other technical indicators to increase your confidence as you apply the Wave Principle in real time. Go to: www.elliottwave.com/wave/ReaderResources.

CHAPTER 17

The Anatomy of Elliott Wave Trading

From Wayne Gorman, Jeffrey Kennedy, and Robert R. Prechter, Jr., *Visual Guide to Elliott Wave Trading* (Hoboken, New Jersey: John Wiley & Sons, 2013), Chapter 1.

Learning Objective Statements

313

- Match the waves as labeled on a chart to the description in the text
- List the waves considered the most advantageous to trade
- Describe trade signals associated with various wave patterns

When teaching the Wave Principle, I begin each class by stating that analysis and trading represent two different skill sets. Although you may be a talented analyst, that does not mean you will be a successful trader and vice versa. I learned the hard way over many years that skilled analysis is a mastery of observation, while successful trading is a mastery of self.

When it comes to trading, there is no right way or wrong way—only your way. One trader's tolerance for risk will be starkly different from another's, just as time frame, portfolio size, and markets traded will also be different. Thus, the guidelines offered within this chapter on how to trade specific Elliott wave patterns are just that—guidelines, but ones that have served me well for many years.

My best advice to you as you look for a trading opportunity is to start your search by asking the question, "Do I see a wave pattern I recognize?" You should look for one of the five core Elliott wave patterns: impulse wave, ending diagonal, zigzag, flat, or triangle. These forms will become the basis of all your trade setups once you learn to identify them quickly and with confidence.

An even simpler question to ask is, "Do I see either a motive wave or a corrective wave?" Motive waves define the direction of the trend. There are two kinds of motive waves: impulse waves and ending diagonals. Corrective waves travel against the larger trend. The three kinds of corrective waves are zigzags, flats, and triangles. If all you do is identify a motive wave versus a corrective wave correctly, you can still identify some useful trade setups.

> **KEY POINT**
> Analysis is a mastery of observation, while successful trading is a mastery of self.

In this chapter, we will examine how to use key components of analysis and trading to help you become a better Elliottician and a consistently successful trader. Specifically, we will examine how the Wave Principle improves trading, which waves are the best to trade, which guidelines to use for trading specific Elliott wave patterns, and why the psychology of trading and risk management—what I call the neglected essentials—are important.

■ How the Wave Principle Improves Trading

Every trader, every analyst, and every technician has favorite techniques to use when trading. Let's go over why the Wave Principle is mine.

How the Wave Principle Improves Upon Traditional Technical Studies

There are three categories of technical studies: trend-following indicators, oscillators, and sentiment indicators. Trend-following indicators include moving averages, Moving Average Convergence-Divergence (MACD), and Directional Movement Index (ADX). A few of the more popular oscillators many traders use today are stochastics, rate-of-change, and the Commodity Channel Index (CCI). Sentiment indicators include put-call ratios and Commitment of Traders report data.

Technical studies like these do a good job of illuminating the way for traders, yet they each fall short for one major reason: They limit the scope of a trader's understanding of current price action and how it relates to the overall picture of a market. For example, let's say the MACD reading in XYZ stock is positive, indicating the trend is up. That's useful information, but wouldn't it be more useful if it could also help to answer these questions: Is this a new trend or an old trend? If the trend is up, how far will it go?

Most technical studies simply don't reveal pertinent information such as the maturity of a trend and a definable price target—but the Wave Principle does.

Five Ways the Wave Principle Improves Trading

Here are five ways the Wave Principle can benefit you and improve your trading:

1. The Wave Principle identifies the trend.
2. It identifies countertrend price moves within the larger trend.

3. It determines the maturity of the trend.
4. It provides high-confidence price targets.
5. It provides specific points of invalidation.

1. Identifying the Trend

". . . action in the same direction as the one larger trend develops in
five waves. . . ."

—Elliott Wave Principle by Frost and Prechter

The Wave Principle identifies the direction of the dominant trend. A five-wave advance identifies the overall trend as up. Conversely, a five-wave decline determines that the larger trend is down. Why is this information important? Because it is easier to trade in the direction of the dominant trend, since it is the path of least resistance and undoubtedly explains the saying, "The trend is your friend." I find trading in the direction of the trend much easier than attempting to pick tops and bottoms within a trend, which is a difficult endeavor and one that is virtually impossible to do consistently.

2. Identifying the Countertrend

". . . reaction against the one larger trend develops in three waves. . . ."

—Elliott Wave Principle by Frost and Prechter

The Wave Principle also identifies countertrend moves. The three-wave pattern is a corrective response to the preceding impulse wave. Knowing that a recent move in price is merely a correction within a larger trending market is especially important for traders because corrections give traders opportunities to position themselves in the direction of the larger trend of a market.

Being aware of the three basic Elliott wave corrective patterns—zigzags, flats, and triangles—enables you to buy pullbacks in an uptrend and to sell bounces in a downtrend, which is a proven and consistently successful trading strategy. Know what countertrend price moves look like, and you can find opportunities to rejoin the trend.

3. Determining the Maturity of a Trend

As R.N. Elliott observed, wave patterns form larger and smaller versions of themselves. This repetition in form means that price activity is a fractal, as illustrated in Figure 17.1. Wave (1) subdivides into five small waves yet is part of a larger five-wave pattern. How is this information useful? It helps traders recognize the maturity of a trend. If, for example, prices are advancing in wave 5 of a five-wave advance and wave 5 has already completed three or four smaller waves, a trader knows that this may not be the best time to add long positions. Instead, it may be time to take profits or at least to raise protective stops.

Since the Wave Principle identifies trend, countertrend, and the maturity of a trend, it's no surprise that the Wave Principle also signals the return of the dominant trend. Once a countertrend move unfolds in three waves (A-B-C), this structure can

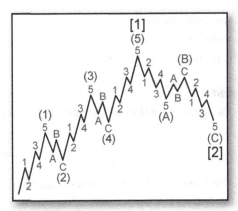

FIGURE 17.1

Source: Elliott Wave Principle.

signal the point where the dominant trend has resumed, namely, once price action exceeds the extreme of wave B. Knowing precisely when a trend has resumed brings an added benefit: It increases the likelihood of a successful trade, which is further enhanced when accompanied by traditional technical studies.

4. Providing Price Targets   What traditional technical studies simply don't offer— high-confidence price targets—the Wave Principle again provides. When R.N. Elliott wrote about the Wave Principle in *Nature's Law*, he stated that the Fibonacci sequence was the mathematical basis for the Wave Principle. Elliott waves, both impulsive and corrective, adhere to specific Fibonacci proportions. For example, all three motive waves tend to be related by Fibonacci mathematics, whether by equality, 1.618, or 2.618 (whose inverses are .618 and .382). See Figures 17.2, 17.3, and 17.4.

Also, corrections often retrace a Fibonacci percentage of the preceding wave. These Fibonacci-derived regions allow traders to set profit-taking objectives and identify areas where the next turn in prices will likely occur (see Figures 17.5 and 17.6).

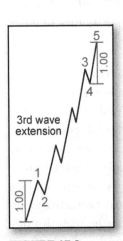

FIGURE 17.2

Source: Elliott Wave Principle.

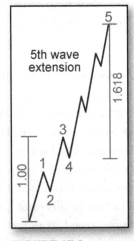

FIGURE 17.3

Source: Elliott Wave Principle.

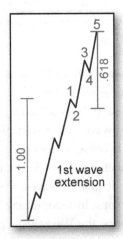

FIGURE 17.4

Source: Elliott Wave Principle.

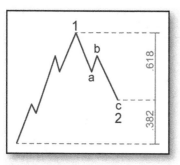

FIGURE 17.5

Source: *Elliott Wave Principle*.

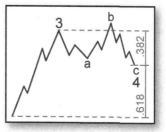

FIGURE 17.6

Source: *Elliott Wave Principle*.

> **KEY POINT**
>
> Knowing when you're wrong on a trade is as important as knowing when you're right.

5. Providing Specific Points of Invalidation   Wave analysis provides a specific point of invalidation, which is the level at which an interpretation is no longer viable. Knowing when you are wrong is perhaps a trader's most important piece of information.

At what point does a trade fail? Many traders use money management rules to determine the answer to this question, because technical studies simply don't offer the answer. Yet the Wave Principle does—in the form of these three Elliott wave rules for impulse waves:

Rule 1: Wave 2 can never retrace more than 100 percent of wave 1.

Rule 2: Wave 4 may never end in the price territory of wave 1.

Rule 3: Out of the three impulse waves (waves 1, 3, and 5), wave 3 can never be the shortest.

A violation of any of these rules implies that the operative wave count is incorrect. How can traders use this information? If a technical study warns of an upturn in prices, and the wave pattern is a second-wave pullback, the trader knows specifically at what point the trade will fail: a move beyond the origin of wave 1. That kind of guidance is difficult to come by without a framework such as the Wave Principle.

■ The Four Best Waves to Trade

Here's where the rubber meets the road. Waves 3, 5, A, and C are the most advantageous to trade, because they are oriented in the direction of the one larger trend. Odds favor traders who are long in bull markets (and short in bear markets) versus short sellers in bull markets (and buyers in bear markets). Overall, trading in the direction of the trend is the path of least resistance.

The Wave Principle helps to identify these high-confidence trades in place of lesser-confidence setups that traders should ignore. Remember, five-wave moves

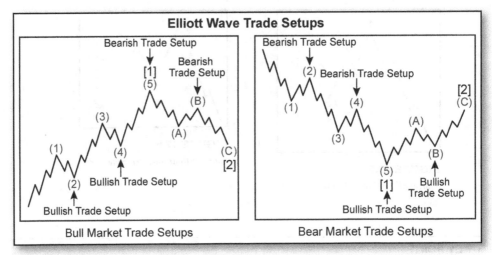

FIGURE 17.7

determine the direction of the larger trend, while three-wave moves offer traders an opportunity to join the trend. So in Figure 17.7, waves (2), (4), (5), and (B) are actually setups for high-confidence trades exploiting waves (3), (5), (A), and (C).

For example, a wave (2) pullback provides traders an opportunity to position themselves in the direction of wave (3), just as a wave (5) rally offers them a shorting opportunity for wave (A). By combining the Wave Principle with traditional technical analysis, traders can improve their trading by increasing the likelihood of a successful trade.

Technical studies can pick out many trading opportunities, but the Wave Principle helps traders discern which ones are more likely to be successful. This is because the Wave Principle is the framework that provides history and context, current information, and a peek at the future.

■ Elliott Wave Trade Setups

This next chart (see Figure 17.7) shows bullish and bearish versions of trade setups. In each, waves (2), (4), (5), and (B) are trade setups that introduce the four primary Elliott-based trading opportunities. These corrective waves offer the trader an opportunity to rejoin the larger trend. In such trend trading, a trader buys pullbacks in uptrends and sells bounces in downtrends.

■ When to Trade Corrections

Corrective waves offer less desirable trading opportunities because of their potential complexity. Impulse waves are trend-defining price moves in which prices typically travel far. Conversely, corrective wave patterns fluctuate more and can unfold slowly while taking a variety of shapes, such as a zigzag, flat, expanded flat, triangle, double zigzag, or combination. Corrections generally move sideways and are often erratic, time-consuming, and deceptive. Thus, it is emotionally exhausting to trade corrections, and the odds of executing a successful trade during this type of price action are low.

Even though I view corrective waves and patterns as providing low-confidence trade setups, there are times when I would consider trading them—but it depends on the potential duration of the correction. If I count five waves up, for example, on a 15-minute price chart of Crude Oil, I do not consider waves 2 or 4 to be viable trading opportunities. I prefer, instead, to wait for waves 2 and 4 to terminate before entering a position. Let's say, though, that we have a market that has also formed an impulse wave, but it has taken weeks or months to do so. In this instance, waves 2 and 4 would form over many weeks and might offer traders many short-term trading opportunities.

■ Guidelines for Trading Specific Elliott Wave Patterns

Before we review guidelines for trading specific Elliott wave patterns, here is my most important analytical and trading rule: **Let the market commit to you before you commit to the market**. In other words, look for *confirming price action*. Just as it is unwise to pull out in front of an oncoming car on the basis of its turn signal alone, it is equally unwise to take a trade without confirmation of a trend change.

The following guidelines incorporate this idea and benefit the trader in two ways. First, waiting for confirming price action tends to decrease the number of trades executed. One of the biggest mistakes traders make is overtrading. Second, it focuses attention on higher-confidence trade setups. If a trader believes that a particular market is topping—and appropriate price action does indeed corroborate this belief—then the trader is more likely to execute a successful trade.

> **Smart Investor Tip**
> Let the market commit to you before you commit to the market.

> **Smart Investor Tip**
> Waiting for confirming price action allows traders to use an evidence-based approach and to focus their attention on high-confidence trade setups.

Impulse Waves

Whenever an impulse wave is complete, the Elliott wave guideline regarding the depth of corrective waves applies:

> "[C]orrections, especially when they themselves are fourth waves, tend to register their maximum retracement within the span of travel of the previous fourth wave of one lesser degree, most commonly near the level of its terminus."
>
> —*Elliott Wave Principle* by Frost and Prechter

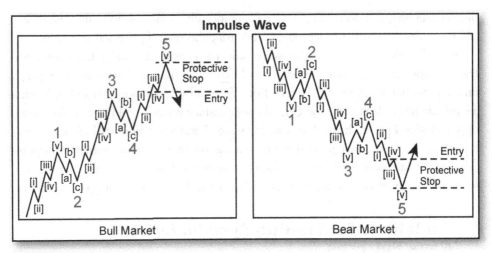

FIGURE 17.8

Although that guideline may sound complicated, it's easy to follow in real trading. The trading technique is to enter on a break below the extreme of wave (iv) of 5 (see Figure 17.8). Doing so prevents top picking and requires the market to take out a prior swing low to act as initial evidence that the impulse wave is indeed finished. Set the initial protective stop at the extreme of the price move.

Ending Diagonal

The guidelines for entry and initial protective stops for ending diagonals are similar to those for impulse waves: Wait for a break of the extreme of wave 4 before taking a position, and place the initial protective stop at the extreme of the price move (see Figure 17.9).

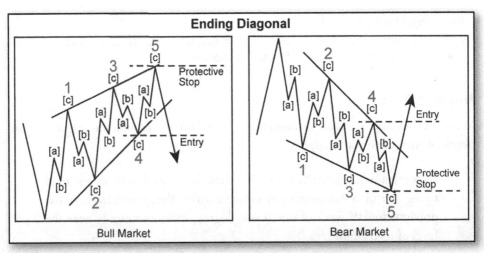

FIGURE 17.9

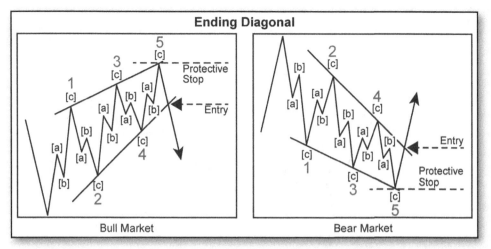

FIGURE 17.10

Remember, these entry techniques demonstrate a conservative approach that I think of as "ready, aim, aim, aim . . . fire" trading. But if you are a more aggressive trader, how do you enter an ending diagonal trade setup? One approach is to enter on a decisive close beyond the trendline that connects the extreme of waves 2 and 4. In this instance, the initial protective stop placement is the same, the extreme of the pattern (see Figure 17.10).

If you define yourself as an out-and-out aggressive trader, here's an entry technique for you. More often than not, wave 3 of an ending diagonal is shorter than wave 1. When this is the case, the rules state that wave 5 cannot be longer than wave 3, since even within an ending diagonal, wave 3 may never be the shortest wave among waves 1, 3, and 5. Thus, you can begin acquiring positions or scale into a position as wave 5 is forming. The protective stop under this aggressive entry technique would be the point at which wave 5 becomes longer than wave 3, since the Wave Principle identifies that as a specific point of invalidation.

Zigzag

The first of two guidelines for entering a trade during a zigzag is on a break of the extreme of wave [iv] of C, provided this level is beyond the termination of wave A (see Figure 17.11).

A second entry guideline is to wait for the extreme of wave B to give way before taking action (see Figure 17.12). The initial protective stop is then the extreme of wave C. This conservative approach prevents picking tops or bottoms without sufficient evidence.

Ideally, traders will take these guidelines and adapt them to their own specific trading style. In fact, using a zigzag as an example, an even more conservative trader could wait a bit longer before entering and demand a five-wave move through the extreme of wave B followed by a corrective wave pattern.

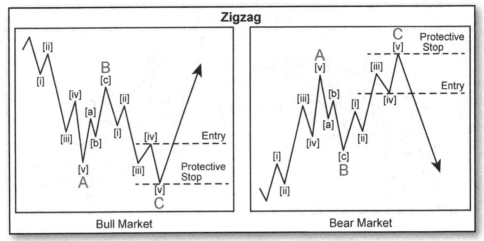

FIGURE 17.11

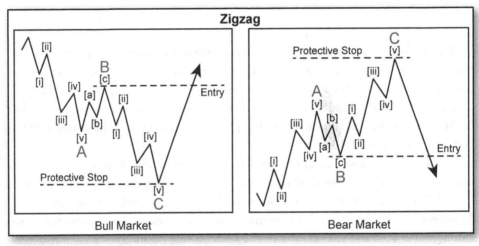

FIGURE 17.12

Flat

Since the final wave of a flat correction subdivides into five waves, the recommended entry technique is similar to that of an impulse wave: Wait until prices exceed the extreme of wave (iv) of C to enter a trade (see Figure 17.13). This approach is not used with zigzags—where wave C also subdivides into five waves—because in a bullish zigzag, for instance, wave (iv) of a C terminates *below* the extreme of wave A, whereas in a bullish flat, it tends to form *above* the extreme of wave A.

Triangle

The final guideline applies to triangles (see Figure 17.14). A triangle is a sideways price move—typically bounded by converging trendlines—that subdivides into waves A, B, C, D, and E. The entry guideline is to wait for prices to break the extreme of wave D and place an initial protective stop where wave E terminates. I

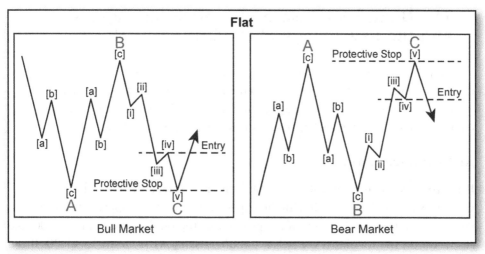

FIGURE 17.13

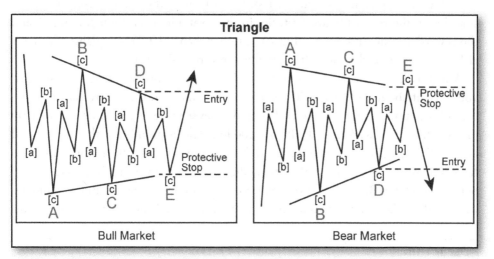

FIGURE 17.14

do not endorse a more aggressive entry technique because triangles are sometimes deceptive: Since they can form in the wave 4, B, or X wave positions, what may appear to be a bullish fourth-wave triangle could actually be a bearish triangle B wave.

Smart Investor Tip

The psychology of the individual is the key to becoming a consistently successful trader.

A trader with a more aggressive trading style will most likely enter a position well before prices penetrate the termination point of wave D. If so, I recommend using the extreme of wave A as an initial protective stop rather than the end of wave C. It is not uncommon in equities or thinly traded markets for intraday price action to exceed the extreme of wave C and reverse.

■ The Neglected Essentials—Risk Management and the Psychology of Trading

When discussing how to become a consistently successful trader, two subjects you don't hear enough about are risk management and the psychology of trading.

Because the topic of risk management is critically important to the success and longevity of a trader, let's briefly discuss risk-reward ratios and trade size.

Risk-Reward Ratio

Risk to reward is a ratio that quantifies the risk versus the reward of a trade. If you buy XYZ stock at $50.00 with the expectation that it will appreciate to $51.00, your expected reward is $1.00. If the protective stop on this position is $49.00, the risk-reward ratio for this trade is 1:1—you're risking $1.00 to make $1.00. If the protective stop is $49.90, then the risk-reward ratio is 10:1.

Note: Even though it's called a risk-reward ratio, the ratio is conventionally stated with the reward figure first. So, in this example, even though risk is 1 and the reward 10, the ratio is stated as 10:1, rather than 1:10. This explains why a 3:1 risk-reward ratio is desirable. It's actually a reward-risk ratio.

A high risk-reward ratio is desirable as a function of probabilities. Let's say that you're right about the market 70 percent of the time, and the risk-reward ratio on each of your trades is 1:1. Thus, out of 10 trades, seven trades were closed with a $1.00 profit, while three were exited with a $1.00 loss. The bottom line is that you walked away with $4.00. What do you think will happen if we increase the risk-reward ratio from 1:1 to 3:1 and decrease the probability of being right from 70 percent to 40 percent? With this 3:1 ratio, for the same $1.00 profit, four winning trades would net $12.00. If we then subtract $6.00 in losing trades, we walk away with a $6.00 profit.

> **DEFINITION:**
> **Risk to reward**
> Risk-Reward Ratio is a ratio used to compare expected returns against the amount of risk taken. In line with market convention, risk-reward ratios are expressed in terms of total reward per one unit of risk.

This difference shows how important the risk-reward ratio is—by decreasing the probability of winning trades from 70 percent to almost half (i.e., 40 percent) while increasing the risk-reward ratio, you increase profitability by 50 percent. A misconception about trading is that a trader need be right only on the direction of the market to make money. This is not entirely correct. As you've just seen, a trader can be right as little as 40 percent of the time and still succeed, provided he or she keeps an eye on the risk-reward ratio.

> **Smart Investor Tip**
> Trades that offer less than a 3:1 risk-reward ratio should be avoided.

Trade Size

How large a position should a trader take? The risk on a single trade should never exceed 1 to 3 percent of the total portfolio size. Retail traders tend to balk at these small percentages, while professional traders embrace them. Thus, at 1 percent, for every $5,000 a trader has in a trading account, he or she should risk only $50 on each position. For example, a trader with $10,000 in his account can take either two trades where the risk is $50 apiece or one trade in which the risk is $100. Many traders fail at trading because they simply don't have sufficient capital in their trading accounts to take the positions they want to take.

If you do have a small trading account, though, you can overcome this challenge by trading small. You can trade fewer contracts, trade e-mini contracts, or even penny stocks. Bottom line, on your way to becoming a consistently successful trader, you must realize that *longevity* is key. If your risk on any given position is small relative to your total capital, then you can weather a losing streak. Conversely, if you risk 25 percent of your portfolio on each trade, after four consecutive losers, you're out of business.

■ The Psychology of Trading

While I consider risk management to be an essential component of successful trading, the true key is psychology—that is, your individual psychology. Let's review a number of psychological factors that prevent traders from becoming consistently successful: lack of methodology, lack of discipline, unrealistic expectations, and lack of patience.

Whether you are a seasoned professional or just thinking about opening your first trading account, it is critically important to your success that you understand how your personal psychology affects your trading results.

Lack of Methodology

If you aim to be a consistently successful trader, then you *must* have a defined trading methodology—a simple, clear, and concise way of looking at markets. In fact, having a method is so important that EWI founder Robert Prechter put it at the top of his list in his essay, "What a Trader Really Needs to Be Successful." Guessing or going by gut instinct won't work over the long run. If you don't have a defined trading methodology, then you don't have a way to know what constitutes a buy or sell signal.

Smart Investor Tip

Successful trading requires a methodology and the discipline to follow the methodology.

How do you overcome this problem? The answer to this question is to write down your methodology. Define in writing what your analytical tools are and, more important, how *you* use them. It doesn't matter whether you use the Wave Principle, point and figure charts, stochastics, RSI, or a combination of all of these. What *does* matter is that you actually make the effort to define what constitutes a buy, a sell, your trailing stop, and instructions on exiting a position. The best hint I can give you about defining your trading methodology is this: If you can't fit it on a 3" × 5" card, it's probably too complicated.

Lack of Discipline

Once you have clearly outlined and identified your trading methodology, you *must* have the discipline to follow the system. A lack of discipline while trading is the second common downfall of many aspiring traders. If the way you view a price chart or evaluate a potential trade setup today is different from how you did it a month ago, then you either have not identified your methodology or you lack the discipline to follow the methodology you have identified. The formula for success is to consistently apply a proven methodology.

> **Smart Investor Tip**
> Stick with realistic expectations. For instance, the goal for every trader the fi rst year should be not to lose money. In other words, shoot for a 0 percent return during your fi rst year.

Unrealistic Expectations

Nothing makes me angrier than those commercials that say something like, "$5,000 properly positioned in Natural Gas can give you returns of over $40,000." Advertisements like this are a disservice to the financial industry as a whole and end up costing uneducated investors a lot more than $5,000. In addition, they help to create the psychologically sabotaging mind-set of having unrealistic expectations.

Yes, it is possible to experience above-average returns trading your own account. However, it's difficult to do it without taking on above-average risk. So, what is a realistic return to shoot for in your first year as a trader—50 percent, 100 percent, 200 percent? Whoa, let's rein in those unrealistic expectations. In my opinion, the goal for every trader the first year out should be *not to lose money*. In other words, shoot for a 0 percent return your first year. If you can manage that, then in year two, try to beat the Dow or the S&P. These goals may not be flashy, but they are realistic.

Lack of Patience

The fourth psychological pitfall that even experienced traders encounter is a lack of patience. According to Edwards and Magee in their seminal book, *Technical Analysis of Stock Trends*, markets trend only about 30 percent of the time. This means that the other 70 percent of the time, financial markets are not trending.

This small percentage may explain why I believe that, for any given time frame, there are only two or three really good trading opportunities. For example, if you're a long-term trader, typically only two or three compelling tradable moves in a market present themselves during any given year. Similarly, if you are a short-term trader, only two or three high-quality trade setups present themselves in a given week.

All too often, because trading is inherently exciting (and anything involving money usually is exciting), it's easy to feel that you're missing something if you're not in a trade. As a result, you start taking trade setups of lesser and lesser quality and begin overtrading.

How do you overcome this lack of patience? Remind yourself that every week there will be another "trade of the year." In other words, don't worry about missing an opportunity today, because there will be another one tomorrow, next week, and next month . . . I promise.

■ For More Information

Learn more at your exclusive Reader Resources site. You will find a free online edition of *Elliott Wave Principle* by Frost and Prechter, plus lessons on Elliott wave analysis, how to trade specific patterns, and how to use Fibonacci and other technical indicators to increase your confidence as you apply the Wave Principle in real time. Go to: www.elliottwave.com/wave/ReaderResources.

Test Yourself

Answer the following True/False questions:

1. Analysis and trading employ the same skill set.
2. Wave analysis identifies the direction of the trend, based on the direction of the impulse wave.
3. The Wave Principle offers traders points of invalidation where they can re-evaluate where their analysis may have gone wrong.
4. Wave 2 can sometimes retrace more than 100 percent of wave 1.
5. A complete Elliott wave cycle consists of nine waves.
6. From origin to termination, waves 2 and 4 offer high-confidence trading opportunities.
7. An aggressive approach to trading an ending diagonal is to wait for the extreme of wave 4 to give way.
8. If you look for confirming price action, then you are letting the market commit to you before you commit to the market.
9. The entry guideline for trading a zigzag is to wait for the extreme of wave **B** to give way.
10. A risk to reward ratio of 1:1 is ideal.

Answers: 1. False 2. True 3. True 4. False 5. False 6. False 7. False 8. True 9. True   10. False

CHAPTER 18

Measuring Market Strength

From Charles D. Kirkpatrick II and Julie R. Dahlquist, *Technical Analysis: The Complete Resource for Financial Market Technicians,* 3rd Edition (Old Tappan, New Jersey: Pearson Education, Inc., 2016), Chapter 8.

Learning Objective Statements

- Explain the concept of divergence
- Define market breadth
- Identify signals of change in market breadth using the advance-decline line
- Describe other measures of internal stock-market strength such as McClellan's calculations
- Explain the use of volume in measuring stock-market strength
- Identify measures of stock-market strength from new high and new low data
- Describe measures of stock-market strength based on the number of stocks priced above their moving average

In addition to measuring the attitudes of market players, the technical analyst needs to look at the internal strength of a market. By looking at data specific to each market, the analyst determines whether the internal strength of the respective market is improving or deteriorating. In this chapter, we examine how the analyst looks at market data such as the number of stocks advancing and declining, the volume of the winners and losers, the new 52-week highs and lows, and the position of the averages relative to moving averages. These measures help to gauge the stock market's underpinnings. The data needed to calculate the indicators studied in this chapter is publicly available in most financial newspapers.

BOX 18.1 WHAT IS A DIVERGENCE?

The most important technical concept for confirmation of a trend is called a **divergence.** As long as an indicator—especially one that measures the rate of change of price or other data (called **momentum**)—corresponds with the price trend, the indicator is said to "confirm" the price trend. When an indicator or oscillator fails to confirm the trend, it is called a **negative divergence or positive divergence,** depending on whether peaks or bottoms, respectively, fail to confirm price peaks or bottoms. A divergence is an early warning of a potential trend change. It means the analyst must watch the price data more closely than when the indicators and oscillators are confirming new highs and lows. Divergence analysis is used between almost all indicators and prices; a divergence can occur more than one time before a price reversal.

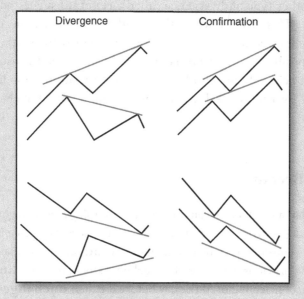

As an example, one of the tenets used in analyzing trading volume is that in a rising trend, volume should expand with the price rise. If at a new short-term peak in prices the trading volume fails to expand above its earlier, time-equivalent high, a negative divergence has occurred that should warn the analyst that the new price high is occurring on less enthusiasm, as measured by volume, and that the uptrend may soon be ending.

It should be noted that knowledge of a wide array of technical indicators does not make an analyst valuable or cause him to profit, but knowing when to apply which indicator does. Because it is almost impossible to understand all indicators, the technical analyst should select just a few and study them intently.

When looking at indicators, the analyst is generally looking for confirmation or divergence. Confirmation occurs when prices are rising and these indicators rise, signaling strong market internals. Confirmation also occurs when falling prices are accompanied by an indication of weak market internals. In other words, confirmation occurs when price movement and market internals appear to agree.

When a market indicator does not support the direction of price movement, the analyst has a strong warning that the trend may be in the process of reversing. This lack of confirmation is referred to as a **divergence**.

One quick example is an indicator called the rate of change indicator (ROC). It is merely a plot of the ratio or difference between today's closing price and the closing price at some specified time in the past, such as 20 days. When the market or stock is hitting a new high and the 20-day ROC is hitting a new high, we have a confirmation of the price action. Should the ROC not be hitting a new high at the same time as the market or stock, we have a negative divergence, a warning that the upward momentum in price is slowing down.

There is another type of divergence called a **reversal** suggested by Constance Brown (1999). This occurs when the oscillator or indicator, in a **positive reversal**, reaches a second low that is not confirmed by another new low in prices. The opposite, the **negative reversal**, occurs when the oscillator reaches a new high but prices do not. Both cases are just variations of a divergence, and as in a normal divergence, each occurrence signals a potential change in market direction.

■ Market Breadth

On any given day, a stock price can do one of three things: close higher, close lower, or remain unchanged from the previous day's close. If a closing price is above its previous close, it is considered to be advancing, or an **advance**. Similarly, a stock that closes below the previous day's close is a declining stock, or a **decline**. A stock that closes at the exact price it closed the day before is called **unchanged**.

Prior to July 2000, all less than one dollar (or point) changes in common stock prices were in fractions based on the pre-Revolutionary practice of cutting Spanish Doubloons into eighths to make change. By February 2001, the old system of quarters, eighths, and sixteenths was replaced with the decimal system. The use of decimals may have affected some historic relationships. The resulting smaller bid-ask spreads may have reduced the number of stocks that are unchanged at the day's end.

Advance/decline data is called the **breadth** of the stock market. The indicators we focus on in this section measure the internal strength of the market by considering whether stocks are gaining or losing in price. In this section, we consider the cumulative breadth line, the advance-decline ratio, the breadth differences, and the breadth thrust.

Before we begin looking more closely at these particular indicators, we must, however, mention a change that has recently occurred. Since 2000, the parameters of many breadth indicators thought to provide accurate signals have changed significantly. Applying standards that had excellent records for identifying stock market reversals now proves to be less than satisfactory. There is likely more than one reason for this sudden change, and some reasons are unknown.

One factor that has caused the old parameters to change is the proliferation on the New York Stock Exchange of ETFs, bond funds, real estate investment trusts (REITs), preferred shares, and American depository receipts (ADRs) of foreign stocks. These do not represent domestic operating companies and, therefore, are not directly subject to the level of corporate economic activity. They are subject to a variety of influences not necessarily connected with the stock market, which means they are not reflecting the market's traditional discounting mechanism.

Another possible factor is the implementation of the aforementioned decimalization. Many of the indicators using advances and declines are calculated as they were before decimalization even though their optimal parameters may have changed. Another possibility, one more likely, is that the aberrant indicators were tested mostly during the long bull market from 1982 through 2000 or later during the recent bull market from 2009 through today (2015). The important lesson for the technical analyst, however, is that indicators do not remain the same. Parameters for known indicators change over time and with structural changes in the markets. The analyst must frequently test indicators and make appropriate adjustments in the types and parameters used.

The Breadth Line or Advance-Decline Line

The breadth line, also known as the advance-decline line, is one of the most common and best ways of measuring breadth and internal market strength. This line is the cumulative sum of advances minus declines. The standard formula for the breadth line is as follows:

$$\text{Breadth Line Value}_{\text{Day T}} = (\text{\# of Advancing Stocks}_{\text{Day T}} - \text{\# of Declining Stocks}_{\text{Day T}}) + \text{Breadth Line Value}_{\text{Day T}-1}$$

On days when the number of advancing stocks exceeds the number of declining stocks, the breadth line will rise. On days when more stocks are declining than advancing, the line will fall.

A breadth line can be constructed for any index, industry group, exchange, or basket of stocks. In addition to being calculated using daily data, it can be calculated weekly or for any other period for which breadth data is available. It is not often applicable to the commodity markets where baskets or indices of commodities rarely are traded, although this is changing with the advent of the Commodities Research Bureau (CRB), Goldman Sachs, and Dow Jones futures index markets.

Ordinarily, the plot of the breadth line should roughly replicate the stock market averages. In other words, when the stock market averages are rising, the breadth line should rise. This indicates that a market rally is associated with the majority of the stocks rising.

The importance to technical analysts of the breadth line is the time when it fails to replicate the averages and, thus, diverges. For example, if the stock market average is rising but the advance-decline line is falling, only a few stocks are fueling the rally, but the majority of stocks are either not participating or declining in value.

Analysts point to several reasons why breadth divergence might not be as powerful of an indicator in the future as it has been in the past. The first reason is the previously discussed proliferation of nonoperating company listings. To deal with the issue of the bias from including stocks that do not represent ownership in operating companies, technical analysts often use only those breadth figures from common stocks that represent companies that actually produce a product or a service. For example, the New York Stock Exchange also reports breadth statistics for only common stocks, disregarding the numerous mutual funds, preferred stocks, and so on. This additional breadth information is available daily in most financial newspapers. The breadth line derived from this list of common stocks generally has been more reliable than the one including all stocks.

However, a major change recently occurred in the way the NYSE reports breadth statistics for common stocks. Beginning in February 2005, the NYSE decided to include only those stocks with three or fewer letters in their stock symbols and those that are included in the NYSE Composite Index, its common stock list. Because of this change, figures since that decision will be incompatible with the prior figures.

Instead of relying on the publicly available statistics, proprietary breadth statistics also are available on a subscription basis. For example, Lowry's Reports, Inc. (www .lowryresearch.com) calculates proprietary breadth statistics that eliminate all the preferred stocks, ADRs, closed-end mutual funds, REITs, and others representing nonproductive companies.

Another difficulty with the breadth has arisen since the year 2000 according to Colby (2003) and others using data up through 2000. Trading rules used with the publicly available breadth statistics before then, despite the known problems with the types of stocks listed, showed relatively attractive results. However, using those same rules since the year 2000, we find much less attractive results in many of these indicators. Indeed, the difference is so large and consistent throughout the trading methods mentioned by Colby that it could not be attributed to the trading rules themselves or to problems connected with optimizing. The difference between then and more recently must have to do with a change in background, character, leadership, or historic relationships.

Why this change? The most obvious economic change is that of the decoupling of the stock market from long-term interest rates. From the Great Depression of the 1930s to the last decade of the previous century, the business cycle was characterized by the bond market and the stock market reaching bottoms at roughly the same time, and the bond market reaching peaks earlier than the stock market reached peaks. In the late 1990s, this business-cycle relationship broke down, switching to almost the exact opposite relationship, whereby the bond market tended to trend oppositely from the stock market. Because the breadth statistics include a large number of interest-related stocks that are not included in the popular averages, this change in relationship may be the cause for the difference in trading rules using breadth, giving the breadth line more strength at tops and more weakness at bottoms.

In the Nasdaq, a cumulative breadth line constructed of only Nasdaq stocks advances, declines, and unchanged has been declining at least since 1983 (earlier figures are difficult to obtain), and even when looked at over shorter periods it seems to have a very strong negative bias. This negative bias is likely due to the "survivor effect," whereby from 1996 to 2015, stocks listed on the Nasdaq declined from 6,136 to 3,005. The loss of issues from the list suggests that a large number of listings went broke during that time and were trending downward even when the larger survivors were advancing and were unavailable during the rebound in stock prices from 2009 through 2015. The Nasdaq index is a capitalization-weighted index where the survivors have considerable influence on price but little influence on breadth. This weighting bias implies that a Nasdaq breadth line is useless as a divergence indicator in its absolute form and must be analyzed instead for changes in acceleration rather than direction.

Several indicators using the advance-decline line concept appear in the classic technical analysis literature. Although these indicators have not performed well in recent market conditions, it is important for the student of technical analysis to be aware of these traditional indicators because they may become productive sometime in the future.

Double Negative Divergence

When the averages are reaching new price highs and the breadth line is not, a **negative divergence** is occurring (see Figure 18.1). This signals weak market internals and that the market uptrend is in a late phase and may soon end. In 1926, Colonel Leonard P. Ayres (1940) of the Cleveland Trust Company was one of the first to calculate a breadth line and the first to notice the importance of a negative breadth

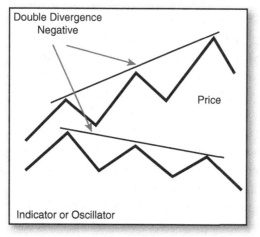

FIGURE 18.1   What Does Negative Divergence Look Like?

divergence from the averages. His theory was that highly capitalized stocks influence the averages, while the breadth line includes all stocks regardless of capitalization. Sometimes at the end of a bull market, the large stocks continue to rise, and the smaller stocks begin to falter.

Other market analysts, such as James F. Hughes (Merrill, *Stocks and Commodities Magazine* V6: 9, p. 354–355), argued that the rise in interest rates accompanying an economic expansion reflected in the stock market causes the interest-related stocks—such as utilities, which have large capital borrowing costs and of which there are many—to falter and, thus, causes the breadth line to lose momentum. Regardless of the cause, since May 1928, when a negative breadth divergence warned of the 1929 crash more than a year later, the observance of a negative divergence has invariably signaled an impending stock market top.

Although a negative divergence signals a market top, a primary stock market top can occur without a divergence. In other words, a breadth divergence is not necessary for a market peak. The peaks in 1937 and 1980, for example, occurred without a breadth divergence. After a sizable, lengthy advance, participants should be on guard and use a breadth divergence to help spot a potential market reversal. However, an analyst should not be adamant about requiring a breadth divergence to occur prior to a market peak.

At market bottoms, especially those that are characterized by climactic price action, a positive divergence in the cumulative breadth line rarely has been reliable in signaling a major reversal upward. However, there have been positive breadth divergences on either tests of major lows or so-called secondary lows that were useful signals of increasing market strength.

A characteristic of the breadth line that the analyst needs to recognize is that there is a downward bias to the line. Therefore, a new cumulative breadth line—one that has no relationship to the previous breadth line—begins once the market reaches a major low. For example, calculating a historical cumulative breadth line for the NYSE data resulted in an all-time peak in 1959. Although the cumulative breadth line never reached the same 1959 level for 40 years, there was a considerable rise in the market averages through 2000. This does not indicate a very large negative divergence over a 40-year time span, although some might argue that the 2007–2009 decline of more than 50% was a generational correction worthy of such a divergence. For our purposes, however, the cumulative breadth line, for divergence analysis, starts again once a major decline has occurred. When the market declines into a major low, one of the four-year plus varieties, analysis of the cumulative breadth line begins anew, and the line has no relationship to the peak of the previous major market cycle. It is as if a major decline wipes out the history of past declines, and the market then begins a new breadth cycle and new history.

A negative divergence, although not being required, has been the most successful method over the past 50 or more years for warning of a major market top. As with most indicators, different technicians use the breadth indicators in slightly different ways. For example, James F. Hughes, who published a market letter in the 1930s, learned of the breadth divergence concept from Col. Ayres (Harlow, 1968; Hughes, 1951). He used the negative breadth divergences as a major input to his stock market forecasting. Hughes required that at least two consecutive negative breadth divergences, called **double divergences** (see Figure 18.1), must occur before a major top was signaled. This requirement prevented mistakes in forecasting from the appearance of a single minor divergence that could later be nullified by a new high in both the averages and the breadth line. Often, more than two divergences occur at major market tops.

When the double breadth divergence warning occurs, it traditionally signals an actual market price peak within a year. Beginning with 1987, for example, a double breadth divergence correctly anticipated the 1987 crash when the breadth line peaked in April 1987, and five months later, in September, the market peaked and then collapsed. The breadth line peaked in the fall of 1989 followed by a peak in the average in July 1990. The most recent breadth peak signaled by a double breadth divergence was the 2007 peak in breadth and the 2008 peak in the averages, as shown in Figure 18.2, that foretold the coming stock market collapse in 2008–2009. The lag between the divergence and the final low is not constant, but the theory of a double divergence warning of a major market decline is still valid.

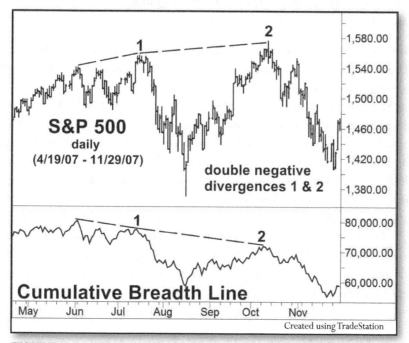

FIGURE 18.2   S&P 500 versus Breadth Line, Double Negative Divergence at 2007 Market Peak (daily, April 19, 2007–November 29, 2007)

Traditional Advance-Decline Methods That No Longer Are Profitable

Over the past ten years the market has changed, rendering the old methods of using moving averages and reversals as signals no longer reliable. Consider the following evidence that traditional advance-decline methods are no longer profitable:

- **Advance-decline line moving average**—Colby mentions this as a profitable method prior to 2000. It is calculated by calculating a 30-day moving average of both the Standard & Poor's 500 and the breadth line. When both the index and the line are above their moving averages, the market is bought, and vice versa, when they are both below their moving averages. In testing this thesis, we found that the 30-day moving average period peaked in profitability in 1998 and by 2000 was bankrupt. Its performance has continued to be negative since then. The optimal moving average value was 2 days, which produced 4,645 roundtrip trades in the 50 years and was less profitable than the buy-and-hold.

- **One-day change in advance-decline line**—The simplest signal occurs when the advance-decline line changes direction in one day. However, in looking back 50 years, we found this method peaked in February 2002 and did not begin profiting until 2009. Using an optimization program, we found that reversals after 75 days proved the most profitable but only beginning in 2003 and still producing an annual return less than the buy-and-hold.

This is useful information in that it warns students of the markets that the methods of analysis are fluid, are constantly changing, and should be thoroughly tested before being implemented in an investment plan.

John Stack, in an interview with Technical Analysis of Stocks & Commodities (Hartle, 1994) mentions using an index that compares the breadth line and a major market index. His purpose is to reduce the necessity of looking at an overlay of an indicator on the price chart to discern when a divergence has occurred. Instead, he calculates an index that tells whether breadth is improving or diverging from the market index and, thus, whether a warning of impending trouble is developing. Arthur Merrill (1990) also devised a numerical method to determine the relative slope of the breadth line versus a market index. By following the slope over time, we can calculate periods in which the breadth line is gaining or losing momentum. The advantageous aspect of this type of indicator is that it also measures the relative momentum when prices are declining.

Advance-Decline Line to Its 32-Week Simple Moving Average

Analysts have developed several variations of using the advance-decline line. One method is to compare it with its own moving average to give buy and sell signals for the market and, thus, create an oscillator. Ned Davis Research, Inc. used a ratio of the NYSE advance-decline line to its 32-week simple moving average. It found that from 1965 to 2010 when the ratio rises above 1.04, the per annum increase in stock prices as measured by the NYSE Composite Index was 19.3%, and when it declined below 0.97, the stock market declined 11.2% per annum. This oscillator is pictured in Figure 18.3.

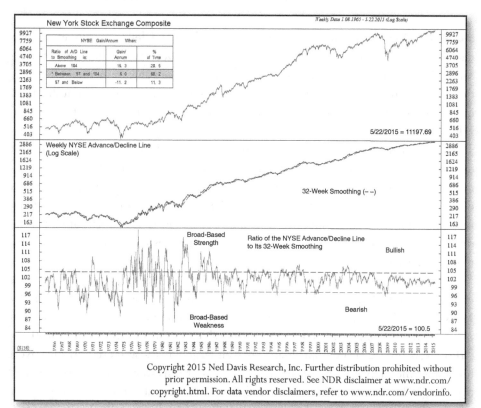

FIGURE 18.3   Advance-Decline Line to Its 32-Week Simple Moving Average versus NYSE Composite Index (weekly, January 8, 1965–May 22, 2015)

Breadth Differences

Indicators using breadth differences are calculated as the net of advances minus declines, either with the resulting sign or with an absolute number. The primary problem with using breadth differences is that the number of issues traded has expanded over time. For example, in the 40-year time period from 1960 to 2000, the number of issues on the New York Stock Exchange doubled from 1,528 issues to 3,083 issues. By 2015, the number had increased to 3,287 issues. More issues means larger potential differences between the number of advances and declines. Any indicator using differences must, therefore, have its parameters periodically adjusted for the increase in issues traded. Examples of useful indicators using breadth differences are listed next.

BOX 18.3 WHAT IS AN EQUITY LINE?

An **equity line** is a graph of a potential account value beginning at any time adjusted for each successive trade profit or loss. It is used to measure the success of a trading system. Ideally, each trade is profitable and adds to the value of the account each time a trade is closed. Any deviation from the ideal line is a sign of drawdown, volatility, or account loss, all of which are unavoidable problems with any trading or investment system. For profitable systems, the equity line should rise from left to right with a minimum number of corrections.

McClellan Oscillator   In 1969, Sherman and Marian McClellan developed the McClellan Oscillator. This oscillator is the difference between two exponential moving averages of advances minus declines. The two averages are an exponential equivalent to a 19-day and 39-day moving average. Extremes in the oscillator occur at the +100 or +150 and −100 or −150 levels, indicating respectively an overbought and oversold stock market.

The rationale for this oscillator is that in intermediate-term overbought and oversold periods, shorter moving averages tend to rise faster than longer-term moving averages. However, if the investor waits for the moving average to reverse direction, a large portion of the price move has already taken place. A ratio of two moving averages is much more sensitive than a single average and will often reverse direction coincident to, or before, the reverse in prices, especially when the ratio has reached an extreme.

Mechanical signals occur either in exiting one of these extreme levels or in crossing the zero line. A test of the zero crossing by the authors for the period May 1995 to May 2015, to see if the apparent changes in the breadth statistics had any effect on the oscillator, proved to be unprofitable. A test of crossing the +100 and −100 levels proved to be unprofitable as well largely because these extremes were not always met. Divergences at market tops and bottoms were informative. The first overbought level in the McClellan Oscillator often indicates the initial stage of an intermediate-term stock market rise rather than a top. Subsequently, a rise that is accompanied by less breadth momentum and, thus, a lower peak in the oscillator is suspect. At market bottoms, the opposite appears to be true and reliable. Finally, trend lines can be drawn between successive lows and highs that, when penetrated, often give excellent signals similar to trend line penetrations in prices.

McClellan Ratio-Adjusted Oscillator   Because he recognized that the use of advances minus declines alone can be influenced by the number of issues traded, McClellan devised a ratio to adjust and to replace the old difference calculation. This ratio is the net of advances minus declines divided by the total of advances plus declines. As the number of issues changes, the divisor will adjust the ratio accordingly. This ratio is usually multiplied by 1,000 to make it easier to read. The adjusted ratio is then calculated using the same exponential moving averages as in the earlier version of the oscillator.

In a study of the usefulness of this oscillator, we optimized the possible overbought and oversold levels and found that +4/+2 was the best level. This produced over the period August 1995–May 2015 a 404.4% return for the period over a buy-and-hold profit of 262.9%. The annual rate of return was 8.17%. Figure 18.4 shows the equity line for this study.

McClellan Summation Index   The McClellan summation index is a measure of the area under the curve of the McClellan Oscillator. It is calculated by accumulating the daily McClellan Oscillator figures into a cumulative index. The McClellans found that the index has an average range of 2,000 and added 1,000 points to the index

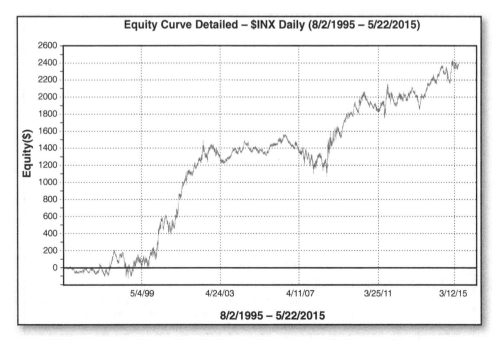

FIGURE 18.4   Equity Line of McClellan Ratio-Adjusted Oscillator with +4/+2 Overbought/Oversold

such that it now oscillates generally between 0 and 2,000; neutral is at 1,000. Originally, the summation index was calculated with the differences between advances and declines, but to eliminate the effect of increased number of issues, the adjusted ratio is now used. This is called the ratio-adjusted summation index (RASI). It has zero as its neutral level and generally oscillates between +500 and −500, which the McClellans consider to be overbought and oversold, respectively. Although no mechanical signals are suggested, the McClellans have mentioned that overbought readings are usually followed by a short correction that is followed by new highs. A failure to reach above the overbought level is a negative divergence and, thus, a sign that a market top is forming. Colby reports that only on the long side do intermediate-term signals profit (with an average holding of 172 days) given when the summation index changes direction.

Ned Davis Research, Inc., uses an overbought/oversold thrust-type signal to identify buy levels in the McClellan Summation Index (see Figure 18.5). A **thrust** buy signal occurs when an oscillator noticeably exceeds its boundaries and rises or falls by a larger amount than usual. The parameters are above 2,000 or below −350. Either signal is valid. The logic is that at a major market price bottom, the steep decline to the bottom is usually a panic and causes an extreme oversold condition.

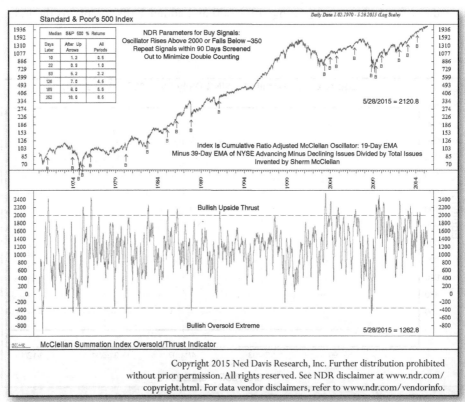

FIGURE 18.5 **McClellan Summation Index Oversold/Thrust Indicator**
(daily, January 2, 1970–May 28, 2015)

However, coming off the bottom, the market usually rebounds strongly, having formed a "V" pattern, and the upside motion, a thrust, is the greatest time to buy. The best case is when an oversold signal is followed within a short time by an overbought signal. This occurred at the major lows in 1970, 1974, and 2009.

Plurality Index   This index is calculated by taking the 25-day sum of the absolute difference between advances and declines. Because the calculation accounts only for the net amount of change independent of the directional sign, it is always a positive number. The stock market has a tendency to decline rapidly and rise slowly. Therefore, high numbers in the plurality index are usually a sign of an impending market bottom, and lower numbers suggest an impending top. Most signals have been reliable only on the long side because lower readings can occur early in an advance and give premature signals. Traditionally, the signal levels for this indicator were 12,000 and 6,000, but the increase in the number of issues has made these signal numbers obsolete (Colby, 2003). Colby uses a long-term (324-day) Bollinger Band breakout of the upper two standard deviations for buys and below two standard deviations for a sell to close. This method produced admirable results and has continued to do so since 2000. There are few signals, and a 15- or 30-day time stop should be used for longs only.

One additional suggestion for eliminating the effect of the increase in the number of issues listed over time is to use the McClellan ratio method of dividing the numerator by the sum of the advances and declines. Thus, the 25-day plurality index raw number becomes the absolute value of the advances minus declines divided by the sum of the advances and declines. This can then be summed over 25 days. The authors attempted to optimize the ratio Plurality Index over a period of 20 years. Although results of 7% to 8% annual returns were possible, the drawdowns in the hypothetical portfolio were greater than 50%, making the indicator useless for most analysts.

Absolute Breadth Index   Whereas the Hughes breadth oscillator uses a ratio of the raw difference between advances and declines divided by the total issues traded, the absolute breadth index uses the **absolute difference** of the advances minus declines divided by the total issues traded. Thus, the index is always a positive number. By experiment, Colby (2003) found that from 1932 to 2000, a profitable signal was generated when this index crossed the previous day's 2-day exponential moving average plus 81%. His report for longs only, which were held for an average of 13 days, only beat the buy-and-hold by 35.1% over the entire 68-year period, without commissions or slippage. Ned Davis Research, Inc., found a 9.1% annual gain versus a buy-and-hold gain of 8.3% per annum in long trades only between February 1977 and May 2015 using a thrust-style 10-day moving average in a thrust-style oscillator signal. Because the crossing of moving averages is often different with buys and short sales, instead of using only one moving average, the authors experimented with and optimized a system similar to the Colby's method using two moving averages: one

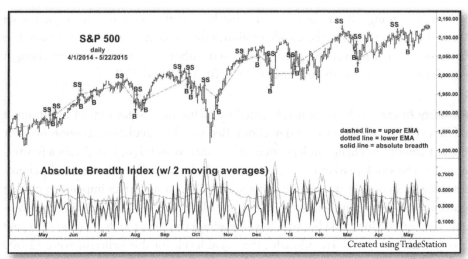

FIGURE 18.6 Absolute Breadth Index and S&P 500 (April 1, 2014–May 22, 2015)

for buys and one for short-sales. The outcome (see Figure 18.6) was moderately favorable with a 505.8% return over the buy-and-hold return of 279.8% for 20 years and a 9.10% annual return with only a 4% drawdown. The parameters were 4 days for the short-sale moving average and 48 days for the buys with an add-on to both of 63%.

Unchanged Issues Index The unchanged issues index uses a ratio of the number of unchanged stocks to the total traded. The theory behind it is that during periods of high directional activity, the number of unchanged declines. Unfortunately, with the decimalization of the stock quotes, the number of unchanged has declined, and the ratio now appears to have almost no predictive power. Testing this indicator, we have found negative results in almost all instances since April 2000.

Breadth Ratios

Instead of using the difference between daily or weekly advances and declines, which can be overly influenced by the increase or decrease in the number of issues listed, breadth ratios use a ratio between various configurations of advances, declines, and unchanged to develop trading indicators and systems for the markets. Using ratios has the advantage of reducing any long-term bias in the breadth statistics. These ratios usually project short-term market directional changes and are of little value for the long-term investor. They have also changed character and reliability since the year 2000.

Advance-Decline Ratio This ratio is determined by dividing the number of advances by the number of declines. The ratio or its components are then smoothed over some specific time to dampen the oscillations. Using daily breadth statistics between 1947 and 2000, Ned Davis Research, Inc., found 30 buy signals were

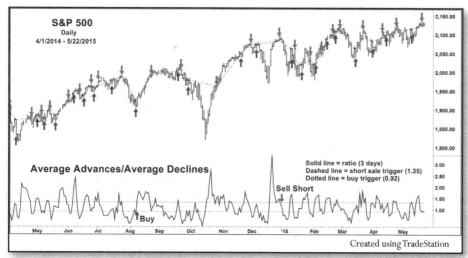

FIGURE 18.7 Optimized Ratio of a Moving Average of Advances to a Moving Average of Declines and Signals and S&P 500 (daily, April 1, 2014–May 22, 2015)

generated when the ratio of ten-day advances to ten-day declines exceeded 1.91. These signals averaged a 17.9% return over the following year. In only one of the 30 instances did the signal fail, and the loss then was only 5.6%. The authors decided to again use two signal lines and optimized the Advance-Decline ratio (see Figure 18.7). We constructed an average of all the advances and an average of all the declines and then divided the advance average by the decline average. Two signal lines were established for buys and short sales. The optimized result over a period of 20 years was a 429.0% return versus a 279.7% return for buy-and-hold. The annual rate of return was 8.51%, but the maximum drawdown was more than 37%, making the system one that most traders would not suffer through.

Colby (2003) reports that taking a one-day advance-decline ratio and buying the Dow Jones Industrial Average (DJIA) when the ratio crossed above 1.018 and selling it when the ratio declined below 1.018, in the period from March 1932 to August 2000, would have turned $100 into $884,717,056, assuming no commissions, slippage, or dividends. Turnover, of course, would have been excessive—an average of one trade every 3.47 days—but the results were excellent for both longs and shorts. We tested this system for the period from April 1995 to May 2015 and found that until February 2002, the results were still credible. However, since 2002, the equity line has collapsed. This negates, for now, the one-day method of trading the advance-decline ratio.

Breadth Thrust

A **thrust** is when a deviation from the norm is sufficiently large to be noticeable and when that deviation signals either the end of an old trend or the beginning of a new trend.

Martin Zweig devised the most common breadth thrust indicator, calculating a ten-day simple moving average of advances divided by the sum of advances and declines. Traditionally, the long-only signal levels in this oscillator were to buy when the index rose above 0.659 and sell when it declined below 0.366. With these limits, however, this method has not had profitable signals since 1994. In optimizing the calculation, we found that rather than using the horizontal line for a buy signal, a standard deviation band about a moving average of the advance/decline ratio, as defined earlier, gave relatively good performance but with a substantial drawdown. This testing and optimizing method is better than the horizontal line because the moving average drifts with the longer trend and thus adjusts for other factors affecting the ratio's trend. As of this writing the average is 39 days, and the two standard deviation multipliers are 1.15 and 0.32 (see Figure 18.8). The return from the best model was 521.7% versus the buy-and-hold return of 272.8% for 20 years. The annual rate of return was 9.25%, even with the 18.3% drawdown. Again, these changes are excellent examples of why the analyst must frequently review the reliability of any indicator being used. When the best of the best is subpar, it usually is a method that can be avoided.

Summary of Breadth Indicators

It appears that since 1995, a period of longer-term volatility in stock prices, the breadth indictors for short-term signals that had previously had admirable records mostly failed. These failures are why technical analysts must constantly test and review their indicators. Many changes occur in the marketplace, both structurally—as, for example, the change to decimalization and the inclusion of many nonproducing stocks in the breadth statistics—and marketwise—as, for example, the disconnection between stock prices and interest rates. No indicator remains profitable forever, both because of these internal changes and because of the overuse by technical

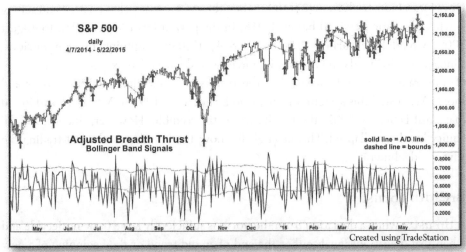

FIGURE 18.8 Adjusted Zweig Breadth Thrust and S&P 500 (April 7, 2014–May 22, 2015)

analysts who recognize their value. Apparently, the best remaining breadth usage is the old Ayres-Hughes double negative divergence analysis and the breadth thrust. They have had minimal failures for more than 60 years. Before an indicator is used in practice, however, it must be tested objectively. No indicator should be used just because it has demonstrated positive results in the immediate past.

■ Up and Down Volume Indicators

Breadth indicators assess market strength by counting the number of stocks that traded up or down on a particular day. An alternative way to gauge market internals is to measure the up volume and down volume. Up volume is the volume traded in all advancing stocks, and down volume is the total volume traded in declining stocks. Up and down volume figures are reported in most financial media.

Considering the volume, rather than only the number of shares traded, places more emphasis on stocks that are actively trading. With the breadth indicators, a stock that moves up on very light trading is given equal importance to one that moves up on heavy trading. By adding volume measures, the lightly traded stock does not have as much influence on the indicator as a heavily traded stock. The one caveat with using volume is that occasionally an enormous trade in a low-priced stock will upset the daily figures. This happened on December 9, 2009, when 3.76 billion Citigroup shares traded. The up and down volume statistics for that day were useless. Finally, the use of dark pools, off-exchange trading, and other methods of avoiding the reporting of transactions as well as the increase in trading in stocks that are part of ETFs and index futures have upset the earlier balance between volume and the individual investor. Many stocks are traded today as commodities in an index, for example, not because they are worthwhile investments but only because they are in the index. Volume as a statistic has, thus, become another aspect of change in the marketplace, and its use for technical indicators is changing and should be approached with caution.

The Arms Index

One of the most popular up and down volume indicators is the Arms Index, created by Richard W. Arms, Jr. (winner of the MTA 1995 Annual Award). The Arms Index (Arms, 1989), also known by its quote machine symbols of TRIN and MKDS, is reported daily in the financial media.

The Arms Index measures the relative volume in advancing stocks versus declining stocks. When a large amount of volume in declining stock occurs, the market is likely at or close to a bottom. Conversely, heavy volume in advancing stocks is usually healthy for the market. The Arms Index is actually a ratio of two ratios, as follows:

$$\text{Arms Index} = \frac{\dfrac{\text{Advances}}{\text{Declines}}}{\dfrac{\text{UpVolume}}{\text{DownVolume}}}$$

The numerator is the ratio of the advances to declines, and the denominator is the ratio of the up volume to the down volume. If the absolute number of advancing shares increases on low volume, the ratio will rise. This higher level of the Arms Index would indicate that, although the number of shares advancing is rising, the market is not strong because there is relatively low volume to support the price increases. This ratio, thus, travels inversely to market prices (unless plotted inversely), tending to peak at market bottoms and bottom at market peaks. This inverse relationship can initially be confusing to the chart reader.

Similar to breadth ratios, the Arms Index can be smoothed using moving averages and tested for parameters at which positions can be entered. An Arms Index greater than 1.0 is considered to be a bearish signal, with lower levels of the index indicating a more favorable market outlook. In our experiments, however, for the period February 2003 through May 22, 2015, we found that when the Arms Index rose above 1.0, it was a short-term buy signal rather than the expected sell signal. The equity curve is shown in Figure 18.9. Note that profits declined right from the beginning and never recovered. This is not the way to use the Arms Index.

Colby (2003) introduced a number of models that showed promise until the year 2000. A long-standing panic signal, devised by Alphier and Kuhn (1987), is to buy the stock market when the Arms Index exceeds 2.65 and hold it for a year. It basically worked well until 2009 when it had a 46% drawdown. It recovered from that in 2011 and went on to profit, but such a drawdown is unacceptable to most investors and a warning of what might occur in the future. When we shortened the holding period rather than using the original 252 days, the performance of the signals improved, but the large drawdown in 2009 remained.

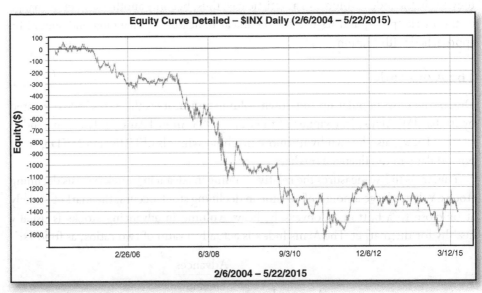

FIGURE 18.9 **Equity Line of Arms Index Buy on Crossing over 1.0 and S&P 500 (daily, March 28, 2003–May 22, 2015)**

Volume Thrust with Up Volume and Down Volume

Using up volume and down volume only and forming an oscillator that is a moving average of the ratio of one to another produces an oscillator that has an excellent history of producing profitable thrusts, especially on the Nasdaq. Shown is a chart (Figure 18.10) that represents the specific method devised by Ned Davis Research, Inc. It is a ratio of the 10-day up volume to the 10-day down volume with thresholds at 1.48, above which is a thrust buy, and 1.00, below which is a sell. The performance is measured by the prospects for the market when the ratio is in one of three ranges. Above 1.48, the Nasdaq advanced for an annualized gain of 38.9%; between 1.48 and 1.00, the annualized gain declined to a positive 12.9%; and below 1.00, it produced a loss of 7.4% annualized.

Ninety Percent Downside Days (NPDD)

Paul F. Desmond, in his Charles H. Dow Award paper (Desmond, 2002), presents a reliable method for identifying major stock market bottoms that uses daily upside and downside volume as well as daily points gained and points lost. The volume figures are reported in the financial media, as are the stock tables. Unfortunately, the sum of points gained and lost is not reported publicly and requires considerable

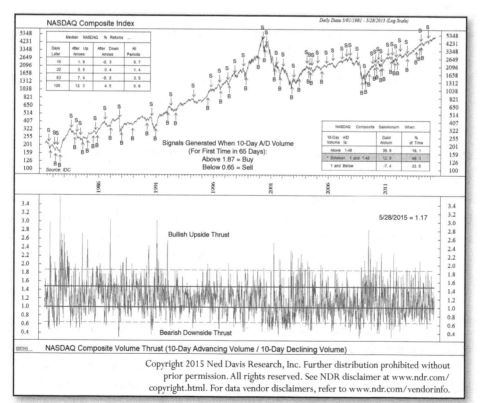

FIGURE 18.10 Volume Thrust and Nasdaq Composite (daily, May 1, 1981–May 28, 2015)

handwork or a computer. A 90% downside day occurs when, on a particular day, the percentage of downside volume exceeds the total of upside and downside volume by 90% *and* the percentage of downside points exceeds the total of gained points and lost points by 90%. A 90% upside day occurs when both the upside volume and the points gained are 90% of their respective totals. What he found was that

- An NPDD in isolation is only a warning of potential danger ahead, suggesting, "Investors are in a mood to panic" (Desmond, 2002, p. 38).

- An NPDD occurring right after a new market high or on a surprise negative news announcement is usually associated with a short-term correction.

- When two or more NPDDs occur, so do additional NPDDs, often 30 trading days or more apart.

- Big volume rally periods of two to seven days often follow an NPDD and can be profitable for agile traders but not for investors.

- A major reversal is signaled when an NPDD is followed by a 90% upside day or two 80% upside days back-to-back.

- In half the cases, the upside reversal occurred within five trading days of the low. The longer it takes for the upside day reversal, the more skeptical the investor should be.

- Investors should be careful when only one of the two upside components reaches 90%. Such rallies are usually short.

- Back-to-back 90% upside days are relatively rare but usually are long-term bullish.

10-to-1 Up Volume Days and 9-to-1 Down Volume Days

Whereas Desmond combines breadth and volume for his panic indicator, Ned Davis Research, Inc. studied up and down volume alone without confirmation from breadth. Ned Davis Research, Inc.'s rules are a little complicated, a sign that the analyst should beware. Complicated rules are usually those that are constructed from curve fitting and might not be viable in the future because they only fit past data. However, the results of these studies were impressive and demonstrated the contrary opinion thesis that panics are often times to buy and sharp, steep rises from lows especially often signal the end of a decline.

Specifically what they found was that roughly six months after a 10-to-1 up volume day, the market was 9% higher (see Figure 18.11). Similarly, after roughly six months following a 9-to-1 down volume day, the market was 6% higher (see Figure 18.12). Shorter periods after each signal were also higher but not by the same percentage. In other words, each of these events suggested a panic bottom.

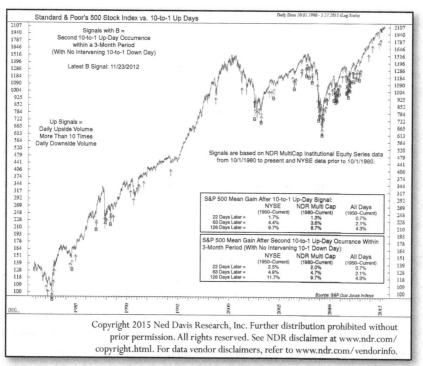

FIGURE 18.11 **10-to-1 Up Days and S&P 500 (daily, October 1, 1980–May 22, 2015)**

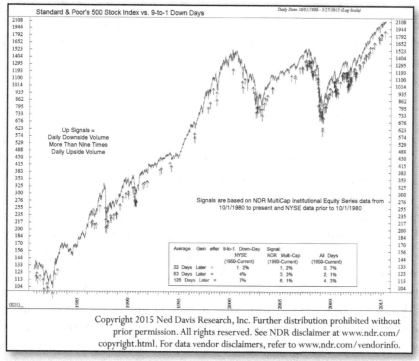

FIGURE 18.12 **9-to-1 Down Volume Days and S&P 500 (daily, October 1, 1980–May 22, 2015)**

◼ Net New Highs and Net New Lows

When the stock market is rising, it is only reasonable to assume that individual stocks are making new highs. Conversely, stock market declines are associated with stocks making new lows.

Generally, a stock is considered to reach a new high if the day's price is higher than the price has been over the past year. Prior to 1978, new highs and new lows were measured from January of the current year only, but in 1978, the New York Stock Exchange began determining new highs and new lows based on trailing 52-week prices. Other exchanges also adjusted their reporting at that time for consistency with the NYSE figures. Thus, a stock reaches a new high when the price is higher than it has been anytime during the previous 52 weeks, not necessarily when it has reached a new all-time high.

The financial press reports 52-week highs and lows, but the period of 52 weeks is not sacred. Analysts calculate many other periods based on their individual investment horizons. For short-term breakouts, for example, 10 or 21 days are used. In any case, the number of new highs and new lows is a useful measure of the number of stocks participating in an advance or decline. It is, thus, an indicator of a continuing trend and usually subject to divergence analysis, similar to breadth statistics.

The raw data of new highs and new lows is subject to the same problems as breadth in that the number of issues listed on an exchange will often change over time and make indicators using differences between highs and lows unreliable and subject to constant change in indicator parameters. As in breadth indicators, the way around this difficulty is to divide the difference between the new highs and lows by the total issues traded on the exchange, thus eliminating any bias from the changing number of listings.

New Highs versus New Lows

The most straightforward, and probably useful, index is to buy when the number of new highs exceeds the number of new lows on a daily basis and to sell when the opposite occurs. Colby (2003) reports favorable results on both sides of the market, long or short, but the holding period is relatively short. One interesting aspect of net new weekly highs and lows is that they generally peak before the market peaks, similar to the breadth line. This extremely reliable observation can warn us when we see a negative divergence in weekly high-low data that a correction is due soon. (The average lead is 33 weeks with a wide error.)

Figure 18.13 shows Ned Davis Research, Inc.'s method of utilizing new highs and lows. It is a 55-day exponential moving average of the daily new highs divided by the sum of the new highs plus new lows. The buy signal is when the oscillator rises above 21%, and the sell signal is when the oscillator declines 40.5 points from the latest peak. The results show a 9.3% annual return versus a 6.6% return in the buy-and-hold.

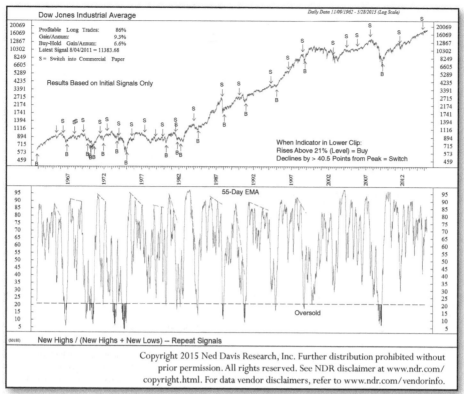

FIGURE 18.13 New Highs / (new lows + new highs) and Dow Jones Industrial
Average (daily, November 9, 1962–May 28, 2015)

High Low Logic Index

Norman Fosback (1976) is the developer of the high-low logic index. This index is
defined as the lesser of two ratios: the number of weekly new highs to total issues
or the number of weekly new lows to total issues. Low index levels tend to suggest
a strongly trending market. A low number would indicate that either a low number
of new highs or a low number of new lows is occurring. A high index level implies
mixed market because the index can only be high when the number of both new
highs and new lows is large.

Analysts traditionally smooth this index over ten weeks with a moving average.
With either the raw or smoothed data, levels are then determined at which a signal
is generated. Generally, high levels are bearish and low levels are bullish. In the first
edition of *The Encyclopedia of Technical Market Indicators*, authors Robert Colby and
Thomas Meyers (1988) reported that from 1937 to 1987, the results from such
indicators were highly significant to the 99.9% confidence level. Their thresholds for
raw data were above 0.020 for a down market one to three months later and below
0.002 for an up market one to six months later. For the ten-week smoothed index,
a downward market was signaled above 0.058 for three months, and an upward

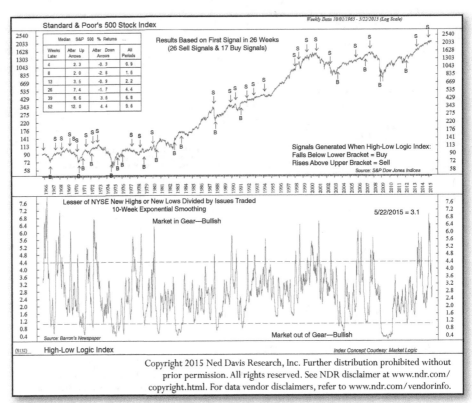

FIGURE 18.14 High-Low Logic Index and S&P 500 (October 1, 1965–May 22, 2015)

market was signaled below 0.005 for three and twelve months later. Figure 18.14 shows Ned Davis Research, Inc. data and its thresholds for buying and selling. It is obvious that the buys are more reliable than the sells.

Hindenburg Omen

Many indicators use a combination of other indicators to derive a signal. The Hindenburg Omen described by Morris (2005) is such an indicator (see Figure 18.15). Similar to Fosback's high-low logic index, the original indicator was devised by the late Jim Mikkea, former editor and publisher of the *Sudbury Bull and Bear Report* and was named by the late Kennedy Gammage (Colby, 2003) after the Hindenburg Dirigible disaster of 1937. Obviously, it signals a market reversal downward. The several descriptions of the current version are found at either (1) Morris (2005), (2) McClellan Financial Publications (http://www.mcoscillator.com), or (3) Robert McHugh (2014). The variables and parameters are individual but all produce approximately the same results:

■ The 52-week highs and lows are each greater than 2.2% (or 2.8%) of total issues.

■ The small number of new highs or new lows is greater than 75.

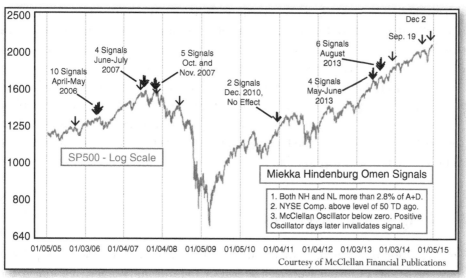

FIGURE 18.15 Hindenburg Omen and S&P 500 (January 5, 2005–January 5, 2015)

- The NYSE index is higher than 50 day previous. An alternative condition is for the 10-week (50-day) moving average of the NYSE to be higher than ten weeks earlier.

- The McClellan Oscillator is negative.

- New highs cannot be more than two times the number of new lows

- Confirmation, defined as two or more occurrences within a 30–36-day period, exists.

The signal is valid for 30 to 36 days and active only when the McClellan Oscillator is negative. Strength of the signal is proportional to the number of early occurrences within the 30–36 day limit.

> "The rationale behind the indicator is that, under normal conditions, either a substantial number of stocks establish new annual highs or a large number set new lows—but not both." When both new highs and new lows are large, "it indicates the market is undergoing a period of extreme divergence—many stocks establishing new highs and many setting new lows as well. Such divergence is not usually conducive to future rising prices. A healthy market requires some semblance of internal uniformity, and it doesn't matter what direction that uniformity takes. Many new highs and very few lows is obviously bullish, but so is a great many new lows accompanied by few or no new highs. This is the condition that leads to important market bottoms." (Peter Eliades, September 21, 2005, Daily Update, www.stockmarketcycles.com)

This indicator reportedly occurred prior to every major crash since 1985 (including the 1987 crash). Twenty-five confirmed omens have occurred, with only two failing to be followed by a decline of 2% or more. The other subsequent declines were not crashes because the omen often gives false signals for crashes. However, the odds of a crash (down more than 15%) are about 24% after a confirmed signal. One major problem with the derivation of this indicator is that it is so complex. As mentioned earlier, complexity usually comes from curve fitting and is, thus, potentially unreliable. The Hindenburg Omen, however, is based on technical logic and is certainly something to follow.

■ Using Moving Averages

The indication of a trending stock usually is gauged by whether the stock price is above or below a moving average. The longer the moving average, the longer the trend the relationship represents. Looking at how many stocks are trending gives us a measure of market strength.

Coppock Curve

In October 1965, a quasi-economist named Edwin "Sedge" Coppock wrote an article in *Barron's Magazine* describing a long-term momentum oscillator he had discovered. It was based on a study he had performed for his church that had asked him to invest their funds. His premise was that the period of a moving average or rate of change should be related to human psychology, and the closest analogy he could come up with after talking with the local bishop was the time it took a person to get over bereavement of a lost friend or relative. The bishop reportedly mentioned 11 to 14 months, and these became the basis of Coppock's Index or Curve. It is calculated as the 10-month, weighted-moving average of the sum of an 11-month rate of change and a 14-month rate of change in a market index such as the S&P 500. Using the original parameters between June 1963 and April 2015, we found its performance between a buy signal and subsequent market peak to average 64.2% for on average 35.2 months. When we included the times when the index crossed below zero for short sales, we found the performance about even with the buy-and-hold. In line with the thinking that market tops are long and often flat whereas bottoms are sharp and short, the sell-short criteria caused the Coppock Index to sell far too soon; thus, it lost the performance potentially gained if it had remained invested longer.

To optimize the parameters (see Figure 18.16), we decided to leave the 11- and 14-month rate of change as is (the reasoning is too good) and optimized the moving averages (one for buys and one for short-sales) and the breakpoint for each moving average. The parameters turned out to be 1 and 9 for the buy and short-

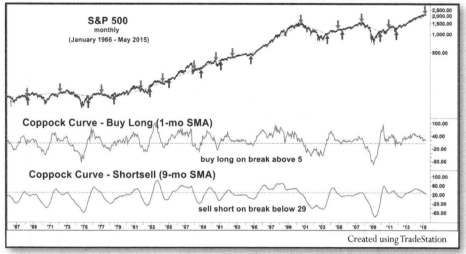

FIGURE 18.16 Optimized Parameters for Coppock Curve and S&P 500
(January 1966–May 2015)

sale moving averages respectively and 5 and 29 for the breakpoints respectively. The
annual rate of return was 7.13%, and the total return was 3,707% versus 2,367%
for the buy-and-hold.

Number of Stocks Above Their 30-Week Moving Average

One indicator of overbought and oversold markets, as pictured in Figure 18.17,
is the number of stocks above or below their 30-week moving averages. This indicator essentially measures the number of stocks in uptrends and downtrends.
It is a contrary indicator, however, in that when the percentage of stocks above
their 30-week moving averages reaches above 70%, the market is inevitably overbought and ready for a correction. Conversely, when the percentage of stocks
below their 30-week moving average declines below 30%, the market is at or
close to a bottom. Investors Intelligence, Inc. popularized this indicator. It has
developed other rules for action between the 30% and 70% levels that follow
intermediate-trend turns.

The 80/60 Rule   One interesting variation in the use of stocks above their 30-week
moving average is the 80/60 rule. This rule states that when the percentage of stocks
above their 30-week moving average has been greater than 80% and then declines
below 60%, the percentage will decline to or close to 30%. In other words, a serious decline will likely follow such a signal. Figure 18.18 by Ned Davis Research, Inc.
suggests that of the 20 instances of this occurring since 1968, 17 resulted in a general
market decline.

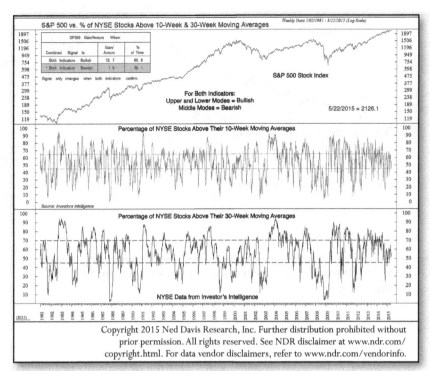

FIGURE 18.17 Percentage of NYSE Stocks above Their 10- and 30-Week Moving Averages (January 2, 1981–May 22, 2015)

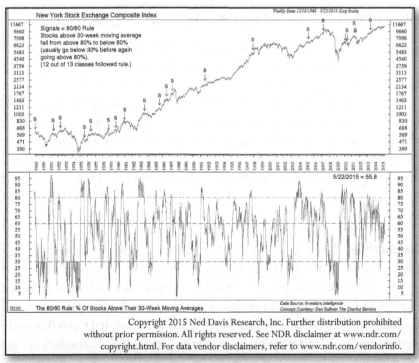

FIGURE 18.18 The 80/60 Rule in Stocks above Their 30-Week Moving Average (December 13, 1968–May 22, 2015)

■ Very Short-Term Indicators

Although market sentiment indicators generally focus on spotting long-term trend reversals, the concept of sentiment can be used as a short-term contrarian indicator. Let's look at a few ways in which following these indicators might provide clues to short-term trading opportunities.

Breadth and New Highs to New Lows

Although breadth and new high-low data tend to be indicators of trend, and divergence analysis is useful in determining when a known trend may be reversing, short-term readings of breadth and new high-low data are often contrary indicators. For example, when the daily breadth ratio of advances to declines rises to 2/1 or 3/1, the subsequent market direction is more often down than up. The opposite is also true for days in which the advance-decline ratio is 2/1 or 3/1 on the downside. It often provides excellent buying opportunities for the short term (that is, the next week).

New highs and new lows show the same results. Trading with the longer-term trend is the best method of maximizing profits. Entering the trend right after it has been recognized, however, is often not profitable, at least until prices have retraced from their initial reaction. Thus, for example, if the market is above its 200-day moving average and is presumably in a longer-term uptrend, whenever the averages break to new 10-day lows is an excellent time to go long. Oppositely, when the market is below its 200-day moving average (and thus in a longer-term downtrend) and rallies take prices above their 10-day highs, you have the best opportunity to sell short. In this manner, the use of new highs and new lows can be used as a contrary signal within the major trend and a way of profiting from price dispersions from the mean trend.

Net Ticks

Ticks represent actual trades. When a stock changes price, even by the smallest amount, either an uptick or a downtick is produced. If the stock trades at its previous price, a zero-tick is produced. By summing at any one instant the number of upticks versus downticks, the day trader has an indicator of market action across the board. It is similar to an advance-decline ratio or difference except that it is based on much more sensitive intraday data.

Generally, tick data is used as a contrary indicator because it measures short-term bursts of enthusiasm or fear. Extreme readings may indicate a longer-term change in trend, but usually the tick ratio oscillates within bounds throughout the day. When it is oversold, traders will buy into the short-term fear, and when it is overbought, they will sell into the temporary enthusiasm. Ratios and moving averages are used with this data in a similar manner to breadth statistics. Ticks can also be calculated for averages and indices such as the Dow Jones Industrial, where only the stocks included in the average are measured.

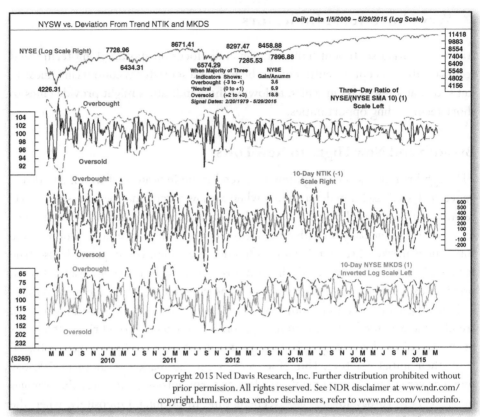

FIGURE 18.19 Short-Term Signals from Tick and Arms (MKDS) Indicators and NYSE Composite (January 5, 2009–May 29, 2015)

Closing ticks can also be used similar to daily breadth statistics. Closing ticks represent the trading action just at the close of trading and show whether traders are anxious or ambivalent. In Figure 18.19, a ten-day moving average of net ticks shows oscillations in line with the averages. Combining this indicator with one of the Arms Index (MKDS) and the NYSE Composite, Ned Davis Research, Inc. found specific levels at which significant market moves could develop.

■ Conclusion

In this chapter, we focused on the measurement of market internal strength. One important factor in measuring market internals is the calculation of market breadth line (advance-decline line). Market breadth is a measure of how widely a market move is spread throughout the stock market. In other words, measuring breadth tells the analyst whether an increase in the market index is characterized by a large increase in the price of a few stocks or a smaller increase in the price of the majority of the market stocks. Is the typical stock moving the same way that the market index (which can be influenced by big moves in a few stocks) is moving? If so, the market direction is confirmed by the internals. If not, the internals and the index are diverging, indicating that internal strength is changing.

Another way of looking at internal market strength is to look at up and down volume. Instead of looking at the number of issues that advanced or declined on a particular day, look at up and down volume measures. Using this type of measure, each stock issue is not given equal weight. Instead, stocks with heavy trading volume are given more weight and play a more important role in gauging internal market strength.

A third major way to gauge internal market strength is to compare the current price of each stock with its historical price. Looking at how many stocks are being traded at price extremes can do this—that is, looking at stocks trading at new highs and new lows. Alternatively, it can be done simply by comparing the current price with a historical average price of each issue to see how many stocks seem to be moving in the same direction as the market index.

Whatever method is being used, the indicators presented in this chapter are designed to measure whether there is enough strength internally to predict that the market trend will continue in the direction it has been. Understanding how internal strength relates to broader market movement is important. Unfortunately, we have seen many of the traditional indicators perform poorly during the past few years. Only time will tell if the traditional indicators with their traditional parameters will perform satisfactorily in the future. In the meantime, analysts continue to develop, test, and refine ways to measure market internal strength. It is the job of the technician to find what works best for the appropriate trading or investment time horizon.

■ References

Alphier, James and B. Kuhn. "A Helping Hand from the Arms Index." *Technical Analysis of Stocks & Commodities* 5, no. 4 (1987): 142–143.

Arms, Richard W., Jr. *The Arms Index: An Introduction to the Volume Analysis of Stock and Bond Markets*. Homewood, IL: Dow Jones-Irwin, 1989.

Ayres, Leonard P. *Turning Points in Business Cycles*. New York, NY: The Macmillan Company, 1940.

Brown, Constance W. *Technical Analysis for the Trading Professional*. New York, NY: McGraw-Hill, 1999.

Colby, Robert W. *The Encyclopedia of Technical Market Indicators*. New York, NY: McGraw-Hill, 2003.

Colby, Robert and Thomas Meyers. *The Encyclopedia of Technical Market Indicators*. New York, NY: McGraw-Hill, 1988.

Davis, Ned. *Being Right or Making Money*. Venice, FL: Ned Davis Research Inc., 2000.

Desmond, Paul F. "Identifying Bear Market Bottoms and New Bull Markets." *Journal of Technical Analysis* (formerly *The Market Technicians Association Journal*) 57 (2002): 38–42.

Fosback, Norman. *Stock Market Logic: A Sophisticated Approach to Profits on Wall Street*. Chicago, IL: Dearborn Financial Publishing, Inc., 1976 (1933 edition).

Harlow, Charles V. *An Analysis of the Predictive Value of Stock Market "Breadth" Measurements*. Larchmont, NY: Investors Intelligence, 1968.

Hartle, Thom. "James B. Stack, Big Sky Investor." *Technical Analysis of Stocks & Commodities* 12, no. 7 (July 1994): 294–302.

Hughes, James F. "The Birth of the Climax-Breadth Method." *Analysts Journal*, 3rd quarter (1951): 25–35.

McClellan, Sherman and Marian McClellan. *Patterns for Profit*. La Canada, CA: Trade Levels, Inc., 1970.

McHugh, Robert. "We Got an Official Confirmed Hindenburg Omen on December 2nd, 2014." www.safehaven.com, 2014.

Merrill, Arthur A. "Negative Volume Divergence Index." *Technical Analysis of Stocks & Commodities*, vol. 8, no. 10 (1990): 396–397.

Merrill, Arthur A. "Advance-Decline Divergences as an Oscillator." *Stocks & Commodities Magazine* 6, no. 9 (September 1988): 354–355.

Morris, Gregory L. *The Complete Guide to Market Breadth Indicators: How to Analyze and Evaluate Market Direction and Strength*. New York, NY: McGraw-Hill, 2005.

ADVANCED CONCEPTS IN CHARTING AND TREND ANALYSIS

CHAPTER 19

Foundations of Cycle Theory

Kyle Crystal, CMT, CFTe

Learning Objective Statements

- Name the two types of cycles
- Identify the three defining characteristics of a cycle
- List and define Hurst's seven Principles of Commonality
- Define a composite wave
- Identify left and right translation
- Describe a dominant cycle
- Recall the tools that aid in cycle identification

■ Cycle Characteristics

Cycles excel at answering the question of "when?" better than most, if not all, other forms of market analysis. There are two broad classes of cycles:

1. *Fixed cycles*, also known as linear cycles
2. *Sequences*, also known as nonlinear cycles

This chapter focuses almost entirely on fixed cycles. Sequences will be addressed in the next chapter.

A word of caution before we begin. It is not recommended that cycles be used alone. Cycles must be used in conjunction with other noncorrelated technical tools that provide confirmation of cycle lows and highs. Momentum oscillators, Elliott Wave analysis, and Andrews Pitchforks are just some of the tools and methodologies that can and should be integrated with cycle analysis.

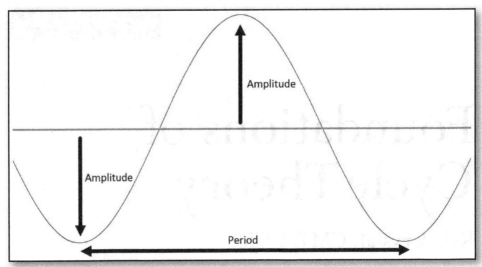

FIGURE 19.1 Cycle Characteristics
Source: Timing Solution.

What Is a Cycle? Three Defining Characteristics

In the context of technical analysis, a cycle refers to a simple oscillation of price movement from a trough to a peak and back lower to another trough. As illustrated in Figure 19.1, it takes three variables to define a cycle: period, amplitude, and phase. In other words, two cycles with the same period, amplitude, and phase are identical.

- *Period:* The unit of time between two consecutive troughs of the same cycle.

- *Amplitude:* The height between a cycle's midpoint and crest or trough.

- *Phase:* The position of a cycle relative to its most recent trough.

It should be noted that the terms "wavelength" and "frequency" are commonly used when discussing cycles. *Wavelength* is the distance between two consecutive troughs. The term is similar to "period," but is not referencing a specific unit of time, such as hours, days, or weeks. *Frequency* is defined as the reciprocal of the period. The simple way to conceptualize frequency is to think of the number of periods that fit into the 360° rotation of a cycle. For instance, a cycle with a period of 90 days has a frequency of around four cycles per year, or about ⅓ of a cycle per month:

$$\frac{365}{90} = 4.1 \text{ cycles per year}$$

$$\frac{(365/90)}{12} = .34 \text{ cycles per month}$$

Principles

J.M. Hurst outlined the principles of cycle theory in his book *Profit Magic of Stock Transaction Timing.* He set forth seven Principles of Commonality that apply to cycle analysis of all financial markets:

1. *Cyclicality:* All financial markets are composed of cycles.
2. *Harmonicity:* A cycle's harmonics are related by multiples of two and three.
3. *Summation:* Price is a composite wave of the sum of individual cycles.
4. *Synchronicity:* Cycle lows tend to bottom in tandem.
5. *Proportionality:* A cycle's period is proportional to its amplitude.
6. *Nominality:* Some wave periods are more common than others.
7. *Variation:* Financial markets will not obey theoretical perfection.

We are now going to explore each of these principles in more detail.

Cyclicality   All financial markets are affected by cycles. We use the same principles, tools, and logic whether we are analyzing equities, fixed income, commodities, or foreign exchange markets.

Harmonicity   A dominant cycle will produce harmonics that are related by small whole numbers, most commonly multiples of two or, less common, multiples of three. These are known as the 2nd and 3rd harmonics, respectively. They may also be reciprocals of small whole numbers, commonly ½ or, less common, ⅓. These are known as the ½ and ⅓ harmonics, respectively. Figure 19.2 displays the interaction of the dominant cycle and its 2nd and 3rd harmonics. This illustration disregards the principle of proportionality, explained below, to emphasize only the harmonics.

Harmonic Relationships

A 100-day dominant cycle produces smaller harmonics through division:
2nd harmonic = 100/2 = 50 days
3rd harmonic = 100/3 = 33.33 days
4th harmonic = 100/4 = 25 days
as well as larger harmonics through multiplication:
1/2 harmonic = 100×2 = 200 days
1/3 harmonic = 100×3 = 300 days
1/4 harmonic = 100×4 = 400 days
Not all harmonics will be present at any one time.

FIGURE 19.2   Cycle Harmonics
Source: Timing Solution.

Be sure to understand that in the example above, all of the harmonics are related to the dominant cycle, and therefore are all part of the same "mathematical family." Their presence confirms the dominant cycle and they may be used to fine-tune a cycle model.

Also, be aware that markets can have more than one cycle (and its respective harmonics) present at the same time. This is often the case with many of the grain markets and helps to explain their often noisy, whipsaw character.

Summation In cycle theory, price is viewed as a *composite wave*, a summation of individual cycles as well as the trend. All cycles are equally weighted within a theoretical cycle model. Study the bottom panel in Figure 19.3, which shows a dominant cycle and its 2nd harmonic. The two cycles add together to create the composite wave above. Note that the summation of the two cycles creates a dip where one would expect to find the dominant cycle's peak. This is an important cycle signature referred to as the "mid-cycle dip." This illustration disregards the principle of proportionality, explained below, to emphasize only the summation of the dominant cycle and 2nd harmonic cycle.

Synchronicity An even harmonic will always bottom in tandem with its next larger period cycle. Read that sentence again. To illustrate, study Figure 19.4. A dominant cycle and its 2nd and 4th harmonics are overlaid in the lower panel. Above that is the

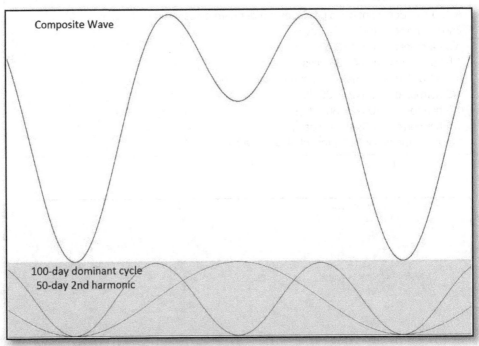

FIGURE 19.3 2nd Harmonic Composite Wave
Source: Timing Solution.

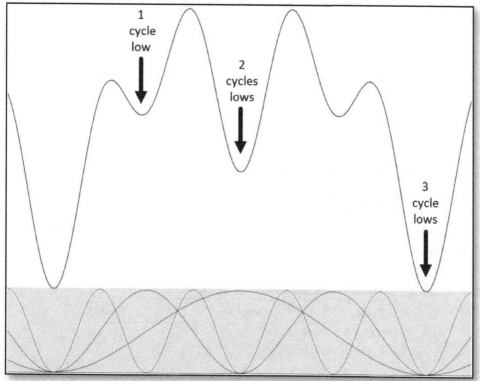

FIGURE 19.4   Principle of Synchronicity
Source: Timing Solution.

summation composite wave of the three cycles. Note how the smaller cycle always bottoms in tandem with its next larger cycle.

This knowledge aids an analyst in properly phasing a chart; that is, understanding where current prices fit into the cycle model. Now, look again and note how there is a direct relationship between the number of cycles bottoming and the magnitude of the decline and degree of the low. The more cycles bottoming, the greater the magnitude of the decline and depth of the ensuing low. As in previous illustrations, the principle of proportionality is ignored to emphasize only the synchronicity of related cycles.

Proportionality   A cycle's period is proportionally related to its amplitude. In other words, longer cycles create the trend for smaller cycles to ride. This principle fits with the fractal nature of various forms of technical analysis, including the Elliott Wave Principle. Figure 19.5 illustrates the Principle of Proportionality because the 2nd harmonic is half the amplitude of the dominant cycle.

Nominality   Some cycle periods are more common than others. Hurst used nominal periods as a guide for cycle analysis. While the specific periods are interesting to note, it is more important to understand that the relationships of the periods are ruled by the Principle of Harmonicity.

FIGURE 19.5 Principle of Proportionality
Source: Timing Solution.

The specific period of a dominant cycle for any market may be materially different than the period in the nominal model; that is both acceptable and expected. The goal of cycle analysis is to create what Hurst referred to as a "current cyclical model." This is a written model detailing the period and phase of each cycle affecting a market.

As presented in *The Profit Magic of Stock Transaction Timing,* below is J.M. Hurst's nominal model.

Hurst's Nominal Model Variation #1

Years	Months	Weeks
18		
9		
4.5		
3		
1.5	18	
1.0	12	
.75	9	
.50	6	26
.25	3	13
	1.5	6.5
	.75	3.25
	.375	1.625

"*The 26- and 13-week components often appear in data as a combined effect of 18-week nominal duration."

Source: The Profit Magic of Stock Transaction Timing.

Variation Cycles in financial markets are messier than the perfection found in cycle theory. While we use the term "fixed cycles" to describe cyclical activity, troughs in financial markets are commonly made slightly early or late of expectations. The term for this is *translation*. A cycle that is described as *right translated* implies price is bottoming later than expectations. A *left translated* cycle bottoms earlier than expectations.

Another example of the Principle of Variation is the fact that cycles and their harmonics will disappear and reappear over time. Generally, the longer a fixed cycle has been in effect, the more likely it is to stop working. As a guideline, fixed cycles become visible after three iterations and tend to repeat for 6 to 12 iterations before shifting.

Variation is also present regarding the Principle of Proportionality. A cycle's amplitude is oftentimes disproportionate to its period. A fundamental shock or news event can result in the amplitude of a smaller harmonic cycle overpowering a larger cycle.

What Is a Dominant Cycle?

A *dominant cycle* is the most visually evident cycle on a chart. An analyst should first try to identify the dominant cycle with his or her eye by looking for sine wave patterns within the price action. Keep in mind that the sine wave will often have a mid-cycle dip due to the 2nd harmonic. After visually examining the chart, an analyst will confirm the dominant cycle with the aid of a spectrogram (discussed later in this chapter). Once identified, the dominant cycle becomes the pulse through which price and other harmonics interact.

■ Fixed Cycle Tools

The following section discusses various tools employed to aid in identifying a dominant cycle and any active harmonics. Spectrograms and wavelet diagrams are useful for visual, objective examination of a cyclical landscape. The Fisher Transform will be of particular interest to quantitative analysts looking to incorporate cycle analysis into their algorithms.

Spectrograms

The French mathematician Fourier discovered the law of harmonic motion, which says every complex vibration can be broken down into a series of simple pendular motions of $\frac{1}{2}, \frac{1}{3}, \frac{1}{4}, \frac{1}{5}, \frac{1}{6}, \frac{1}{7}, \frac{1}{8}, \frac{1}{9}, \frac{1}{10}$ ad infinitum. This discovery led to the development of spectral analysis, otherwise known as harmonic analysis.

A spectrogram is used to visualize the results of spectral analysis. It is a graph in which the *y*-axis displays a cycle's amplitude and the *x*-axis represents a cycle's period. The output of the analysis is commonly displayed as a series of spikes. The taller and skinnier the spike, the more important the cycle is to that market. J.M. Hurst developed a custom spectrogram he referred to as a "periodogram" for this activity.

The spikes of the spectrogram identify and map the harmonic relationships present within a market. The dominant cycle is commonly the tallest spike, or one of the tallest, within the graph. Harmonics are commonly smaller spikes that are mathematically related to the dominant cycle by small whole numbers. Again, harmonics work to confirm the presence of a dominant cycle. The spectrogram's spikes are like a mathematical puzzle that leads to a current cycle model.

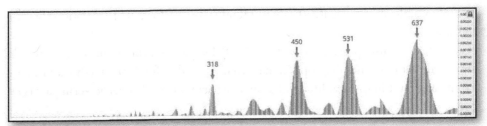

FIGURE 19.6 Spectrogram of VanEck Vectors Oil Services ETF (Ticker: OIH)

Source: Optuma.

Before moving on, a word of advice. It is necessary to be flexible when interpreting the mathematical relationships between cycles. Figure 19.6 shows an example of a spectrogram. Note the 637-day cycle is the tallest spike. It is verified as a dominant cycle by the 2nd harmonic spike at 318.5 days (637/2=318.5). Be aware that an analyst would still accept harmonic verification of the dominant cycle had the harmonic's spike appeared at 315 days or 323 days, for example. There are no exact guidelines on how much variation is acceptable. The experience and judgment of the analyst are important.

Wavelet Diagrams

Wavelet diagrams map cyclical activity over defined periods of time. The results are interpreted in a graph in which the *y*-axis represents the period of a cycle and the *x*-axis tracks the date. The presence and strength of a cycle is typically displayed as a color. In Figure 19.7, lighter colors are used to indicate the presence and intensity of cyclical activity while darker areas represent the absence of cyclical activity. This type of graph is useful in determining how long a cycle has been present. Also, note that Figure 19.7 demonstrates that cycles disappear and reappear over time.

Fisher Transform

Created by J.F. Ehlers, the Fisher Transform is a complex mathematical solution to automating cycle analysis. The formula transforms price into a nearly Gaussian probability density function by normalizing prices, resulting in the ability to identify peaks and troughs.[1] The indicator consists of the Fisher Transform and a "trigger line" designed to provide action signals. The behavior of the Fisher Transform is similar to a momentum oscillator with less lag. It may be used to generate mechanical buy-and-sell signals, as well as more sophisticated bullish and bearish divergences. It is also useful for confirmation of a cycle high or low.

Figure 19.8 places the Fisher Transform on a daily chart of February 2018 lean hogs futures. A 28-day dominant cycle is identified by the arcs. Numbers are placed

---

[1] John F. Ehlers, "Using the Fisher Transform," *Stocks & Commodities Magazine* 40, no. 11 (2002, November): 40–42.

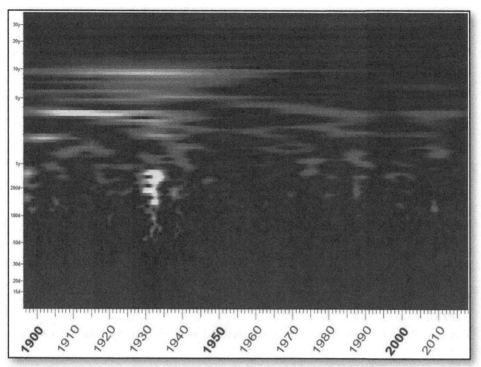

FIGURE 19.7 Wavelet Diagram of the Dow Jones Industrial Average
Source: Timing Solution.

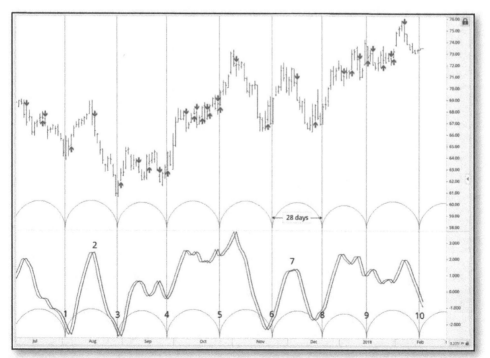

FIGURE 19.8 Fisher Transform on February 2018 Lean Hogs Futures
Source: Optuma.

next to troughs and crests of interest. Down arrows mark where the Fisher's trigger line gives sell signals while up arrows identify where the trigger line gives buy signals. Note how the price action at points 6, 7, and 8 forms a clean sine wave pattern. The Fisher Transform does a great job of confirming that the expected cycle lows and highs have passed. This is also the case with points 1, 2, and 3.

Now study the choppier points in time where the arrows are whipping back and forth between sell and buy. This behavior appears as the indicator picks up on the smaller harmonics taking hold of price during bull market corrections.

■ References

Ehlers, John F. "Using the Fisher Transform." *Stocks & Commodities Magazine* 40, no. 11 (2002, November): 40–42.

Garrett, William C. *Investing for Profit with Torque Analysis*. Spokane, WA: Investment Book Publishers, 1973.

Hurst, J.M. *The Profit Magic of Stock Transaction Timing*. Englewood Cliffs, NJ: Prentice-Hall, 1970.

Kaufman, Perry J. *New Trading Systems and Methods*. 4th ed. Hoboken, NJ: John Wiley & Sons, 2005.

Wilkinson, Chris. "Jim Tillman." From *Technically Speaking: Tips and Strategies from 16 Top Traders* (pp. 387–422). Greenville, SC: Traders Press, 1997.

CHAPTER 20

Basics of Cycle Analysis

Kyle Crystal, CMT, CFTe

Learning Objective Statements

- Explain how the annual cycle conforms to cycle theory
- Describe two methods of detrending price data
- Restate common seasonal tools
- Memorize notable economic cycles and their periods
- Recall some sequences/nonlinear cycles

■ Natural Cycles

Natural cycles follow the same Principles of Commonality found within traditional fixed cycles. Theoretically, they function in the same manner as any cycle previously discussed. What is different is that we allow nature to dictate the periods of the nominal model. The table below is a list of the planets and their heliocentric cycle periods. The term "heliocentric" refers to the time it takes for a planet to complete one orbit around the sun. Even harmonics are present between Mercury, Earth, and Mars. Venus is a separate cycle, as it is not related by a small whole number. Interestingly, it is related through a Fibonacci relationship: 61.8% of the Earth's dominant cycle. Can you identify a simple harmonic relationship between the heliocentric periods of Uranus, Neptune, and Pluto?

Heliocentric Cycle Periods

Planet	Years	Month	Days	Rough Harmonic Equivalent
Mercury	.24	2.89	87.97	4th Harmonic
Venus	.62	7.38	224.70	
Earth	1.00	12.00	365.26	Dominant Cycle
Mars	1.88	22.57	686.98	1/2 Harmonic
Jupiter	11.86	142.34	4,332.59	
Saturn	29.45	233.48	10,759.20	
Uranus	84.02	1008.14	30,685.93	
Neptune	164.78	1977.38	60,187.64	
Pluto	248.03	2981.0	90,737	

Source: Timing Solution.

The term "synodic" refers to the time it takes for a planet to return to the same position with reference to the earth and the sun. These are also periods of interest.

Synodic Cycle Periods

Planet	Month	Days
Mercury	3.81	115.87
Venus	19.19	583.92
Earth	—	—
Mars	25.63	779.93
Jupiter	13.11	398.80
Saturn	12.42	378.10
Uranus	12.12	369.66
Neptune	12.06	367.49
Pluto	12.05	366.74

Source: Timing Solution.

While we are not going to explore natural cycles in depth, there are many interesting cyclic ideas that come from the interaction of these periods. These methods are worthy of deeper study outside of this text.

Seasonality

Seasonality, also known as the annual cycle, is the cycle of the sun. It is the most common natural cycle analyzed as it is present in almost all markets. It heavily influences commodity markets and is present, though less influential, within forex, fixed income, and equities.

Before we move on to practical analysis, note that seasonality follows all of J.M. Hurst's Principles of Commonality but does have some unique features specific to this cycle. First, observe how the solstices and equinoxes divide the year into four seasons that are even harmonics of the annual cycle. Technically, the vernal equinox, around March 21st, marks 0 degrees and the start of the cycle. As seen in this text, some software programs will display seasonal information starting from the calendar year for the sake of convenience.

Keep in mind that while seasonality is a relatively stable market cycle, it still adheres to the Principle of Variation. The annual cycle, like all cycles, is prone to shift over time. Special care should be taken to confirm which pieces of the cycle are stable and correlated. This will be addressed further in this chapter.

Seasonal Tools   The following section will focus on two types of seasonal charts: a cumulative line chart and a monthly performance chart. Each approach offers a different perspective on the annual cycle.

Seasonality Charts   The best way to get a broad overview of a market's seasonal cycle is with a line chart like Figure 20.1, displaying the seasonal pattern of cash wheat over the past 10 years. Why 10 years? Because cyclical patterns shift over time and we want relevant data. The "calculation style" within the properties of the chart is set to "median" to filter out the influence of any statistical outliers present within the data. The calculation style is defined as "percentage" to normalize price movement over longer periods of time. Now study the line chart and visualize the pattern as circular, where the right edge of the chart leads immediately to the left edge of the chart. The clear takeaway from the seasonal pattern below is that cash wheat commonly forms a major high around April/May that leads to a strong decline into a major August/September low.

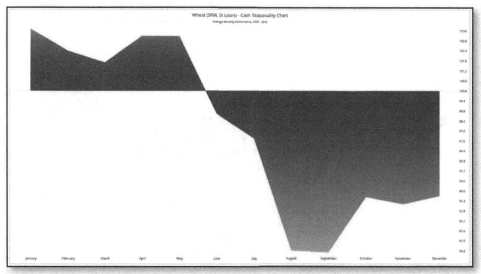

FIGURE 20.1   CBOT (SRW) Cash Wheat Seasonality Cumulative Line Chart, 2009–2018

Source: Optuma.

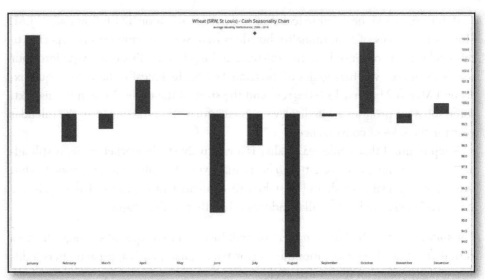

FIGURE 20.2   CBOT (SRW) Cash Wheat Seasonality Monthly Performance Bar Chart, 2009–2018

Source: Optuma.

Another way to display seasonality is with a monthly performance bar chart like Figure 20.2. Compare this chart to the line chart in Figure 20.1 to visualize the differences. A monthly performance chart helps answer the question, "Which months offer the greatest opportunity for long or short positions?"

As an example of the Principle of Variation at work, study the seasonal line chart of CBOT SRW cash wheat from 1980 to 2018 in Figure 20.3 and compare the chart to Figure 20.1 showing seasonality of the same market from 2009 to 2018. Changing

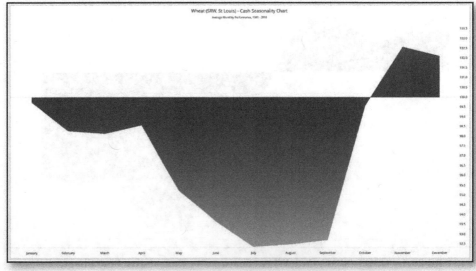

FIGURE 20.3   CBOT (SRW) Cash Wheat Seasonality Line Chart, 1980–2018

Source: Optuma.

the time period being analyzed allows the analyst to identify seasonal shifts over time. As one can see, the August/September low is a product of a seasonal shift over the past 10 years. Figure 20.3 shows that the traditional seasonal low used to appear in June/July.

Composite Chart   A composite chart breaks up historical price action into different slices of time according to a common period and overlays them on top of each other. An average is usually displayed with a thicker line to reinforce the cycle's general pattern. This is most commonly done with a one-year period in order to observe seasonal correlation. Figure 20.4 shows a composite chart of CBOT SRW cash wheat from 2009 to 2018. Studying a market's seasonal cycle this way gives an analyst a more realistic feel for the correlation levels within an individual year. Keep in mind that the previous seasonality charts imply a major seasonal high in April–May that falls to the major seasonal low in August–September. Can you identify pieces of the seasonal cycle that are more correlated and sections that are less correlated?

Detrending

Detrending is the act of removing the trend from a time series with the goal of isolating cyclical activity. Detrending can be utilized to isolate any cycle but is most commonly employed with seasonal analysis. Why would we choose to detrend data? Because trending markets tend to suppress cycles. By removing the trend, we allow cyclical activity to shine through. Keep in mind that sometimes it is not necessary to detrend data. For example, the VIX is unable to trend and so the raw data is adequate for cycle analysis.

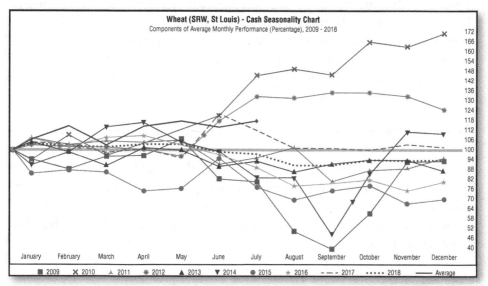

FIGURE 20.4   CBOT (SRW) Cash Wheat Seasonality Composite Chart, 2009–2018
Source: Optuma.

You are referred to Perry Kaufman's *New Trading Systems and Methods* for a thorough examination of numerous detrending techniques.[1] Within his text, Kaufman notes that detrending can be accomplished using any of the following methods: average price, median price, percentage change, linear regression, moving averages, first differences, link relatives, and X-11. The output of each of these methods is subtly different and it is necessary to understand which variables can erroneously influence the results.

Variables to Consider First, statistical outliers damage the results of detrending. A black swan event should be assimilated into a model but should not be allowed to overly influence the data. Use a median instead of a mean in the calculations to improve detrending results and reduce the effect of statistical outliers.

Second, be aware that significant changes in price levels over periods of time can erroneously influence detrending results. This is an important problem to address for markets with long periods of price history as well as continuous futures contracts that retroactively adjust historical price levels. Note that the average price and median price methods of detrending fail to account for changing price history. An analyst should be aware that methods such as percentage change, linear regression, moving average detrending, and first differences minimize this issue.

As mentioned previously, detrending is most commonly employed to calculate a market's seasonal cycle. Perry Kaufman's *New Trading Systems and Methods* identifies four basic methods of detrending specifically for calculating seasonality: average price, median price, percentage change from the previous month, and moving average deseasonalizing (detrending). This chapter discusses two methods: percentage change and moving average detrending.

In the following examples, the issue of statistical outliers is addressed by using the mean of each month's price range as opposed to the close. The monthly mean is defined as the monthly high plus the monthly low divided by two. I have also chosen to use cash cotton prices as opposed to a continuous contract to avoid any retroactive adjustments to historical data. Furthermore, the percentage change method and moving average detrending both minimize the effects of changing price levels over time.

Percentage Change Method Figure 20.5 lists cash cotton's mean monthly price from 2006 to 2017.

Figure 20.6 calculates the percentage change in the monthly mean from the previous month. The average (mean) monthly percentage change for each calendar month is then calculated in row 16. The percentage of months with a positive return is listed in row 17 to help get a feel for the consistency of returns. Row 20 turns the values into a seasonal index.

---

[1] Perry J. Kaufman, *New Trading Systems and Methods*, 4th ed. (Hoboken, NJ: John Wiley & Sons, 2005), 403–446.

	A	B	C	D	E	F	G	H	I	J	K	L	M
1		Jan	Feb	Mar	Apr	May	Jun	Jul	Aug	Sep	Oct	Nov	Dec
2	2006	52.44	52.89	50.79	49.61	47.86	47.97	47.60	49.72	47.47	46.84	47.54	50.97
3	2007	50.46	49.44	50.06	47.01	45.03	51.25	58.75	54.42	58.66	59.92	59.94	60.11
4	2008	64.63	69.69	72.81	64.67	60.86	63.93	64.10	62.39	57.58	46.99	40.06	41.82
5	2009	45.04	41.75	39.08	46.12	53.51	51.53	54.88	54.31	56.47	60.48	66.60	69.99
6	2010	68.52	70.54	76.66	76.76	75.82	75.76	78.62	85.86	95.56	110.96	128.87	136.73
7	2011	148.50	179.90	195.38	177.87	152.41	148.22	116.70	103.48	103.37	98.79	94.29	87.09
8	2012	90.06	86.66	84.84	84.76	74.81	69.44	68.50	70.27	69.69	70.22	68.36	71.86
9	2013	75.25	78.68	84.95	82.46	81.02	84.79	82.69	85.91	82.56	78.38	75.27	79.26
10	2014	83.11	84.97	87.85	87.16	85.19	80.39	71.10	66.17	65.08	63.10	60.63	59.86
11	2015	58.53	62.36	61.78	63.86	63.45	64.19	63.37	63.02	60.28	61.19	62.80	63.79
12	2016	61.92	59.53	57.19	61.67	62.74	64.55	69.13	70.48	68.84	68.65	70.56	71.82
13	2017	73.37	74.58	75.13	74.43	79.41	71.33	67.02	68.34	71.55	68.30	70.00	74.98

FIGURE 20.5   Cash Cotton Mean Monthly Prices, 2006–2017

Source: Excel; data from Optuma.

	O	P	Q	R	S	T	U	V	W	X	Y	Z	AA
1		Jan	Feb	Mar	Apr	May	Jun	Jul	Aug	Sep	Oct	Nov	Dec
2	2006	0.05	0.01	-0.04	-0.02	-0.04	0.00	-0.01	0.04	-0.05	-0.01	0.02	0.07
3	2007	-0.01	-0.02	0.01	-0.06	-0.04	0.14	0.15	-0.07	0.08	0.02	0.00	0.00
4	2008	0.08	0.08	0.04	-0.11	-0.06	0.05	0.00	-0.03	-0.08	-0.18	-0.15	0.04
5	2009	0.08	-0.07	-0.06	0.18	0.16	-0.04	0.07	-0.01	0.04	0.07	0.10	0.05
6	2010	-0.02	0.03	0.09	0.00	-0.01	0.00	0.04	0.09	0.11	0.16	0.16	0.06
7	2011	0.09	0.21	0.09	-0.09	-0.14	-0.03	-0.21	-0.11	0.00	-0.04	-0.05	-0.08
8	2012	0.03	-0.04	-0.02	0.00	-0.12	-0.07	-0.01	0.03	-0.01	0.01	-0.03	0.05
9	2013	0.05	0.05	0.08	-0.03	-0.02	0.05	-0.02	0.04	-0.04	-0.05	-0.04	0.05
10	2014	0.05	0.02	0.03	-0.01	-0.02	-0.06	-0.12	-0.07	-0.02	-0.03	-0.04	-0.01
11	2015	-0.02	0.07	-0.01	0.03	-0.01	0.01	-0.01	-0.01	-0.04	0.02	0.03	0.02
12	2016	-0.03	-0.04	-0.04	0.08	0.02	0.03	0.07	0.02	-0.02	0.00	0.03	0.02
13	2017	0.02	0.02	0.01	-0.01	0.07	-0.10	-0.06	0.02	0.05	-0.05	0.02	0.07
14													
15	Month	Jan	Feb	Mar	Apr	May	Jun	Jul	Aug	Sep	Oct	Nov	Dec
16	Average	0.030	0.026	0.015	-0.003	-0.018	-0.001	-0.010	-0.005	0.002	-0.008	0.005	0.029
17	%+ months	0.66	0.66	0.58	0.25	0.25	0.42	0.33	0.50	0.33	0.42	0.50	0.75
18													
19	Month	Jan	Feb	Mar	Apr	May	Jun	Jul	Aug	Sep	Oct	Nov	Dec
20	Indexed	102.96	105.61	107.17	106.82	104.94	104.79	103.70	103.20	103.40	102.59	103.09	106.11

FIGURE 20.6   Percentage Change Detrending Cash Cotton, 2006–2017

Source: Excel; data from Optuma.

Figure 20.7 shows the output from the percentage change method to detrend cash cotton. The graph on the left plots the monthly percentage change while the graph on the right shows the seasonal pattern as an index or equity curve.

Moving Average Method   Next, we are going to apply a moving average approach to detrending the same cash cotton data. Study the worksheet in Figure 20.8. Column F is the mean of column C (the monthly price high) and column D (the monthly price low). We then create a 12-month moving average of that data point. Note the

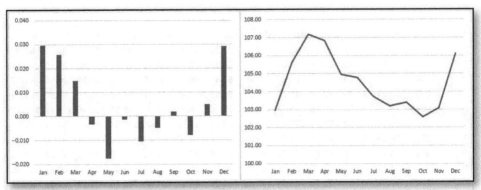

FIGURE 20.7 Monthly Percentage Change and Seasonal Pattern of Cash Cotton, 2006–2017

Source: Excel; data from Optuma.

arrow at G325 shows the current moving average for the previous 12 inputs from column F. We then take the value from column G and displace it back in time to create a centered moving average (CMA). Since there are an even number of data points, 12 in this case, we cannot technically center the moving average between the sixth and seventh data points. As per Kaufman's suggestion, averaging the sixth and seventh data point is a sufficient shortcut. Column I shows the "average of two adjacent CMAs" placed in the time period of the 6th data point. It is from this value that we can then detrend the data by subtracting column F, resulting in the "Seasonal adj factor" in column J. The "seasonal index" in column K is the ratio of column F divided by column I.

The "seasonal index" output from column K of Figure 20.8 is arranged in Figure 20.9 in the traditional seasonal format. The mean and median of each column is calculated in rows 16 and 18.

	A	B	C	D	E	F	G	H	I	J	K
1	Date	Open	High	Low	Close	Avg of range	12month MA	12 month CMA	Average of two adjacent CMAs	Seasonal adj factor	Seasonal index
314	1/1/2006	52.24	53.57	51.31	52.22	52.44	49.19	49.63	49.71	2.73	1.055
315	2/1/2006	52.37	54.00	51.77	52.19	52.89	49.89	49.91	49.77	3.11	1.063
316	3/1/2006	52.11	52.11	49.47	50.40	50.79	50.05	49.80	49.86	0.93	1.019
317	4/1/2006	50.32	51.72	47.50	48.47	49.61	49.95	49.37	49.58	0.03	1.001
318	5/1/2006	48.32	49.30	46.42	47.94	47.86	49.79	49.22	49.30	-1.44	0.971
319	6/1/2006	49.35	49.70	46.23	47.20	47.97	49.79	49.31	49.27	-1.30	0.974
320	7/1/2006	46.25	49.65	45.55	49.20	47.60	49.63	49.14	49.22	-1.62	0.967
321	8/1/2006	50.48	51.08	48.36	49.55	49.72	49.91	48.85	49.00	0.72	1.015
322	9/1/2006	48.56	48.73	46.20	46.20	47.47	49.80	48.79	48.82	-1.36	0.972
323	10/1/2006	45.97	48.54	45.13	47.03	46.84	49.37	48.58	48.68	-1.85	0.962
324	11/1/2006	46.53	49.25	45.83	49.25	47.54	49.22	48.34	48.46	-0.92	0.981
325	12/1/2006	49.68	53.21	48.73	52.44	50.97	49.31	48.61	48.48	2.49	1.051
326	1/1/2007	51.14	51.31	49.60	50.25	50.46	49.14	49.54	49.08	1.38	1.028
327	2/1/2007	49.82	50.88	48.00	50.07	49.44	48.85	49.93	49.74	-0.30	0.994
328	3/1/2007	49.95	50.81	49.30	49.82	50.06	48.79	50.87	50.40	-0.35	0.993
329	4/1/2007	49.49	49.51	44.51	44.51	47.01	48.58	51.96	51.41	-4.40	0.914
330	5/1/2007	43.47	47.14	42.92	47.05	45.03	48.34	52.99	52.47	-7.44	0.858
331	6/1/2007	46.48	56.50	45.99	56.50	51.25	48.61	53.75	53.37	-2.13	0.960
332	7/1/2007	56.65	61.49	56.00	56.80	58.75	49.54	54.93	54.34	4.40	1.081
333	8/1/2007	57.50	58.10	50.73	56.12	54.42	49.93	56.62	55.78	-1.36	0.976
334	9/1/2007	56.70	62.17	55.15	60.50	58.66	50.87	58.52	57.57	1.09	1.019
335	10/1/2007	60.61	61.90	57.93	61.08	59.92	51.96	59.99	59.25	0.66	1.011
336	11/1/2007	60.74	62.42	57.46	57.46	59.94	52.99	61.31	60.65	-0.71	0.988
337	12/1/2007	57.45	62.76	57.45	62.76	60.11	53.75	62.36	61.83	-1.73	0.972

FIGURE 20.8 12-Month CMA Detrending Cash Cotton, 2006–2017

Source: Excel; data from Optuma.

	P	Q	R	S	T	U	V	W	X	Y	Z	AA	AB
1													
2		Jan	Feb	Mar	Apr	May	Jun	Jul	Aug	Sep	Oct	Nov	Dec
3	2006	1.055	1.063	1.019	1.001	0.971	0.974	0.967	1.015	0.972	0.962	0.981	1.051
4	2007	1.028	0.994	0.993	0.914	0.858	0.960	1.081	0.976	1.019	1.011	0.988	0.972
5	2008	1.033	1.104	1.148	1.029	0.990	1.067	1.099	1.108	1.071	0.911	0.793	0.842
6	2009	0.923	0.869	0.820	0.957	1.073	0.988	1.011	0.962	0.953	0.974	1.036	1.057
7	2010	1.004	1.000	1.043	0.994	0.926	0.868	0.842	0.848	0.863	0.925	1.012	1.024
8	2011	1.075	1.281	1.380	1.258	1.093	1.091	0.888	0.827	0.887	0.914	0.934	0.922
9	2012	1.010	1.010	1.022	1.054	0.957	0.909	0.911	0.947	0.943	0.951	0.924	0.960
10	2013	0.989	1.017	1.082	1.039	1.012	1.052	1.018	1.050	1.004	0.949	0.908	0.956
11	2014	1.011	1.050	1.107	1.117	1.110	1.067	0.967	0.925	0.936	0.935	0.924	0.935
12	2015	0.929	0.997	0.993	1.031	1.024	1.032	1.013	1.008	0.969	0.988	1.016	1.032
13	2016	0.997	0.950	0.903	0.964	0.971	0.989	1.046	1.049	1.004	0.983	0.993	0.997
14	2017	1.016	1.035	1.042	1.031	1.101	0.987	0.923	0.936	0.974	0.923	0.938	0.991
15													
16	Average detrended seasonal change (mean)	1.006	1.031	1.046	1.032	1.007	0.999	0.981	0.971	0.966	0.952	0.954	0.978
17	Indexed mean	100.579	103.078	104.603	103.245	100.720	99.863	98.056	97.072	96.623	95.226	95.391	97.820
18	Average detrended seasonal change (median)	1.010	1.014	1.032	1.030	1.001	0.989	0.989	0.969	0.970	0.950	0.959	0.981
19	Indexed median	101.020	101.376	103.226	102.983	100.110	98.879	98.895	96.866	97.037	95.042	95.948	98.132

FIGURE 20.9 12-Month CMA Detrending Cash Cotton, 2006–2017

Source: Excel; data from Optuma.

Figure 20.10 shows the output of the moving average detrending method. The mean calculation on the left shows less detail than the median calculation on the right.

Comparison of Seasonal Detrending Methods Figure 20.11 contains the output of the two methodologies, percentage change and moving average detrending. As one can see, the results show differences but the takeaway of the study is clear. Cash cotton commonly forms its major seasonal high around March and declines into the major seasonal low around October. Note that in *New Trading Systems and Methods,* Perry Kaufman points out that the percentage change method commonly leads to

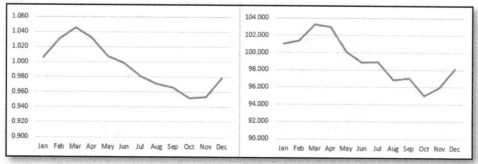

FIGURE 20.10 12-Month CMA Detrended Cash Cotton, No. 2 Seasonal Pattern, 2006–2017

Source: Excel; data from Optuma.

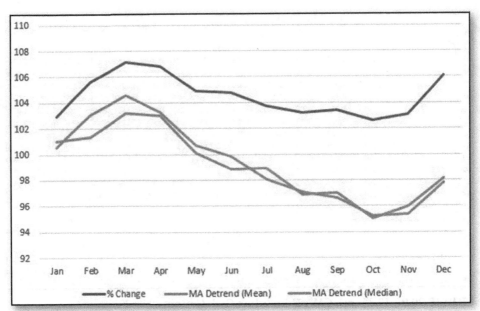

FIGURE 20.11 Seasonal Methodology Comparison of Cash Cotton, No. 2, 2006–2017

Source: Excel; data from Optuma.

other detrending approaches because it picks up on changes in momentum, similar to a traditional oscillator.[2]

■ Notable Cycles

"Fixed" Economic Cycles

Students of financial markets should be familiar with the major economic cycles. The K-wave, Kuznets cycle, Juglar cycle, Presidential cycle, and Kitchin cycle are summarized here.

Kondratieff Wave Russian economist Nikolai Kondratieff identified a long-term cycle of 52–53 years (the range is sometimes broadened to 45–60 years) within the developed Western economies of England, France, and the United States. He observed the cycle in a variety of things including interest rates and commodities. Figure 20.12 shows a spectrogram of world GDP growth rates from 1870 to 2007, showing the presence of the Kondratieff wave, or K-wave, as well as some of the other cycles discussed in the chapter. The spikes labeled "1" and "2" mark the K-wave. (Line 1 is the spectrogram of the initial GDP series. Line 2 is the GDP series with corrected values for the World War periods.)

[2] Perry J. Kaufman, *New Trading Systems and Methods*, 4th ed. (Hoboken, NJ: John Wiley & Sons, 2005), 424.

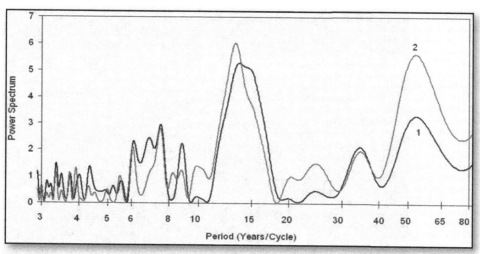

FIGURE 20.12 Spectral Analysis of World GDP, 1870–2007

Source: Andrey V. Korotayev; Sergey V. Tsirel.

Kuznets Cycle Lasting between 15 and 20 years, the Kuznets cycle was first identified by Nobel Prize Laureate Simon Kuznets (1901–1985). The cycle is attributed to investments in housing and building construction and is sometimes referred to as the "building cycle" or "infrastructure cycle."

Juglar Cycle First identified in 1862 by French economist Clemente Juglar (1819–1905), the Juglar cycle has a period of approximately 7–11 years (averaging 9 years). It is sometimes referred to as the "fixed investment" cycle. Juglar's studies produced evidence that crises are periodical and not random.

Presidential Cycle The Presidential cycle is defined by the four-year election cycle in the United States. The cycle is phased according to every fourth November. The most recent election cycle began in November of 2016. Note that this cycle can be further sliced and diced by Republican versus Democratic presidencies.

Kitchin Cycle Discovered in the 1920s by Joseph Kitchin (1861–1932), this cycle approximates a 40-month period (3.33 years) and is slightly shorter than the Presidential cycle. It is sometimes referred to as the "inventory cycle."

Economic Cycles in the Dow Jones Industrial Average Figure 20.13 is a wavelet diagram of the DJIA dating back to the late 19th century. The Juglar, Presidential, and Kitchin cycles are clearly identifiable. Note the Juglar cycle was strong from about 1900–1965. It is barely detectable in today's market. Unlike the Juglar cycle, the Presidential and Kitchin cycles are clearly present within the wavelet diagram. The lightly colored area indicates the cycle is active and worthy of further exploration.

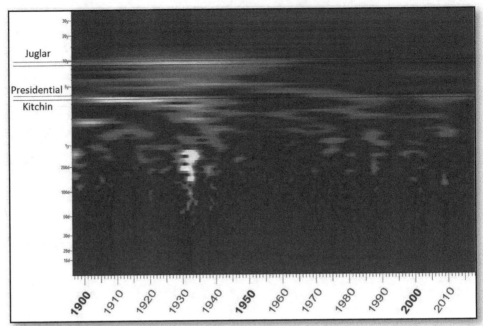

FIGURE 20.13 Economic Cycles within the DJIA, 1900–2018

Source: Timing Solution.

Sequences (Nonlinear Cycles)

A sequence, or nonlinear cycle, is any time-based pattern that does not conform to traditional fixed cycles. The following list provides some examples of common sequences and is by no means exhaustive.

Fibonacci and Lucas Leonardo Pisano, also known as Fibonacci, is credited with many mathematical innovations, one of which is the discovery of a natural growth function known as "phi." Fibonacci mathematics are more commonly utilized in technical analysis as a ratio, but the pure sequence is sometimes found within markets as well. The Fibonacci sequence is referred to as a "summation series" because each number is the result of the sum of the two previous numbers:

$$0,1,1,2,3,5,8,13,21 \ldots \text{etc.}$$

Mathematician Francois Edouard Anatole Lucas helped bring attention to another summation series that produces a different sequence:

$$0,2,1,3,4,7,11,18,29 \ldots \text{etc.}$$

Keep in mind that sequences can apply to bars, calendar days, weeks, months, and so forth.

Natural Squares   A natural square is the product of any number multiplied by itself:

$$1 \times 1 = 1$$
$$2 \times 2 = 4$$
$$3 \times 3 = 9$$
$$4 \times 4 = 16$$

This creates the following sequence:

$$1, 4, 9, 16, 25, 36, 49 \dots \text{etc.}$$

Like the Fibonacci and Lucas sequences, the natural square sequence can be applied to bars, calendar days, weeks, months, and so on.

Spiral Calendar   Chris Carolan discovered a fascinating growth sequence that is detailed in his book, *The Spiral Calendar*. Carolyn identifies that historical pivots within financial markets are sometimes related by a natural nonlinear cycle: the relationship between the Fibonacci sequence and lunar cycles.[3] The idea of applying a growth function, in this case the Fibonacci series, to a natural cycle is an interesting topic for further study outside of this text.

Benner   Samuel Benner was an Ohio farmer and a student of market cycles. In his 1884 book, *Benner's Prophecies of Future Ups and Downs in Prices*, he details numerous nonlinear cycles active within different commodity markets. Figure 20.14 illustrates a nonlinear sequence within the pig-iron market.[4] Note the lows repeat with a pattern of 9, 7, and 11 years between troughs. The cycle highs repeat a sequence of 8, 9, and 10 years between peaks.

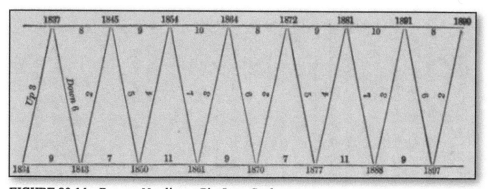

FIGURE 20.14   Benner Nonlinear Pig-Iron Cycle
Source: Samuel Benner, *Benner's Prophecies of Future Ups and Downs in Prices* (Cincinnati, OH: Robert Clarke & Co., 1884).

---

[3] Christopher Carolan, *The Spiral Calendar and Its Effect on Financial Markets and Human Events* (Gainesville, GA: New Classics Library, 1992).

[4] Samuel Benner, *Benner's Prophecies of Future Ups and Downs in Prices* (Cincinnati, OH: Robert Clarke & Co., 1884), 45.

■ References

Benner, Samuel. *Benner's Prophecies of Future Ups and Downs in Prices*. Cincinnati, OH: Robert Clarke & Co., 1884.

Carolan, Christopher. *The Spiral Calendar and Its Effect on Financial Markets and Human Events*. Gainesville, GA: New Classics Library, 1992.

Dewey, Edward R. and Og Mandino. *Cycles: The Mysterious Forces That Trigger Events*. New York, NY: Hawthorn Books, 1971.

Hurst, J.M. *The Profit Magic of Stock Transaction Timing*. Englewood Cliffs, NJ: Prentice-Hall, 1970.

Kaufman, Perry J. (2005). *New Trading Systems and Methods* (4th ed.). Hoboken, NJ: John Wiley & Sons.

Korotayev, Andrey V. and Sergey V. Tsirel. "A Spectral Analysis of World GDP Dynamics: Kondratieff Waves, Kuznets Swings, Juglar, and Kitchin Cycles in Global Economic Development, and the 2008–2009 Economic Crisis." *Journal of Structure and Dynamics* 4, no.1 (2010). Retrieved from https://escholarship.org.

MARKETS AND VOLATILITY

Questioner: What, sir, do you think the market will do?

Famous financier: I believe the market will fluctuate.

**—Attributed variously to John D. Rockefeller,
J.P. Morgan, and others**

Regardless of whether technical analysis originated in the rice markets of Japan, in the stock market of the United States, or in trading markets elsewhere, its use in analyzing financial markets and managing risk is global. Practitioners may be found wherever there are markets with freely moving prices, readily available data, and open access.

This section provides a primer on financial markets that lend themselves most to technical analysis. Equities, exchange-traded products, currencies, commodities, and others are covered here. This introduction is presented to assure that the student new to technical analysis has a basic working knowledge of these markets. Beyond that, critical aspects of these markets as they relate to technical analysis are emphasized including futures settlement prices and open interest, the nature of currency pairs, and the special challenges presented by price data in different markets. Nascent markets in cryptocurrencies are also given their due as technicians monitor their evolution and recalibrate their tools for trading in these new assets.

This section also includes an introduction to options contracts and the options market. This is essential to understanding the section's final topic: modern measures of volatility and volatility indexes, integral facets of today's markets, and technical analysis.

CHAPTER 21

Markets, Instruments, Data, and the Technical Analyst

Michael Kahn, CMT

Learning Objective Statements

- Name four asset classes amenable to technical analysis
- List five tradeable instruments that a technician is likely to employ
- Describe data-handling issues with which a technician should be familiar

■ Tradable Markets

While there are many different tradable assets in many different marketplaces all over the world, the technical analyst generally focuses on a subset. That does not mean that any market with a regular price settlement or fixing cannot be charted but rather that true technical analysis of a market requires certain characteristics for activity and liquidity.

For the vast majority of technical analysis, there are four major types of asset classes:

1. Stocks (equities)
2. Bonds (fixed income and short-term interest rates)
3. Currencies (foreign exchange)
4. Commodities (hard or physical assets)

And there are five major types of tradable instruments that a technical analyst should know:

1. Cash (or spot): the price to buy or sell an asset right now
2. Futures: a contract to buy or sell an asset at a defined time in the future
3. Options: a contract to buy or sell an asset at or during a defined time and at a defined price
4. Index: a mathematical average of the prices of an underlying basket of assets
5. Exchange-traded product (ETP): a basket of underlying assets trading as a unit

While all instrument types are available for each asset type, not all are actively traded. Therefore, only some of them will be of interest to a technical analyst. For example, while options premiums per se might not be the subject of technical analysis, the technician should be familiar with the data generated in that marketplace as it is a rich source of information about sentiment and market conditions.

The following provides a visual representation of the relationships between asset types and instrument types. In other words, it highlights where technical analysts will typically focus their activities. Even so, an individual instrument must still pass the requirements for robust activity and price history.

Asset ↓ Instrument →	Cash	Futures	Options	Index	ETP
Stocks	x			x	x
Bonds		x		x	x
Currencies	x				x
Commodities		x		x	x

It may be quite possible to perform technical analysis on an asset and instrument combination not highlighted here as long as there is robust activity and price history. The following chapters will discuss these asset types and instrument types, including what they are and what types of data are important to know.

■ Behind the Scenes of Market Data

Market data arrives at a technical analyst's workstation in many ways, so it is important to know how it moves from the trade to the analyst's screen. Whether data is contributed from a foreign exchange dealer as they adjust their bids or as the result of a trade flowing through a formal exchange, once that price is created it has a long journey ahead.

During that journey, it is subject to reporting errors that create "price spikes," out-of-order reporting, and data cleaning. None of this matters to a technical analyst until an erroneous data point reaches the chart.

Data Filters

Most vendors receive their feeds from exchanges and dealers, attempt to put trades in time order, and then try to filter out bad data. The problem is in knowing what data is bad.

For example, if a stock trades at 25.21, 25.20, 25.21, and then 26.50, was that last trade an error? Most vendors have a filter through which they pass successive trades that take place within a range they select. If a trade is outside that range, they may wait to see if the following trade is close to that supposedly out-of-range trade. If it is, both trades pass along to the end user. If it is not, the out-of-line trade is rejected. How well a vendor does this depends on their infrastructure and the rules applied to each market.

Unless the technical analyst uses very small intraday intervals, this probably will not be an issue. However, when a filter allows a bad trade through or rejects a valid trade it might affect the high or low for that interval. An errant high or low may affect trendlines and indicators.

Late Trades

Vendors may differ on how they handle the open of a market session and the close. With the latter, on active days, the "tape" may run late. In other words, trades are reported after the official close. Where in the chart does the vendor put them, particularly related to intraday intervals?

Although the details will not always matter, the technical analyst should be aware of these conditions.

Intraday analysts should also consider how intraday intervals are built. Do trades at 12:00, for example, go into the 12:00 hour or the 11:00 hour?

These are issues to consider but not worry about too much. However, it does suggest the technical analyst verify critical data with two or more sources. Market data vendors are good but not infallible.

CHAPTER 22

Equities

Michael Kahn, CMT

Learning Objective Statements

- Define equity securities and primary data types
- Describe the benefits of equities for investors
- Identify the effect of corporate actions on price data
- Classify sectors, capitalization, and other ways to segment the market

■ What Are Equities?

The terms "equities" and "stocks" have different origins but, in practice, are interchangeable. Both represent an ownership share or portion of the value of a company. There are no implied guarantees other than sharing in the fortunes of the company, good or bad.

Contrast this with debt, which carries a promised rate of return. Equities have unlimited upside potential whereas debt is limited to a stream of defined payments.

Both equities and debt have claims on the liquidation value of a company should it become bankrupt or otherwise insolvent. However, debt and liens must be paid first before shareholders are eligible for any monies.

Investors buy and sell stocks on formal exchanges or over the counter. The former has a centralized trading and clearing operation while the latter depends on dealers trading from their own inventories. However, from a technical analysis point of view, it does not matter where or how a stock trades if certain key information—most notably price and volume—is available after each and every trade is executed. That does not mean trading in each type of venue is identical. There are subtle differences, perhaps in transparency and liquidity, but for plotting and analyzing a chart it really does not matter.

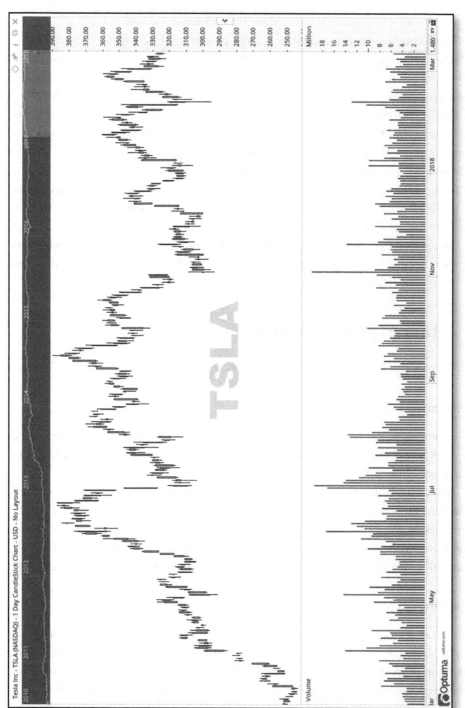

Tesla Inc - TSLA (NASDAQ) - 1 Day CandleStick Chart - USD - No Layout

Volume

FIGURE 22.1 Chart of Tesla, Inc.

■ Benefits for Investors

Investors own stocks for three reasons. The first is capital gains. Over time, it is expected that companies grow and their stocks increase in value.

The second reason is for income. A large percentage of companies pay dividends, which may increase from time to time, to their shareholders.[1] Companies that do not pay dividends may choose to spend whatever free cash they generate on expanding their businesses. This, in turn, theoretically increases growth and their stock price.

Finally, the third reason to own a stock is in order to have a voice in the management of the company. Holders of stock, or more accurately common stock, have voting rights that allow them to select directors of the company and vote on certain initiatives brought forth by management or other shareholders.

Companies have other methods to return value to shareholders. They may choose to buy back some of their own shares. The reduction in the supply of shares tends to increase the value of the remaining shares outstanding.

Companies may also choose to issue special dividend payments to shareholders. These one-time payments may skew the action on a chart but they are too infrequent to change the efficacy of chart analysis.

■ Other Forms of Equity

Aside from stock and bonds, companies may issue other securities.

Warrants

These are usually issued with stock and give the holder the right to buy more shares of stock at a certain price by a certain date. These are similar to options, which are introduced in Chapter 28.

The major difference between warrants and options is how they are created. Warrants are issued by companies. Options are written by other traders. Typically, warrants have longer maturities than options. In addition, when an option is exercised, one trader delivers existing shares to the other. When a warrant is exercised, the company issues new shares, which increases the total number of shares outstanding.

Preferred Stock

This class of stock is a hybrid of common stock and bonds. Preferred shares usually pay a higher dividend than common stock, their dividends must be paid before common stock dividends, and they rank higher than common stock in a bankruptcy. Preferred shares do have capital gains potential but do not carry voting rights.

---

[1] MarketWatch reported on October 3, 2017, that 82.6% of the companies in the S&P 500 paid dividends; https://www.marketwatch.com/story/sp-500-dividend-payouts-hit-a-record-in-the-third-quarter-2017-10-03.

There are several reasons why a company issues preferred stock but the most important is that preferred shares give it the ability to raise large sums of money quickly. This is because institutions have special tax treatment and tend to buy larger blocks of preferred stock. Individuals are not likely to have tax advantages but may still benefit from higher dividend yields and stronger, that is, safer, status in a bankruptcy.

Also, some preferred stock is convertible to shares of common stock under certain conditions. The downside is that some preferred stock is callable, meaning the company can buy back shares at face value under certain conditions.

Convertible Bonds

These are debt securities and for the most part act like them, but under certain conditions the holder may convert, or exchange, the bonds for stock. They carry no voting rights unless converted. And as long as they remain bonds, they have a higher status in a bankruptcy than any stocks.

Investors might buy convertible bonds because they protect their principal on the downside but allow them to participate in the upside gains should the issuing company grow. Startup companies might be ideal issuers.

Companies can also issue convertible bonds to lower their borrowing costs. These bonds carry a built-in premium for the conversion feature that results in a lower interest rate.

■ What Does a Technical Analyst Need?

There are several types of data important for a technical analyst but only two kinds are used in most applications—price and volume. Most indicators derive from these two items.

Price: Open, High, Low, and Close refer to those actual traded prices for any given time interval (minute, hour, day, week, etc.).

Volume: Number of shares changing hands in a specific trade or summed over an interval. Sometimes, if an instrument does not have volume data—foreign exchange, for example—technical analysis might substitute trade count, the number of transactions regardless of the size of the transactions.

Traders would also be interested in the following:

Bid/Ask: Current prices buyers are willing to pay and sellers are willing to accept (from the exchange or market markers).

Size: The limit to the number of shares the maker of a bid or offer will trade.

Time: The time the trade took place.

52-week high and low: The highest and lowest prices traded over the past year.

Market capitalization: The value of all publicly available shares of stock in a company. It is the product of price multiplied by the number of shares outstanding.

Tesla, Inc. (TSLA)
NasdaqGS - NasdaqGS Real Time Price. Currency in USD

301.85 -1.30 (-0.43%)
As of 9:57AM EDT. Market open.

Previous Close	303.150	Market Cap	51.862B
Open	302.000	Beta	0.83
Bid	302.14 x 900	PE Ratio (TTM)	N/A
Ask	302.45 x 800	EPS (TTM)	-16.138
Day's Range	299.00 - 305.29	Earnings Date	Oct 30, 2018 - Nov 5, 2018
52 Week Range	244.590 - 389.610	Forward Dividend & Yield	N/A (N/A)
Volume	1,029,564	Ex-Dividend Date	N/A
Avg. Volume	10,207,960	1y Target Est	322.38

FIGURE 22.2 Typical Stock Quote Information
Source: Yahoo! Finance.

While technical analysis does not directly consider the following, they can affect the price action. These fall loosely under the umbrella of **corporate actions**, or events driven by the company itself and not the market.

Ex-dividend: Ex-dividend refers to the date that determines who is entitled to the dividend payment. Investors purchasing the stock on or after that date are not entitled to the upcoming dividend payment. They literally buy the stock "without the dividend." Buyers of the stock before the ex-dividend date are entitled to the upcoming dividend payment, even if they sell their shares before the dividend is actually paid.

Splits: A company may split its shares for a number of reasons but it only changes the number of shares outstanding. The value of the shares remains the same as the price also adjusts; for example, a stock trading at 90 euros splits three for one. The result is three times as many shares trading at 30 euros per share.

This change then propagates back in time on the chart. Therefore, if the stock traded 300 shares at 90 euros last week (300 × 90 euros = 27,000 euros), after the split, the data for that date would read 900 shares at 30 euros (900 shares × 30 euros = 27,000 euros). The value of the trading that day remains the same.

Reverse splits create a higher price for a stock with lower volume. Again, the value remains the same. This usually occurs when a stock falls below a threshold price needed to remain listed on an exchange.

Secondary offering: Whereas an initial public offering (IPO) creates a public company for the first time, a secondary offering is the issuance of new shares in an existing public company. This necessarily dilutes the value of previously existing shares. Companies do this to raise more capital but rather than issuing debt, they issue equity.

Restricted shares: In new or startup companies, insiders such as directors and key employees may be rewarded with shares of stock when the company goes public. One of the restrictions on these employees is that they must hold the shares for a period of time called a lock-up period. When that period ends, the potential for a surge in selling by these insiders increases and the stock price may sag, at least temporarily.

■ Segmenting the Market for Analysis

The old saying is, "The stock market is a market of stocks." This means that each stock has its own unique trading profile and peculiarities, even though all forms of market analysis look at indexes and averages to distill all the action into one single forecast.

However, there are many ways to slice and dice the market. Analysts look at individual stocks. They look at stocks within one industry—computer software, for example. They look at sectors in the market—technology or health care. And they may look at all stocks within a region (e.g., Latin America) or country. They even segregate the market by capitalization or value of the company such as "small caps" and "large caps."

How do technical analysts segment the market for analysis? They look at a plethora of indexes covering each of these areas. Examples would be the Russell 2000 index of small stocks, the SOXX-50 of Pan-European blue-chip stocks, and the KBW Banking Index.

This is addressed in more detail in Chapter 23 (Indexes), but it is important to know in which segment(s) of the market a particular stock falls. It does not affect price analysis but it could determine intermarket relationships, an important tool for the technical analyst to use.

Further, studies have shown that the price performance of an individual stock depends heavily on the performance of its sector. The theory is that if there is sufficient business to spread around in an industry—a housing boom, for example—chances are that even a weak competitor in that sector can capture some of that business.

Here is a summary of some of the different ways to group individual stocks.

Sectors and industries	Banks, oil drillers, healthcare providers, gold miners, etc.
Capitalization	Large, medium, small, and micro
Geography	Country or an entire region in the world. S&P 500, Kospi, DAX, Pan-European, Asia Tigers, Emerging Africa, World
Other	Examples include growth and value, defensive and aggressive.

See Chapter 23 for more detail.

Indexes

Michael Kahn, CMT

Learning Objective Statements

- Identify major global equity indexes
- Name common nonequity indexes used by technical analysts
- Explain weighting methods used in major indexes
- Define "survivorship bias"

■ What Are Indexes?

Indexes are representations of the value of a subset of the market, whether that subset is very small or almost an entire market. Using several different methods, they compute an average price for gauging the performance of all components they cover as a group.

The primary asset class for indexing is the stock market because there are so many stocks traded. However, indexes do exist in other asset classes and function in nearly the same way.

Consider an index to be a summarizing technique. Rather than analyze each of the 30 stocks in the Dow Jones Industrial Average, for example, the technical analyst can chart the index itself to find trends and other patterns on the chart.

When someone asks, "How did the market do today?" they really mean, "How did the Dow (or Shanghai Composite, or IBEX-35) do today?" An index is a representation of the market or segment of the market it covers.

The most helpful aspect of indexes, especially in the equities markets, is that they help the technical analyst drill down from the country level to the sector level to the industry group level. In this way, the universe of potential investments is narrowed and targeted for analysis.

Country level: Indexes represent entire markets in a country. Most often, technical analysts operating in one country will only track the benchmark in other countries rather than an entire series of market-segmenting indexes such as small stocks or industry sectors. Below is the global list published in the *Wall Street Journal* with additional African and Mideast indexes.

Asia Pacific	Europe	Americas
All Ordinaries (Australia)	ATX (Austria)	S&P 500 (U.S.)
S&P/ASX 200 (Australia)	Bel-20 (Belgium)	S&P/TSX Comp (Canada)
Dow Jones China 88 (China)	Prague PX (Czech Republic)	Merval (Argentina)
Shanghai Composite (China)	OMX Copenhagen (Denmark)	Sao Paulo Bovespa (Brazil)
Hang Seng (Hong Kong)	OMX Helsinki (Finland)	Santiago IPSA (Chile)
S&P BSE Sensex (India)	CAC 40 (France)	IPC All-Share (Mexico)
Jakarta Composite (Indonesia)	DAX (Germany)	
Nikkei 225 (Japan)	BUX (Hungary)	**Africa/Middle East**
Topix Index (Japan)	FTSE MIB (Italy)	Tel Aviv (Israel)
FTSE Bursa KLCI (Malaysia)	AEX (Netherlands)	FTSE/JSE All-Share (South Africa)
S&P/NZX 50 (New Zealand)	Oslo Bors All Share (Norway)	Tadawul All Share (Saudi Arabia)
PSEi (Philippines)	WIG (Poland)	EGX 30 (Egypt)
Straits Times (Singapore)	PSI 20 (Portugal)	All Share Index (Nigeria)
Kospi (South Korea)	RTS Index (Russia)	MASI (Morocco)
Colombo Stock Exch (Sri Lanka)	IBEX 35 (Spain)	
Weighted (Taiwan)	OMX Stockholm (Sweden)	
SET (Thailand)	Swiss Market (Switzerland)	
	BIST 100 (Turkey)	
	FTSE 100 (U.K.)	

Regional level: There are even indexes that seek to represent markets on each continent or the entire global equities market.

EAFA: Europe, Australia, Asia, and the Far East. Includes stocks from developed countries excluding the United States and Canada.

The Global Dow: Tracks 150 leading companies from around the world.

Latin America 40: Tracks 40 of the largest Latin American equities.

STOXX Europe 600: Covers 600 companies of all sizes in 17 European countries. Includes 90% of the free-float market capitalization of the European stock market.

Market capitalization (value): Within a country, indexes can represent stocks by their market capitalization, or market value. Using just the Russell indexes as examples, the Russell 3000 index tracks virtually the entire U.S. stock market, containing 98% of its market value. The Russell 1000 tracks the top one-third, by market value, of those stocks. The Russell 2000 tracks the bottom two-thirds and is a benchmark index for small stocks in the United States.

Sector: Within many global stock markets, indexes track different sectors of the economy such as financial, technology, consumer staples, energy, and utilities.

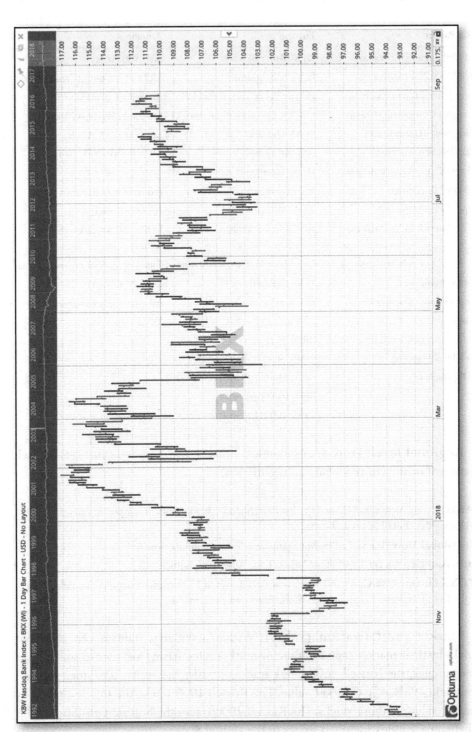

FIGURE 23.1 Chart of KBW NASDAQ Bank Index

Industry: Sectors may further break down into individual industries, such as banks, insurance companies, computer software, computer hardware, automakers, retail stores, and gold miners.

Other: Some markets may also have indexes segregating so-called growth stocks and value stocks. Others may make distinctions between typical stocks and high-risk "venture" stocks.

■ Benefits for Investors

The main benefit for investors is the ability to monitor or analyze a segment of the market with one instrument. There is no need to track the data from dozens or even hundreds of underlying stocks.

Investors can also rank sector or country performance and chart relative performance on a single chart. In this way, they can determine when one index starts to outperform or lag another.

■ Other Indexes

While the stock market is rife with indexes of all types, other asset classes also have indexes. They serve the same function of segmenting their respective markets to allow for analysis of the cross currents flowing beneath the prices of each component.

The following is just a small sample of the types of nonstock indexes available, listed by asset class or function. Each has at least a closing or settlement value each trading day so the technical analyst may chart them. Volume data is rare.

U.S. Dollar Index

This popular index seeks to track the value of the U.S. dollar versus a trade-weighted basket of other currencies. Typically, this index answers the question, "What did the U.S. dollar do today?"

The euro accounts for more than half of this index as the European Union is a major trading partner with the United States. Other currencies include the Japanese yen, British pound, Canadian dollar, Swedish krona, and Swiss franc.

CRB Index

The Commodities Research Bureau index changed owners and formulations several times over the years since it was first created as a basket of futures contracts. It covered energy, industrial, agricultural, and precious metals markets and served as a representation of "what commodities are doing."

Various iterations, names, and formulas exist: Thomson-Reuters CRB Index, Reuters/Jefferies CRB index, and continuous futures index.

Competing commodities indexes also exist, including the Bloomberg Commodities Index. There are also more focused indexes such as the DBIQ Diversified Agriculture Index, which tracks only agricultural commodities.

Real Estate

The technical analyst will likely focus on real estate prices as represented by Real Estate Investment Trusts (REITs). Here, the primary index is the FTSE NAREIT U.S. Real Estate Index.

Baltic Dry Index (BDI)

This is an index of shipping and trade prices created by the London-based Baltic Exchange. It serves as a measure of the cost of transporting various raw materials. It is further broken down by shipping size but technical analysts typically look only at simple price charts of the BDI to assess major trends and economic health.

Note that, as a dry index, it does not cover the costs of transporting wet products such as crude oil.

LIBOR

Standing for London Interbank Offered Rate, LIBOR is a benchmark short-term interest rate charged by banks when they borrow from each other. Many other rates are priced off LIBOR, from mortgages to swap transactions.

While LIBOR is the global standard, there are similar rates available in local markets. HIBOR, TIBOR, and SIBOR are but a few and represent standards in Hong Kong, Tokyo, and Singapore, respectively.

LIBOR is important for a technical analyst because it replaced eurodollars in the TED spread. Originally U.S. Treasuries minus eurodollars, the TED spread measures perceived risks in the short-term interest rate market. When the spread between risk-free three-month Treasury bills and riskier three-month eurodollars increases, analysts surmise a "flight to safety" in the market. Traders' and investors' attitudes toward risk turn negative, and global markets may be under pressure. During the financial crisis of 2008, the TED spread, now represented by Treasuries minus LIBOR, soared.

As of this writing, controversy over the process of setting and reporting LIBOR has given rise to other rate indexes that may take LIBOR's place. One such index gaining widespread acceptance is called SONIA (Sterling Overnight Interbank Average Rate); another is SOFR (Secured Overnight Financing Rate).

Bonds

Bond indexes can cover a country market or a subset of that country's bond market. They can be grouped by region, such as a Euro Bond Index or an emerging-markets bond index.

A few examples are the Bloomberg Barclays U.S. Aggregate Bond Index, Markit iBoxx USD Liquid High Yield Index (junk bonds), and the Citi Emerging Markets Broad Bond Index.

■ Index Construction and Weighting

There are many ways to construct an index and each has its benefits and drawbacks. Here are the most commonly used methods.

Capitalization-Weighted (Value-Weighted)

Most indexes use this method. The value of each individual stock in the index is weighted by its relative market capitalization (price multiplied by shares outstanding). In other words, (price × shares outstanding)/total market capitalization of all stocks in the index.

	Market Cap	Percent
Stock AAA	24 billion	38.71
Stock BBB	20 billion	32.25
Stock CCC	18 billion	29.03
	62 billion	100.00

Usually, the index begins its life set at a round number rather than the actual mathematical value derived on day one. However, each day's change will then depend on the weightings.

Modified Capitalization-Weighted

In this weighting scheme, the calculations are the same as for regular capitalization-weighted indexes but there is a limit set for how big any individual stock's contributions can be. For example, the index might require that no stock be allowed to grow to represent more than 10% of the index's movements.

Equal-Weighted (Unweighted)

In this weighting scheme, each stock in the index carries the same percentage weight. Therefore, the largest stocks cannot unduly influence the index's movements. The drawback is that movements in small, illiquid stocks have the same importance as those of a market's most important benchmarks.

Price-Weighted

The most notable index using this scheme is the Dow Jones Industrial Average. Price-weighted indexes are the easiest to calculate. However, their biggest drawback is that they ignore market values completely and are greatly affected by stock splits.

Splits force the index sponsor to change the divisor used to create the price average. In the case of the Dow, each split of a member stock forces the divisor to get smaller, and in 2018 it stood at 0.14523396877348. Aside from an unwieldy number of decimal places, it magnifies the movements of the index. For example, each 1-point move in a stock results in a change to the index of 6.89 points. For a stock trading at 200 and a stock trading at 25, the same percentage move will result in eight times more impact for the stock trading at 200.

■ Survivorship Bias

Sponsors of indexes add and remove stocks from their products periodically. For example, a stock falls below a capitalization threshold and is removed from an index. A different stock is then elevated to membership in that index because the original stock is in decline and the new stock is presumably doing well. Therefore, the fortunes of the index change for the better, even if only by a small amount, and the market or segment it represents looks strong.

Unless the investor or analyst makes the effort, they do not hear much about the removed stock with regard to the performance of the index. The surviving index continues on its way.

This aspect of survivorship bias can have significant impact on backtesting done on index data. Such backtests are not representative of testing or trading the individual components. The process of removing failing companies from an index mitigates the impact the weak performers would have had on a trading system.

There are also biases in indexes based on how stocks are initially selected to become members of an index. Index sponsors have a vested interest in the survival of the index itself and may choose stocks toward that end. They may overlook some otherwise qualified stocks for future performance reasons.

For stocks that do make it into indexes, weighting methodology introduces other biases. For example, the bigger the stocks become within a capitalization-weighted index, the more influence they have on the index performance. Therefore, the index "cares" more about its winners and less about its losers, giving an additional upward bias to its performance.

Price-weighted indexes are biased toward their highest-priced members regardless of their importance to the economy. While a company may split its shares or otherwise change its price, it cannot change its value. This introduces other distortions in the way the index represents its market segment.

There is a story told about how an unscrupulous stock broker would guarantee returns to customers. He would send a stock pick to half of an acquired mailing list of prospects and also send a recommendation to the other half to sell short that same stock.

If the stock moves higher, prospects who received the recommendation to buy are happy and those who received the recommendation to sell dismiss the broker.

Now the broker sends a new buy recommendation to half of the remaining list and a short recommendation for the same stock to the other half. Again, when the stock moves, let's say lower this time, half of the new list is impressed by the broker's stock-picking prowess.

The process may repeat a few more times until a subset of the original mailing list thinks the broker is a genius. What disappears from consideration is that along the way most prospects were dealt poor recommendations. That is survivorship bias.

We also see it in less nefarious areas. For example, it exists in mutual fund companies where winning funds survive and losing funds are shut down and fade from memory along with their poor track records.

■ Using Indexes

Indexes do not trade in the cash market, but exchanges and/or data vendors calculate their values throughout the trading day. Therefore, a technical analyst can chart and analyze them like any traded instrument.

While one can build a portfolio comprised of the same components and weights as in a specific index, it is usually not practical. Therefore, to directly trade an index, traders turn to other instruments designed to track them. These can be futures or options based on the underlying index. Or they can be actual portfolios of stocks maintained by companies and sold to investors as ETFs.

Why analyze indexes? Because almost everyone trading in a given market—Australian stocks, for example—looks at the major market indexes there. These indexes reflect the overall trend of that market or sector of that market. Derivatives based on them, such as futures, are also the focus of activity, and active buying and selling creates a very liquid market where technical analysis excels.

As long as the index is actively calculated and reported, technical analysis applies. Some data vendors may even provide a form of index volume by summing underlying stock volume and possibly weighing it as it does the index price itself. A bonus when analyzing ETFs as a proxy for an underlying index is that ETFs have their own volume data.

■ Data Types Available

Indexes are calculated from the values of their underlying stocks using their selected weighting or averaging method. Since they do not directly trade there is no volume data. Some services may provide volume based on the underlying stock volumes, either summed or averaged according to the same weighting method used for the index price.

Most indexes will provide intraday data (price and time), so there will be open, high, and low data. Others will only calculate a close value at the end of each trading day.

Dow Jones Transportation Averag (^DJT)
DJI - DJI Real Time Price. Currency in USD

11,318.38 +8.58 (+0.08%)

As of 10:23AM EDT. Market open.

Previous Close	11,309.80	Day's Range	11,275.40 - 11,324.37
Open	11,305.65	52 Week Range	9,237.46 - 11,475.74
Volume	4,679,362	Avg. Volume	488,527

FIGURE 23.2 Typical Index Quote Information
Source: Yahoo! Finance.

As with stocks, 52-week high and low data is often useful to see where an index currently stands within a range.

There are a few potential problems with index prices, with the most important being changes in the underlying components. Some indexes reevaluate their components quarterly. This could cause slight jumps in the index price on the day of the change, although it is less likely in indexes with large numbers of stocks.

Another important issue is a problem with a major component. For example, a stock suffers an unusually large miss on earnings or it has a legal issue that sends its price sharply lower. This local problem propagates to the index or even market level. On the plus side, it may be the target of a surprise takeover bid that sends its price soaring.

Finally, some stocks may not open on time with the rest of the market. This will cause the index to calculate using previous close prices or not calculate at all.

■ What Does a Technical Analyst Need?

Indexes are simple in terms of charting. A technical analyst needs the close price and probably the open, high, and low. While volume data may be available, it may not always be reliable.

Unlike many other instruments, nonprice data is also important, especially the industry, sector, market, capitalization, and country it represents. A utilities index will trade differently from a biotech index. An emerging country index will trade differently from a developed country index. Finally, small cap indexes will trade differently from large cap indexes.

CHAPTER 24

Fixed Income/ Bonds

Michael Kahn, CMT

Learning Objective Statements

- List the major types of issuers of debt securities
- Identify the basic terms of a debt instrument: issuer, coupon, maturity
- State the ways in which debt prices are expressed
- Explain the relationship between price and yield
- Define "yield curve"
- Describe the importance of U.S. government debt in the pricing of other debt securities: "yield (or credit) spread"

■ What Are Bonds?

While there may be subtle differences, investors and traders use the terms *debt securities*, *bonds*, and *fixed income securities* interchangeably. A "bond" got its name because it was a bond between borrower and lender. Fixed income refers to the typical bond paying a fixed payment over its life, no matter what happens to its market price.

While the names may be different, the characteristics of a bond follow several defined rules.

First and foremost, a bond is a loan made by an investor to a borrowing entity. It is a promise to pay back the amount borrowed at a later date, with interest. The borrower is bound to this agreement, hence the term "bond."

Why would a borrowing entity issue a bond? Most likely, a bank or financial institution cannot or will not lend it the amount needed or will not make the loan at an acceptable interest rate. In the case of a sovereign government, the amount of a loan could be in the hundreds of millions of dollars or other currency, far greater than the lending capacity of a single lender.

Therefore, the borrower turns to the public capital markets to raise the needed funds. They may enlist the services of an investment bank, or a consortium of investment banks, to manage the deal.

The most important relationship for a technical analyst to know is that yields and bond prices move inversely to each other. The reason is that an existing bond with a fixed interest rate must compete with new bonds for investor capital when interest rates change.

For example, a bond with a stated 5% interest, or coupon, rate will drop in value when interest rates rise to 6%. The reason is that it must offer a lower price to a buyer in order to compete with a newly issued 6% bond. Therefore, the buyer of the old bond will theoretically enjoy the same yield on their investment (called yield-to-maturity) by way of both interest payments and capital gains when they redeem their bond at face value at maturity.

Don't worry about the terms just yet. Explanations are below so focus only on the fact that bond prices and interest rates necessarily move in different directions.

■ Benefits for Investors

Investors own bonds mainly to collect their interest payments, though there is also the possibility of capital gains. As fixed income investments, investors know in advance when they will receive payments of interest, how much they will receive and when they will get their original investment back. The payment stream is known but limited.

Bonds are also debt instruments so they have a higher place in the hierarchy for payment should an issuing company become insolvent.

In a portfolio, bonds help to smooth the returns of more uncertain assets, such as stocks. And bonds and stocks often move in different directions, further adding to the smoothing effects of bonds.

■ Major Issuers of Bonds

The major issuers of bonds are essentially *governments* and *corporations*.

In the government sector, bonds range from national or sovereigns, to state and regional and down to local municipalities. At the national or federal level, bonds are usually backed by the full faith, credit, and taxing power of the government that issued them.

There are cases where certain bonds are issued by other entities and backed by their government. In the United States, the mortgage bond market is the best example.

Unique to the United States is the municipal bond market. All bonds issued by state and local governments fall into this category. The distinction is important due to the tax treatment of municipal bonds. Interest on state and local bonds are exempt from federal income taxation. And likewise, interest on federal bonds are exempt from local income taxation. Some states also exempt interest from all bonds issued by municipalities within their state from their own local income taxation.

However, capital gains are taxable at all levels.

Another unique feature of the municipal bond market is the revenue bond. Bonds issued by state and local governments are backed by their respective full faith and credit. Revenue bonds, however, are issued by state and local governments on behalf of a private company working on a project for "the public good," or for a specific project by that government. They are backed by the revenues of that project.

In the corporate sector, bonds are issued by individual corporations to finance their own needs. Typically, they are segmented by their quality ratings, where bonds from top-rated issuers are called "high grade" or "investment grade" bonds. Bonds from the weakest and most speculative companies are colloquially called "junk" bonds or simply "high-yield" bonds, due to their higher interest rates.

Issuer Type	Common Names
Independent countries	Sovereign, federal, national
State, province, local governments	State, provincial, local
State, county, city (United States only)	Municipal, tax-exempt
Corporations	High grade, investment grade, junk, high yield

Sovereign bonds in each country may also have individual names. Here are a few of the majors:

United States	Treasury bonds, notes, bills
Germany	Bunds, Bobls, Schatz
France	Oats, BTFs, BTANs
United Kingdom	Gilts
Japan	JGBs (Japanese Government Bonds)

The different names within each country depend on the maturity, or life, of the bond. Many countries do not have special names—Canada Bond, for example.

A technical analyst is likely to track only a few benchmark issues, such as the 10-year maturity, in any given country and analyze the futures contracts based on them.

■ Components of a Bond

Because bonds are loans made by bond holders to bond issuers, they do not offer any ownership, or equity, in the issuing entity. The terms of that loan include the issuer, principal amount, interest rate, price, date of maturity, and the frequency and amount of interest payments made to the bond holder.

Principal (Face Value)

The principal of the bond is the amount of the face value, or the amount that will be returned to the investor when the bond matures. Typically, in the United States it is in units of $1,000 or $5,000 and similar for other currencies. The actual price of the bond depends on conditions in the market the day it is purchased and can be higher or lower than the face value.

Maturity

The maturity of a bond is the date at which the issuer returns the principal back to the bond holder. Bonds typically have maturities longer than 10 years. If they are shorter, they might be called notes instead. Maturities can be as short as overnight and one week or as long as 30 years, or even 100 years in rare cases.

Coupon

The coupon is the periodic interest payment made to the bond holder. It is the income portion of the name fixed income. Decades ago, bonds were issued as physical certificates with attached coupons that investors clipped to present for payment. This process is now all electronic.

For example, a bond priced in euros with a 4% coupon will pay 4%, or 40 euros per year in interest per bond, assuming 1,000 euros face value. If interest rates change, the value of the bond will go up or down but it will still pay the same 40 euros per year.

The coupon rate is set when the bond is issued and depends on the interest rates of the day, as well as the characteristics of the issuer. For investors, the coupon divided by the price paid for the bond is their current yield, or income yield. If the price of the bond is par, then the current yield is the same as the coupon rate.

Par Value

Par value refers to the nominal, or face value of a bond but in percentage terms. A bond trading at par has the same market value as its face value. Typically, a bond represents 1,000 units of currency ($1,000 for U.S.). For example, a bond trading at 102 would cost $1,020 for each $1,000 bond. That is 102% of par.

Traders might quote a bond at par, meaning it trades at 100% of its face, or par, value. For example, a bond has a nominal value of 1,000 euros and is trading at that same level would be priced at par. A quote of par and a half means the bond trades at 100.50, or 100.5% of face value, or a market value of 1,005.00. A quote of 97.25 means the bond's value is 972.50.

Yield-to-Maturity

A bond's yield-to-maturity includes the periodic interest payments, any capital gains or losses and the eventual return of principal (face value) when the bond matures.

Basically, it is the interest rate used to calculate the net present value of all cash flows—both in amounts and times received.

Most bonds are priced off a risk-free benchmark, such as the 10-year U.S. Treasury rate. It is then adjusted higher to compensate for the risk of the issuer, length of maturity, structure of the cash flows, and simple supply and demand. This is called the yield spread or spread to the benchmark. The term may also be applied to the spread, or difference, in yield between two other types of bonds, such as high-grade corporate bonds and speculative "junk" bonds.

Typically, the sovereign debt is used as a benchmark because it theoretically has zero default risk. Indeed, the debt of the U.S. government may even be used as a benchmark for other sovereign debt.

A speculative corporate bond would have a higher interest rate than a bond with the same maturity issued by a blue-chip company. And that bond would have a higher interest rate than one issued by its sovereign government. Of course, that is not always true for economically weak countries where corporations could have better credit scores.

For example, if the 10-year Treasury note yields 4%, a 10-year AAA-rated corporate in the U.S. might yield 4.5%. An A-rated corporate bond might yield 5.0%.

Thirty-year bonds typically yield more than 10-year notes. Bonds of longer maturities normally have higher rates than those due in only a few years. (See "Yield Curve" below.)

Many bonds do not have these simple characteristics. Those issued with coupon rates below the market rate for a bond of similar quality and maturity are also issued at a price below face value. The investor pays less for a lower income stream but still receives the full face value of the bond at maturity. The name for such bonds is original issue discount (OID). Tax treatment may be different than for standard bonds, especially in the municipal bond market.

If an investor buys a bond in the secondary market and interest rates are higher than they were when the bond was issued, the price of the bond will be below par. This is because bond prices and interest rates have an inverse relationship. And in practical terms, an investor would not buy a bond with a below-market interest rate when he or she can buy one with a market rate. They would demand to buy it at a lower price so that the yield-to-maturity for each bond would be similar.

Figure 24.1 shows a typical bond quote in the cash or spot market.

Duration

Bond analysts also consider a bond's duration, which is the time it takes for the holder to recoup the original investment and is based on the net present value of all cash flows. It is also a measure of a bond's price sensitivity to changes in interest rates. The greater the duration, the more the price changes as market interest rates change.

An extreme example would be a 10-year zero-coupon bond. In this case, the duration would be the time to maturity.

Treasury Yields

NAME	COUPON	PRICE	YIELD	1 MONTH	1 YEAR	TIME (EDT)
GB3:GOV 3 Month	0.00	2.06	2.09%	+7	+110	10:58 AM
GB6:GOV 6 Month	0.00	2.21	2.27%	+7	+119	10:58 AM
GB12:GOV 12 Month	0.00	2.37	2.44%	+3	+123	10:58 AM
GT2:GOV 2 Year	2.63	99.98	2.64%	-3	+131	10:59 AM
GT5:GOV 5 Year	2.75	100.07	2.73%	-11	+103	10:59 AM
GT10:GOV 10 Year	2.88	100.30	2.84%	-12	+73	10:58 AM
GT30:GOV 30 Year	3.00	100.30	2.99%	-10	+26	10:59 AM

FIGURE 24.1   U.S. Treasury Prices

A more realistic example, although simplified with round numbers, would be a bond with 10 years left to maturity, a 10 percent coupon and a price of par, or face value. The duration would be 6.75 years.

Keep in mind that cash flows received now are more valuable than cash flows received later. Duration would necessarily be less than the maturity of the bond.

A technical analyst does not have to worry too much about these specifics because they do not directly affect technical analysis. Typically, the analysis will focus on futures markets where bond contracts have standardized features. However, it is important to know that the price of a discounted bond has a natural bias to the upside as maturity approaches.

Rating

Bonds carry quality ratings to let investors know a bit more about the company or government behind them. Ratings agencies consider primarily an investor's risks for getting their money back, and interim interest payments, after loaning it in the form of bonds.

Ratings ranges are either investment grade or non-investment grade. Each ratings agency has its own method for assigning these ratings but the three major independent agencies—Moody's, Standard & Poor's (S&P), and Fitch—are all similar.

For example, AAA, AA, A, and BBB are the various levels of investment grade, using S&P nomenclature. Each is modified by "+" and "−."

Anything lower than that is considered non-investment grade, although that runs the gamut from simply not good enough for investment grade to extremely speculative to imminent default.

Miscellaneous Characteristics

Some corporate bonds have other features such as convertibility and calls. Convertible bonds include the right to exchange debt (bonds) for equity (stocks) under certain conditions.

Callable bonds allow the issuer to "call back" or pay off the debt early at a fixed price. Typically, an issuer would do that if interest rates fall sharply, giving it a chance to refinance at a lower rate. The bond holder may receive a premium over face value but loses the chance for price appreciation as rates fall.

■ Typical Information in a Bond Quote

Issuer

The issuer is the entity issuing the debt. It could be a government (country, state, province, city) or a corporation.

Coupon

The coupon is the stated interest rate based upon the face value of the bond. For example, a 6% coupon pays 6% annually based on 100% of par value. Typically, this means $60 per $1000 face value.

Maturity

The maturity date is the date the bond matures and the principal must be repaid. Interest no longer accrues after that date, unless specifically stated in the bond contract.

Bid/Ask/Last

As with other traded items, bonds have bid and ask prices, as well as last trade prices. These are denoted in units specific to the bond type. They could be in basis points (.01) or a fractional representation, such as eighths (1/8), sixteenths (1/16) or thirty-seconds (1/32).

Each bond type also has a specific nomenclature to denote the fractions. For example, U.S. Treasury bonds trade in 32nds so a quote of 92.07, often presented as 92'07, means 92 7/32.

A "+" appended to that adds a 64th. Therefore, 92.07+ means 92 15/64.

Some short-term debt may be priced in discounted yield. In the United States, Treasury bills might be quoted as 3.07. This represents the annualized yield, based on a 360-day year, when the investor buys the bill below par and redeems it at maturity at par. No interest payments are otherwise made.

Net

As with other traded items, this is the change in price from the previous trading day. Even intraday charts will show this format, rather than change from last hour or last 15-minute period.

From this data, a trader might calculate the yield-to-maturity, which considers all interest payments and eventual repayment of principal. He or she may also calculate the current yield, which is the income stream (coupon payment) divided by the price paid for the bond.

■ Yield Curve

The yield curve is simply a listing of a country's interest rates across the spectrum of maturities in which it issues debt. Typically, the rates are plotted on a yield versus time-to-maturity chart and the slope of the curve suggests conditions about the underlying economy of that country.

One way a technical analyst can keep track of a yield curve is simply by plotting the difference between two maturities' yields over time. In the United States, the 10-year yield minus the 2-year yield is a popular proxy for the U.S. yield curve.

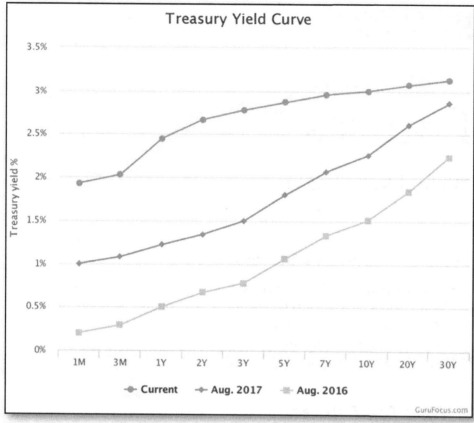

FIGURE 24.2 U.S. Treasury Yield Curve
Source: GuruFocus.com.

An upward sloping yield curve, with interest rates for longer maturities above those for shorter maturities, is normal. A flat or downward sloping yield curve means short-term rates are higher than long-term rates.

■ What Does a Technical Analyst Need?

In the cash bond market, aside from the specific characteristics of the bond (coupon, maturity, rating), the last price is important along with the high and low. Volume is likely not a factor, as it is often unreported.

There is one other consideration relating to liquidity. As bonds age, they become less active, mostly because they get "put away." This means they exist in smaller and smaller lots and often in retail accounts that tend to hold them rather than trade them. Also, bonds are somewhat fungible in that a similar issuer, coupon, and maturity will be good enough for most investors to buy.

The majority of technical analysis on bonds and fixed income occurs in the futures markets or on indexes created from yields.

CHAPTER 25

Futures

Michael Kahn, CMT

Learning Objective Statements

- Explain the purpose of futures markets
- Classify various futures markets as industrial, agricultural, financial, and so on
- List the major terms of a futures contract
- Define open interest in futures
- Describe challenges technicians face when using futures market data

■ What Are Futures?

Futures are contracts to buy or sell a specific quantity of commodities, financial instruments, or currencies for delivery on future dates. Originally designed to reduce uncertainty, they allow individuals and institutions to lock in prices in the future.

The benefit to hedgers or commercial producers is that they will know for sure the prices they will receive for products delivered or the prices paid for products purchased. Speculators often take the other side of those transactions, hoping to profit from movement in those underlying products.

For example, an airline believes that oil prices will be higher in six months than they are now. While it does not use crude oil directly in its operations, it does use jet fuel, which is derived from crude oil. Therefore, it purchases crude oil futures for delivery in six months. This essentially locks in the current price so the company can properly budget its business for later.

Conversely, a farmer believes corn prices are at risk of decline due to any number of factors from ample rain, falling demand, and a strong downtrend. He or she sells corn futures to lock in the sale price, thereby reducing risk from volatility and falling prices.

In all markets speculators will disagree about, for example, whether oil will rally or corn will fall. Therefore, speculators will be on opposite sides of the trades, providing liquidity to the market and facilitating the risk management trades of the hedgers.

■ Benefits for Investors

Futures are standardized contracts that trade on exchanges and go through a clearing mechanism that guarantees the trades. Central clearing offers the advantage of mitigating counterparty risk.

Another benefit of futures is that they are liquid instruments. A vast majority of futures contracts are closed or offset before maturity, and so do not necessarily culminate in the actual delivery of the underlying asset.

Another benefit for investors is the ability to trade on relatively small margins. This allows the investor to participate with a lower layout of capital and to leverage returns, although risks are also leveraged.

Finally, futures offer the means to hedge the underlying asset. For example, commercial organizations that know they will need to purchase a commodity in the future might lock in the price now in the futures market. Conversely, a miner or farmer can lock in prices now to deliver at a later date.

■ Futures Terminology

Maturity: The date at which the futures contract ceases trading.

Volume: The number of contracts traded each day.

Open Interest: The number of futures contracts outstanding in each delivery month. Unlike equities, the number of outstanding futures contracts can vary from day to day. The level and trend in open interest is another measure of market mood.

Front month: Also called spot month or nearby month. This is the nearest delivery month.

Active month: Usually the front month but the activity in some futures markets changes to a later delivery month before the front month matures.

Continuous contract: A synthetic price series of futures contracts used to provide long-term price analysis.

Settlement: Futures may settle in the physical delivery of the underlying asset or in cash based on the value of the underlying asset.

Settlement price: The official final price of the trading day used for determining margin requirements. It is not necessarily the final traded price but rather an average price over a specific window of time.

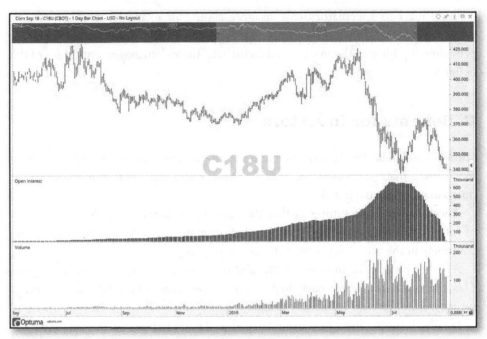

FIGURE 25.1   CBOT Corn Futures, September 2018

Commitments of Traders (COT): This is a weekly report from the Commodity Futures Trading Commission (CFTC) showing the aggregate holdings (open interest) of different types of participants in the U.S. futures market. Participants include commercials (hedgers), small speculators, and large speculators. Sentiment indicators look at extremes in bullishness and bearishness among the groups for analysis.

Basis: This is the relationship between prices in the cash or spot market and prices in the futures market. Basis is an important value to track for hedging and arbitrage. It is affected by different factors for markets as disparate as stock indexes, metals, and agricultural products.

Contango: An upward-sloping curve for contract maturities. Near-month prices are lower than far-month prices.

Backwardation: A downward-sloping curve for contract maturities. Near-month prices are higher than far-month prices. Also called inversion.

Futures contracts are derivative instruments because their prices depend on the prices of underlying assets. For example, an investor or trader can buy coffee in the cash market or in the futures market. A portfolio manager can buy a basket of stocks in the cash market or a stock index, such as the Nikkei 225 or FTSE-100, in the futures market.

Figure 25.2 shows a typical futures quote.

Month	Options	Charts	Last	Change	Prior Settle	Open	High	Low	Volume	Hi / Low Limit	Updated
SEP 2018	OPT		827'0	+7'4	819'4	816'0	828'6	816'0	4,182	895'4 / 745'4	10:28:41 CT 31 Aug 2018
NOV 2018	OPT		839'4	+8'0	831'4	834'0	841'2	828'6	51,726	906'4 / 756'4	10:29:53 CT 31 Aug 2018
JAN 2019	OPT		853'0	+8'0	845'0	847'0	854'2	842'0	12,967	920'0 / 770'0	10:29:57 CT 31 Aug 2018
MAR 2019	OPT		865'4	+7'2	858'2	859'4	867'0	855'4	7,695	933'2 / 783'2	10:29:57 CT 31 Aug 2018
MAY 2019	OPT		877'0	+6'4	870'4	872'4	879'0	867'6	2,233	945'4 / 795'4	10:29:18 CT 31 Aug 2018
JUL 2019	OPT		888'4	+7'4	881'0	882'6	889'6	878'2	2,218	956'0 / 806'0	10:29:57 CT 31 Aug 2018
AUG 2019	OPT		888'2	+3'2	885'0	887'4	888'2	887'4	56	960'0 / 810'0	10:27:48 CT 31 Aug 2018
SEP 2019	OPT		892'0	+7'6	884'2	888'6	892'0	888'6	23	959'2 / 809'2	10:27:48 CT 31 Aug 2018
NOV 2019	OPT		894'4	+8'0	886'4	885'0	895'6	884'2	1,487	961'4 / 811'4	10:27:48 CT 31 Aug 2018

FIGURE 25.2   CBOT Soybean Futures
Source: CME Group.

■ Futures Markets by Asset Class

The term "futures market" can describe futures trading for a single commodity, financial instrument or currency, or it can describe trading for the entire class of instruments in all asset types.

However, because futures exchanges specialize in the futures of some assets and/or they simply segregate the information, the technical analyst should understand the categories.

Agriculture: This group contains commodities that are grown, raised, and harvested including grains, seeds, livestock, lumber, softs (coffee, sugar, cocoa), fibers (cotton), and by some definitions, biofuels.

Energy: Includes Brent crude oil, West Texas crude, refined products (heating oil, gasoline, jet fuel), natural gas, propane, coal, electricity, and some biofuels.

Equity and equity index: Single stocks, global indexes (S&P 500, DAX, Russell, ASX 200, China 50, IBEX 35, and many more).

Foreign exchange: Major currencies including euro, Japanese yen, British pound, Swiss franc, Australian dollar, Canadian dollar, New Zealand dollar, Swedish krona. Emerging markets such as Mexican peso, Brazilian real, Indian rupee, and Russian ruble. Also includes cross-rates, which are direct currency-to-currency trades not involving the U.S. dollar.

Interest rates: This is a broad category including all fixed income markets from short-term to long-term U.S. Treasury debt. It also includes short sterling, eurodollars, gilts, bunds, BTPs, JGBs, and swaps.

Metals: Most metals trading refers to precious metals and copper. However, industrial metals (aluminum, zinc, lead, and more) have an active home in London.

Other: Freight, environmental, real estate, weather, and more.

■ What Does a Technical Analyst Need?

Open, high, low, and last prices, with open interest and volume are important. The prices of additional futures deliveries beyond the active contract are also used for spreads and to identify if a market is in contango or backwardation.

For some futures markets, most notably indexes, analysts also look at the cash index price for spreading and arbitrage purposes.

■ Challenges for a Technician

The biggest problem a technical analyst faces in the futures market is that futures contracts expire. This makes long-term charting for most markets difficult, if not impossible.

To overcome this problem, there are several methods used to stitch together successive futures contracts into "continuous contracts." Each data vendor may choose to use every available contract month or just those traditionally most active. Also, each vendor may choose to use the front month or the most active month, which are not always the same.

FIGURE 25.3   CME Live Cattle Futures, Unadjusted Continuous Contract, Time Rollover Method. *Note:* Large gaps appear where the data is rolled from one contract to the next.

FIGURE 25.4 CME Live Cattle Futures, Adjusted Continuous Contract,
Time Rollover Method. *Note:* This is the same period covered in Figure 25.3.

Time rollover: This method simply splices together successive contracts.
When the current contract reaches its last day of trading, the data series changes
to the next contract. Each data point is a true traded price but the chart tends to
jump at rollover. This renders indicators, averages, and other technical studies
less useful.

Another problem is that it uses trading from the very last days of the current
contract, which may be less active and less liquid. To overcome this specific issue,
vendors may choose a date several weeks before contract expiration to roll to the
next contract.

Activity rollover: Similar to the time rollover method, the data vendor creates
an algorithm that changes from the near contract to the next contract when the latter
acquires higher volume, open interest, or both. In this method, the most important
contract—the most active—is always charted. However, the same problem with
price jumps remains.

Rollover with adjustment: Using either of the two methods for deciding when
to roll to the next contracts, this method adjusts previous trading data so that the end
of one contract's reporting matches the start of the new contract's reporting. While
this creates a smooth chart, all data prior to the current month's data is not real.

Smoothing: With this method, the vendor creates a synthetic continuous contract
that both smooths the chart and gradually assigns more weight to the most active

contract. Using either the time or activity rollover method, the vendor calculates the continuous contract value as a moving, weighted average of the near two contracts.

For example, with 20 days left until rollover date, the current contract has a 20 weighting and the next contract has a zero weighting. The value of the continuous contract would be the same as the current contract.

With 19 days left, the current contract has a 19 weighting and the next contract has a 1 weighting.

By the rollover date, the current contract has a zero weighting and the next contract has a 20 weighting.

The data vendor decides what contracts to use, when to roll them over, and how far in advance it wants to start weighting the next contract.

The benefit is a smooth chart with good highs, lows, trendlines, and studies. The downside is that very few of the data points are real, actually traded prices.

CHAPTER 26

Exchange-Traded Products (ETPs)

Michael Kahn, CMT

Learning Objective Statements

- Define an exchange-traded product (ETP)
- Review differences between exchange-traded funds (ETFs) and exchange-traded notes (ETNs)
- Describe the uses for leveraged ETPs

■ What Are Exchange-Traded Products?

Investors are taught to diversify their portfolios to spread out single stock (or any other asset) risk. However, a portfolio of more than just a few positions gets difficult to manage, especially when it comes time to rebalance them or replace stocks due to splits and bankruptcies.

Mutual funds were the popular solution as one purchase gave the investor a share in the fund and exposure to the stocks within its portfolio. Still, mutual funds had their limitations, from significant transaction costs to the inability to trade them intraday. In order to sell them, investors have to enter orders during the day but then wait for the market to close to find out the price for the day. That price, calculated at the end of each day, is called the net asset value (NAV) and it is the only data point available to technical analysts.

Exchange-traded products were introduced to overcome these problems, stream-line the process, reduce costs, and gain more favorable tax treatment as a bonus. Because they trade just like stocks, ETPs do not have published net asset values at the end of each trading day. Their last prices are their final values.

The most popular ETPs are exchange-traded funds (ETFs), which are essentially mutual funds that trade on exchanges. The sponsor of the ETF, or its contracted

Energy Select Sector SPDR ETF (XLE)
NYSEArca - Nasdaq Real Time Price. Currency in USD

74.22 -0.80 (-1.07%)
As of 12:16PM EDT. Market open.

Previous Close	75.02	Net Assets	19.3B
Open	74.79	NAV	77.05
Bid	0.00 x 1000	PE Ratio (TTM)	N/A
Ask	0.00 x 900	Yield	3.00%
Day's Range	74.14 - 74.81	YTD Return	8.22%
52 Week Range	62.91 - 79.42	Beta (3y)	1.02
Volume	3,447,729	Expense Ratio (net)	0.14%
Avg. Volume	12,564,293	Inception Date	1998-12-16

FIGURE 26.1 Typical ETP Quote Information
Source: Yahoo! Finance.

agent, owns shares of the underlying stocks, or other assets, and makes shares of that portfolio available to the public.

ETP quotes look very similar to stock quotes (Figure 26.1).

Benefits for Investors

Benefits depend on the specific ETP. Some allow the investor to "own" an entire sector of the market rather than having to choose and purchase many individual stocks. Other ETPs enable the investor to access markets that were previously difficult to enter. These include emerging markets and commodities.

Another benefit is automated tracking of changes to the underlying index. The ETP sponsor adds and subtracts components and adjusts weights so the investor does not have to worry about doing it.

ETFs versus ETNs

The major difference between exchange-traded funds (ETFs) and exchange-traded notes (ETNs) is what the fund and the investors actually own. ETFs own the underlying assets and investors own shares in that ownership. ETNs are structured products that are issued as senior debt notes. The holder of an ETN owns shares in a bond backed by those assets.

FIGURE 26.2 SPDR S&P 500 and S&P 500 Index

In terms of technical analysis, the difference is negligible. However, should the products fail, the holders of each have very different remedies.

Many ETFs track stock indexes, such as the SPDR S&P 500 ETF (SPY). Others track specific sectors or areas of the market, such as the iShares PHLX SOX Semiconductor Sector Index Fund (SOXX). The fund typically uses the same weighting method on the stocks it owns as does the index it seeks to track.

Exchange-traded notes (ETNs) evolved to solve other problems, typically in nonequity markets. These are a type of unsecured, unsubordinated debt security based on the performance of a market index. There are no payments (dividends or interest) and no protection of principal, therefore they are similar to unsecured loans made to the ETN sponsor (typically a bank). The payoff is the change in the price of the underlying from ETN purchase to sale less the fees paid to the very bank to which the unsecured loan was made.

Leveraged and Inverse ETFs

ETFs generally track the performance of an underlying basket or index. However, to increase their utility and allow "long only" investors to express bearish opinions, the industry created inverse ETFs, which rise in price when their underlying basket or index declines in price.

Further, ETF sponsors created many ETFs to give both regular and inverse ETF investors the ability to apply leverage. It is now possible to purchase an ETF that moves twice as fast as the underlying index and in the opposite direction.

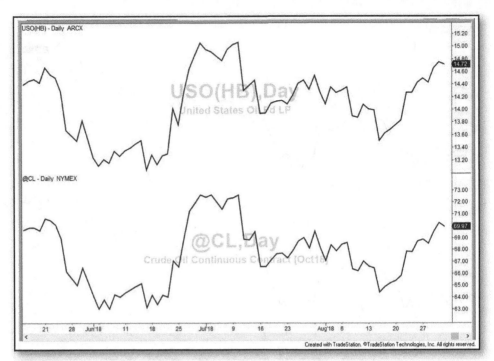

FIGURE 26.3 United States Oil Fund LP ETF and NYMEX WTI Crude Oil Continuous Contract

There are $2\times$, $3\times$, and even $4\times$ ETFs that really boost potential risks and rewards. All these engineered ETFs (leveraged, inverse, and leveraged inverse) are meant for short-term trading only. Because they are rebalanced at the end of each trading day, they have a natural downward bias in price.

For example, if the basket opens at 1,000, falls 10% today to 900, and gains 10% tomorrow, the value will be 990.

However, a $2\times$ ETF will open at 1,000, falls 20% to 800, and then rallies 20% tomorrow to 960.

Of course, this is an exaggerated example, but carried over time, the ups and downs in a leveraged ETF will naturally cause price decay. Therefore, they are useful only for intraday or perhaps a few days' speculation.

No Risk-Free Basket

The astute analyst might think that constructing a short portfolio of a regular $2\times$ or $3\times$ ETF and its inverse counterpart would result in a risk-free profit as both decay over time. This would be true if there were no trends or very shallow trends in the underlying basket.

During a strong trend, the ETF with the correct directional bias will profit according to its leverage. The other ETF will decay but most likely not enough to offset the gains in its counterpart.

FIGURE 26.4 ProShares UltraShort Technology ETF

The higher the volatility in the market, the greater the time decay of leveraged ETFs.

Real Estate Investment Trusts (REITs)

Real estate investment trusts (REITs) represent another packaged product offered to investors. They represent interest in a portfolio of income-producing real estate, such as office buildings and shopping centers, or other interests in real estate financing. Just as with stocks and ETPs, they trade on exchanges so technical analysis here is similar.

However, the way they handle tax issues, including dividend passthroughs, is different. Any investor who buys and holds them will have to check with a tax advisor to determine suitability. However, for a technical analyst, as long as the REIT remains viable, the analysis is similar to other instruments.

■ What Does a Technical Analyst Need?

Analysis of ETPs is very similar to that of stocks, mainly because ETPs trade on the same exchanges. Price and volume data are readily available.

Away from the charts, and similar to indexes, the technical analyst should be aware of what is tracked by a particular ETP. For example, two different ETFs tracking the same sector might contain different stocks. Further, if some of the same stocks within each ETF have different weightings, then performance of the ETFs will differ.

CHAPTER 27

Foreign Exchange (Currencies)

Michael Kahn, CMT

Learning Objective Statements

- Identify the base and quote currencies in a pair
- Classify currency pairs as "major" or "cross"
- Discuss the impact on technical analysis of the "dealer market" system of currency trading
- Explain the data used in building currency charts
- Describe cryptocurrencies

■ What Is Foreign Exchange?

Foreign exchange, FX, forex, and *currency* are interchangeable terms for international money changing. To make a purchase in another country, the buyer must convert his or her money from the home currency to the foreign currency. For example, a buyer in the United States wanting to make a purchase in Italy must exchange U.S. dollars for euros. If the exchange rate is $1.20 per euro, the exchange rate called euro/U.S. dollar would be 1.2000.

To exchange the euros back to dollars, assuming the exchange rate stays the same and there is no commission, one euro would fetch $1.20.

Another way to state this exchange rate would be through the currency pair euro/U.S. dollar. It is the currency pair that trades on world markets.

Because the U.S. dollar is considered to be the reserve, or anchor, currency for the world, the bulk of currency trading is based on the dollar—for example, dollar/ Indian rupee, dollar/Swiss franc, and dollar/Russian ruble. Euro and Japanese yen are also considered to be major currencies and even serve as the de facto reserve currencies in their respective regions of the world. The most active trading typically occurs in these pairs, known as "majors": dollar/yen, euro/dollar, as well as sterling/dollar.

FIGURE 27.1   Euro/U.S. Dollar (EURUSD)

However, there is also active trading between many currencies directly with one another without having to exchange to U.S. dollars first. These are U.S.-centrically called cross rates and the most widely traded are euro/Japanese yen and euro/British pound. Of course, any currency may be crossed with any other if there are buyers and sellers.

■ Benefits for Investors

Aside from pure speculation on exchange rates, the major benefit of currency markets for investors is allowing them to participate in the changing exchange rates between countries via a liquid and leveraged market.

Also, to invest in a local asset, it may be necessary to do so in the asset's home currency. For example, to buy a German bond, one would need euros. And in business, to buy a manufacturing plant in Australia, one would need Australian dollars.

■ Base Currency

The base currency is the first currency appearing in a currency pair quote. The second currency is called the quote currency. Therefore, a quote for the euro, as base currency, against the U.S. dollar would be EURUSD reported in units of dollars.

For the standard quote on the Japanese yen, the base currency is the U.S. dollar. Therefore, the currency pair reads USDJPY and is reported in yen.

FIGURE 27.2   EURUSD Quote Information
Source: DailyFX.

By convention, trading in euro/dollar and pound/dollar puts the U.S. dollar as the quote currency. However, the dollar is the base currency for dollar/yen.

While not a regulation or rule, there is a currency hierarchy in common use in traded currency markets:

Euro
British pound sterling
Australian dollar
New Zealand dollar
United States dollar
Canadian dollar
Swiss franc
Japanese yen

This means that most trading takes place with the higher ranked currency as the base and the lower ranked currency as the quote. For example, GBPAUD for British pound/Australian dollar, which is quoted in Australian dollars, the quote currency. For CHFJPY, or Swiss franc/Japanese yen, the quote is in Japanese yen.

A quick way to remember what the chart says is to keep in mind that when a currency pair rises in value, it is the base currency that is stronger.

Pips and Spreads

The pip is the smallest amount a price can move in any currency quote. The name is an acronym for percentage in point.

Most major currencies are quoted in four decimal places so a pip would be 0.0001 units of the quote currency. The yen is an important exception because it trades in two decimal places. A pip for the yen would be 0.01. Most currencies trade within a range of 100 to 150 pips a day.

The difference between the bid and the ask is called the spread and it is quoted in pips. Therefore, a quote for euro/U.S. dollar of 1.2105/09 would have a spread of 4 pips.

A pip seems to be an insignificant amount, but in the forex markets, trade sizes are often very large. Therefore, a movement of just a few pips can mean a large profit or loss.

Available Data

Cash forex markets are over-the-counter and do not have a central reporting mechanism. Vendors have arrangements with many forex trading desks to capture their bids and offers, but there is no volume reported. Since there is no trade volume, some technical analysts substitute trade count, which is based on bid changes.

Most vendors distribute bids and asks but not actual traded prices. Therefore, by convention, charts plot bids. The close would be the final bid of a given interval. This could have implications for indicators and is something that must be considered when using such data for backtesting and monitoring trading systems.

■ Cryptocurrency

Cryptocurrencies, or "cryptos," are virtual currencies that are not issued by any government and exist only in computers. There are no physical coins or paper bills.

Cryptos solve a big problem with fiat, or government-issued currencies in that nobody can manipulate them. Prices only move in the free and open market based on supply and demand.

While they are theoretically unencumbered by government interference, that has proved to be untrue in practice. Governments now limit some trading and allowable uses of cryptocurrencies. New futures contracts may be a useful method for trading and, along with indexes, for tracking cryptocurrencies.

The most attractive feature of cryptos is anonymity because cryptocurrency trades and ownership information are kept in encrypted, distributed networks. Critics claim that this is the perfect environment for nefarious uses such as money laundering and illegal trafficking.

On the downside, there is nothing real backing them up. They are not based on gold or even the promises of a nation. Therefore, there are no real fundamentals to analyze.

The first cryptocurrency was Bitcoin, which was launched in 2009 under mysterious circumstances by an individual or group known by the pseudonym Satoshi Nakamoto. Since then, more than 1,000 other coins appeared, including Litecoin, Ethereum, and even BananaCoin.

Coins are mined in computers loosely similar to gold mined from the ground. The miner must solve complex mathematical equations to bring new coins into existence. This turned out to be an energy intensive process and some mining demands more power than an entire small country.

Blockchain

Many coins, including Bitcoin, are based on blockchain technology, which records all transactions that ever occurred in blocks on a distributed network. Transactions are recorded in blocks and one block then attaches to the previous—hence the term blockchain. All participants in the network agree on a common set of rules that validate the transactions. The result is a single chain of verified data that cannot be disputed later.

■ What Does a Technical Analyst Need?

Price reporting in currencies often substitutes the bid price for the traded price, but charting and analysis will still be able to use the open, high, low, and last. There are no volume figures in the cash market, but trade count can be a good proxy.

Cryptos that trade on exchanges offer pricing data. Technical analysis here is like that for equities but without consideration of any fundamentals.

CHAPTER 28

Options

Michael Kahn, CMT

Learning Objective Statements

- Explain the purpose of options markets
- List the major terms of an option contract
- Describe "the Greeks"
- Define implied volatility

■ What Are Options?

Options contracts, or simply options, are agreements that give the holder the right, but not the obligation, to buy or sell a specific amount of an underlying security at a specified price at or until a defined time in the future.

Options are derivative instruments because their value depends on the value of their underlying asset. Further, options are "decaying" or "wasting" assets because, all other things being equal, their value will decline over time until they expire.

All assets depend on some definition of value, which is then modified by supply-and-demand factors established by buyers and sellers. However, options depend on many other variables, the most notable being their strike prices and time left until they expire.

This chapter discusses these factors so that a technical analyst understands them. Although technical analysis may be applied to the asset's underlying options, technical analysis itself is not effective in forecasting options prices. But these concepts and terms are needed to understand some technical indicators and analyses employed by technicians.

■ Benefits for Investors

There are two major benefits for options investors. The first is leverage, or the ability to gain price exposure to a given amount of assets for a lower initial cost. The second is hedging a position in the spot market.

For a small premium, the options investor has the right to buy or sell an asset at a specific price. They will have to pay that full price (or deliver the full amount of assets) at some time in the future, but they can choose to close out their position before that happens. Therefore, they can profit from the move in the underlying asset for a lower cost, and therefore lower risk.

■ Options Terminology

Call option: A call gives the holder the right, but not the obligation, to buy a defined amount of the underlying security at a certain price at or by a certain date.

Put option: A put gives the holder the right, but not the obligation, to sell a defined amount of the underlying security at a certain price at or by a certain date.

Strike price: This is the price at which the holder of the option may buy or sell the underlying security. For example, a call option with a strike price of 50 gives the holder the right to buy the underlying stock at that price no matter what the price of the stock may be at that time.

If the stock trades below 50, the option is "out-of-the-money" and the holder will not exercise it.

Expiration: The date at which the option holder no longer has any rights and the option no longer has value.

Premium: The price paid for the option.

Open interest: The number of options contracts outstanding per strike/ expiration combination.

Exercise: Using the rights acquired under the option to buy or sell the underlying security.

In-the-money: A call option with a strike price below the price of the underlying; a put option with a strike price above the price of the underlying.

Out-of-the-money: A call option with a strike price above the price of the underlying; a put option with a strike price below the price of the underlying.

At-the-money: An option with a strike price at or very close to the price of the underlying.

Implied volatility: The calculated expectation of future volatility.

Options writer: A writer creates a new option by selling to a buyer. Writing and selling are used interchangeably, although selling to close out a position is not called writing.

American style: Options that may be exercised at any time up to and including their expiration date.

European style: Options that may be exercised only at expiration.

Options prices contain both an intrinsic value and a time value. The intrinsic value is the value the option would have if it were to expire now. The more in-the-money the option, the higher the intrinsic value. Out-of-the-money options have no intrinsic value.

Time value is the speculative component. The longer an option has until it expires, the greater the chance that it will move into profitability. That is why a call option with a strike price of 100 has some value even if the underlying security trades at 20. If there is time left before expiration, there is still a chance that it can rally enough, small though it might be, to make the option profitable.

Typically, options with the same strike price but expirations further in the future have higher prices than those with nearby expirations. And the closer to expiration, the faster the time decay.

■ Using the Options Market

There are many reasons why an investor or trader trades options. The main reasons, as with other derivatives markets, is to hedge another position or to speculate on the performance of the underlying security.

Hedging: A hedge is like an insurance policy in that it can help to mitigate risk for a small fee. For example, a portfolio manager buys a large position in Company A stock for its long-term price appreciation potential but is worried that the next earnings report will show short-term issues.

He or she can buy put options on that stock that will increase in value if the price of the stock falls on its earnings news. If the stock rallies instead, the options may expire worthless but, again as with an insurance policy, the holder prefers that the negative event never happens.

Options also allow the holder to hedge against an unexpected increase in price or even a lack of movement in the price of the underlying.

Speculation: Options allow both buyers and sellers to capitalize on their market forecasts, whether they are bullish, bearish, or neutral. However, because options prices depend on many factors, including market volatility, traders can profit from increases or decreases in those factors as well.

For example, a stock trades sideways for months and its volatility declines to historically low levels. An options trader can create a strategy to profit from an increase in volatility, even if the underlying stock remains in a trading range. In other words, bullish, bearish, and neutral traders can all profit from increases in volatility.

■ Major Components of Options Prices

Options quotes include the standard pricing and volume data of other instruments. Open interest, bid, ask, and size figures are often displayed along with implied volatility.

AAPL18071225 (2018 Sep 225.00 Call)			LAST 4.20	CHANGE +1.64 (+64.06%)
Last Sale	4.20	Tick		Down
Time of Last Sale	08/31/2018 13:40	Exchange		
Net Change	+1.64	Previous Close		2.56
Open	3.30	High		5.12
Bid	4.15	Low		3.10
Ask	4.20	Volume		18681
Open Interest	15820	Expiration Date		09/07/2018

FIGURE 28.1 Typical Option Quote Information

Source: Cboe.

AAPL(APPLE INC) Options Chain

Exchange: Cboe ▼   Options Range: Near the Money ▼   Size: 2x4   Expiration: 2018 September ▼   View Chain

Aug 31, 2018 @ 14:03 ET   Bid: 227.91   Ask: 227.93   Vol: 25695732   Last 227.92   Change +2.89

Calls

SEPTEMBER 2018 (EXPIRATION: 09/07)

Strike	Last	Net	Bid	Ask	Vol	Int
AAPL18071225-E	4.17	+1.58	4.15	4.25	4817	15820
AAPL18071227.5-E	2.64	+1.09	2.62	2.75	3607	8882
AAPL18071230-E	1.61	+0.72	1.58	1.63	11605	14576
AAPL18071232.5-E	0.90	+0.36	0.91	0.94	3009	5758

Puts

SEPTEMBER 2018 (EXPIRATION: 09/07)

Strike	Last	Net	Bid	Ask	Vol	Int
AAPL1807U225-E	1.32	-1.03	1.19	1.24	3589	9254
AAPL1807U227.5-E	2.19	-1.61	2.14	2.22	1909	6989
AAPL1807U230-E	3.60	-2.10	3.50	3.65	249	4447
AAPL1807U232.5-E	5.07	-1.93	5.35	5.50	181	424

Calls

SEPTEMBER 2018 (EXPIRATION: 09/14)

Strike	Last	Net	Bid	Ask	Vol	Int
AAPL18141225-E	5.66	+1.71	5.60	5.70	720	6266
AAPL18141227.5-E	4.35	+1.66	4.15	4.30	494	3536
AAPL18141230-E	3.06	+1.13	3.05	3.15	1463	3842
AAPL18141232.5-E	2.22	+0.86	2.20	2.27	713	1205

Puts

SEPTEMBER 2018 (EXPIRATION: 09/14)

Strike	Last	Net	Bid	Ask	Vol	Int
AAPL1814U225-E	2.59	-1.02	2.54	2.58	532	1302
AAPL1814U227.5-E	3.75	-1.45	3.55	3.70	3119	643
AAPL1814U230-E	5.15	-0.92	4.90	5.10	429	141
AAPL1814U232.5-E	6.39	-2.26	6.55	6.70	3	23

Calls

SEPTEMBER 2018 (EXPIRATION: 09/21)

Strike	Last	Net	Bid	Ask	Vol	Int
AAPL18211225-E	6.57	+1.79	6.50	6.60	1244	16708
AAPL18211227.5-E	5.11	+1.54	5.10	5.25	1012	5248
AAPL18211230-E	3.99	+1.31	3.95	4.05	2412	16323
AAPL18211232.5-E	3.04	+1.05	3.00	3.05	695	4871

Puts

SEPTEMBER 2018 (EXPIRATION: 09/21)

Strike	Last	Net	Bid	Ask	Vol	Int
AAPL1821U225-E	3.48	-0.85	3.35	3.40	938	5013
AAPL1821U227.5-E	4.50	-1.14	4.40	4.50	710	1378
AAPL1821U230-E	5.80	-1.47	5.70	5.85	163	1779
AAPL1821U232.5-E	7.40	-2.00	7.25	7.40	36	331

Calls

SEPTEMBER 2018 (EXPIRATION: 09/28)

Strike	Last	Net	Bid	Ask	Vol	Int
AAPL18281225-E	7.65	+2.21	7.20	7.45	99	2244
AAPL18281227.5-E	6.37	+2.14	5.80	6.00	543	1336
AAPL18281230-E	4.77	+1.42	4.65	4.75	814	3473
AAPL18281232.5-E	4.05	+1.68	3.65	3.75	34	438

Puts

SEPTEMBER 2018 (EXPIRATION: 09/28)

Strike	Last	Net	Bid	Ask	Vol	Int
AAPL1828U225-E	4.04	-0.89	3.95	4.05	52	813
AAPL1828U227.5-E	5.17	-0.17	5.05	5.20	33	446
AAPL1828U230-E	6.40	-1.44	6.30	6.50	88	132
AAPL1828U232.5-E	7.84	-0.25	7.80	8.00	6	13

FIGURE 28.2 Typical Option Chain
Source: Cboe.

While traders can look at individual options data, a very widely used display called an "options chain" lists all options, or a subset, available for a given expiration month. In other words, it shows the pricing, volume, and open interest for all puts, all calls, or both arranged by strike price.

Options analysts also look at derivatives of price that measure how fast their prices decay over time, how fast their prices change with a given change in the price of the underlying and more. These derivatives are designated with Greek letters such as delta and gamma, so options traders simply call them "the Greeks."

- **Delta** measures how much an option price changes for a one-point move in the underlying. Its value ranges between 0 and 1 for calls and between −1 and 0 for puts.

- **Gamma** measures the rate of change in delta. It is essentially the second derivative of price. Values are highest for at-the-money options and smallest for those far in- or out-of-the-money.

- **Vega** measures the risk from changes in implied volatility. Higher volatility makes options more expensive since there is a greater chance that the underlying security price will move above the strike price for a call, or below the strike price for a put.

- **Theta** measures the rate of time-value decay and is always a negative number as time moves in only one direction.

- **Rho** measures the impact of changes in interest rates on an option's price. Since interest rates do not change very frequently, this Greek does not get the same exposure as the others.

■ Implied Volatility (IV)

Implied volatility is the estimated volatility of a security's price and is critical in the pricing of options. Although not a guarantee, implied volatility tends to increase while the market in the underlying security is bearish. Conversely, when the underlying security is bullish, implied volatility tends to decrease. This is due to the common belief that bear markets are riskier than bull markets.

The most important concept is that implied volatility is an estimate of the future volatility, or fluctuations, of a security's price.

While levels of implied volatility are associated with bullish and bearish markets in the underlying security, it really does not predict market direction. It only forecasts the sizes of potential price swings. In other words, high volatility means a large price swing, but it could be higher or lower, or both. Low volatility suggests that price probably will not experience broad, unpredictable changes.

Implied volatility is not the same as historical volatility, also known as realized volatility or actual volatility. Historical volatility measures past market changes in the price of the underlying asset.

Different quotation systems might label implied as "vol" or denote it by another Greek letter, sigma, "σ."

■ Options Strategies

There are many different ways options are combined to create bullish, bearish, or neutral strategies.

For example, a trader may believe the underlying security is about to have a very large move but does not know which way it will be. A long straddle position, utilizing a call and a put, will let the trader profit if the underlying does, in fact, move significantly in either direction. One option will increase and the other will expire worthless. The risk is that the underlying does not move and the trader loses on both options.

Combinations of options can create risk-and-reward profiles that either limit risk or exploit specific options characteristics such as volatility and time decay.

Some combinations, such as spreads, allow the trader to speculate on the direction of the underlying with lower cost by buying one option and selling a different option. The tradeoff is that it limits profit potential.

■ Pricing Models

There are three common pricing models in use that take into account interest rates, the price of the underlying security, volatility, and the time to expiration. This is a complex area of discussion and is best left to an options course.

However, technical analysts should know the names of these models. They are Black-Scholes and the Black model, the Cox-Rubinstein Binomial, and the Monte Carlo model.

■ Warrants

Warrants are not options but they are very similar. Usually issued on stocks, they give the holder the right, but not the obligation, to buy shares in the underlying company by a certain date. Therefore, they are essentially call options with one major difference. Whereas call options are written by the public, a warrant is only written, or created, by the company issuing the stock.

Typically, warrants have longer maturities than options. In addition, when an option is exercised, one trader delivers existing shares to the other. When a warrant is exercised, the company issues new shares, which increases the total number of shares outstanding.

■ What Does a Technical Analyst Need?

Although they can certainly chart the prices of options over time, technical analysts do not really analyze options. What is most important is understanding implied volatility because it is one of the primary concepts used in technical analysis. In succeeding chapters, the reader will learn about the Chicago Board Options Exchange volatility index, known by its trading symbol "VIX."

CHAPTER 29

Understanding Implied Volatility

From Russell Rhoads, *Trading VIX Derivatives: Trading and Hedging Strategies Using VIX Futures, Options, and Exchange-Traded Notes* (Hoboken, New Jersey: John Wiley & Sons, 2007), Chapter 1.

Learning Objective Statements

- Explain the difference between historical and implied volatility
- Describe the concept of put-call parity
- Discuss how implied volatility may be used to estimate price movement
- State how to calculate single-day implied volatility

In this book, we will discuss the ins and outs of a popular market indicator, or index, that is based on implied volatility. The indicator is the Cboe Volatility Index®, widely known by its ticker symbol, VIX. It should come as no surprise that a solid understanding of the index must begin with a solid understanding of what implied volatility is and how it works.

Implied volatility is ultimately determined by the price of option contracts. Since option prices are the result of market forces, or increased levels of buying or selling, implied volatility is determined by the market. An index based on implied volatility of option prices is displaying the market's estimation of volatility of the underlying security in the future.

■ Historical versus Forward-Looking Volatility

There are two main types of volatility discussed relative to securities prices. The first is historical volatility, which may be calculated using recent trading activity for a stock or other security. The historical volatility of a stock is factual and known. Also, the historical volatility does not give any indication about the future movement of a stock. The forward-looking volatility is what is referred to as the implied volatility. This type of volatility results from the market price of options that trade on a stock.

The implied volatility component of option prices is the factor that can give all option traders, novice to expert, the most difficulty. This occurs because the implied volatility of an option may change while all other pricing factors impacting the price of an option remain unchanged. This change may occur as the order flow for options is biased more to buying or selling. A result of increased buying of options by market participants is higher implied volatility. Conversely, when there is net selling of options, the implied volatility indicated by option prices moves lower.

Basically, the nature of order flow dictates the direction of implied volatility. Again, more option buying increases the option price and the result is higher implied volatility. Going back to Economics 101, implied volatility reacts to the supply and demand of the marketplace. Buying pushes it higher, and selling pushes it lower.

The implied volatility of an option is also considered an indication of the risk associated with the underlying security. The risk may be thought of as how much movement may be expected from the underlying stock over the life of an option. This is not the potential direction of the stock price move, just the magnitude of the move. Generally, when thinking of risk, traders think of a stock losing value or the price moving lower. Using implied volatility as a risk measure results in an estimation of a price move in either direction. When the market anticipates that a stock may soon move dramatically, the price of option contracts, both puts and calls, will move higher.

A common example of a known event in the future that may dramatically influence the price of a stock is a company's quarterly earnings report. Four times a year a company will release information to the investing public in the form of its recent earnings results. This earnings release may also include statements regarding business prospects for the company. This information may have a dramatic impact on the share price. As this price move will also impact option prices, the option contracts usually react in advance. Due to the anticipation that will work into option prices, they are generally more expensive as traders and investors buy options before seeing the report.

This increased buying of options results in higher option prices. There are two ways to think about this: the higher price of the option contracts results in higher implied volatility, or because of higher implied volatility option prices are higher. After the earnings report, there is less risk of a big move in the underlying stock and the options become less expensive. This drop in price is due to lower implied volatility levels; implied volatility is now lower due to lower option prices.

A good non-option-oriented example of how implied volatility works may be summed up through this illustration. If you live in Florida, you are familiar with hurricane season. The path of hurricanes can be unpredictable, and at times homeowners have little time to prepare for a storm. Using homeowners insurance as a substitute for an option contract, consider the following situation.

You wake to find out that an evacuation is planned due to a potential hurricane. Before leaving the area, you check whether your homeowners insurance is current. You find you have allowed your coverage to lapse, and so you run down to your agent's office. As he boards up windows and prepares to evacuate inland, he informs you that you may renew, but the cost is going to be $50,000 instead of the $2,000 annual rate you have paid for years. After hearing your objections, he is steadfast. The higher price, he explains, is due to the higher risk associated with the coming storm.

You decide that $50,000 is too much to pay, and you return home to ride out the storm. Fortunately, the storm takes a left turn and misses your neighborhood altogether. Realizing that you have experienced a near miss, you run down to your agent's office with a $50,000 check in hand. Being an honest guy, he tells you the rate is back down to $2,000. Why is this?

The imminent risk level for replacing your home has decreased as there is no known threat bearing down on your property. As the immediate risk of loss or damage has decreased tremendously, so has the cost of protection against loss. When applying this to the option market, risk is actually risk of movement of the underlying security, either higher or lower. This risk is the magnitude of expected movement of the underlying security over the life of an option.

When market participants are expecting a big price move to the upside in the underlying security, there will be net buying of call options in anticipation of this move. As this buying occurs, the price of the call options will increase. This price rise in the options is associated with an increase risk of a large price move, and this increase in risk translates to higher implied volatility.

Also, if there is an expectation of a lower price move, the marketplace may see an increase in put buying. With higher demand for put contracts, the price of puts may increase resulting in higher implied volatility for those options. Finally, if put prices increase, the result is corresponding call prices rising due to a concept known as put-call parity, which will be discussed in the next section.

■ Put-Call Parity

Put and call prices are linked to each other through the price of the underlying stock through put-call parity. This link exists because combining a stock and put position can result in the same payoff as a position in a call option with the same strike price as the put. If this relationship gets out of line or not in parity, an arbitrage opportunity exits. When one of these opportunities arises, there are trading firms that will quickly buy and sell the securities to attempt to take advantage of this mispricing. This market activity will push the put and call prices back in line with each other.

Put and call prices should remain within a certain price range of each other or arbitragers will enter the market, which results in the prices coming back into parity. Parity between the two also results in a similar implied volatility output resulting from using these prices in a model to determine the implied volatility of the market.

TABLE 29.1	Put, Call, and Stock Pricing to Illustrate Put-Call Parity	
Stock/Option		**Price**
XYZ Stock		$50.00
XYZ 50 Call		$1.00
XYZ 50 Put		$2.00

Stated differently, increased demand for a call option will raise the price of that call. As the price of the call moves higher, the corresponding put price should also rise, or the result will be an arbitrage trade that will push the options into line. As the pricing of the option contracts are tied to each other, they will share similar implied volatility levels also.

For a quick and very simple example of how put-call parity works, consider the options and stock in Table 29.1.

Using the XYZ 50 Put combined with XYZ stock, a payout that replicates being long the XYZ 50 Call may be created. The combination of owning stock and owning a put has the same payout structure as a long call option position. With the XYZ 50 Call trading at 1.00 and the XYZ 50 Put priced at 2.00, there may be a mispricing scenario. Table 29.2 compares a long XYZ 50 Call trade with a combined position of long XYZ stock and long a XYZ 50 Put.

The final two columns compare a payout of owning XYZ stock from 50.00 and buying the XYZ 50 Put at 2.00 versus buying an XYZ 50 Call for 1.00. Note that at any price at expiration, the long call position is worth 1.00 more than the combined stock and put position. With this pricing difference, there is the ability to take a short position in the strategy that will be worth less and buy the strategy that will be worth more at expiration. The payout diagram in Figure 29.1 shows how the two positions compare at a variety of prices at expiration.

The lines are parallel throughout this diagram. The higher line represents the profit or loss based on buying the 50 call. The lower line represents the payout for the spread combining a long stock position and a long 50 put position. At any price at expiration, the combined position has less value than the long 50 call. Knowing this outcome, it is possible to benefit from the 1.00 spread, which will exist at any price at expiration for two positions that are basically the same.

Due to put-call parity and the mispricing between the 50 Call and 50 Put, the call may be purchased combined with a short position in the stock and put option. A quick

TABLE 29.2	Payout Comparison for Long Call and Long Stock + Long Put Trade			
XYZ at Expiration	**Long XYZ Stock**	**Long XYZ 50 Put**	**Long Stock + Long Put**	**Long XYZ 50 Call**
45.00	−5.00	3.00	−2.00	−1.00
50.00	0.00	−2.00	−2.00	−1.00
55.00	5.00	−2.00	3.00	4.00

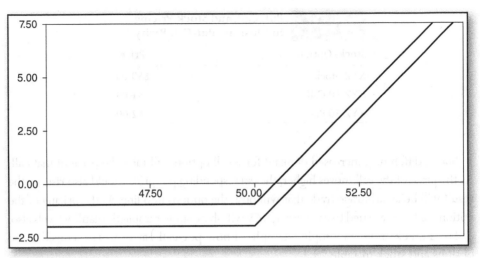

FIGURE 29.1 Payout Diagram Comparison

transaction using the prices in the example would result in a profit of 1.00 upon options expiration. This 1.00 profit would be realized regardless of the price of the stock
at expiration. Firms would attempt to take advantage of this opportunity through buying the cheaper call option and selling the comparable more expensive put option. The
market activity of these participants is what keeps put and call option prices in line with
each other and the implied volatility of both put and call contracts at the same level.

■ Estimating Price Movement

What the implied volatility of an option projects onto the underlying security is the expected range of price movement over a certain period of time. This estimation of price
movement is based on statistics and the bell curve. The implied volatility of an option is
the projection of an annualized one standard deviation move in the underlying stock over
the life of the option. According to statistics and using implied volatility as a guide, the
price of a stock should land between up and down one standard deviation at option expiration. The closing price should land in this range 68.2 percent of the time.

This 68.2 percent comes from statistics and what is referred to as a normal distribution. Statistics like this reveal that 68.2 percent of the time a stock should be between up
one standard deviation and down one standard deviation a year from today. A formula
may also be used to take this annualized number and narrow down the projection to a
single day. The normal distribution also indicates that there is a 95.4 percent expectation
of the stock landing between up two standard deviations and down two standard deviations. Finally, at three standard deviations, the probability reaches 99.7 percent.

With a stock trading at $50 and the underlying option prices indicating 20 percent
implied volatility, the result is a one standard deviation price move equal to $10
(20 percent of $50). In other words, the stock is expected to close between $40
(down $10) and $60 (up $10) with 68.2 percent certainty a year from today. A two
standard deviation price move would be equal to $20. This is calculated by simply

multiplying 2 times a single standard deviation. Using two standard deviations, it can be projected out that the stock should land between $30 and up $70, with a confidence of 95.4 percent. At three standard deviations, there is a 99.7 percent chance of the stock closing between $20 and $80 a year from the date of the calculation.

■ Valuing Options: Pricing Calculators and Other Tools

An option pricing calculator is a tool that allows a user the ability to input the pricing variables that determine the value of an option with the result being a theoretical option price. Ultimately the market determines the price of an option through buying and selling forces. However, when analyzing and investigating option trades, using an option pricing calculator with certain assumptions gives an idea where an option may be trading in the future. Also, using an option pricing calculator is an excellent way to become familiar with the price action of option contracts. The Cboe has a free option calculator available on its website at www.cboe.com/tradtool; it is a valuable tool for option pricing.

The value of an option contract is derived from a variety of inputs. Inputs into an option pricing model include the price of the underlying security, the strike price of the option, the type of option, dividends, interest rates, and time to option expiration. The final input into an option pricing model is the implied volatility of the option. These inputs may be used in a model to determine the value of an option.

Table 29.3 demonstrates how an option pricing model is used to determine the value of an option. The inputs are at the top of the table, with the value of the option showing up as the only output. Option pricing models calculate a variety of pieces of useful information, such as the impact of changes in pricing factors. These outputs are known as the option Greeks. However, to keep focus on the topic at hand, implied volatility, only the necessary outputs are going to be demonstrated in this example of an option calculator.

TABLE 29.3 Option Pricing Calculator–Option Value Output	
Factor	**Input**
Call/Put	Call
Underlying Price	44.75
Strike Price	45.00
Implied Volatility	30%
Days to Expiration	30
Interest Rate	1.00%
Dividends	0.00%
Output	**Result**
Option Value	1.45

The option price in the model is determined from a stock trading at 44.75 with implied volatility of 30 percent and a risk-free interest rate of 1.00 percent. The result is a call option value with a strike price of 45 and 30 days to expiration would be valued at 1.45 based on the inputs used in this model. Keep in mind that this is a pricing model, not the actual market trading price of the option. Again, the inputs in the model are assumptions, not just the market price. Just because using these inputs results in a value of 1.45 for this 45 Call does not mean it can be traded at this level. In fact, the market price of this option will vary if the market consensus differs from the inputs used in this model.

The real value of an option at any given time is actually determined by the price that it may be bought or sold in the market. In the case of this 45 Call, even though the inputs into the model result in a 1.45 value, when checking market quotes for this option we find that the current trading price is 1.70. The reason for the difference between our model's value and the market price is the result of different implied volatility levels being used. The previous model, in Table 29.3, takes inputs and the result in a difference in option values based on the inputs.

The pricing factors in an option pricing model are for the most part set in stone. The exception of this is the implied volatility input. For the model, the assumption of 30 percent implied volatility was used. However, the market is pricing in a higher implied volatility level. This is determined before any numbers or formulas have been run just by comparing the option market price and the option value assumption that resulted from the model. The market price of the option is higher than the pricing model output. Seeing this, it is pretty certain that the implied volatility based on market prices is higher than what was entered into the model. There is a direct correlation between high and low relative option prices and higher or lower implied volatility.

Table 29.4 is an option pricing model that uses the market price as an input with the sole output being implied volatility. This implied volatility level is being indicated by the 1.70 market price of the 45 Call. The higher option price here is a higher implied volatility than what was used in the first pricing model. As the option price in this model is higher than the option value that resulted from a 30 percent implied

TABLE 29.4 Option Pricing Calculator—Implied Volatility Output	
Factor	Input
Call/Put	Call
Underlying Price	44.75
Strike Price	45.00
Option Price	1.70
Days to Expiration	30
Interest Rate	1.00%
Dividends	0.00%
Output	**Result**
Implied Volatility	35%

TABLE 29.5	Impact of a 5 Percent Increase in Implied Volatility	
Implied Volatility	30%	35%
Option Price	1.45	1.70

volatility, the expectation would be a higher implied volatility result. Using 1.70 as the price of the option actually results in the implied volatility that is being projected by this option price to be 35 percent. Professional traders generally start with the market price of an option to calculate implied volatility as that is where the implied volatility of an option is ultimately determined.

Another method of demonstrating the impact of different implied volatility levels on option prices appears in Table 29.5. Instead of a comparison of what the model output was versus the option price based on model outputs, consider the previous option prices in a different way. Consider the two option prices and implied volatility differences as changes based on an increase in demand for the option. Both prices represent the market and the option price increases from 1.45 to 1.70. This option price rise occurs due to an increase in buying of the call option while all other factors that influence the option price stay the same.

Since the price of the option contract has increased, the resulting implied volatility output from an option model has also increased. Higher option prices, whether put or call prices, will result in a higher implied volatility output with no changes in any of the other option pricing factors.

To recap, there is a direct link between the demand for option contracts and their prices in the marketplace. This is regardless of changes occurring in the underlying stock price. With demand in the form of buying pressure pushing option prices higher or an increase in selling occurring due to market participants pushing option prices lower, the implied volatility of an option is dictated by market forces.

■ Fluctuations Based on Supply and Demand

As mentioned in the first section of this chapter, implied volatility does fluctuate based on supply and demand for options. This leads to the question, "What exactly causes the supply and demand for options to fluctuate?" The short answer is the near-term expected price changes that may occur in the underlying stock. These moves are usually the result of information that has influenced the fundamental outlook for a stock. The best example of this type of information would be a company's quarterly earnings reports.

Every publicly traded company in the United States reports its earnings results four times a year. The date and timing (generally before the market opens or after the market closes) are usually known well in advance of the actual announcement. Along with the earnings results, other information is disseminated, such as the company's revenues and the source of those revenues. Many companies offer a possible outlook regarding the prospects for their business conditions, and most will hold a public conference call to answer professional investors' questions. These events often have a dramatic impact, either positive or negative, on the price of a stock.

Again, the date that these results are announced is public knowledge and often widely anticipated by analysts and traders. As the date draws near, there is usually trading in the stock and stock options that is based on the anticipated stock price reaction to the earnings announcement. The result is usually net buying of options as there is speculation regarding the potential move of the underlying stock. The net option buying results in higher option prices and an increase in the implied volatility projected by the options that trade on this stock. Usually this increase impacts only the options with the closest expiration and strike prices that are close to where the stock is trading. An excellent example of this can be seen in the option prices and resulting implied volatility levels for Amazon stock shown in Table 29.6.

These are market prices from just before the close of trading on July 22, 2010. Amazon's earnings were reported after the market close on the 22nd with weekly options that expire on the 23rd having only one trading day until expiration after the news was released. The difference in implied volatility between the options that have one trading day left and those that have just under a month left is pretty significant.

This difference stems from the options that market participants would use as a short-term trading vehicle related to Amazon's earnings announcement. This would be the same for hedgers and speculators alike. Both would focus on the strike prices that are closest to the trading price of the stock as well as the options with the least amount of time to expiration.

Option contracts that have the closest expiration to a known event that occurs after the event are the contracts that will have the most price reaction before and after the event occurs. With Amazon reporting earnings the evening of July 22 and an option series expiring on July 23, the July 23 options are the contracts that will see the most price action based on the stock price reaction to the earnings release.

The stock price is very close to the 120 strike price when the option first listed and just before the earnings announcement. Using the 120 strike options, implied

TABLE 29.6 Amazon Option Implied Volatility and Option Prices Minutes Prior to an Earnings Announcement

AMZN @ 120.07				
Call Strike	July 23 Call	July 23 Call IV	Aug 21 Call	Aug 21 Call IV
115	7.00	163%	9.25	48%
120	3.92	156%	6.25	45%
125	1.82	148%	4.05	45%
Put Strike	July 23 Put	July 23 Put IV	Aug 21 Put	Aug 21 Put IV
115	1.92	159%	4.05	48%
120	3.82	155%	6.20	47%
125	6.75	148%	8.90	45%

volatility for both the put and call options that expire the following day is around 155 percent. This indicates that on an annualized basis the option market is pricing in a 155 percent price move over a single day. This is much more dramatic sounding than it is in reality. Annualized implied volatility of 155 percent for an option with a single trading day left translates to a one-day move of around 9.76 percent. The math behind this is (see the following feature on calculating single-day implied volatility):

$$9.76\% = 155\%/15.87$$

This single-day implied volatility can be interpreted as being a single standard deviation range of expected price movement of the stock on that day.

CALCULATING SINGLE-DAY IMPLIED VOLATILITY

Assuming there are 252 trading days in a year, the denominator of this formula turns out to be the square root of the number of trading days for the year.

1 Day Movement = Implied Volatility/Square Root of 252

Amazon did report its earnings, and the initial price reaction was pretty close to what the option market was pricing in. The NASDAQ opening price the day after the company reported earnings was down 11.76 percent from the previous day's close. The market was forecasting a 9.76 percent move based on option pricing.

As a refresher from college statistics: One standard deviation in statistics indicates there is a 68.2 percent chance that an outcome is going to land between up and down one standard deviation. So this single-day implied volatility indicates the market is expecting Amazon's stock to trade within up or down 9.76 percent with a 68.2 percent level of confidence in the next day.

Table 29.7 shows the increase in the implied volatility of the 120 Call projected by Amazon option prices as the earnings announcement approaches. Implied volatility for other options rises in the same way, since 120 is the closest strike to the stock price when the option started trading and just before earnings were announced. Also, the options contract is a weekly expiration option that begins trading on a Thursday morning and expires on the following week's Friday close. This particular

TABLE 29.7	Implied Volatility Changes Approaching Amazon Earnings		
Date	AMZN	120 Call	120 Call IV
July 15	120.13	4.80	71%
July 15	122.06	5.92	78%
July 16	118.49	4.00	84%
July 19	119.94	4.33	87%
July 20	120.10	3.95	90%
July 21	117.43	2.73	111%
July 22	120.07	3.92	155%

option started trading on July 15 with the last trading day being July 23 or what is called a weekly option that has only eight trading days from listing to expiration.

The first row is the opening price for the weekly option and underlying price for the option. When the option first traded it had an implied volatility level of 71 percent. This compares to non-earnings-period implied volatility levels, which are usually in the mid 30 percent range for Amazon options.

Over the next few days, the earnings announcement draws closer and the stock stays in a fairly tight range. The implied volatility of the option contracts continues to rise as time passes. By the time the announcement is imminent, the implied volatility of the 120 Call has more than doubled.

This illustration of how implied volatility climbs in front of a potentially market-moving event is a bit magnified by the options only having one day of time value remaining before the announcement. However, it is a good illustration of how option prices, through the implied volatility component, discount a potential market-moving event when the timing of this event is a known entity.

■ The Impact on Option Prices

Implied volatility is commonly considered an indication as to whether an option is cheap or expensive. This determination may be made through examining past implied volatility levels for the options of a particular stock or index and comparing present values.

Demand for options pushes up the price of an option contract and results in higher implied volatility. However, other factors such as the underlying price, time to expiration, and interest-rate levels also determine the price of an option. These other factors are not impacted through the buying and selling pressure on option contracts. Only implied volatility will fluctuate based on market buying and selling pressure.

The goal of any directional trading strategy should be to buy low and sell high. If the market considers any trading vehicle inexpensive, there will be participants that take advantage of this through purchasing the instrument. On the other hand, if something appears expensive it may be sold. Implied volatility is a measure that option traders use to define whether options are overvalued or undervalued.

As a simple example, take the option prices and implied volatility levels in Table 29.8. The data in this table represent a stock trading at 24.00 per share, and the value of a 25 Call with 90 days until expiration. The different option prices are based on various implied volatility levels. Note that as the option price increases so does the implied volatility of the 25 Call.

TABLE 29.8	Implied Volatility Levels and Option Prices	
Stock Price	**25 Call**	**Implied Volatility**
24.00	0.80	20%
24.00	1.05	25%
24.00	1.30	30%

If options for the underlying stock usually trade with an implied volatility of 25 percent, then when the option could be purchased for 0.80 it may be considered undervalued or inexpensive. At 0.80 the option had an implied volatility level of 20 percent. When implied volatility rose to 30 percent and the option was trading for 1.30, the option may be considered expensive. At 1.05 with an implied volatility of 25 percent, the historical norm, the 25 Call may be considered fairly valued.

Of course, using implied volatility as a measure of how expensive or cheap an option is must be done in the context of some external factors. Remember, if the company is preparing to announce quarterly earnings, the implied volatility would be expected to be high relative to other periods of time. In that case, a comparison to implied volatility behavior around previous earnings announcements would be a more accurate analysis of whether the options appear cheap or expensive.

◼ Implied Volatility and the VIX

The VIX will be further defined, but the concepts in this chapter should be tied to the VIX before moving forward. The VIX is a measure of the implied volatility being projected through the prices of S&P 500 index options. The VIX can be used to indicate what type of market movement option prices are projecting on the S&P 500 over the next 30 days or even a shorter time. Since the VIX is measuring implied volatility of S&P 500 index options and since implied volatility is a measure of risk projected by option pricing, the VIX is considered a gauge of fear in the overall market.

CHAPTER 30

About the VIX Index

From Russell Rhoads, *Trading VIX Derivatives: Trading and Hedging Strategies Using VIX Futures, Options, and Exchange-Traded Notes* (Hoboken, New Jersey: John Wiley & Sons, 2007), Chapter 2.

Learning Objective Statements

- Describe the components of the VIX index
- Explain the implications of a rising or falling VIX index
- State how to calculate expected 30-day market movement

Officially known as the Cboe Volatility Index, the VIX is considered by many to be a gauge of fear and greed in the stock market. A more accurate description of what the VIX measures is the implied volatility that is being priced into S&P 500 index options. Through the use of a wide variety of option prices, the index offers an indication of 30-day implied volatility as priced by the S&P 500 index option market.

Before diving further into the calculation that results in the VIX, this chapter will cover the history of exactly how this index was developed followed by an overview of how the VIX is determined. Then for interested parties there is a more in-depth discussion of how the VIX is calculated. The VIX index has historically had an inverse relationship to performance of the S&P 500, and this often results in questions from traders who are new to the VIX.

Finally, there are a handful of VIX-related indexes based on other equity-market indexes. The S&P 100–related VIX is still calculated using the old method to maintain some continuity for historical comparisons. Finally, there are also VIX indexes calculated on options based on the NASDAQ 100, Russell 2000, and Dow Jones Industrial Average, which are discussed toward the end of the chapter.

■ History of the VIX

The concept behind the VIX index was developed by Dr. Robert Whaley of Vanderbilt University in 1993. His paper "Derivatives on Market Volatility: Hedging Tools Long Overdue," which appeared in the *Journal of Derivatives*, laid the groundwork for the index. The original VIX was based on pricing of S&P 100 (OEX) options and used only eight option contracts to determine a volatility measure.

TABLE 30.1	S&P 500 Industry Weightings	
Industry		**Weighting**
Consumer discretionary		9.10%
Consumer staples		11.70%
Energy		11.40%
Financials		15.40%
Health care		13.40%
Industrials		10.00%
Information technology		18.50%
Materials		3.40%
Telecom services		3.30%
Utilities		3.80%

At the time, OEX options were the most heavily traded index option series that reflected performance of the stock market in the United States. This volatility index was based on a limited number of options and was slightly disconnected from the overall stock market due to the narrower focus of the S&P 100 versus the S&P 500.

In 2003 there was a new methodology for calculation of the VIX index that was developed through work done by the Cboe and Goldman Sachs. Although the calculation was altered, the most important aspect to this change for individuals is that the underlying options changed from the OEX to options trading on the S&P 500. Another significant change was an increase in the number of options that were used in the index calculation. Through a wider number of option contract prices feeding the formula to calculate the VIX, a true 30-day implied volatility level that is being projected on the S&P 500 by the options market is realized.

The S&P 500 index is considered by professional investors to be the benchmark for the performance of the stock market in the United States. The members of the index are 500 of the largest domestic companies in the United States that meet criteria based on market capitalization, public float, financial viability, liquidity, type of company, and industry sector. Companies are usually dropped from the index when they have violated membership criteria or have ceased to operate due to a merger or acquisition.

The industry representation of the S&P 500 index appears in Table 30.1. With a broad distribution of companies in the index, there is no industry that dominates the index's performance. This diversification across industries is a major reason the S&P 500 is considered a performance benchmark by most professional investors.

■ Calculating the VIX

After the VIX index was introduced, the Cboe moved forward with the first exchange listed volatility derivative instruments. Through the Cboe Futures Exchange (CFE®), the Cboe introduced futures contracts based on the VIX. Other instruments have followed, and more are in development.

There are two ways to explain how the VIX is determined. First, it can be explained using simple nonmathematical terms. Then, for those interested in an in-depth discussion of the formula and calculation, a more detailed overview will follow. Having a basic understanding of how the VIX is determined is more than enough to move forward with trading. However, for those with more interest in the VIX calculation, the more comprehensive description is included.

The Nonmathematical Approach

The VIX is an indicator of 30-day implied volatility determined through the use of S&P 500 index option prices. The option price used in the formula is actually the midpoint of the bid-ask spread of relevant at and out of the money actively traded S&P 500 index options. Using the midpoint of the spread is a more accurate price description than the last price for an option contract. Also, the contracts used are the S&P 500 index options that trade to the next two standard expirations with at least eight days to expiration. When a series reaches this eight-day point, it is not used anymore in the calculation and the options that expire farther in the future then start to contribute to the VIX calculation.

All of these S&P 500 options are then used to create a synthetic at the money option that expires exactly 30 days from the very moment of the calculation. This time variable to the formula is constantly being updated to weight the balance of the two expiration series in the formula. Using a wide number of actively quoted S&P 500 index options, a synthetic 30-day option is created and the VIX is the implied volatility of that option. This results in implied volatility of the synthetic option contract, which is then reported as the VIX.

The Formula and Calculations

It is possible to trade the VIX with a cursory understanding of how the index is determined. Those who are satisfied with their understanding of the VIX and what it represents may skip ahead. However, readers who are more interested in how the VIX is calculated should be interested in the remainder of this section.

The input for calculating the VIX index comes from all actively quoted S&P 500 index options for the next two standard option expirations that have at least eight days remaining until expiration. Eliminating the nearer term expiration options that have only a week to expiration takes out some of the end-of-contract volatility that can occur in the market.

The option contracts from these two expiration series are the at and out of the money put and call options. The series of options used extends out of the money until there are two consecutive option strikes that have no bid-ask market posted. Again, the midpoint of the bid-ask spread for the options is used in the calculation.

The time to expiration part of the calculation is very specific, down to the second. This is constantly being updated to change the weighting between the two series of options feeding into the calculation. Although S&P 500 index options cease trading on a Thursday for Friday morning settlement, the time to expiration is based on the market opening time, 8:30 A.M. central time, on the Friday of expiration.

There is also a forward price for the S&P 500 that is calculated using the closest at the money options in conjunction with put-call parity. This S&P 500 forward price is the underlying security price and strike price used to price the synthetic option used in the calculation. The implied volatility of that option is what is quoted at the VIX.

Finally if there is interest in using Microsoft Excel© to replicate calculating the VIX, a paper produced by Tom Arnold and John H. Earl Jr. of the University of Richmond is useful. In a very short study, 10 pages, they lay out the groundwork for using Excel to replicate the calculation of the VIX (to read the full paper, go to http://papers.ssrn.com/sol3/papers.cfm?abstractid=1103971). Also, once the template has been set up, changing the time frame and underlying instrument is simple. Using the template, the VIX methodology may be applied to a variety of instruments or time frames with little effort.

■ The VIX and Put-Call Parity

Many traders and investors often ask why there appears to be an inverse relationship between the direction of stock prices and the VIX. The relationship may be broken down to the nature of purchasing options. When the market is under pressure, there is a net buying of put options, which will result in higher implied volatility. This rapid increase in demand for put options pushes the implied volatility for both put and call contracts higher; the reason behind this is called put-call parity.

Put-call parity states that the prices of put and call options that have the same strike price and expiration are related. This relationship exists due to the ability to create synthetic positions in one option through combining the other option with the underlying stock. With this possibility, if the price of one option differs enough from the price of the other, an arbitrage opportunity may present itself.

For instance, in a zero-interest-rate environment, a put and call price should have the same value if the stock is trading at the strike price. As the options are related in price, the implied volatility of these options is also related. This is unrealistic, but it is a good method of demonstrating put-call parity. The prices in Table 30.2 may be used to demonstrate what can happen when put-call parity breaks down.

It is possible to replicate the payout of a long call through combining a put option and a stock position. Stated another way, a long stock position along with owning a put will result in the same payout structure as being long a call option. So, if the same payout may be created in two methods, the pricing of these two should be equivalent. If they are not equal, the lower priced one may be bought while the higher

TABLE 30.2	Prices to Demonstrate Put-Call Parity
Security	**Price**
XYZ Stock	45.00
XYZ 45 Call	2.50
XYZ 45 Put	2.00

TABLE 30.3	Long XYZ 45 Call versus Long XYZ 45 Put + Long XYZ at Expiration			
XYZ	Long XYZ Stock	Long XYZ 45 Put	Long Stock + Long Put	Long XYZ 45 Call
35	−10.00	8.00	−2.00	−2.50
40	−5.00	3.00	−2.00	−2.50
45	0.00	−2.00	−2.00	−2.50
50	5.00	−2.00	3.00	2.50
55	10.00	−2.00	8.00	7.50

priced one is simultaneously sold. This is known as an arbitrage trade, in which an instant profit may be realized through a pricing difference in two equivalent securities.

If the XYZ 45 Put is purchased and shares of XYZ stock are also bought, the resulting position at expiration will be the same as owning the XYZ 45 Call. Above 45.00, the call option would result in a long position in XYZ; below 45.00, the call would not be exercised and there would be no position in XYZ. With a long 45 put position combined with a long position in the stock, if the stock is below 45.00 at expiration, the put option will be exercised and the stock sold. The result would be no position in XYZ. Above 45.00, the stock would still be owned, as the XYZ 45 Put would not be exercised. Regardless of the stock price at expiration, the resulting position in XYZ will be the same. Due to the different prices between the 45 Call and 45 Put, there is a difference in profit or loss of the position at expiration. Table 30.3 demonstrates this at a variety of price points at expiration.

The column Long Stock + Long Put represents the position payout at expiration of the combined long stock–long put position. Note at all price levels the combined long stock and long put position is worth 0.50 more than the long call position. If at all price levels at expiration the long call position will be worth less than stock plus put position, then an arbitrage opportunity exists.

The arbitrage trade would be to purchase the stock and put option while taking a short position in the call option. At any price level for XYZ at expiration, this trade would result in a profit of 0.50. Table 30.4 displays the outcome through buying XYZ at 45.00 and purchasing the XYZ 45 Put for 2.00 along with selling the XYZ 45 Call at 2.50.

TABLE 30.4	Long XYZ Stock + versus Long XYZ 45 Put + Short XYZ 45 Call at Expiration			
XYZ	Long XYZ Stock	Long XYZ 45 Put	Short XYZ 45 Call	Combined Profit/Loss
35	−10.00	8.00	2.50	0.50
40	−5.00	3.00	2.50	0.50
45	0.00	−2.00	2.50	0.50
50	5.00	−2.00	−2.50	0.50
55	10.00	−2.00	−7.50	0.50

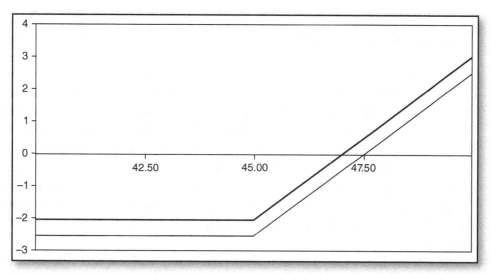

FIGURE 30.1 Payoff Comparison

Admittedly this is an overly simplistic example, but the hope here is to get across the idea of put-call parity and what happens when put and call prices get out of line relative to each other. Execution of this combined position with the result of a riskless profit would involve transaction costs and a cost of capital. For individuals this might be prohibitive, but for professional trading firms this is an opportunity. When option prices get out of line to a point where a professional firm may take advantage through placing orders to buy and sell the instrument that are mispriced, then orders to take advantage of this mispricing will be executed. These trades will quickly push markets back into line and eliminate the arbitrage profit.

Figure 30.1 is a payoff diagram that compares the payout of the long call and combined long put–long stock position. The higher line represents the combined long put–long stock position. The lower line shows the profit or loss for the long call position. Note the lines are parallel—the only difference is the profit or loss. This difference shows an arbitrage profit that may be realized by shorting the long call and buying the other two instruments, then holding the positions to expiration.

The put-call parity formula has many components and is beyond the scope of this book. However, the formulas in Table 30.5 illustrate on a position basis what the equivalent single-position result is from different combinations of a put, call, or stock.

TABLE 30.5	Variety of Positions Created through Put-Call Parity
Position	**Combination**
Long call	Long stock + long put
Short call	Short stock + short put
Long put	Short stock + long call
Short put	Long stock + short call
Long stock	Long call + short put
Short stock	Short call + long put

A comparable payout of any single long or short position with a put, call, or stock may be created using a combination of the other two securities. Although it may seem like this does not relate to the VIX, there is a point to this exercise.

The relationship between put and call prices that results in put-call parity does have an impact on the VIX index. The level of the VIX is based on the implied volatility of a variety of both put and call options. The indicated implied volatility of option contracts rises and falls based on market forces. The specific market force that impacts implied volatility is the net buying or selling of options. This increase in demand is not necessarily purchase of either all call or all put options buy just net buying of option contracts. Since strong demand for call options will result in higher put prices and demand for puts will result in higher call prices, higher demand for either type of contract results in higher implied volatility for both put and call contracts.

The VIX has historically had an inverse relationship with the S&P 500 index. The reason behind this inverse relationship relates to the type of option activity that occurs during bullish markets versus bearish markets. When markets rally, there is rarely a rush by investors to purchase call options. Therefore when the market is rising, there is rarely dramatically higher options purchasing versus options selling.

When the S&P 500 comes under pressure, especially in very turbulent times, there is often a panic-like demand for put options. This demand for protection results in increased purchasing of put options. The result is a fast move higher in implied volatility for both S&P 500 put and call options. This higher demand then results in an increase in implied volatility and finally a move higher in the VIX index.

In summary, the VIX moves higher when there is more demand for S&P 500 options, this demand tends to increase when there is nervousness about the overall market. This concern about the market will result in increased demand for put options. Put-call parity is the reason the implied volatility of both types of options moves together. The result of this increased demand for puts is higher implied volatility indicated by the pricing of S&P 500 options and a move higher in the VIX.

■ The VIX and Market Movement

Again, the VIX is a measure of 30-day implied volatility as indicated by the pricing of S&P 500 index options. The VIX is expressed as an annualized volatility measure, but it may actually be used to determined shorter-term market-price movements. Recall the example with Amazon reporting earnings. The implied volatility of the at-the-money options that only had a day left to expiration could be used to determine the magnitude of movement expected from Amazon stock the day following the company's earnings release. The implied volatility of those options was expressed as an annualized number.

The VIX is the 30-day implied volatility of the S&P 500, but it is also expressed as an annual figure. When the VIX is quoted at 20, this can be interpreted as SPX

MARKETS AND VOLATILITY

options pricing in an annualized move, up or down, of 20 percent in the S&P 500 index over the next 30 days. Using the VIX index, the anticipated movement of the underlying market may also be interpreted. The formula for determining the expected magnitude of market movements based on the VIX index is shown in the following section.

CALCULATING EXPECTED 30-DAY MARKET MOVEMENT

The formula for determining expected 30-day market movement is simple:

30-Day Movement = VIX/Square Root of 12

To determine the anticipated 30-day movement of the stock market as defined by the VIX involves dividing the VIX by the square root of 12. The implied volatility for a stock is used to interpret the expected one-day move for the stock. The square root of 12 is a convenient number as 30 days is the average month and there are 12 months in the year. In a similar manner to breaking down what implied volatility was indicating about movement in Amazon stock, the VIX may be used to determine the anticipated 30-day move for the S&P 500.

If the VIX is quoted at 20, the result would be the market expecting movement of about 5.77 percent over the next 30 days. Following the formula for determining 30-day market movement, the math would be:

$$5.77\% = 20/3.46$$

At times the VIX has reached some extreme points with the index actually reaching over 100 intraday. Table 30.6 shows what different VIX levels indicate about anticipated stock market movement.

The VIX may also be used as an indication of what magnitude of daily price movement is being expected for the S&P 500.

TABLE 30.6 VIX and Expected 30-Day Movement of the S&P 500

VIX	Expected 30-Day Move
3.46	1%
6.92	2%
10.40	3%
13.85	4%
17.32	5%
20.78	6%
24.25	7%
27.71	8%
31.18	9%
34.64	10%

In the VIX trading arena, the option and futures traders take the level for the VIX and divide it by 16 to get a rough estimate of what sort of daily move is expected in the stock market based on the level of the VIX. For example, the denominator of the formula is the square root of 252 or about 15.87. The traders round this up to 16 to get their denominator. So the VIX at 16 would indicate S&P 500 index options are anticipating daily price movement of 1 percent (16/16). A VIX of 32 would be interpreted as the S&P 500 option market anticipating a daily price move of 2 percent (32/16).

The math behind this method is not exact, but this is a pretty good rule of thumb. In 2008 when the VIX was trading in the mid-60s, this may be taken as the option market expecting a daily price move of 4 percent. Using a more common stock market index, this translates to the Dow Jones Industrial Average (DJIA) at 10,000 points being expected to trade in a 400-point range on a daily basis. Four-hundred-point days in the DJIA usually result in the stock market getting more than just professional investor's attention during the day. Those sort of moves generally grab headlines.

■ Equity Market Volatility Indexes

In addition to an index based on S&P 500 volatility, the Cboe has developed a handful of other volatility measures based on other common stock market indexes. Table 30.7 is a list of indexes based on index volatility that the Cboe has developed. There are also some quotes and strategy based and alternative-asset-based volatility indexes the Cboe has developed.

Cboe DJIA Volatility Index

The Cboe DJIA Volatility Index is calculated in a similar fashion as the VIX. Quotes for this index are disseminated using the symbol VXD. The index was created in 2005, and the index was introduced on March 18 of that year. The index indicates the market's expectation of 30-day implied volatility based on index option prices on the Dow Jones Industrial Average (DJX).

The DJX is one of the oldest stock indexes and is one of the most commonly quoted indicators of the overall stock market. Charles Dow, the publisher of the *Wall Street Journal*, created the index in order to bring more attention to his newspaper. The DJIA was first quoted on May 26, 1896. On days the stock market is open, at some point on the national

TABLE 30.7 Cboe Equity Market Volatility Indexes

Index	Ticker	Underlying	Website
Cboe Volatility Index	VIX	SPX	www.cboe.com/vix
Cboe DJIA Volatility Index	VXD	DJX	www.cboe.com/vxd
Cboe NADSAQ-100 Volatility Index	VXN	NDX	www.cboe.com/vxn
Cboe Russell 2000 Volatility Index	RVX	RUT	www.cboe.com/rvx
Cboe S&P 100 Volatility Index	VXO	OEX	www.cboe.com/vxo
Amex QQQ Volatility Index	QQV	QQQ	www.nyse.com

Sources: www.cboe.com and www.nyse.com.

news how the DJX did on the day will be mentioned. Some other common names for the DJX are the DJIA, Dow Jones, or just the Dow. For a person who pays little attention to the stock market or even for most investors, the Dow Jones Industrial Average is what they think of when they think of the stock market.

The DJX is composed of 30 stocks that represent a wide variety of industries and some of the largest companies in the United States. The stocks appear in Table 30.8. The small concentration of companies does take something away from the index being representative of the overall economy, but it continues to be the most commonly quoted index.

TABLE 30.8 **Members of the Dow Jones Industrial Average**

Company	Symbol
Alcoa Inc.	AA
American Express Company	AXP
AT&T Corp.	T
Bank of America Corp.	BAC
Boeing Co.	BA
Caterpillar Inc.	CAT
Chevron Corp.	CVX
Cisco Systems	CSCO
Coca-Cola Co.	KO
E.I. Du Pont de Nemours	DD
Exxon Mobil Corp.	XOM
General Electric Company	GE
Hewlett-Packard Co.	HPQ
Home Depot Inc	HD
Intel Corp.	INTC
International Business Machines Corp.	IBM
Johnson & Johnson	JNJ
J.P. Morgan Chase Company	JPM
Kraft Foods Inc.	KFT
McDonald's Corp.	MCD
Merck & Co. Inc.	MRK
Microsoft Corp.	MSFT
Minnesota Mining & Mfg. Co.	MMM
Pfizer Inc.	PFE
Procter & Gamble Co.	PG
The Travelers Companies	TRV
United Technologies Corp.	UTX
Verizon Communications Inc.	VZ
Wal-Mart Stores Inc.	WMT
Walt Disney Co.	DIS

TABLE 30.9	Dow Jones Industrial Average Industry Weightings	
Sector	**Weighting**
Basic materials	3.75%
Consumer goods	10.52%
Consumer services	13.24%
Financials	10.80%
Health care	7.78%
Industrials	22.46%
Oil and gas	9.83%
Technology	17.64%
Telecommunications	3.98%

Note that although the index is referred to as an industrial index, a variety of industries are represented by the DJX. For example, Wal-Mart and Home Depot are major retailers, Pfizer is a pharmaceutical company, and The Travelers Companies specializes in financial services. The industry weightings for the DJX appear in Table 30.9.

The highest weighting of stocks in the DJX is represented by industrial companies, but only about a quarter of the performance of the index will be attributed to this market sector. A variety of other industries contribute to the DJX, which does result in an index that is representative of the overall economy in the United States. For instance, when consumer goods and services are combined, this area of the market represents about another quarter of the index's performance.

Finally, the CFE does not currently trade futures based on the VXD. However, from April 2005 to the middle of 2009, futures contracts based on this index did trade at the exchange.

Cboe NASDAQ-100 Volatility Index

Using quotes for options that trade on the NASDAQ-100 Index (NDX), the Cboe NASDAQ-100 Volatility Index is an indication of implied volatility on the NASDAQ-100 index. Trading with the symbol VXN, the index displays 30-day implied volatility for the NDX.

The NASDAQ-100 is an index composed of the 100 largest companies not involved in the financial sector that trade on the NASDAQ. The NASDAQ marketplace opened in 1971 as an alternative exchange to the traditional floor-based exchanges like the New York Stock Exchange. In 1985 the NASDAQ developed two market indexes to promote their exchange, one of which is the NASDAQ-100.

Table 30.10 shows the industry sector weightings that comprise the NDX. What is unique regarding this market index is the lack of financial and health care stocks in the index. The result is a focus on other industries with a very large weighting in the technology sector. In fact, the index is dominated by technology- and communications-oriented stocks, which when combined make up almost 75 percent of the index. Also, the SPX has approximately a 20 percent weighting in the financial sector, which results in the NDX and SPX having disparate performance at times.

TABLE 30.10	NASDAQ-100 Sector Weightings
Sector	**Weighting**
Basic materials	0.40%
Consumer cyclical	8.40%
Communications	24.40%
Consumer noncyclical	16.80%
Energy	0.50%
Industrial	3.10%
Technology	46.40%

Futures were also traded on the VXN from 2007 to 2009. As this index may experience higher volatility than some other market indexes, the demand for a return of these contracts may result in them being relisted at some point.

Cboe Russell 2000 Volatility Index

The Russell 2000 Index is composed of the 2,000 smallest companies that are in the Russell 3000 Index. Although representing two-thirds of the companies in the Russell 3000, which is composed of 3,000 of the largest publicly traded companies in the United States, the Russell 2000 only represents about 8 percent of the market capitalization of the Russell 3000. The Russell 2000 index is composed of small-cap companies, which mostly focus on domestic markets. This index has a great niche as a representation of domestic economic trends in the United States.

Russell Investments also calculates the Russell 1000 index, which consists of the 1,000 largest companies in the Russell 3000. The top third of those companies represents 92 percent of the market capitalization of the Russell 3000.

The ticker symbol RUT represents option trading on the index and, like the previous volatility-related indexes, the Russell 2000 Volatility Index (RVX) attempts to show what the market is pricing in 30-day implied volatility for the index. At times the Russell 1000, Russell 2000, and Russell 3000 names are not entirely accurate. When, due to an acquisition, merger, or dissolution, a company ceases to exist as it had in the past, it may be replaced by a new company in a market index. These Russell indexes are actually reconfigured once a year at the end of June, with the number of stocks in each index taken back to the proper number.

Also, there is a minimum capitalization level for a company to be a member of the Russell 1000. When the indexes are rebalanced, the number of stocks in the Russell 1000 and Russell 2000 is very close to their respective numbers, but it may not be equal to the expected number of stocks in each index. For instance, after the 2010 rebalance, the Russell 1000 consisted of 988 stocks and the Russell 2000 consisted of 2,012 stocks. The total of the two indexes results in all the stocks that make up the Russell 3000. The Russell 3000 makes up 99 percent of the market capitalization of the U.S. stock market.

Between the index restructuring dates, companies that cease to exist will be deleted from the indexes, but no replacement will necessarily be put in their place.

However, company spinoffs and initial public offerings may be added between the June reconstruction dates. Those stocks are added on a quarterly basis.

RVX futures traded at the Cboe from 2007 through early 2010.

Cboe S&P 100 Volatility Index

When the VIX was originally quoted by the Cboe, the calculation was based on the implied volatility of the S&P 100 Index (OEX), not the S&P 500. When the calculation was altered in 2003, it was done so with part of the revision resulting in a focus on the S&P 500 as opposed to the S&P 100 index.

The Cboe S&P 100 Volatility Index (VXO) is actually the original VIX index, which was created in 1993. It continues to be calculated using the original methodology based on OEX options. Introduced in 1983 by the Cboe, OEX was the first equity index option product. Originally the index name was the Cboe 100 Index. Loosely translated, OEX could mean Option Exchange 100. The OEX and options listed on the index were so innovative that entire books were written on trading OEX options.

The OEX represents 100 of the largest companies in the United States. This results in the combined components of the OEX being close to 45 percent of the total market capitalization of publicly traded stocks in the United States. Also, almost 60 percent of the S&P 500 market capitalization is represented by the 100 stocks in the OEX.

Even with just 100 names, the OEX is a diversified index with all industry sectors being covered. Table 30.11 is a summary of the industry weightings of the OEX. Note the industry weightings of the OEX are as diversified as the S&P 500 even though there are fewer stocks in the index.

■ Amex QQQ Volatility Index

The Amex QQQ volatility index is another measure of implied volatility of the Nadsaq market. The method behind this index is similar to the original volatility index calculation used for the VXO. The index indicates the forward-looking volatility for

TABLE 30.11	S&P 100 Index Industry Weightings
Industry	Weighting
Consumer discretionary	6.25%
Consumer staples	15.32%
Energy	15.86%
Financials	11.06%
Health care	15.40%
Industrials	10.59%
Information technology	17.35%
Materials	1.03%
Telecom services	5.30%
Utilities	1.86%

the QQQ based on option prices. To get a true option contract value, the midpoint of the bid-ask spread is used as the option price input for the calculation.

The Cboe and CFE currently trade options and futures only on the VIX index. However, these alternate VIX indexes may be used to gain insight into market activity. The VIX and other index-related volatility indexes are excellent representations of what sort of near-term volatility is expected from the overall stock market according to the implied volatility of index options. Each of the indexes that have VIX representation have slightly different components and may indicate that there is higher expected volatility in one sector as opposed to others.

BEHAVIORAL FINANCE AND OTHER THEORIES OF MARKET DYNAMICS

Analogies, it is true, decide nothing, but they can make one feel more at home.

—Sigmund Freud

Technicians have long been aware of the human dynamic in price movement. How do people think about what is "cheap" or "expensive"? What is the "real" value of an asset? How do fear and greed—the traditional two-headed demon with which all traders do battle—affect sober and rational judgment?

Recent decades have brought serious scholarship to the study of behavioral finance. This has generated a framework and vocabulary for learning how people interact with prices. And it has fully opened the discussion related to efficient markets and technical analysis: If it is possible to calculate the "correct" value of an asset, what explanations are there for divergence from that value?

This section begins with a summary of the Efficient Market Hypothesis and its strengths and vulnerabilities. Technical traders are introduced as "noise traders" who do not make decisions based on traditional information or valuation. An illuminating reconciliation of these theories follows with discussion of the Adaptive Market Hypothesis.

This section also highlights sentiment and its measures as employed by technicians. This, too, reflects the human component of price movement. This includes data from opinion polls to Commitments of Traders to short interest. Technicians are always focused on what fuels price movement and the attempt to qualify and quantify the data.

CHAPTER 31

What Is the Efficient Market Hypothesis?

From Edwin T. Burton and Sunit N. Shah,
Behavioral Finance (Hoboken, New Jersey:
John Wiley & Sons, 2013), Chapter 1.

Learning Objective Statements

- Identify the basic concept of the Efficient Market Hypothesis (EMH)
- Describe the three forms of the EMH
- Explain the characteristics of stock prices as a martingale
- Describe how randomly generated output can appear non-random and how that might relate to asset prices and returns
- Identify the three areas in which behavioral finance challenges the EMH

467

The efficient market hypothesis (EMH) has to do with the meaning and predictability of prices in financial markets. Do asset markets "behave" as they should? In particular, does the stock market perform its role as economists expect it to? Stock markets raise money from wealth holders and provide businesses with that money to pursue, presumably, the maximization of profit. How well do these markets perform that function? Is some part of the process wasteful? Do prices reflect true underlying value?

In recent years, a new question seems to have emerged in this ongoing discussion. Do asset markets create instability in the greater economy? Put crudely, do the actions of investment and commercial bankers lead to bubbles and economic catastrophe as the bubbles unwind? The great stock market crash of October 19, 1987, and the financial collapse in the fall of 2008 have focused attention on bubbles and crashes. These are easy concepts to imagine but difficult to define or anticipate.

Bubbles usually feel so good to participants that no one, at the time, really thinks of them as bubbles; they instead see their own participation in bubbles as the inevitable payback for their hard work and virtuous behavior—until the bubbles burst in catastrophe. Then, the attention turns to the excesses of the past. Charges of greed, corruption, and foul play accompany every crash.

If the catastrophe and the bubble that precedes it are the result of evil people doing evil things, then there is no reason to suppose that markets are themselves to blame. Simple correctives, usually through imposition of legal reforms, are then proposed to correct the problem and eliminate future bubbles and catastrophes. Casual empiricism suggests this approach is not successful.

What if markets are inherently unstable? What if bubbles and their accompanying catastrophes are the natural order of things? Then what? If prices do not, much of the time, represent true value and if the markets themselves breed excessive optimism and pessimism, not to mention fraud and corruption, then the very existence and operation of financial markets may cause instability in the underlying economy. Prices may be signaling "incorrect" information and resources may be allocated inefficiently. The question of whether asset markets are efficiently priced, then, is a fundamental question. The outcome of this debate could shed light on the efficiency of the modern, highly integrated economies in which a key role is played by financial institutions.

It is important to agree on a definition of market efficiency, but there are many such definitions. Practitioners in the everyday world of finance often use market efficiency in ways that are different than the textbook definitions. We delimit the most common definitions in the next two sections of this chapter.

■ Information and the Efficient Market Hypothesis

The EMH is most commonly defined as the idea that asset prices, stock prices in particular, "fully reflect" information.[1] Only when information changes will prices change. There are different versions of this definition, depending on what kind of information is assumed to be reflected in current prices. The most commonly used is the "semistrong" definition of the EMH: *Prices accurately summarize all publicly known information.*

This definition means that if an investor studies carefully the companies that he/she invests in, it will not matter. Other investors already know the information that the studious investor learns by painstakingly poring over public documents. These other investors have already acted on the information, so that such "public" information is already reflected in the stock price. There is no such thing, in this view, as a "cheap" stock or an "expensive" stock. The current price is always the "best estimate" of the value of the company.

In particular, this definition implies that knowing past prices is of no value. The idea that past stock price history is irrelevant is an example of the weak form of the EMH: *Knowledge of past prices is of no value in predicting future stock prices.*

The semi-strong form implies the much weaker version of the EMH embodied in the weak form of the EMH. It is possible that the weak form is true but that the semi-strong form is false.

The weak form of the EMH is interesting because it directly attacks a part of Wall Street research known as "technical" research. In technical research, analysts study past prices and other historical data in an attempt to predict future prices. Certain patterns of stock prices are said by "technicians" to imply certain future pricing paths. All of this means, of course, that by studying past prices you can predict when

---

[1] See Eugene Fama's definition in "Random Walks in Stock Market Prices," *Financial Analysts Journal* 21, no. 5 (May 1965):55–59.

stock prices are going to go up and when they are going to go down. Put another way, technical research is an attempt to "beat the market" by using historical pricing data. The weak form says that this cannot be done.

Unlike other versions of the EMH, the weak form is especially easy to subject to empirical testing, since there are many money managers and market forecasters who explicitly rely on technical research. How do such managers and forecasters do? Do they perform as well as a monkey randomly throwing darts at a newspaper containing stock price names as a method of selecting a "monkey portfolio"? Do index funds do better than money managers who utilize technical research as their main method of picking stocks? These questions are simple to put to a test and, over the years, the results of such testing have overwhelmingly supported the weak form version of the EMH.

The semi-strong version of the EMH is not as easy to test as the weak form, but data from money managers is helpful here. If the semi-strong version is true, then money managers, using public information, should not beat the market, which means that they should not beat simple indexes that mirror the overall market for stocks. The evidence here is consistent and overwhelming. Money managers, on average, do not beat simple indexes. That doesn't mean that there aren't money managers who seem to consistently outperform over small time samples, but they are in the distinct minority and hard to identify before the fact. Evidence from institutional investors, such as large pensions funds and endowments, are consistent with the view that indexing tends to produce better investment results than hiring money managers.

If this were all we knew, then the EMH would be on solid ground. But we know more. There is growing evidence that there are empirical "regularities" in stock market return data, as well as some puzzling aspects of stock market data that seem difficult to explain if one subscribes to the EMH.

We can identify three main lines of attack for critics of the semi-strong form of the EMH:

1. Stock prices seem to be too volatile to be consistent with the EMH.
2. Stock prices seem to have "predictability" patterns in historical data.
3. There are unexplained (and perhaps unexplainable) behavioral data items that have come to be known as "anomalies," a nomenclature begun by Richard Thaler.[2]

The evidence that has piled up in the past 20 years or so has created a major headache for defenders of the EMH. Even though money managers don't necessarily beat the indexes, the behavioralists' research suggests that perhaps they should.

There is a third form of the EMH that is interesting but not easy to subject to empirical validation. The third form is known as the strong form of the EMH: *Prices accurately summarize all information, private as well as public.*

The strong form, of course, implies both the semi-strong and the weak forms of the EMH. However, both the semi-strong and weak forms can be true while the strong definition can be false. The strong form includes information that may be

---

[2] See Richard Thaler, *Winner's Curse: Paradoxes and Anomalies of Economic Life* (New York, NY: Free Press, 1992).

illegally obtained—or, perhaps, information that is legally obtained but illegal to act upon. Needless to say, those breaking the law are not likely to provide performance data to researchers attempting to ascertain whether they are beating the market.

There seems to be a general consensus that the strong form of the EMH is not likely to be true, but one should not rush to such a conclusion simply because relevant data may be hard to come by. What little data we have from those who have obtained illegal information and then acted upon it is mixed. Sometimes crooks win; sometimes they appear to lose. When Ivan Boesky, probably the most famous insider information trader in history, concluded his investment activities and was carted off to jail, it was clear that investors who owned index funds made better returns than investors in Boesky's fund, even before the legal authorities got wise to Boesky's activities. If Boesky couldn't beat the market with inside information, it does give one pause.

Of the three informational definitions of the EMH, it is the semi-strong hypothesis that commands most interest. It is widely believed that the weak form is likely to be true, and it is commonly assumed that the strong form is not likely to be true, so interest focuses mainly on the semi-strong hypothesis. Information determines prices and no one can really exploit publicly known information—that is the content of the semi-strong EMH hypothesis.

■ Random Walk, the Martingale Hypothesis, and the EMH

There is an alternative, mathematical view of the stock market related to the EMH. The mathematical version begins with the idea that stock prices follow a process known as *random walk*. The idea of the random walk is sometimes taken by wary observers as the idea that stock price behavior is simply arbitrary, but that is not what random walk means.

Imagine a coin flip where the coin is completely "fair" in the sense that a heads or tails flip is equally likely to occur. Suppose you start with $100 in wealth before beginning a series of coin flips. Suppose further that if you flip a heads, you receive $1, and if you flip a tails, you have to give up $1. After the first flip, for example, you will have either $101 (if you flip a heads) or $99 (if you flip a tails). Your total wealth over time, in this simple example, is following a process known as a random walk. A random walk is a process where the next step (flip outcome, in this example) has a fixed probability that is independent of all previous flips.

What does random walk rule out? If knowing the results of previous coin flips is useful in predicting future coin flips, then the process is not a random walk. Imagine that there have been five flips of heads in a row with no flips of tails. Does this mean it is more likely that the next coin flip will be tails? If so, then the process is not a random walk. The likelihood of a heads or a tails on the next coin flip must be independent of the history of previous flips for the process to be a random walk.

Does this mean, as some assume, that the results are arbitrary? No. We know a lot about this process. What we can't do, however, is predict the next coin flip with any high degree of certainty. If the coin is a fair coin, the heads or tails are equally likely on the next flip regardless of its history.

The coin-flipping game is a good example of a *martingale*. A martingale has the following property:

$$E[X_{t+s} \mid X_1, X_2, \ldots, X_t] = X_t \text{ for any } t, s > 0 \tag{31.1}$$

What does the above equation mean? X_t is the value at time t of some variable X. It might be helpful to think of X as your wealth, so that X_t is the value of your wealth at time t. X_{t+s} is then your wealth at some future date, $t+s$. The E in the equation is the expectation operator. The simplest way to think about E is that $E[X_{t+s} \mid X_1, X_2, \ldots, X_t]$ is what, on average, you expect the value of your wealth to be at a future date, $t+s$, given your knowledge of your wealth historically.

So, back to our example. You start on date t with $100 and you flip a coin that is equally likely to be a heads flip as a tails flip. What do you expect your wealth to be s periods from today, t? Since you are just as likely to gain $1 as to lose $1 on each flip, your wealth at any future period is expected to be the same as it is today. Thus, this process satisfies the martingale property. If your wealth is totally in stocks, and if stocks follow a martingale, so will your wealth. On average, you will neither make nor lose money.

But this is not a very satisfying theory of how stocks behave. Why would anyone own stocks if, on average, they could not be expected to increase their wealth? We need to modify our simple coin-flipping experiment to allow for wealth to increase, but in a way consistent with our martingale assumption. Suppose your wealth grows at $0.20 per period on average, so that $E[X_{t+s} \mid X_1, X_2, \ldots, X_t] = X_t + \$0.20 \times s$. Then, your wealth is no longer a martingale.

To transform it into a martingale, define a new variable, Y_t:

$$Y_t = X_t - \{t \times \$0.20\} \tag{31.2}$$

Y_t is a martingale since:

$$
\begin{aligned}
E[Y_{t+s}] &= E[X_{t+s}] - \{(t+s) \times \$0.20\} \\
&= X_t + \{s \times \$0.20\} - \{(t+s) \times \$0.20\} \\
&= X_t - \{t \times \$0.20\} = Y_t
\end{aligned}
\tag{31.3}
$$

Even though wealth is growing over time, we have converted the wealth variable into another variable that is a martingale.

If stock prices follow a random walk, then past stock prices cannot be used to predict future stock prices. Random walk doesn't mean we know nothing or that the result of the process is arbitrary. Instead, one of the implications of random walk is that the outcome on any specific future date cannot be known with certainty. By a simple conversion, similar to what was shown earlier, we can convert the wealth accumulation process into a martingale.

Why all the effort? A martingale is a process whose value at any future date is not predictable with certainty. While X_t is the best estimate of any future value of X after X_t, we still cannot know with any degree of certainty what that value will be.

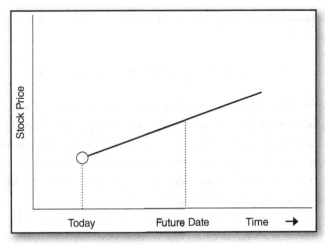

FIGURE 31.1 Expected Future Stock Price

The idea of a martingale captures the informational definitions given in the previous section in a mathematical statement. Given the information available today, the best estimate of a future stock price is today's price (possibly with a risk-adjusted trend over time). This process is described in Figure 31.1.

Of course, the actual prices will not be on the solid line in Figure 31.1. Instead, they will bound around randomly, but trend upward in a pattern suggested by the bold solid line. The actual price movement might appear (or be expected to appear) as the lighter line that bounces around the solid line in Figure 31.2.

What makes the martingale an appropriate model for the EMH is that on any date, past information offers no real clue to predicting future prices. It is the absence of predictability that is the single most important feature of the martingale process.

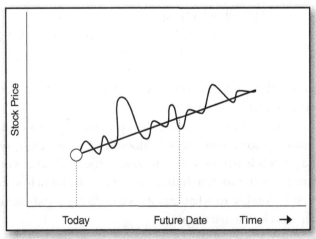

FIGURE 31.2 Actual Future Stock Price

■ False Evidence against the EMH

There are always, at any point in time, legendary money managers who have arguably beaten the market over their respective lifetimes. Warren Buffett comes to mind as one of the more prominent examples. Is the existence of money managers with long track records of having beaten indices evidence against the EMH? To give this question some perspective, conduct a simple thought experiment. Imagine a group of 10,000 people engaged in a coin-flipping experiment. In each period, each of these 10,000 people flips a coin and notes the result. What would we expect if the coins were, in all cases, fair coins? The likelihood of heads or tails is identical and equal to 50 percent on each and every coin toss.

In the first trial, you would expect, on average, about half of the 10,000 folks to flip heads and about half to flip tails. This would mean 5,000 flipped heads and 5,000 flipped tails. This wouldn't be the exact outcome, but it serves as a useful approximation to the actual outcome. Now, flip again. After the second trial, you would expect about one-fourth of the participants (2,500) to have flipped two heads in a row and one-fourth (2,500) to have flipped two tails in a row. Continue on in this manner through eight coin flips and what would you have? On average, you would expect about 39 flippers to have flipped eight heads in a row and about the same to have flipped eight tails in a row. Are these 39 flippers evidence that there is something to the science of coin flipping?

What about the number of folks who flipped heads seven out of eight times? There should be about 312 of those folks on average. That makes over 350 people who flipped heads at least seven out of eight times. Isn't that evidence that these people are good head flippers?

No, clearly such evidence is useless. If coin flipping is completely random, with a 50 percent chance each time of either flipping heads or tails, you will still get a significant number of extreme outcomes, even after repeated trials. In fact, failure to get the extremes of eight in a row or seven out of eight a reasonable number of times would be evidence that the flipping was not truly random. The same is true of evidence from money management. If money management outcomes are completely random and no one is really any good at stock picking, then a small percentage of money managers will, nevertheless, appear to be good on the basis of their track records.

One of the anomalies the behavioralists have uncovered is that things that are random often appear not to be random. That is, they don't look random. There seems to be an expectation by observers that if a random process is creating a data series, then that data series should have a random appearance. It turns out that there are many more ways for the outcome of a randomly generated data series to look like a pattern than there are ways for it to look random. Put another way, output from a randomly generated process will typically exhibit trends, repetition, and other patterns even though the results are generated by a truly random process.

■ What Does It Mean to Disagree with the EMH?

Behavioral finance argues that the EMH is false and that academic finance needs to rethink its foundations. What does it mean for the EMH to be false? There are three different ways that behavioralists have waged warfare against the EMH: the first is logical, the second is psychological, and the third is empirical. The logical argument is what economists call *economic theory*. The psychological arguments are derived mostly from experiments in human psychology that throw doubt on the realism of the assumptions that underlie finance theory. Finally, the empirical arguments exhibit patterns of "predictability" in financial data that belie the assumed "nonpredictability" of future asset prices.

The three different ways to confront the EMH correspond to casual observations that have persisted and echoed through financial markets since their beginning. These observations were dismissed just as casually by finance economists as minor and unscientific. Until very recently, the preponderant view among finance economists was that markets were efficient and that casual observers were wrong. Sometimes, it was argued the casual observers had a vested interest in their assertions that the market was inefficient. After all, virtually the entire money management industry is built on the proposition that intelligent and diligent research and thinking can produce investment returns that exceed random stock picking or indexing, contrary to the semi-strong hypothesis of the EMH.

In the chapters that follow, we consider each of the three ways that the EMH has been challenged in the academic literature. A natural question is: if not the EMH, then what? What paradigm would supplant the EMH if the behavioralists succeed in undermining it? We look at that question after considering the behavioralist critique.

CHAPTER 32

The Forerunners to Behavioral Finance

From Edwin T. Burton and Sunit N. Shah,
Behavioral Finance (Hoboken, New Jersey:
John Wiley & Sons, 2013), Chapter 3.

Learning Objective Statements

- Explain momentum strategies and mean-reversion strategies
- Define the general concept of value investing
- Describe why value investing is similar to a mean-reversion approach
- Explain how value investing (Graham and Dodd) conflicts with the EMH

Academics were reasonably content with the efficient market hypothesis (EMH) until sometime toward the end of the twentieth century. The year 1987 was critical in undermining faith in the EMH. U.S. stock market behavior in 1987 was bizarre. The year began with the Dow Jones Industrial Average at slightly above 2,200, and it ended the year in that general area. If all you knew were the beginning and ending stock market averages, then 1987 would seem to be a ho-hum type of year. But in between the beginning and ending averages, there was an incredible rally and a historic collapse. The market's behavior can be summarized in Figure 32.1.

The interesting question about 1987's stock market performance is: why? What news and information were there that led to a 30 percent rally in the first half of the year, followed by October 19, 1987, the worst single-day percentage loss in U.S. equity market history? The year 1987 should be called the "Rip Van Winkle" year. If you fell asleep in early January and awoke in late December, you would not know that much of anything had happened.

When you ask observers what happened to cause the big rally and big decline, almost everyone will provide an answer, especially those who consider themselves savvy about financial markets. But the answers are all over the map, and no single explanation has gained enough currency to gain widespread acceptance. There are plenty of one-off explanations, but none that command any real authority. The

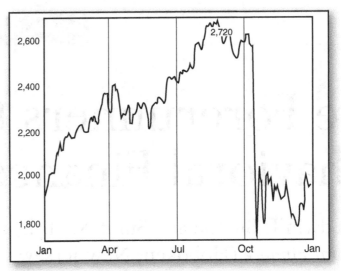

FIGURE 32.1 Summary of Market Behavior

Wall Street Journal had a special edition the day after the 509-point, 22 percent historic sell-off on October 19, 1987. In that edition, they surveyed the various top executives of the largest and most prestigious Wall Street firms as to their opinions regarding the cause of the stock market crash. The opinions varied widely with no particular consistency. Even among market professionals who commune with one another regularly and drink at the same watering holes, there was no consensus as to what had happened and a blithering variety of different views espoused.

If you lived through the 1987 crash, then you are likely still wondering what happened. The very few who guessed that the crash was coming (and predictably there should be a few who guessed right) built careers and fortunes out of their prescient views. Paul Tudor Jones was one such individual and created the highly successful Tudor Management on the back of his accurate prediction of the 1987 crash. But did he really know what caused it? Perhaps.

■ The Folklore of Wall Street Traders

The first modern bull market in common stocks was in the United States in the 1920s. This was also the first time that nonprofessional investors, ordinary citizens, began to take an active participatory role in the public financial markets. A lot of speculative activity took place during this period and financial "traders" became mythic actors on the Wall Street stage. There were a number of books published during the 1920s that described "trading the market" that suggested that the market was "predictable," if one simply followed a few set and time-tested rules. Of course, different books had different rules, but there were some common themes.

The most famous of these books grew out of a series of articles that began appearing in 1922 in the *Saturday Evening Post* written by financial journalist Edwin Lefèvre. In 1923, the collection of articles was recast as a book published that year by Lefèvre entitled *Reminiscences of a Stock Operator*.[1] The book chronicles the trading activity of a fictitious character named Lawrence Livingston. It has long been assumed that the real trader, whose activities are described in this book, was Jessie Livermore, known early in his career as the "Boy Plunger." The book described all sorts of trading activities including the use of short selling and conducting short squeezes. For our purposes, the significance of Lefèvre's book and others of this genre is that the book suggests that there are ways for the speculative trader to "beat the market." Some of the activities spelled out in this book became illegal under reform legislation in the 1930s. But many of the strategies discussed were based on understanding the emotional sentiment factors that, according to the book, create important stock market moves.

In the 1920s, there wasn't any real academic interest in the stock market, so ideas like the EMH were not discussed in any serious way. Indeed, one of the leading academic economists in the United States, Yale's Irving Fisher, published a book in 1929 (bad timing) that suggested that stocks were unlikely to ever go down again. John Maynard Keynes, one of the most famous economists in history, was, in the 1920s, busily speculating on currency markets, the metals markets, and stock markets. Keynes was to later describe the market as being dominated by "waves of pessimism and optimism" in his classic *The General Theory of Employment, Interest and Money,* published in 1935.[2] Even leading economists suggested, by their behavior, that financial markets were predictable. Behavioral finance did not exist as an academic discipline, nor did any particular finance curriculum exist anywhere in academia during this period, but it is clear from what economists were saying that the EMH would not have ruled the roost among academic economists.

What is interesting about all of this is that trading folklore and the activities of leading academic economists fit the behavioral finance point of view, not the EMH point of view. Economists who were actively discussing and acting in financial markets seemed of the opinion that markets were predictable, which is a key tenet of modern behavioral finance.

There were generally two trading strategies that circulated in the folklore. The first strategy was what we today call a *momentum* strategy. If you see a stock going up dramatically, then hop on board because it will likely continue going up. If everyone hops on board and you can perceive that everyone is on board, then you should hop off. The "hopping off" is more akin to what we call today *mean reversion*. Mean reversion is the idea that if a stock has been doing really well for a long time and people seem to love the stock, then you should sell on the premise that the stock will not do well in the future. So, two trading strategies, mildly conflicting, permeated a lot of the folklore, including Lefèvre's book:

1. In the short term, stocks that are going up will continue that trend; stocks that are going down will continue that trend.

---

[1] Edwin Lefèvre, *Reminiscences of a Stock Operator* (Hoboken, NJ: John Wiley & Sons, 2006; originally published in 1923).

[2] John Maynard Keynes, *The General Theory of Employment, Interest and Money* (New York, NY: Harcourt, Brace and World, Inc., 1935). See especially Chapter 12, pages 154 and 155.

2. In the long run, stocks that have done well for a long time will do poorly in the future, and vice versa.

The first strategy is known today as *short-term momentum,* and the second strategy is still known as *mean reversion.* The central ideas behind these strategies were known and discussed openly by traders in the 1920s. Sixty and 70 years later, academic economists would pick up these ideas and begin to research their validity under the banner of behavioral finance. Because of the ready availability of data, by the time these researchers began to look at the data, it was relatively easy to document data trends such as those suggested by momentum and mean reversion. We look at this in some detail later in this book. Our point here is that Wall Street trading folklore had long believed in these strategies, even if there was no serious research to test their validity.

■ The Birth of Value Investing: Graham and Dodd

In 1934, Benjamin Graham and David Dodd, both business school professors, coauthored a book entitled *Security Analysis*[3] that focused investor attention on the financial statements of public companies. The timing for publishing this book could not have been better. The Securities Acts of 1933 and 1934 required all public companies to publish detailed financial statements at least every three months (10-Q quarterly filings). This meant that investors had ready access to the data that Graham and Dodd were now saying could be used to beat the market.

Graham and Dodd argued in their famous book that investors could profit by studying a company's financial statements, income statements, and balance sheet statements to ascertain its value. They implicitly and explicitly decried the "horse race" character of the public markets and said the conscientious investor could beat the crowd by painstakingly studying the "true value" of a company, which could, they argued, be gleaned from the company's financial statements.

The Graham and Dodd approach came to be known as *value investing.* Many modern-day investors hearken back to Graham and Dodd as their inspiration. Warren Buffett is one such Graham and Dodd admirer. The idea is that an investor should buy out-of-favor stocks with strong "fundamentals." The fundamentals are ascertained by poring over income statements and balance sheets to uncover what could best be described as diamonds in the rough. The clear message was don't buy the stocks that other people like; buy the stocks that other people shun. Look for value among the stocks beaten down and overlooked.

This theme meant that markets could be beaten, which is the opposite of the theme of the EMH. Value investing also seemed to be similar to the message of mean reversion. Stocks that had not done well might be the best "values" because investors overreact emotionally to a string of bad news without necessarily considering the

[3] Benjamin Graham and David Dodd, *Security Analysis* (New York, NY: Whittlesey House, 1934).

underlying fundamentals. Stocks that had done well for a long time were likely to not be good buys because market participants may not have looked closely at deteriorating fundamentals.

The 1930s destroyed much of the public's interest in the stock market, but when interest returned in the 1950s, value investing became a big business, with money managers professing adherence to Graham and Dodd's message. Over time, empirical support seemed to develop for value investing, culminating in a landmark research paper published in 1992 by two academic economists, Eugene Fama and Kenneth French. The research by Fama and French appeared to validate the idea that value investing could beat the market.

The main message of Graham and Dodd reinforced the common perception in the 1930s and 1940s that there were ways to beat the market and that stock price movements were, in principle, predictable.

■ Financial News in a World of Ubiquitous Television and Internet

In modern financial markets, there is constant news reporting on television and the Internet describing the ups and downs of individual securities and aggregated indices as well as all the news that seems relevant to their movements. Traders, eager to have the latest information, keep tuned minute-by-minute to the constant barrage of information that emanates from modern electronic sources. But what kind of information is being conveyed? Most often, the information is opinion as opposed to facts, and the facts that are reported are typically already publicly known facts. One word that could aptly fit the modern financial news that is reported is *noise*. What about the audience? No doubt, many in the audience could be described as "noise traders." If listeners rush out and buy and sell stocks based on outdated facts or random opinions, then such listeners are—by definition—noise traders, because they are not trading on true information but, much of the time, on stale and bogus information.

These news outlets are constantly trumpeting ideas such as "year-end rallies" and the like, which have no relationship to the fundamental drivers of company value. Rational traders would have no interest in year-end rallies. Notions of "support" and "resistance" levels of prices permeate the daily drumbeat of financial news. But a rational trader would find no meaning in these concepts. Yet someone is listening, and no doubt, someone is trading off the noise that is ever-present in the financial news reporting media.

CHAPTER 33

Noise Traders and the Law of One Price

From Edwin T. Burton and Sunit N. Shah, *Behavioral Finance* (Hoboken, New Jersey: John Wiley & Sons, 2013), Chapter 4.

Learning Objective Statements

- Define "fungibility" in the context of financial markets
- Explain "arbitrage"
- Describe "noise" vs. "information"
- Define "noise trader"

One of the very first things a student learns in beginning economics is that if two commodities are identical, then they will command identical prices in the marketplace. If the price of the two commodities should ever diverge, buyers will buy the cheaper of the two, and sellers will sell the more expensive of the two, pushing the divergent prices toward each other. It is likely that someone will try to buy the commodity in the cheap market and sell it in the more expensive market and earn an arbitrage profit. Thus, the law of one price emerges: two identical commodities must have the same price almost all the time.

■ The Law of One Price and the Case of Fungibility

All of this seems simple enough, as long as we are comfortable with the definition of identical. What if two things are identical, but we refer to them by different names? Are they still identical? Do they still command the same price in the marketplace? Imagine a factory that produces baseballs. Suppose that every second baseball produced is called a hardball, whereas all others produced are called *baseballs*. But

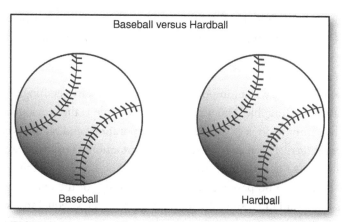

FIGURE 33.1 Can These Two Have Different Prices?

suppose in every respect there is absolutely no physical difference between a hardball and a baseball. They are the exact same thing except for their differing names. Can a hardball have a different price than a baseball? (See Figure 33.1.)

The two items above are not strictly identical because they have different names. This difference in name allows for the possibility that market participants may see them as truly different and that it may be possible for these two physically identical items to have different prices. If we think of these as assets, then we could say that the efficient market hypothesis (EMH) requires that these two items have identical prices since all information about them is the same. A *behavioral economist* might argue otherwise. The different names might lead to different prices, even when the items themselves are physically indistinguishable.

Imagine a baseball-hardball machine that costlessly converts hardballs into baseballs and baseballs into hardballs, one for one in each case. If the price of baseballs and hardballs were to differ, then one should buy the cheaper of the two, feed it into the machine, and out would come the other, which could then be sold at a profit. This is a simple example of arbitrage. This type of costless conversion is known as *fungibility*.

There are many examples of fungibility in financial markets. Options in certain combinations and most futures contracts are completely fungible into the underlying instruments from which they derive their value. Owning a gold future is simply another way of owning gold, and if the owner of a gold future does not sell the future, then delivery of gold will take place on the future's delivery date. In this manner, the gold future owner becomes the owner of actual gold. This is an example of fungibility. The simple arbitrage of the baseball-hardball machine example is possible in the options and futures markets, though in a more complicated fashion.

What happens if the hardball and the baseball are not fungible? An easy way to make them not fungible is to put an indelible label on each. Each hardball would have the label *hardball* imprinted on it, and each baseball would have the label *baseball* imprinted on it. Then the arbitrage process might fail.

Suppose hardballs have the higher price. A buyer of hardballs might hold out for the product with the preferred label, even though, except for labeling, there is absolutely no physical difference. In the absence of fungibility, there is a clear possibility that the prices of two "identical" things might command different prices (almost all the time). There is no simple arbitrage that produces a guaranteed profit in finite time by buying one and selling the other. In principle, nothing forces the prices to equality, absent fungibility.

The reason fungibility is an important issue is that many seemingly identical pairs of securities are not fungible. The most famous example is the stock pair consisting of Royal Dutch common stock (a Netherlands corporation) and Shell common stock (a British corporation).[1] This pair represents different amounts of ownership in the same company. The former is entitled to 40 percent of all the earnings of the company, while the latter is entitled to 60 percent of all of the earnings of the company. The price of three shares of Royal Dutch should always be approximately equal to the price of two shares of Shell, if the law of one price holds. There simply is no difference between three shares of Royal Dutch and two shares of Shell regarding their economic claims on the company. But, as is well known, Royal Dutch and Shell rarely trade at a 1.5 ratio and can diverge from that ratio by substantial margins and for indefinite periods of time.

Why doesn't the law of one price work in this case? The answer is lack of fungibility. You cannot buy three shares of Royal Dutch Shell and convert those shares into two shares of Shell (British). If you buy shares in either company, the only available method of disposal is to sell them.

If you could convert the cheaper shares into the more expensive shares at a three-to-two ratio, then simple arbitrage would bring the prices together, but you cannot do the conversion. No machine is available. The only thing available is the marketplace. That lack of fungibility has, in practice, meant that those who purchase the cheaper of the Shell stocks and an offsetting position[2] in the more expensive (on a three-to-two ratio) have lingered in that transaction with no particular tendency for the prices to equalize.

If two commodities are identical and fungible (in the sense that one could be converted into the other and vice versa at minimal cost), then the law of one price should hold. But if fungibility is not present, then it is an open question whether the prices of two identical but not fungible assets will converge. The famous example of Royal Dutch and Shell is a very public example of identical things that lack fungibility for which the law of one price doesn't seem to hold.

What If Identical Things Are Not Fungible?

Now let us imagine two identical assets that cannot be transformed one into another except by selling one and buying the other. This is the truly interesting case for the EMH. The fungibility case has a mechanical way of resolving itself and is more an exception than the norm in financial markets. Things that seem almost identical in financial markets are typically not fungible one into the other.

---

[1] See the exposition of the twin Shell stocks by Andrei Shleifer in *Inefficient Markets* (New York, NY: Oxford University Press, 2000), Chapter 2.

[2] Offsetting position means a short sale, or borrowing the stock from a holder and selling it, planning to repurchase the stock at a later date and return it to its original owner.

Can prices of two identical, but not fungible, things, like our baseball and hard-ball, diverge and maintain that divergence for a significant period of time, perhaps even indefinitely? The EMH would say that the prices of two things, even if not fungible, should be identical or virtually identical most of the time. That sounds vague, but it is nonetheless a demanding requirement, as we shall see.

If prices in the marketplace are not right, then someone has to be buying and selling at these incorrect prices. There have to be buyers willing to pay too much or sellers willing to sell for too little in order to keep prices from being the right prices. What does the phrase "right prices" mean? It means the prices that rational, knowledgeable participants would be willing to buy or sell something for.

One can easily imagine that there might be individuals who think that our baseballs and hardballs are different things. Individuals perhaps lack the knowledge to know that the baseball and hardball are identical. But, in time, surely they would learn that they are not truly different. Then, it becomes hard to imagine that anyone would pay more for one than the other. But what if there were people who could never be convinced that these two identical items were identical? Perhaps they don't learn, or perhaps they think the fact that they are labeled differently is enough to constitute a true difference.

Can two identical things with different names be different? For our purposes, the answer is no. They should be considered the same thing. But the deeper question is: can they have different prices? If they cannot have different prices, then the EMH, at least for this case, is validated. If different prices can prevail for products that differ only by label, then much other economic theorizing, not just the EMH, could be challenged as well.

How could these prices be different? Someone has to be willing to pay a higher price for one than for the other.

The Friedman View

Milton Friedman provided an argument in the context of currency markets that amounted to a defense of the EMH:

> Despite the prevailing opinion to the contrary, I am very dubious in fact that speculation in foreign exchange would be destabilizing. . . . People who argue that speculation is generally destabilizing seldom realize that this is largely equivalent to saying that speculators lose money, since speculation can be destabilizing only if speculators on the average sell when the currency is low in price and buy when it is high.[3]

Friedman was discussing whether speculators were a destabilizing influence in currency markets. He is arguing that speculators, traders who move prices away

[3] Milton Friedman, *Inefficient Markets* (Chicago, IL: University of Chicago Press, 1953), 175.

from efficiency, will lose money, suggesting that *smart* traders will push prices back toward efficiency while they take the opposite positions and that such speculators will eventually lose all of their capital.

The modern version of Friedman's argument introduces the notion of noise traders, which would include not only Friedman's speculators but other market participants as well. Friedman's argument, updated, would be that noise traders as a group would lose money as they foolishly buy at high prices and sell at low prices.

But Noise Traders, if Sufficiently Diverse, May Not Matter

Imagine some individuals who are irrationally willing to pay more for a baseball than a hardball. Isn't it reasonable to suppose that there may be other individuals who are irrationally willing to pay more for a hardball than a baseball? Perhaps degrees of irrationality are randomly distributed about the true rational outcome. Then, such irrational individuals may offset one another. A kind of law of large numbers might come into play that has the baseball lovers counterbalanced by the hardball lovers so that the prices of the two remain approximately identical—offsetting irrationality, we might suppose. Eugene Fama made precisely this argument in his defense of the EMH[4] against the argument that noise traders would disrupt matters.

The Noise Trader Agenda

It has long been known that there are many, often silly, reasons that people buy and sell stocks. No one pretends that all traders and investors are completely rational; common observation suggests that is not the case. But the very existence of noise traders is not sufficient to invalidate the EMH. In order to show that the EMH is in trouble, at least two conditions must be met. We will call these two conditions the *noise trader agenda*:

1. Noise trader behavior must be systematic. Noise traders must be shown not to simply cancel one another out. If some are too optimistic and others are too pessimistic, then one group may simply cancel out the effect of the other. Instead, there must be something like herd activity, such that a large group of noise traders, or a small group with a large amount of assets, behave in a similar manner.

2. Noise traders need to survive economically for a significant period of time. If all noise traders do is lose money through their noise trading, then their impact will be limited. Noise traders need to make substantial and persistent profits under some conditions. Otherwise, noise traders are simply cannon fodder, as Friedman suggests, for the smart traders.

---

[4] Eugene Fama, "Efficient Capital Markets: A Review of Theory and Empirical Work," *Journal of Finance* 25, no. 2 (May 1970): 383–417.

■ Noise

Where does the term *noise trader* come from, and what does it mean? Noise trading is normally defined by what it is not. A noise trader is not the rational, knowledgeable trader or investor who is commonly assumed in finance theory. The noise trader is doing something else. A noise trader could be as harmless as a year-end tax seller, paying no attention to values at the moment of sale. It could be a grandmother buying a present of stock for a grandchild, where the main interest in the stock is that the company produces something appealing to children, regardless of the inherent investment merits of the company itself.

Fischer Black's 1985 Presidential Address to the American Finance Association

The concept of noise in a financial market context has its first modern expression in Fischer Black's address to the American Finance Association meetings in December 1985. Black's talk on that occasion was simply entitled "Noise."[5] Noise, in a scientific context, almost invariably refers to "white noise" or "Brownian motion." Intuitively, this notion of noise is describing something that bounces around with no particular direction. But the bouncing around is stable. Figure 33.2 is a typical depiction of white noise.

Notice that the pattern is continuous but erratic. Modern financial theory uses white noise to characterize the pattern of stock prices,[6] so Black's lecture was aimed at an audience that was familiar with this notion of noise.

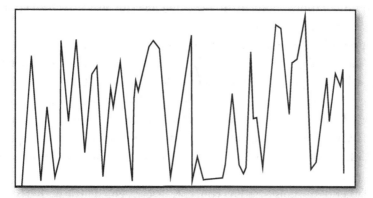

FIGURE 33.2 White Noise.

---

[5] See Fischer Black, "Noise," *The Journal of Finance* 41, no. 3 (July 1986); Papers and Proceedings of the Forty-Fourth Annual Meeting of the American Finance Association, New York, NY, December 28–30, 1985, 529–543.

[6] Salih Neftci, *An Introduction to the Mathematics of Financial Derivatives* (New York, NY: Academic Press, 1996). Neftci gives a simple explanation of Brownian motion and its equivalent, a Wiener process, on pages 148–149. Neftci's book is an intuitive and easy-to-read description of the role that white noise plays in modern finance.

Fischer Black was both an academic and a practitioner. At least half of his working days were spent in Wall Street or Chicago security trading operations. Black was intimately familiar with the diversity of trader motives and activities. He describes a variety of different types of noise traders. The definition of a noise trader is elusive in Black's talk (as it is in the entire literature), but Black provides the following definition: "Noise trading is trading on noise as if it were information."[7] That definition begs the question as to what exactly is noise, which Black elsewhere in the talk describes as something characterized by "a large number of small events." It is not completely clear what Black means here, but the talk is descriptive of many aspects of trading markets that those who trade for a living would quickly recognize.

Following are the opening lines of Black's presentation:

> I use the word "noise" in several senses in this paper. In my basic model of financial markets, noise is contrasted with information. People sometimes trade on information in the usual way. They are correct in expecting to make profits from these trades. On the other hand, people sometimes trade on noise as if it were information. If they expect to make profits from noise trading, they are incorrect.[8]

Black defines noise traders indirectly by what they are not. A noise trader is someone who is not trading on *information*. By information, Black implicitly means relevant and true information such as might be useful in predicting the future earnings of a publicly traded company. It is not clear from Black's description what a noise trader actually does, but it is clear what a noise trader doesn't do. Black's noise trader is not the rational, information-seeking investor that is typically portrayed in the efficient market paradigm.

In the preceding section, we defined a noise trader as someone willing to buy or sell at "incorrect" prices. In the hardball/baseball story, a noise trader would be someone willing to pay a different amount for a hardball than for a baseball even though they are the same asset. Someone who doesn't use information would fit both Black's definition and our definition. There is no way around the idea that if you want the EMH to be violated, you will need to have models that incorporate noise traders. Without them, you simply can't get identical, nonfungible things to trade at different prices.

As the father of the noise-trading concept, Black seemed little bothered by the implications of noise trading: "Noise makes financial markets possible, but also makes them imperfect."[9]

---

[7] Black, "Noise," 531.
[8] Ibid., 529.
[9] Ibid., 530.

But Black goes on to say, "With a lot of noise traders in the market, it now pays for those with information to trade. . . . Most of the time, the noise traders will lose money by trading, while the information traders as a group will make money."[10]

After a description of how information traders move prices back to their correct value, Black concludes: "I think almost all markets are efficient almost all of the time. 'Almost all' means at least 90 percent."[11]

Fischer Black's talk paradoxically introduced the notion of noise trading, but concludes that the EMH withstands the impact of noise traders. But Black was not the first to see things this way.

It is clear that Black shares the Friedman view, outlined earlier, and that his talk in 1985 can be interpreted as an update of the earlier Friedman position with one important caveat. Black left open the door to critics of the EMH when he observed: "In other words, I do not believe it makes sense to create a model with information trading but no noise trading where traders have different beliefs and one trader's beliefs are as good as any other trader's belief."[12]

Behavioral finance would look back to the following remark as a prescient preview of the direction noise trader research would take: "Noise makes financial markets possible, but also makes them imperfect."[13]

Friedman would not have agreed with Black that noise traders played a positive and essential role in financial markets. Friedman saw such activity as foolish and mostly as a nuisance. Friedman seemed to feel that noise traders were simply sitting ducks for rational traders to take money from. Other than that, noise traders need not be considered and could not influence asset prices in any significant way. It is clear that Black's presidential address moves away from Friedman by asserting that noise traders are essential to financial markets, that they impact prices constantly, and that they cannot be left out of any serious financial market theorizing.

The Friedman-Black Path for Noise Traders

The arguments advanced by Milton Friedman and Fischer Black suggest the pathway ahead for critics of the EMH. Inserting noise traders into models of the financial system, as Black insisted upon, and dealing with what we earlier referred to as the *noise trader agenda,* could enable the existence of noise traders to pose a challenge to the presumed efficiency of financial markets.

---

[10] Black, "Noise," 530.

[11] Ibid., 533.

[12] Ibid., 531.

[13] Ibid., 530.

CHAPTER 34

Noise Traders as Technical Traders

From Edwin T. Burton and Sunit N. Shah,
Behavioral Finance (Hoboken, New Jersey:
John Wiley & Sons, 2013), Chapter 7.

Learning Objective Statements

- Explain why technical traders are considered a specific type of noise trader
- Describe the actions of technical traders as noise traders in the context of market valuation

When watching contemporary news accounts of financial market activity, one frequently hears expressions that have no explicit role in traditional finance theory but seem to mean something to the audience of the news commentators. Examples include:

"The market is forming a bottom."
"A very oversold market rallied today."
"The market broke through resistance today."
"The market dropped through support today."
"The market acts well."
"The market looks tired."

These expressions have meaning in the trading world, but they are not part of the received financial theory, and the efficient market hypothesis (EMH) predicts that none of these remarks has any real truth embodied in them. All of these expressions and many more like them are descriptions of technical analysis. If *fundamental analysis* can be defined as basing stock analysis on things taken from accounting statements and projections of accounting statements, then *technical analysis* is based on things that explicitly eschew considerations of profits, cash flow, dividends—any of the tools of fundamental analysis.

The most popular form of technical analysis is the charting of stock prices. There is a big business in providing investors with stock price charts both in printed form and in computer-accessible online form. Armed with pricing history, many traders

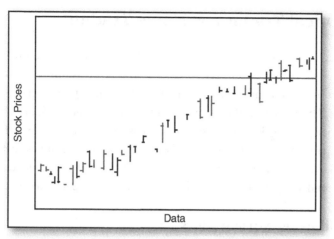

FIGURE 34.1　Stock Price Chart

base their stock buys and sells on how they interpret stock price patterns from historical data. An example of a stock price chart is given in Figure 34.1.

Dates are plotted on the horizontal axis and stock prices are plotted vertically. The horizontal line indicates a particular stock price that the charting pattern suggests is significant. That stock prices have surpassed the value indicated by the horizontal line is taken to be important in determining the future path of the price of the stock.

Academics once scoffed at technical traders as akin to believing in voodoo dolls, but technical trading by the turn of the twenty-first century had gone mainstream. The CMT Association, by 2020, boasted a membership of 4,500 "market analyst professionals in over 137 countries around the globe."[1] The CMT Association boasts that it offers a certification program to become a Chartered Market Technician (CMT), achievable by passing a set of examinations that test applicants on their knowledge of technical analysis. It has three levels of the CMT exam, much like its much revered ancestor, the Chartered Financial Analyst certification, pioneered by the CFA Institute.[2]

Besides attracting the interest of individual traders, technical analysis was available from mainstream stockbrokers for their clients' usage. Large pools of hedge fund money, by 2012, were invested in trading strategies solely based on past stock price histories. The National Futures Association counts among its members 4,500 firms and 55,000 associates, the vast majority of whom are actively involved in some form of technical trading. All of this activity, of course, runs counter to the EMH, which says that technical analysis activity represents wasted motion and wasted money. But regardless of the calumny heaped upon technical analysis by adherents of the EMH, it is an undeniable fact that technical trading underlies a very large amount of actual trading in modern financial markets.

Many common strategies in technical trading involve projecting past pricing trends into the future. This type of trading, if widespread, can create and sustain a pricing bubble. We will refer to such occurrences as *herd instinct* trading. In the latter part of this chapter, we consider some examples of the herd instinct and bubble literature.

---

[1] Information taken from www.cmtassociation.org.
[2] Details available at www.cfainstitute.org.

■ Technical Traders as Noise Traders

Since technical traders are not rational traders in the sense of the EMH, they can instead be thought of as a specific type of noise trader. To simplify matters, think only about that subset of technical analysis that involves nothing more than the use of stock price charts. There are two things that are intriguing about stock price chart analysis: (1) stock price charting is widely used, and (2) users tend to agree on what many stock price chart patterns mean. The first of these considerations implies that noise traders who are price chart traders represent a significant part of the actual trading community. The second suggests that their behavior in the marketplace may be systematic.

Trend-Following Noise Traders

One of the most widely believed patterns observable in stock price charts is that if a trend is portrayed by the chart, the trend will continue. If the stock price has been rising over time, then the prediction is that it will continue to rise. If the stock price has been falling over time, then the prediction is that it will continue to fall. This idea that price trends, once in place, will continue seems to be a prevailing view in other markets besides financial markets. Many participants in the housing market seem to have expectations of future prices that are a straightforward projection of recent pricing trends.

One simple way to model a noise trader would be an extrapolative model that forecasts future prices as a straightforward projection of the trend implicit in most recent prices (see Figure 34.2). A noise trader using the extrapolative expectations, such as depicted in Figure 34.2, might pay little or no attention to fundamentals. Bad news would not matter to such a noise trader, unless the bad news changed the pattern of stock prices so the extrapolation would lead to some different forecast.

If there is a large number of noise traders defined in this way, then one would expect some self-fulfilling aspect of such trading behavior. Expecting current trends to continue could lead to a higher or lower demand for a stock than might be warranted

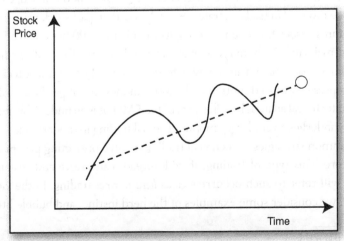

FIGURE 34.2 Predicted Stock Price Based on Trend Projection

by the fundamentals. This characterization of a noise trader is consistent with the Shleifer model since overoptimism or overpessimism could easily result from trend following. Such traders might even be more profitable than rational traders, at least for a while, for the reasons given in that model.

Reversal Patterns in Stock Prices

Somewhat more complicated is what stock price charts might tell us about market reversals. A market reversal takes place when a rising (falling) price trend becomes a falling (rising) price trend. What stock price patterns predict reversals? There are many.

One of the most interesting stock price patterns that technical traders subscribe to is known as the *island reversal*. The island reversal requires that a stock price jumps from one price to a substantially different price either immediately or during a trading halt, which could be nothing more than close of market on one day and the opening of the market on the next trading day. The gap in the price creates an island, as shown in Figure 34.3.

According to some versions of the island reversal signal, whenever a stock price gaps it must go back and fill in the gap, so that some future reversal in price is predicted by the island reversal phenomenon.

Another popular reversal pattern is the *head-and-shoulders* pattern. Sometimes this is called either a head-and-shoulders top or a head-and-shoulders bottom, depending on whether it is forecasting a fall in future stock prices or an increase in future stock prices. A head-and-shoulders top is pictured in Figure 34.4, together with its forecast of declining prices. In Figure 34.4, the head-and-shoulders pattern has formed and is now suggesting that stock prices will fall, reversing the previous uptrend in prices that had been in place before the formation of the head-and-shoulders pattern.

Head-and-shoulders patterns were studied extensively by Carol Osler[3] and later by Osler and Kevin Chang.[4] Osler's 1998 study reported that strategies based on head-and-shoulders patterns in U.S. equity markets proved to be unprofitable. The Osler-Chang results, published a year later and based on data from currency markets, found the opposite. Head-and-shoulders trading in currency markets was profitable, according to Osler and Chang.

> The head-and-shoulders trading rule appears to have some predictive power for the German mark and yen but not for the Canadian dollar, Swiss franc, French franc, or pound. Taken individually, profits in the markets for yen and marks are also substantial when adjusted for transactions costs, interest differentials, or risk. These results are inconsistent with virtually all standard exchange rate models, and could indicate the presence of market inefficiencies.[5]

---

[3] Carol Osler, "Identifying Noise Traders: The Head-and-Shoulders Pattern in U.S. Equities," Federal Reserve Bank of New York, 1988.

[4] Kevin P.H. Chang and Carol Osler, "Methodical Madness: Technical Analysis and the Irrationality of Exchange-Rate Forecasts," *Economic Journal* 109, no. 458 (October 1999): 636–661.

[5] Ibid., abstract.

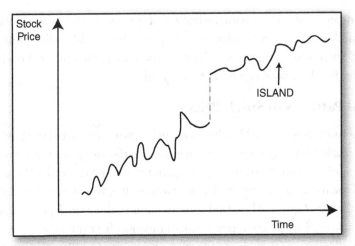

FIGURE 34.3   Price Island

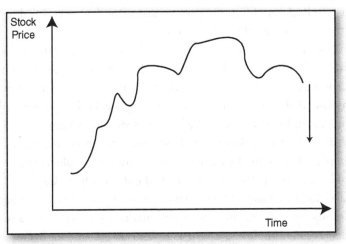

FIGURE 34.4   A Head-and-Shoulders Top

A final example of reversal patterns are the twin concepts of *base building* and *forming a top*. Base building occurs when a stock has dropped over a period of time but seems to have stabilized at a lower level and has traded in a narrow range around that lower level (see Figure 34.5).

The dotted line represents the base that is forming. Forming a top is a similar pattern, flipping the chart upside down so that forming a top is ultimately predicting a future decline in prices, while base building is suggested to lead to prices headed higher at some future date.

The Systematic Issue

Stock price charts are easy to construct and the simple patterns that we just discussed can be discerned from the data with minimal effort. Simple algorithms can

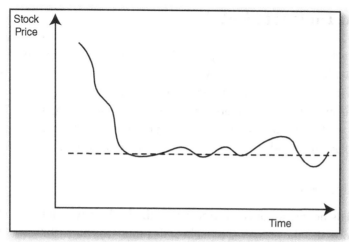

FIGURE 34.5 **Base Building**

be employed—not necessarily all identical—to take advantage of any profit opportunities that stock price charts might have embedded in them. Trend following can be seen as a version of herd mentality. A price is going up rapidly, and everyone jumps on board and buys the stock whose price is rising. A frenzy develops as the price rises higher and higher, and future prices are extrapolated to be even higher still. This line of reasoning suggests that trend following is likely to be systematic. Defenders of the EMH argue that noise traders will tend to cancel one another out, and something like the Law of Large Numbers will take hold, so that, in the aggregate, noise trader activity won't matter. But if the noise traders are all doing pretty much the same thing, then the cancel-out argument no longer applies.

Technical trading is a broader approach than simply stock price charting. Besides other stock market information such as volume, various trading statistics, seasonal trading patterns, and the like, technical trading also encompasses many other considerations with the common characteristic that none of these considerations involve fundamental company information such as dividends, earnings, and so forth. Since there is such a variety of different things that are encompassed under the umbrella of technical trading, the cancel-out criticism is likely to apply to much of technical trading. But the cancel-out phenomenon will not apply to strategies that are widely followed by a large number of traders and investors and for which there are not some obvious counterstrategies that seek to do the opposite.

The term *herd instinct* has been applied to models that have systematic behavior. This could be one application of the technical trading strategies, when such strategies are characterized by a large number of investors and traders pursuing similar strategies. Robert Shiller developed a herd instinct model in 1984 that was overlooked until much later, when the idea of systematic noise trading behavior found a more accepting home in the finance literature.

■ Herd Instinct Models

Herd instinct models[6] are motivated by observing financial market booms and busts. They are typically highly aggregative, and the herd behavior is usually summarized by a single-agent model representing the herd. Market practitioners have observed cycles in financial markets that are often described as a "feeding frenzy." A price of a particular asset begins to rise then develops a momentum of its own, seemingly independent of any real fundamental change in the things that should determine its price.

The Shiller Model

Shiller builds his model of stock returns on the back of two different observations. First, he notes that the prevailing thought at that time (the mid-1980s) was that the lack of forecastability in stock returns implied investor psychology could not have much impact in financial markets. The logic was that investor fads should be predictable, so if they impacted stock prices, price movements should be somewhat predictable as well.

Second, he notes that firms generally announce dividend movements in advance, implying that dividend movements are somewhat forecastable. Since dividends should certainly have some impact on stock prices, but price movements are not very forecastable, the prices themselves must anticipate future dividend movements. With investor psychology already ruled out as a factor, that leaves an optimal forecast of dividends as the only possible determinant of stock prices.

Consequently, he models returns on stock prices as:

$$E_t R_t = \delta \tag{34.1}$$

where δ represents a constant, E_t represents the mathematical expectation conditional on all known information at time t, and R_t is defined as

$$R_t = \frac{P_{t+1} - P_t + D_t}{P_t} \tag{34.2}$$

with P_{t+1} and P_t representing next period's and this period's prices, respectively, and D_t representing this period's dividend. The fact that δ is a constant reflects the idea that, in equilibrium, prices adjust so as to equate all stocks' expected returns.

One can solve this equation recursively to obtain a representation of a given stock's price at any time t:

$$P_t = \sum_{k=0}^{\infty} \frac{E_t D_{t+k}}{(1+\delta)^{k+1}} \tag{34.3}$$

---

[6] These models are normally part of bubble models. For an excellent account of what we know and don't know about bubbles, see Rodney Sullivan, "Taming Global Village Risk II: Understanding and Mitigating Bubbles," *Journal of Portfolio Management* 35, no. 4 (2009): 131–141.

In other words, Shiller argues that the EMH implies that the price of a stock at any point in time is simply an optimal forecast of the future stream of dividends. Consequently, if the price of a given stock moves, more often than not that movement should reflect movement in future dividends from that stock.

However, the data does not bear out such a finding. If investor psychology cannot be a factor in price movements according to the EMH, Shiller argues that that leaves only anticipation of dividend movements as a driver of stock prices, so that stock price movements should generally be followed by changes to dividends. The fact that empirical evidence does not support that conclusion, he argues, casts doubt on the EMH as a complete model of stock price movements.

In response, Shiller proffers a slightly adapted version of the EMH that includes irrational investors. This model has rational, or smart-money, investors, as well as investors Shiller calls "ordinary," which represent noise traders. Smart-money investors have the following demand for a given stock as a proportion of total shares outstanding:

$$Q_t = \frac{(E_t R_t - \rho)}{\varphi} \tag{34.4}$$

where $E_t R_t$ is defined as above, ρ is the expected return level at which there is no smart-money demand for the asset, and φ represents the risk premium smart-money investors would require to hold all the shares of the given stock.

Ordinary investors, however, are assumed to demand a total value of stock defined as Y_t. Market equilibrium requires that

$$Q_t + \frac{Y_t}{P_t} = 1 \tag{34.5}$$

from which one can solve recursively to arrive at the expression for the price of the stock:

$$P_t = \sum_{k=0}^{\infty} \frac{E_t D_t + \varphi E_t Y_{t+k}}{(1 + \rho + \varphi)^{k+1}} \tag{34.6}$$

This is simply an adjusted form of equation (34.3). Noise traders have their impact through the Y_t terms, so that as φ goes to zero, noise traders have no impact and the formula reverts to (34.3), and as φ goes to infinity, noise traders drown out smart-money investors and the market price is $P_t = Y_t$.

Shiller then goes through several specifications for Y_t and examines the resulting effect on price. First, he postulates what would happen if ordinary investors are driven by fads for stocks. Y_t would then have a hump-shaped pattern, rising as the stock comes into fashion, leveling off for a while, and then tapering back down towards its original level. The effect on price would depend on the how long the pattern takes to evolve. A relatively short fad would have little effect, since price includes a weighted sum of all future ordinary investor demands, so that a brief fad would get attenuated significantly in its effect on price. Essentially, smart-money investors would simply take the opposite position of ordinary investors, selling the stock high while it is in vogue and then buying it back at lower prices as it goes out of style, so that overall price movements would be minimal.

However, a long-developing fad would have a significant impact on price, with smart-money investors slowly buying in as Y_t rises toward its peak, knowing prices will be higher in the future. The price would peak shortly before Y_t does, then decline as future Y_t values are set to decline as well. Shiller argues that such a phenomenon could explain the lack of forecastability in stock prices.

He then looks at a couple of extreme views on Y_t, namely that Y_t responds directly to either past returns or current and past dividends, and argues that both would imply that a stock's price might overreact to dividends relative to what the EMH would predict. To test this theory, he looks at historical data on the relevant metrics for the Standard & Poor's Index, and finds that stock prices have historically overreacted to dividends. The excess volatility of prices relative to dividends could therefore be explained by an irrational investor model such as this one.

Shiller does, however, caution about reading too much into his results. The specifications of his model are rather restrictive and make strong assumptions about the impact of irrational investors. Further, even if the model's assumptions are correct, Shiller admits that the observed relationship could have other explanations, such as firm dividend behavior responding to the same social dynamics that influence the society at large. Regardless, it is difficult to look at the evidence presented and come away without some additional doubt about the validity of the EMH.

Abreu-Brunnermeier Model

Abreu and Brunnermeier (2003)[7] provide a noise trader model designed to deal specifically with bubbles and crashes. The Abreu-Brunnermeier (AB) model has the interesting feature that even arbitrage traders may find it in their interest to ride the wave of the bubble. Arbitrage traders, the so-called rational traders, are aware that there are noise traders out there and that they can impact prices, perhaps in the manner suggested by Shiller in his model. AB assume that prices begin to diverge from efficient prices without any particular reason and the arbitrageurs observe the divergence. Not all arbitrageurs notice the divergence at the same time. Once an arbitrageur observes the divergence, the arbitrageur will not necessarily trade against the divergence. Some will trade against it, but others might be tempted to ride the wave. The model permits the bubble to be burst by the combined action of the arbitrageurs, but it doesn't provide any certainty that the combined action of the arbitrageurs will ever successfully burst the bubble. Instead, AB use an arbitrary stopping time by which the bubble will burst, no matter what actions the noise traders and the arbitrageurs may be taking. The authors describe this arbitrary stopping date as based on "exogenous reasons." The interpretation of the arbitrary stopping date is that an unforeseen event of significance occurs that changes things and bursts the bubble.

---

[7] Dilip Abreu and Markus K. Brunnermeier, "Bubbles and Crashes," *Econometrica* 71, no. 1 (January 2003): 173–204.

The AB model is successful in capturing the idea that people join bandwagons and get off of bandwagons and such herding activity can prolong a bubble as well as end it. The model is less successful in explaining why this herding activity takes place. The model is descriptive more than insightful. The idea that arbitrageurs might ride the wave of the bubble even when they are perfectly aware that the market is in a bubble phase is an interesting feature of the AB model. There seems some casual evidence that even those who are aware that market prices are beyond what can be supported by fundamentals often will participate anyway on the grounds that they can rationally expect the bubble to continue. This changes the usual definition of an arbitrageur in a way that could prove troublesome for supporters of the EMH.[8]

AB assumes that a divergence between market price and efficient price emerges and then is observed. An econometric study by Gurkaynak[9] suggests that such observations may be difficult to accomplish in practice. The old adage that you only know you were in a bubble when it is over seems borne out by Gurkaynak's statistical tests.

■ Conclusion

Bubbles are still not well understood. As Reinhart and Rogoff[10] note in their landmark work on financial crises, most economists treat bubbles largely as narratives, as if they are a part of economic history but not much a part of economic theory. We don't really understand how bubbles begin or end, and we are not sure how one can detect bubbles until after the fact. What we do seem to know is that technical trading and herd instinct trading likely play a role in bubbles. Technical traders who herd together and follow simple trend-following strategies can serve to prolong a bubble by simple feedback from price increases to expectations of future price increases.

One of the most interesting questions about bubbles is whether bubbles are an inherent feature of modern financial systems. Are the seeds of the next bubble ever present? Minsky[11] is the most well-known proponent of the view that bubbles inevitably arise from financial markets. Minsky argues that Keynesian economics, properly interpreted, is about bubbles and collapses and quotes Keynes extensively in his own research. Policy makers seem to have the opposite view. After bubble crashes, policy makers rush to enact reforms that will prohibit future bubbles. This may be foolhardy if Minsky's inevitability arguments are correct.

---

[8] A similar point is made in Taisei Kaizojiand and Didier Sornette, "Market Bubble and Crash," reprinted in Rama Cont, *Encyclopedia of Quantitative Finance* (Hoboken, NJ: John Wiley & Sons, 2009).

[9] Refet S. Gurkaynak, "Econometric Tests of Asset Price Bubbles: Taking Stock," *Journal of Economic Surveys* 22, no. 1 (2008): 166–186.

[10] Carmen M. Reinhart and Kenneth Rogoff, *This Time Is Different: Eight Centuries of Financial Folly* (Princeton, NJ: Princeton University Press, 2009).

[11] Hyman Minsky, "The Financial Instability Hypothesis," The Jerome Levy Economics Institute of Bard College, Working Paper No. 74, May 1992.

CHAPTER 35

Academic Approaches to Technical Analysis

From Andrew W. Lo and Jasmina Hasanhodzic, *The Evolution of Technical Analysis: Financial Prediction from Babylonian Tablets to Bloomberg Terminals* (Hoboken, New Jersey: John Wiley & Sons, 2010), Chapter 8.

Learning Objective Statements

- Describe how technical analysis remains relevant despite the EMH
- Discuss how the Adaptive Market Hypothesis reconciles the EMH with technical and behavioral factors

Big strides have been made toward the standardization of technical analysis in recent years.[1] The impetus for statistically evaluating technical analysis naturally comes from academia, with studies yielding evidence of its validity in wide-ranging areas, such as moving averages (Brock, Lakonishok, and LeBaron, 1992), genetic algorithms to discover optimal trading rules (Neely, Weller, and Dittmar, 1997), and the Dow theory (Brown, Goetzmann, and Kumar, 1998), to name a few. In their quest to quantify technical analysis, academics have turned, too, to the most controversial of its techniques: geometric patterns. Finding patterns in price charts is a subjective endeavor that relies on the natural smoothing filter of the human eye (which, needless to say, is vastly more sophisticated than a moving average); therefore, a main challenge in quantifying the patterns lies in modeling the way in which eyes smooth the data they view. Academics such as Chang and Osler (1994) and Lo, Mamaysky, and Wang (2000) take on this challenge by smoothing the data using statistical filtering techniques. They then develop algorithms to automatically identify technical patterns in those data and finally evaluate the information content of the patterns thus found; these works, too, find proof of the potential value of technical analysis.

In this chapter we survey these and other relevant works. Our purpose is to review the main trends rather than provide an all-inclusive encyclopedia of academic research.

■ Theoretical Underpinnings

While the idea that stock market prices follow a random walk was anticipated in the nineteenth-century popular investment literature by French authors such as Henri Lefèvre, the steps toward its mathematical formalization were first made in 1900 by the French graduate student Louis Bachelier (1870–1946) in his doctoral dissertation, *Théorie de la Spéculation*. Unfortunately, the dissertation, now deemed the "origin of mathematical finance," fell into oblivion until the statistician L. J. Savage rediscovered his thesis and contacted Paul A. Samuelson, who immediately recognized its significance.[2]

A great deal of research has been devoted ever since to formulating theoretically the efficient market hypothesis, building up market efficiency—the idea that "prices fully reflect all available information"—into one of the most important concepts in economics. Since Samuelson's and Fama's landmark papers, many others extended their original framework, yielding a "neoclassical" version of the efficient market hypothesis, where price changes, properly weighted by aggregate marginal utilities, must be unforecastable.[3] In markets where, according to Lucas (1978), all investors have "rational expectations," prices do fully reflect all available information and marginal-utility-weighted prices follow martingales. Market efficiency has been extended in many other directions, including the incorporation of nontraded assets such as human capital, state-dependent preferences, heterogeneous investors, asymmetric information, and transaction costs.[4] But the general thrust is the same: Individual investors form expectations rationally, markets aggregate information efficiently, and equilibrium prices incorporate all available information instantaneously.[5]

But the EMH is not the unassailable edifice it is often made out to be. For example, consider situations of asymmetric information. It has been argued that even if market inefficiencies could be induced by asymmetric informedness of market participants, they would be instantly eliminated. In Fischer Black's (1986) presidential address to the American Finance Association, he argued that financial market prices were subject to "noise," which could temporarily create inefficiencies that would ultimately be eliminated through intelligent investors competing against each other to generate profitable trades. Since then, many authors have modeled financial markets by hypothesizing two types of traders—informed and uninformed—where informed traders have private information better reflecting the true economic value of a security, and uninformed traders have no information at all, but merely trade for liquidity needs.[6] In this context, Grossman and Stiglitz (1980) suggest that market efficiency is impossible because if markets were truly efficient, there would be no incentive for investors to gather private information and trade, and DeLong et al. (1990, 1991) provide a more detailed analysis in which certain types of uninformed traders can destabilize market prices for periods of time even in the presence of informed traders.[7]

More direct evidence against the EMH and in favor of technical analysis emerged in the work of Treynor and Ferguson (1985), who show that it is not only the past prices, but the past prices plus some valuable nonpublic information, that can lead to profit. A more basic challenge to market efficiency was proposed by Lo and MacKinlay (1988), who strongly reject the efficient market hypothesis for weekly stock market returns by using a simple volatility-based specification test.

■ Empirical Evaluation

The early empirical testing of the EMH turned out in its favor, though this was as much due to the cultural attitudes toward technical analysis as to the scientific results. For example, in their important study, Fama and Blume (1966) investigate whether one can exploit the degree of dependence between successive price changes of individual securities by following a mechanical trading rule. Independence here refers to a situation where successive price changes are independent in a probabilistic sense. For example, if today's price is higher than yesterday's, that makes it neither more nor less likely for tomorrow's price to be higher than today's. If, on the other hand, a positive price change increases the likelihood of observing a positive (negative) price change in the future, that is called positive (negative) dependence. The trading rule they consider is known as Alexander's filter technique, and they measure its profitability by comparing its expected returns to those of a passive buy-and-hold strategy. More precisely, in their 1966 paper, "Filter Rules and Stock-Market Trading," Fama and Blume investigate whether the random walk model of price movements is meaningful from an investor's viewpoint. They start by noting that the degree of dependence between successive price changes of individual securities may simultaneously be meaningful to some and insignificant to others—it all depends on the specific case. For example, for an investor, the independence assumption becomes meaningful if it can make expected profits from some mechanical trading rule greater than those of a buy-and-hold strategy.

With this in mind, the authors evaluate Alexander's filter technique, a mechanical trading rule developed by Sidney Alexander to test whether or not prices move in trends. According to the filter of size *x* percent, if the daily closing price of a particular security moves up at least *x* percent, one buys and holds the security until its price moves down at least *x* percent from a subsequent high, at which time one sells and goes short and maintains the short position until the price moves up at least *x* percent above a subsequent low, at which time one covers and buys.

The authors apply Alexander's filter technique to a series of daily closing prices for each of the individual securities of the Dow Jones Industrial Average from 1956 to 1962 using various values for *x*. They find that even when the commissions are omitted, the average returns from the filter rules are inferior to the returns from the buy-and-hold strategy. This stands in contrast to the findings of Alexander, who, according to the authors, wrongly concluded that the filter rule was superior to the buy-and-hold rule. The reason for his misinterpretation lies in his improper adjustment for dividends, Fama and Blume explain. They also point out that even if the filter technique were restricted to the more profitable long positions, it would not consistently outperform the buy-and-hold strategy, and that, naturally, the inclusion of commissions further emphasizes the superiority of the buy-and-hold strategy. Fama and Blume hence conclude that "even on extremely close scrutiny" the results "[do] not yield evidence of dependence."[8]

The authors do find, however, that slight amounts of both positive and negative dependence are present in the price changes. Specifically, for the filter sizes of 0.5 percent, 1.0 percent, and 1.5 percent, the average returns per security on long positions are greater than the average return from buy-and-hold, and the average losses on short positions are smaller than the gains from buy-and-hold. The opposite is true for filter sizes that are larger than 1.5 percent and smaller than 5 percent, constituting evidence for positive dependence in very small movements of stock prices and for the negative dependence in the intermediate movements. However, the authors deemphasize this evidence by arguing that the degree of the dependences is so small that it is easily offset by the transaction costs, making it impossible, even for a floor trader, to profit from the filter rule. Since the marginal transaction costs of the floor trader are the minimum trading costs, the authors again conclude that the market is indeed efficient and that, even from an investor's viewpoint, the random walk model is an adequate description of the price behavior. Such conclusions rule out the possibility that technical analysts, whose principal assumption is that past prices contain information for predicting future returns, can add value to the investment process. Consequently, for a long time technical analysis has been largely discredited in the academic world, with Burton G. Malkiel, the author of the influential *A Random Walk Down Wall Street* (1973), concluding that "under scientific scrutiny, chart-reading must share a pedestal with alchemy."

To this day many academics remain critical of the discipline. However, an increasing number of studies suggest, either directly or indirectly, that "technical analysis may well be an effective means for extracting useful information from market prices."[9] A growing number of finance academics are coming to recognize that efficient markets are not an adequate model of reality. Thus, a crack in the door has been opened for academic considerations of technical analysis.

An early (though in its time largely ignored) study by Granger and Morgenstern (1963) finds that the random walk model ignores the possibly important low-frequency (long-run) components of the time series of stock market prices. Specifically, in their 1963 paper, "Spectral Analysis of New York Stock Market Prices," Granger and Morgenstern test how well the random walk model fits the specified sample of New York Stock Exchange prices and also promote the idea that "the most appropriate statistical techniques to be used [in the analysis of stock market data] are the recently developed spectral methods."[10] Spectral analysis, in this case, refers to a statistical procedure known as the Fourier transform, which, loosely speaking, decomposes a time series into cycles of different frequencies. This procedure is used to obtain a frequency spectrum of the time series—its representation in the frequency domain—which shows how much of the series lies within different frequency bands over a range of frequencies.

The authors start by suggesting that the random walk model may ignore the possibly important low-frequency (long-run) components of the time series. For example, let $\{X_t\}$ denote a time series of prices generated by a random walk model, ω a small frequency value, and a some constant term. Then, the first differences of $\{X_t\}$ are virtually indistinguishable from the first differences of $\{Y_t\}$, where $Y_t = X_t + a \cos(\omega t)$, even though the latter contains a low-frequency (long-run) component specified by a cosine of a small ω. The authors then test whether their data contain long-run components of greater importance than the random walk hypothesis would imply. They hence estimate the frequency spectrum of the data and compare them to the expected spectrum if the random walk hypothesis were true. They find that, while most of the frequency bands of the estimated spectra parallel their expected counterparts, certain bands are significantly greater than what the random walk model would lead us to expect. The authors conclude that the random walk model, "although extremely successful in explaining most of the spectral shape, does not adequately explain the strong long-run (24 months or more) components of the series."[11]

The controversy of the EMH in the theoretical literature has also paved the way for more direct studies of the validity of various technical analysis techniques and systems: The natural starting point was the most readily quantifiable of them, such as technical trading systems and moving averages. For example, Pruitt and White (1988) test the performance of a technical trading system and conclude that it does better than a simple buy-and-hold strategy to an extent that could not be attributed to chance alone.

And in their 1992 paper, "Simple Technical Trading Rules and the Stochastic Properties of Stock Returns," Brock, Lakonishok, and LeBaron test "two of the simplest and most popular trading rules"—moving average and trading range break—based on the data of the Dow Jones Index from 1897 to 1986. Two moving average varieties are considered: the "variable length moving average," which initiates buy (sell) signals when the short moving average is above (below) the long moving average by an amount larger than the specified band, and the "fixed length moving average," which initiates buy (sell) signals when the short moving average cuts the long moving average from below (above) and keeps that position for the next 10 days. In a trading range break-out rule, a buy (sell) signal is generated when the price penetrates the resistance (support) level, as defined by a local maximum (minimum). It is found that the buy signals select periods with higher conditional returns and lower volatilities, while the sell signals select periods with lower conditional returns and higher volatilities; the fact that the higher returns for buys do not arise during riskier periods indicates that the difference in returns between buys and sells is not easily explained by risk.

Overall, these results indicate that the technical rules explored do possess some predictive power. Consistently, buy (sell) signals provided by the trading rules generate returns that are higher (lower) than unconditional returns. Moreover, the returns generated from the buy and sell signals are unlikely to be generated by the random walk or other popular null models, suggesting that the empirical foundations of the EMH may not be as strong as is generally believed.

Attention turned next to the most controversial of technical analytic practices, chart-pattern reading, for patterns are the most subjective and hardest to quantify of technical indicators. One of the first rigorous studies of patterns was initiated by Charles Kirkpatrick, who convinced his then employer, Arthur Little Corporation, to hire Robert Levy to conduct the study. The results are summarized in Levy's 1971 paper, "The Predictive Significance of Five-Point Chart Patterns." Studying 32 possible forms of five-point chart patterns in the daily closing prices of 548 New York Stock Exchange securities from 1964 to 1969, Levy finds that after accounting for transaction costs none of the patterns show profitable forecasting ability. He concedes that changing the parameters of his pattern definitions and the type of data on which they are based, and most significantly specifying patterns not only in terms of price but also in terms of volume, may alter the conclusions.

The next important step in this direction was made by Chang and Osler, who in their pioneering work, "Evaluating Chart-Based Technical Analysis: The Head-and-Shoulders Pattern in Foreign Exchange Markets," evaluate the predictive power of the head-and-shoulders pattern using daily dollar exchange rates of the dollar vs. the yen, mark, Canadian dollar, Swiss franc, French franc, and pound during what at the time constituted the entire floating rate period, from March 1973 to June 1994. Chang and Osler's head-and-shoulders pattern identification algorithm starts by tracing out a zigzag pattern in the data, then scans the thus smoothed data for the evidence of the defining characteristics of the head-and-shoulders pattern. Importantly, the position is entered after the breaking of the neckline and exited when a new peak or a new trough is reached, and the profits are calculated as the gain or loss between entry and exit. The results indicate that the profits are significantly greater than what a random walk model would suggest, albeit only for the mark and the yen. Nonetheless, this suggests that the head-and-shoulders pattern has some predictive power. The authors also note that while profitable for the mark and the yen, the head-and-shoulders pattern is "extremely risky." Namely, the standard deviation of returns across positions ranged from 2 to 4 times the mean return. However, Chang and Osler argue that it is still likely that investors would find the profits from the head-and-shoulders pattern attractive in the context of a diversified portfolio, given that they are often more concerned with systematic risk than with absolute risk.

Further work in the pattern quantification was done by Lo, Mamaysky, and Wang (2000), who in an attempt to transform the "art" of technical analysis into more of a science, propose in their paper, "Foundations of Technical Analysis: Computational Algorithms, Statistical Inference, and Empirical Implementation," an algorithm which aims to formalize and automate the highly subjective and controversial practice of detecting, with the naked eye, the geometric patterns that appear in price charts and are believed to have predictive value. They start by recognizing that the evolution of prices over time is not random, but that it contains certain regularities or patterns, and they then attempt to identify, or extract, these nonlinear patterns from the historical time series of prices. Here it is important to realize that identifying patterns directly from the raw price data would not be sensible. When professional technicians study a price chart, their eyes naturally smooth the data, while their cognitive faculties discern regularities. Moreover, many would argue that much of this process takes place on an intuitive and subconscious level, making it even harder to quantify. Hence, natural candidates for modeling the process by which technicians look for patterns in a price chart are pattern-recognition techniques known as smoothing estimators, which estimate nonlinear relationships by averaging the data in sophisticated ways to reduce the observational errors. In particular, Lo, Mamaysky, and Wang (2000) automate technical analysis using a smoothing estimator known as kernel regression.

In an attempt to answer the question of whether or not this aspect of technical analysis "works," they apply kernel regression to the daily returns of individual NYSE/AMEX and Nasdaq stocks from 1962 to 1996. The kernel regression function is then analyzed for the occurrence of each of the 10 technical patterns under consideration in the experiment: head-and-shoulders, triangles, rectangles, broadening and double formations, and their inverse or "bottom" counterparts. After the technical patterns have been obtained, their information content is examined by comparing the unconditional empirical distribution of returns with the corresponding conditional empirical distribution, conditioned on the occurrence of a technical pattern. If technical patterns are informative, conditioning on them should alter the empirical distribution of returns; in other words, if the information contained in such patterns has already been incorporated into returns, there should not be much difference between the conditional and unconditional distribution of returns.[12]

They find that certain technical patterns, when applied to many stocks over many time periods, do provide incremental information, especially for Nasdaq stocks, supporting the claim that technical analysis can add incremental value to the investment process.[13] The authors conclude that although there will probably always be demand for talented technical analysts, the benefits of transparency and low cost associated with its automation suggest that algorithms should play some role in an investor's portfolio and may also bring technical analysis closer to other forms of systematic financial analysis. The same conclusions are reached by Hasanhodzic (2007), who conducts the robustness test of the Lo, Mamaysky, and Wang results by replacing the kernel regression smoothing algorithm with the neural network one.

"The proof is in the pudding," respond successful technicians when faced with skepticism about their craft. Rather than simply dismissing as exception bias the track records of winning technicians, some academics have evaluated them statistically. One such technician, the legendary early-twentieth-century Dow theorist William Hamilton, is the subject of Brown, Goetzmann, and Kumar's 1998 paper, "The Dow Theory: William Peter Hamilton's Track Record Reconsidered." In particular, Brown, Goetzmann, and Kumar reevaluate Alfred Cowles's (1933) test of the Dow theory, which provided "strong evidence" against the ability of the theory to forecast stock market prices. The authors test whether Hamilton's interpretation of the Dow theory can predict stock market movements and attempt to uncover the rules of the Dow theory (as interpreted by Hamilton) and to understand its implications for the EMH. To this end, they label as bullish, bearish, neutral, or indeterminate the 255 editorials Hamilton published in *The Wall Street Journal* during his tenure as its editor from 1902 to 1929, and then calculate the frequency with which the Dow theory beats the risk-free rate (assumed to be at 5 percent per annum) over the interval following an editorial, conditional upon bull or bear call.

Brown, Goetzmann, and Kumar (1998) find that the proportion of successful up calls is greater than the proportion of the failed up calls, and that the proportion of successful down calls is much greater than the proportion of failed down calls. In fact, their contingency table analysis shows strong evidence of an association between Hamilton's calls and subsequent market performance. In addition, the proportion of correct bear calls is found to be much higher than what could be attributed to chance alone. To make these observations more concrete, they simulate a trading strategy based on Hamilton's editorials—going long the market on a bullish signal and shorting the market on a bearish one. They find that over the 27-year period under consideration, the Hamilton strategy yields a very similar average annual return to the Standard & Poor's Composite Index but with lower volatility, resulting in a superior risk-adjusted return.

To test the validity of Hamilton's forecasts out of sample (that is, for the Dow Jones Industrial Average from 1930 to 1997 for which Hamilton did not generate any forecasts), Brown, Goetzmann, and Kumar (1998) first reduce the dynamics of past price series to basic trend shapes such as rising trends, falling trends, head-and-shoulders, and resistance levels. These trend shapes are then used as inputs to a neural network that is trained on the 27 years' worth of Hamilton editorials data to identify a nonlinear mapping from features to Hamilton's recommendation.

The success of the in-sample performance (that is, for the 1902–1929 period for which Hamilton's forecasts are available) of the neural network indicates that Hamilton did rely on structures that resemble positive and negative trends and reversals. The out-of-sample performance is evaluated on the September 1930–December 1997 period, and returns of the buy-and-hold strategy are compared to those of the "next day Hamilton strategy" and the "second day Hamilton strategy." The "next day Hamilton strategy" refers to investing at the opening-of-the-day prices of the day on which the neural network forecast comes out—for example, an investor who bought the paper before the opening of the market can take advantage of the signal immediately or as soon as the market opens. And the "second day Hamilton strategy" refers to investing at the close-of-the-day prices of the day on which the neural network forecast comes out—for example, an investor who bought the paper before the opening of the market cannot take advantage of the signal until the end of the day. The authors find that while the returns of the second day strategy are almost exactly equal to the buy-and-hold returns (but would be less than that after transaction costs), they do exhibit less variance and lower systematic risk compared to the buy-and-hold.

Such results are comparable to those obtained during Hamilton's lifetime: returns that are close to a buy-and-hold strategy, but that are characterized with lower levels of risk. The next-day Hamilton strategy has much higher returns than the second-day Hamilton strategy; however, even the next-day strategy does not dominate buy-and-hold in the 1980s. The results suggest that the Dow theory is not entirely consistent, and it would not be able to generate large excess returns due to transaction costs and other trading frictions. However, these results also indicate that the Dow theory was more than random decision making on the part of Hamilton. In particular, the Hamilton strategy appears to reduce portfolio volatility and, in the case where the immediate execution of the sell signal is possible, to yield profits that are higher than those of the buy-and-hold. Again, this implies that the empirical foundations of the EMH may not be as strong as long believed.

The observation that human nature never changes, and that consequently technical indicators designed to measure the reflection of human nature in market prices never change either, is a notable argument in favor of technical analysis, but one that at the same time underscores its main shortcoming: Technical analysis has not kept up with technological advances. Of course, charting and data collection have become automated, but most popular patterns and heuristics of today were developed in the precomputing age when calculating a simple moving average was a formidable task. For example, the 10-day moving average became popular not because it was optimal, but simply because it was trivial to compute. The 10-day moving average remains in common use today in spite of the fact that computers can calculate a moving average for *any* time scale with equal ease.

Suboptimal parametrization is only a symptom of a chronic disease afflicting technical analysis: Its static nature cannot account for the ever-changing character of financial markets. In the past, when execution was manual and costly, and financial systems were far less connected and complex, "static" used to be a prerequisite for practical use; now it is more often a recipe for failure. As markets evolve and trading strategies become more sophisticated, the need for new, dynamic indicators is apparent. Never has this need been more urgent than now, in the wake of the financial crisis of 2007–2009.

Some authors have taken steps in this regard by investigating the form of an optimal trading rule that can be revealed by the data themselves, rather than evaluating the commonly used technical indicators. For example, in their 1997 paper, "Is Technical Analysis on the Foreign Exchange Markets Profitable? A Genetic Programming Approach," Neely, Weller, and Dittmar use genetic programming to discover trading rules that are most profitable given the data with which they are dealing. The purpose of such an approach is to reduce the risk of the out-of-sample bias, which arises when the trading rules are selected ex post, rather than at the beginning of the sample period (the authors claim that the results of previous studies that sought to document the existence of excess returns to various types of trading rules in the foreign exchange market are all biased in this way). Six exchange rate time series are considered: dollar/German mark, dollar/yen, dollar/pound, dollar/Swiss franc, German mark/yen, and pound/Swiss franc, and the rules are obtained over the period 1975–1980.

When the performance of these rules is examined over the period 1981–1995, strong evidence of economically significant out-of-sample excess returns after the adjustment for transaction costs is found for each of the six exchange rates. Since technical analysts commonly claim that their rules exploit general features of financial markets, rather than being specific to any particular market, the authors run the dollar/German mark rules on the data of other markets under consideration and conclude that there is a significant improvement in performance in the vast majority of cases.

Finally, the trading rules that emerge from their research approximate well the rules commonly used by technical analysts, they argue. The rules that at first sight might appear complicated are often highly redundant; for example, the rule that was represented by a tree with 10 levels and 71 nodes turned out to be equivalent to the following simple advice: "Take a long position at time t if the minimum of the normalized exchange rate over periods $t - 1$ and $t - 2$ is greater than the 250-day moving average."[14]

■ Adaptive Markets and Technical Analysis

Even though the craft of technical analysis is deeply rooted in human civilization, serious efforts to formalize and statistically evaluate it have been launched only in the last two decades. The cultural biases of finance academics are, at least in part, responsible. In his autobiography, *Education of a Speculator*, the renowned trader and one-time finance professor, Victor Niederhoffer, paints an irreverent picture of the kind of forces at work in creating such biases at the University of Chicago where he was a finance Ph.D. student in the 1960s:

> This theory and the attitude of its adherents found classic expression in one incident I personally observed that deserves memorialization. A team of four of the most respected graduate students in finance had joined forces with two professors, now considered venerable enough to have won or to have been considered for a Nobel Prize, but at that time feisty as Hades and insecure as kids on [their] first date. This elite group was studying the possible impact of volume on stock price movements, a subject I had researched. As I was coming down the steps from the library on the third floor of Haskell Hall, the main business building, I could see this Group of Six gathered together on a stairway landing, examining some computer output. Their voices wafted up to me, echoing off the stone walls of the building. One of the students was pointing to some output while querying the professors, "Well, what if we really do find something? We'll be up the creek. It won't be consistent with the random walk model." The younger professor replied, "Don't worry, we'll cross that bridge in the unlikely event we come to it."

I could hardly believe my ears—here were six scientists openly hoping to find no departures from ignorance. I couldn't hold my tongue. "I sure am glad you are all keeping an open mind about your research," I blurted out. I could hardly refrain from grinning as I walked past them. I heard muttered imprecations in response.[15]

One reason the EMH took such a stronghold in the academic community is because it was the first to be formalized and operationalized; although economists, including Nobel laureates, have proposed behavioral theories of financial markets—such as Simon's theory of bounded rationality—over half a century ago, their ideas were not as directly implementable using the mathematical and computational tools available at the time. Now that the notions of adaptive markets and computationally bounded algorithms are available, a reinterpretation of market efficiency in evolutionary and computational terms might be the key to reconciling this theory with the possibility of making profits based on past prices alone. From an engineer's perspective, the efficiency of a device or system is rarely an all-or-nothing condition, but is more likely to be a continuum that captures the degree to which energy is transformed from one type to another. Just as air conditioners and hot-water heaters have efficiency ratings that fall somewhere between 0 and 100 percent—with higher ratings implying better cooling and heating abilities per unit of input power—financial markets differ in their ability to transform information into market prices, with more efficient markets impounding greater information into prices over a fixed time interval. The relevant question is not whether a market is efficient, but rather what its *relative degree of efficiency* is when compared to other alternatives.

Moreover, it makes little sense to talk about market efficiency without taking into account that market participants have bounded resources and adapt to changing environments. Instead of saying that a market is "efficient," we should say, borrowing from theoretical computer science, that a market is efficient with respect to certain resources, such as time or memory, if no strategy using those resources can generate a substantial profit. Similarly, it may be misleading to say that investors act optimally given all the available information; rather, they act optimally within their resources. This allows for markets to be efficient for some investors but not for others; for example, a computationally powerful hedge fund may extract profits from a market that looks very efficient from the point of view of a day trader who has fewer resources at his disposal—arguably the status quo.[16]

Human behavior is central to the limitations of the EMH, but the debate between disciples of market efficiency and proponents of behavioral finance have created a false dichotomy between the two schools of thought—in fact, both perspectives contain elements of truth, but neither is a complete picture of economic reality. Markets do function quite efficiently most of the time, aggregating vast amounts of disparate information into a single number—the price—on the basis of which millions of sound decisions are made. This remarkable feature of capitalism is an example of Surowiecki's (2004) "wisdom of crowds." But every so often, markets can break down, and the wisdom of crowds can quickly become the "madness of mobs."

Why do markets break down? Animal spirits! Recent neuroscientific research has shown that what we consider to be "rational" behavior is the outcome of a delicate balance among several distinct brain functions, including emotion, logical deliberation, and memory.[17] If that balance is upset—say, by the strong stimulus of a life-threatening event—then reason may be cast aside in favor of more instinctive behaviors like herding or the fight-or-flight response. Although few of us encounter such threats on a daily basis, much of our instincts are still adapted to the plains of the African savannah 50,000 years ago, where survival was a full-time occupation. Brain scans have shown that these same instincts can be triggered by more modern threats such as shame, social rejection, and financial loss. And as social animals, humans will react en masse if the perceived threat is significant enough, occasionally culminating in lynch mobs, riots, bank runs, and market crashes. Markets are not always efficient, nor are they always irrational—they are adaptive.

This "adaptive markets hypothesis" of Lo (2004, 2005)—essentially an evolutionary biologist's view of market dynamics—is at odds with the current economic orthodoxy, which has been heavily influenced by mathematics and physics (see, for example, Lo and Mueller, 2010). This orthodoxy has emerged for good reason: Economists have made genuine scientific breakthroughs, including general equilibrium theory, game theory, portfolio optimization, and derivatives pricing models. But any virtue can become a vice when carried to an extreme. The formality of mathematics and physics, in which mainstream economics is routinely dressed, can give outsiders—especially business leaders, regulators, and policymakers—a false sense of precision regarding our models' outputs (recall Samuelson's admonition that "macroeconomists have predicted 5 out of the past 3 recessions"). From an evolutionary perspective, markets are simply one more set of tools that *Homo sapiens* has developed in his ongoing struggle for survival. Occasionally, even the most reliable tools can break or be misapplied.

The adaptive markets hypothesis offers an internally consistent framework in which the EMH and behavioral biases can coexist. Behavior that may seem irrational is, instead, behavior that has not yet had sufficient time to adapt to modern contexts. For example, the great white shark moves through the water with fearsome grace and efficiency, thanks to 400 million years of natural selection. But take that shark out of water and onto a sandy beach, and its flailing undulations will look . . . irrational! The origins of human behavior are similar, differing only in the length of time we have had to adapt to our environment (about 2 million years) and the speed with which that environment is now changing.

Like the six blind monks who encountered an elephant for the first time—each monk grasping a different part of the beast and coming to a wholly different conclusion as to what an elephant is—disciples of the EMH and behavioral finance have captured different features of the same adaptive system.

The implications of the adaptive markets hypothesis for technical analysis are significant. Markets can be trusted to function properly during normal times, but when humans are subjected to emotional extremes (either pleasure or pain), animal spirits may overwhelm rationality, even among seasoned investors. Therefore, fixed investment rules that ignore changing environments will almost always have unintended consequences, and pattern recognition—in any form—may yield important competitive advantages.

Languishing for too long in the murky waters of part art, part science, technical analysis is finally starting to develop a more rigorous foundation. Although the fortress walls separating technicians from the adherents of modern finance still stand tall, they are not insurmountable, and we hope that the recognition of the thousands-of-years-long legacy of technical analysis and the role it has played in shaping the behavioral theory of financial markets will awaken some of the skeptics and open the door for a more constructive dialogue between the two communities.

■ Notes

1. See, for example, D. Aronson, *Evidence-Based Technical Analysis: Applying the Scientific Method and Statistical Inference to Trading Signals* (Hoboken, NJ: John Wiley & Sons, 2007) and C. Kirkpatrick and J. Dahlquist, *Technical Analysis: The Complete Resource for Financial Market Technicians* (Upper Saddle River, NJ: FT Press, 2006).

2. J.-M. Courtault, Y. Kabanov, B. Bru, P. Crepel, I. Lebon, and A. Le, "Louis Bachelier: On the centenary of 'Théorie de la Spéculation,'" *Mathematical Finance* 10, no. 3 (2000) 339–353.

3. See, for example, S. F. LeRoy, "Risk Aversion and the Martingale Property of Stock Returns," *International Economic Review* 14, no. 2 (1973), 436–446; M. Rubinstein, "The Valuation of Uncertain Income Streams and the Pricing of Options," *Bell Journal of Economics* 7 (1976), 407–425; R. Lucas, "Asset Prices in an Exchange Economy," *Econometrica* 46 (1978), 1429–1446.

4. See A.W. Lo, ed., *Market Efficiency: Stock Market Behaviour in Theory and Practice, Volumes I and II.* (Cheltenham, UK: Edward Elgar Publishing Company, 1997), 50–67 for a representative collection of papers in this literature.

5. See A.W. Lo, "Efficient Markets Hypothesis," in L. Blume and S. Durlauf, eds., *The New Palgrave: A Dictionary of Economics*, 2nd ed. (New York, NY: Palgrave McMillan, 2007) for a more detailed summary of the market efficiency literature in economics and finance.

6. See, for example, S. Grossman and J. Stiglitz, "On the Impossibility of Informationally Efficient Markets," *American Economic Review* 70 (1980), 393–408; D.W. Diamond and R.E. Verrecchia, "Information Aggregation in a Noisy Rational Expectations Economy," *Journal of Financial Economics* 9 (1981), 221–235; A.R. Admati, "A Noisy Rational Expectations Equilibrium for Multi-Asset Securities Markets," *Econometrica* 53, no. 3 (1985), 629–657; A.S. Kyle, "Continuous Auctions and Insider Trading," *Econometrica* 53, no. 6 (1985), 1315–1336; and J. Y. Campbell and A.S. Kyle, "Smart Money, Noise Trading and Stock Price Behavior," *Review of Economic Studies* 60 (1993), 1–34.

7. More recently, studies by G. Luo, "Evolution and Market Competition," *Journal of Economic Theory* 67 (1995), 223–250; G. Luo, "Market Efficiency and Natural Selection in a Commodity Futures Market," *Review of Financial Studies* 11 (1998), 647–674; G. Luo, "Natural Selection and Market Efficiency in a Futures Market with Random Shocks," *Journal of Futures Markets* 21 (2001), 489–516; G. Luo, "Evolution, Efficiency and Noise Traders in a One-Sided Auction Market," *Journal of Financial Markets* 6 (2003), 163–197; D. Hirshleifer and G. Luo, "On the Survival of Overconfident Traders in a Competitive Securities Market," *Journal of Financial Markets* 4 (2001), 73–84; and L. Kogan, S.A. Ross, J. Wang, and M.M. Westerfield, "The Price Impact and Survival

of Irrational Traders," *Journal of Finance* 61 (2006), 195–229 have focused on the long-term viability of noise traders when competing for survival against informed traders. While noise traders are exploited by informed traders as expected, certain conditions do allow them to persist, at least in limited numbers, these authors argue.

8. E. Fama and M. Blume, "Filter Rules and Stock Market Trading," *Journal of Business* 39 (1966), 236.

9. A.W. Lo, H. Mamaysky, and J. Wang, "Foundations of Technical Analysis: Computational Algorithms, Statistical Inference, and Empirical Implementation," *Journal of Finance* LV, no. 4 (August 2000), 1705.

10. C.W.J. Granger and O. Morgenstern, "Spectral Analysis of New York Stock Market Prices," *Kyklos* XVI (1963), 3.

11. Granger and Morgenstern, "Spectral Analysis," 11.

12. The distance between the two distributions is measured in two ways: (1) by a goodness-of-fit test, which compares the deciles of conditional returns with their unconditional counterparts, and (2) by the Kolmogorov-Smirnov test.

13. It is important here to distinguish between evaluating the "profitability" of technical trading rules and evaluating the "information content" of technical analysis; the former necessitates the modeling of the trading implementation and risk management, whereas the latter detects supply/demand imbalances regardless of whether one can profitably act on that information.

14. C. Neely, P. Weller, and R. Dittmar, "Is Technical Analysis in the Foreign Exchange Market Profitable? A Genetic Programming Approach," *Journal of Financial and Quantitative Analysis* 32 (1997), 405–426, p. 420.

15. V. Niederhoffer, *Education of a Speculator* (New York, NY: John Wiley & Sons, 1997), 270.

16. J. Hasanhodzic, A.W. Lo, and E. Viola, "A Computational View of Market Efficiency," Available online at http://arxiv.org/abs/0908.4580 (2009).

17. A. Damasio, *Descartes' Error: Emotion, Reason, and the Human Brain* (New York, NY: Avon Books, 1994).

■ BIBLIOGRAPHY

Bachelier, L. *Théorie de la Spéculation*, trans. A. J. Boness, Paris: Gauthiers-Villars, 1900. In P.H. Cootner, ed., *Random Character of Stock Market Prices*. Cambridge, MA: MIT Press, 1964.

Black, F. "Noise." *Journal of Finance* 41 (1986): 529–544.

Brock, W. A., J. Lakonishok, and B. LeBaron. "Simple Technical Trading Rules and the Stochastic Properties of Stock Returns." *Journal of Finance* 47 (1992): 1731–1764.

Brown S. J., W. N. Goetzmann, and A. Kumar. "The Dow Theory: William Peter Hamilton 's Track Record Reconsidered." *Journal of Finance* 53, no. 4 (1998): 1311–1333.

Chang, K. and C. Osler. "Evaluating Chart-Based Technical analysis: The Head-and-Shoulders Pattern in Foreign Exchange Markets." Federal Reserve Bank of New York Working Paper (1994).

DeLong, B., A. Shleifer, L. Summers, and M. Waldman. "Noise Trader Risk in Financial Markets." *Journal of Political Economy* 98 (1990): 703–738.

DeLong, B., A. Shleifer, L. Summers, and M. Waldman. "The Survival of Noise Traders in Financial Markets." *Journal of Business* 64 (1991): 1–19.

Fama, E. and M. Blume. "Filter Rules and Stock Market Trading." *Journal of Business* 39 (1966): 226–241.

Granger, C. W. J. and O. Morgenstern. "Spectral Analysis of New York Stock Market Prices." *Kyklos* XVI (1963): 1–27.

Grossman, S. and J. Stiglitz. "On the Impossibility of Informationally Efficient Markets." *American Economic Review* 70 (1980): 393–408.

Hasanhodzic, J. "Investments Unwrapped: Demystifying Technical Analysis and Hedge-Fund Strategies." Massachusetts Institute of Technology Ph.D. thesis (2007).

Lo, A. W. "The Adaptive Markets Hypothesis: Market Efficiency from an Evolutionary Perspective." *Journal of Portfolio Management* 30 (2004): 15–29.

Lo, A. W. "Reconciling Efficient Markets with Behavioral Finance: The Adaptive Markets Hypothesis." *Journal of Investment Consulting* 7 (2005): 21–44.

Lo, A. W. and A. C. MacKinlay, 1988. "Stock Market Prices do not Follow Random Walks: Evidence from a Simple Specification Test." *Review of Financial Studies* 1, no. 1 (1988): 41–66.

Lo, A. W., H. Mamaysky, and J. Wang. "Foundations of Technical Analysis: Computational Algorithms, Statistical Inference, and Empirical Implementation." *Journal of Finance* LV, no. 4 (2000): 1705–1765.

Lo, A. W. and M. Mueller. "WARNING: Physics Envy May Be Hazardous To Your Wealth." *Journal of Investment Management* 8 (2010): 13–63.

Lucas, R. "Asset Prices in an Exchange Economy." *Econometrica* 46 (1978): 1429–46.

Malkiel, B. G. *A Random Walk Down Wall Street*. New York: W.W. Norton & Co., 1973.

Neely, C., P. Weller, and R. Dittmar. "Is Technical Analysis in the Foreign Exchange Market Profi table? A Genetic Programming Approach." *Journal of Financial and Quantitative Analysis* 32 (1997): 405–426.

Pruitt, S. and R. White. "The CRISMA Trading System: Who Says Technical Analysis Can't Beat the Market?" *Journal of Portfolio Management* 14 (1988): 55–58.

Surowiecki, J. *The Wisdom of Crowds: Why the Many Are Smarter Than the Few and How Collective Wisdom Shapes Business, Economies, Societies and Nations*. New York: Little, Brown, 2004.

Treynor, J. and R. Ferguson. "In Defense of Technical Analysis." *Journal of Finance* 40 (1985): 757–773.

CHAPTER 36

Market Sentiment and Technical Analysis

Michael Carr, CMT, CFTe

Learning Objective Statements

- Define "sentiment" as it relates to financial markets
- Discuss the importance of the "crowd"
- Describe the challenges of using sentiment indicators

◼ Sentiment Drives Market Prices

Analysts have spent decades searching for a formula to define a stock's value. For example, the discounted cash flow (DCF) model is one of many used as the basis for investment decisions. Yet there may be a fundamental flaw in this process.

Using this example, DCF analysis provides an estimate of a company's value found by discounting the company's expected future free cash flows. This means it requires developing estimates of sales, costs, inflation rates, company growth rates, and other variables for several years. Those values are then stated in current dollars under the assumption that inflation erodes buying power over time and a dollar today therefore has more value than that same dollar will have in 10 years.

DCF and other such models provide an estimate of the company's fair value. Formally, this is the net present value of the future cash flows. If the stock price is below the estimated value, the stock is considered a buy.

Left unanswered in this process is the question of why the price of the stock would be different from what this or other models generate. Remember, markets are assumed to be efficient, which means the stock should be trading at the "correct" price.

But, the current price rarely equals the estimated fair value. That is, at least in part, because a factor related to sentiment pushes the price of the stock above or below its fair value. This factor is shown in the following formula.

$$P = \sum_{k=0}^{n} V \times \sum_{k=0}^{n} \omega$$

where P is the current market price

V is the estimated value of the stock found with DCF or another model

ω is the value of the sentiment factor

The summations indicate that each market opinion carries its own estimate of the stock's value and of the sentiment factor. This sentiment factor is roughly defined as how each market participant feels about a stock. It attempts to explain why a company like Netflix can trade with a price-to-earnings (P/E) ratio of more than 400 when the average P/E ratio is less than 20. This is shown in Figure 36.1.

Traders believe that Netflix will grow and so bid the stock up above the fair value indicated by the models. The stock price can remain above its fair value so long as sentiment remains bullish, even though the fundamentals do not justify the high price.

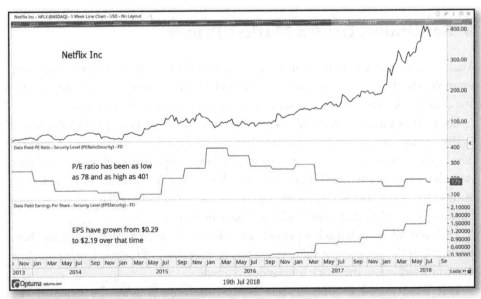

FIGURE 36.1   NFLX and Sentiment.

Note: Sentiment is the only explanation for the large swings in Netflix's valuation.

◾ The Crowd Determines Sentiment

Sentiment explains whether the market price is above or below the estimated fair value. When the market price is above the estimated value, sentiment is bullish. Bearish sentiment forces the market price below the estimated fair value of the stock.

The formula presented earlier depicts sentiment as both an individual function and a group function. Each market participant will determine their level of bullishness or bearishness. Combined, those individual opinions drive the market. Of course, some opinions will carry more weight than others.

In the current market environment, there is a large group of investors that owns stocks without regard to value and without an opinion about the company. These are index funds and they represent a significant portion of the market.

Among investors with an opinion, institutional managers are important for two reasons. One is that they control large amounts of money. In the simplest terms, large amounts of buying push prices up and large amounts of selling push prices down. The large funds have a significant impact on the trends of prices.

Large managers also affect the sentiment of individual investors. They are interviewed on CNBC, speak to reporters at Bloomberg, and express their thoughts via other media outlets. Their opinions are often available to individual investors and that contributes to the sentiment of individual investors.

Individual investors form their own opinions on their investments as well. Using Netflix as an example, some will avoid the stock because they believe it is overvalued while others will own the stock because they believe it is a disruptive technology.

Notably, some will believe it is overvalued but will buy it anyway because they recognize that it is going up, driven to higher and higher prices by the crowd's buying. They might believe they will be able to spot when the top is forming and be able to get out before the decline sets in. In this case, the investors understand that the crowd's sentiment is an important factor in determining the direction of the trend.

The concept of the crowd has been important to investors since at least 1841 when Charles Mackay first published *Extraordinary Popular Delusions and the Madness of Crowds*.[1] Mackay cited stock market bubbles as an example of the madness of crowds. Ever since, crowds have unfairly been associated with irrational beliefs.

In 1954, Humphrey Neill clearly explained why it is important to understand the role of the crowd in the markets. In his book, *The Art of Contrary Thinking*,[2] Neill noted that the crowd must be wrong at important turning points.

Consider a market top. The size of the crowd builds as the market rises. As the crowd becomes increasingly bullish, investors are committing more and more funds to their investments.

---

[1] Charles Mackay, *Extraordinary Popular Delusions and the Madness of Crowds* (Amherst, NY: Prometheus Books, 2001).

[2] Humphrey B. Neill, *The Art of Contrary Thinking: It Pays to Be Contrary* (Caldwell, ID: Caxton Printers, 2004).

In this way, the crowd determines the direction of the trend. When a majority of investors are buying, prices are rising in response to their demand. When the majority is selling, prices are falling in response to the increase in the supply of shares created by the sell orders.

At extreme highs, the market, in effect, runs out of buyers. In other words, as the crowd becomes increasingly bullish and commits more and more funds to the market, the supply of new investment capital decreases. Eventually, when it seems as if everyone in the crowd is bullish, the market tops.

On the downside, the opposite scenario plays out. The crowd becomes increasingly bearish and sell orders flood the market. When the bears are done selling, the market will rally.

In both cases, extremes in sentiment mark the end of the trend. In Neill's formulation, it is profitable to take a position contrary to the crowd at extremes. However, it is important to be on the same side of the market as the crowd while the trend is building to an extreme.

The logic of the crowd theory of prices is sound and fairly simple. But while the concept is simple, the price value of the sentiment factor of the market can never be precisely known.

However, there are useful indicators that help analysts estimate the sentiment factor. Broadly speaking, these indicators are based on either market data and trading statistics or on data from outside the markets, such as opinion surveys of professionals and individual investors.

CHAPTER 37

Sentiment Measures from Market Data

Michael Carr, CMT, CFTe

Learning Objective Statements

- Describe the VIX as a sentiment measure
- Explain the use of options volume and open interest as sentiment indicators
- Describe the use of futures open interest in gauging sentiment
- Identify the three primary groups in the *Commitments of Traders* report
- Define short interest
- Explain insider activity as a sentiment indicator

■ *Commitments of Traders* Data

The Commodity Futures Trading Commission (CFTC) is the federal agency charged with oversight of the futures markets. To ensure transparency in the markets, the CFTC requires large traders to report their positions on a weekly basis. This data is distributed in the *Commitments of Traders* (COT) reports.

The report shows the number of open positions in a futures market, known as open interest, for futures and options on futures markets in which 20 or more traders hold positions equal to or above the reporting levels established by the CFTC. The reporting level is determined by the regulators to ensure that large positions in each market are known to the CFTC.

Open interest is measured in futures and options contracts and is defined as the number of existing contracts that are open in a market and it changes from day to day. This is an important difference between options and futures markets as compared to the stock market, since the number of outstanding shares of a company's stock remains relatively constant and is controlled by the company.

In futures and options markets, for each long position there must be a corresponding short position. Therefore, the open interest is evenly balanced between longs and shorts.

For example, one investor may want to open a position by buying a contract in the futures market while another investor believes prices will fall and is interested in opening a short position. If they both enter the market at the same time and both initiate a new position of one contract, open interest will increase by one contract.

But buyers may also enter the market while other investors are looking to exit a position. In this case, with a buyer opening a long position while a seller offsets a long position, open interest would remain unchanged. If both a long and short position are closed at the same time in the market, open interest decreases.

The COT report allows analysts to determine which groups of participants are opening and closing positions in different markets and allows analysts to track those changes over time.

Market participants are assigned to one of four categories. For physical commodities such as agricultural and energy markets, the categories are:

1. Producer/Merchant/Processor/User
2. Swap Dealers
3. Managed Money
4. Other Reportables

In financial markets including futures on stock market indexes and Treasury securities, the categories are:

1. Dealer/Intermediary
2. Asset Manager/Institutional
3. Leveraged Funds
4. Other Reportables

The CFTC also provides legacy reports that separate the participants into commercial, non-commercial (large speculators), and nonreportable positions (small speculators). This classification is more popular among technical analysts. An example of the report is shown in Figure 37.1.

This information is often aggregated by data providers and can be analyzed over time as shown in Figure 37.2. It is common to summarize the open interest of each of the groups in terms of the number of contracts "net long" or "net short."

In general, this data is analyzed in terms of "smart money" and "not-so-smart money." The smart money is the commercials who are the producers and users of the commodity. In the wheat market, commercials could include farmers and food companies that require wheat. Commercials know the market well and are likely to sell when prices are high and buy when prices are low. This will show in the chart as extreme net short and net long positions, respectively, held by commercials.

The not-so-smart money is considered to be the small speculators who are often individual investors and are expected to be wrong at important turning points.

```
WHEAT-SRW - CHICAGO BOARD OF TRADE                                          Code-001602
Commitments of Traders - Futures Only, August 28, 2018
----------------------------------------------------------------------------------------
        :  Total  :              Reportable Positions                 :  Nonreportable
        :--------------------------------------------------------------:  Positions
        :  Open   :     Non-Commercial     :  Commercial    :   Total     :
        : Interest :  Long  :  Short : Spreading: Long  : Short :  Long  : Short :  Long  : Short
----------------------------------------------------------------------------------------
        :        : (CONTRACTS OF 5,000 BUSHELS)                        :
        :        :
All   : 456,974: 162,377   98,477   90,331  165,752  222,007  418,460  410,815:  38,514   46,159
Old   : 378,607: 143,165   95,681   63,927  141,468  185,109  348,560  344,717:  30,047   33,890
Other :  78,367:  31,734   15,318   13,882   24,284   36,898   69,900   66,098:   8,467   12,269
        :        :
        :        :     Changes in Commitments from: August 21, 2018       :
        : -36,653: -23,564   -8,103  -17,013    6,167  -12,441  -34,410  -37,557:  -2,243      904
        :        :
        :        :  Percent of Open Interest Represented by Each Category of Trader  :
All   : 100.0  :   35.5     21.5     19.8     36.3     48.6     91.6     89.9:    8.4     10.1
Old   : 100.0  :   37.8     25.3     16.9     37.4     48.9     92.1     91.0:    7.9      9.0
Other : 100.0  :   40.5     19.5     17.7     31.0     47.1     89.2     84.3:   10.8     15.7
        :        :
        :# Traders :           Number of Traders in Each Category           :
All   :  407  :    140      100      131       99      130      310      309:
Old   :  392  :    138      101      111       91      124      288      284:
Other :  205  :     53       43       34       42       89      115      153:
        :-------------------------------------------------------------------
        :        :  Percent of Open Interest Held by the Indicated Number of the Largest Traders
        :        :            By Gross Position                 By Net Position
        :        :  4 or Less Traders   8 or Less Traders    4 or Less Traders   8 or Less Traders
        :        :   Long:   Short     Long     Short:     Long     Short     Long     Short
        :-------------------------------------------------------------------
All   :             14.3     13.5     22.0     22.5      11.1     12.1     18.0     19.5
Old   :             15.7     14.7     24.9     24.7      12.0     13.8     19.8     22.3
Other :             23.5     18.7     36.3     28.7      22.7     16.5     29.9     23.6
```

FIGURE 37.1   COT Data for CBOT Wheat

Source: CFTC, https://www.cftc.gov/dea/futures/deacbtlf.htm.

Large speculators include hedge funds and other large investors who are often trend followers and their positions will often mirror the long-term price trend.

The idea of smart money extends to the stock market as well. In that market, insiders and large investors are considered the smart money and regulators also require these investors to report their buying and selling activities.

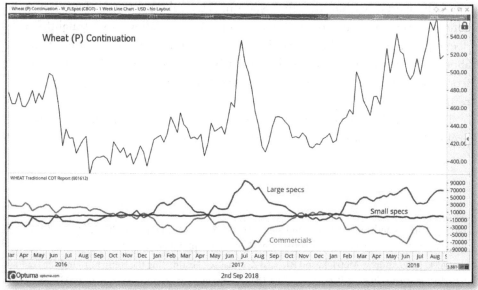

FIGURE 37.2   Net Positions of Each of the Three Legacy Groups Over Time

■ Insider Trading

The Securities and Exchange Commission (SEC) requires corporate insiders—meaning a company's officers and directors, and any beneficial owners of more than 10% of a class of the company's equity securities—to notify the SEC of all purchases and sales.[1]

The initial filing is done on Form 3, which must be filed within 10 days of becoming an officer, director, or beneficial owner. Changes in ownership are reported on Form 4 and must be reported to the SEC within two business days. If they miss one of these deadlines, the insider will need to file a Form 5 as soon as possible.

Insider trading, following the signals shown on Form 4, has been shown to be a profitable strategy. In developing a strategy, analysts should consider:

- Buying is generally more significant than insider selling. Sellers can sell for a variety of reasons including estate planning or covering personal expenses. Sales are not normally a sign of trouble unless multiple insiders are selling large positions at around the same time. However, buying is done only because the insiders believe the market is undervaluing the stock.
- Open market purchases are more significant than those made at discounts to the market via the exercise of stock options.
- The size of the trade offers important information. An executive doubling their position is making a large commitment of their personal funds.

Although analyzing insider trading activity can be a difficult task, there are potential rewards. One study found that "the purchase portfolio earns abnormal returns of more than 50 basis points per month. About one-quarter of these abnormal returns accrue within the first five days after the initial transaction, and one-half accrue within the first month. The sale portfolio does not earn abnormal returns. Our portfolio-based approach also allows for straightforward decompositions of performance by various characteristics; we find that the abnormal returns to insider trades in small firms are not significantly different from those in large firms, and that top executives do not earn higher abnormal returns than do other insiders."[2]

This research confirms that what insiders do with their money can provide profitable insights into the state of their companies.

---

[1] U.S. Securities and Exchange Commission, "Forms 3, 4, 5," January 15, 2013, https://www.sec.gov/fast-answers/answersform345htm.html. Accessed September 3, 2018.

[2] Leslie A. Jeng, Andrew Metrick, and Richard Zeckhauser, "Estimating the Returns to Insider Trading: A Performance-Evaluation Perspective," *Review of Economics and Statistics* 85, no. 2 (2003): 453–471. doi:10.1162/003465303765299936.

◾ VIX

Another indicator to help read what investors are doing with their money and their market sentiment is the VIX Index. Traders and analysts often call the VIX the "fear index" because the indicator tends to move up as the S&P 500 moves down.

Technically, VIX is a calculation designed to produce a measure of constant, 30-day expected volatility of the U.S. stock market, derived from real-time, mid-quote prices of S&P 500 Index call and put options.[3]

VIX and the S&P 500 are shown in Figure 37.3. Notice the VIX does tend to spike as the S&P 500 forms short-term bottoms.

While VIX is useful to some analysts, the chart shows the difficulty of interpreting the indicator. There is no way to know in real time when VIX is high enough to signal a market bottom.

Another shortcoming of VIX is the fact that it cannot be traded directly. VIX is tradable with options, futures contracts, options on futures, and other derivative products. These markets provide another tool for analysts to gauge market sentiment.

◾ Open Interest

Analysis of the open interest in futures and options markets also offers insight into the sentiment of traders. Remember that open interest is the total number of outstanding derivative contracts that have not been settled by an offsetting trade or by exercise or delivery.

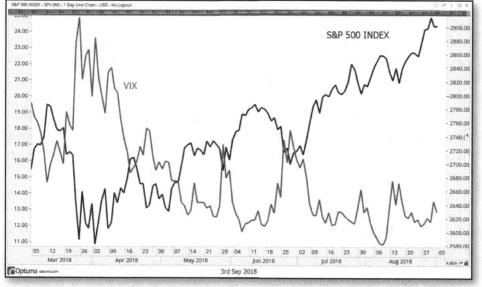

FIGURE 37.3   VIX and the S&P 500

---

[3] Cboe, "VIX Options," VIX FAQs, www.cboe.com/vixOptions.

Futures

For each long position in a futures market there must be a short position. From the time the buyer and seller open the contract until it is closed, that contract is considered "open."

In general, an increase in open interest indicates that new money is entering the market. This would indicate that the trend is likely to continue. A decline in open interest shows that money is leaving the market as traders exit positions and the trend is likely to reverse. If open interest is steady for some time, the trend is likely near a reversal point, but in most cases steady open interest is an early warning indicator and not an urgent call to action.

These general tendencies can be summarized in Table 37.1.

TABLE 37.1 Open Interest and Trend		
Direction of Trend	Change in Open Interest	Interpretation
Up	Increasing	Uptrend likely to continue.
Up	Decreasing	Uptrend likely to reverse.
Down	Increasing	Downtrend likely to continue.
Down	Decreasing	Downtrend likely to reverse.

Options

Open interest in options markets is also of interest to technical analysts. Of course, a distinction between calls and puts must be made when tracking open interest in options. But having open interest and volume data on both those types of options also opens opportunities to measure sentiment by comparing these statistics for calls and puts.

One indicator that provides information about sentiment is the put/call (P/C) ratio. The P/C ratio compares the volume or the open interest of puts to calls. Figure 37.4 shows the P/C volume ratio for equity options traded on the Cboe as the bear market began in 2008.

The long-term average of the ratio is 0.65, indicating that volume in puts is about 65% of the volume of calls on a typical trading day. The ratio moves above 1 when traders are buying more puts than calls, an indication that traders, as a group, are unusually bearish. Readings below 0.5 indicate traders are unusually bullish.

The P/C ratio is interpreted in a contrarian manner. High readings, indicating a high level of bearishness among traders, are considered to be bullish in the short run. Low readings, indicating traders are buying fewer puts than usual, are bearish in the short run. This indicator is a short-term market timing tool because the most actively traded options are the ones that are expiring within the next month.

Open interest ratios are also interpreted in a contrarian manner. The put/call open interest ratio compares the open interest in put options to the open interest in call options. Analysts will generally combine all contracts with the same expiration date to calculate open interest.

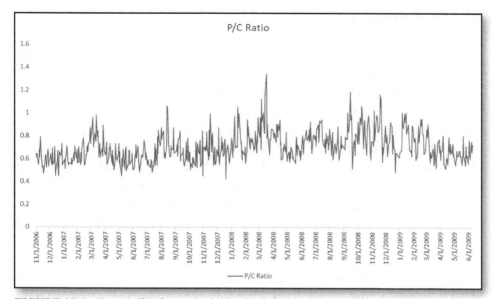

FIGURE 37.4 Put/Call Volume Ratio for Equities

Source: Cboe, www.cboe.com/data/historical-options-data/volume-put-call-ratios.

For equities, the open interest in calls will generally be greater than the open interest in puts. However, the open interest in options for indexes and for exchange-traded funds (ETFs) shows the opposite behavior. Buying put options on indexes is a popular strategy to hedge a portfolio. The long-term average of the P/C open interest ratio for options on indexes is 1.2, indicating that traders generally own more puts than calls on indexes.

The P/C open interest ratio for index options is shown in Figure 37.5. Low readings tend to indicate extreme bullishness and are generally buying opportunities.

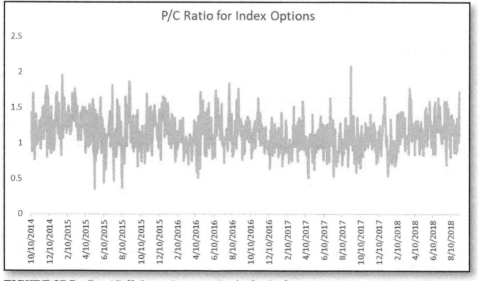

FIGURE 37.5 Put/Call Open Interest Ratio for Indexes

Source: Cboe, www.cboe.com/data/historical-options-data/volume-put-call-ratios.

■ Short Interest

Another measure of investor activity that analysts apply to the stock market is short interest. Short selling is selling a security that the seller does not own. By selling before buying, the trader hopes to benefit from a price decline.

Typically, a short sale involves the sale of a security at the current price, which is settled with shares lent to the short seller by a third party. The seller makes the short sale on the assumption that the price of the security will go down. If this occurs, the short seller will purchase shares to lock in a profit and replace the shares previously borrowed. Of course, if the stock rises in price and the short seller elects to close out the position through a purchase, the short seller will absorb the resulting loss.

Brokerage firms are required to report their short positions on the 15th of each month and the exchanges publish compilations of these reports eight business days later.

Short interest is the total number of shares of a security that have been sold short by customers and securities firms that have not yet been repurchased to settle outstanding short positions in the market.

Many analysts track an indicator known as Days to Cover. It is calculated as the aggregate short interest for the month divided by the average daily share volume. This is also known as the short interest ratio.

The short interest ratio is an indicator of the market sentiment of a specific stock. If the short interest ratio is very high, that means investors are shorting a large share of a company's outstanding stock, indicating many investors expect the stock to fall in price.

This can be interpreted in a contrarian manner. If the short interest ratio is high, traders with short positions will suffer losses if the stock rallies. They may choose to cover shorts by buying shares of the company, cutting losses, and adding to the buying pressure in the stock. For this reason, some analysts view a high short interest ratio as a bullish indicator.

A report from the New York Stock Exchange is shown in Figure 37.6.

LARGEST NEGATIVE CHANGES

GO TO: Biggest Short Positions | Largest Positive Changes | Largest % Increases | Largest % Decreases | Shorts As A Percentage of Float | Days To Cover

Friday, August 24, 2018

	Company	Symbol	8/15/18	7/31/18	Chg	% Chg	% Float	Days to cover	Avg daily volume
1	Alibaba Group Holding Limited	BABA	104,805,856	141,518,165	-36,712,309	-25.9	4.1	4	25,678,361
2	iShares MSCI Emerging Markets	EEM	103,810,963	124,646,079	-20,835,116	-16.7	...	2	60,558,808
3	AT & T Inc.	T	72,648,177	88,569,189	-15,921,012	-18.0	1.0	3	25,214,597
4	Sprint Corporation	S	112,937,261	125,745,921	-12,808,660	-10.2	21.4	8	14,670,024
5	Kinder Morgan, Inc.	KMI	35,365,854	46,170,287	-10,804,433	-23.4	1.9	3	12,427,930
6	Chesapeake Energy Corp.	CHK	140,275,900	150,756,605	-10,480,705	-7.0	15.7	5	27,940,626
7	Gerdau S.A.	GGB	39,931,984	48,876,115	-8,944,131	-18.3	...	4	9,592,948
8	J.C. Penney Company, Inc.	JCP	131,239,763.0	139,657,455	-8,417,692	-6.0	42.8	10	13,054,910
9	VALE S.A.	VALE	46,968,266	55,084,008	-8,095,742	-14.7	...	2	21,101,721
10	Two Harbors Investment Corp.	TWO	5,558,908	12,843,789	-7,284,881	-56.7	3.2	2	3,276,121

FIGURE 37.6 Short Interest Statistics

Source: The *Wall Street Journal*, www.wsj.com/mdc/public/page/2_3062-nyseshort-highlites.html#shortC.

In this example, the large short interest in J.C. Penney Company (NYSE: JCP) could be of interest. More than 42% of the company's outstanding shares are out as shorts and it would take 10 days of average trading to cover those positions. If the stock rallies at all, shorts may choose to cover their positions, possibly creating a sharp rally in the stock as they buy.

CHAPTER 38

Sentiment Measures from External Data

Michael Carr, CMT, CFTe

Learning Objective Statements

- Describe the use of news and advisories as sentiment measures
- Explain the concept of contrary opinion
- Indicate how mutual fund cash and other funds measures are used to gauge sentiment

■ AAII

Many analysts use surveys to gauge sentiment. A popular and readily accessible survey is conducted by the American Association of Individual Investors (AAII). This survey measures the sentiment of individual investors. Other surveys track the opinions of investment advisers and other groups.

The AAII Investor Sentiment Survey is a weekly survey asking individual investors whether they are bullish, bearish, or neutral over the next six months. The survey question is shown in Figure 38.1.

AAII has conducted the survey every week since July 1987. The most recent data is available free of charge at the AAII website. Results are summarized in a diagram, and historical data is available as a spreadsheet that can be downloaded. Figure 38.2 shows the results of the survey.

From the diagram, we can see that generally about 35% of individuals are bullish, 25% are bearish, and 40% are neutral.

Some analysts consider rare signals near the extremes to be actionable. For example, when bulls or bears account for 70% or more of the sample, they may

AAII Investor Sentiment Survey

"I feel that the direction of the stock market over the next 6 months will be:"

- ○ Up — Bullish
- ○ No Change — Neutral
- ○ Down — Bearish

[Submit]

FIGURE 38.1 AAII Survey Question

Source: AAII, www.aaii.com/SentimentSurvey?a=homepageSentimentSurvey.

Survey Results for Week Ending 7/18/2018

Data represents what direction members feel the
stock market will be in next 6 months.

HISTORICAL AVERAGE: 38.5%

BULLISH
34.7%

-8.4 Percentage point change from last week

HISTORICAL AVERAGE: 31.0%

NEUTRAL
40.4%

+12.6 Percentage point change from last week

HISTORICAL AVERAGE: 30.5%

BEARISH
24.9%

-4.2 Percentage point change from last week

Note: Numbers may not add up to 100% because of rounding.

FIGURE 38.2 AAII Survey Results for Week Ending 7/18/2018

Source: AAII, www.aaii.com/SentimentSurvey?a=homepageSentimentSurvey.

view that as a contrarian signal. While this is a typical way to use the data, it might not be the most useful.

In June 2014,[1] AAII published research that showed:

> The best contrarian signal occurred not when investors were unusually optimistic or pessimistic, but rather when they described themselves as being neutral (defined by the survey as expecting stock prices to be unchanged over the next six months). Unusually high levels of neutral sentiment have been followed by a median 26-week rise in the S&P 500 of 8.6% and a median 52-week rise in the S&P 500 of 17.7%. In contrast, the S&P 500 had a median return of 5.2% and 10.7%, respectively, over all 26-week and 52-week periods throughout the survey's history.

The study also noted that large-cap stocks were up 83% of the time six months after neutral sentiment reached an extreme. A year after neutral readings reached an extreme value, large caps were up 88% of the time.

That is an important insight. Indecision is the best indicator to watch for. When a large number of investors are neither bullish nor bearish, the market tends to deliver the best results. This is actually in line with the popular saying on Wall Street that the market's job is to confound the maximum number of investors at any given time. When a large number of investors have no idea what will happen, stocks tend to soar. This ensures the maximum number of investors will be wrong.

In addition to AAII's survey, analysts also have access to other surveys.

■ Investors Intelligence

One example is Investors Intelligence, which has published the *Advisors' Sentiment Report* since 1963. This report surveys the market views of over 100 independent investment newsletters (those not affiliated with brokerage houses or mutual funds) and reports the findings as the percentage of advisers that are bullish, bearish, and expecting a correction. An example of this indicator is shown in Figure 38.3.

The report is interpreted as a contrarian indicator. Contrarians go against popular opinion. A large number of bulls is considered to be bearish and a high bearish reading is considered bullish.

In Figure 38.3, when the number of bullish advisors topped 60%, a market pullback was likely. This indicator rarely identifies market bottoms. Investors Intelligence notes that bottoms occur when at least 55% of advisors are bearish, an event that has happened just 10 times since 1987.[2]

---

[1] Charles Rotblut, "Analyzing the AAII Sentiment Survey Without Hindsight," AAII: The American Association of Individual Investors, www.aaii.com/journal/article/analyzing-the-aaii-sentiment-survey-without-hindsight.touch.

[2] Investors Intelligence Global, "Advisors' Sentiment: A Contrarian Approach to Market Timing," www.investorsintelligence.com/x/advisors_sentiment.html.

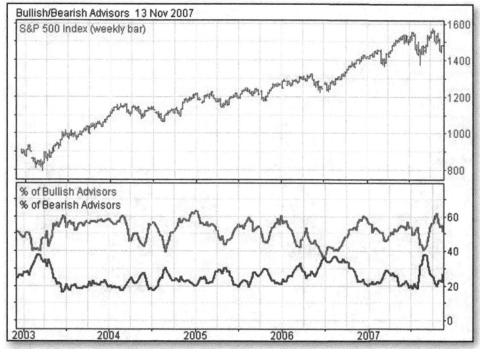

FIGURE 38.3   Bullish and Bearish Advisors

Source: "Advisors' Sentiment: A Contrarian Approach to Market Timing," InvestorsIntelligence.com, www.investorsintelligence.com/x/advisors_sentiment.html.

■ Magazine Covers

Another contrary indicator is the use of the news, or the "magazine cover indicator." This indicator is based on the idea that when an idea is popular enough to be on the cover of a magazine, the trend is about to reverse. If a popular magazine proclaims a bull market, for example, the magazine cover indicates the bull market is near an end.

There's a logic to this rationale. Magazine editors design covers to attract attention. If investors are enthusiastic about the prospects of the stock market, they will react positively to the cover. That should generate sales for the magazine. But the public's enthusiasm for the market comes after they have bought stocks. The cover reflects the fact that investors are already invested in stocks and tells us there is unlikely to be a lot of cash on the sidelines. That is why it is a contrarian indicator.

The most famous example of the magazine cover indicator is *BusinessWeek*'s proclamation of the "Death of Equities" in 1978. It is shown in Figure 38.4 with a more recent example of a cover that preceded a real estate market crash.

The Death of Equities cover proved to be wrong. After a 13-year bear market in stocks that preceded the cover, an historic bull market would push the S&P 500 up by more than 1,400% in the next 20 years.

The real estate magazine cover shown in Figure 38.4 also preceded a major trend reversal. Home prices would fall almost 30% in the four years after that cover appeared as shown in Figure 38.5.

FIGURE 38.4 Notable Magazine Covers

Source: "The Crowd Is Wrong at Turning Points," AllStarCharts.com, May 8, 2012, https://allstarcharts.com/the-crowd-is-wrong-at-turning-points/.

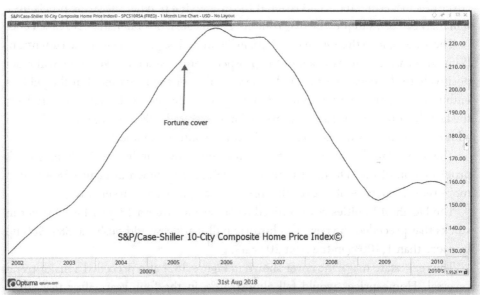

FIGURE 38.5 S&P Case-Shiller 10-City Composite Home Price Index

In the real estate market, the principle for a contrarian indicator is similar to the idea in the stock market. When a number of investors are on the same side of a trade, there is a high probability they are fully invested and there is only a small amount of cash in reserve waiting to be put to work in the market. A lack of buying power will then lead to an end of the rally.

Similarly, during market declines, investors become increasingly bearish and they decrease exposure to the market. The result is that as the level of bearishness increases, selling increases until there are few sellers left in the market. The absence of sellers allows the decline to end and the trend to reverse.

Because the amount of money that buyers have in reserve on the sidelines offers potentially profitable insights, a number of indicators have been developed to track that concept.

■ Mutual Fund Cash/Assets Ratio

For many years, a popular indicator involved tracking the amount of cash mutual fund managers held. The size of the mutual fund market is large, as shown in Figure 38.6.

Equity funds held more than $21 trillion at the end of 2017, an amount that almost doubled in the bull market that began in 2009.

Fund managers will normally hold a small amount of their assets under management (AUM) in cash to meet expenses and to fund redemptions. However, they will generally want to be invested in equities to achieve returns that match or exceed the benchmark average.

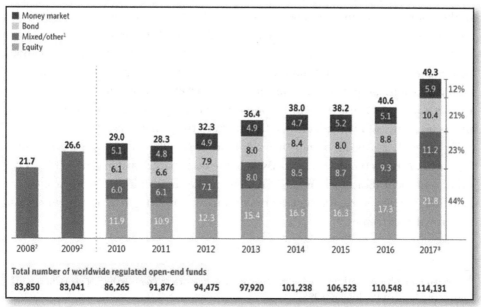

FIGURE 38.6 Total Net Assets of Worldwide Regulated Funds

Source: 2018 Investment Company Fact Book, Investment Company Institute (ICI), www.icifactbook.org/ch1/18_fb_ch1.

Norman Fosback found that tracking the amount of cash held in reserve by fund managers could offer profitable insights into market timing. Fosback focuses on the difference between a fund's actual cash level and what we would otherwise expect that level to be, given prevailing interest rates.[3]

He explained this indicator, which he called the Fosback Index, in 2009: "When interest rates are high, as in the 1970s and 1980s, the funds earn a high risk-free return in the money market and have an obvious risk-reward incentive to own those securities. Similarly, when money rates are lower, as in the late 1990s and throughout this decade, the profit incentive on cash is correspondingly less. This is why the [Mutual Fund] Cash/Assets Ratio was high in the earlier periods and is ultra-low today."[4]

At that time, in the early days of the bull market, Fosback was bullish, demonstrating the value of this indicator.

Unfortunately, market changes have made this information less meaningful. In addition to mutual funds, investors have trillions of dollars invested in exchange-traded funds (ETFs) and mutual fund managers have developed strategies using derivatives to track benchmark indexes. While the mutual fund cash/assets ratio could still be useful, it may not be as reliable in the future as it was in the past.

■ Money Market Fund Assets

Another source of potential buying power is the amount of assets in money market funds. Money market funds seek to maintain a stable net asset value by investing in short-term, high-grade securities sold in the money market. The average maturity of their portfolios is limited to 60 days or less. This makes the funds a cash substitute since investors in money market funds expect their funds to be safe.

As investors sell stocks or other assets in a brokerage account, they generally hold proceeds in a money market fund. By holding the funds in a brokerage account, the cash can readily be put to work in the stock market. That is why assets in money market funds are considered to be potential buying power that could push stock prices up as investors' confidence in the market's trend increases.

In general, assets in money market funds rise when investors are nervous. Figure 38.7 shows the sharp rise in assets in the bear market that began in 2008. Like other sentiment indicators, assets in money market funds rarely provide a signal in isolation. Furthermore, the signals are contrarian, indicating it is best to go against the crowd at extremes.

---

[3] Norman G. Fosback, *Stock Market Logic: A Sophisticated Approach to Profits on Wall Street* (Chicago, IL: Dearborn Financial Publishing, 1998).

[4] Mark Hulbert, "More Bullish than Any Time since Early 1990s," *MarketWatch*, November 17, 2009, https://www.marketwatch.com/story/mutual-funds-cash-levels-are-quite-high-2009-11-17. Accessed September 3, 2018.

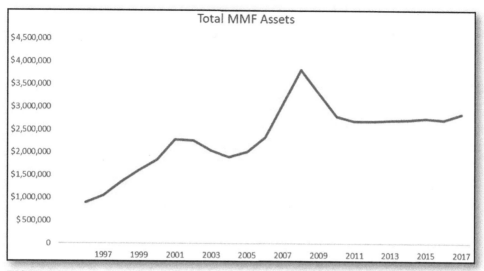

FIGURE 38.7   Total Money Market Fund Assets, in Millions

Source: 2018 Investment Company Fact Book, Investment Company Institute,
www.icifactbook.org/data/18_fb_data#section4.

BASIC STATISTICS FOR THE TECHNICAL ANALYST

Baseball is 90% mental and the other half is physical.

—Yogi Berra

The community of technical analysts is an amalgam of scientists and artists. It may well be that the most insightful technicians are those that are ambidextrous: able to brainstorm creatively yet also adept with the modern tools of math and computing power.

Whether examining market returns, performance metrics, or common indicators, technical analysts must discern between statistical validity and, well, useless vapidity. Of course, we all use computers to do the heavy lifting of calculations. But a solid understanding of statistical terms and methods points the way to the best uses—and the appropriate skepticism—for statistical results.

This section is an introduction to statistics designed for technical analysts. It covers two critically important topics: descriptive statistics and probability, specifically as they relate to the technician's work.

Descriptive statistics provide much of the language we use in characterizing the body of data called price. Probability studies offer methods for making informed judgments about what might be expected from markets and trading systems over time.

Bear in mind that the material in this section will be important as you delve into trading system development and evaluation, indicator construction, and portfolio allocation.

CHAPTER 39

Introduction to Descriptive Statistics

Jonas Elmerraji, CMT

Learning Objective Statements

- Describe the three most common measures of central tendency: mean, median, and mode
- Discuss alternative methods of calculating the mean and their uses
- Describe what is meant by "measures of dispersion"
- Explain two measures of dispersion: standard deviation and variance
- State the value of data visualization as a complement to descriptive statistics

■ Introduction

FIGURE 39.1
Source: xkcd.com.

Statistics is the science of learning from data.

If that sounds like a broad and far-reaching definition, it should. Statistics touches every field of study, from physics to social sciences to finance. Simply put, it is the set of tools that helps us separate fact from fiction.

Statistical measures are also a core ingredient in many popular classical and modern technical indicators and trading strategies. All that makes statistical analysis a crucial part of the modern technical analyst's toolbox.

Understanding statistical analysis is also what separates professional technical analysts from hobbyists dabbling with trading. We live in an increasingly data-driven and quantified world. Even if your own approach to the markets does not make you a "quant," knowing how to look at the markets from a statistical vantage point can provide important perspective and context for your analysis.

Statistics can help technicians answer difficult questions, such as:

Is the ascending triangle still an effective price pattern in 2019?

Is a strategy that has generated 10% average annual returns over the past five years the result of a powerful predictive signal? Or might those kinds of results be due to random chance?

Likewise, one of the reasons statistical analysis is so crucial to understand is because all is not always what it seems in the financial world. In a 2014 paper published in the *Journal of Portfolio Management,*[1] Professors Harvey and Liu made a jarring revelation:

> Most of the empirical research in finance, whether published in academic journals or put into production as an active trading strategy by an investment manager, is likely false. Second, this implies that half the financial products (promising outperformance) that companies are selling to clients are false.

That does not necessarily mean that a large swatch of financial practitioners is trying to deceive; the statistical tools and procedures many of them have been using for years are flawed.

Along those same lines, the proliferation of exchange-traded funds (ETF) has made getting exposure to various asset classes, investment factors, and investment styles easier than ever before. The challenge is that a growing collection of research has shown that many, many ETFs fail to capture the very exposures they are de-signed to capture.[2] Simply put, the onus is on market participants to validate that the conclusions made by others are sound.

[1] C.R. Harvey and Y. Liu, "Evaluating Trading Strategies," *The Journal of Portfolio Management Special 40th Anniversary Issue* 40, no. 5 (2014): 108–118. DOI: https://doi.org/10.3905/jpm.2014.40.5.108

[2] W. Gray, "Academic Factor Exposure versus Fund Factor Exposure" [Web log post] (April 26, 2017), https://alphaarchitect.com/2017/04/26/academic-factor-exposure-versus-fund-factor-exposure/.

As a modern technician, you have access to amounts of data that Charles Dow could not even have imagined when he penned the basis of Dow Theory a century ago. Statistics can help you make sense of those data points.

This content is designed to provide you with an introduction (or refresher, in many cases) to key statistical concepts through the lens of the technical analyst.

■ Descriptive Statistics

At a high level, statistics is often broken into two subdomains: descriptive statistics and inferential statistics. As the name implies, descriptive statistics is about describing or summarizing data using quantitative or visual tools. For this reason, the term "summary statistics" is often used to describe common descriptive statistics.

Inferential statistics, on the other hand, builds on descriptive statistics to draw conclusions or inferences based on that data.

Descriptive statistics serve an incredibly important role for investors in particular: they summarize large, unruly datasets into more understandable pieces. This should not sound like anything new. As a technical analyst, you have already been exposed to many tools that help to summarize the enormous datasets that comprise price action.

Take, for instance, a popular stock like Apple, Inc., which by itself trades an average of 26.5 million shares on a given day, as of 2018. That volume of data adds up across the whole market. As of this writing, a single day of raw textual trading data for the S&P 500 can take up approximately 2GB of storage space!

Most investors, professional and amateur alike, simply could not handle the sheer volume of raw data generated by a single stock, let alone many of them. Because of this, most of us use a summary of the price action over a set time frame, such as daily or hourly price data and charts.

Even then, it can be impossible to keep track of what is happening in the thousands of stocks that make up the market. You can think of stock market indexes like the S&P 500 as a descriptive statistic of sorts for the market as a whole. It provides an imperfect (but very useful) summary of what is happening in the market.

The descriptive statistics we will explore in these pages are much like stock market indexes, only they generalize to more applications than just the stock market.

Specifically, we will look at two major classes of descriptive statistics: measures of central tendency and measures of variability.

Measures of Central Tendency

Measures of central tendency look at where the bulk of the data lies. In other words, averages.

Averages play an important role for the technical analyst because they are a key building block of many technical indicators, most notably moving averages. It is worth noting that from an academic finance perspective, measures of central tendency are

TABLE 39.1 Dow Jones Industrial Average Returns by Year

Year	Dow Return
2007	6%
2008	−34%
2009	19%
2010	11%
2011	6%
2012	7%
2013	27%
2014	8%
2015	−2%
2016	13%
2017	25%

Source: Bloomberg.

used to determine expected returns, E[R]. This concept will come into play later in this section.

To aid in understanding measures of central tendency, it makes sense to take a practical example from finance. We will look at the annual performance of the Dow Jones Industrial Average between 2007 and 2017, rounded to the nearest whole percentage. This can be found in Table 39.1.

One thing that is important to note is that there is no panacea when it comes to picking a measure of central tendency—each method has pros and cons. To find the ideal summary statistics, you need to have a solid understanding of your data's quirks and characteristics.

Mean The most common measure of central tendency is the mean. While the technical term for this statistic is the arithmetic mean (a way of differentiating from other approaches to calculating the mean), this is the stat most people are talking about when they use the term "average" or "mean."

The mean is simply the sum of the observations divided by the number of observations. In mathematical notation, the formula for mean looks like this:

$$\overline{x} = \frac{1}{n}\sum_{i=1}^{n} x_i$$

where, n is the number of observations we are averaging, and x_i is the ith observation. By convention, the mean is referred to as $\overline{x}$ (pronounced x-bar).

With our Dow Jones Industrial Average example introduced above, the mean annual return would be the sum of each of the annual returns, divided by 11:

$$\frac{(6\% + -34\% + 19\% + 11\% + 6\% + 7\% + 27\% + 8\% + -2\% + 13\% + 25\%)}{11}$$

The answer is 7.8%. Bear in mind that the exact number may not show up in our annual return data (although a couple of years are very close). Even so, that 7.8% number summarizes the Dow's performance over that 11-year stretch.

It is important to note a couple of characteristics of the arithmetic mean. First, this statistic is heavily impacted by outliers. Second, each observation counts equally. These characteristics can present problems. For instance, you may believe that more recent observations should carry more significance than Dow returns a decade ago. We will look at ways to handle this situation later in this chapter.

Median The median is the middle number in a dataset. In other words, if you randomly mixed up the Dow return numbers from Table 39.1 in a hat, any number you drew from that hat would have an equal chance at being above or below the median of the group.

To determine the median for our Dow dataset, we first arrange our returns in order from smallest to largest, and then eliminate one entry from each end of the series until we end up with a single final value. Note that this only works when we have an odd number of observations in our dataset. If we have an even number, we take the mean of the final two observations.

For our Dow dataset, the median return is 8%:

~~−34%~~, ~~−2%~~, ~~6%~~, ~~6%~~, ~~7%~~, 8%, ~~11%~~, ~~13%~~, ~~19%~~, ~~25%~~, ~~27%~~

The biggest benefit of the median is that it is not influenced by large outliers. If 2008 had been a −60% year, the median would remain at 8%, while the mean return would have been pulled lower. This is one reason why the median is often used to summarize datasets with exceptionally large outliers, such as income surveys.

The median is also a better measure of central tendency when our data is skewed. (More detail about skewness is given in Chapter 40.)

Mode The mode is the observation that occurs most often in a dataset. In the Dow returns example from Table 39.1, the mode is 6%, the only return value that appears twice. The mode is the least common of the three major measures of central tendency in terms of popularity, but it does have quite a bit of value when looking at categorical data. For instance, when looking at a dataset of car sales, if we group unit sales by car model, the mode will identify which specific model is the most popular.

Note that it is possible for there to be no mode or even more than one mode in a given dataset. For instance, if the next year brought another 11% move in the Dow, the data would become bimodal, with modes at 6% and 11%.

Geometric Mean   The geometric mean is a less-common average outside of the finance world, but this measure of central tendency is incredibly useful for investors. The geometric mean is unique in that it can be used to find an average across items that have different scales. In other words, the observations in a geometric mean are *scaling factors*, not absolutes. This is useful in applications like portfolio construction.

For instance, the geometric mean of a portfolio's various returns over a set number of periods gives us the rate that portfolio would need to return to produce the same final value if each return was the same. Or, put more simply, its compound rate of return.

Why is the geometric mean so important to investors? It is because time series datasets ruin the interpretability of the arithmetic mean.

Let us look at a simple example.

Imagine a stock whose return is −50% the first year, and 75% the second year. In this situation, the arithmetic mean of the two returns is simply $(−0.5 + 0.75)/2 = .125$, or 12.5%. Clearly, a 12.5% return is not close to being representative of the investment's actual performance. Worse, if you had invested $100 in that stock, you'd end up with $50 after year one, and $87.50 after year two—ultimately a losing investment, despite the positive return the simple average gave us!

The geometric mean can help us account for those issues. The geometric mean can be calculated using the following equation:

$$GM = \left(\prod_{i=1}^{n} x_i \right)^{1/n}$$

Once again, n is the number of observations we are averaging, and x_i is the ith observation.

That equation is actually very similar to the arithmetic mean. Instead of summing the observations in our dataset and dividing by the number of observations, we find their product by multiplying them together. Then, we take the nth root.

(That large *pi* symbol signifies product notation—it behaves much like the summation notation used in the equation for simple mean, except it signifies that we are multiplying each x_i observation instead of adding.)

Because the observations in our dataset are really scaling factors when we use a geometric mean, they do not play nicely with zeros or negative numbers, both common results when dealing with investment returns. To cope with that, we add 1 to each of our returns before plugging them into the equation, then subtract it at the end.

For our imaginary stock example, we can calculate our geometric mean as follows:

$$GM = (0.5 \times 1.75)^{1/2} = \sqrt{0.875} = 0.9354$$
$$0.9354 - 1 = -0.0646$$

Computing the geometric mean above gives us a compound annual return of −6.46%. It is no coincidence that is the average annual rate that would turn our $100 investment into $87.50 over two years. In other words, using the geometric mean preserves the compound nature of investment returns.

Weighted Arithmetic Mean   One final type of average that technical analysts need to be aware of is a variant of the simple arithmetic mean we discussed at the start of this section: the weighted arithmetic mean, better known as the weighted average.

The weighted arithmetic mean is a way to cope with one of the major limitations of the simple mean: the idea that all observations count equally. One clear application of this for technicians is the moving average.

With a 200-day simple moving average, the price of the stock yesterday has the same impact on the 200-day moving average as the price of the stock almost a year ago. Depending on the instrument and what it has done in the intervening months, it might be more appropriate to put a greater weight on more recent prices and a lower weight on older prices.

The solution is to use a weighted average.

A weighted average multiplies each observation in a dataset by some weighting factor before adding it to subsequent observations, then divides the result by the sum of the weights:

$$\overline{x} = \frac{\sum_{i=1}^{n} W_i x_i}{\sum_{i=1}^{n} W_i}$$

where n is the number of observations we're averaging, x_i is the ith observation, and W_i is the weighting factor for that ith observation.

The actual weighting factor (W_i) for a given observation can vary. For instance, a portfolio's returns can be calculated by simply multiplying each stock's individual return by its weight in the portfolio and summing the results.

For the purposes of moving averages, the popular exponential moving average is actually just a weighted arithmetic mean of prices, where another separate equation is used to decrease weighting factors exponentially as the age of the data increases.

One of the simplest examples of a weighted mean in technical analysis is the linearly weighted moving average. It simply weights each observation so that the oldest observation is weighted by 1 and the newest is weighted by the number of observations. For instance, a 200-day linearly weighted moving average would multiply today's price by 200, yesterday's price by 199, and so on.

Imagine we want to compute a 5-day linearly weighted moving average for the following price data at a given point in time.

TABLE 39.2   **Five Days of Stock Prices**

Days Ago	1 (Most Recent Price)	2	3	4	5
Price	282.38	280.86	281.33	279.95	281.42

The equation to calculate the linearly weighted moving average for that day would be:

$$\frac{(5 \times 282.38 + 4 \times 280.86 + 3 \times 281.33 + 2 \times 279.95 + 1 \times 281.42)}{5 + 4 + 3 + 2 + 1}$$

$$= \frac{4220.65}{15} \approx 281.38$$

By weighting our moving average, we assign greater value to more recent observations in our dataset.

Measures of Dispersion

Thinking back to our Dow price return data from Table 39.1, the various averages we have looked at *do* help us figure out where the bulk of the returns ended up, but they are missing a very important element. They fail to give us any idea of how the observations are spread out.

For instance, we have already figured out that the mean return of the Dow between 2007 and 2017 was 7.8%. But that number alone leaves out the fact that the Dow plunged 34%, or that it rallied 25% or more twice in just five years. The mean does not tell us anything about how volatile the Dow's returns are—for that, we need another factor. That other factor, called dispersion, is a critical piece of the puzzle when summarizing a dataset.

Just like measures of central tendency correspond to expected returns in academic finance, there is a similar mapping for dispersion: volatility, or risk. In fact, the notion that statistical dispersion equals risk is so deeply ingrained in the investment community that we actually use dispersion measures like standard deviation as a stand-in for risk itself.

This should make sense intuitively. If the Dow's mean is an approximation of its typical return in a given year in our dataset, dispersion can help us measure the risk that it missed that mark for any given year. In other words, dispersion measures the volatility of the return series around the average.

Standard Deviation and Variance Standard deviation and variance are the two most common measures of dispersion. It makes sense to talk about them as a unit because they are so closely related.

Standard deviation, generally represented as σ, measures how far a set of observations are scattered from their average. For any given sample of observations, standard deviation is calculated with the following equation:

$$\sigma = \sqrt{\frac{\sum_{i=1}^{n}(x_i - \overline{x})^2}{n-1}}$$

where, x_1 through x_n are our observations, $\overline{x}$ is the mean value of the observations, and n is the number of observations.

Stated simply, the equation finds the average squared difference of the group, then takes the square root. The variance, usually represented as σ^2, simply leaves out the square root. In other words, variance is the square of standard deviation.

Because of this relationship, standard deviation and variance both effectively measure the same thing. The difference is that standard deviation is measured on the same scale as the mean, which gives it better interpretability.

Getting a Fuller Picture

While the descriptive statistics we have looked at in this chapter can go a long way toward summarizing datasets, they still fall short of providing a complete picture. Thankfully, as a technical analyst, you are already familiar with an extremely effective way of summarizing data: visual methods.

Consider the four distinct datasets graphed in Figure 39.2. These four groups of points are called Anscombe's quartet; they were constructed in 1973 by English

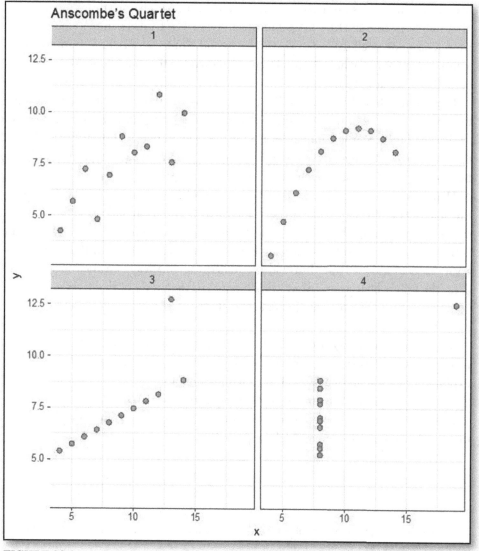

FIGURE 39.2 Anscombe's Quartet

statistician Francis Anscombe. At a glance, the datasets could not look much more different—which is why it may come as such a surprise that the four plots of points actually have *the exact same summary statistics*.[3]

In fact, the summary statistics that all four datasets have in common actually go beyond what we have looked at in these pages so far. In addition to identical means and variances, the four datasets also have identical correlations, regression lines, and coefficients of determination. Looking purely at those values, it would be tempting to conclude that the four datasets are very similar to one another. But, of course, the scatterplots in Figure 39.2 paint a very different picture.

Looking at data graphically can provide an instant snapshot of what is really happening in that data. The idea of using visual methods to summarize relationships between data was popularized in the science world by the well-known statistician John Tukey in his 1977 book *Exploratory Data Analysis*. But technical analysts have been using charts to summarize market data for centuries before that.

Going back to our Dow Jones Industrial Average returns example (Table 39.1), we can take our small dataset of Dow returns and plot them on a histogram to create a visual summary of what a "typical" annual return for the index looks like. We have done this in Figure 39.3.

Histograms show how data is distributed across a single variable. Each bar cuts the possible returns of the Dow into 5% increments. At a glance, Figure 39.3 shows us that the most common annual return for the Dow between 2007 and 2017 fell in the 2.5% to 7.5% range. If we are trying to get a grasp on what a "typical" year looks like for the Dow, this simple chart packs a lot of insight.

Histograms also summarize data by sorting observations into bins. Changing the size of the bins can change the shape of the histogram and provide some insights that may not otherwise be readily apparent. In Figure 39.3, the tallest bin is the one that holds returns ranging from 2.5% to 7.5%. You can think of this as a variation of mode. If the bin-width equaled the smallest unit measured in our data, the tallest histogram bar would be equal to the mode of the dataset. We will come back to a variation of this chart in the next chapter, when we delve into probability.

You already know how useful charting techniques like candlestick charts can be at conveying information. As it turns out, a very similar-looking chart can be useful for exploratory data analysis as well. It is called the boxplot.

The boxplot graphically shows a dataset's quartiles, which break each dataset into four subsets with equal numbers of observations. A bigger box on a boxplot means that the data points are more widely scattered.

[3] F. Anscombe, "Graphs in Statistical Analysis," *The American Statistician* 27, no. 1 (1973), 17–21, DOI:10.2307/2682899.

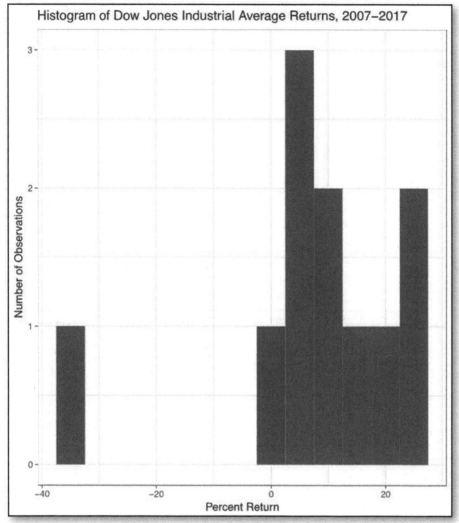

FIGURE 39.3   A Histogram of Dow Returns, 2007–2017

Figure 39.4 shows a boxplot of daily stock returns for the group of large technology stocks often referred to as the "FAANGs": Facebook, Amazon.com, Apple, Netflix, and Alphabet. While similar, one of the five stocks is not quite like the others: Netflix has a much wider range for daily returns than its peers during this time frame; it is a more volatile stock.

Exploratory data analysis can also be useful in telling us when there is no exploitable relationship. While all five FAANG stocks have slightly different-sized boxes, they are all approximately centered around the same (slightly positive) daily return. That is an indication that none of the FAANG stocks systematically outperformed the rest of the pack during this time frame.

Both the histogram and boxplot look at a single variable: in our examples, we used annual and daily returns, respectively. We can also look at relationships between multiple variables.

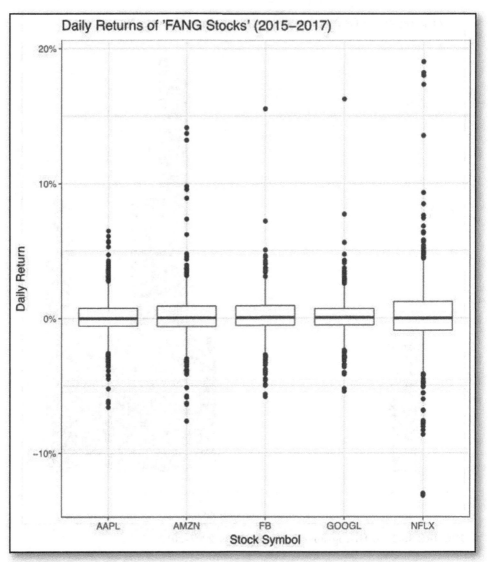

FIGURE 39.4 **A Boxplot of Returns for Apple, Amazon, Facebook, Alphabet, and Netflix, 2015–2017**

Using our FAANG data on a scatterplot, we can graph the daily returns of Amazon against Alphabet to see how daily returns of one stock on a given day affect the daily returns of the other. This is shown in Figure 39.5.

At a glance, Figure 39.5 shows that there is a relationship between Amazon and Alphabet. In general, higher returns in one stock tend to correlate with higher returns in the other. This sort of information may be useful when deciding on stock exposures, for example. Owning too many highly correlated stocks could make exposure to an adverse event bigger than it otherwise appears.

Likewise, identifying conditions that cause outlier points on the scatterplot could be the jumping-off point for identifying an exploitable market phenomenon when the relationship between the two stocks breaks down.

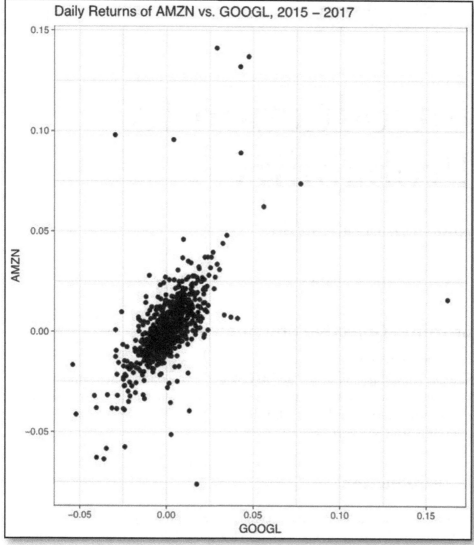

FIGURE 39.5 A Scatterplot of Daily Returns for AMZN versus GOOGL

The types of charts presented in this chapter are by no means an exhaustive list of the graphical techniques for summarizing statistics. They should be seen as a starting point for technicians who wish to use their skills at visual pattern identification on statistical data.

We live in a data-centric world today. According to analytics firm IDC, more data will be created in the next two years than in the entire history of the human race.[4] Some of that mountain of data undoubtedly contains profitable investment signals. The challenge is organizing and summarizing that data in a way that makes sense to market participants. Descriptive statistics give us the tools to summarize investment data in useful ways.

[4] IDC, *The Digital Universe of Opportunities: Rich Data and the Increasing Value of the Internet of Things* [White paper] (2014), https://www.emc.com/leadership/digital-universe/2014iview/executive-summary.htm.

CHAPTER 40

Introduction to Probability

Jonas Elmerraji, CMT

Learning Objective Statements

- Define probability
- Explain the impact of the law of large numbers on a series of outcomes
- Define random variable and the phrase "independent and identically distributed"
- Describe a normal probability distribution
- Identify skew and kurtosis

▉ Introduction

Odds are you have at least a passing familiarity with probability.

You may be less familiar, however, with how probabilities relate to the investment world. This section was written to provide you with some probabilistic intuition about financial markets.

If I told you that I could virtually guarantee flipping any fair coin and getting 10 heads in a row, you would think that I was cheating somehow. After all, if the odds of heads or tails are 50-50, the odds of getting a streak of 10 heads in a row are slim to none.

Or, specifically, the odds are about 1 in 1,024. That is a probability of less than one tenth of 1%. But what if I told you that I could just about guarantee a run of 10 straight heads?

Flip any fair coin 4,713 times, and you will almost certainly see a run of 10 heads—in fact, there is less than a 1% chance you will not! (And whether the run of 10 heads shows up in the first 10 coin flips or afterward just boils down to random chance.)

There are a couple of important takeaways from this coin-flip example. The first is that the famous line from British economist Ronald Coase holds true here: "If you torture the data long enough, it will confess." Even incredibly unlikely events can be forced by playing with the statistics. The other important takeaway from this example is the significance of randomness, even in situations where we understand the probabilities well.

Pure chance dictates where the run of 10 heads falls within our 4,713-flip experiment. Furthermore, flipping a coin 4,713 times doesn't even *totally* guarantee we will see a run of 10 heads; while the probabilities tell us that it will happen 99 times out of every 100, randomness can still hand you that 1-in-100 scenario that does not work out. In the world of statistics, there are no certainties, only confidence intervals.

And if that randomness is not accounted for, it can wreak havoc on our investment results. The purpose of this section is to introduce you to some of the basics of probability—and the challenges that make it difficult to apply them to the financial markets.

■ The Search for the High-Probability Trade

As a technical analyst, it is likely you have already been exposed to the idea of a probabilistic approach to the financial markets. After all, even the newest trader understands that there is no guarantee that a given trade will be profitable—even if it is a so-called "high-probability trade."

Because financial markets are incredibly noisy from a statistical standpoint, randomness can play a large role in investment returns.

That poses a challenge to investment managers because it means that even valid trading systems can produce prolonged streaks of underperformance. Just like extremely improbable events like runs of 10 straight heads become highly likely across many coin flips, statistically profitable investment strategies can produce surprising runs of prolonged underperformance across many trades.

If those runs happen to present themselves in the early stages of a strategy's performance, a manager may be met with a drawdown that takes many years to recover from, or that even prompts unsurvivable redemptions from investors.

On the other hand, a result of the noisy nature of the markets that is less often acknowledged is the fact that positive performance due to randomness can lead to false discoveries—that is, employing strategies that make money due to luck alone.

Is a strategy that has generated 10% average annual returns over the past five years the result of a powerful predictive signal? Or might those kinds of results be the result of random chance?

How about 20% returns? Or 40% returns?

While we will not spend much time on those specific questions in this section, it is important to realize that those questions are rarely easy to answer. Like our coin-flip example at the start of this chapter, there are no certainties, only confidence intervals.

■ Properties of Probability

Before we dive into the properties of probability, we should define it. Probability measures the extent to which an event is likely to occur. Probabilities are measured on a scale between 0 and 1. A probability of 0 indicates that an event is more or less impossible, while a probability of 1 indicates proximate certainty. Practically speaking, the majority of probabilities we are concerned with fall somewhere in between.

For a given event (E) with N mutually exclusive and equally likely outcomes, the probability of E is classically defined by:

$$P(E) = \frac{N_E}{N}$$

In other words, the probability of E is the number of potential outcomes that result in the event divided by the number of total possible outcomes. For instance, with our coin flip example, the probability of flipping heads on a fair coin is $P(H) = \frac{Heads}{Heads\ or\ Tails} = \frac{1}{2}$.

The outcome of our coin toss is an example of a random variable because the result is dictated by a random phenomenon. While we know that our coin flip will end up resulting in either heads or tails, the result we get on any given flip is random. Over many coin flips, though, the law of large numbers dictates that the average of the results will end up close to the expected probability of 0.5.

Figure 40.1 shows the occurrence of heads in a simulation of 500 flips of a fair coin. While the outcome of any given flip is random, the occurrence of heads over the entire experiment (the empirical probability of flipping a head) ultimately converges with the theoretical probability of flipping a head as the number of coin flips increases.

What this suggests is that, assuming a true high-probability trading strategy (that is, one where the alpha generated is not due purely to chance), the outcome of any single trade might be random, but the probabilistic expectation is that over a large number of trades, the observed win rate converges with the true win rate of the strategy.

One important assumption being made in our coin toss example and many other prototypical probability examples is that our random variables are independent and identically distributed (often abbreviated i.i.d.). Independence means that the occurrence of one event does not affect the probability of the occurrence of the other. With a coin flip, independence means that the event of flipping heads is not impacted by how many heads were flipped in prior coin tosses. This can be a hard concept for many people to grasp—even after flipping nine heads, the probability of flipping heads on the 10th toss is still 0.5.

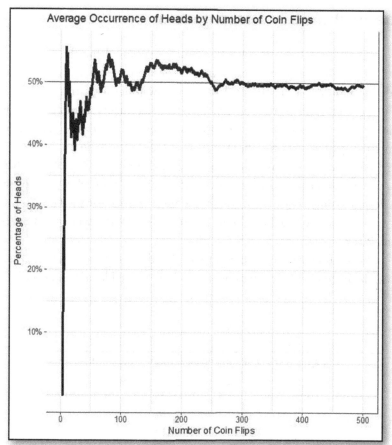

FIGURE 40.1 **Average Occurrence of Heads by Number of Coin Flips**

(Casinos' roulette tables generally display the results of previous roulette spins on a tote board for this very reason. Gamblers often feel compelled to bet based on those prior winning spins even though the odds of the next spin are not affected by what has happened before.)

Identically distributed variables are variables with the same probability distribution. For example, if we flip two identical coins back-to-back, each has the same probability of resulting in heads. If, however, one coin has a different probability of heads coming up than the other, then the two coins are not identically distributed. It is important to note that identically distributed does not necessarily mean that outcomes must be equally probable; two coins that each have a 70% probability of resulting in heads would be identically distributed.

The i.i.d. assumption is a key assumption of many statistical calculations. This is important to be aware of, because a large body of academic research has shown that financial return series data is not an i.i.d. process.

■ The Probability Distribution

Recall our Dow Jones Industrial Average return example from the previous chapter.

Figure 36.3 shows a histogram of returns for the Dow between 2007 and 2017. If we add more observations to our dataset of Dow Jones Industrial Average returns, we start to get a clearer picture of how the Dow's annual returns are distributed.

Figure 40.2 is a histogram of Dow Jones Industrial Average returns from 1921 through 2017. Just as with the shorter span of Dow returns in the previous chapter (Figure 36.3), the dataset shown in the histogram in Figure 40.2 of this chapter can provide us with descriptive statistics that summarize a "typical" return for the Dow. In fact, despite being longer by 86 years, the mean return for the Dow in the longer dataset is 7.95%, a mere 0.14% difference from the 7.81% average return between 2007 and 2017.

One interesting takeaway from Figure 40.2 is that as the number of observations increases, the histogram of returns begins to look more like a "bell curve." This is an

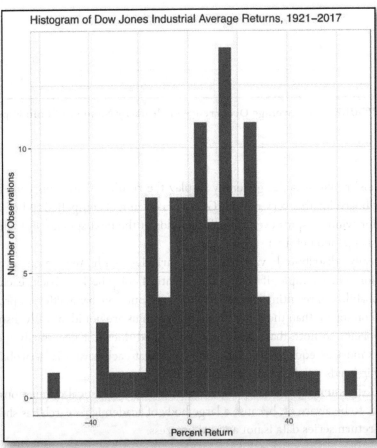

FIGURE 40.2   A Histogram of Dow Returns, 1921–2017

example of a probability distribution, a function that provides the probabilities of occurrences of different possible outcomes for a random variable.

In other words, a probability distribution helps us understand what is likely given some amount of randomness.

The Normal Distribution

The best-known bell curve is the normal distribution (also sometimes called a Gaussian distribution). The normal distribution can be found in many applications; for instance, human height and weight across a population tend to be more or less normally distributed (Figure 40.3).

We can also plot on our distribution the descriptive statistics that we discussed in the previous chapter in order to get a better visual sense of where our data lie, as well as how probable a given observation is within the context of the distribution.

This is useful when evaluating strategy performance as well as understanding the likelihood behind surprising events, like the deep drawdowns the Dow took in 2008.

A variation of the normal distribution is the log-normal distribution, which refers to a random variable whose logarithm is normally distributed. This is a commonly used distribution in finance because in some markets it has been found to be a better approximation of return distributions.

Before moving on, it is important to address the commonly repeated observation that stock price returns do not follow a normal distribution. Academic studies have repeatedly shown[1] that the actual return distributions empirically exhibited by stock prices are not normally distributed. This is one reason why price shocks occur far more frequently than academic models would suggest.

One of the consequences of this is that the assumption of normality made by many indicators (such as those using standard deviation) means that they do not necessarily do what investors think they do.

For example, under a normal distribution, we expect that observations will only exceed two standard deviations above or below the mean 5% of the time. However, in 2008, daily returns for the S&P 500 exceeded this threshold by almost a factor of three.

Many statistics have a normality assumption in their interpretation. Likewise, many academic models have some assumption of normally distributed returns baked in. For that reason, it is wise for technical analysts to use caution when relying on common statistical tools (particularly complex ones) to draw a conclusion.

Other Common Distributions

The normal distribution is far from the only probability distribution—it is merely the best known. Another (even simpler) type of distribution is the uniform

[1] C.D. Kirkpatrick and J.R. Dahlquist, *Technical Analysis* (Upper Saddle River, NJ: FT Press, 2007).

distribution, which represents a situation where all intervals of the same length on the distribution are equally probable. For instance, a series of rolls of dice follow a uniform distribution (Figure 40.4).

The uniform distribution is sometimes used to detect fraud by examining the rightmost digits of a study or investment return series where the numbers are reported with a very high degree of precision. In these cases, the rightmost digit of the number is effectively random, and follows a uniform distribution. Spotting cases where certain digits appear more frequently than is likely under the uniform distribution can be a tip off that the numbers were fabricated.

Another useful distribution is the binomial distribution, which is used to measure probabilities of events with two distinct outcomes. For instance, a trading strategy with a 70% win rate could be modeled as a binomial distribution with $P(\text{win}) = 0.7$ and $P(\text{loss}) = 0.3$. Of course, this naively assumes that our wins and losses don't have the same statistical issues that returns do, but it can still be a useful model to have available.

Skewness and Kurtosis

For the modern investor, it has become important to be familiar with the terms skewness and kurtosis. While these words were once the exclusive domain of statisticians, the increasing quantification of investment performance using statistical tools has made them a common sight in the investment world.

Skewness and kurtosis are statistics that describe the way a probability distribution looks.

Skewness is the degree to which returns are asymmetric around the mean. Figure 40.3 shows a symmetric normal distribution with a skewness of zero. The return histogram for the Dow Jones Industrial Average shown in Figure 40.2, however, exhibits some negative skew. The skewness is positive when the right "tail" of the distribution is larger than the left side (that is, it is stretched to the right).

A comparison of a normal probability density function versus one with negative skew is shown in Figure 40.5.

All things being equal, positive skewness is preferred because it means that deviations from the mean tend to average higher returns; there is more area on the right side of the density curve. One important side effect of high levels of skewness is that conventional measures of risk that assume symmetric distributions (such as standard deviation) no longer do a good job of assessing risk.

Kurtosis, on the other hand, measures the degree to which returns show up in the tails of a distribution. Looking at Figure 40.2, the Dow's returns do not tail off at zero occurrences as a normal distribution might suggest—instead, there are small "fat tails" at the return extremes.

A normal distribution, such as the one in Figure 40.3, has kurtosis of 3. Distributions with higher kurtosis have more returns out in the tails. Kurtosis is often measured relative to the normal distribution—in this case, a distribution with

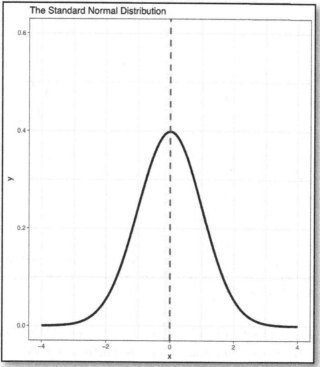

FIGURE 40.3 The Standard Normal Distribution:
Mean = 0 and Standard Deviation = 1

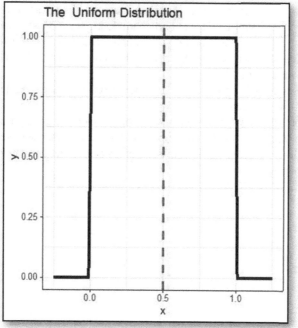

FIGURE 40.4 The Uniform Distribution

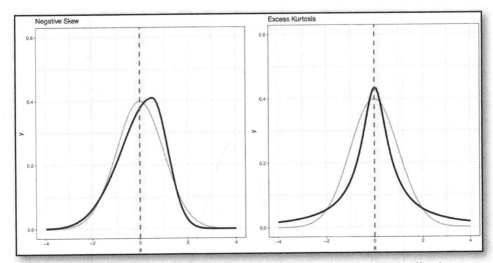

FIGURE 40.5 Negative Skew, Positive Excess Kurtosis, and Normal Distribution.

Note: (Left) A distribution with negative skew. (Right) A distribution with positive excess kurtosis. Normal distributions shown in gray.

excess kurtosis of 1 would actually have kurtosis of 4. The right panel of Figure 40.5 shows a probability density function with excess kurtosis of 1.95.

Generally speaking, lower kurtosis is seen as a good thing because the size and occurrence of "tail events" are lower.

How Can I Do This Myself?

Reading about statistical tools is one thing, but actually implementing them is another.

As you read this section on statistical analysis, you may find yourself wondering how to actually implement the statistics, tests, and charts found here. Most of the tools found in these pages can be replicated using common spreadsheet software, such as Microsoft Excel. Excel's free Analysis ToolPak add-in provides many statistical tools not found in the base version of the program.

Trading software, such as Optuma or TradeStation, can also calculate statistics on securities as well as portfolios.

Even more sophisticated end-to-end analysis can be done using programming languages such as R and Python and the free and open-source data science libraries and packages maintained by their respective communities. All of the charts and simulations shown in this section were generated from R code.

PERSPECTIVES ON TECHNICAL TRADING SYSTEMS

It is common sense to take a method and try it. If it fails, admit it frankly and try another. But above all, try something.

—**Franklin Delano Roosevelt**

Many technical analysts and traders believe that systematic trading is the pinnacle application of technical analysis. In this age of information, we have the power to make an incredible number of calculations in the blink of an eye, based on both historical and real-time data. At the least, applying the logical structures required by a trading system to trading methods forces the analyst/trader to a more rigorous and empirical game. This section introduces many of those logical processes in theory and in practice.

The discussion begins with a vocabulary and framework for testing technical signals. This ranges from the definition of a "rule" to variations and inversions of traditional rules. Properly performing such tests offers the technician insights into what might contribute, or be extraneous, to the success of a trading methodology.

The section goes on to identify both the critical mindset the developer needs to do the challenging work of building trading models and examples of integrating "internal" and "external" indicators into a single model.

Finally, this section, and the book, closes with a chapter that ties one of technical analysis' most venerated methods, relative strength, to the modern tools of empirical testing and investment.

CHAPTER 41

Objective Rules and Their Evaluation

From David Aronson, *Evidence-Based Technical Analysis* (Hoboken, New Jersey: John Wiley & Sons, 2006), Chapter 1.

Learning Objective Statements

- Describe objective and subjective methods in technical analysis
- Define "rule" as used in trading systems
- Explain binary rules as well as individual and multiple thresholds
- Identify traditional rules and inverse rules
- Discuss the importance of benchmarking in evaluating trading rules
- Describe the key components of "trading costs"
- Describe the value of using detrended prices

This chapter introduces the notion of objective binary signaling rules and a methodology for their rigorous evaluation. It defines an evaluation benchmark based on the profitability of a noninformative signal. It also establishes the need to detrend market data so that the performances of rules with different long/short position biases can be compared.

■ The Great Divide: Objective versus Subjective Technical Analysis

Technical analysis (TA) divides into two broad categories: objective and subjective. Subjective TA is comprised of analysis methods and patterns that are not precisely defined. As a consequence, a conclusion derived from a subjective method reflects the private interpretations of the analyst applying the method. This creates the possibility that two analysts applying the same method to the same set of market data may arrive at entirely different conclusions. Therefore, subjective methods are untestable, and claims that they are effective are exempt from empirical challenge. This is fertile ground for myths to flourish.

In contrast, objective methods are clearly defined. When an objective analysis method is applied to market data, its signals or predictions are unambiguous. This makes it possible to simulate the method on historical data and determine its precise level of performance. This is called back testing. The back testing of an objective method is, therefore, a repeatable experiment which allows claims of profitability to be tested and possibly refuted with statistical evidence. This makes it possible to find out which objective methods are effective and which are not.

The acid test for distinguishing an objective from a subjective method is the *programmability criterion: A method is objective if and only if it can be implemented as a computer program that produces unambiguous market positions (long,[1] short,[2] or neutral[3]).* All methods that cannot be reduced to such a program are, by default, subjective.

■ TA Rules

Objective TA methods are also referred to as mechanical trading rules or trading systems. In this book, all objective TA methods are referred to simply as *rules*.

A rule is a function that transforms one or more items of information, referred to as the rule's input, into the rule's output, which is a recommended market position (e.g., long, short, neutral). Input(s) consists of one or more financial market time series. The rule is defined by one or more mathematical and logical operators that convert the input time series into a new time series that consists of the sequence of recommended market position (long, short, out-of-the-market). The output is typically represented by a signed number (e.g., $+1$ or -1). This book adopts the convention of assigning positive values to indicate long positions and negative values to indicate shorts position. The process by which a rule transforms one or more input series into an output series is illustrated in Figure 41.1.

A rule is said to generate a *signal* when the value of the output series changes. A signal calls for a change in a previously recommended market position. For example a change in output from $+1$ to -1 would call for closing a previously held long position and the initiation of a new short position. Output values need not be confined to $\{+1, -1\}$. A complex rule, whose output spans the range $\{+10, -10\}$, is able to recommend positions that vary in size. For example, an output of $+10$ might indicate that 10 long positions are warranted, such as long 10 contracts of copper. A change in the output from $+10$ to $+5$ would call for a reduction in the long position from 10 contracts to 5 (i.e., sell 5).

Binary Rules and Thresholds

The simplest rule is one that has a *binary output*. In other words, its output can assume only two values, for example $+1$ and -1. A binary rule could also be designed to recommend long/neutral positions or short/neutral positions. All the rules considered in this book are binary long/short $\{+1, -1\}$.

An investment strategy based on a binary long/short rule is always in either a long or short position in the market being traded. Rules of this type are referred to as *reversal rules* because signals call for a reversal from long to short or short to long.

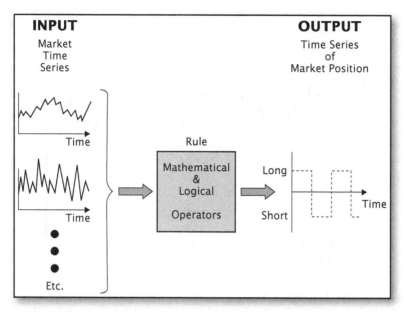

FIGURE 41.1 TA Rule Transforms Input Time Series into a Time Series of Market Position

Over time a reversal rule produces a time series of +1's and −1's that represent an alternating sequence of long and short positions.

The specific mathematical and logical operators that are used to define rules can vary considerably. However, there are some common themes. One theme is the notion of a *threshold*, a critical level that distinguishes the informative changes in the input time series from its irrelevant fluctuations. The premise is that the input time series is a mixture of information and noise. Thus the threshold acts as a filter.

Rules that employ thresholds generate signals when the time series crosses the threshold, either by the rising above it or falling beneath it. These critical events can be detected with logical operators called *inequalities* such as *greater-than* (>) and *less-than* (<). For example, if the time series is greater than the threshold, then rule output = +1, otherwise rule output = −1.

A threshold may be set at a fixed value or its value may vary over time as a result of changes in the time series that is being analyzed. Variable thresholds are appropriate for time series that display trends, which are large long-lasting changes in the level of the series. Trends, which make fixed threshold rules impractical, are commonly seen in asset prices (e.g., S&P 500 Index) and asset yields (AAA bond yield). The moving average and the Alexander reversal filter, also known as the zigzag filter, are examples of time series operators that are commonly used to define variable thresholds.

The moving-average-cross rule is an example of how a variable threshold is used to generate signals on a time series that displays trends. This type of rule produces a signal when the time series crosses from one side of its moving average to the other. For example:

If the time series is above its moving average, then *the rule output value* = +1, *otherwise the rule output value* = −1.

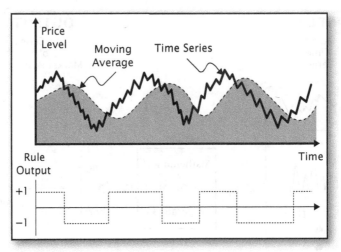

FIGURE 41.2   Moving-Average-Cross Rule

This is illustrated in Figure 41.2.

Because it employs a single threshold, the signals generated by the moving-average-cross rule are, by definition, mutually exclusive. Given a single threshold, there are only two possible conditions—the times series is either above or below[4] the threshold. The conditions are also exhaustive (no other possibilities).[5] Thus, it is impossible for the rule's signals to be in conflict.

Rules with fixed value thresholds are appropriate for market time series that do not display trends. Such time series are said to be *stationary*. There is a strict mathematical definition of a stationary time series, but here I am using the term in a looser sense to mean that a series has a relatively stable average value over time and has fluctuations that are confined to a roughly horizontal range. Technical analysis practitioners often refer to these series as *oscillators*.

Time series that display trends can be *detrended*. In other words, they can be transformed into a stationary series. Detrending frequently involves taking differences or ratios. For example the ratio of a time series to its moving average will produce a stationary version of the original time series. Once detrended, the series will be seen to fluctuate within a relatively well-defined horizontal range around a relatively stable mean value. Once the time series has been made stationary, fixed threshold rules can be employed. An example of a fixed threshold rule using a threshold of value of 75 is illustrated in Figure 41.3. The rule has an output a value of +1 when the series is greater than the threshold and a value of −1 at other times.

Binary Rules from Multiple Thresholds

As pointed out earlier, binary rules are derived, quite naturally, from a single threshold because the threshold defines two mutually exclusive and exhaustive conditions: the time series is either above or below threshold. However, binary rules can also be derived using multiple thresholds, but employing more than one threshold creates the possibility

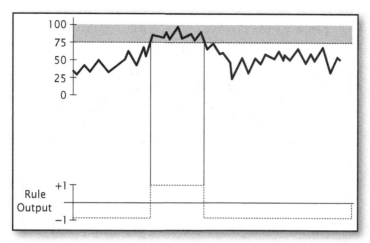

FIGURE 41.3 Rule with a Single Fixed Threshold

that the input time series can assume more than two conditions. Consequently, multiple threshold rules require a more sophisticated logical operator than the simple inequality operator (greater-than or less-than), which suffices for single threshold rules.

When there are two or more thresholds, there are more than two possible conditions. For example, with two thresholds, an upper and lower, there are three possible conditions for the input time series. It can be above the upper, below the lower, or between the two thresholds. To create a binary rule in this situation, the rule is defined in terms of two mutually exclusive events. An event is defined by the time series crossing a particular threshold in a particular direction. Thus, one event triggers one of the rule's output values, which is maintained until a second event, which is mutually exclusive of the first, triggers the other output value. For example, an upward crossing of the upper threshold triggers a +1, and a downward crossing of the lower threshold triggers a −1.

A logical operator that implements this type of rule is referred to as a *flip-flop*. The name stems from the fact that the rule's output value *flips* one way, upon the occurrence of one event, and then *flops* the other way, upon the occurrence of the second event. Flip-flop logic can be used with either variable or fixed threshold rules. An example of a rule based on two variable thresholds is the moving average band rule. See Figure 41.4. Here, the moving average is surrounded by an upper and lower band. The bands may be a fixed percentage above and below the moving average, or the deviation of the bands may vary based on of the recent volatility of the times, as is the case with the Bollinger Band.[6] An output value of +1 is triggered by an upward piercing of the upper threshold. This value is retained until the lower threshold is penetrated in the downward direction, causing the output value to change to −1.

Obviously, there are many other possibilities. The intent here has been to illustrate some of the ways that input time series can be transformed into a time series of recommended market positions.

Hayes[7] adds another dimension to threshold rules with *directional modes*. He applies multiple thresholds to a stationary time series such as a diffusion[8] indicator. At a given point in time, the indicator's mode is defined by the zone it occupies and its

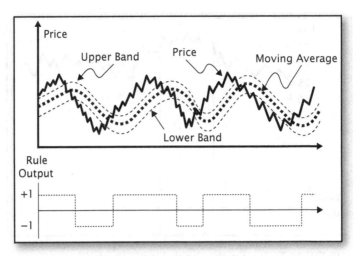

FIGURE 41.4   Moving Average Bands Rule

recent direction of change (e.g., up or down over the most recent five weeks). Each zone is defined by an upper and lower threshold (e.g., 40 and 60). Hayes applies this to a proprietary diffusion indicator called Big Mo. With two thresholds and two possible directional modes (up/down), six mutually exclusive conditions are defined. A binary rule could be derived from such an analysis by assigning one output value (e.g., +1) to one of the six conditions, and then assigning the other output value (i.e., −1) to the other five possibilities. Hayes asserts that one of the modes, when the diffusion indicator is above 60 and its direction is upward, is associated with stock market returns (Value Line Composite Index) of 50 percent per annum. This condition has occurred about 20 percent of the time between 1966 and 2000. However, when the diffusion indicator is > 60, and its recent change is negative, the market's annualized return is zero. This condition has occurred about 16 percent of the time.[9]

■ Traditional Rules and Inverse Rules

Part Two of this book is a case study that evaluates the profitability of approximately 6,400 binary long/short rules applied to the S&P 500 Index. (Ed. note: The full study is not published in this text.) Many of the rules generate market positions that are consistent with traditional principles of technical analysis. For example, under traditional TA principles, a moving-average-cross rule is interpreted to be bullish (output value +1) when the analyzed time series is above its moving average, and bearish (output value of −1) when it is below the moving average. I refer to these as *traditional* TA rules.

Given that the veracity of traditional TA maybe questionable, it is desirable to test rules that are contrary to the traditional interpretation. In other words, it is entirely possible that patterns that are traditionally assumed to predict rising prices may actually be predictive of falling prices. Alternatively, it is possible that neither configuration has any predictive value.

This can be accomplished by creating an additional set of rules whose output is simply the opposite of a traditional TA rule. I refer to these as *inverse* rules. This is

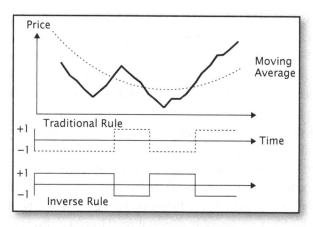

FIGURE 41.5 Traditional Rules and Inverse Rules

illustrated in Figure 41.5. The inverse of the moving-average-cross rule would output a value of −1 when the input time series is above its moving average, and +1 when the series is below its moving average.

There is yet another reason to consider inverse rules. Many of the rules tested in Part Two utilize input series other than the S&P 500, for example the yield differential between BAA and AAA corporate bonds. It is not obvious how this series should be interpreted to generate signals. Therefore, both up trends and down trends in the yield differential were considered as possible buy signals.

■ The Use of Benchmarks in Rule Evaluation

In many fields, performance is a relative matter. That is to say, it is performance relative to a benchmark that is informative rather than an absolute level of performance. In track and field, competitors in the shot-put are compared to a benchmark defined as best distance of that day or the best ever recorded in the state or world. To say that someone put the shot 43 feet does not reveal the quality of performance, however if the best prior effort had been 23 feet, 43 feet is a significant accomplishment!

This pertains to rule evaluation. Performance figures are only informative when they are compared to a relevant benchmark. The isolated fact that a rule earned a 10 percent rate of return in a back test is meaningless. If many other rules earned over 30 percent on the same data, 10 percent would indicate inferiority, whereas if all other rules were barely profitable, 10 percent might indicate superiority.

What then is an appropriate benchmark for TA rule performance? What standard must a rule beat to be considered good? There are a number of reasonable standards. This book defines that standard as the performance of a rule with no predictive power (i.e., a randomly generated signal). This is consistent with scientific practice in other fields. In medicine, a new drug must convincingly outperform a placebo (sugar pill) to be considered useful. Of course, rational investors might reasonably choose a higher standard of performance but not a lesser one. Some other benchmarks that could make sense would be the riskless rate of return, the return of a buy-and-hold strategy, or the rate of return of the rule currently being used.

In fact, to be considered good, it is not sufficient for a rule to simply beat the benchmark. It must beat it by a wide enough margin to exclude the possibility that its victory was merely due to chance (good luck). It is entirely possible for a rule with no predictive power to beat its benchmark in a given sample of data by sheer luck. The margin of victory that is sufficient to exclude luck as a likely explanation relates to the matter of *statistical significance*.

Having now established that the benchmark that we will use is the return that could be earned by a rule with no predictive power, we now face another question: How much might a rule with no predictive power earn? At first blush, it might seem that a return of zero is a reasonable expectation. However, this is only true under a specific and rather limited set of conditions.

In fact, the expected return of a rule with no predictive power can be dramatically different than zero. This is so because the performance of a rule can be profoundly affected by factors that have nothing to do with its predictive power.

The Conjoint Effect of Position Bias and Market Trend on Back-Test Performance

In reality, a rule's back-tested performance is comprised of two independent components. One component is attributable to the rule's predictive power, if it has any. This is the component of interest. The second, and unwanted, component of performance is the result of two factors that have nothing to do with the rule's predictive power: (1) the rule's long/short position bias, and (2) the market's net trend during the back-test period.

This undesirable component of performance can dramatically influence back-test results and make rule evaluation difficult. It can cause a rule with no predictive power to generate a positive average return or it can cause a rule with genuine predictive power to produce a negative average return. Unless this component of performance is removed, accurate rule evaluation is impossible. Let's consider the two factors that drive this component.

The first factor is a rule's *long/short* position bias. This refers to the amount of time the rule spent in a $+1$ output state relative to the amount of time spent in a -1 output state during the back test. If either output state dominated during the back test, the rule is said to have a position bias. For example, if more time was spent in long positions, the rule has a long position bias.

The second factor is the *market's net trend* or the average daily price change of the market during the period of the back test. If the market's net trend is other than zero, and the rule has a long or short position bias, the rule's performance will be impacted. In other words, the undesirable component of performance will distort back-test results either by adding to or subtracting from the component of performance that is due to the rule's actual predictive power. If, however, the market's net trend is zero or if the rule has no position bias, then the rule's past profitability will be strictly due to the rule's predictive power (plus or minus random variation). This is demonstrated mathematically later.

To clarify, imagine a TA rule that has a long position bias but that we know has no predictive power. The signals of such a rule could be simulated by a roulette wheel. To create the long position bias, a majority of the wheel's slots would be allocated to long positions (+1). Suppose that one hundred slots are allocated as follows: 75 are +1 and 25 are −1. Each day, over a period of historical data, the wheel is spun to determine if a long or short position is to be held for that day. If the market's average daily change during this period were greater than zero (i.e., net trend upward), the rule would have a positive expected rate of return even though the signals contain no predictive information. The rule's expected rate of return can be computed using the formula used to calculate the expected value of a random variable (discussed later).

Just as it is possible for a rule with no predictive power to produce a positive rate of return, it is just as possible for a rule with predictive power to produce a negative rate of return. This can occur if a rule has a position bias that is contrary to the market's trend. The combined effect of the market's trend and the rule's position bias may be sufficient to offset any positive return attributable to the rule's predictive power. From the preceding discussion it should be clear that the component of performance due to the interaction of position bias with market trend must be eliminated if one is to develop a valid performance benchmark.

At first blush, it might seem as if a rule that has a long position bias during a rising market trend is evidence of the rule's predictive power. However, this is not necessarily so. The rule's bullish bias could simply be due to the way its long and short conditions are defined. If the rule's long condition is more easily satisfied than its short condition, all other things being equal, the rule will tend to hold long positions a greater proportion of the time than short positions. Such a rule would receive a performance boost when back tested over historical data with a rising market trend. Conversely, a rule whose short condition is more easily satisfied than its long condition would be biased toward short positions and it would get a performance boost if simulated during a downward trending market.

The reader may be wondering how the definition of a rule can induce a bias toward either long or short positions. This warrants some explanation. Recall that binary reversal rules, the type tested in this book, are always in either a long or short position. Given this, if a rule's long (+1) condition is relatively easy to satisfy, then it follows that its short condition (−1) must be relatively difficult to satisfy. In other words, the condition required for the −1 output state is more restrictive, making it likely that, over time, the rule will spend more time long than short. It is just as possible to formulate rules where the long condition is more restrictive than the short condition. All other things being equal, such a rule would recommend short positions more frequently than long. It would be contrary to our purpose to allow the assessment of a rule's predictive power to be impacted by the relative strictness or laxity of the way in which its long and short conditions are defined.

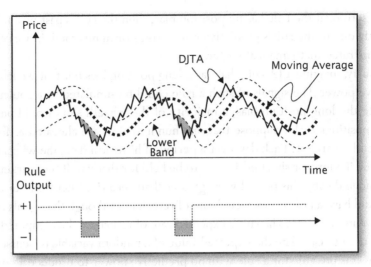

FIGURE 41.6   Rule with Restrictive Short Condition and Long Position Bias

To illustrate, consider the following rule, which has a highly restrictive short condition and, therefore, a relatively lax long condition. The rule, which generates positions in the S&P 500 index, is based on the Dow Jones Transportation Average.[10] Assume that a moving average with bands set at +3 percent and −3 percent is applied to the DJTA. The rule is to be short the S&P 500 while the DJTA is below the lower band, by definition a relatively rare condition, and long at all other times. See Figure 41.6. Clearly, such a rule would benefit if the S&P were in an uptrend over the back-test period.

Now let's consider the back test of two binary reversal rules which are referred to as rule 1 and rule 2. They are tested on S&P 500 data over the period January 1, 1976 through December 2004. During this period of approximately 7,000 days, the S&P 500 had an average daily return of +0.035 percent per day compounded, or +9.21897 percent annualized. Assume that rule 1 was in a long state 90 percent of the time and rule 2 was in a long state 60 percent of the time. Also, suppose that neither rule has predictive power—as if their output values were determined by a roulette wheel with 100 slots. The output for rule 1 is based on a roulette wheel with 90 slots assigned a value of +1 and the remaining 10 assigned a value of −1. The output for rule 2 is based on a wheel with 60 slots assigned a +1 value and 40 a value of −1. By the Law of Large Numbers, it is reasonable to expect that over the 7,000 days, rule 1 will be long very close to 90 percent of the time and rule 2 will be long approximately 60 percent of the time. Although the rules have different long/short biases, they have equal predictive power—none. However, their expected rates of return will be quite different over this segment of market history.

The expected return of a rule depends upon three quantities: (1) the proportion of time the rule spent in long positions, (2) the proportion of time spent in short positions (1 minus the proportion of time long), and (3) the market's average daily price change during the historical test period. The expected return (ER) is given by the following equation.

$$ER = [p(L) \times ADC] - [p(S) \times ADC]$$

Where

p(L) – probability of long position (proportion long)

p(S) – probability of short position (proportion short)

ADC: average daily change in market traded

Based on this calculation, the expected return for rule 1 is .028 percent per day or 7.31 percent annualized.[11] The expected return for rule 2 is 0.007 percent per day or 1.78 percent annualized.[12] This demonstrates that the rules' historical performance misleads us in two ways. First, both rules generate positive returns, yet we know that neither has any predictive power. Second, rule 1 appears to be superior to rule 2 even though we know they have equal predictive power—none.

When testing actual trading rules, one way to remove the deceptive effect due to the interaction of position bias and market trend would be to do the following: Subtract the expected return of a nonpredictive rule with the same position bias as the rule tested from the observed return of the tested rule. For example, assume that we did not know rules 1 and 2 had no predictive power. Simply by knowing their historical position bias, 90 percent long for rule 1 and 60 percent for rule 2, and knowing the market's average daily return over the back-test period, we would be able to compute the expected returns for rules with no predictive power having these position biases using the equation for the expected return already shown. The expected returns for each rule and would then be subtracted from each rule's observed performance. Therefore, from rule 1's back-tested return, which was 7.31 percent, we would subtract 7.31 percent, giving a result of zero. The result properly reflects rule 1's lack of predictive power. From rule 2's return of 1.78 percent, we would subtract a value of 1.78 percent, also giving a value of zero, also revealing its lack of predictive power.

The bottom line is this: by adjusting the back-tested (observed) performance by the expected return of a rule with no predictive power having an equivalent position bias, the deceptive component of performance can be removed. In other words, one can define the benchmark for any rule as the expected return of a nonpredictive rule with an equivalent position bias.

A Simpler Solution to Benchmarking: Detrending the Market Data

The procedure just described can be quite burdensome when many rules are being tested. It would require that a separate benchmark be computed for each rule based on its particular position bias. Fortunately there is an easier way.

The easier method merely requires that the historical data for the market being traded (e.g., S&P 500 Index) be detrended prior to rule testing. It is important to point out that the detrended data is used only for the purpose of calculating daily rule returns. It is not used for signal generation if the time series of the market being traded is also being used as a rule input series. Signals would be generated from actual market data (not detrended).

Detrending is a simple transformation, which results in a new market data series whose average daily price change is equal to zero. As pointed out earlier, if the market being traded has a net zero trend during the back-test period, a rule's position bias will have no distorting effect on performance. Thus, the expected return of a rule with no predictive power, the benchmark, will be zero if its returns are computed from detrended market data. Consequently, the expected return of a rule that does have predictive power will be greater than zero when its returns are computed from detrended data.

To perform the detrending transformation, one first determines the average daily price change of the market being traded over the historical test period. This average value is then subtracted from each day's price change.

The mathematical equivalence between the two methods discussed, (1) detrending the market data and (2) subtracting a benchmark with a equivalent position bias, may not be immediately obvious. If you think about it, you will see that if the market's average daily price change during the historical testing period is equal to zero, then rules devoid of predictive power must have an expected return of zero, regardless of their long/short position bias.

To illustrate this point, let's return to the formula for computing the expected value of a random variable. You will notice that if the average daily price change of the market being traded is zero, it does not matter what p(long) or p(short) are. The expected return (ER) will always be zero.

$$ER = [p(long) \times avg.\ daily\ return] - [p(short) \times avg.\ daily\ return]$$

For example, if the position biases were 60 percent long and 40 percent short, the expected return is zero.

$$0 = [0.60 \times 0] - [0.40 \times 0] \quad \text{Position Bias: 60 percent long, 40 percent short}$$

If, on the other hand, a rule does have predictive power, its expected return on detrended data will be greater than zero. This positive return reflects the fact that the rule's long and short positions are intelligent rather than random.

Using Logs of Daily Price Ratio Instead of Percentages

Thus far, the returns for rules and the market being traded have been discussed in percentage terms. This was done for ease of explanation. However, there are problems with computing returns as percentages. These problems can be eliminated by computing daily returns as the logs of daily price ratios, which is defined as:

$$Log \left(\frac{current\ day's\ price}{prior\ day's\ price} \right)$$

The log-based market returns are detrended in exactly the same way as the percentage changes. The log of the daily price ratio for the market being traded is computed for each day over the back-test period. The average is found, and then this average is deducted from each day. This eliminates any trend in the market data.

■ Other Details: The Look-Ahead Bias and Trading Costs

It is said the devil lives in the details. When it comes to testing rules, this truth applies. There are two more items that must be considered to ensure accurate historical testing. They are (1) the look-ahead bias and the related issue, assumed execution prices, and (2) trading costs.

Look-Ahead Bias and Assumed Execution Prices

Look-ahead bias,[13] also known as "leakage of future information," occurs in the context of historical testing when information that was not truly available at a given point in time was assumed to be known. In other words, the information that would be required to generate a signal was not truly available at the time the signal was assumed to occur.

In many instances, this problem can be subtle. If unrecognized, it can seriously overstate the performance of rule tests. For example, suppose a rule uses the market's closing price or any input series that only becomes known at the time of the close. When this is the case, it would not be legitimate to assume that one could enter or exit a position at the market's closing price. Assuming this would infect the results with look-ahead bias. In fact, the earliest opportunity to enter or exit would be the following day's opening price (assuming daily frequency information). All of the rules tested in Part Two of this book are based on market data that is known as of the close of each trading day. Therefore, the rule tests assume execution at the opening price on the following day. This means that a rule's daily return for the current day (day_0) is equal to the rule's output value ($+1$ or -1) as of the close of day_0 multiplied by the market's change from the opening price of the next day (open day_{+1}) price to the opening price on day after that (open day_{+2}). That price change is given as the log of the ratio defined as opening price of day_{+2} divided by the opening price on day_{+1}, as shown in the following equation:

$$Pos_0 \times Log \left[\frac{O_{+2}}{O_{+1}} \right]$$

Where:

Pos_0 = Rule's market position as of the close of day_0

O_{+1} = Open S&P 500 on day_{+1}

O_{+2} = Open S&P 500 on day_{+2}

This equation does not show the detrended version of rule returns, as shown here:

$$\text{Pos}_0 \times \left[\text{Log} \left[\frac{O_{+2}}{O_{+1}} \right] - \text{ALR} \right]$$

Where:

Pos_0 = Rule's market position as of the close of day_0

O_{+1} = Open S&P 500 on day_{+1}

O_{+2} = Open S&P 500 on day_{+2}

ALR = Average Log Return over Back Test

Look-ahead bias can also infect back-test results when a rule uses an input data series that is reported with a lag or that is subject to revision. For example, the back-test of a rule that uses mutual fund cash statistics,[14] which is released to the public with a two-week delay, must take this lag into account by lagging signals to reflect the true availability of the data. None of the rules tested in this book use information reported with a lag or that is subject to revision.

Trading Costs

Should trading costs be taken into account in rule back-tests? If the intent is to use the rule on a stand-alone basis for trading, the answer is clearly yes. For example, rules that signal reversals frequently will incur higher trading costs than rules that signal less frequently and this must be taken into account when comparing their performances. Trading costs include broker commissions and slippage. Slippage is due to the bid-asked spread and the amount that the investor's order pushes the market's price—up when buying or down when selling.

If, however, the purpose of rule testing is to discover signals that contain predictive information, then trading costs can obscure the value of a rule that reverses frequently. Since the intent of the rule studies conducted in this book are aimed at finding rules that have predictive power rather than finding rules that can be used as stand-alone trading strategies it was decided not to impose trading costs.

■ Notes

1. A long position in a security means the investor owns the security and hopes to benefit by selling it in the future at a higher price.
2. A short position in a security means the investor has sold the security without owning it but is obligated to buy it back at a later point in time. The holder of a short position therefore benefits from a subsequent price decline, thereby permitting the repurchase at a lower level than the selling price, earning a profit.

3. *Neutral* refers to the case where the investor holds no position in the market.

4. It is assumed that all market information required by the method is known and publicly available at the time the method produces the recommendation.

5. The possibility of the time series being equal to the moving average is eliminated by computing the value of the moving average to a greater degree of precision than the price level.

6. J. Bollinger, *Bollinger on Bollinger Bands* (New York, NY: McGraw-Hill, 2002).

7. T. Hayes, *The Research Driven Investor: How to Use Information, Data and Analysis for Investment Success* (New York, NY: McGraw-Hill, 2001), 63.

8. A diffusion indicator is based on an analysis of numerous market time series within a defined universe (e.g., all NYSE stocks). The same rule, such as a moving average cross, is applied to all the series comprising the universe. Each series is rated as in an uptrend or downtrend, depending on its position relative to its moving average. The value of the diffusion indicator is the percentage of time series that are in an upward trend. The indicator is confined to the range 0 to 100.

9. This analysis does not make clear how many rule variations were explored to attain this level of discrimination. It is impossible to evaluate the significance of these findings without information on the amount of searching that led to the discovery of a rule.

10. Many of the rules tested in this book use data series other than the S&P 500 to generate signals on the S&P 500.

11. $(0.9) \times 0.035\% - (0.1) \times 0.035\% = 0.028\%$ per day or 7.31% annualized.

12. $(0.60) \times 0.035\% - (0.40) \times 0.035\% = 0.007\%$ per day or 1.78% annualized.

13. The look-ahead bias is discussed by Robert A. Haugen, *The Inefficient Stock Market: What Pays Off and Why* (Upper Saddle River, NJ: Prentice-Hall, 1999), 66.

14. The percentage of fund portfolios invested in interest-bearing cash instruments such as T-bills, commercial paper, and so forth.

CHAPTER 42

Being Right or Making Money

From Ned Davis, *Being Right or Making Money*, 3rd Edition (Hoboken, New Jersey: John Wiley & Sons, 2014), Chapter 1.

Learning Objective Statements

- List the four key characteristics Ned Davis claims are common to successful investors
- Describe the importance of having plans to persevere through mistakes and losses
- Identify Ned Davis' nine rules to consider when building a timing model
- Discuss the theory behind "contrary opinion"

■ Bad News about Forecasting (Being Right)

There are a number of factors—including a potential cyclical bear market, demographics, and the U.S. energy renaissance—that could be game changers, and might help forecast the future. I hope you will find my perspectives useful, even though after studying forecasting for over 40 years I realize I do not always know what the market is going to do.

You may have heard of the Texan who had all the money in the world but who had an inferiority complex because he felt he wasn't very bright. When he heard about a brilliant doctor who was offering brain transplants, he immediately consulted him to find out if it were true and how much it would cost. The doctor told him it was indeed true that he could boost intelligence quotient (IQ) levels. The doctor had three types of brains in inventory: lawyer brains for $5 an ounce, doctor brains at $10 an ounce, and stock-market guru brains for $250 per ounce. The Texan asked, "Why in the world are the stock-market guru brains so much more expensive or valuable than those of doctors or lawyers?" And the doctor replied, "Do you have any idea how many gurus it takes to get an ounce of brain?"

People laugh at that joke because unfortunately there is a lot of truth to it. I don't know in what direction the markets will go, and neither does Janet Yellen or

Barack Obama. Even George Soros, whose modest $1 billion take-home pay of a few years ago qualifies him as a bona fide market guru, says in his book *The Alchemy of Finance*,[1] "My financial success stands in stark contrast with my ability to forecast events . . . all my forecasts are extremely tentative and subject to constant revision in the light of market developments."

While 95 percent of the people on Wall Street are in the business of making predictions, the super successful Peter Lynch, in his book *Beating the Street*,[2] says, "Nobody can predict interest rates, the future direction of the economy, or the stock market. Dismiss all such forecasts. . . ." And as Mark Twain once observed, "The art of prophecy is difficult, especially with respect to the future."

I think it was Alan Shaw, one of the more successful practitioners of technical analysis, who said, "The stock market is man's invention that has humbled him the most." Fellow legendary technician Bob Farrell warned, "When all the experts and forecasts agree—something else is going to happen."[3]

Economist John Kenneth Galbraith put it this way, "We have two classes of forecasters: those who don't know and those who don't know they don't know."

Financial theorist William Bernstein described it similarly, but with an even darker message: "There are two types of investors, be they large or small: those who don't know where the market is headed, and those who don't know that they don't know. Then again, there is a third type of investor—the investment professional, who indeed knows that he or she doesn't know, but whose livelihood depends upon appearing to know."[4]

Despite my realization that forecasting is difficult, I haven't become a spoilsport and turned away from predicting the market's course entirely, because I've had my share of really good forecasts. Perhaps recounting how I came to distrust "being right" and instead embraced techniques that allowed me to make money consistently will be helpful.

Like nearly all novice investors and analysts, back in 1968 I was convinced that all I had to do was discover the way the investment world worked, develop the best indicators available to forecast changes in the markets, have the conviction to shoot straight, and gather my profits. And my record of forecasting stock prices from 1968 to 1978 was so good that during a *Wall $treet Week* broadcast in 1978 Louis Rukeyser said, "Ned Davis has had an outstanding record in recent years . . . and has been absolutely right about most of the major ups and downs. . . ."

The only problem was that at the end of each year, I would total up my capital gains and unfortunately I would not owe Uncle Sam much money. Before someone else could question me, I asked myself, "If you are so smart, why aren't you rich?" It was about that time (1978–1980) that I began to realize that smarts, hard work, and even a burning desire to be right were really not my problems, or the solution to my problems. My real problems were a failure to cut losses short, a lack of discipline and risk management, letting my ego color my market view (which made it difficult to admit mistakes), and difficulty controlling fear and greed. *It was thus a lack of proper investment strategy and good money management techniques, not poor forecasting, that was holding me back.*

I dealt with those problems, and by 1985 *Barron's* magazine was interviewing me and saying on its cover: "No Bum Steers from This Raging Bull: Ned Davis Has Been Dead Right on the Market."

Over the years I have seen scores of very bright investment advisors turn into hugely successful gurus who blaze into the investment business with spectacular forecasts. Yet, I've watched each and every one of them crash back to earth when a big subsequent forecast inevitably proved wrong. The Bible says, "Live by the sword, die by the sword." As my late friend Marty Zweig and I watched these forecasting gurus fail, we often said to each other, "Live by the forecast, die by the forecast."

Before examining indicators, I'd like to discuss the record of some professional forecasters. Perhaps the biggest myth in financial markets is that experts have expertise or that forecasters can forecast. The reality is that flipping a coin would produce a better record. Therefore, relying on consensus economic forecasts to provide guidance for investment strategy is almost certain to fail over the long run.

What is my evidence? Consider forecasts from the Survey of Professional Forecasters released by the Federal Reserve Bank of Philadelphia and shown in Figure 42.1 (solid line). The dashed line shows real GDP. The chart shows seven recessions (shaded zones) since 1970. As a group, professional economic forecasters did not correctly call a single one of these recessions. In fact, they have never predicted a recession, period. Since the first edition of *Being Right or Making Money* was published in 2000, on average economists have been 59 percent too high in their 12-month forecasts (predicted growth: 3.1 percent; actual growth: 1.9 percent).

Well, what about the experts at the Federal Reserve? They are supposed to be independent. They have a lot of money to spend on research, a full professional staff, and they have expanded their projections from a year or so to five years ahead. Two years ago the initial projection for 2013 was 4.15 percent real growth. In Figure 42.2 we plot the wide range of projections by the Fed (not the central tendency or specific point forecast) and then see how real GDP performed since 2000. And as shown,

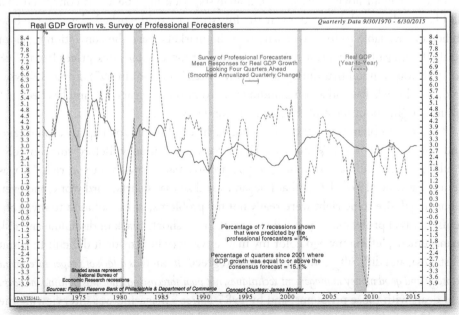

FIGURE 42.1   Real GDP Growth versus Survey of Professional Forecasters

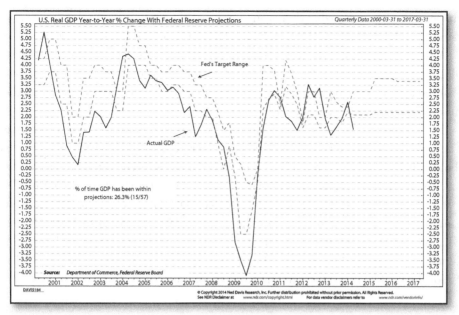

FIGURE 42.2 Real Year-to-Year Percentage Change in U.S. GDP versus Federal Reserve Projections

the Fed was actually correct (actual GDP fell within the Fed's wide range) just 26.3 percent of the time!

The last word I'll offer on predictions is from the Fed's leader during much of the period covered by the chart. In October 2013 Alan Greenspan said, "We really can't forecast all that well. We pretend we can, but we can't."

Forecasting the economy and the investment markets consistently and reliably is very difficult. In fact, consensus predictions often contain the seeds of their own destruction by altering human actions. Most crowds are usually wrong at sentiment extremes as I will discuss later in this chapter.

■ Good News about Making Money

After studying winners in the investment world over many years, I found some good news. While *nobody was right* year in and year out, a number of advisors and investors did in fact *make money* year in and year out. I decided I would follow their advice on how to make money consistently.

In 1980 I acquired a computer and a good program, and started building timing models that I felt would give me the objectivity, discipline, flexibility, and risk management that I needed to make consistent profits. And since 1980 the Ned Davis Research Group has been dedicated to building timing models that do not forecast, but are simply designed to make money. These models have made a real and substantial change in my investment profits, and both Uncle Sam and I are now much better off. As far as my forecasting of the market goes: if anything, it suffered. Timing models that make money invariably are less cocky than a crystal-ball guru. The models are so

BEING RIGHT OR MAKING MONEY

concerned with minimizing disastrous risks that they try to hit singles and doubles rather than home runs. And they definitely limit the number of strikeouts.

Again, my financial well-being improved significantly, and the humility and discipline that the timing models forced upon me relieved me of a lot of stressful anxiety. I shifted my focus from gaining glory and prestige to designing a business focused on making money while managing risk.

Timing models have permitted me to make money on a more consistent basis. Throughout my career I have followed a number of renowned market winners, and though their methods do not all include timing models, these winners share certain investment-strategy characteristics that we have tried to incorporate into our models.

I found winners such as Marty Zweig, Dan Sullivan of *The Chartist*,[5] and Value Line,[6] who have consistently made money since 1980 (according to Mark Hulbert, who rates advisors). I found investment legends who consistently win, including John Templeton, Warren Buffett, Peter Lynch, George Soros, Stan Druckenmiller, Paul Tudor Jones, Bill Gross, and Jim Stack. What commonalities do these winners share?

■ Being Right and Other Investment Techniques Are Overrated and Are Not the Keys to Success

It's not the markets they trade or even the techniques they use. These are people who rely on different philosophies, ranging from Ben Graham's long-term valuation techniques to in-and-out technical commodity trading . . . from dollar-cost averaging to market timing . . . from buying high-yielding stocks to buying relatively strong stocks with almost no yield. Clearly, a variety of techniques can make money. I find it exciting that numerous techniques can make money, as investors can choose the technique that best fits their own psyches.

The winning methods of successful professional investors are even sometimes contradictory. For example, in the book *Market Wizards*[7] the successful pro Jim Rogers is quoted as saying that he often examines charts for signs of "hysteria," and also that "I haven't met a rich technician." In the same book an equally successful pro, Marty Schwartz, is quoted as saying, "I always laugh at people who say, 'I've never met a rich technician.' I love that! It is such an arrogant, nonsensical response. I used fundamentals for nine years and then got rich as a technician." If you think that is confusing, in the book *What I Learned Losing a Million Dollars*[8] the legendary John Templeton is quoted as saying, "Diversify your investments." In the same book, the equally legendary Warren Buffett says, "Concentrate your investments. If you have a harem of forty women, you never get to know any of them very well."

So as I studied other long-term winners on Wall Street, I found that instinctively or otherwise, they had come to the same conclusions that I had. While the methods of Warren Buffett, Peter Lynch, and John Templeton are very different from my risk-management, asset-allocation, market-timing orientation, all of these men have been exceedingly humble, made multiple mistakes, and rarely (if ever) get headlines about a spectacular call. Yet they all use objective methods for picking stocks, their investment philosophy is disciplined and designed to limit risks, and they are flexible when they must be.

This book is not designed to challenge those of you who are long-term fundamentalists or short-term technicians. Instead, we offer some tools that hopefully will help you to be more right more often. But much more importantly, this book will show you that being right is not really where it's at, since at least as much of your focus should be on risk management, a disciplined strategy, and flexibility.

■ The Four Real Keys to Making Money

As I continued studying legendary investors, I discovered that all of these winners shared four key characteristics, some of which I had already learned by the time I completed kindergarten.

1. **Objective indicators:** These legendary investors all used *objectively determined indicators* rather than gut emotion. We have a little riddle about this. In a room there were three people: a high-priced lawyer, a low-priced lawyer, and the tooth fairy. In the middle of the room was a $100 bill. Suddenly the lights went out, and when they came back on the $100 bill was gone. Who took it? The answer, of course, is the high-priced lawyer—because the other two are figments of the imagination. We want to make sure that what our indicators say is factual and not a figment of our imaginations. As our teachers tried to help us understand in kindergarten, it is critical to learn what is real and what is imaginary.

What is an objective indicator? It must be mathematical, with long historical analysis to demonstrate its effectiveness. One example might be the rate of inflation. Perhaps it is because the Fed is supposed to control inflation, or perhaps it is because bond yields have an inflation premium, but inflation is one of the best macroeconomic indicators to use to call the stock market.

But in all of the noisy data, how much does inflation need to rise or fall on a monthly basis to be important? The chart in Figure 42.3 looks at the year-to-year rate of inflation relative to a five-year moving average. In the 41.3 percent of the time since 1952 that the year-to-year inflation rate was at least 0.5 of a percentage point below the five-year average, the S&P 500 shot up at a 13.5 percent annual rate— almost double the 62-year buy-and-hold average of 7.2 percent. And when inflation was more than one percentage point above the five-year average, one actually lost money in stocks.

2. **Discipline:** All the winners are very *disciplined*, remaining faithful to their systems through good and bad times. I sometimes compare investing to classical Greek tragedies, in which the hero is inevitably ruined by some character flaw. My own biggest flaw in investing, as noted earlier, is letting my ego get involved in my market view. This makes it very difficult to admit mistakes. Thus, to shift from concentrating on being right to making money, I had to learn discipline. That is how I came up with the idea of using computer-derived mathematical

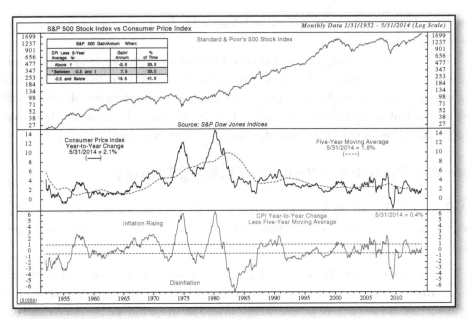

FIGURE 42.3 S&P 500 Index versus Consumer Price Index

models for stock-market timing that would *force* discipline upon me. That discipline may not have made me more right over the past 40 years, but it did control my mistakes and allowed me to be a much more successful investor. In June 1998 Dan Sullivan said in his *The Chartist* newsletter, "Successful investors have several things in common. First, they have patience. Second, successful investors are like great athletes, they adhere to a strict discipline." As my teacher taught me in kindergarten, there will be chaos if you don't have discipline.

3. **Flexibility:** While disciplined, these winners were *flexible* enough to change their minds when the evidence shifted, even if they did not understand why. In his book *Winning on Wall Street*,[9] Marty Zweig talks about how bearish he was during a sell-off in February and March 1980: "I was sitting there looking at conditions and being as bearish as I could be—but the market had reversed. Things began to change as the Fed reduced interest rates and eased credit controls. Even though I had preconceived ideas that we were heading toward some type of 1929 calamity, I *responded* to changing conditions." In conclusion he states, "The problem with most people who play the market is that they are not flexible . . . to succeed in the market you must have discipline, flexibility, and patience."

Barton Biggs once called Stan Druckenmiller "the investment equivalent of Michael Jordan. . . . He is the best consistent macro player." Biggs said, "He is a combination of being very intellectual and analytical, but also using technical analysis." In *Market Wizards*, author Jack Schwager writes of Druckenmiller:

> Another important lesson . . . is that if you make a mistake, respond immediately! Druckenmiller made the incredible error of shifting from short to 130 percent long on the very day before the massive

October 19, 1987, stock crash, yet he finished the month with a net gain. How? When he realized he was dead wrong, he liquidated his entire long position during the first hour of trading on October 19 and actually went short. . . . The *flexibility* [emphasis added] of Druckenmiller's style . . . is obviously a key element of his success.

So as I learned in kindergarten: expect surprises. Things change.

4. **Risk Management:** Finally, all of these successful investors were *risk managers*. I asked Paul Tudor Jones once what he does at work all day, and he answered, "The first thing I do is try to figure out what is going to go wrong, and then I spend the rest of the day trying to cover my butt." In *Market Wizards*, Paul says, "I am always thinking about losing money as opposed to making money." And he is widely known as a risk taker!

Nearly all of the pros I have studied are clear about one thing: *they want to control their losses*. In *Market Wizards*, fundamentalist Jim Rogers says, "Whenever I buy or sell something, I always try to make sure I'm not going to lose any money first . . . my basic advice is don't lose money." In the same book, technician Marty Schwartz says, "Learn to take the losses. The most important thing in making money is not letting your losses get out of hand." In his book, *Pit Bull*,[10] Schwartz says, "Honor thy stop . . . exiting a losing trade clears your head and restores your objectivity." Controlling losses is one lesson I wished I had learned in kindergarten. They did tell me to be careful, but it wasn't until much later that it sunk in. I learned this from Warren Buffett, who once stated his two favorite rules for successful investing: Rule #1: Never lose money. Rule #2: Never forget Rule #1. In *What I Learned Losing a Million Dollars*, the legendary Bernard Baruch is quoted as saying, "Don't expect to be right all the time. If you have a mistake, cut your loss as quickly as possible."

In *Reminiscences of a Stock Operator*,[11] the hero (widely believed to be the legendary trader Jesse Livermore) says, "A loss never bothers me after I take it. I forget it overnight. But being wrong—not taking the loss—that is what does the damage to the pocketbook and to the soul." Echoing that sentiment, Druckenmiller in *The New Market Wizards*[12] says of George Soros, "Soros is also the best loss taker I've ever seen. He doesn't care whether he wins or loses on a trade. If a trade doesn't work, he's confident enough about his ability to win on other trades that he can easily walk away from the position." Finally, the last word on the subject of taking losses (and making money) goes to Leo Melamed, chairman emeritus of the Chicago Mercantile Exchange. In the book *The Inner Game of Trading*,[13] in response to the question, "What do you think are the primary psychological barriers that prevent most traders from being successful?" Leo answered: "One of them is the ability to take a loss. You've got to know that no risk taker is going to be right all the time. As a matter of fact, I figured out when I was trading that I could be wrong 60 percent of the time and come out a big winner. The key is money management. You must take your losses quickly and keep them small and let your profits run and make them worthwhile. . . ."

In the December 12, 2013, edition of *The Chartist Mutual Fund Letter* was a list of seven insights from John Bogle, founder of the Vanguard Mutual Fund Group, that I found helpful in making money. He says:

1. Balancing of return and risk is the task of intelligent investing.
2. Predicting stock-market returns has a very high margin of error.
3. Impulse is your enemy.
4. There is no escaping risk; a well-diversified portfolio should provide remarkable growth over the long term.
5. Investing is simple, but it is not easy. It requires discipline, patience, steadfastness, and common sense.
6. Be patient and ignore the crowd. If you can't resist temptation, you absolutely must not manage your own money.
7. The secret to investing is there is no secret.

So, in conclusion, what I've learned after all these years is that *we are in the business of making mistakes*. I've never heard Peter Lynch give an interview where he didn't point out some mistake he has made. And he has said, "If you are right half of the time (in the markets), you have a terrific score. It is not an easy business." So if we all make mistakes, what separates the winners from the losers? The answer is simple—*the winners make small mistakes*, while the losers make big mistakes.

■ The Battle for Investment Survival and Handling Mistakes

When I first became professionally involved in the stock market, a book by Gerald M. Loeb, who was called "the dean of Wall Street," made a big impression on me. The book is *The Battle for Investment Survival*.[14] I have battled in the marketplace daily for over 40 years and in my opinion Loeb was right—*investment survival* is everything. In 1994, the hugely successful George Soros said in his book *The Alchemy of Finance*, "If I had to sum up my practical skills, I would use one word: survival." He writes about how his father, who lived through the Russian Revolution as an escaped prisoner of war, taught his son "the art of survival." I don't think you need to be a prisoner of war to be successful on Wall Street, but I do think you often need to react as a survivor would.

In a recent *Business Week Investor* interview, successful money manager Michael Orkin said, "Have caution and respect for the market. The first job is survival."

I feel I have been a fairly high achiever in my life, and yet as I reflect on my successes, I also see failure after mistake after failure. Being a survivor means you must be able to handle these mistakes. I usually pick myself up and say: you have done the best you can; that's all you can ask of yourself—period, end of discussion. I also tell myself that failure is just the opportunity to start over with a lot of important new information. Another lesson I have learned during the ups and downs of my career is that when someone criticizes me, I let it go to my head because there may be something constructive I can learn from it. But I never ever let criticism go to my heart, where it can hurt me. Likewise, when people compliment me, I let it go to my heart, but I try not to let praise go to my head. Being caught up in the manic-depressive crowd psychology world of the stock market, it is important to have a balanced view of both successes and mistakes.

Here is a recent example of my personal struggle with making mistakes. On March 12, 2013, I authored a commentary *Hotline* entitled "Stubborn on Gold." I said:

> This is a commentary *Hotline*, as it is not my usual objective, disciplined analysis. As you know, I like to have both the Fed and the tape together to make a strong bet. I also look at sentiment and macro factors, like inflation.
>
> In the case of gold, I've largely lost the tape. Gold is in a major consolidation. It has not broken support around 1530, but it sure rallies poorly. I think it would need to break its downtrend line to get a more hopeful tape message. Moreover, while I think of gold as a currency hedge, history also argues it has served as an inflation hedge, and inflation has been very, very quiet. It may not stay quiet, but for now it is not at all a trigger for gold.
>
> So I am left with just the friendly Fed and some sentiment factors. Nevertheless, I am a little stubborn on gold, and I am convinced that it is going quite a bit higher in the long run . . . [due to Fed monetary-base growth] . . . my opinion is that a gold insurance position, relative to *global* money-printing, is still a prudent investment.

I bring up this mistake in hopes that eating some humble pie will prove a useful lesson. Even after 40 years in this business and preaching about being open-minded and disciplined, it is still very easy and very human, to fall into a stubborn desire to be right. Ouch!

In listing the personal qualities it takes to succeed in his book, *One Up on Wall Street*, [15] Peter Lynch does not mention being smart or being right, but rather he lists things like patience, persistence, humility, flexibility, and a *willingness to admit to mistakes*.

Paul Tudor Jones puts a positive spin on mistakes in *Market Wizards*, saying, "One learns the most from mistakes, not successes." He talks about a very intense gut-wrenching loss on a disastrous cotton trade he made early in his career, saying that his experience altered his whole trading style in terms of risk. He first called himself Mr. Stupid and said, "I am not cut out for this business; I don't think I can hack it much longer." But "that was when I first decided I had to learn discipline and money management. It was a cathartic experience for me, in the sense that I went to the edge, questioned my very ability as a trader, and decided that I was not going to quit. I was determined to come back and fight. I decided that I was going to become very disciplined and businesslike about my trading."

I have heard Paul tell another story that contains a critical message. He says that one time when he was trapped in a losing trade, he went to a pro for advice as to whether he should honor his stops. The pro said, "The markets are going to be here 20 and 30 years from now; the real question is, will you be?"

■ Stories of Five Successful Winners

I thought about calling this section of the book "Being Wrong and Making Money." My experience tells me investors will be right enough that the profits will take care of themselves (being right and making money), but the key is how you handle your losses and your mistakes. So I thought telling stories about five successful winners in the investment world might help illustrate the point. I talked about three of them in the previous edition of this book, when all were near the top of their fields. Also, all five are and were successful money managers who approach the market as I do, as a market timer or tactical asset allocator. All have been hugely successful on Wall Street. They are Marty Zweig, Paul Tudor Jones, Dan Sullivan, Chris Cadbury, and James Stack.

Before and during the 1987 crash, Marty Zweig was widely labeled as a prominent gloom-and-doomer due to his vocal warnings that there might be a 1929-style crash, followed by an economic depression. His forecasts were ubiquitous on television and in major media newsmagazines. I had talked to Marty several times during the crash, and if anything, he was more bearish than he was being portrayed.

Thus, I was surprised when a few days after the crash he told me he was going to turn all out bullish. I asked him why, given his concerns about a depression. He said, "I have spent the last 20 years of my life building indicators and most of them are flashing buys—what is the use of building them if you aren't going to follow them?" Thus, his keen mind was so *flexible* that he was able to forget his *deep-seated worries* and follow his indicator rules, correctly turning bullish very quickly. This kind of flexibility, an ability to let his prior stance be and thus shift with the indicators, made Marty one of the top investment advisors from July 1980 until he quit publishing his investment newsletter in December 1997. He never had a down year. When I asked Marty why he changed a position, he simply said, "I'm just trying to stay out of trouble." He turned his nervous, worrying nature into a profitable risk-management virtue. To sum up, Marty was hardly ever 100 percent in or out of the stock market, rarely forecasted where stocks were going, rarely achieved the number one advisory spot in a single year, only took small risks, and paid a lot of commissions since he often shifted his stance. Yet over the long run, he ended up well ahead of other advisors and many hedge funds.

As for Paul Tudor Jones, $1,000 invested in his Tudor Futures Fund on September 18, 1984, would have been worth $669,670 on December 31, 2013, a gain of 668.67 percent in just over 29 years, or a whopping 24.8 percent per annum, perhaps one of the greatest money-management success stories ever achieved. The Tudor Futures Fund has *never* had a losing calendar year since its launch in September 1984. This record led *Barron's* to feature Paul in its year-end list of experts for many years. In a *Barron's* Roundtable discussion at the start of 1989, Paul was quoted as being very bearish on both the U.S. stock market ("The fact is I think the stock market is a low-risk short.") and the Japanese market ("I couldn't sleep at night if I were long the Japanese market.") However, he was very wrong on both counts (although a year later, his call on Japan proved prophetic). But this super speculator was so good at money management, flexibility, and cutting losses short, and so adept at being objective and disciplined, that he ended 1989 making 42 percent for his investors and returning some $200 million to his partners.

Lest you think that was a fluke, Paul spoke at a Ned Davis Research (NDR) investment conference in early 1991. His number one trade for the year was to short the Dow and buy gold. Again, he was wrong. Paul recently told me *the* reason for *all* the Wall Street success stories he knew was clear—"money management, money management, money management." I am certain that Paul has been right many times and has made much money when he was right, but these stories show that the top pros can be wrong and still make money!

The Chartist has been highly ranked by the *Hulbert Financial Digest*[16] for returns for over 21 years. In a letter, Dan Sullivan, *The Chartist*'s editor, once said:

> For the year-to-date, the Actual Cash Account, which buys and sells in sync with our consensus Model, has lost $22,525, −3.71 percent. The Aggressive Account has lost $12,849, −6 percent. . . . To be absolutely candid, the losses we have sustained, given the high standards we have always set for ourselves, border on disastrous. . . . While no one enjoys taking losses, there are times when to do so is absolutely essential. One of the main planks in our stock-market methodology is the preservation of capital. This involves taking losses quickly, before they become unmanageable.

The September 12, 2013, issue of *The Chartist* newsletter listed four negative behaviors and attitudes that can lead to poor investment returns:

1. Failing to take losses.
2. Being overly fearful at market bottoms and overly optimistic at market tops.
3. Failing to take responsibility for your own money.
4. Not following a disciplined strategy.

And it has worked. *The Chartist Mutual Fund Letter* (February 13, 2014) says:

> The Actual Cash Account now stands at $1,327,947, still another record high on a monthly basis. Per our usual policy, a month-by-month performance of the Actual Cash Account since its inception is available to any subscriber. The Actual Cash Account has outperformed the benchmark S&P 500 with dividends factored in since we started it with an original $100,000 back in August of 1988. What we are most proud of is the fact that the profitable results have been accomplished with considerably less risk than buy and hold because this real money account has the ability to move to the sidelines during adverse periods. We are using basically the

same methodology that we deployed when we started this newsletter some 25 years ago. It has stood the test of time.

Since our philosophy is somewhat like Sullivan's, I'd like to quote a few of the things he has written. On January 17, 1991, after having just sold a group of stocks at a loss and before correctly turning bullish again to catch the 1991 bull market, Sullivan observed:

> Here's what you get with *The Chartist*. We are not going to be right all of the time, but be assured that we back our recommendations with our own money. We're not going to ask our subscribers to take any risks that we are not willing to take ourselves. When we are wrong, we are going to admit it flat out. You're not going to see us loaded up with a portfolio of losing stocks for an extended period of time, hoping that the market is going to bail us out.
>
> As stated previously, our philosophy is to cut losses quickly. At the outset of a buying campaign, we think "short-term." If the stocks we select are not living up to their expectations, we act quickly to cut losses. However, once we find ourselves on the profit side of the ledger, you will not find us all that anxious to sell. In essence, we are quite willing to risk paper profits. Most investors are too slow to cut losses and too quick to take profits, which is the exact opposite of our approach to the market.
>
> The market is going to be there tomorrow and it will present us with many opportunities in the future. It is not the slightest blow to our ego or self-esteem to tell you that our timing was off the mark. We were wrong. But, that is how we do it here at *The Chartist*.

Winners like Dan Sullivan are very flexible and very disciplined, and they're risk managers. While I am not trying to knock the importance of study, hard work, and being right in terms of investment success, the key is how to make money. If you choose not to follow my exact rules, or even if you decide to throw out market timing altogether, I still believe that objectivity, flexibility, discipline, and risk management are the keys to making money, and this book can help your understanding of the importance of those factors.

I am including two advisors who did not appear in the last edition. Only one is still practicing. But I wanted to include both because their general approach is similar to mine. Again, I am not trying to push my investment strategy on anyone. It just so happens that I have the psyche of a hedge-fund trader, and so I sought out winners who used tools similar to those I use to make money consistently.

The differences between Chris Cadbury and Jim Stack are striking. Cadbury's approach was very short-term, and Stack's is more cyclical. Cadbury, who recently retired, was more focused on mean reversion, sentiment, and overbought/oversold indicators, while Stack is more technical-trend and macro-oriented. Personally, I try to fuse all of these factors. Yet, both have made money by cutting risks short and letting profits run.

Cadbury was ranked number one in the United States by *Timer Digest* at some point each year from 2002 to 2011, according to the one-year performance metrics used by that publication. He had more than 45 years of trading experience. In 2011 *Timer Digest* said:

> In terms of performance, as measured by *Timer Digest*, Chris Cadbury has distinguished himself across multiple time horizons and in response to various market environments.
>
> He ranked No. 1 for both 5- and 10-year periods ending on December 31, 2010, as well as No. 2 for 3 years and No. 3 for 8 years. Over the 10-year horizon, the market has essentially gone nowhere. And within that time period, there have been several difficult bull and bear cycles to negotiate.

When the market gets oversold and excessive pessimism exists, Cadbury likes to go contrary to sentiment extremes with buy signals. But once he buys (for example, the S&P 500 futures), he generally sets a five-point stop-loss. I have seen him be wrong with several five-point losing trades in a row, but he will stay with his indicators. I've seen him go from three or four small losses to a 100-point gain. Cadbury is also quite flexible. He can lean bearish for an extended period (1987 and 2007–2008) and then flip and lean bullish (since 2009). This flexibility is rare for market-letter writers.

Jim Stack publishes a newsletter called *InvesTech Research* and conducts his research from Whitefish, Montana, far from the madding crowd on Wall Street. He uses objective indicators, historical research, and a disciplined safety-first approach to investing that has been successful for over 30 years.

Besides "objectivity," Stack lists "humility" and "integrity" as fundamental principles for survival in this business. Mark Hulbert rates Stack as a market timer, but Stack prefers to think of himself as more of a risk manager (as I prefer to think of myself). Stack says:

> The April [2013] issue of the *Hulbert Financial Digest* released its latest Stock Market Timers Honor Roll. As described by Mark Hulbert, making it onto their honor roll requires producing above-average performance in both up and down markets.
>
> In our view, managing risk through portfolio and sector allocation isn't the same as market timing, so we don't consider ourselves to be market timers. Yet we are honored to be included in the 4 percent of advisors who made this respected list. In the performance Scoreboard of the same issue, the InvesTech Research Portfolio Strategy was the only service to make it into the top five in risk-adjusted ranking over the past 5-, 10-, and 15-year time periods.[17]

While Cadbury and Marty Zweig both used stop-loss strategies effectively to move into cash and manage risks, Jim Stack does not use published stops and feels he manages risks simply by following his indicators in a disciplined, patient manner. He basically uses the trend as a stop-loss. I saw him turn mostly optimistic too soon, before the 2009 lows, but he maintained his position, thanks to numerous historical studies that showed an "upcoming buying opportunity of a lifetime."[18] Again, after seeing him squirm in the tumultuous year of 2012, I thought his description of risk management was insightful and useful:

> Managing risk will be increasingly important as this bull market matures. But risk management does not mean jumping into a high-cash position every time fearful headlines appear or one becomes nervous because of a market correction. If that was the case, one would have moved to cash and been whipsawed at least four times since this bull market began.
>
> Managing risk requires setting aside one's emotions and relying on discipline. That's easy to say, but very difficult to do without time-tested technical models and extensive historical knowledge. This bull market, like every predecessor, will someday draw to a close. And while there are no guarantees, we are confident that our tools and 33 years of analytical experience will help us recognize the warning flags when they start to appear.

Objective risk management can take different forms, but it works.

■ Making Our Own Reality

I've often wondered why the crowd and popular forecasts are so often wrong. My favorite theory is that crowd psychology and liquidity (potential demand) are inversely related. For another explanation, in the foreword to Charles Mackay's book *Extraordinary Popular Delusions and the Madness of Crowds*,[19] the legendary Bernard Baruch says that "all economic movements by their very nature, are motivated by crowd psychology. . . . Without due recognition of crowd thinking (which often seems crowd-madness) our theories of economics leave much to be desired." But listen to how he views crowd thinking, "Schiller's dictum: Anyone, taken as an individual, is tolerably sensible and reasonable—as a member of a crowd, he at once becomes a blockhead."

Baruch, who wrote this foreword in October of 1932, prescribes a "potent incantation" to use against crowd thinking:

> I have always thought that if, in the lamentable era of the "New Economics," culminating in 1929, even in the very presence of dizzily spiraling prices, we had all continuously repeated, "two and two still make four," much of the evil might have been averted. Similarly, even in the general moment of gloom in which this foreword is written, when many begin to wonder if declines will never halt, the appropriate abracadabra may be: They always did.

Some other quotes I like regarding crowds, reality, and human nature are these:

Jonathan Swift: "Truths languish, while myths flourish."

Bennett Goodspeed: "Man is extremely uncomfortable with uncertainty. To deal with his discomfort, man tends to create a false sense of security by substituting certainty for uncertainty. It becomes the herd instinct."

Edwin Lefèvre, *Reminiscences of a Stock Operator*: "The speculator's chief enemies are always boring from within. It is inseparable from human nature to hope and to fear."

Or as Shakespeare put it in *Julius Caesar*: "The fault, dear Brutus, is not in our stars / But in ourselves, that we are underlings." Or as Pogo said, "We have met the enemy and they are us."

Additionally, I have become fascinated with the concept that we all *create our own realities*.

An important truth is that people will view reality according to how they *want* to perceive it or believe it *should be*. I found a powerful illustration of this principle in a human-relations class I was taking, in which we read a quote from a long-serving warden of New York's infamous Sing Sing prison. According to the warden, "Few of the criminals in Sing Sing regard themselves as bad men. They are just as human as you and I. So they rationalize, they explain. . . . Most of them attempt by a form of reasoning, fallacious or logical, to justify their anti-social acts even to themselves . . . the desperate men and women behind prison walls *don't blame themselves for anything*." *Rationalization is a powerful coping mechanism.*

People who seemingly *have to* gamble provide another good example of the human tendency to create our own realities. Despite the fact that casinos make hundreds of millions of dollars every year, I've almost never met a gambler who claimed to have been a loser. Gamblers will look you straight in the eye when they tell you that. It is my belief that the pain of losing is so great, they actually forget the losses. *Denial is a powerful defense mechanism.*

Yet another illustration: in listening to the sexual harassment testimony given during the Clarence Thomas confirmation hearing, I found that it was impossible for me to discern who was telling the truth and who was lying, but clearly, I believed, he or his accuser had to be lying. That is, until I heard a wise psychiatrist say that she thought that both of them were telling the truth. At least it was the *truth as far as each of them saw it. Illusion or delusion is a powerful psychological force.*

Some time ago I read a fascinating magazine interview with actor Ralph Fiennes, who played the evil Nazi Amon Goeth in the film *Schindler's List*. He said, *It's not a rational thing, but it's an instinctive thing.* . . . If you're playing a role, you are immersing yourself in thinking about that character—how he moves, how he thinks. In the end he *becomes an extension of your own self. You like him.* It just throws up all kinds of question marks about acting, about human behavior, about how evil is probably a lot closer to the surface than we like to think."

When asked whether there was an emotional residue from the experience of playing a character he views as obscene and sick, after a long pause Fiennes answered softly, "I think there was a price to pay for this one. When you're investigating behavior that is so negative, so intensely for three months, then you feel sort of peculiar because you might have at moments enjoyed it and at the same time you feel slightly soiled by it. . . ."[20]

A person's mind can sometimes get badly twisted under intense emotional pressure.

Then there's the O. J. Simpson case. Was he guilty? Two-thirds of whites said yes. Three-fifths of blacks said no. William Raspberry, the black Pulitzer Prize–winning journalist, asked: "How can that be? Are white people, less invested in Simpson's fate, being objective, while blacks are being emotional? Have we come to the point where color is of such importance as to override every other consideration, to render us, black and white, *incapable* of a *shared reality*?"[21]

The recent trial of George Zimmerman, a white man, for the death of Trayvon Martin, a black teenager, provides similar examples:

Washington Post, July 22, 2013

Among African Americans, 86 percent say they disapprove of the verdict—with almost all of them saying they strongly disapprove—and 87 percent saying the shooting was unjustified. In contrast, 51 percent of whites say they approve of the verdict while just 31 percent disapprove. There is also a partisan overlay to the reaction among whites: 70 percent of white Republicans but only 30 percent of white Democrats approve of the verdict.

Gallup, April 5, 2012

U.S. public opinion about the Trayvon Martin case in Florida reflects the same type of racial divide found in 1995 surveys asking about the murder trial of O. J. Simpson in Los Angeles. In one Gallup poll conducted Oct. 5–7, 1995, for example, 78 percent of blacks said the jury that found Simpson not guilty of murder made the right decision, while only 42 percent of whites agreed.

Pew Research Center poll, July 22, 2013

Younger Americans express far more dissatisfaction over the Zimmerman trial verdict than do older Americans. Among those under 30, 53 percent say they are dissatisfied with the verdict and just 29 percent are satisfied. The balance of opinion is the reverse among those ages 65 and older: 50 percent are satisfied and just 33 percent dissatisfied.

Finally, as an avid basketball fan, my favorite example of imagination distorting reality comes while watching games. And I'm willing to admit to being guilty of succumbing to this particular distortion myself. Almost always, the vast majority of home fans at a game will swear that the referees favored the opposing team (many even proclaiming that the other team has paid off the refs), even though their home team won the game, and even though objective statistics generated by academics based upon NBA games show that if there is a bias, the calls in an average game favor the home team. Crowd psychology is contagious and can influence even what we see with our own eyes. *One's perception equals one's reality.*

So the bottom line is that *people often create their own realities*, based upon things that may have happened to them as far back as the very early years of life. We are all subject to that condition. We are human. This means what feels right and easy and obvious in your gut is quite often wrong.

The reason I believe people make their own realities and see and hear what they want to see and hear is not that they are not looking for reality, but rather that they are hardwired to have a certain nature. Shown a half glass of water, many people simply will describe it as half full while others insist it is half empty. A lot of us just get up in the morning as natural-born optimists or pessimists. On the other hand, I would probably look at the glass and ask, are we sure that is indeed water? I am a natural-born skeptic. One needs to know one's nature, but to make money consistently in stocks, one must also be able to be an optimist or a pessimist when the objective indicator evidence so dictates.

■ The Ned Davis Research Response to All This

To avoid being swept up by the crowd, and to prevent our own reality from becoming badly distorted, we need an unbiased, objective standard that weighs the evidence and passes judgment devoid of emotionalism. In applying this concept to the financial markets, Ned Davis Research builds *objective, mathematical timing models*, which we believe are the best tools to overcome emotional rationalizations.

Ned Davis Research has two mandates—we are trying to make money and we are trying to stay out of big trouble. Thus, we tell our clients that the *art* of forecasting is something we do only for fun, but that making money is something about which we are serious, and we approach it in as *scientific* and *quantitative* a manner as is possible.

I like to think of *money management* today as similar to the beginning of the European Renaissance. While there were many invaluable contributions to the arts during that period from men such as Michelangelo and Rembrandt, much of what has shaped the world since then came from those who were bold enough to venture forward with scientific investigation, including da Vinci, Galileo, and Newton.

So while we are in an industry that often blends art and science, our preference is to have a strongly objective, scientific, and quantitative bias to our work.

Most technicians look at stock charts and see patterns that, unfortunately, exist only in the eyes of the beholder (just as many observers of art can find many different meanings in a painting). Most fundamentalists look at a company and profess to be able to envision earnings way into the future. We simply try to get into harmony with the impartial reality from the numbers (the weight of the evidence) available today.

■ Timing Models

I developed my basic approach to the stock market when studying high school economics. The teacher said that prices are determined by supply and demand. So when I got into the business, I tried to focus on areas of analysis that give one clues about the forces that drive those variables. The three areas I found were the tape, the Fed, and crowd psychology.

Since prices are the equilibrium points between supply and demand, it follows that if prices are rising broadly, demand must be stronger than supply, and vice versa. Since it controls interest rates and the amount of money available, the Fed should never be ignored when trying to ascertain supply and demand. Likewise, extremes in crowd sentiment can tell us if demand is largely satisfied or if nervous holders of stock have mostly sold out.

In an effort to make money, we build timing models that we will explain in this book. But first, let's discuss five key rules we use when we build our models, which include the three areas that give clues about supply and demand.

The primary rule that we use in our models is something I modestly call Davis' Law.

Davis' Law
The degree of unprofitable anxiety in an investor's life corresponds directly to the amount of time one spends dwelling on how an investment should be acting, rather than the way it actually is acting.

Rule No. 1. Don't fight the tape. We do not like to fight the harsh reality of the tape (market trend), and we try to get in harmony with the cold, bloodless verdict of the market. To enforce Davis' Law, our models are at least 50 percent price- or trend-sensitive, which we believe means we can never be fully invested during a vicious bear market or never miss the bulk of a roaring bull market.

As Marty Zweig said in *Winning on Wall Street*: "To me, the tape is the final arbiter of any investment decision. I have a cardinal rule: never fight the tape. . . . I'm a trend follower, not a trend fighter." We think our emphasis on trend- and price-sensitive indicators means that if we make a mistake, the trend will change and bail us out with a small mistake, and if we are right and it turns out to be a big move, we are almost guaranteed to get a good part of that large gain. In other words, dwell on the reality of market action rather than hopes, wishes, and imagination.

A key point on the tape/trend. In the 2010 edition of *Reminiscences of a Stock Operator*, there are some thoughts from Paul Tudor Jones. He talks about many of the disasters from the bubbles over the past decade or so, but he ends up with this conclusion: "The whole point of *Reminiscences* was that all of those very serious economic issues should be largely irrelevant to a great operator. Yes, they are interesting to debate, important to know, but always secondary to the tale the tape tells us on a continual basis."

In the next chapter, we will feature many of the indicators in our timing models. But, in each section, I also wanted to illustrate what I am talking about through indicator examples that are not in the models. For example, Figure 42.4 looks at price trends in the Dow Jones Industrial Average (DJIA) and Dow Jones Transportation Average (DJTA). The results, shown in the box in the top clip, go back 114 years, to 1900. As can be seen, the market has advanced at double-digit rates of gain

FIGURE 42.4 DJIA and DJTA Above/Below Their 200-Day Moving Averages

The figure contains the following table:

1900-08-29 to 2014-07-01		
DJIA Performance When DJIA and DJTA are:	% Gain/ Annum	% of Time
* Both Above Their 200-Day MA	11.27	53.18
One Above / One Below Their 200-Day MA	2.83	18.15
Both Below Their 200-Day MA	-3.20	28.67

(dividends not included) in the 53 percent of the time demand was above supply, as measured by when both the DJIA and DJTA are above their respective 200-day average prices. One actually lost money on the DJIA when both were below their smoothed 200-day trend.

As I learned in kindergarten: don't pick fights with bullies (the tape).

Rule No. 2. Don't fight the Fed. We are not pure technicians. Why stand on one foot, when two feet give you better balance? So we also try not to fight city hall—the Federal Reserve Board. The Fed often writes the script for Wall Street.

In *Winning on Wall Street*, Marty Zweig said, "The major direction of the market is dominated by monetary considerations, primarily Federal Reserve policy and the movement of interest rates." Like Zweig and Ned Davis Research, Dan Sullivan of *The Chartist*, who along with Zweig has consistently outperformed in the Hulbert Advisory Service rankings since 1980, puts most of his emphasis on market trends, market momentum, and monetary conditions. Sullivan says, "The Monetary Model gauges the direction of interest rates. There is a direct correlation between the movement of interest rates and stock prices. Favorable monetary conditions (declining rates) provide the catalyst for bull markets. Conversely, rising rates hinder the upward movement of stock prices as fixed-rate investments become more attractive to investors."

One classic indicator of Fed easing or tightening is the yield curve, featured in Figure 42.5. By forcing the T-bill yields (which the Fed largely controls) above T-bond yields, the Fed can push up long-term interest rates that compete with stock dividend yields. And in the 58.5 percent of the time in which the central bank has

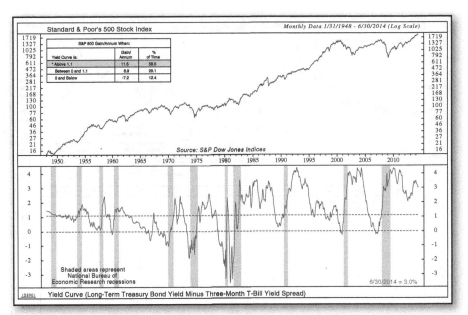

FIGURE 42.5 *Top*, S&P 500 Index; *Bottom*, Yield Curve (long-term Treasury bond yield minus three-month T-bill yield spread)

pushed short-term rates well below long-term rates, the S&P 500 has shot ahead at double-digit rates, as you can see on the chart.

One example of the availability of money can be seen on Figure 42.6. All of the net gains in stocks since 1925 have come when the Fed was providing monetary-base growth above 0.5 of a percentage point on a real basis (above inflation). The Fed has a definite impact on supply and demand for stocks.

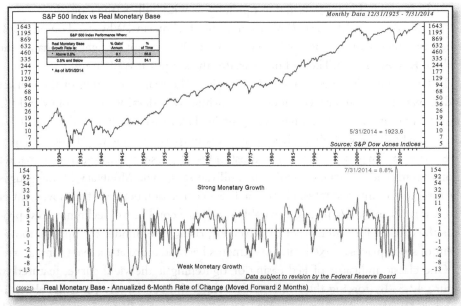

FIGURE 42.6 *Top*, S&P 500 Index; *Bottom*, Real Monetary Base: Annualized Six-Month Rate of Change (moved forward two months)

As we learned in kindergarten, try to be friends with the biggest kid in class—in this case, the Fed.

Rule No. 3. Be wary of the crowd at extremes. I believe that the stock market is a fairly efficient mechanism. If you are good at controlling your losses, the market presents you with the likelihood of about a 9 to 10 percent gain per year over the long run. To beat that return—to beat the efficient market—you are going up against not only some of the smartest people around, but also some of the most sophisticated technology.

Much of the time, the crowd is right. Yet almost by definition, the only way to beat the majority is by selectively taking a position against them. So we use numerous ways to measure majority crowd sentiment, to gauge market risk. For example, we monitor valuation and sentiment indicators, such as new-issue speculation, advisory-service sentiment, put/call ratios, the Dow earnings yield, and mutual fund cash/assets ratios to measure emotional moves in and out of the market. What distinguishes our philosophy from others is that our indicators are generally built to go *with* the majority flow until the indicators reach extreme readings and begin to *reverse*. It is at that point that it usually pays to be contrary.

In *Beating the Street* Peter Lynch said, "Over the past three decades, the stock market has come to be dominated by a herd of professional investors. Contrary to popular belief, this makes it easier for the amateur investor. You can beat the market by ignoring the herd."

Even Max Lucado, best-selling author, writer, and preacher, points out, "A man who wants to lead the orchestra must turn his back on the crowd."

In *Winning on Wall Street* Marty Zweig said, "Just because 51 percent of the crowd is bullish and 49 percent bearish is no reason the market cannot go higher. In fact, it probably will advance at that point. The time to be wary of crowd psychology is when the crowd gets extraordinarily one-sided. . . . The idea is: Beware of the crowd when the crowd is too one-sided."

Warren Buffett said one of his secrets to success is "we simply attempt to be fearful when others are greedy and to be greedy only when others are fearful." And this value investor explains the connection between sentiment and values:

> The most common cause of low prices is pessimism—sometimes pervasive, sometimes specific to a company or industry. We want to do business in such an environment, not because we like pessimism, but because we like the prices it produces.[22]

Technical analyst Joe Granville said, "If it is obvious, it is obviously wrong." I think what he meant is that what everybody knows is already priced into stocks (discounted), and it is, thus, not worth knowing.

The last word on sentiment goes to another very successful investor, Sir John Templeton, who ostensibly invested based upon fundamentals and values. He said, "Bull markets are born on pessimism, grow on skepticism, mature on optimism, and die on euphoria."

As I learned in kindergarten, if you want good reports or the teacher's praise, you need to be able to stand out from the crowd. It is not always good to follow the other kids, especially when they're really emotional.

■ What Is Contrary Opinion and How to Use It

If you want to try to be a genius and catch major market turning points, you can start with contrary opinion—wait for majority opinion to reach an extreme and then assume the opposite position. At turning points, contrary sentiment indicators are nearly always right. Almost by definition, *a top in the market is the point of maximum optimism and a bottom in the market is the point of maximum pessimism.*

To better understand how contrary opinion operates, think of money as financial liquidity. And think of an extreme in liquidity as the direct opposite of an extreme in psychology. If everyone decided that the Dow Industrials would rise by 25 percent, for instance, they would rush out and buy stocks. Everyone would become fully invested, the market would be overbought, and nobody would be left to buy, in which case the market wouldn't be able to go any higher. *When optimism is extreme, liquidity is low.*

On the other hand, if everyone was pessimistic and thought the Dow would drop by 25 percent, the weak and nervous stockholders would sell, the market would be sold out, and nobody would be left to sell, in which case the market wouldn't go down any more. Whereas increasing optimism and confidence produce falling liquidity, rising pessimism and fear result in rising liquidity.

My favorite way to describe this inverse relationship is to compare liquidity to a car's shock absorbers. As you drive down the road, you will inevitably encounter some potholes—some random, unpredictable, negative events. If your car has good shocks (abundant liquidity), you will be able to continue merrily along your journey after encountering a pothole. But if your car has poor shocks (no liquidity), you may crash.

Another way of looking at contrary opinion is to compare stockholders to nuts in a tree. An investor once wrote to me, asking, "How do you get nuts out of a nut tree?" The answer, he said, is through a nut-shaking machine, which is hooked to the nut tree. The machine rattles the tree, and the nuts drop until all of the nuts have fallen out. In other words, when there is enough fear in the market, all of the weak holders are shaken out, and there is no selling left to be done. "Have the nuts been shaken out," the contrarian asks, "or are all of the speculative traders fully invested?"

The impact of contrary opinion can also be illustrated by comparing the market to a theater. If someone yelled "*fire*" in a theater full of people, panic would break out and people would get crushed in the ensuing rush to the door. But if someone yelled "*fire*" in a theater with very few people, the people would be more likely to walk out in an orderly manner. In looking at any market, it is important to determine the degree to which it is crowded.

What makes contrary opinion really valuable is that it opens your mind and keeps you from being swept up in the crowd. With an open mind, you can say to yourself, "I know the majority is right, and I know the world is going to hell in a handbasket, but what if the minority is right? What if there is a silver lining in the cloud out there?"

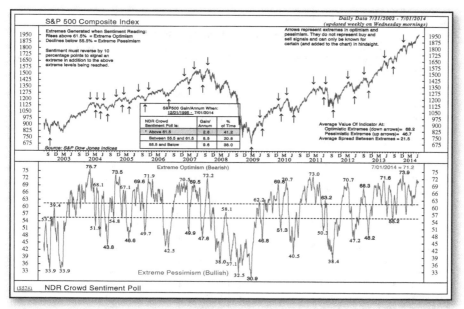

FIGURE 42.7 *Top*, S&P 500 Composite Index; *Bottom*, Crowd Sentiment Poll (2002–2014)

Contrary opinion allows you to be flexible, enabling you to turn your emotions inside out, and to act when you need to act.

Psychology plays into the supply-demand equation through valuation and emotional buying and selling when greed or fear takes over. To show clients why they should be wary of the crowd at extremes, many years ago I put together a composite of seven sentiment indicators and called it the NDR Crowd Sentiment Poll. The record can be seen in Figures 42.7 and 42.8, and in Table 42.1.

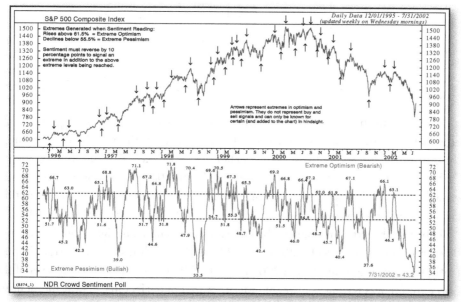

FIGURE 42.8 *Top*, S&P 500 Composite Index; *Bottom*, Crowd Sentiment Poll (1995–2002)

TABLE 42.1 Crowd Sentiment Poll

NDR CROWD SENTIMENT POLL (S574)

Date	Extreme Pessimism	Extreme Optimism	S&P 500	S&P Point Profit/Loss	Crowd Right	Crowd Wrong	Date	Extreme Pessimism	Extreme Optimism	S&P 500	S&P Point Profit/Loss	Crowd Right	Crowd Wrong
1/15/1996	51.7		600	-61		x	9/21/2001	37.6		966	-207		x
2/12/1996		66.7	661	-24		x	1/4/2002		66.1	1173	-77		x
4/12/1996	45.2		637	-32		x	2/8/2002	46.5		1096	-68		x
5/17/1996		63.0	669	-38		x	3/8/2002		63.1	1164	-387		x
7/29/1996	42.3		631	-126		x	10/9/2002	33.9		777	-371		x
11/29/1996		65.1	757	-36		x	1/21/2004		75.7	1148	-39		x
12/16/1996	51.6		721	-56		x	3/25/2004	51.9		1109	-36		x
1/20/1997		68.8	777	-19		x	4/12/2004		68.1	1145	-51		x
4/4/1997	39.0		758	-194		x	5/21/2004	47.3		1094	-47		x
7/30/1997		71.1	952	-32		x	6/30/2004		66.6	1141	-76		x
9/15/1997	51.7		920	-63		x	8/13/2004	43.8		1065	-119		x
10/7/1997		67.2	983	-77		x	11/18/2004		73.5	1184	-13		x
11/12/1997	44.6		906	-78		x	1/28/2005	55.4		1171	-39		x
12/5/1997		64.8	984	-27		x	2/15/2005		67.1	1210	-57		x
1/26/1998	51.8		957	-122		x	4/19/2005	46.6		1153	-91		x
3/16/1998		71.8	1079	-2		x	8/2/2005		69.6	1244	-66		x
6/15/1998	47.9		1077	-107		x	10/18/2005	49.7		1178	-90		x
7/16/1998		70.4	1184	-210		x	11/25/2005		71.9	1268	-28		x
9/4/1998	33.5		974	-214		x	7/21/2006	42.5		1240	-191		x
11/23/1998		69.6	1188	-47		x	1/17/2007		70.5	1431	-44		x
12/14/1998	54.7		1141	-134		x	3/16/2007	49.9		1387	-126		x
1/8/1999		70.5	1275	-49		x	5/9/2007		69.5	1513	-102		x
3/2/1999	51.8		1226	-124		x	8/16/2007	47.6		1411	-151		x
4/13/1999		67.3	1350	-44		x	10/12/2007		72.2	1562	-879		x
4/20/1999	55.3		1306	-62		x	3/6/2009	30.9		683	-262		x
5/13/1999		66.8	1368	-74		x	6/11/2009		62.2	945	-44		x
6/14/1999	48.7		1294	-125		x	7/13/2009	46.8		901	-246		x
7/16/1999		65.3	1419	-165		x	1/11/2010		69.8	1147	-71		x
10/18/1999	42.4		1254	-196		x	2/12/2010	51.3		1076	-136		x
1/13/2000		69.2	1450	-97		x	4/15/2010		70.7	1212	-152		x
2/24/2000	51.5		1353	-174		x	7/7/2010	40.5		1060	-283		x
3/24/2000		66.8	1527	-145		x	2/18/2011		73.0	1343	-71		x
5/25/2000	46.0		1382	-128		x	6/17/2011	50.3		1272	-72		x
7/17/2000		66.4	1510	-90		x	7/8/2011		63.2	1344	-220		x
7/28/2000	54.5		1420	-101		x	10/4/2011	38.4		1124	-286		x
9/1/2000		67.2	1521	-147		x	3/19/2012		70.7	1410	-124		x
10/13/2000	48.7		1374	-58		x	6/5/2012	47.2		1286	-175		x
11/6/2000		62.0	1432	-117		x	9/19/2012		68.3	1461	-108		x
12/26/2000	45.7		1315	-59		x	11/15/2012	49.5		1353	-302		x
1/30/2001		61.9	1374	-223		x	5/22/2013		71.6	1655	-15		x
3/16/2001	40.4		1151	-158		x	9/3/2013	55.2		1640	-201		x
5/22/2001		67.1	1309	-343		x	12/30/2013		73.9	1841			?
							Average	46.7	68.2	Total	-10501		

Ned Davis Research Group   S574_IND.RPT

When I built the NDR Crowd Sentiment Poll, my main goal was to prove to clients that the crowd was *usually* wrong at extremes in sentiment. We tried to judge the extremes objectively by defining certain levels as excessive and looking for big shifts. But as proven by the historical record (1996–2013), shown in Table 42.1, the crowd has yet to be right even *once* at extremes in sentiment. In fact, following the crowd at extremes would have cost one over 10,000 S&P 500 points since 1996.

To be fair, the extremes can *only* be known for certain in hindsight, and the optimistic extreme of 71.6 percent bulls on May 22, 2013, was almost correct. More importantly, the extreme pessimism in 2008 and early 2009 was largely correct, even if the *exact* extreme was wrong. Sentiment indicators are not perfect in runaway momentum moves, but they can help one keep a clear head when the crowd is fearful or euphoric.

■ History and Risk Management

Two other rules we use in building timing models are these:

1. When I asked in kindergarten why we needed to study boring old history, the teacher said, "Those who do not study history are condemned to repeat its mistakes." Ned Davis Research takes great pride in our large historical database. We are able to take our models back as far in history as possible, so they have a chance to adjust to as many different environments as possible.

   We also conduct many historical studies for investor perspective. Two real-time examples follow.

   Table 42.2 is a little subjective for my taste, but it is also one of the studies of which I am proudest. I put it out on the morning of 9/11, right after the

---

TABLE 42.2 Crisis Events, DJIA Declines, and Subsequent Performance

| NED DAVIS RESEARCH, INC. | CHART OF THE DAY | 11 SEPTEMBER 2001 |

Our updated table of crisis events is featured in the table below (study T_900). It shows that the DJIA has dropped by a median of 5% during crisis events, but has rallied afterwards. The table's implication is that after an initial negative reaction to today's tragic events, a recovery could be expected. Of course, the list is subjective, and even the reaction dates are subject to interpretation in some cases. Please let us know if you would like to see the table modified in any way. Future NDR publications will have more details and perspectives, including statistics on the performance of other assets during and after previous crises.

CRISIS EVENTS, DJIA DECLINES AND SUBSEQUENT PERFORMANCE

Event	Reaction Dates	Date Range % Gain/Loss	DJIA Percentage Gain Days After Reaction Dates 22	63	126
Fall of France	05/09/1940 - 06/22/1940	-17.1	-0.5	8.4	7.0
Pearl Harbor	12/06/1941 - 12/10/1941	-6.5	3.8	-2.9	-9.6
Truman Upset Victory	11/02/1948 - 11/10/1948	-4.9	1.6	3.5	1.9
Korean War	06/23/1950 - 07/13/1950	-12.0	9.1	15.3	19.2
Eisenhower Heart Attack	09/23/1955 - 09/26/1955	-6.5	0.0	6.6	11.7
Sputnik	10/03/1957 - 10/22/1957	-9.9	5.5	6.7	7.2
Cuban Missile Crisis	10/19/1962 - 10/27/1962	1.1	12.1	17.1	24.2
JFK Assassination	11/21/1963 - 11/22/1963	-2.9	7.2	12.4	15.1
U.S. Bombs Cambodia	04/29/1970 - 05/26/1970	-14.4	9.9	20.3	20.7
Kent State Shootings	05/04/1970 - 05/14/1970	-4.2	0.4	3.8	13.5
Arab Oil Embargo	10/18/1973 - 12/05/1973	-17.9	9.3	10.2	7.2
Nixon Resigns	08/09/1974 - 08/29/1974	-15.5	-7.9	-5.7	12.5
U.S.S.R. in Afghanistan	12/24/1979 - 01/03/1980	-2.2	6.7	-4.0	6.8
Hunt Silver Crisis	02/13/1980 - 03/27/1980	-15.9	6.7	16.2	25.8
Falkland Islands War	04/01/1982 - 05/07/1982	4.3	-8.5	-9.8	20.8
U.S. Invades Grenada	10/24/1983 - 11/07/1983	-2.7	3.9	-2.8	-3.2
U.S. Bombs Libya	04/15/1986 - 04/21/1986	2.6	-4.3	-4.1	-1.0
Financial Panic '87	10/02/1987 - 10/19/1987	-34.2	11.5	11.4	15.0
Invasion of Panama	12/15/1989 - 12/20/1989	-1.9	-2.7	0.3	8.0
Gulf War Ultimatum	12/24/1990 - 01/16/1991	-4.3	17.0	19.8	18.7
Gorbachev Coup	08/16/1991 - 08/19/1991	-2.4	4.4	1.6	11.3
ERM U.K. Currency Crisis	09/14/1992 - 10/16/1992	-6.0	0.6	3.2	9.2
World Trade Center Bombing	02/26/1993 - 02/27/1993	-0.5	2.4	5.1	8.5
Russia Mexico Orange County	10/11/1994 - 12/20/1994	-2.8	2.7	8.4	20.7
Oklahoma City Bombing	04/19/1995 - 04/20/1995	0.6	3.9	9.7	12.9
Asian Stock Market Crisis	10/07/1997 - 10/27/1997	-12.4	8.8	10.5	25.0
U.S. Embassy Bombings Africa	08/07/1998 - 08/10/1998	-0.3	-11.2	4.7	6.5
Russian LTCM Crisis	08/18/1998 - 10/08/1998	-11.3	15.1	24.7	33.7
Mean		**-7.1**	**3.8**	**6.8**	**12.5**
Median		**-4.6**	**3.9**	**6.7**	**12.1**

Days = Market Days

T_900 9/11/2001

TABLE 42.3

TABLE 42.3 Percentage Gain per Annum for Stocks, Industrial Production, Inflation, Bonds, and the U.S. Dollar by Party of President and Majority Party in Congress, 1901–2014

GAIN/ANNUM (%) FOR STOCKS, INDUSTRIAL PRODUCTION, INFLATION, BONDS, AND U.S. DOLLAR ($) BY PARTY OF PRESIDENT AND MAJORITY PARTY* IN CONGRESS (03/04/1901 - 07/01/2014)						
	Stocks (DJIA)	Industrial Production	Inflation (CPI)	Since: Real Stock Returns	1925 Long-Term Gov't Bonds	1971 Fed's U.S. Dollar
Democratic President	7.97	5.18	4.35	3.47	3.53	-0.25
Republican President	3.02	1.80	1.80	1.20	7.74	-1.39
Democratic Congress	6.21	4.45	4.29	1.85	5.28	-1.21
Republican Congress	3.62	1.45	0.65	2.95	6.39	-0.23
Dem. Pres., Dem. Congress	7.53	6.14	4.48	2.92	2.57	-2.38
Dem. Pres., Rep. Congress	9.76	1.11	3.78	5.76	8.12	3.93
Rep. Pres., Rep. Congress	1.70	1.56	-0.37	2.07	5.48	-4.24
Rep. Pres., Dem. Congress	4.46	2.05	4.01	0.43	8.99	-0.52
All Periods Buy/Hold	5.28	3.38	2.99	2.22	5.57	-0.94
*Majority Party = Party with average of % control in House and % control in Senate greater than 50%.						

Ned Davis Research, Inc.   T_50.RPT

horrible attacks on the World Trade Center. It shows how the study of history can provide perspective and help one stay grounded.

Using history for perspective and keeping one's mind open and flexible is critical for investment success. Nearly all surveys of Wall Street investors show that they lean Republican, so it is widely believed that the stock markets prefer Republicans. And, in fact, the market and economy performed very well under Eisenhower and Reagan.

When President Obama was elected in late 2008, many wealthy investors got out of stocks, predicting disaster. They were particularly upset with Obama's calls to sharply raise taxes on the top 2 percent, a group that happens to be large holders of stock. The market did continue to decline sharply in early 2009. However, I wrote a *Hotline* arguing that in order to make money in stocks consistently, I believed that one should analyze them with an apolitical mindset. In fact, I featured Table 42.3, and wrote, "The historical record shows the stock market doing better under Democratic presidents, but also with more inflation."

No matter how things eventually turn out or what one thinks about President Obama, certainly a study of history provides a useful perspective. I believe the record since 1901 suggests stressing factual reality over Wall Street myths. Also, while people fret about a gridlocked government, the limited historical examples suggest that this, too, has not been a big problem for stocks.

President Harry S. Truman once said, "My choice early in life was either to be a piano player in a whorehouse or a politician. And to tell the truth, there's hardly any difference." Regardless of what people think about politicians, I still try to respect people's political beliefs. But the study of history tells me that investing based upon politics is a poor way to make money.

2. Despite all our efforts to build models that will provide good gains going forward, we realize that we will never find the Holy Grail, and thus, we try to build *good money management* into our timing models by attempting to cut losses short and letting profits run. There are periods, historically, in which model indicators tend to fail or stay wrong against a major move. Accordingly, we put stop-losses in the indicators, where the indicator weight goes to zero until the indicator gives a new signal. As we learned in kindergarten, sometimes doo-doo happens, so we need to be prepared.

Finally, we see ourselves as risk managers. Here's a story about risk management I want to share with you.

Two cowboys, having lost their jobs, went into a bar to drown their sorrows. Over the bar was a sign that said, Bear Hides $25. When they asked the bartender what that meant he said, "It means what it says," so the two cowboys went out, came back with two bear hides, and received $50. One of the cowboys was a capitalist and he said, "All we need now is inventory," so they got on their horses and rode deep into bear country. It was dark out, so they put up their tent and went to sleep. Early the next morning they heard a rumble, so one cowboy looked outside to see what it was. When he opened the tent he saw 10,000 growling bears. He looked at all the bears and then looked at the other cowboy, and with a grin said, "We're rich!"

One good definition of the difference between professionals and amateurs is that amateurs ask what the potential rewards are, while professionals ask what the risks are. Take our composite timing models, for example. If we have a model composed of 10 indicators, all of which are bullish, we would obviously be extremely bullish. But let's say two of these 10 reliable indicators turn bearish. Obviously, with eight bullish indicators and just two bearish indicators, we would stay with the investment, but we might take 20 percent of our chips off the table out of respect for the higher risks. This is not a black-and-white world that we live in. It's beautifully composed of shades of gray and degrees of bullishness and bearishness.

Thus, the bottom line at Ned Davis Research is that our timing models, at every stage of development, are designed with one thought foremost in mind, and that is *controlling big mistakes*.

The Nine Rules of Ned Davis Research Group

The nine rules that follow are a teaching aid for new NDR employees.

1. Don't Fight the Tape

   The tape provides a stop-loss for should-be beliefs.

   The trend is your friend (smoothings, slopes, and stop-losses).

   Go with Mo (momentum, breadth thrusts, signs of churning).

   Listen to the cold, bloodless verdict of the market (pay special notice to indicators on the leading edge of the market like volume, new highs or lows, the Dow Utilities, bonds, relative strength, etc.).

   Moves with a lot of confirmation are the healthiest, and huge moves are often global in nature.

2. Don't Fight the Fed

   Remain in harmony with interest-rate trends (rates dropping is good; rates rising is bad).

   Money moves markets. Stay in line with monetary trends (especially money less economic demands equals liquidity left over for financial markets).

   Economic strains: inflationary pressures lead to Fed tightness (up commodities, up gold, down dollar, rising real interest rates).

   Economic ease: disinflation leads to Fed ease.

3. Beware of the Crowd at Extremes

Go with the flow until it reaches a psychological extreme and begins to reverse. At that point, it pays to take a contrary approach (reverse inverted brackets).

Key relationship: liquidity and psychology are inversely related.

Extreme optimism equals low cash. Extreme fear equals high cash.

Liquidity is like shock absorbers on a car.

Is the theater crowded or empty?

Top is the point of maximum optimism. Bottom is the point of maximum pessimism.

Valuation measures long-term extremes in psychology.

4. Rely on Objective Indicators

Rather than using gut emotions to determine the supply and demand balance, use the weight-of-the-evidence approach (computer-derived mathematical measurements).

5. Be Disciplined

Our mandate is to follow our models, forcing us to be *disciplined*.

Benchmark or anchor composite model determines core invested position.

6. Practice Risk Management

We are in the business of making mistakes. Winners make small mistakes, losers make big mistakes. We focus on a risk management strategy to keep mistakes small (use stop-losses and a heavy dose of technical trend-sensitive indicators).

7. Remain Flexible

Indicators change and data is revised. Scenarios change. Use dynamic modeling, such as standard deviation brackets. Review models on an objective and timely basis.

8. Money Management Rules

We are more interested in making money than being right.

Be humble and flexible (be ready to turn emotions upside down and thus be open-minded).

Let profits run, cut losses short.

Think in terms of risks, including the risk of missing a bull market.

Buy on the rumor, sell on the news.

Consider cyclical, seasonal, progressive trading patterns that do not add to models (for fun).

9. Those Who Do Not Study History Are Condemned to Repeat Its Mistakes

Go back as far as possible. Use bull, bear, and neutral cycles.

■ Notes

1. George Soros, *The Alchemy of Finance* (New York: John Wiley & Sons, 1987).
2. Peter Lynch and John Rothchild, *Beating the Street* (New York: Simon & Schuster, 1993).

3. Jonathan Burton, "Learn a Lesson—Before You Get One" summarized from Bob Farrell's 10 "Market Rules to Remember," *MarketWatch* (June 11, 2008).

4. William Bernsetin, *The Intelligent Asset Allocator* (New York, NY: McGraw-Hill, 2000).

5. *The Chartist*, P.O. Box 758, Seal Beach, CA 90740.

6. Value Line, 220 East 42nd Street, New York, NY 10017.

7. Jack D. Schwager, *Market Wizards* (New York, NY: New York Institute of Finance, 1989).

8. Brendan Moynihan and Jim Paul, *What I Learned Losing a Million Dollars* (Nashville, TN: Infrared Press, 1994).

9. Martin Zweig, *Winning on Wall Street* (New York, NY: Warner Books, 1986).

10. Martin Schwartz, *Pit Bull* (New York: Harper Business, 1998).

11. Edwin Lefèvre, *Reminiscences of a Stock Operator* (Larchmont, NY: George H. Doran, 1923).

12. Jack D. Schwager, *The New Market Wizards* (New York, NY: Harper Business, 1992).

13. Howard Abell and Robert Koppel, *The Inner Game of Trading* (Chicago, IL: Probus Publishing, 1994).

14. Gerald M. Loeb, *The Battle for Investment Survival* (New York, NY: Simon & Schuster, 1935).

15. Peter Lynch and John Rothchild, *One Up on Wall Street* (New York, NY: Simon & Schuster, 1989).

16. *Hulbert Financial Digest*, 8001 Braddock Road #107, Springfield, VA 22151.

17. James B. Stack, *InvesTech Research* (May 31, 2013).

18. James B. Stack, "A Buying Opportunity of a Lifetime?," *InvesTech Research* (March 13, 2009).

19. Charles Mackay, *Extraordinary Popular Delusions and the Madness of Crowds* (New York, NY: Barnes & Noble, 1989).

20. John Darnton, "Self-Made Monster: An Actor's Creation," *New York Times*, February 14, 1994.

21. William Raspberry, "Does This Poll Mean That Skin Color Is Everything?" (Washington Post Writers Group, 1994).

22. Warren Buffett, "1990 Chairman's Letter," Berkshire Hathaway Chairman's Letters to Shareholders.

CHAPTER 43

The Model-Building Process

Sam Burns

Updated by Ned Davis from *Being Right or Making Money*, 3rd Edition (Hoboken, New Jersey: John Wiley & Sons, 2014), Chapter 2.

Learning Objective Statements

- Describe "internal" and "external" indicators
- Explain the use of valuation indicators as sentiment measures
- Describe the basic relationships of economic growth, Fed policy, and money supply
- Discuss the use of moving average signals based on "crossings" and "slopes"
- Explain the use of price momentum and indicator momentum
- Identify the problem of curve-fitting, or overoptimization

Earlier we described the types of indicators we use to try to manage risk in the stock market in general. This chapter will further outline our model-building process.

■ The Model-Building Process

A market-timing model can form the basis of an investor's market outlook by providing a benchmark for adjusting exposure to different types of assets. By using objective, quantitative information and testing its predictive value against historical data, an investor can avoid making decisions based on emotion, gut feel, or the pronouncements of the market guru *du jour*. A model with a variety of indicators, which individually have value in highlighting risk and reward, can offer a more stable, predictable, and reliable reflection of the market than any single indicator can. Such a model can anchor the investment/asset-allocation process.

■ Where to Start: Model Inputs

Any model is only as good as its inputs, and if those inputs contain errors, aren't timely, or are simply irrelevant, the model will provide little benefit. So the first thing investors who want to build or maintain a quantitative timing model must do is make sure that they have clean (error-free), reliable data that is updated regularly. One must also take into account data revisions, which are common in economic reports, and make sure that the information used is consistent over time. At Ned Davis Research, we devote a lot of time and effort to making sure our data is as clean, as reliable, and as up-to-date as possible.

The next thing an investor building a timing model should investigate is which data series, out of the innumerable possible sets out there, are the most useful or relevant for asset-allocation and market-timing purposes. Some data is best suited for aggressive, short-term trading, while other data is best suited for long-term asset allocation and risk control. Finding out what is useful is the biggest challenge the investor faces and is a primary goal of our analysts. To help narrow the possibilities and provide some structure for those looking to use or develop models, we offer some of the results of our research and the ways we categorize data.

One distinction we often make is between "internal" and "external" indicators.

Internal indicators are based on the market itself. They include price trend and momentum, as well as corollary indicators, such as the number of stocks rising versus the number falling on a given day (a.k.a. *breadth*). Internal indicators are generally designed to ensure that we keep our eye on the ball by focusing the model on the actual market whose future we are trying to predict, and that we do not allow the model to become too far removed from that market's primary underlying trend. Our goal is to be in harmony with that trend. Because we have found that the trend in market prices is perhaps the most important factor to consider, internal measures typically account for half (or more) of the indicators in our timing models.

External indicators aren't derived from the market directly, but are known (or thought) to significantly influence it. The best example of an important external indicator is interest rates. History shows that their level and direction have a major impact on the direction of stock prices. So we try to include indicators based on interest rates in our stock-timing models.

The following sections describe the various categories of indicators we have found useful in constructing models.

■ Sentiment and Valuation Indicators

While many analysts consider sentiment and valuation indicators to be quite separate and distinct, we put the two together because we often view valuation indicators as simply another way of measuring investor sentiment. Investor psychology plays a crucial role in how stock prices behave, and so monitoring what most investors are thinking and doing is very important. There are several regularly updated polls or surveys of various investors, including market newsletter writers, futures traders, and individuals. These polls typically just ask the respondents whether they have a bullish (positive) or a bearish (negative) view on stocks and then aggregate the responses to give the percentage of the group that is bullish or bearish at any given time. When a great majority of investors have the same view of the market, it is typically a warning to expect a reversal contrary to the majority opinion. In addition to watching the surveys, we also consider data related to valuation, such as price/earnings (P/E) ratios, as a sentiment indicator. Why? Because the price investors are willing to pay for a stock, relative to its underlying assets or earnings, indicates their level of confidence or optimism about the prospects for that stock (or in the aggregate, the market). When investors are very optimistic they will pay higher prices, as reflected in high price/earnings or price/book value ratios, while pessimistic investors will buy only at low valuation levels. We see how much investors are paying for current valuations and compare that to historical norms. This has the added benefit of reflecting what investors are actually *doing*, as opposed to what they are *saying* in response to polls.

An example of a sentiment and valuation indicator is the results of the weekly poll of its members by the American Association of Individual Investors, and the price/earnings ratio of the S&P 500 (see Figures 43.1 and 43.2).

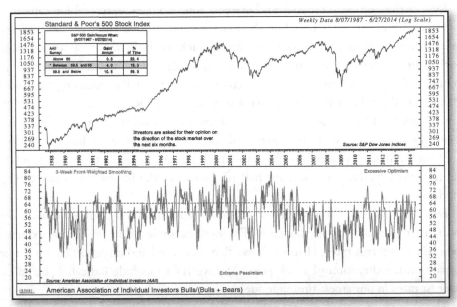

FIGURE 43.1 *Top*, S&P 500 Index; *Bottom*, American Association of Individual Investors: Bulls/(Bulls + Bears)

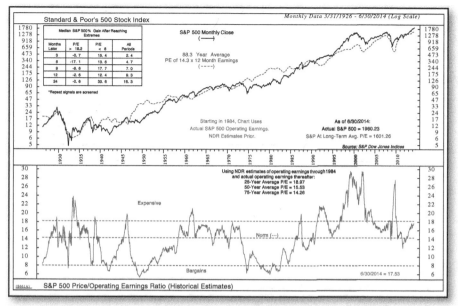

FIGURE 43.2 *Top*, **S&P 500 Index;** *Bottom,* **S&P 500 Price/Operating Earnings Ratio (historical estimates)**

■ Monetary Indicators

Some of the most important external indicators are monetary indicators. These reflect what is happening to the *price* of money (interest rates) and the *supply* (availability) of money. Interest rates are a primary driver of stock returns, because high rates make debt securities relatively more attractive than equities to investors, and also drive up businesses' cost of raising capital. So indicators based on the level and trend of interest rates (or bond prices, which are inversely related to rates) are common in our stock-market models. Of course, bond prices and interest rates appear in our bond-market models as well, but they are considered internal indicators in that context. We also use indicators based on the growth of the money supply, since changes in that often influence interest rates, the stock market, and the economy as a whole. We do this by tracking M1, M2, and M3, which are monetary aggregates defined and watched carefully by the Federal Reserve. Figure 43.3 shows how such indicators can be used.

One of the principles that we adhere to at Ned Davis Research is *don't fight the Fed*. The Fed, of course, is the Federal Reserve Board, which acts as the nation's central bank and largely controls the money supply and short-term interest rates. It has a great deal of influence over the banking system, the economy, and the financial markets, and its primary goal is to achieve price stability (a very low inflation rate) and sustainable economic growth. Because it is concerned, first and foremost, with keeping inflation low and economic growth reasonable (not too strong and not too weak), the Fed uses its influence on interest rates and

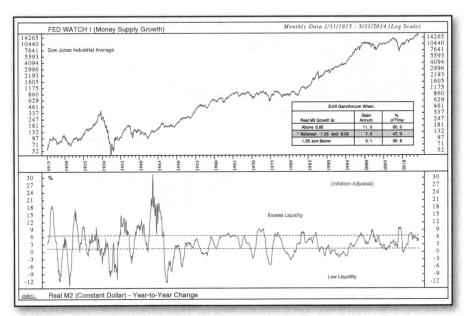

FIGURE 43.3 Fed Watch I (money supply growth): *Top*, DJIA; *Bottom*, Year-to-Year Change in Real M2 (constant dollars)

the money supply to stimulate the economy when it is too weak and restrain the economy when it appears to be growing at an unsustainable rate. Excessively high growth often leads to higher inflation, as demand for goods and services exceeds the economy's ability to produce them. The resulting scarcity boosts prices. Thus, when the Fed decides it needs to restrain the economy, it raises rates and reduces the money supply to limit consumers' purchasing power. But higher interest rates and slower money-supply growth are bad for stock prices. So whenever the Fed is in a restrictive monetary posture, it also ends up restraining stock prices as well. When we see evidence that the Fed is turning more restrictive we become more cautious toward stocks. This is why we place considerable weight on the monetary indicators in our stock-market timing models.

A simple but effective monetary indicator can be constructed by determining the momentum, or rate of change, of interest rates. For example, one can simply compute the year-to-year change in the average yield on Baa-rated corporate bonds, as shown in Figure 43.4. When the current yield is materially higher than it was one year earlier it sends a negative warning signal for stock prices, as it implies that interest rates have risen enough to become restrictive. Conversely, when rates have fallen noticeably below the level of a year earlier that's a positive for stocks, because falling rates can stimulate the economy and offer less competition for investors' capital. For a more sensitive indicator, one could use a six-month, rather than a one-year, rate of change. This simple kind of monetary indicator can go a long way toward making sure that an investor is not swimming against the tide . . . and the Fed.

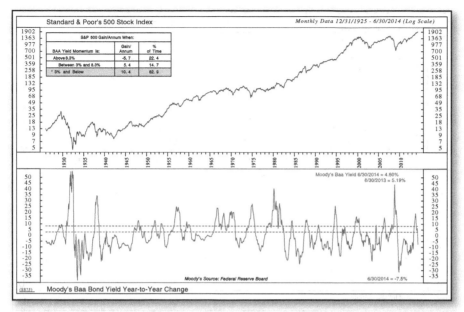

FIGURE 43.4 *Top,* S&P 500 Index; *Bottom,* Moody's Year-to-Year Change in Baa Bond Yield

Economic Indicators

A broader category of external indicators can be classified simply as economic indicators. These track economic vitality or inflation. Examples are gross domestic product (GDP), the consumer price index (CPI), and surveys showing current and expected economic conditions (such as the monthly polls underlying The Conference Board's index of consumer confidence and the Institute for Supply Management's report on business activity). These indicators typically have the most effect on bond prices and interest rates, and thus on the actions of the Federal Reserve and on stock prices. In many cases, good economic news—such as high growth, high employment, or high confidence—is bad for bonds and stocks. Conversely, news of slower economic, wage, or employment growth, or lower consumer confidence can be good for both. Why this perverse reaction? Because strong economic reports are likely to prompt the Fed to worry about rising inflation, leading it to cool off the economy by raising rates and curbing money-supply expansion. That, in turn, would make stocks and bonds less attractive (see Figure 43.5).

Internal Indicators

All of these external indicators can be useful when applied correctly, but because they are, in effect, once or twice removed from the stock market itself, we don't rely exclusively on them. Because economic data is often revised, subject to estimation errors, or released with a lag, we typically want to anchor our models with data straight from the source—the price, breadth, and volume readings from the market itself. As noted earlier, we call all of the indicators based on stock prices and volume

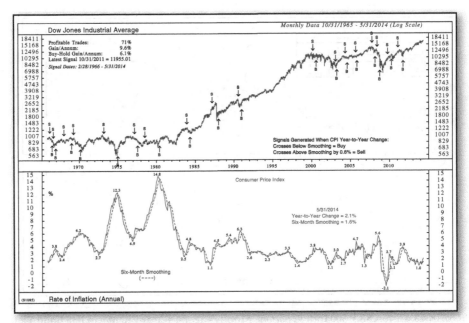

FIGURE 43.5 *Top*, DJIA with Buy/Sell Signals; *Bottom*, Annual Rate of Inflation

internal. But to get a really solid view of what is happening in the market, we might also use other types of internal indicators, along with various signal-generation techniques. The same principles apply to indicators for any other market as well (bonds, commodities, and so on).

■ Moving Averages

One well-known way to get a handle on the underlying trend in stock prices is to use a *moving average (MA)*. This is simply an average of the last, say, 50 days of prices. It's updated each day, by dropping the price from 51 days earlier and adding in the most recent day's quote. Then the average is recalculated.

When plotted on a chart, this continuously updated fixed-period average *moves*, along with the actual price data; hence the name. What this technique does is smooth out the largely random short-term wiggles in the price of a stock or a market index, revealing the underlying trend. One can calculate a moving average using any number of periods. But the longer the time frame is, the more smoothing will occur and the less sensitive the results will be to the latest price changes. A short-term trader might use a five-day moving average to pick up the near-term trend, while a long-term investor might use a six-month moving average to pick up only larger, longer term moves and ignore shorter term fluctuations.

The moving average I just described (known as a simple moving average) has a potential drawback in that it applies equal weight to all of the prices it includes. But if the more recent data is the most important, one may want to use an average that applies more weight to the newest information and less to the older numbers. This is achieved by using a weighted moving average or an exponential moving average. Both calculate a moving average by placing more weight on recent observations. The actual calculations are a bit complicated and are available in many reference books. The important point is that, in some cases, variations on an indicator can improve performance. So, we use variations in our models as well.

■ Crossings and Slopes

Once we have calculated a moving average, how can it be used to objectively generate signals about the direction of prices? One way is to just see if the current stock or index price is above or below the current moving average value. If it is above that value the trend can be considered up, and if the current price is below the moving average the trend can be considered down. We call this a *crossing* indicator. However, the price can whip back and forth around the moving average and thus change its signal too frequently. To get around that, a model can be built that recognizes signals, up or down, only if they're based on moves of a certain minimum size. Or, one can use both short- and longer term averages together. The short-term average smooths out the very short-term blips in prices but remains responsive to the latest price action, while the longer term average indicates the underlying trend. A change in trend is signaled when the short-term average (rather than the price itself) crosses above or below the longer term average. This reduces the frequency of *whipsaws*, or short-term signals caused by random volatility in prices (see the table in the top section of Figure 43.6, which shows how the 50- and 200-day moving averages impact DJIA performance going back to 1900).

Another approach is to ignore the latest price and just watch the direction of the moving average itself. We consider this a *slope* indicator because we are measuring

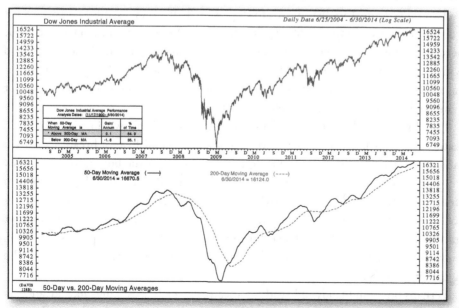

FIGURE 43.6   *Top*, DJIA 2004–2014; *Bottom*, 50-Day versus 200-Day Moving Averages

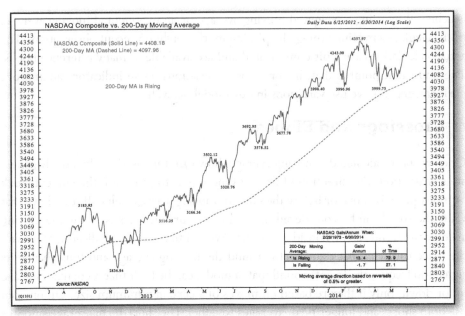

FIGURE 43.7 NASDAQ Composite versus 200-Day Moving Average

the moving average's direction or slope (when plotted on a chart). When the moving average rises a specified amount from a low (say, 5 percent), an uptrend is in place, while a decline of a specified amount from a peak indicates a downtrend. (Figure 43.7 shows a moving-average direction with a small slope for the NASDAQ.) By varying the length of the moving average and the amount that it must rise or fall to give a signal, the analyst can dictate the indicator's sensitivity (e.g., by making it send frequent signals for short-term traders or less frequent signals for longer term investors). We often use some combination of these moving-average indicators in our models.

Two other indicators that illustrate slope signals are very useful. Figure 43.8 uses a 5.5 percent rise on the NASDAQ 100 Index (NDX) to get a buy signal, and a 6.8 percent decline from a high to get a sell signal. Only 48 percent of the trades made with this indicator were profitable, but it cuts losses short and lets profits run, so it has made good money. Figure 43.9 uses a similar slope analysis on interest rates to generate buy and sell signals on the S&P 500.

One breadth indicator I have had good luck with is shown in Figure 43.10. I featured this on January 7, 2013, following a buy signal from a breadth thrust on January 4. Historically, it showed *no* losses one year after the buy signal. The indicator gives a buy whenever 90 percent of our database of institutional grade common stocks rises above their 50-day moving average. We call this a *breadth-thrust* buy signal. In my *Hotline* I said, "I generally try to 'trust the thrust' with such strong momentum, and I am very careful with overbought readings or excessive optimism when big momentum is strong on the upside." As can be seen on the chart, that January 4 buy signal hit a real bull's-eye!

Perhaps the granddaddy of breadth indicators, which uses things like advance and decline lines, new highs or new lows, up and down volume, and so on, is shown on

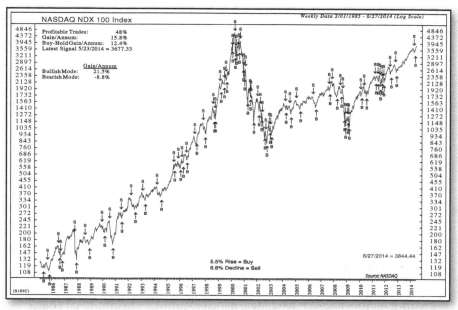

FIGURE 43.8   NASDAQ NDX 100 Index

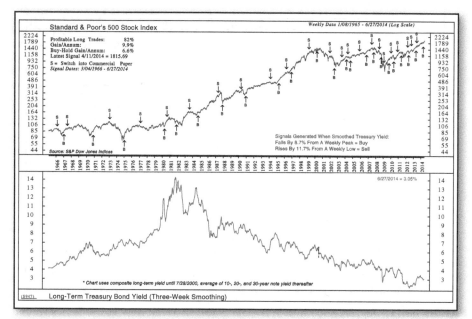

FIGURE 43.9   *Top*, S&P 500 Index with Buy/Sell Signals; *Bottom*, Long-Term Treasury Bond Yield (three-week smoothing)

Figure 43.11. It just tracks the number of NYSE issues at new 52-week lows each week as a percentage of issues traded. It goes back all the way to 1940! When there are a lot of new lows, the market has declined, on average. And when there are very few new lows, the market has little downside leadership and good breadth; in that case, the S&P 500 has advanced at double-digit rates more than 50 percent of the time. Make the breadth trend your friend.

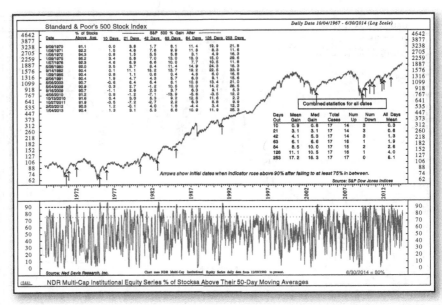

FIGURE 43.10 *Top*, S&P 500 Index; *Bottom*, Multi-Cap Institutional Equity Series Percentage of Stocks above Their 50-Day Moving Averages

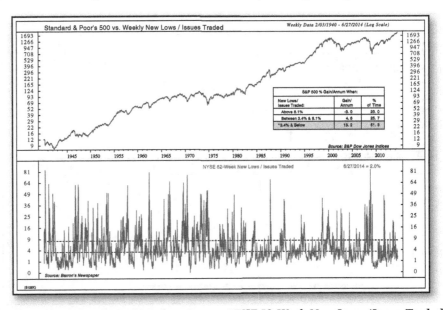

FIGURE 43.11 *Top*, S&P 500 Index; *Bottom*, NYSE 52-Week New Lows/Issues Traded

■ Momentum

Another important type of internal indicator is *momentum*. The term typically applies to physical objects, and, indeed, stock prices exhibit characteristics similar to those of objects that are in motion. Momentum is typically measured as a rate of change, as in the distance an object travels in a given period, or the amount by which stock prices rise or fall in a given time span. To calculate a 10-day

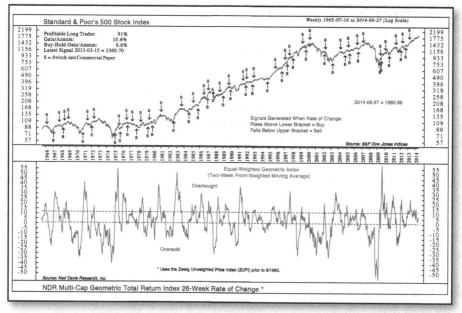

FIGURE 43.12 NASDAQ Composite versus 200-Day Moving Average

momentum, simply divide the current price by the price 10 days ago and subtract 1 from the result. A positive value indicates that the price trend is up, and a negative value implies a downtrend. We also look at how high or low the momentum is, because when a market shows a significant *thrust*, or sharp movement in one direction (an extremely high or low momentum reading), it often indicates that prices will continue in the same direction for a while, much as an object hurled into the air will keep rising for a while due to its momentum before it slows and tumbles back to earth (see Figure 43.10). So a very high momentum reading implies that prices will continue on an upward path for some time, while a very low (negative) reading implies that a downtrend is under way. The chart waits for a clear reversal from extreme readings to show an objective change in momentum (see Figure 43.12).

Momentum can be applied to external indicators, too. We can use the momentum of bond prices to give signals for stocks, or the momentum of the CRB (Commodity Research Bureau) Commodity Price Index to give signals for bonds or stocks. Also, because extreme momentum cannot be maintained indefinitely, and extreme readings are often followed later by reversals, we can use *brackets*, or specified levels of momentum (up or down), to indicate when an extreme has been reached. An extreme by itself may be useful for signals, or we can set up the indicator so that it gives a signal when an extreme has been hit *and then reverses* back below the bracket level to indicate that the momentum has been spent and a reversal is likely.

■ Putting Indicators Together

We've now seen a variety of indicators that can be used in a market-timing or asset-allocation model. As mentioned, no single indicator or data series can consistently provide a reliable view of something as complex as the stock or bond market. So in the same way that companies are often run by a group of informed directors, we put a variety of individual indicators into a model to produce a *consensus* (composite) view of the market. That way, if any one indicator is ineffective or gets out of sync with the market it won't throw the investor completely off course, since the other indicators in the model will likely override the erroneous one.

The simplest way to create a model from a collection of separate indicators, and the way we often do it at Ned Davis Research, is to just determine whether each indicator is bullish, bearish, or neutral. Then we assign a +1 for each bullish indicator, a −1 for each bearish indicator, and 0 for the neutral indicators, and add up the results. If a model has 20 individual indicators and 12 are bullish, 6 are bearish, and 2 are neutral, the composite model reading would be +6. The analyst could then test the model's readings over time against the market's performance and determine if it provides good signals and what the optimum parameters are for taking action. For example, testing might indicate that it's best to buy shares when the model rises to +2 or more, and to sell only when it falls to −2 or below.

Ideally, a composite model will include a variety of indicators, including trend, monetary, and sentiment gauges, so that a complete picture of market conditions emerges, and no single type of indicator carries too much weight. Thus, building a model is a bit like building an investment portfolio; it's generally wise to diversify. At Ned Davis Research, our experience and long-standing focus on risk control and avoiding major losses has led us to usually require that at least half of a composite model's indicators be trend-oriented, or internal. This ensures that the model will always be forced to stay with the trend of the market itself.

One key issue that a model builder must consider is *overoptimization* or excessive *curve-fitting*. With enough data and many permutations and combinations of indicators, a determined analyst with a computer can find some mixture of indicators that appears to predict the stock market (or almost anything else) with very high accuracy *in hindsight* (meaning the information *fits the curves* of past stock price movements very closely). But because the future never looks exactly like the past, indicators or models that are created (*fitted*) based on the exact sequence of prices seen in the past invariably perform much worse in the future, as they haven't picked up a real, repeatable pattern or trend. Because computers can try literally millions of possible data combinations and match them to a set of historical prices, a few indicators will pop up, purely by chance, that will show extraordinarily good results and seem to be the holy grail of investing. But any results that fit the past too perfectly are unlikely to fit the future nearly so well. They should be examined very carefully or discarded.

One way to try to avoid overfitting indicators or models is to analyze and test them on a subset of the available historical data (such as the first 10 years of a 20-year span), set the indicator's parameters, and then test it on a different subset (the next 10 years) to see if both results are similar. If they are, the indicator is more likely to be reliable. If they aren't, the correlation with past data probably has been found by chance. The indicator is more lucky than good.

Other ways to determine if an indicator's or model's results are likely to be repeated in the future is to examine all of the signals it gives. One thing to check is whether a good performance is due entirely to one or a few big gains. An example would be an indicator that just happened to be out of the stock market, or short the market, during the historic stock market crash of October 19, 1987. If the indicator's other signals weren't particularly good, one would have much less confidence in its ability to provide consistently accurate future results. Similarly, any indicator that gives only a very few signals over the historical testing period must be used with caution, even if the results look good. The fewer the signals, the higher the probability that the results are due to luck.

Ideally an indicator or model should provide useful information during *any* period of reasonable length, rather than just in certain periods or under specific conditions. However, an indicator that works only under certain circumstances can still be useful, so long as one does not rely on it too much. Measures designed to highlight extremes, for example, such as very high or low price momentum or investor sentiment readings, can be very valuable *when they are flashing a signal*. But during periods when the indicator is not at an extreme and is just sitting in the middle of its typical range, it should be ignored. This is why it's important to create a composite model that aggregates the readings of many different indicators, and why we often allow individual indicators within a model to be neutral or have no influence when they have nothing to say.

■ Conclusion

Our primary goal in creating a model is to offer investors a testable anchor for measuring risk and reward and making sound asset-allocation decisions. Using objective, quantitative information limits the potential for letting psychological biases (which everyone has) block the correct choices. Subjective opinions and gut feel are often erroneous, inconsistent, and unreliable over time. It's very easy for an individual to get trapped in a subjective market view and stubbornly refuse to do the smart thing. A good model can provide the discipline and confidence needed to navigate the perilous waters of investing.

In summary, the main elements of creating and using a market-timing/asset-allocation model are:

■ Gather as much objective, quantitative data as possible.

■ Make certain that the information is accurate and can be updated in a relatively timely manner.

- Test individual data series and the various manipulations of the data mentioned above against the market to determine if they have any potential predictive value. Make sure not to overfit the data to historical prices.

- Select different types of indicators (e.g., trend, monetary, sentiment, etc.) based on their historical reliability and their ability to complement one another.

- Combine the indicators into a model that gives a single composite reading. The indicators can be weighted equally or by their relative importance or historical accuracy.

- Test the resulting model to see if it provides reliable results.

- *Use the model as the basis for disciplined investing.*

CHAPTER 44

Relative Strength as a Criterion for Investment Selection

From Robert A. Levy, "Relative Strength as a Criterion for Investment Selection," *The Journal of Finance* 22, Issue 4 (1967): 595–610.

President, Computer Directions Advisors, Inc., Silver Spring, Maryland

Learning Objective Statements

- Define relative strength
- Explain the value of relative strength in analyzing stock price movements
- List several relative strength ratios that may be calculated
- Identify some of the limitations of relative strength in investment decisions

■ I. Introduction

An extensive body of literature has recently emanated from scholarly sources stating that successive stock market price changes are statistically independent (i.e., that the study of past price trends and patterns—known in the trade as technical analysis—is no more useful in predicting future price movements than throwing a dart at the list of stocks in a daily newspaper). Most of the empirical tests to date of this random walk theory have employed some variation of serial correlation or runs analysis. The results have been both consistent and impressive. As stated by Eugene F. Fama:

> I know of no study in which standard statistical tools have produced evidence of *important* dependence in series of successive price changes.

In general, these studies (and there are many of them) have tended to uphold the theory of random walks.[1]

There is, however, at least one important technique of technical analysis that has not been extensively tested—correction for the "co-movement" of stock prices. Benjamin F. King, Jr., in his unpublished Ph.D. dissertation, concluded that a large part of the movement of the price of a stock can be viewed as co-movement, not independent of what happens to the prices of other stocks.[2] King's conclusion was supported in a statement by John M. Birmingham, Jr.

> One . . . analysis, as yet only privately circulated, does indicate that the portfolio planning students are on the right track when they talk about intercorrelation of stock prices. It strongly suggests that the majority of individual stock price changes are controlled by more dominant "general market" and industry tendencies. In other words, successive changes in GM may be independent of previous changes for GM stock, but they are not independent of simultaneous changes in all other stocks or, in particular, other auto stocks.[3]

The intercorrelation or co-movement of stock prices could conceal existing dependencies in successive price changes. Perhaps an overly simplified example will illustrate this phenomenon more clearly. Table 44.1 sets forth the prices of Stocks A and B at the beginning of four consecutive time periods.

A serial correlation study (Table 44.2) might attempt to measure the relationship between successive first differences for each stock.

The limited data above certainly offer no preliminary indication that any significant degree of correlation exists between successive price changes.

Notice, however, that Stock B was relatively stronger than Stock A in all three periods. This fact might be revealed by computing the period-by-period percentage change in each stock's price and then ranking these percentage changes, assigning a

TABLE 44.1

| | Price at Beginning of Time Period | | | |
Stock	1	2	3	4
A	$10.00	$12.00	$10.00	$11.00
B	10.00	15.00	14.00	18.00

---

[1] Eugene F. Fama, "Random Walks in Stock Market Prices," *Financial Analysts Journal* XXI, no. 5 (September–October, 1965), 57.

[2] Benjamin F. King, Jr., "The Latent Statistical Structure of Security Price Changes" (unpublished Ph.D. dissertation, University of Chicago, 1964). Cited by Lawrence Fisher, "Outcomes for 'Random' Investments in Common Stocks Listed on the New York Stock Exchange," *Journal of Business* XXXVIII, no. 2 (April, 1965), 159.

[3] John M. Birmingham, Jr., "Random and Rational: Stock Price Behavior and Investment Returns," *Financial Analysts Journal* XXI, no. 5 (September–October, 1965), 53.

TABLE 44.2

| Stock | Successive First Differences by Time Period | | |
	1–2	2–3	3–4
A	+$2.00	−$2.00	+$1.00
B	+ S.00	−1.00	+ 4.00

TABLE 44.3

| Stock | Percentage Change in Price by Time Period | | |
	1–2	2–3	3–4
A	+20.0%	−16.7%	+10.0%
B	+50.0	−6.7	+28.3

| Stock | Performance Ranks by Time Period | | |
	1–2	2–3	3–4
A	2	2	2
B	1	1	1

rank of 1 to the stock with the greatest percentage appreciation (or least percentage depreciation) and a rank of 2 to the stock with the opposite characteristics. The outcome of this process is reported in Table 44.3.

Significantly, a serial correlation study of performance ranks offers far more promise of indicating a close relationship over time than would the same study using successive first differences.

By using ranks that measure *relative* strength, the co-movement of stocks is filtered out. This technique for eliminating the effects of the "general market" will be used for the empirical tests in this study.

■ II. Construction of the Data File

Raw Data The raw data for the tests that follow were the weekly closing prices of 200 stocks listed on the New York Stock Exchange for the 260-week period beginning on Monday, October 24, 1960 and ending on Friday, October 15, 1965.[4] The time period chosen was the most recent and lengthy period for which data were economically available in a form usable on the IBM 7090 and 7094 computers. The stocks were chosen according to the following criteria: (1) as previously mentioned, they had to have been listed on the New York Stock Exchange for the entire test

---

[4] Price data were supplied by Arnold E. Amstutz, Assistant Professor of Management at the Massachusetts Institute of Technology, and were checked extensively against the following sources: "Statistical Section," *Barron's,* October 1961 (XL, nos. 44 through 52, and XLI, no. 1); *ISL Daily Stock Price Index: New York Stock Exchange* (Palo Alto, California: Investment Statistics Laboratory, 1961 annual edition and quarterly editions from 1962 through 3rd quarter 1965); "New York Stock Exchange Transactions," *The Wall Street Journal*, October 4, 11, and 18, 1965.

period; (2) they must have been listed in the May 1965 edition of *Moody's Handbook of Widely Held Common Stocks;*[5] and (3) they must have been included as component stocks in Standard and Poor's Industry Stock Price Indexes as published in the 1964 *Security Price Index Record.*[6] In an effort to assure a representative sampling of the market, the stocks meeting the above three criteria were divided into industry groups, as determined by Standard and Poor's Industry Stock Price Indexes. The final selection of 200 stocks was then made in such a manner that the relative distribution of stocks by industry was approximately the same as in the Standard and Poor Industry Stock Price Indexes. (Although the sampling procedure was *ex post*, the author considers it unlikely that the test results have been materially biased.)

Price Ratios   All price series were adjusted for splits, stock dividends, and for the reinvestment of both cash dividends and proceeds received from the sale of rights.[7] It was then possible to compute various price relationships. Beginning with the 27th week (in order to allow for the compilation of 26 weeks' historical data), the following price ratios were computed weekly for each stock (Table 44.4).

One of the above ratios (C/A26) is "historical" (i.e., it is based upon data originating prior to and including C) and so may be used for purposes of investment selection. The remaining two ratios, 4/C and 26/C, are "future" (i.e., they are based upon data originating subsequent to and including C), and so may be used for purposes of measuring the results of investment selection.

TABLE 44.4

Ratio Designation	Description
C/A26	The price for the current week divided by the average of the series of prices ending with the price for the current week and including the prices for the 26 weeks immediately preceding. (Computed for weeks 27 through 260.)
4/C	The price for the current week divided into the price 4 weeks subsequent to the current week. (Computed for weeks 27 through 256 only.)
26/C	The price for the current week divided into the price 26 weeks subsequent to the current week. (Computed for weeks 27 through 234 only.)

---

[5] *Moody's Handbook of Widely Held Common Stocks* (New York: Moody's Investors Service, May 1965).

[6] *Security Price Index Record* (New York: Standard and Poor's Corp., 1964). Of the 200 stocks, four were not included in the Industry Stock Price Indexes at the beginning of the test period.

[7] Information on splits, stock dividends, cash dividends, and rights offerings were obtained from the following sources: *ISL Daily Stock Price Index, op. cit.,* 1961 annual edition and quarterly editions from 1962 through 3rd quarter 1965; *Moody's Handbook, op. cit.,* quarterly editions, 4th quarter 1960 through third quarter 1965; *Stock Guide* (New York: Standard and Poor's Corp., monthly editions, October 1960 through November 1965). The adjustment for reinvestment of cash dividends and proceeds received from the sale of rights ignored income taxes and brokerage fees.

TABLE 44.5

Week No.	Stock Number	Price Ratios		
		C/A26	4/C	26/C
027	001	1.306	0.906	1.101
027	002	1.212	0.990	0.802
027	003	1.269	1.023	0.918

The specific time periods covered by the ratios were chosen because of their familiarity (i.e., approximately one month and one-half year), and in the case of 26/C, because of the possibility that there might be some measurable effect evolving from the six-month long-term capital gains provision of the federal income tax law.

Moving averages were used for computation of the historical ratio because of their tendency to smooth over temporarily exaggerated price movements, and because of their popularity with market practitioners. Moving averages were not used, however, for the future ratios since the future ratios are intended for the measurement of investment performance rather than for investment selection. Performance measures must be convertible into dollars and cents, and should express the relationship between cost of a given security and proceeds that would have been received upon sale of that security.

Relative Strength Ranks   As explained above, three price ratios were computed, as permitted by available data, for each of 200 stocks for each of 234 weeks (from week number 27 through week number 260). Next, on a week-by-week basis, each set of ratios was ranked by stock. The highest ratio was given a rank of 000 and the lowest a rank of 199. The following illustration, dealing with three stocks for one week, should facilitate an understanding of the ranking process. Price ratios for three stocks at week number 27 could have appeared as in Table 44.5.

Assuming that only three stocks were included in the study, the ranking process would have produced the additional information (shown in Table 44.6).

This same ranking process would have been extended to weeks number 28, 29, 30, etc. (each set of ratios for each week being ranked separately). Of course, 200 stocks were actually included in the study rather than only three, so that the ranks were inclusive over the range 000–199.

Volatility Ranks   Several of the tests that follow make reference to the comparative volatility of the price movements of the individual securities. A measure of volatility known

TABLE 44.6

Week No.	Stock Number	Relative Strength Ranks		
		C/A26	4/C	26/C
027	001	000	002	000
027	002	002	001	·002
027	003	001	000	001

as the coefficient of variation was utilized in this study. The coefficient of variation is the ratio of the standard deviation of a set of numbers to the arithmetic mean of the set. For purposes of price volatility measurement, the relevant "set of numbers" was taken to be the 27 consecutive weekly prices ending with C for any given security.

For each week separately beginning with week number 27, and for each of the 200 stocks, the coefficient of variation for the 27 latest weekly closing prices was determined. On a week-by-week basis, these coefficients were then ranked by stock from 000 to 199, with the highest ratio receiving the lowest rank (a ranking process identical to that used for the price ratios).

Market Ranks   In order to test certain techniques of market timing, long-term (i.e., 26-week) historical market ranks were included in the data file. The computation of these market ranks was relatively simple. The 200 stocks in total were considered to be representative of the entire market. Each week, the sum of the 200 C/A26 ratios was determined in order to indicate the market's performance over the preceding six months. There were 234 C/A26 sums computed (one for every week from week number 27 through week number 260). The long-term market ranks were then arrived at by ranking the C/A26 sums (i.e., the performance of the sample over 234 holding periods) from 001 through 234.

It may be correctly contended that the process described above resulted in the use of hindsight. For example, the rank for week number 27 was only determinable after the results for week number 260 were known. While this is true, it is considered unlikely that the dispersion of six-month market results would be significantly different over say one 234-week period of time as opposed to any other. In other words, the market ranks would probably be about the same no matter whether hindsight were used or whether some time period prior to the period of this study were adopted as a standard of dispersion of six-month market performance. Of course, the use of hindsight solved the critical problem of data availability.

Divergence Ranks   Whereas the market ranks described above measure the historical strength or weakness of the market as a whole, they do not permit a determination of the extent of "speculative excesses" prevalent in the market at any given point in time. To accomplish this purpose, additional market measures, to be called divergence ranks, were computed for each week of the test period.

A possible indicator of speculative excesses, employed by many practitioners, is the comparison of the price movements of the strongest and weakest stocks against the price movements of all stocks in total. The two divergence ranks (long-term strong divergence and long-term weak divergence) were designed respectively to detect exaggerated market conditions by measuring the difference between the performance of the strongest, or weakest, stocks and the performance of the average stock, over 26-week historical time periods.

To illustrate, the computation of the long-term strong divergence rank was as follows: Each week, the average of the C/A26 ratios for the 20 strongest securities was compared to the average of the C/A26 ratios for all 200 securities. The absolute difference (divergence) between the two averages, week by week, was determined. These differences were then ranked, by week, from 001 through 234 with the largest difference receiving the lowest rank. Thus, a long-term strong divergence rank of 001 would indicate a wide divergence between the historical 26-week average price movements of the 20 strongest stocks and the historical 26-week average price movements of all 200 stocks. A rank of 234 would, of course, indicate just the opposite (i.e., a narrow spread between the two averages).

The long-term weak divergence ranks were computed in an identical manner except that the C/A26 ratios of the 20 weakest stocks were substituted for the C/A26 ratios of the 20 strongest stocks. Upon completion of these computations, every week from number 27 through number 260 was assigned two distinct divergence ranks, each ranging from 001 through 234.

The criticism of market ranks, as presented above, also applies to divergence measures. The method utilized for both computations involves hindsight. However, as explained earlier, this criticism is not considered to be of major importance.

III. Relative Strength Continuation: Empirical Results

(The reader should note that the word "historical," in the context used herein, refers to events occurring prior to the time at which a stock is considered for selection; the word "future" refers to events occurring subsequent to selection; the labels "long-term" and "short-term" refer respectively to 26-week and 4-week periods of time; and the words "strong" and "weak" refer to the trend of a stock's price movement relative to the movement of all other stock prices.)

Table 44.7 lists the short-term (4/C) and long-term (26/C) average ratios, by groups of stocks, for the entire test period. The groups were determined by classifying the stocks in accordance with their historical (C/A26) relative strength ranks. Also tabulated are the 4/C and 26/C ranks, listed in the same manner. The 4/C and 26/C average ranks are not affected by extreme price movements of one or more securities. This is not true, however, of the average ratios. Moreover, as discussed above, the computation of average ranks eliminates the sometimes confusing effect that the trend of the general market has on measures of investment performance. Ranks, being a relative measure, are free of general market influence. This applies whether the ranks are historical (C/A26) or future (4/C and 26/C).

Technical analysts contend that stocks that historically have been relatively strong tend to remain relatively strong for some significant period of time. Analysis of the 4/C (short-term) average ranks and ratios in Table 44.7 provides no evidence that this contention is correct. There seems to be no discernible pattern to the results.

However, the 26/C average ranks and ratios clearly support the concept of continuation of relative strength. The stocks that historically were among the 10 per cent strongest (lowest ranked) appreciated in price by an average of 9.6 per cent over a 26-week future period. These same stocks had an average 26/C rank of 90.8.

TABLE 44.7	4-Week and 26-Week Average Investment Performance by Stock Group as Classified According to Historical Relative Strength Ranks			
	4-Week Performance		26-Week Performance	
C/A26 Relative Strength Rank	Average 4/C Ratios	Average 4/C Ranks	Average 26/C Ratios	Average 26/C Ranks
000–019	1.009	102.0	1.096	90.8
020–039	1.009	99.6	1.074	94.2
040–0S9	1.010	98.0	1.066	97.2
060–079	1.009	99.8	1.060	99.3
080–099	1.009	99.1	1.062	98.5
100–119	1.010	99.4	1.057	101.4
120–139	1.009	99.4	1.061	99.2
140–159	1.010	97.9	1.061	99.5
160–179	1.010	98.0	1.057	101.6
180–199	1.008	101.8	1.029	113.3
All Stocks	**1.009**	**99.5**	**1.062**	**99.5**

On the other hand, the stocks that historically were among the 10% weakest (highest ranked) appreciated in price an average of only 2.9% over a 26-week future period; and the average 26/C rank of these latter stocks was 113.3.

There appears to be good correlation between past performance groupings and future (26-week) performance groupings. This is easily discerned when the C/A26 relative strength rank group numbers are compared to performance indicators based upon 26/C average group ratios and ranks (Table 44.8).

The correlation coefficient between the C/A26 rank group numbers (column 1) and the 26/C ratio group numbers (column 2) is .87. The correlation coefficient between the C/A26 rank group numbers and the 26/C rank group numbers (column 3) is .92.

TABLE 44.8		
C/A26 Relative Strength Rank Group Number	Group Performance Indicator Based Upon	
	26/C Average Group Ratios	26/C Average Group Ranks
1	1	1
2	2	2
3	3	3
4	7	6
5	4	4
6	8	8
7	5	5
8	6	7
9	9	9
10	10	10

The relationship tabulated above was not confirmed when weekly correlation co-efficients between C/A26 and 26/C ranks were computed. The 208 correlation coefficients ranged from .37 to −.21, with an average of .08. (The corresponding range of 230 correlation coefficients between C/A26 and 4/C ranks was .51 to −.47, with an average of .00.) This minimal degree of relationship is not, however, inconsistent with dependence of the kind argued.

The conclusion to be drawn from Table 44.7 is that relative strength does, as technicians have claimed, tend to continue over the longer (26-week) period. This does not appear to be the case, however, for the shorter (4-week) period. The apparent unpredictability of the short-term (4/C) results seems to corroborate the results of the numerous serial correlation studies and runs analyses that have shown *short-term* price movements to be random.

The average price appreciation of the historically strongest securities (9.6% over 26 weeks, or approximately 20.1% per annum) provides some preliminary evidence of non-randomness in price changes. The annual price appreciation of all stocks, computed from the average 26/C ratio at Table 44.7, was 12.8%. Even allowing 4% per annum in brokerage fees (assuming a 1% one-way transaction cost, and two turnovers of the portfolio per year), the profits attainable by purchasing the historically strongest stocks are superior to the profits from random selection.

■ IV. The Effect of Stock Price Volatility

In an effort to delve deeper into the data presented in Table 44.7 and in order to improve the potential investment results, several subclassifications of Table 44.7 were made. One of these subclassifications was to first divide the securities each week into three groups based upon their historical volatility ranks. Those stocks with a volatility rank of 000 through 049 (the 25% most volatile stocks) were placed in the first group. Those stocks with a volatility rank of 150 through 199 (the 25% least volatile) were placed in the third group. All other stocks (50% of the total) were assigned to the middle group.

After subclassifying the stocks in this manner, computations identical to those reported in Table 44.7 were performed for each of the three volatility groups. The results are set forth at Table 44.9. (The 4/C results are omitted in Table 44.9 and in succeeding tables in this paper. There does not appear to be a discernible pattern in these short-term results.)

The best results were obtained when dealing with the most volatile stocks. The average 26-week price appreciation for the most volatile group ranged from 10.4% for those stocks with the 10% strongest C/A26 relative strength ranks, to 2.5% for those stocks with the 10% weakest C/A26 ranks; and the respective 26/C average ranks ranged from 85.7 to 117.3.

As shown in Table 44.9 the most volatile stock group shows a wider dispersion of both 26/C average ranks and 26/C average ratios than either of the less volatile groups. Clearly, the employment of the continuation of relative strength concept appears to be most effective with regard to the most volatile securities. Moreover, the

Volatility Ranks						
000–049		050–149		150–199		All
Average 26/C Ratios	Average 26/C Ranks	Average 26/C Ratios	Average 26/C Ranks	Average 26/C Ratios	Average 26/C Ranks	Average 26/C Ratios
1.104	85.7	1.063	103.7	1.100	110.3	1.096
1.078	90.7	1.063	97.4	1.107	93.9	1.074
1.081	93.2	1.057	99.0	1.078	96.8	1.066
1.060	99.4	1.064	99.1	1.046	100.1	1.060
1.073	96.1	1.071	98.3	1.038	99.7	1.062
1.069	103.4	1.069	99.1	1.035	104.3	1.057
1.076	105.6	1.071	97.3	1.046	100.3	1.061
1.090	103.5	1.064	98.0	1.048	100.4	1.060
1.068	111.1	1.050	98.6	1.061	101.3	1.057
1.025	117.3	1.030	109.1	1.036	115.4	1.029
1.076	97.2	1.061	99.6	1.051	101.7	1.062

historically strongest stocks in the most volatile group realized an implied average annual appreciation of 21.9% (based upon their average 26/C ratio). (Of course, the market practitioner interested in risk aversion may prefer not to invest in those stocks that historically have been most volatile.)

Table 44.9 also indicates an excellent spread in 26/C average ratios as between the historically strong stocks and the historically weak stocks in the least volatile group. However, the 26/C average ranks for that group show no discernible pattern. In fact, the 10% historically strongest stocks in the least volatile group have both a high 26/C ratio (1.100) and a high 26/C rank (110.3), thus implying that the market was extraordinarily strong for the 26 weeks succeeding those time periods during which the strongest stocks were also the most stable.

The general conclusion to be drawn from Table 44.9 is that, over the entire test period, the selection of securities that historically had been both relatively strong and relatively volatile produced profits superior to those attainable from random selection.

■ V. Market Ranks: A First Attempt at Timing

The second subclassification of the results reported in Table 44.7 was by historical market ranks. All of the stocks at those weeks that had a market rank of 001 through 058 (the weeks at which the strongest historical market trends had been recorded) were placed in the first market group. The stocks at those weeks that had a market rank of 177 through 234 (the weeks at which the weakest historical market trends

TABLE 44.10

TABLE 44.10   Average Investment Performance by Stock Group as Classified According to Historical Relative Strength Subclassified According to Historical Long-Term Market Ranks

Long-Term Market Ranks						
001–058		059–176		177–234		All
Average 26/C Ratios	Average 26/C Ranks	Average 26/C Ratios	Average 26/C Ranks	Average 26/C Ratios	Average 26/C Ranks	Average 26/C Ratios
1.150	83.8	1.086	88.6	1.056	104.4	1.096
1.102	95.8	1.060	93.7	1.075	93.7	1.074
1.101	97.0	1.043	98.9	1.077	93.4	1.066
1.085	102.1	1.042	99.5	1.072	95.6	1.060
1.088	100.2	1.044	99.0	1.074	95.2	1.062
1.087	102.0	1.033	103.3	1.076	96.0	1.057
1.090	100.1	1.042	99.3	1.072	98.0	1.061
1.084	102.3	1.043	99.2	1.071	96.9	1.060
1.090	99.5	1.044	99.9	1.048	108.0	1.057
1.061	112.2	1.011	113.6	1.034	113.9	1.029
1.094	99.5	1.045	99.5	1.065	99.5	1.062

had been recorded) were placed in the third group. Remaining stocks (approximately 50% of the total) were assigned to the middle group.

The purpose of this subclassification was to indicate the extent to which historical market ranks could be used to facilitate market timing. The results of the subclassification by long-term historical market rank are presented in Table 44.10.

The stocks that had the 10% strongest C/A26 relative strength ranks, and that were in the strongest (lowest-ranked) long-term historical market rank group, recorded an average 26/C ratio of 1.150 and an average 26/C rank of 83.8. An average 26/C ratio of 1.150 implies an average annual price appreciation of 32.3%. However, the weeks included in this first market group covered only about 25% of the test period. The average annual rate of return for the entire test period would depend on the results achieved during the remaining 75% of the time (i.e., for the second and third market rank groups).

The second long-term historical market rank group (covering approximately 50% of the time period) supported the continuation of relative strength concept as did the first group. The 10% historically strongest stocks in the second group yielded an average 26/C ratio of 1.086 and an average 26/C rank of 88.6.

The third long-term historical market rank group (covering the weeks at which the weakest historical 26-week market trends had been recorded) did not support the concept of relative strength continuation. The most profitable stocks (based on average 26/C ranks and ratios) in the third market group were those stocks with a C/A26 rank ranging from 020 through 159. The historically strongest stocks did not produce the most satisfactory 26/C results. It is noteworthy, however, that even during the 26-week period following those weeks in the third market rank group, the stocks with the poorest C/A26 ranks (180–199) continued to produce the poorest C/A26 ranks and ratios.

Table 44.10 leads to the conclusion that the utilization of the continuation of relative strength concept produces superior profits during all periods except those periods immediately succeeding a comparatively weak market. Stocks with moderately strong C/A26 ranks seem to perform better during these latter periods.

It is also indicated by Table 44.10 that the best results are attainable by buying stocks in a market that historically had been comparatively strong. This implies that strength in the market tends to be followed by additional strength (i.e., continuation of relative strength seems to be applicable to the market as a whole as well as to individual securities).

■ VI. Divergence Ranks: A Second Attempt at Timing

The two divergence ranks described above also served as the basis for subclassifying the information presented at Table 44.7. The subclassifications were determined as follows: (1) all stocks at those weeks that had a divergence rank of 001–058 (the weeks at which the greatest historical divergence had been recorded) were placed in the first of three groups; (2) the stocks at those weeks that had a divergence rank of 177–234 (the weeks at which the least historical divergence had been recorded) were placed in the third group; and (3) remaining stocks (approximately 50% of the total) were assigned to the middle group. Table 44.11 sets forth the results of the subclassification by the long-term strong divergence ranks; and Table 44.12 presents the outcome of the subclassification by long-term weak divergence ranks.

Tables 44.11 and 44.12 indicate that the greatest 26-week rates of return are attained when selecting the 10% historically strongest stocks from the third divergence rank group; and the poorest returns (among the 10% historically strongest securities) arise from selecting those stocks in the first divergence rank group. With respect to Table 44.11 this principle is borne out by the average 26/C ratios (although not by the 26/C ranks); whereas, for Table 44.12 the average 26/C ranks are more indicative.

The stocks in the first divergence rank group do not appear to adhere very closely to the continuation of relative strength concept. Perhaps the historically strongest stocks that had shown the greatest divergence may have temporarily exhausted their upward momentum. On the other hand, those securities in the middle and third groups are quite consistent in following the patterns forecasted by their C/A26 relative strength ranks.

As between the two tables, the long-term weak divergence ranks at Table 44.12 produce the most outstanding results. For the 26-week periods following those weeks that evidenced least historical divergence (the third group), the 26/C average ratios ranged from 1.156 for the 10% historically strongest stocks to 1.029 for the 10% historically weakest; and the 26/C average ranks had a corresponding range of 77.6 to 122.0. This represents the best of the results yet investigated. However,

TABLE 44.11 26-Week Average Investment Performance by Stock Group as Classified According to Historical Relative Strength Ranks and Subclassified According to Historical Long-Term Strong Divergence Ranks

C/A26 Relative Strength Rank	Long-Term Strong Divergence Ranks						All Stocks	
	001–058		059–176		177–234			
	Average 26/C Ratios	Average 26/C Ranks	Average 26/C Ratios	Average 26/C Ranks	Average 26/C Ratios	Average 26/C Ranks	Average 26/C Ratios	Average 26/C Ranks
000–019	1.032	96.5	1.116	86.1	1.123	95.4	1.096	90.8
020–039	1.008	102.7	1.088	90.5	1.116	93.4	1.074	94.2
040–059	1.010	99.6	1.071	97.2	1.119	94.7	1.066	97.2
060–079	1.008	99.7	1.064	100.0	1.110	97.2	1.060	99.3
080–099	1.013	96.8	1.064	100.4	1.114	95.8	1.062	98.5
100–119	1.005	100.5	1.061	102.0	1.106	101.0	1.057	101.4
120–139	1.021	92.4	1.063	101.7	1.102	101.2	1.061	99.2
140–159	1.011	96.8	1.064	100.7	1.105	99.8	1.060	99.5
160–179	1.008	98.8	1.065	101.3	1.093	105.3	1.057	101.6
180–199	0.981	111.2	1.032	115.1	1.078	111.3	1.029	113.3
All Stocks	1.010	99.5	1.069	99.5	1.107	99.5	1.062	99.5

TABLE 44.12 26–Week Average Investment Performance by Stock Group as Classified According to Historical Relative Strength Ranks and Subclassified According to Historical Long-Term Weak Divergence Ranks

Long-Term Weak Divergence Ranks

C/A26 Relative Strength Rank	001–058		059–176		177–234		All Stocks	
	Average 26/C Ratios	Average 26/C Ranks	Average 26/C Ratios	Average 26/C Ranks	Average 26/C Ratios	Average 26/C Ranks	Average 26/C Ratios	Average 26/C Ranks
000–019	1.086	104.7	1.080	88.3	1.156	77.6	1.096	90.8
020–039	1.081	101.4	1.062	91.7	1.097	91.0	1.074	94.2
040–059	1.080	100.7	1.049	96.4	1.092	94.6	1.066	97.2
060–079	1.077	101.8	1.046	97.9	1.074	99.8	1.060	99.3
080–099	1.088	96.7	1.044	99.0	1.075	99.4	1.062	98.5
100–119	1.080	100.9	1.039	101.4	1.071	101.9	1.057	101.4
120–139	1.090	95.8	1.046	99.0	1.062	104.7	1.061	99.2
140–159	1.092	94.2	1.038	101.7	1.073	101.0	1.060	99.5
160–179	1.093	95.3	1.034	104.3	1.068	102.8	1.057	101.6
180–199	1.076	103.5	1.008	115.2	1.023	122.0	1.029	113.3
All Stocks	1.084	99.5	1.045	99.5	1.079	99.5	1.062	99.5

since they are only attainable for approximately 25% of the time, the over-all rate of return would depend upon the profits achieved for the remaining 75%.

Also of significance, the sum total of all securities in the first divergence rank group at Table 44.11 yields an average 26/C ratio as low as 1.010. This implies that long-term strong divergence ranks might be an effective means of forecasting long-term (26-week) market weakness. The 1% average return over a six-month period, for all stocks in the first group, is quite low when compared to the over-all averages at Tables 44.10 and 44.12. Yet this was the return achieved for the 26 weeks immediately following those periods during which performance of the historically strongest stocks diverged by a relatively large amount from the performance of all 200 stocks. The possibility that long-term strong divergence ranks may possess forecasting significance is a familiar one to the many market practitioners who regularly advise caution whenever the market becomes "speculative" (i.e., whenever a few "high-flyers" or "glamor" issues begin to record extraordinary gains relative to other securities). Of course, these market practitioners do not think in terms of divergence ranks; but they do express conceptually what the long-term strong divergence ranks seek to measure quantitatively.

It might also be expected that, if significant divergence (as measured by the long-term strong divergence rank) precedes a weak market, then a small degree of divergence (measured in the same manner) should forecast a comparatively bullish market. In fact, this supposition is borne out by Table 44.11 where the average 26/C ratio for all stocks in the third divergence rank group is 1.107—higher than any of the overall averages at Tables 44.10 and 44.12.

To summarize, the utilization of divergence ranks appears to facilitate market timing. Tables 44.11 and 44.12 (subclassifications of the information presented at Table 44.7) indicate that return on investment can be significantly improved by selecting the 10% historically strongest securities in the third divergence rank group (i.e., the group covering those weeks for which comparatively little divergence was noted). In the case of the long-term weak divergence ranks (Table 44.12), the results of following this strategy were superior to any results yet investigated. And in the case of the long-term strong divergence ranks (Table 44.11), it was discovered that comparatively weak market periods usually followed those weeks included in the first divergence rank group; and comparatively strong market periods tended to follow those weeks included in the third divergence rank group.

Any conclusions regarding the validity of using market ranks or divergence ranks to facilitate market timing must, however, be of a tentative nature. The studies in this paper fail to relate the various average 26/C ratios to the number of dollars that would be available for investment at various times in the market.

■ VII. Limitations

Although it appears that superior profits can be achieved by investing in securities that historically have been relatively strong in price movement, the random walk hypothesis is not thereby refuted. To the extent that the superior profits are attributable to the incurrence of extraordinary risk, the prices of individual securities could still be said to fluctuate randomly about a trend that is related to the opportunity cost of capital (a function of risk). Thus, only when a technical investment strategy can produce profits that are superior to those attainable by random selection, a risk that is less than that of random selection, can the random walk hypothesis be disproven.[8]

It is therefore necessary to determine the riskiness of the various technical measures tested above. Volatility ranks, while indicative of price stability, are unsatisfactory measures of risk for two reasons. First, since they are based upon the coefficient of variation of *prices* rather than *price changes*, they are more properly related to price action than to risk. While price action is an important variable for technicians to determine, it is not equivalent to risk. For example, stock prices rising sharply and rapidly would have a large coefficient of variation. But if the price series adhered closely to a linear trend, this coefficient of variation would bear no relationship to any common definition of risk. The relevant measure in this case would be either the coefficient of variation of *price changes* or the coefficient of alienation of price regressed on time. However, even these two measures would share with the volatility ranks a second weakness if applied to risk determination. Namely, prospective risk may not be a function of historical risk. It is the realized variance of the resultant rates of return rather than the predictability of past prices that better reflects risk.

Why, then, have the realized variances of the future returns and ranks not been computed? The answer is that there is no satisfactory method of doing so. To illustrate, comparisons of C/A26 ranks and 26/C ranks were made over 208 holding periods, each one commencing and terminating one week later than the previous one. Thus, it is clear that there are only eight non-overlapping 26-week periods analyzed. Consequently, the results are extensively intercorrelated; and the use of standard statistical measures becomes suspect. Only if each holding period were treated independently could the variances be relied upon; and under these circumstances, we would have 208 variances for each historical rank grouping, with no satisfactory method of combining them for analysis.

As a result, this study is limited by omission of statistical tests of significance, and omission of measures of return variability among individual securities and individual holding periods. However, as Paul Cootner commented in discussing his work on the random walk model:

> . . . my own tests . . . suffer from lack of a good statistical test of significance; on the other hand, they come closer to testing for the kind of non-randomness which stock market traders claim exists. It is a foolish sort of statistical reasoning which would suggest we limit our investigations to those hypotheses which are easy to investigate.[9]

---

[8] For a further discussion by the author of the theory of random walks, see "The Principle of Portfolio Upgrading," *Industrial Management Review* IX, no. 1 (Fall, 1967); and "Random Walks: Reality or Myth," *Financial Analysts Journal* XXIII, no. 6 (November–December 1967).

[9] Paul H. Cootner, "Stock Prices: Random vs. Systematic Changes," *Industrial Management Review* III, no. 2 (Spring, 1962), 43.

Page numbers followed by *n* indicate note numbers.